Drugs, Alcohol, and Tobacco

CONTENT

CURRICULUM

Totally Awesome™ *Teaching Strategies*

LIFE SKILLS

Linda Meeks
The Ohio State University

Philip Heit
The Ohio State University

Randy Page
University of Idaho

Everyday Learning Corporation
Editorial, Sales, and Customer Service Office
P.O. Box 812960
Chicago, IL 60681

Project Editor: Mary Baker
Project Assistant: David Baker
Production: Meeks Heit Productions
Production Editor: Ann G. Turpie
Director of Art and Design: Jim Brower
Illustrator: Jennifer King
Director of Marketing: David Willcox
Director of Corporate and School Promotions: Julie DeVillers

Printed in the United States of America.

4 5 6 7 8 9 10 EB 06 05 04 03 02 01 00

Library of Congress Catalog Number: 94-76120

ISBN 0-9630009-5-0

REVIEWERS

Sergeant Joyce Baker
Resource Officer/Staff Instructor
Drug Education Program
Savannah-Chatham County Board of Education
Savannah, Georgia

Reba Bullock, M.Ed.
Health Education Curriculum Specialist
Baltimore City Public Schools
Baltimore, Maryland

Richard Fopeano, Ph.D.
Assistant Professor
Department of Health and Physical Education
Rowan College of New Jersey
Glassboro, New Jersey

Sheryl Gotts, M.S.
Curriculum Specialist
Health and Physical Education
Milwaukee Public Schools
Milwaukee, Wisconsin

Major William Greer
Millen Police Department
Millen, Georgia

Steven Hawks, Ed.D., C.H.E.S.
Assistant Professor of Health Education
Department of Health, Physical Education, and Recreation
Utah State University
Logan, Utah

Janet Henke, B.S.
Middle School Teacher
Baltimore County Public Schools
Towson, Maryland

Russell Henke, M.Ed.
Coordinator of Health
Montgomery County Public Schools
Rockville, Maryland

Larry Herrold, M.S.
Supervisor, Office of Health and
    Physical Education, K-12
Baltimore County Public Schools
Towson, Maryland

Joseph M. Leake, B.S., C.H.E.S.
Health Education Curriculum Specialist
Baltimore City Public Schools
Baltimore, Maryland

Barbara Sullivan, M.S.
Drug Education Facilitator
Baltimore County Public Schools
Towson, Maryland

Bambi Sumpter, Dr. PH
Education Associate
South Carolina Department of Education
Columbia, South Carolina

Bridget Susi, M.S.
Health Education Consultant
Georgia Department of Education
Atlanta, Georgia

Mary Sutherland, Ed.D., MPH, C.H.E.S.
Associate Professor
Department of Curriculum and Instruction
College of Education
Florida State University
Tallahassee, Florida

Edith Thompson, M.Ed.
Assistant Professor
Department of Health and Physical Education
Rowan College
Glassboro, New Jersey

TABLE OF CONTENTS

TABLE OF CONTENTS

TABLE OF CONTENTS

TABLE OF CONTENTS

Section 4
Prevention and Treatment of Drug Abuse

Chapter 15
PREVENTION OF DRUG ABUSE

Chapter 16
TREATMENT FOR DRUG ABUSE

Section 5
Drug Education: Curriculum and Teaching Strategies

Chapter 17
THE DRUG EDUCATION CURRICULUM

Chapter 18
TOTALLY AWESOME TEACHING STRATEGIES

TABLE OF CONTENTS

Chapter 19
TEACHING MASTERS AND STUDENT MASTERS   521

USING TEACHING MASTERS AND
STUDENT MASTERS   521

DRUGS: PROMOTING RESPONSIBLE
AND HEALTHFUL BEHAVIOR

TABLE OF CONTENTS

PREFACE

Happiness is a state of noncontradictory joy—a joy without penalty of guilt, a joy that does not clash with any of your values, and does not work for your own destruction.

Ayn Rand
Atlas Shrugged

Young persons have many decisions to make as they grow and mature. One of the motivating factors in decision making is the desire for happiness. But, what is happiness? Ayn Rand's definition helps to clarify what is meant by true happiness. She believes true happiness is a non-contradictory joy. Educators want young persons to have this type of happiness in their lives. They want young persons to make decisions, engage in relationships, and participate in behaviors that promote true happiness. Thus, effective drug education focuses on differentiating between:

1. drug use that promotes happiness because it is a non-contradictory joy and promotes health and well-being;
2. drug use that interferes with true happiness because it results in penalty of guilt, leads to a clash in values, works for the destruction of self and others, and harms health and well-being.

Drugs, Alcohol, and Tobacco: "Totally Awesome" Teaching Strategies contains everything that educators need in order to implement effective drug education in school and community settings.

Section 1, Drugs and Wellness, provides the foundation for the further study of drugs. It also includes a discussion of violence. In this section, the authors present the theme for this book: education about drugs and violence has as its goal for students to be drug free (avoid the use of harmful and/or illegal drugs), drug informed (use over-the-counter and prescription drugs according to directions), and safe (engage in respectful nonviolent relationships).

Section 2, Drugs: A Factual Account, provides detailed background information for educators on the following topics: drug actions and reactions, stimulant drugs, seda-tive-hypnotic drugs, narcotics, marijuana, hallucinogens, inhalants, over-the-counter drugs, prescription drugs, and anabolic steroids.

Section 3, Alcohol, Tobacco, and Well-Being, provides detailed background information for educators on alcohol and tobacco. The authors believe that these two drugs deserve special emphasis. There is a detailed examination of the pharmacology and acute effects of alcohol, the risks associated with alcohol consumption, patterns of alcohol consumption, alcoholism, causes of alcoholism, treatment modalities, and alcohol and youth. Coverage of tobacco includes a detailed examination of cigarette smoking and youth, trends in smoking, components of tobacco smoke, health effects of tobacco, tobacco and the law, and smoking cessation.

Section 4, Prevention and Treatment of Drug Abuse, examines common approaches used to prevent drug abuse and to treat drug abuse. Various prevention approaches are described and there is an analysis of what works and what does not work in prevention. There is a discussion of community-based drug prevention, parent and family efforts, school-based prevention approaches, and drug prevention in the workplace. Various approaches to drug treatment are described, and there is a discussion of law enforcement strategies.

Section 5, Drug Education: Curriculum and Teaching Strategies, contains everything that is needed to implement drug and violence prevention curricula. There is a copy of The Meeks Heit Drug Education Curriculum that includes goals and philosophy, a responsible decision-making model, a model for using refusal skills, life skills for inner well-being, protective factors that promote resiliency, scope and sequence chart with objectives for grades Pre-K through 12, totally awesome teaching strategies for each of the identified objectives, infusion of drug education into several curriculum areas, violence prevention skills, critical thinking skills, character education, multicultural infusion, inclusion of students with special needs, suggestions for including parents and community leaders, coverage of intervention and treatment, drug policy, and evaluation. There are also numerous student masters and teaching masters designed to be used in educational settings with young persons in grades Pre-K through 12.

Drugs, Alcohol, and Tobacco: "Totally Awesome" Teaching Strategies was conceived, written, and designed by educators for educators who want to work with youth to help them develop a drug-free, drug-informed, and non-violent lifestyle.

DRUGS AND WELLNESS

DRUGS: PROMOTING RESPONSIBLE AND HEALTHFUL BEHAVIOR

Throughout life a person has many decisions to make. One of the motivating factors in decision-making is the desire for happiness. But, what is happiness? Ayn Rand defines happiness in her book *Atlas Shrugged* (Rand, 1957) as "a state of noncontradictory joy—a joy without penalty of guilt, a joy that does not clash with any of your values, and does not work for your own destruction."

Effective drug education focuses on differentiating between:
1. drug use that promotes happiness because it is a non-contradictory joy and promotes health and well-being;
2. drug use that interferes with true happiness because it results in penalty of guilt, leads to a clash in values, works for the destruction of self and others, and harms health and well-being.

This introductory chapter provides the framework for a drug education program that is effective. It examines factors that influence health and well-being; describes factors that influence drug use; examines the prevalence of drug use by youth of all ages; and ultimately focuses on an approach to promoting drug-free youth.

FACTORS THAT INFLUENCE HEALTH AND WELL-BEING

A popular approach to drug education has focused on just saying NO to drug use that is harmful and/or illegal. However, a person will only say NO if (s)he is motivated to do so. Therefore, the focus of drug education is best placed on motivating persons to say YES to something that produces a better reward than the use of harmful and/or illegal drugs. Persons must be convinced that saying YES to health and well-being is rewarding and promotes happiness.

This section of the chapter focuses on factors that influence health and well-being. Topics discussed are wellness and the Wellness Scale; health knowledge; healthful behaviors and risk behaviors; healthful situations and risk situations; healthful relationships and destructive relation-

ships; responsible decision-making skills; resistance skills; self-esteem; model of health and well-being; and the effects of drug use on health and well-being.

Wellness and the Wellness Scale

Wellness is another way to describe the quality of life. **Wellness** is the quality of life that includes physical, mental-emotional, family-social, and spiritual health. The **Wellness Scale** (Fig. 1-1) depicts the ranges constituting the quality of life—from optimal well-being to high level wellness, average wellness, minor illness or injury, major illness or injury, and premature death. At least six factors influence health and wellness:
1. the behaviors a person chooses;
2. the situations in which a person participates;
3. the relationships in which a person engages;
4. the decisions that a person makes;
5. the resistance skills that a person uses;
6. the level of self-esteem that a person develops.

Health status is the sum total of the positive and negative influence of behaviors, situations, relationships, decisions, use of resistance skills, and self-esteem on a person's health and wellness. Each influence that is positive is viewed as a plus (+) while each influence that is negative is viewed as a minus (−). A person's health status fluctuates on the Wellness Scale depending on these influences.

Drug use may have a positive or negative influence on health status depending on how it affects behaviors, situations, relationships, decisions, use of resistance skills, and self-esteem. For example, a person who has high blood pressure or epilepsy may take prescription medicine in order to enhance health status and thus improve the quality of the person's life. A person is **drug informed** when (s)he takes over-the-counter drugs and/or prescription drugs according to directions to promote health. A person is **drug free** when (s)he does not use harmful and illegal drugs. A person may choose not to be drug informed and drug free. A person may choose to drink an alcoholic

Figure 1-1
Wellness Scale Factors That Influence Health and Well-Being

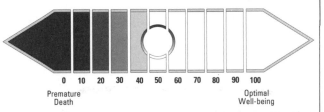

Risk behaviors	Wellness behaviors
Risk situations	Healthful situations
Destructive relationships	Healthful relationships
Irresponsible decision making	Responsible decision making
Lack of resistance skills	Use of resistance skills
Negative self-esteem	Positive self-esteem

0 10 20 30 40 50 60 70 80 90 100

Premature
Death

Optimal
Well-being

Health status is the sum total of the positive and negative influences of behaviors, situations, relationships, decisions, use of resistance skills, and self-esteem.

beverage before driving an automobile. The alcohol may affect the person's judgment and ability to drive. This person is engaging in behavior and decision making that jeopardize his/her health and safety and that of others.

Health Knowledge

Health knowledge consists of facts that are needed to evaluate behaviors, situations, and relationships; to make responsible decisions; to use resistance skills; and to promote positive self-esteem. The following ten areas provide a framework for the content for comprehensive school health education curricula:

1. mental and emotional well-being,
2. family and relationship skills,
3. growth and development,
4. nutrition,
5. personal fitness,
6. substance use and abuse,
7. diseases and disorders,
8. consumer health,
9. safety and injury prevention,
10. community and environment.

The unit on drugs includes factual information and life skills and is taught in the content area of substance use and abuse. Factual information and life skills are also taught within other content areas. For example, the ways in which

specific drugs are used for the treatment of diseases might be taught in the content area of diseases and disorders. Within the content area of consumer health, topics might include reading the labels on containers of prescription drugs and understanding the difference between generic and brand-name drugs. The dangers of using anabolic steroids might be included in the content area of personal fitness. Health knowledge provides a foundation for health and well-being.

Healthful Behaviors and Risk Behaviors

Health knowledge is essential in order to evaluate behavior and to determine whether or not it promotes health status. For example, knowledge about drugs is essential to evaluate whether or not the use of a drug(s) will promote health status. **Healthful behaviors** or **wellness behaviors** are actions that enhance self-esteem; promote health; prevent illness, injury, and premature death; and improve the quality of the environment. Examples of healthful behaviors with regard to drug use include reading and following the directions on a prescription or over-the-counter drug label, discarding old prescriptions, and keeping medicines in a safe place away from children.

Risk behaviors or **harmful behaviors** are voluntary actions that threaten self-esteem; harm health; increase the likelihood of illness, injury, and premature death; and destroy the quality of the environment. Examples of risk behaviors with regard to drug use include taking another person's prescription medicine, deliberately not following the directions on prescription or over-the-counter drugs, taking two drugs at one time without checking with a physician, and injecting anabolic steroids in order to improve appearance and/or athletic performance. Avoiding risk behaviors and choosing healthful behaviors promote health and well-being.

Healthful Situations and Risk Situations

Most persons recognize that health knowledge will assist them in evaluating the consequences of their behavior. Health knowledge also is essential in evaluating the consequences of being in various situations. **Healthful situations** or **wellness situations** are circumstances that enhance self-esteem; promote health; prevent illness, injury, and premature death; and improve the quality of the environment. Examples of healthful situations with regard to drugs include attending drug-free parties, sitting in nonsmoking sections of restaurants, and being a passenger in an automobile with someone who has not been drinking alcohol.

Risk situations or **harmful situations** are circumstances that threaten self-esteem; harm health; increase the likelihood of illness, injury, and premature death; and destroy the quality of the environment. Examples of risk situations involving drug use include attending a party where there are illegal drugs, being in a location where illegal drugs are being sold, and sitting in a room where others are smoking. Avoiding risk situations and choosing healthful situations promote health and well-being.

Healthful Relationships and Destructive Relationships

A current area of emphasis in health knowledge involves the careful examination of how the quality of a person's relationships influences his/her health status. **Relationships** are the connections that people have with each other. **Healthful relationships** are relationships that enhance self-esteem, foster respect, develop character, and promote health-enhancing behaviors and responsible decision making. Examples of healthful relationships with regard to drug use might include those in which persons encourage one another to remain drug free, help one another solve problems and cope with difficult situations, and motivate one another to accomplish goals.

Destructive relationships or **harmful relationships** are relationships that threaten self-esteem, are disrespectful, indicate a lack of character, threaten health, and foster irresponsible decision making. Examples of destructive relationships with regard to drug use might include those in which a person is abusive toward another after drinking alcohol, lies about his/her drug use to another, and/or encourages another to use or sell illegal drugs. Avoiding destructive relationships and choosing healthful relationships promote health and well-being.

Responsible Decision-Making Skills

Another factor influencing health and well-being involves a person's skills in making responsible decisions. The **Responsible Decision-Making Model** (Table 1-2) is a series of steps to follow to assure that the decisions a person makes lead to actions that:
1. promote health,
2. promote safety,
3. protect laws,
4. show respect for self and others,
5. follow guidelines set by responsible adults such as parents and guardians,
6. demonstrate good character and moral values.

With regard to drug use, the responsible decision-making model helps persons know when to say NO. Criteria are

Table 1-2
Responsible Decision-Making Model

1. **Clearly describe the situation you face.**
   If no immediate decision is necessary, describe the situation in writing. If an immediate decision must be made, describe the situation out loud or to yourself in a few short sentences. Being able to describe a situation in your own words is the first step in clarifying the question.
2. **List possible actions that can be taken.**
   Again, if no immediate decision is necessary, make a list of possible actions. If an immediate decision must be made, state possible actions out loud or to yourself.
3. **Share your list of possible actions with a responsible adult such as someone who protects community laws and demonstrates character.**
   When no immediate action is necessary, sharing possible actions with a responsible adult is helpful. This person can examine your list to see if it is inclusive. Responsible adults have a wide range of experiences that can allow them to see situations maturely. They may add possibilities to the list of actions. In some situations, it is possible to delay decision making until there is an opportunity to seek counsel with a responsible adult. If an immediate decision must be made, explore possibilities. Perhaps a telephone call can be made. Whenever possible, avoid skipping this step.
4. **Carefully evaluate each possible action using six criteria.**
   Ask each of the six questions to learn which decision is best.
   a. Will this decision result in an action that will protect my health and the health of others?
   b. Will this decision result in an action that will protect my safety and the safety of others?
   c. Will this decision result in an action that will protect the laws of the community?
   d. Will this decision result in an action that shows respect for myself and others?
   e. Will this decision result in an action that follows guidelines set by responsible adults such as my parents or guardian?
   f. Will this decision result in an action that will demonstrate that I have good character and moral values?
5. **Decide which action is responsible and most appropriate.**
   After applying the six criteria, compare the results. Which decision best meets the six criteria?
6. **Act in a responsible way and evaluate the results.**
   Follow through with this decision with confidence. The confidence comes from paying attention to the six criteria.

included that can be used to evaluate each of the options a person might be considering. For example, a young student might be invited to a friend's home for lunch and know that a parent will not be there. (S)he also might know that the friend will serve wine coolers. Using the responsible decision-making model, the person can evaluate whether or not to accept the invitation. The person might ask: Will going to my friend's house and drinking wine coolers for lunch promote my health? Will it be safe? Will I be obeying school and community laws? Will this show respect for myself and others, such as my friend's parents? Will my parents approve of this decision? Does this decision demonstrate that I have good character and moral values? A careful evaluation of the criteria indicates that the answer to each question is NO. Using carefully designed criteria in decision making is more responsible than making a decision solely on the basis of what a person would like to do at a given moment. Making responsible decisions promotes health and well-being.

Resistance Skills

After developing the skill of responsible decision making, a person recognizes when (s)he must say NO to an action or situation because (s)he wants to say YES to good health. **Resistance skills** or **refusal skills** are skills that are used when a person wants to say NO to an action and/or leave a situation. The **Model for Using Resistance Skills** (Table 1-3) contains a list of suggested ways for effectively resisting pressure to engage in actions that:
1. threaten health,
2. threaten safety,
3. break laws,
4. result in lack of respect for self and others,
5. disobey guidelines set by responsible adults,
6. detract from character and moral values.

With regard to drug use, resistance skills help a person who is pressured. Resistance skills might be used when a person is approached by someone who is selling drugs.

Table 1-3
Model for Using Resistance Skills

1. **Use assertive behavior.**
   There is a saying, "You get treated the way you 'train' others to treat you." Assertive behavior is the honest expression of thoughts and feelings without experiencing anxiety or threatening others. When you use assertive behavior, you show that you are in control of yourself and the situation. You say NO clearly and firmly. As you speak, you look directly at the person(s) pressuring you. Aggressive behavior is the use of words and/or actions that tend to communicate disrespect. This behavior only antagonizes others. Passive behavior is the holding back of ideas, opinions, and feelings. Holding back may result in harm to you, others, or the environment.

2. **Avoid saying, "NO, thank you."**
   There is never a need to thank a person who pressures you into doing something that might be harmful, unsafe, illegal, or disrespectful or which may result in disobeying parents or displaying a lack of character and moral values.

3. **Use nonverbal behavior that matches verbal behavior.**
   Nonverbal behavior is the use of body language or actions rather than words to express feelings, ideas, and opinions. Your verbal NO should not be confused by misleading actions. For example,
   if you say NO to cigarette smoking, do not pretend to take a puff of a cigarette in order to resist pressure.

4. **Influence others to choose responsible behavior.**
   When a situation poses immediate danger, remove yourself. If no immediate danger is present, try to turn the situation into a positive one. Suggest alternative, responsible ways to behave. Being a positive role model helps you feel good about yourself and helps gain the respect of others.

5. **Avoid being in situations in which there will be pressure to make harmful decisions.**
   There is no reason to put yourself into situations in which you will be pressured or tempted to make unwise decisions. Think ahead.

6. **Avoid being with persons who choose harmful actions.**
   Your reputation is the impression that others have of you, your decisions, and your actions. Associate with persons known for their good qualities and character in order to avoid being misjudged.

7. **Resist pressure to engage in illegal behavior.**
   You have a responsibility to protect others and to protect the laws of your community. Demonstrate good character and moral values.

These skills might be used when a person is pressured to become a member of a gang that is involved in drug use. A person might use resistance skills when offered a puff from a cigarette. Being able to resist pressure is important to one's health and well-being.

Self-Esteem

Self-esteem is the personal internal image that a person has about himself/herself. A person has **positive self-esteem** when (s)he believes that (s)he is worthwhile and lovable. A person has **negative self-esteem** when (s)he believes that (s)he is unworthy and unlovable. Why is it so important for a person to have positive self-esteem in order to promote health and well-being? The level of a person's self-esteem seems to have a profound effect on behavior. Persons with positive self-esteem are more likely to avoid self-destructive behavior and to choose self-loving behavior. **Self-loving behavior** is healthful and responsible behavior indicative of a person who believes himself/herself to be worthwhile and lovable.

Suppose a person with positive self-esteem is pressured to buy or sell drugs to be a part of a gang. This person is more likely to resist the pressure because (s)he feels lovable. A person with negative self-esteem might choose to sell the drugs to gain a sense of belonging that (s)he feels is lacking.

Suppose a young child is pressured to take a puff of a cigarette. A young child who has positive self-esteem does not need to succumb to the pressure to smoke to feel worthy. However, a child with negative self-esteem may succumb to the pressure in order to feel important. Developing positive self-esteem is important to one's health and well-being. Positive self-esteem is translated into an internal message that says, "I am too important to harm myself or others."

Model of Health and Well-Being

The **Model of Health and Well-Being** (Fig. 1-4) shows the relationship among the four dimensions of health, the ten areas of health knowledge, and the six factors that influence health status. Three of the dimensions of health—physical health, mental-emotional health, and family-social health—provide the framework for the outside of the model. The fourth dimension of health, spiritual health, is at the core of the Model.

Surrounding the core of the Model is a Well-Being Wheel. The Well-Being Wheel is composed of the ten content areas for which knowledge is needed in order to choose

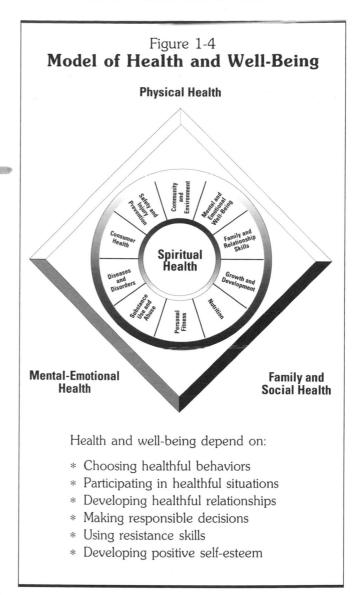

Figure 1-4
Model of Health and Well-Being

Physical Health

Spiritual Health

Mental-Emotional Health

Family and Social Health

Health and well-being depend on:

* Choosing healthful behaviors
* Participating in healthful situations
* Developing healthful relationships
* Making responsible decisions
* Using resistance skills
* Developing positive self-esteem

healthful behaviors, participate in healthful situations, develop healthful relationships, make responsible decisions, use resistance skills, and develop positive self-esteem. The ten areas of health are connected. In turn, they influence the four dimensions of health. The connectedness of the six factors that influence health status with the ten areas of health and the four dimensions of health is called **holistic health**. The **holistic effect** means that a behavior, situation, relationship, decision, resistance skill, and level of self-esteem in any one of the ten areas will affect the other areas and the four dimensions of health.

Effects of Drug Use on Health and Well-Being

To gain a picture of holistic health and the holistic effect, an analogy might be used. Let a large jar of water represent the Well-Being Wheel. The water represents all ten areas of health and the four dimensions of health. Let drops of red food coloring represent positive influences on health status: wellness behaviors, wellness situations, healthful relationships, responsible decisions, the wise use of resistance skills, and positive self-esteem. The red food coloring is used to signify saying YES to good health.

With regard to drug use, the red food coloring might represent one of the following: reading the label of an over-the-counter drug before using it; storing medicines in a safe place away from children; attending drug-free parties; avoiding places where there is drug trafficking; participating in school activities to enhance self-esteem; or spending time with caring persons such as family members.

As drops of the red food coloring are placed in the water in the jar, the water turns red. The food coloring has a holistic effect. Any one of the actions on the aforementioned list might have caused this holistic effect. With regard to drug use, healthful and responsible actions affect the whole person.

This illustration can be repeated using blue food coloring to represent negative influences on health status: risk behaviors; risk situations; destructive relationships; irresponsible decisions; the failure to use resistances skills; and negative self-esteem. The blue food coloring is used to signify saying NO to good health.

With regard to irresponsible drug use and decision making, the blue food coloring might represent one of the following: using another person's prescription drug; keeping medicine in a place within children's reach; attending parties where illegal drugs are used; purchasing illegal drugs; being a passenger in an automobile in which the driver has been drinking alcohol; sitting in the smoking section of a restaurant; or being friends with someone who sells drugs.

As drops of the blue food coloring are placed in the water in the jar, the water turns blue. The food coloring has a holistic effect. Any one of the actions on the aforementioned list might have caused this holistic effect. With regard to drug use, harmful and irresponsible actions affect the whole person.

FACTORS THAT INFLUENCE DRUG USE

If drug education is to be effective, it is essential for educators to understand protective and risk factors. Protective factors increase the likelihood that a young person will say YES to health and say NO to drugs while risk factors increase the likelihood that a young person will say NO

to health and say YES to drugs. This section of the chapter will differentiate between protective factors and risk factors. It will examine the following protective factors associated with resiliency: being reared in a loving, functional family; being involved in school activities; having positive self-esteem; having clearly defined goals and plans to reach them; having close friends who do not abuse drugs; regularly practicing one's faith; feeling a sense of accomplishment at school; having adult role models including parents who do not abuse drugs; having a healthful attitude about competition and athletic performance; being committed to following the rules of the community; and having a plan to cope with life stressors.

There also will be a discussion of the following risk factors associated with irresponsible and harmful drug use: being reared in a dysfunctional family; having negative self-esteem; being unable to resist peer pressure; having difficulty mastering developmental tasks; being economically disadvantaged; lacking faith experiences and fellowship; having a genetic background with a predisposition to chemical dependency; experiencing family disruption; experiencing depression; experiencing pressure to succeed in athletics; having difficulty achieving success in school; having attention deficit hyperactive disorder; having immature character disorder; and having borderline personality tendencies.

Protective Factors and Resiliency

Drug education must provide young people with armor to protect them or keep them from being vulnerable when they are exposed to situations in which they might use drugs. **Protective factors** are characteristics of individuals and their environments that make a positive contribution to development and behavior. Young people who are armed with protective factors are more likely to resist drugs and demonstrate resiliency. **Resiliency** is the ability to recover from or adjust to misfortune, change, pressure, and adversity. Resilient youth are often described as being stress resistant and invincible in spite of adversity. They are able to cope with misfortune without the use of drugs. Any successful drug-education program must focus on protective factors that promote resiliency (Fig. 1-5).

Protective factor 1: Being reared in a loving, functional family. A **loving, functional family** is a family in which feelings are expressed openly and honestly, effective coping skills are practiced, and members show respect for one another. In a loving, functional family, children observe and are taught important lessons that serve as protective factors:

- self-loving behavior;
- healthful attitudes toward sexuality;
- healthful attitudes and practices regarding drug use;
- healthful ways to express feelings and to communicate;
- faith and moral values;
- responsible decision-making skills;
- coping skills with the ability to delay gratification when necessary.

Self-loving behavior is behavior that is healthful and responsible and indicates that a person believes himself/herself to be worthwhile and lovable. It is an outgrowth of the way that a person is treated by parents and/or other significant adults within the family. When a young person is treated in a loving and respectful manner, (s)he feels important. This feeling of importance translates into the message, "I am important and I will treat myself as if I am important." The young person is motivated to care for himself/herself. Thus, there is little motivation for irresponsible and harmful drug use.

Sexuality includes the feelings and attitudes a person has about his/her body, sex role, and sexual orientation as well as his/her feelings and attitudes regarding the bodies, sex roles, and sexual orientation of others. Once again, the parents and/or other significant adults within the family influence a young person's sexuality. When this influence is positive, the young person accepts and embraces his/her sexuality and is comfortable. The young person does not need to be under the influence of drugs to cope with his/her sexuality.

Parents and/or other significant adults also influence the attitudes and practices of a young person regarding drug use through role modeling. A **role model** is a person who is influential and whose behavior and attitudes are learned and copied. Young persons observe parents and/or other significant adults and begin to learn and copy their attitudes and behaviors. If these adults engage in responsible and healthful behavior regarding drugs, younger family members will accept this as appropriate behavior and copy it.

Parents and/or other significant adults are role models for communication styles. **Communication** is the sharing of feelings, thoughts, and information with another person. When young persons learn to communicate effectively, they feel connected to others. This helps them overcome any feelings of loneliness and alienation. They do not need to be under the influence of drugs to feel comfortable in expressing feelings and experiencing closeness to others.

Figure 1-5
Protective Factors That Serve as a Coat of Armor and Promote Resiliency

Protective factors that promote resiliency are:

* Being reared in a loving, functional family
* Being involved in school activities
* Having positive self-esteem
* Having clearly defined goals and plans to reach them
* Having close friends who do not abuse drugs
* Regularly practicing one's faith
* Feeling a sense of accomplishment at school
* Having adult role models including parents who do not abuse drugs
* Having a healthful attitude about competition and athletic performance
* Being committed to following the rules of the community
* Having a plan to cope with life stressors

Parents and/or other significant adults in loving, functional families protect their children from irresponsible and harmful drug use by arming them with strong values and by instilling faith. A **value** is something of great importance to a person. Adults in loving, functional families share their values with their children. Their behavior is consis-

9

tent with their values. For example, they may value hard work. Their behavior demonstrates that they value hard work. Their values are an outgrowth of their faith. **Faith** is the belief system that guides a person's behavior choices and gives meaning and purpose to life. When the family regularly practices faith and discusses its family values, younger family members develop inner strength. They can rely on this inner strength when they need to resist pressure and when they need to differentiate between right and wrong. The loving, functional family operates with clarity rather than confusion.

Children in loving, functional families have the opportunity to observe their parents struggle with difficult situations and make responsible decisions. Parents and/or other significant adults within the family assist children by helping them evaluate choices. They teach them that there are consequences for behaving in irresponsible and harmful ways.

Adults within a loving, functional family teach children coping skills and the need to delay gratification when necessary. Most people will experience a series of difficult life crises as they go through life. Adults in loving, functional families prepare their children for these difficult life crises by teaching them how to cope. They help their children by allowing them to cope under their guidance rather than "fixing" problems for them. This protects children from wanting a quick "fix" such as a drug when they experience a life crisis.

When children are helped to master life crises, they gain confidence. They recognize that if they stay with solving a problem they gain perseverance and confidence in their problem-solving skills. They also experience the pain and experience the stages that persons go through during life crises. Elisabeth Kübler-Ross was a pioneer in the study of coping skills needed for death and dying. She identified five stages that are experienced during this life crisis: denial, anger, bargaining, depression, and acceptance (Kübler-Ross, 1975).

Since her pioneer work, psychologists have recognized that the five stages Kübler-Ross identified are operative in other life crises. In other words, the process of mastering many life crises involves experiencing denial, anger, bargaining, depression, and acceptance. Experiencing this process and mastering it appears to be a key to mental and emotional health. For example, if a child learns that his/her parents are going to divorce, (s)he usually first denies the reality and pretends it will not happen. Then the child becomes very angry. This is followed with bar-

gaining such as, "If I help more around the house, will daddy/mommy stay?" When bargaining is not effective, the child becomes depressed. Eventually, if the child receives support and recognition of feelings, (s)he will accept the divorce even though (s)he did not want it to happen.

Adults who allow children to experience these five stages help them toward emotional maturity. They prevent their children from feeling stuck or living in a constant state of denial, anger, and/or depression. Young persons who feel stuck or young persons who live with persons who feel stuck are more likely to use drugs.

Finally, adults in loving, functional families teach children the importance of delaying gratification when necessary. **Delayed gratification** is allowing oneself to struggle in the present so that a desirable benefit will be achieved in the future. For example, a child may be asked to do homework before watching television or to earn a certain amount of money before purchasing sporting equipment. By doing difficult tasks or work before receiving a reward, delayed gratification is learned. Learning to delay gratification when appropriate is a protective factor because this skill also enables young people to master the art of coping successfully.

In summary, being reared in a loving, functional family is a protective factor because the skills gained in this kind of a family help youth develop an armor to protect themselves against pressures to use drugs.

Protective factor 2: Being involved in school activities. There are at least two reasons that involvement in school activities is beneficial in protecting against the pressures to use drugs in irresponsible and harmful ways. First, participation in school activities such as Boy Scouts, Girl Scouts, Camp Fire Girls, Indian Princesses, plays, yearbook staff, clubs, honoraries, and athletic groups takes time. Participating in such activities leaves youth with less idle time and it helps prevent boredom and monotony. Second, schools usually have eligibility guidelines for participation in school activities. For example, youth who drink alcoholic beverages may be disciplined by the school and may become ineligible to participate in activities such as plays and/or athletic teams. Youth who enjoy such activities do not want to lose the privilege of participation.

Protective factor 3: Having positive self-esteem. As mentioned previously in this chapter, youth with positive self-esteem are more likely to avoid self-destructive behavior and to choose self-loving behavior. An analogy might be used to illustrate the reason. Suppose self-esteem is viewed

10

as a paintbrush used to color life's situations. Youth who have positive self esteem evaluate situations differently than those with negative self-esteem. Their paintbrushes stroke their lives with bright colors and they are unwilling to risk the quality of their lives by choosing harmful and irresponsible drug use.

Protective factor 4: Having clearly-defined goals and plans to reach them. A **goal** is a desired achievement toward which a person works. Goals add meaning and purpose to life. They provide a link from the present to the future. When youth have goals, they are more likely to evaluate the consequences of their actions in terms of the future as well as the present.

Protective factor 5: Having close friends who do not abuse drugs. Friends are especially helpful as protective factors by providing an armor to shield against the pressures to engage in harmful and irresponsible drug use. Suppose a young person temporarily drops his/her armor of protective factors. Then friends who do not abuse drugs can step in and encourage this young person to be drug free and drug informed. In a sense, the friends' armor helps shield the vulnerable young person. There is at least one other reason that it is important to have close friends who do not abuse drugs. When in the presence of friends who are drug free and drug informed, there is less temptation to experiment with drugs.

Protective factor 6: Regularly practicing one's faith. Faith is the belief system that guides a person's behavior and gives meaning and purpose to life. There appear to be important commonalities among the various faiths and belief systems. In each, self-discipline, loving behavior, obedience, and respect are emphasized. Each of these traits plays a role in deterring irresponsible and harmful drug use. **Self-discipline** is the effort or energy with which a person follows through on what (s)he intends or promises to do. A disciplined lifestyle is one of the building blocks needed for a drug-free and drug-informed lifestyle. Loving behavior is important because it helps youth understand that their behavior has consequences not only to themselves but to significant others in their lives. Obedience and respect are involved in responsible decision making. The desire to obey and respect the principles of one's faith most likely means being drug free and drug informed. Encouraging youth to be involved in youth groups involving their faith is an important protective factor. In such groups, values are continually discussed and emphasized in a peer setting.

Protective factor 7: Feeling a sense of accomplishment at school. Youth spend most of their time in the school environment. In this environment, they test some of their beliefs about themselves. They examine their successes and failures and how they measure up alongside their peers. When youth have a sense of accomplishment at school, they develop feelings of self-worth. Feelings of self-worth can be very empowering and tend to build positive self-esteem, another protective factor.

Protective factor 8: Having adult role models including parents who do not abuse drugs. Society is replete with adult role models who subliminally provide the message that drug use is sexy, macho, athletic, and attractive. One only has to watch television a very short time to observe such examples. When youth admire adults who do not abuse drugs, this helps counteract the opposite messages that they are observing.

Protective factor 9: Having a healthful attitude about competition and athletic performance. Participation in athletics benefits young persons in many ways. First, and foremost, participation in athletics affords the opportunity to enhance physical, mental, and emotional health. The level of physical fitness may be improved. There are opportunities to be close to teammates and form positive peer relationships. Involvement in school-sponsored athletics promotes loyalty to the school and to the community. Positive performance in athletics bolsters self-esteem and provides the opportunity for recognition. For some young persons, athletics provide a vehicle by which to earn a scholarship or grant-in-aid to a college or university. Still other young persons aspire to have a career in athletics.

Using one's talents to the best of one's abilities and accepting the results is a prerequisite for healthful competition. It enables youth to keep a healthful perspective about winning. Youth with a healthful attitude about competition and athletic performance focus on their talents and developing these talents. They are not swayed to win at all costs.

Protective factor 10: Being committed to following the rules of the community. A **commitment** is a pledge to do something. All successful relationships involve some form of commitment. Commitment provides for continuity and trust. Commitment is important for cohesion in a community. When persons in a community are committed to one another, they pledge their support for actions that are in the common good. This of course includes supporting rules and laws that promote the health and safety of persons living within the community. When youth are committed to following the rules of the community, they pledge to keep the community safe from drug trafficking and drug abuse that harms individuals. Being involved in the community and in community activities gives youth the feeling of self-worth needed to maintain this commitment.

Protective factor 11: Having a plan to cope with life stressors. All youth experience stress, but youth who regularly use stress-management skills (Chapter 2) have a plan to dissipate the effects of the stress. As a result, these youth have more balanced lives. They are prepared to deal with difficult situations and are not tempted to use and abuse drugs to temporarily lessen the effects of stress.

Risk Factors

Any successful drug education program must focus on skills that lessen the impact of risk factors that tend to make young people vulnerable to irresponsible and harmful drug use (Fig. 1-6). **Risk factors** are characteristics of individuals or environments associated with increased vulnerability to problem behaviors. Risk factors refer only to the statistical probability that youth will engage in irresponsible and harmful drug use. Risk factors are a useful way to identify youth who may need help. They do not predict an adverse outcome for any particular child or adolescent.

Risk factor 1: Being reared in a dysfunctional family. A **dysfunctional family** is a family in which feelings are not expressed openly and honestly, coping skills are inadequate, and members are distrustful of one another. In contrast, the loving, functional family might be depicted as the ideal family in which children observe and are taught the skills needed to resist harmful and irresponsible drug use. The Family Continuum (Table 1-7) might be used to contrast the loving, functional family with the dysfunctional family. Children reared in dysfunctional families may exhibit one or more of the following:
- self-destructive behavior,
- confused attitudes regarding sexuality,
- irresponsible and harmful drug use,
- difficulty communicating and expressing feelings in healthful ways,
- confused value system,
- inadequate decision-making skills,
- inadequate coping skills and reliance on instant gratification.

Being reared in a dysfunctional family is a risk factor because the skills needed to protect and promote health

Figure 1-6
Risk Factors That Make Young Persons Vulnerable to Drug Use

Risk factors are:

* Being reared in a dysfunctional family
* Having negative self-esteem
* Being unable to resist peer pressure
* Having difficulty mastering developmental tasks
* Being economically disadvantaged
* Lacking faith experiences and fellowship
* Having a genetic background with a predisposition to chemical dependency
* Experiencing family disruption
* Experiencing depression
* Experiencing pressure to succeed in athletics
* Having difficulty achieving success in school
* Having attention deficit hyperactive disorder
* Having immature character disorder
* Having borderline personality tendencies

are often not modeled or practiced and learned. A closer examination will explain the reasons.

Self-destructive behavior is behavior that is irresponsible and/or harmful to the self and indicates that a person does not believe himself/herself to be worthwhile and lovable. In most dysfunctional families, the significant adults behave in harmful ways. They may harm themselves by drinking too much alcohol and/or by using other drugs irresponsibly. They may harm one another by being physically, emotionally, or sexually abusive. Young people reared in dysfunctional families begin to copy negative

Table 1-7
The Family Continuum

The Family Continuum depicts the degree to which a family promotes skills needed for loving and responsible relationships.

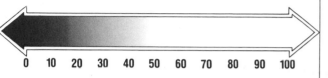

0	10	20	30	40	50	60	70	80	90	100

Dysfunctional Families	Loving, Functional Families
• Self-destructive behavior	• Self-loving behavior
• Confused attitudes regarding sexuality	• Healthful attitudes toward sexuality
• Irresponsible and harmful drug use	• Healthful attitudes and practices regarding drug use
• Difficulty communicating and expressing feelings in healthful ways	• Healthful ways to express feelings and to communicate
• Confused value system	• Faith and moral values
• Inadequate decision-making skills	• Responsible decision-making skills
• Inadequate coping skills and reliance on instant gratification	• Coping skills with the ability to delay gratification when necessary

role models. They begin to behave the same way. A lack of regard for the self makes these youth more vulnerable to using drugs.

Significant adults in dysfunctional families often have difficulty integrating sexuality and love. They may have difficulty accepting their sexuality and forming intimate relationships. Therefore, they are not effective role models for attaining healthful sexuality and forming intimate relationships for their children. When children reach puberty and need to focus on their sexuality and integrate their new sexual feelings with their values, they are ill-equipped. They are vulnerable to trying drugs in order to cope with their emerging sexual feelings.

Significant adults in dysfunctional families often use drugs in irresponsible and harmful ways or respond in harmful ways to others who do so. For example, an adult may be chemically dependent. Another adult in the family may not be chemically dependent, but may demonstrate codependence. **Codependence** is a mental disorder in which a person loses personal identity, has frozen feelings, and

copes ineffectively (Fig. 1-8). Persons who have codependence are called **codependent**. Children reared in families in which adults are chemically dependent and codependent may copy this behavior. They may begin to abuse chemicals such as alcohol or marijuana. They may begin to behave in codependent ways and to lose their personal identity, deny their feelings, and cope ineffectively.

In a dysfunctional family, denial and dishonesty often replace expressions of feelings and truthful explanations. **Denial** is a condition in which a person refuses to recognize what (s)he is feeling because it is extremely painful.

Denial lies largely outside the direct control of a person's conscious awareness. It results from a deep unwillingness to experience feelings that would ensue if those forbidden realities were acknowledged—an unwillingness so deep that the mind blocks any awareness that would lead to these dangerous emotions. It is a very active, if unconscious, process, requiring the constant input of psychic energy to scan the environment so "blinders" can quickly be activated. Denial may be seen as an impaired strategy for achieving security. In the face of a threat, narrowing one's awareness can create the appearance of safety (Cermak, 1986).

How might denial of feelings place young people at risk for drug use? Unfortunately, young people who try to constrict or control their feelings usually work hardest to control those feelings considered to be immature, dangerous, uncomfortable, or just plain bad: anger, fear, sadness, rage, embarrassment, bitterness, and loneliness. One way to control these feelings is to alter them through the use of chemicals.

Another way in which being reared in a dysfunctional family places young people at risk for drug use focuses on the confusion regarding values and the failure to regularly discuss and practice faith within the family setting. Thus, young people are handicapped in situations in which they must discern between right and wrong. They also have not developed the inner strength that they might have developed in a loving, functional family who participated in faith experiences together regularly.

Adults in dysfunctional families usually have poor decision-making skills. If they had responsible decision-making skills, they most likely would not be in the difficult situation in which they are. Often they are not proficient at identifying and evaluating alternatives in order to make responsible decisions. Because they are not proficient in this process, they fail to teach it to the young persons

Figure 1-8
The Roots and Characteristics of Codependence

crisis in this manner, they begin to model this behavior. Whenever they experience a life crisis, they are at risk for using drugs to numb the pain they otherwise would experience as they struggle to master the crisis.

In summary, being reared in a dysfunctional family is a risk factor because young people do not learn the skills necessary to protect themselves against pressures to use drugs.

Risk factor 2: Having negative self-esteem. Earlier in this chapter, self-esteem was defined as the personal internal image that a person has about himself/herself. Youth with negative self-esteem believe that they are unworthy and unlovable. They feel a sense of isolation and alienation. They do not feel close to others and may perceive themselves as unattractive. They are at risk for drug use for several reasons.

First, they may choose drugs as a way of numbing the painful feelings of alienation and failure. The drugs provide them with temporary relief. Second, they may choose to use drugs in order to gain acceptance. Because they feel unworthy and unlovable, they may believe that any connectedness or friendship is better than being alone. When pressured to use drugs, they say YES in order to gain membership into a group or to gain friendship even though the social connections they are gaining are with drug-taking youth. Third, they may use drugs because they do not have the assertiveness and self-confidence required to say NO. Fourth, they may use drugs to cover up uncomfortable feelings. For example, the risk of drug use is particularly high in adolescent females who consider themselves physically unattractive and who also are underweight (Page, 1993). Adolescent males who are shy were found to use illicit drugs more frequently than those who are not shy (Page, 1989).

Any successful drug education program recognizes that the best inoculation against drug use is an inoculation with positive self-esteem.

Risk factor 3: Being unable to resist peer pressure. **Peer pressure** is the pressure that young persons exert on other young persons to encourage them to make similar decisions or behave in similar ways. With regard to irresponsible and harmful drug use, peer pressure might be described as tactics some young persons use to encourage other young persons to use, buy, or sell drugs. There are several reasons that young persons might be vulnerable to peer pressure. The first is closely related to the risk factor previously discussed—negative self-esteem. When

within the family who are then at risk for drug use because they have inadequate skills for identifying and evaluating alternatives with regard to drug use.

Finally, significant adults in dysfunctional families usually have inadequate coping skills. When faced with difficult life crises, they may not have the perseverance needed to struggle and master the crises. They may choose the easy way of instant gratification. **Instant gratification** is choosing a benefit now rather than waiting until a more appropriate time. Obviously, an easy way to dull the pain of dealing with a life crisis is to numb the mind by using drugs. When young people observe adults handling a life

a young person has negative self-esteem, (s)he does not feel worthy or important. One way to feel better is to conform to what others are doing. In essence, peers are saying, "Be like us; use, buy, or sell drugs and you will be accepted." This logic is very persuasive when a young person feels inadequate.

A second reason that a young person might be unable to resist peer pressure focuses on his/her knowledge and skill in using resistance or refusal skills. Wanting to say NO and saying NO are two different issues. The first issue is one of judgment, whereas the second issue is one of assertiveness. A young person may not know how to say NO in an assertive manner and to stick to this decision. This is the reason the teaching of resistance skills or refusal skills is so necessary. Young persons need the opportunity to role-play situations in which they say NO so they can use the skills they have learned when they are in more threatening situations.

Educational efforts also must focus on helping young persons choose friends, particularly their friendship circles or "crowds" to which they belong. Crowd membership often indicates something about adolescents' attitudes toward alcohol and other drugs. While all adolescents are likely to be exposed to drugs, including alcohol, those who identify themselves as members of drug-oriented crowds (druggies, partyers) are at special risk for alcohol and other drug problems. While having one or more friends who use alcohol or other drugs is a significant risk factor, membership in a crowd that uses alcohol or other drugs to define its identity places young persons in the compromised position of having to continue to use alcohol or other drugs to maintain both a social network and a sense of self. For these young persons, giving up alcohol or other drugs may mean giving up a part of their identity.

Risk factor 4: Having difficulty mastering developmental tasks. Robert Havighurst, a sociologist, identified eight developmental tasks of adolescence (Havighurst, 1972):
1. achieving a new and more mature relationship with age-mates of both sexes;
2. achieving a masculine or feminine social role;
3. accepting one's physique and using the body effectively;
4. achieving emotional independence from parents and other adults;
5. preparing for marriage and family life;
6. preparing for an economic career;
7. acquiring a set of values and an ethical system as a guide to behavior—developing an ideology;
8. developing a social conscience.

During adolescence, young persons struggle to master each of these eight developmental tasks. It is essential that they are able to struggle and cope as they learn to master each. Young persons rely on coping skills, responsible decision-making skills, and the perseverance to delay gratification as they progress with the struggle of mastery. They also rely on responsible and nurturing adults to help them with this important process. If they lack skills needed to help them with the mastery of these developmental tasks and are without the support of nurturing adults, they are likely to step off the road of mastery and to become involved with self-destructive behaviors such as drug use.

Risk factor 5: Being economically disadvantaged. The term "high-risk youth" often is used to refer to the truly disadvantaged children in our society—those who are growing up in urban, crime-ridden environments under conditions of poverty, with parents ill-equipped to nurture them, and with little hope of breaking out of a vicious cycle of school failure, delinquency, drug use, teenage pregnancy, and chronic underemployment.

Census data can be used to locate entire districts of young persons who live in extreme poverty and who are likely to suffer disproportionately high levels of prenatal damage, poor health during infancy and childhood, malnutrition, and emotional and physical abuse and neglect. The mothers of these children are often isolated or impaired, lack a decent place to live, and often do not have access to either supportive schools or social services adequate for protecting their children from the effects of difficult life conditions.

Many children who grow up under this unfavorable scenario develop an interrelated pattern of problems in adolescence—doing poorly in school, dropping out, becoming teenage parents, becoming delinquent, and using alcohol and/or other drugs as part of a cycle of misery and hopelessness (Kazdin, 1993). The sheer volume of risk factors these youth endure puts them at high risk for alcohol and other drug problems. However, economic disadvantage places young persons at risk for drug involvement for a variety of reasons that go beyond the simple lack of money. The following factors are highly associated with both economic disadvantage and alcohol and/or other drug use:
1. frequent exposure to alcohol and/or other drug use by peer and adult models—especially if such exposure is accompanied by easy access to substances and pressure to use them;
2. frequent exposure to the sale and distribution of illegal substances by individuals who, through this trade, become models of economic success;

15

3. marital distress and family disruptions;
4. a crisis-laden existence that is experienced as inescapable, tense, and emotionally demanding—one from which alcohol and/or other drug use promises relief, however brief.

High-risk youth are certainly not restricted to those who have a lower socioeconomic status (Dougherty, 1993). However, the educational intervention for those youth who are economically disadvantaged must focus on helping them develop the skills to break out of the vicious cycle of school failure, delinquency, drug use, teenage pregnancy, and chronic underemployment.

Risk factor 6: Lacking faith experiences and fellowship. Youth who do not participate in their faith and who are not involved in fellowship are more at risk for drug use than those who participate and are involved. An obvious reason stands out. Those who do not participate in their faith, especially with their parents, are less likely to be close to their families. And those who are not involved in fellowship with their peers are less likely to have peers who participate in their faith.

But, there is another factor to consider. Participation in faith experiences and fellowship with others provides an important opportunity to examine behavior. Emphasis is placed on behavior that indicates character. This is added reinforcement for choosing a drug-free lifestyle.

Risk factor 7: Having a genetic background with a predisposition to chemical dependency. There is increasing evidence of a genetic predisposition to developing drug problems. As a group, children of parents with alcoholism are likely to show signs of alcohol dependence at a younger age, escalate their use more rapidly, and experience more serious dependence than peers whose parents do not have alcoholism. Studies of twins and the adopted children of biological parents with alcoholism confirm the inheritability of a predisposition to alcohol abuse. Children of parents with alcoholism may also be at substantial risk for other kinds of drug abuse. However, factors such as parenting skills and attitudes must be considered along with genetic vulnerabilty.

More than half of the persons who abuse alcohol and/or other drugs who are in inpatient treatment programs have a family history of alcohol and/or other drug abuse. The general average for vulnerability to alcoholism for all types of children is four to five times the risk for the general population. Sons of fathers with alcoholism may have up to nine times greater probabilty of having alcoholism than sons of fathers without alcoholism.

Children of drug-using parents appear to have a different physiological response to alcohol and/or other drugs compared to the offspring of nonusers. For some individuals, alcohol seems to have increased normalizing, stress reduction, and pleasurable effects. In addition, these individuals appear to experience fewer negative effects of intoxication from the same amount of drugs. Because of these unique effects, genetically-predisposed individuals may experience more reinforcement for continued use. If so, this would help explain a greater susceptibility to alcohol and/or other drug dependency.

Risk factor 8: Experiencing family disruption. The following facts portray some important changes in American families (Steinberg, 1991):
1. The majority of youngsters will spend some time in a single-parent household before the end of adolescence.
2. About half of all children will experience parental divorce or separation.
3. About one-fourth of all children will experience parental remarriage.
4. About one-eighth of all children will experience multiple parental divorces.
5. The vast majority of children will grow up with mothers who are employed outside of the home and, as a consequence, these children will have spent time in non-parental child care during infancy or early childhood.
6. A large number of children need supplementary care during afternoon hours of their elementary or middle school years.

Although a single-parent family is not necessarily dysfunctional, young persons living in single-parent families have only one adult role model living with them and one adult to manage their supervision. As a result, they do not have the opportunity to live with adults who interact in loving ways. They may spend periods of time at home alone without supervision. This is exacerbated by the fact that young persons living in single-parent families are much more likely to be living at poverty levels. Educational efforts in this instance might focus on opportunities for close relationships with adults, especially adults of the opposite sex from that of the parent with whom they are living. Creative ways to supervise these young persons also are important.

Risk factor 9: Experiencing depression. **Depression** is an emotional state characterized by a dysphoric mood, sleep disturbance, withdrawal of interest in environment, feelings of guilt, lack of energy, poor concentration or memory, loss of capacity to experience pleasure, appetite disturbance, and suicidal ideations (Gabe, 1989). **Comorbidity** is a term used by mental health professionals to indicate the presence of drug abuse in combination with a psychiatric illness. The comorbidity of drug abuse and depression is especially common (Belfer, 1993). Young persons may experience one of four types of depression (Gabe, 1989): major depression, physiological or endogenous depression, characterological or lifestyle depression, or depression resulting from chemical dependency.

Major depression is an emotional state that is usually a response to trauma or to a stressor, or a significant loss. The loss that precipitates the depression might be the loss of a parent's job, death of a friend or family member, divorce, change of school, or a move that the young person perceives to be very difficult. Major depression is not the result of drug use but may put a young person at risk for drug use. The young person perceives that drug use might numb the pain for a period of time. To alleviate this risk, educators might intervene and offer assistance when a young person experiences a loss. Discussing the feelings about the loss in a safe environment is important. Helping young persons set goals to move beyond the emotional crisis also is helpful.

Physiological depression or **endogenous depression** is an emotional state that results from physiological changes in the body. This type of depression may occur rapidly over a one-to-four week period with no precipitating event. Research indicates that physiological depression is more common in young persons from families with a history of depression. Young persons who experience physiological depression are at risk for drug-taking behavior because they believe drugs can help them get some control over their depression. They should be referred for psychiatric evaluation. Today, physiological depression is being treated successfully with a combination of medication and counseling.

Characterological depression or **lifestyle depression** is an emotional state characterized by an overriding negative view of the self, others, and life events. In order for depression to be described as characterological in nature, it must be interwoven into the personality and persist for at least one year. Young persons who suffer from characterological depression usually have learned this way of responding to stressors at an early age. They have usually been reared in dysfunctional families in which the expression of anger and hurt have not been tolerated. Often, they have experienced repeated trauma and depression.

This leads them to believe that everything, including relationships and most life events, will always turn out for the worse. They might be described as having catastrophic thinking. For example, a young person with characterological depression might do poorly on a test. This person might immediately assume (s)he will fail the course and not pass in school. This means in the future (s)he will not attend college and get a job. And, of course, no one will ever love him/her. What starts out as one life event, a poor grade on one test, is perceived as a series of failures.

Because young persons who suffer from characterological depression perceive that they have no control over future outcomes, they are at high risk for drug use. Mood-altering substances provide an escape from their perception of reality as punitive and unfulfilling. When they associate with other young persons who use drugs, this perception is reinforced. To dissuade them from being at risk for drug use, counseling is usually needed to help them address their attitudes and to modify the way they perceive themselves, others, and life events.

Depression resulting from chemical dependency is a kind of depression that surfaces during the recovery process. Young persons who are chemically dependent must face the significant losses that have occurred because of their prolonged and problematic substance abuse. When recovery first begins, these young persons begin to stop their denial and face their losses. Depression is common during this phase of recovery. Much support is needed at this time in order for the young person to cope with the feelings of loss that were previously denied. If support is not provided, the young person may return to drug use.

Risk factor 10: Experiencing pressure to succeed in athletics. Unfortunately, for some young persons, participation in athletics exceeds healthful boundaries. These young persons become vulnerable to drug use to enhance their performance. Examples might be used to illustrate how this might happen.

Suppose a young male has low self-esteem and does not feel connected to his family. Perhaps he does not communicate well with his father nor spend much quality time with him. Yet the father attends all of the son's football games. The young male is a very aggressive tackle on the football team. Even though he generally has low self-esteem, he temporarily feels good about himself when his name and number of tackles in the most recent game appear in the newspaper. He also feels a sense of importance knowing his father is in the stands watching him. When he is approached to use anabolic steroids to further enhance his performance, the internal message he hears is, "If I feel good getting X number of tackles, I will feel even better if I get 2X number of tackles." He says YES to drugs and says NO to health because he perceives a benefit to him—recognition from his father.

Suppose a young female is a star athlete in track at her school. She has the opportunity to win the 400 meter event in the state championships. Being the state champion in this event will almost guarantee that she will earn a scholarship to the college of her choice. A local drug pusher approaches her and offers her performance-enhancing drugs. She feels very anxious about the upcoming state championships. She loses her perspective and becomes vulnerable to drug use.

A final example might be that of a young male who has been reared in a climate of poverty. He sees no way out of this environment except to become a professional athlete. He has been encouraged to pursue athletics because he has already demonstrated that he is an adept basketball player. He idolizes some of the players in the NBA. A drug pusher lies and tells him that many of the players in the NBA rely on drugs to enhance their performance. Being young and naive, the young person believes this false information. He begins to believe that the road to success is through taking drugs. He is vulnerable to drug use as a result.

The aforementioned examples focus on youth who mistakenly believe they will receive benefits from drugs. These youth perceive that the benefits outweigh the risks. In each of the examples, there is faulty thinking. Drug education must focus on helping youth challenge perceived benefits derived from faulty thinking.

Risk factor 11: Having difficulty achieving success in school. **Able learners** are young persons who are able to master academics in standard ways without special help. These young persons have the ability to perform with a reasonable amount of success in school. Unfortunately, some young persons do not have that ability. A variety of reasons may explain their substandard performance. There may be personal situations such as an illness or divorce within the family. There may be so much pressure to perform well that they feel frozen and unable to respond well in the learning environment. Regardless of the reason, young persons who struggle with school performance are more at risk for drug use than their peers who are experiencing success in school. For this reason and other reasons, educators need to intervene whenever a young person's achievement is below his/her capabilities. It is

important to find out what the source of the problem is and how to alleviate it so that the young person returns to acceptable school performance.

Young persons who are learning disabled need special help and specific academic strategies in order to learn. To be **learning disabled** means to have difficulty learning a basic scholastic skill because of a disorder that interferes with the learning process. These young persons also need to learn coping strategies because their frustration level is frequently high. They often compare themselves to peers who do not experience difficulty learning.

Some young persons with learning disabilities experience added pressures because they become overly concerned with their future. These young persons are at risk for drug use in order to obtain temporary relief from their difficulties. It is important for educators to understand the needs of young persons with learning disabilities. These young persons need opportunities to relate with their peers in positive ways. They need support and encouragement in order to enhance self-esteem. They need to be integrated into school activities so that they do not feel left out or isolated.

Risk factor 12: Having attention deficit hyperactive disorder. Some young persons who are at risk for drug use have special conditions that require intervention and special direction. One of these conditions is attention deficit hyperactive disorder. Having immature character disorder and having borderline personality tendencies are risk factors discussed later in this chapter. Although the number of young persons with these conditions is small, educators need to understand the dynamics accompanying each in order to reduce the likelihood of drug use.

Attention deficit hyperactive disorder (ADHD) is a disorder characterized by difficulty in focusing attention, high levels of distractibility, problems with filtering out background stimuli, impulsivity, difficulty in delaying gratification, and frequent overarousal. ADHD is commonly believed to be caused by insufficient amounts of neurotransmitters that result in difficulty in auditory processing. There is a breakdown of communication within the brain system that results in these young persons having difficulty in processing information, retrieving auditory messages, auditory discrimination, and logical sequential thinking (Gabe, 1989).

Young persons with ADHD often have been reared in families with a history of alcoholism. One or both parents may have alcoholism and ADHD. The parents themselves are often frustrated, confused, and exhausted. They may admit the difficulty they have raising their child.

The behavior of young persons with ADHD is easy to describe: impulsiveness, difficulty in delaying gratification, short attention span, hyperactive behavior, frequently and easily overstimulated, accident prone, fidgety, and clumsy (Gabe, 1989). The impulsiveness may lead to inappropriate actions such as stealing and/or vandalism followed by denial and lying to cover up behavior.

Young persons with ADHD are usually very immature and have difficulty with their peers. As a result of their immaturity, they often associate with younger persons. Because of their impulsiveness and immaturity, they have difficulty in school. They experience difficulty in learning situations requiring logical sequential thinking, concentration, and auditory processing. Because of their difficulty in learning, they may be placed in special learning environments. In school, they may require an individual education plan (IEP). They may be grouped into classes with other students who experience difficulty in learning. As a result, these young persons may have fewer opportunitites to develop relationships with peers who are experiencing success in school.

Young persons with ADHD are often depressed. Their feelings of failure may be accompanied by bursts of anger. This is often followed by guilt and remorse about their behavior and a desire to relate well with others. Young persons with ADHD want to be connected to others. They usually have a healthful value system and demonstrate compassion for others.

Having information about young persons with ADHD provides educators with clues as to why these students might be at risk for drug use. Several factors play a role: impulsiveness, difficulty in delaying gratification, dishonesty, immature behavior, negative peer interaction, difficulty in school, and bouts of depression. It is important to assist these youth in developing skills to protect them from being vulnerable to drug use. Providing structure and routine is important in alleviating distraction. Allowing enough time for these young persons to process information is important. Using positive rewards instead of punishments helps bolster self-esteem.

Providing opportunities for positive peer interaction both in and outside the classroom is especially important. Being certain to assign specific tasks to these young persons is a necessity.

Risk factor 13: Having immature character disorder. **Immature character disorder** is a condition in which young persons display maladaptive personality characteristics as indicated by a chronic history of antisocial behavior; difficulty maintaining close, compassionate relationships; and refusal to accept the responsibility for the consequences of their behavior. They have a history of inappropriate behavior in which they have broken rules. They tend to choose thrill-seeking experiences. It is not uncommon for them to become involved in shoplifting, reckless driving, speeding, burglary, and cruelty to animals and small children. They are dishonest and lie about what they have done.

Young persons with immature character disorder have difficulty connecting with others. They are not usually warm. When they initiate relationships, they usually are not able to maintain them. Although they are able to perform academically, they often view school as a waste of time and are easily bored and often truant.

Youth with immature character disorder have difficulty with the expression of emotions. They often are unsure of how they feel and imitate the feelings of others. They are very narcissistic and seek immediate gratification rather than struggle. Their narcissism is reflected in their poorly developed value system; they have little regard for the rights and feelings of others.

Many of these young persons were reared in dysfunctional families in which parents and/or significant adults did not adequately nurture them. They may have been overindulged and, as a result, did not learn ways to handle frustration. They are not prepared for relationships or for coping with difficult situations.

It is easy to understand why young persons with immature character disorder are at risk for drug use. They want to engage in behaviors that result in thrill seeking and escaping. Professional help is required to change this behavior. These young persons need to learn a strong value system, responsible decision-making skills, relationship skills, and to develop positive self-esteem. In most cases, the young person's entire family needs professional help if there is to be any change.

Risk factor 14: Having borderline personality tendencies. **Borderline personality tendencies** is a condition in which young persons do not have a stable identity and, as a result, feel an internal void accompanied by deep depression. Most young persons with borderline personality tendencies are female. They may have been reared in a family in which the mother had borderline personality tendencies. Thus, the mother had difficulty establishing identity and now the daughter has the same difficulty.

Other females with borderline personality tendencies may have been reared in a family in which there was a history of traumatic loss and in which there was no tolerance for autonomy and personal identity. As a result, these females have difficulty with their identity. This lack of identity makes it difficult for them to internalize a personal value system. They feel an internal void and become overwhelmed by day-to-day tasks. They may turn to compulsive behaviors such as shopping, eating disorders, addictive relationships, and drugs to compensate for the internal void. They often develop highly dependent relationships yet they fear being engulfed and overwhelmed at the same time. They struggle with intimacy.

It is quite obvious why young persons with borderline personality tendencies may seek drug-taking behaviors. Professional help is needed for a variety of issues in order to prevent these young persons from being at risk.

To summarize, there are numerous protective factors and risk factors that influence drug use. Educators need to be aware of both in order to be effective.

PREVALENCE OF DRUG USE BY YOUTH OF ALL AGES

Despite some reports that drug use is declining, the United States suffers from one of the highest rates of adolescent and young adult substance use in the industrialized world (Johnston, O'Malley, & Bachman, 1991; Kandel & Davies, 1991). The use of drugs is widespread among young people and drug use often begins in the elementary and middle grades (Bush & Iannotti, 1993; Vega et al., 1993). This section of the chapter will examine the prevalence of drug use by young persons and will include discussions of drug use by elementary and middle/junior high youth, drug use by high school youth, demographic factors associated with drug use, and racial/ethnic differences associated with drug use.

Drug Use by Elementary and Middle/Junior High Youth

Today, children begin drinking at an earlier average age than they did in the past. Currently, many children have their first drinking experience at about age 12. In the 1940s and 1950s, the average age for starting to drink was 13 to 14 (Gordon & McAlister, 1982; Kassebaum, 1990). Among eighth graders who have used alcohol, more than

half (55 percent) report first use by grade six (American School Health Association, Association for Advancement of Health Education, & Society for Public Health Education, 1989).

About three-fourths (77 percent) of eighth graders report having used alcohol in their lifetime and one-third within the previous month (ASHA, AAHE, & SOPHE, 1989). More than one-fourth of eighth grade students say that they have had five or more drinks on a single occasion with the past two weeks (Marwick, 1988).

The following findings describing drug use by eighth graders are from the National Adolescent Health Survey (ASHA, AAHE, and SOPHE, 1989):
- More than half (51 percent) report having tried cigarettes, and 16 percent smoke cigarettes regularly;
- 15 percent report having tried marijuana;
- Of students using marijuana, 44 percent tried it for the first time by sixth grade;
- One in five (21 percent) report having used inhalants;
- 61 percent of inhalant users report first use by sixth grade;
- 5 percent report having tried cocaine and approximately 2 percent have tried crack;
- 84 percent report that it is easy to get alcohol;
- 57 percent report that it is easy to get marijuana;
- 27 percent report that it is easy to get cocaine.

Information regarding the prevalence of drug use among elementary school students is scant. However, pressure to use drugs begins early (National Commission on Drug-Free Schools, 1990). An elementary school survey conducted by the National Parents' Resource Institute for Drug Education (1988) revealed that pressure to use substances begins around the fourth grade. Between fourth and sixth grades, reported experimentation with alcohol (usually beer and wine coolers) increased from 6 percent to 17 percent. Also, nearly 2 percent of sixth graders reported having experimented with marijuana and 5 percent of students in grades seven to nine were daily tobacco users.

Children in grades four through six felt that the most important reason for using alcohol and marijuana was to "fit in with others," followed by the "desire to feel older" (Weekly Reader Publications, 1987). Over 30 percent of sixth graders reported peer pressure to try cocaine or crack and marijuana. About 45 percent felt peer pressure to try wine coolers, and more than half felt pressure to drink beer or wine and to smoke cigarettes. This survey also revealed that students in fourth through sixth grades felt

20

that television and movies made alcohol and other drugs seem attractive.

Drug Use by High School Youth

In a recent national school-based survey, the Youth Risk Behavior Survey (Centers for Disease Control, 1991), over 11,000 U.S. high school students were asked if they had used marijuana, alcohol, and any form of cocaine during their lifetime and during the 30 days preceding the survey (current use). Students in grades 9–12 were also asked if during the 30 days preceding the survey they had had five or more drinks on one occasion. Results from this survey are presented in Table 1-9 and Table 1-10.

Overall, nearly nine of ten high school youth (88.1 percent) reported ever drinking alcohol (lifetime use) and six of ten (58.6 percent) reported drinking alcohol at least once within the past 30 days prior to the survey (current use). Current and lifetime use of alcohol increased with grade level. For example, the proportion of current users of alcohol increased from half (50.1 percent) of 9th graders to nearly two-thirds of 12th graders (65.6 percent). Male students (62.2 percent) were more likely to report current alcohol use than female students (55.0 percent).

Heavy drinking (consuming five or more drinks of alcohol on at least one occasion during the 30 days preceding the survey) was reported by 36.9 percent of high school students. Heavy drinking was more common for male students (43.5 percent) than for female students (30.4 percent). Heavy drinking also increased by grade level. Of 9th graders, 27.7 percent reported heavy drinking. The proportion of heavy drinkers increased to 35.7 percent of 10th graders, 39.6 percent of 11th graders, and 44.0 percent of 12th graders.

Current use of marijuana in this national sample of 9th to 12th graders was reported by 13.9 percent of students, and lifetime use was reported by 31.4 percent of the students. Current cocaine use was reported by 2.1 percent of all students, and lifetime use by 6.6 percent of students. A higher percentage of males used these two substances than females. The use of cocaine and marijuana also was more common among students in the highest grades.

One drawback of school-based drug-use surveys, such as the Youth Risk Behavior Survey, is the underrepresentation of school dropouts as well as students who are chronically absent, are in juvenile detention centers, or are homeless or runaways. Drug-use rates among these underrepresented groups appear to be higher than among

Table 1-9
High School Students* Reporting Lifetime Use of Substances by Gender and Grade—1990 Youth Risk Behavior Survey

Student Category	Substance		
	Alcohol (%)	Marijuana (%)	Cocaine (%)
Gender			
Male	89.5	35.9	8.1
Female	86.7	27.0	5.2
Grade			
9th	82.6	20.6	3.6
10th	87.0	27.9	5.8
11th	90.1	34.7	7.6
12th	92.4	42.2	9.3
Total	88.1	31.4	6.6

Source: Centers for Disease Control. (1991). Alcohol and other drug use among high schools students—United States, 1990. *Morbidity and Mortality Weekly Report*, 40:776–777.
*Unweighted sample size = 11,631 students in grades 9–12.

those in school populations of adolescents (USDHHS, 1991). Thus, the reported figures are likely to underestimate actual use in the total adolescent population (Morrison, 1991).

Demographic Factors Associated with Drug Use

A number of demographic factors are associated with drug use. Age and gender are key demographic factors for young people.

Age. Involvement with substances becomes increasingly likely as children approach adolescence. A most important predictor of risk for drug abuse is age at initial use. Use initiated before the age of 15 is a major risk factor for serious drug-abuse problems. Onset of use after that time is associated with fewer problems and a greater likelihood that individuals will discontinue use on their own.

Adolescent drug use follows a predictable developmental sequence, such that earlier stages in the sequence predict later stages. Alcohol use typically precedes marijuana use which, in turn, precedes use of other illicit drugs. Yet, despite the rather high prevalence of substance use among

Table 1-10
High School Students* Reporting Current[a] Use of Substances by Gender and Grade—1990 Youth Risk Behavior Survey

Student Category	Substance			
	Alcohol (%)	Heavy Drinking[b] (%)	Marijuana (%)	Cocaine (%)
Gender				
Male	62.2	43.5	16.9	3.3
Female	55.0	30.4	11.1	1.0
Grade				
9th	50.1	27.7	9.5	1.1
10th	57.0	35.7	13.5	2.4
11th	61.2	39.6	13.9	2.5
12th	65.6	44.0	18.5	2.3
Total	58.6	36.9	13.9	2.1

Source: Centers for Disease Control. (1991). Alcohol and other drug use among high schools students—United States, 1990. *Morbidity and Mortality Weekly Report*, 40:776–777.
*Unweighted sample size = 11,631 students in grades 9–12.
[a] Use during the 30 days preceding the survey.
[b] Consumed five or more drinks on at least one occasion during the 30 days preceding the survey.

youth, only a small percentage of adolescents go on to become abusers.

Young adults ages 18–29 years use alcohol and drugs more than any other age group. One exception to this is alcohol use among African-Americans. Young adult African-Americans use less alcohol than their parents or grandparents. It has been proposed that this may occur because parents are "second generation" African-Americans who moved to the city and had few opportunities for good housing and jobs. The young adults now are "third generation" African-Americans with better community connections and opportunities.

Gender. In general, higher percentages of males than females are involved in adolescent illicit drug use, especially heavy drug use. Overall, the percentage of those ever having used marijuana is only slightly higher among males, but daily use of marijuana is three times as frequent among males. Adolescent males also have considerably higher prevalence rates of most other illicit drugs. Annual prevalence rates tend to be one and one-half to two and one-half times as high among males as among females for nitrites, LSD, PCP, heroin, cocaine and crack cocaine, inhalants, and ice. Also, males report much higher use rates of steroids than females. Compared to females, males report somewhat higher rates of use for opiates other

than heroin, barbiturates, and stimulants. Only in the case of tranquilizers and methaqualone do the annual prevalence rates for females match or exceed those for males (Johnston, O'Malley, & Bachman, 1991).

Frequent use of alcohol tends to be disproportionately concentrated among males. Daily use, for example, is reported by 5.2 percent of high school senior males compared with only 1.9 percent of females. Also, males are more likely than females to drink large quantities of alcohol on a single occasion; 39 percent of males report taking five or more drinks in the past two weeks compared with 25 percent of females (Johnston, O'Malley, & Bachman, 1991).

In recent years, there were modest sex differences in smoking rates among high school seniors, with more females smoking. Although equivalent proportions of both sexes report any smoking in the past month (29 percent), slightly more males report smoking at the rate of half pack or more per day than females (11.6 percent vs. 10.8 percent) (Johnston, O'Malley, & Bachman, 1991).

Racial/Ethnic Differences Associated with Drug Use

Drug use prevalence varies across adolescent racial/ethnic groups. American Indian high school seniors report the highest prevalence rates for most illicit drugs, alcohol, and cigarettes. White American students report the next highest rates for use of most drugs. The lowest rates of use are among Asian-American youth, with African-American youth next to the lowest (except for marijuana). For the most part, substance use prevalence among Hispanic/Latino youth is in the intermediary range. One exception, however, is the relatively high level of cocaine use among Hispanic males (Bachman et al., 1991). Prevalence figures among adolescents for alcohol, marijuana, and cocaine use for each of these racial/ethnic groups are included in Table 1-11 and Table 1-12. Racial and ethnic differences in drug-use frequency, however, are often obscured by differences in social and environmental differences (Fullilove, 1993; Lillie-Blanton et al., 1993). This needs to be kept in mind when examining the following data.

Drug use by African-American youth. Several national and local surveys have shown lower rates of youth drug use among African-Americans than white Americans (Edmonds, 1990; Page & Allen, 1993). Lower use by African-American youth than white American youth contrast with the fact that African-American youth are overrepresented in public drug treatment programs, hospital admissions for drug problems, drug-related mortality, and arrests with drug-positive urine samples. Rates of drug use by African-American youth do not appear to exceed those of white Americans until middle adulthood (Bachman et al., 1991). Thus, it is possible that there is a greater frequency of late-onset drug-abuse behaviors on the part of African-

Americans. A recent study of sixth and seventh grade students showed that although African-American students had lower lifetime prevalence of drug use than white American and Hispanic students, they had a higher prevalence of drug use risk factors (Vega et al., 1993).

One explanation for lower rates of reported drug use by African-American youth could be greater inclination to provide socially desirable responses to survey questions about drug use than white American (majority) youth. African-American youth may feel more threatened by the perceived consequences of their acknowledgment of drug use. Further, they may have less trust in researchers (Mensch & Kandel, 1988). The current findings regarding low rates of drug use among African-American youth might be summarized as follows (Bachman et al., 1991):

. . . we are confronted with (at least) two worlds of drug-use data. On the one hand, the findings from general population and school-based surveys clearly and consistently show relatively low levels of drug use by most non-white youth, especially African-Americans and Asian-Americans. On the other hand, the public health statistics on mortality, morbidity, and treatment provide a somewhat different perspective. So perhaps our most important conclusion must be that neither form of data provides a complete picture of drug use. However, that should not overshadow the other important conclusion: the majority of non-white youth do complete high school,

Table 1-11
Use of Alcohol, Marijuana, and Cocaine in the Past 30 Days by Male High School Seniors*

| | *Substance* | | | |
Group	Alcohol (%)	Heavy Drinking[a] (%)	Marijuana (%)	Cocaine (%)
White American Males	72.3	48.1	25.0	5.6
African-American Males	49.2	24.0	18.5	2.6
Mexican-American Males	65.0	45.3	22.0	8.2
Puerto Rican & Other Latin-American Males	55.4	31.4	18.9	8.1
Asian-American Males	43.7	19.4	9.7	1.8
American Indian Males	69.0	48.1	27.6	7.3

Source: Adapted from Bachman, J.G., Wallace, J.M., O'Malley, P.M., Johnston, L.D., Kurth, C.L., and Neighbors, H.W. (1991) Racial/ethnic differences in smoking, drinking, and illicit drug use among American high school seniors, 1976–89. *American Journal of Public Health*, 81:372–377.

*The sample for this data consists of 73,527 high school seniors from the Monitoring the Future project conducted by the University of Michigan's Institute for Social Research. This data reflects the results of annual, nationally representative surveys conducted 1985–1989.

[a]Had five or more drinks in a row in the last two weeks.

Table 1-12
Use of Alcohol, Marijuana, and Cocaine in the Past 30 Days by Female High School Seniors*

	Substance			
Group	Alcohol (%)	Heavy Drinking[a] (%)	Marijuana (%)	Cocaine (%)
White American Females	66.6	31.3	19.8	4.1
African-American Females	32.8	9.3	9.9	1.3
Mexican-American Females	50.5	23.6	13.6	3.0
Puerto Rican & Other Latin-American Females	43.0	14.5	9.6	2.9
Asian-American Females	34.2	10.7	8.1	2.6
American Indian Females	60.2	33.7	23.9	9.2

Source: Adapted from Bachman, J.G., Wallace, J.M., O'Malley, P.M., Johnston, L.D., Kurth, C.L., and Neighbors, H.W. (1991) Racial/ethnic differences in smoking, drinking, and illicit drug use among American high school seniors, 1976–89. *American Journal of Public Health,* 81:372–377.

*The sample for this data consists of 73,527 high school seniors from the Monitoring the Future project conducted by the University of Michigan's Institute for Social Research. This data reflects the results of annual, nationally representative surveys conducted 1985–1989.

[a]Had five or more drinks in a row in the last two weeks.

and among most of these individuals, usage rates for both illicit and licit drugs are lower than average.

Drug use by Asian-American youth. The term "Asian-American" encompasses a diverse population of peoples who come from Japan, China, Korea, India, the Philippines, Vietnam, and other Asian countries. Thus, the label Asian-American is an oversimplification because it represents more than 60 disparate ethnic subgroups with differing nationalities, languages, cultures, religions, customs, and histories. Asian-Americans are one of the nation's fastest-growing ethnic groups and are expected to comprise 4 percent of the total U.S. population by the year 2000. Those born within the U.S. and established there for generations are virtually undistinguishable from the population as a whole. Two-thirds of Asian-Americans are foreign-born.

There is little data on the prevalence of drug use among Asian-Americans and more particularly on Asian-American youth. The limited data that does exist hints that relative to other groups, Asian-American youth report very low levels of drug use (Table 1-11 and Table 1-12). Among high school seniors, substantially lower proportions of Asian-American males used cocaine, marijuana, and alcohol than white American, African-American, Hispanic, and American Indian males. Low levels of drug use also were reported by Asian-American females relative to other racial/ethnic groups. Because of lower-than-average dropout rates among Asian-Americans, there appears to be a higher proportion of Asian-

American youth who were surveyed as high school seniors. Thus it is possible that Asian-Americans might even have lower drug-use rates compared to other groups when taking into account the higher dropout rates of these groups (Bachman et al., 1991). There is a definite need for research to delineate drug-use patterns among the various and diverse groups that comprise the Asian-American population.

One study showed lower use rates of heroin, PCP, amphetamines, and Valium among Chinese-American youth than other groups. However, Chinese-American youth reported using Quaaludes twice as often as white American and Hispanic/Latino youth, and five times as often as African-American youth (Austin, Lee, & Prendergast, 1989).

Asian-Americans as a whole have the lowest level of alcohol consumption and alcohol-related problems of all the major racial/ethnic groups. This low rate of alcohol consumption and abuse may be attributed partly to cultural factors and partly to the flushing response, which occurs in a high proportion of Asian peoples. This physiological reaction is characterized by facial flushing, headaches, dizziness, rapid heart rate, itching, and other discomforting symptoms. Traditionally, drinking among Asians takes place in a controlled setting and rarely do Asians drink alone. Moderation is strongly encouraged (Chi, Lubben, & Kitano, 1989; National Institute on Alcohol Abuse, 1990). Some researchers contend that alcohol and other drug problems may be greater than what is reported in surveys or indicated by the number entering drug-treatment services. Thus, drug-prevention programs should attempt to lower the stigma that Asian-Americans may attach to seeking professional help (Austin, Lee, & Prendergast, 1989).

Drug-prevention programs also need to consider the several hurdles that Asian-American youth face when they immigrate to the United States. Under great pressure to succeed, they may have limited language and social skills. Conflicts often arise as Asian-American youth become "Americanized" more quickly than their parents. Some youth may turn to alcohol and other drugs in response to the stress they experience in adjusting to a new culture. As a result, these youth need adequate support as they learn strategies for dealing with acculturation problems (Austin, Lee, and Prendergast, 1989).

Drug use by Hispanic/Latino youth. The proportion of Hispanic/Latino youth who drink alcohol is similar to that of white American youth. However, there is evidence that the Hispanic/Latino youth who do drink, drink larger quantities as they grow older, subsequently causing more drinking problems. Despite increases in drinking among Hispanic/Latino females, Hispanic/Latino males are more likely to begin drinking at a younger age and to drink more heavily than Hispanic/Latino females. If current trends continue, the gender gap in drinking between Hispanic/Latino males and females may shrink.

With regard to other drugs, it appears that the level of use is comparable to, or just below, that of white American youth. However, Hispanic/Latino youth are more likely to have tried cocaine than white American or African-American youth. Also, as with alcohol, Hispanic/Latino youth are more likely than white American youth to experience problems related to drug use.

Machismo among Hispanic/Latinos is culturally-expected conduct for males. Generally, males are expected to be dominant, strong, protective, brave, and authoritarian. Although several of these cultural characteristics are positive, the ideal of machismo for many Hispanic/Latino males also includes drinking large quantities of alcohol without showing ill effects—"holding liquor like a man." Even though heavy drinking is often considered masculine by Hispanics/Latinos, alcoholism is usually viewed as a weakness in moral character when it entails a loss of self-control (Office of Substance Abuse Prevention, 1990).

Conversely, Hispanic/Latino females are expected to abstain or drink very lightly, if they drink at all. The cultural expectation for Hispanic/Latino females has been

for them to act like virtuous ladies—to submit to the males in their lives and to serve their families selflessly. Traditionally, drinking has been seen as a behavior verging on impropriety. Since females are to be very moral, it is not surprising that Hispanic/Latino females are more likely than white American and African-American females to abstain from alcohol use. Of those who drink, the vast majority are light drinkers. However, this situation is changing as Hispanic/Latino females undergo acculturation or adjustment to U.S. society (Office of Substance Abuse Prevention, 1990).

The few studies on Hispanic/Latinos' knowledge, attitudes, or practices concerning alcohol and other drugs indicate that (Bogan, 1991):

- Hispanic/Latinos in general may have lower rates than non-Hispanic white Americans of lifetime use of alcohol, PCP, hallucinogens, and stimulants;
- Hispanic/Latino youth ages 12–17 may have higher rates of cocaine use than non-Hispanic youth of the same age;
- Puerto Rican and Cuban youth may have the highest rates of cocaine use among Hispanic/Latinos;
- Mexican-American youth ages 12–17 may have higher rates of marijuana use than non-Hispanic white Americans;
- Hispanic/Latino children have extensive exposure at an early age to alcohol and other drug use;
- Younger Hispanic/Latino females in general use alcohol much less than Hispanic/Latino males;
- Younger Hispanic/Latino females use alcohol more than the females in their parents' generation, perhaps as a result of acculturation;
- Hispanic/Latinos often feel that drinking is an innocent way to celebrate and have fun;
- At the same time, Hispanic/Latinos may believe that drinking is a primary cause of inappropriate behavior.

Drug use by American Indian youth. American Indian youth experience high rates of drug use in comparison to other racial/ethnic groups of youth (Table 1-11 and Table 1-12). Among American Indians, alcohol and other drug abuse results in large numbers of preventable deaths, injuries, and illnesses, especially among adolescents and young adults. Most tribes consider alcohol and other drug problems to be their most important health issue.

Drinking is prevalent among American Indian adolescents and even younger American Indian children. Heavy drinking is also prevalent among American Indian youth; reports of blacking out or being extremley intoxicated are common. American Indians have the highest prevalence of alcohol problems among U.S. population groups. Therefore, it is not surprising that the rate of alcohol-related birth defects is higher among American Indians than any other racial/ethnic group. Despite this, it is important to remember that many American Indians do not drink at all or drink very little. Also, there are marked intertribal differences in alcohol-consumption patterns and rates of alcohol-related health problems, such as cirrhosis of the liver and fetal alcohol syndrome (Office of Substance Abuse Prevention, 1989).

Another substance abuse problem among American Indian youth that is of concern is a high rate of inhalant use. Inhalants are among the easiest mind-altering drugs to obtain. In addition, inhalants are cheap and reportedly offer a "high" of short duration, making it possible for users to experience several "highs" in a brief period of time. A few American Indian children as young as six years of age report using inhalants, although the usual age to start is about ten years of age. The dangers of inhalant drugs are discussed in Chapter 9.

Drug use by white American youth. Any beliefs that substance use is restricted to minority youth are erroneous. Table 1-11 and Table 1-12 present data showing that high proportions of white American youth use alcohol and drugs relative to African-American, Hispanic/Latino, and Asian-American youth. The high prevalence of white American youth who drink alcohol illustrates the prominent degree to which drug use, especially alcohol use, is ingrained and embedded into the majority youth culture. It will be discouraging if the acculturation of minority groups leads to an acculturation to higher alcohol and other drug use to the normative levels of the majority youth culture.

We have discussed the possibility of differences in tendencies between white American and minority youth in divulging drug-use behavior to researchers. Thus, it is plausible that a factor in explaining higher drug use by white American youth could be reporting differences. Another factor that needs to be investigated by researchers is the degree to which absenteeism and dropping out of school influences school-based drug surveys.

Society cannot afford to be misled into regarding drug use as a minority problem. Substance use and abuse affects youth from all demographic and socio-economic sectors of society. Those who maintain a view that substance abuse is some other group's problem are sadly wrong. No community or school is immune. Substance abuse destroys the lives of young people, affecting youth of all walks of life.

To summarize, drug use by young persons in the elementary, middle/junior high, and high school is a challenging problem for educators. Awareness of the prevalence of drug use forces educators to give drug education a top priority. Understanding racial/ethnic differences in drug use helps educators provide the best interventions possible.

PROMOTING DRUG-FREE YOUTH

One aim of the National Education Goals is to have every school in the United States free of drugs as a means of offering school environments that are conducive to learning by the year 2000 (National Education Goals Panel, 1991). Several of the year 2000 national health objectives target reductions in the use of alcohol and other drugs (United States Department of Health and Human Services, 1991). These objectives include:

- increasing the average age of first use of addictive substances;
- reducing occasions of heavy drinking by young people;
- reducing use of alcohol, marijuana, and cocaine by school age children and youth ages 18–25;
- reducing alcohol-related motor vehicle crash deaths;
- increasing awareness of the harmful effects of addictive substances;
- facilitating better access to treatment services;
- policy development and implementation to reduce minors' access to alcohol.

How might this overwhelming task be accomplished? What type of educational program might be implemented to promote drug-free youth and drug-free schools? This section of the chapter discusses drug education that focuses on inner well-being and describes the organization and purpose of this book.

Drug Education and Inner Well-Being

Drug education must provide skills that enable young persons to become strong, have a sense of self, and resist external pressures. In developing a concrete philosophy for drug education and the drug-education curriculum, the authors of this book have given these thoughts much consideration.

Thus, the authors have developed a drug-education program/curriculum that includes content, objectives, life skills and totally awesome teaching strategies that focus on helping young persons become actively involved in developing inner well-being (Fig. 1-13). **Inner well-being** is a condition that results from:

- having positive self-esteem,
- managing stress effectively,

Figure 1-13
Drug Education and Inner Well-Being

Inner well-being is a condition that results from:

* Having positive self-esteem
* Managing stress effectively
* Choosing healthful behaviors
* Choosing healthful situations
* Engaging in healthful relationships

* Making responsible decisions
* Using resistance skills when appropriate
* Demonstrating character
* Participating in the community
* Abiding by laws

---

* choosing healthful behaviors,
* choosing healthful situations,
* engaging in healthful relationships,
* making responsible decisions,
* using resistance skills when appropriate,
* demonstrating character,
* participating in the community,
* abiding by laws.

About This Book

This book is designed for drug education professionals who are engaged in helping young persons develop inner well-being and choose a drug-free and drug-informed lifestyle. A **drug-free lifestyle** refers to a lifestyle in which persons do not use harmful and illegal drugs. A **drug-informed lifestyle** refers to a lifestyle in which persons

use legal drugs such as over-the-counter drugs and medicines according to directions.

This book is divided into five sections:
* Section 1: Drugs and Wellness,
* Section 2: Drugs: A Factual Account,
* Section 3: Alcohol, Tobacco, and Well-Being,
* Section 4: Prevention and Treatment of Drug Abuse,
* Section 5: Drug Education: Curriculum and Teaching Strategies.

Section 1: Drugs and Wellness focuses on philosophy and includes discussions of promoting responsible and healthful behavior with regard to drugs and promoting respectful, nonviolent relationships. These discussions help the drug professional gain insight into the purposes of education for a drug-free and drug-responsible lifestyle and a nonviolent lifestyle.

Section 2: Drugs: A Factual Account provides factual information for the professional on several topics: drug actions and reactions, stimulant drugs, sedative-hypnotic drugs, narcotics, marijuana, hallucinogens, inhalants, over-the-counter drugs, prescription drugs, and anabolic steroids.

Section 3: Alcohol, Tobacco, and Well-Being focuses on factual information regarding alcohol and tobacco. These two drugs are included in a separate part of the book because of their widespread use.

Section 4: Prevention and Treatment of Drug Abuse focuses on factual information regarding strategies for prevention and various treatment models. Prevention is key in order to influence young persons not to begin to use harmful drugs. Treatment is highlighted in order to examine ways

to assist those young persons who have used harmful drugs and need to recover and plan a new lifestyle.

Section 5: Drug Education: Curriculum and Teaching Strategies contains everything the professional needs to implement a curriculum that helps young persons develop inner well-being and a lifestyle that is drug free, drug informed, and nonviolent. A framework for a drug curriculum that can be used by a school district is presented. Suggestions for implementing this curriculum include the use of totally awesome teaching strategies, blackline masters, and student handouts. Suggestions for implementing the curriculum through infusion into health, language arts, mathematics, science, social studies, art, and music are included. Infusion brings a broader mix of teachers into the drug-education program and reinforces the importance of teaching young persons skills they need in order to be drug free, drug informed, and nonviolent. Many of the strategies contain suggestions for inclusion of students with special needs and infusion of multicultural education.

BIBLIOGRAPHY

American School Health Association, Association for Advancement of Health Education, and Society for Public Health Education. (1989) *The National Adolescent Health Survey: A Report of the Health of America's Youth.* Oakland, CA: Third Party Publishers.

Austin, G.A., Lee, H.H., & Prendergast, M.L. (1989) *Substance Abuse Among Asian-American Youth: Prevention Research Update Number 5.* Los Alimitos, CA: Western Center for Drug-Free Schools and Communities.

Bachman, J.G., Wallace, J.M., O'Malley, P.M., Johnston, L.D., Kurth, C.L., & Neighbors, H.W. (1991) Racial/ethnic differences in smoking, drinking, and illicit drug use among high school seniors, 1976–1989. *American Journal of Public Health*, 81:372–377.

Belfer, M.L. (1993) Substance abuse with psychiatric illness in children and adolescents: Definitions and terminology. *American Journal of Orthopsychiatry*, 63:70–79.

Bogan, W.A. (1991) Reaching Hispanic/Latino youth. *Communicating About Alcohol and Other Drugs: Strategies for Reaching Populations at Risk.* In E.B. Arkinand & J.E. Funkhouser (Eds.), 171–209. Office for Substance Abuse Prevention Monograph-5. DHHS Publication No. (ADM)90-1665. Washington, D.C.: U.S. Government Printing Office.

Bush, P.J., Iannotti, R.J. (1993) Alcohol, cigarette, and marijuana use among fourth-grade urban schoolchildren in 1988/1989 and 1990/1991. *American Journal of Public Health*, 83:111–114.

Centers for Disease Control. (1991) Alcohol and other drug use among high school students—United States, 1990. *Morbidity and Mortality Weekly Report*, 40:776–777, 783–784.

Cermak, T.L. (1986) *Diagnosing and Treating Co-Dependence.* Minneapolis: Johnson Institute Books.

Chi, I., Lubben, J.E., & Kitano, H.H. (1989) Differences in drinking behavior among three Asian-American groups. *Journal of Studies on Alcohol*, 50:15–33.

Dougherty, D. (1993) Adolescent health: Reflections on a report to the U.S. Congress. *American Psychologist*, 48:193–201.

Edmonds, J.T. (1990) Reaching black inner-city youth. *Communicating About Alcohol and Other Drugs: Strategies for Reaching Populations at Risk.* In E.B. Arkinand & J.E. Funkhouser (Eds.), 121–170. Office for Substance Abuse Prevention Monograph-5. DHHS Publication No. (ADM)90-1665. Washington, D.C.: U.S. Government Printing Office.

Fullilove, M.T. (1993) Perceptions and misperceptions of race and drug use. *Journal of the American Medical Association*, 269:1034.

Gabe, Janice. (1989) *A Professional's Guide to Adolescent Substance Abuse.* Springfield, IL: Academy of Addictions Treatment Professionals.

Gordon, N.P., & McAlister, A. (1982) Adolescent drinking: Issues and research. *Promoting Adolescent Health: A Dialogue in Research and Practice.* In T. Coates (Ed.), 201–210. New York: Academic Press.

Havighurst, R. (1972) *Developmental Tasks and Education.* New York: David McKay Company, Inc.

Johnston, L.D., O'Malley, P.M., & Bachman, J.G. (1991). *Drug Use Among American High School Seniors, College Students, and Young Adults, 1975–1990.* DHHS Publication No. (ADM)91-1813. Washington, D.C.: National Institute of Drug Abuse.

Kandel, D.B., & Davies, M. (1991) Decline in the use of illicit drugs by high school students in New York State: A comparison with national data. *American Journal of Public Health,* 81:1064–1067.

Kandel, D.B., & Yamaguchi, K. (1985) Developmental patterns of the use of legal, illegal, and medically prescribed psychotropic drugs from adolescence to young adulthood. *Etiology of Drug Abuse: Implications for Prevention.* In C.L. Jones and R.J. Battjes (Eds.), 193–120. NIDA Research Monograph 56. DHHS Publication No. (ADM)85-1335. Washington, D.C.: U.S. Government Printing Office.

Kassebaum, P. (1990) Reaching families and youth from high-risk environments. *Communicating About Alcohol and Other Drugs: Strategies for Reaching Populations at Risk.* In C.L. Jones & R.J. Battjes (Eds.), 11–120. Office for Substance Abuse Prevention Monograph-5. DHHS Publication No. (ADM)90-1665. Washington, D.C.: U.S. Government Printing Office.

Kazdin, A.E. (1993) Adolescent mental health: Prevention and treatment programs. *American Psychologist,* 48:127–141.

Kübler-Ross, Elisabeth. (1975) *Death: The Final Stage of Growth.* Englewood Cliffs, NJ: Prentice Hall.

Lillie-Blanton, M., Anthony, J.C., & Schuster, C.R. (1993) Probing the meaning of racial/ethnic group comparisons in crack cocaine smoking. *Journal of the American Medical Association,* 269:993–997.

Marwick, C. (1988) Even "knowing better" about smoking and other health risks may not deter adolescents. *Journal of the American Medical Association,* 260:1512–1513.

Mensch, B.S., & Kandel, D.B. (1988) Underreporting of substance use in a national longitudinal youth cohort. *Public Opinion Quarterly,* 52:110–124.

Morrison, M.A. (1991) Overview: Kids and Drugs. *Psychiatric Annals,* 21(2):72–73.

National Commission on Drug-Free Schools. (1990) *Toward a Drug-Free Generation: A Nation's Responsibility.* Washington, D.C.: National Education Goals Panel.

National Education Goals Panel. (1991) *Measuring Progress Toward the National Education Goals: Potential Indicators and Measurement Strategies—A Discussion Document.* Washington, D.C.: National Education Goals Panel.

National Institute on Alcohol Abuse. (1990) *Alcohol and health: Seventh special report to the U.S. Congress.* DHHS Publication No. (ADM)90-1656. Washington, D.C.: U.S. Government Printing Office.

National Institute on Drug Abuse. (1991) *Drug Abuse and Drug Abuse Research: The Third Triennial Report to Congress from the Secretary, Department of Health and Human Services.* DHHS Publication No. (ADM)91-1704. Washington, D.C.: U.S. Government Printing Office.

National Institute on Drug Abuse. (1991) *Drug Abuse Curriculum for Employee Assistance Program Professionals.* DHHS Publication No. (ADM)90-1587. Rockville, MD.

National Parents' Resource Institute for Drug Education. (1988) *Drug Usage Prevalence Questionnaire: 1986–87.* Atlanta.

Office for Substance Abuse Prevention. (1989) *The Fact Is Alcohol and Other Drug Problems Are a Major Concern in Native American Communities.* Rockville, MD: National Clearinghouse for Alcohol and Drug Information.

Office for Substance Abuse Prevention. (1990) *The Fact Is Reaching Hispanic/Latino Audiences Requires Cultural Sensitivity.* Rockville, MD: National Clearinghouse for Alcohol and Drug Information.

Page, R.M. (1989) Shyness as a risk factor in adolescent substance abuse. *Journal of School Health,* 59:432–435.

Page, R.M. (1993) Perceived physical attractiveness and frequency of substance use among male and female adolescents. *Journal of Alcohol and Drug Education,* 38:81–91.

Page, R.M., & Allen, O. (1993) Differences in indicators of psychosocial well-being in black and white adolescents (Abstract). *Research Quarterly for Exercise and Sport,* 64 (Supplement): A-63.

Rand, Ayn. (1957) *Atlas Shrugged.* New York: NAL Dutton.

Steinberg, L. (1991) Adolescent transitions and alcohol and other drug prevention. *Preventing Adolescent Drug Use: From Theory to Practice.* In E.N. Goperlund (Ed.), 91–1725. Office for Substance Abuse Prevention Monograph-8. DHHS Publication No. (ADM). Rockville, MD: Office for Substance Abuse Prevention.

United States Department of Health and Human Services. (1991) *Healthy People 2000: National Health Promotion and Disease Prevention Objectives.* Publication No. PHS 91-50213.

Vega, W.A., Zimmerman, R.S., Warheit, A.E., & Gil, A.G. (1993). Risk factors for early adolescent drug use in four ethnic and racial groups. *American Journal of Public Health,* 83:185–189.

Weekly Reader Publications. (1987) *The Weekly Reader National Survey: Drugs and Drinking.* Middletown, CT: Field Publications.

DRUGS AND VIOLENCE: PROMOTING RESPECTFUL RELATIONSHIPS

Violence in America is a nationwide tragedy and an international embarrassment (Callahan & Rivara, 1992). The United States is truly the most violent nation in the world; the violence affects both urban and rural America (Hall et al., 1993: McAnarney, 1993). **Violence** is the use of force with the intent to harm oneself or another person. Violence takes many forms including homicide, suicide, assault, rape, domestic violence, and child abuse (Children's Safety Network, 1991). Several years ago, the incidence of violence in the United States was approximately 1 per 1,000. Today, the incidence is nearly 75 per 1,000. Americans are in agreement that something must be done to promote respectful relationships and stop violent actions that harm the self and others. This chapter focuses on factors that promote respectful relationships, factors that increase the risk of violence, types of violence, and promoting nonviolent behavior in youth.

FACTORS THAT PROMOTE RESPECTFUL RELATIONSHIPS

Protective factors are characteristics of individuals and their environments that make a positive contribution to development and behavior. With regard to violence, protective factors motivate persons to strive for respectful, caring, and nonviolent relationships with others. This section of the chapter includes a discussion of factors that motivate persons to strive for those kinds of relationships with others (Fig. 2-1): identifying high-quality relationships, developing relationship skills, demonstrating self-loving behavior, expressing feelings in healthful ways, using stress-management skills, developing conflict-resolution skills, and being drug free.

Identifying High-Quality Relationships

Relationships are the connections that people have with each other. Although the quality of relationships varies, they are vital to our existence. Some relationships are fulfilling: they are a source of happiness and joy. Other relationships are depletive; they are a source of sadness and pain and endanger a person's ability to function.

Inspiriting relationships are relationships that lift the spirit and contribute to a sense of well-being. Inspiriting relationships make a person feel worthwhile, important, and high in self-esteem (Jourard, 1970). When a person's spirits are lifted, (s)he experiences joy, enthusiasm, passion, hope, and satisfaction.

Dispiriting relationships are relationships that lower a person's spirit and make a person feel unimportant, worthless, isolated, and frustrated. They contribute to feelings of low self-esteem.

Developing Relationship Skills

It is important to learn how to be successful in relationships, to get along well with others, and to respect their rights. Success in relationships is determined by the skills a person possesses as well as a person's knowledge, attitudes, values, and behaviors. Skills that enhance relationships include being able to show care and concern for others, being able to express feelings in healthful ways, to articulate values, to make responsible decisions, and to effectively cope in difficult situations. Additional skills are being able to set goals and to delay gratification if necessary in order to meet those goals.

Relationship skills can be learned. Because a person is first exposed to relationships in his or her family, the family is the primary source of learning relationship skills. A **family** is a system consisting of interconnecting people in which each person affects the others in profound and hidden ways (Forward, 1989). Because of the natural bonds in a family, familial relationships have a powerful effect on a person.

The importance of role models. Parents or other significant adults who serve as role models in a family are the most influential persons in a family. They might be compared to coaches. Just as coaches help their players develop skills in a particular sport, parents or other significant adults who "parent" have the responsibility of helping children

Figure 2-1
Protective Factors Motivate Persons to Strive for Respectful, Caring, and Nonviolent Relationships

The following skills serve as protective factors:

* Identifying high-quality relationships
* Developing relationship skills
* Demonstrating self-loving behavior
* Expressing feelings in healthful ways
* Using stress-management skills
* Developing conflict-resolution skills
* Being drug free

in a family develop the skills they will need in order to experience success in their relationships.

Spirit-relationship continuum. Parents have different qualifications as well as varied strengths and weaknesses as they interact with their children as role models and

"coaches." Most relationships, including those in families, do not have the extreme effects of being either dispiriting or inspiriting. Most relationships fall somewhere in between and can be evaluated by using a continuum. A **spirit-relationship continuum** is a set of values that includes a range of dispiriting descriptors at the lower end and a range of inspiriting descriptors at the higher end (Table 2-2). The continuum is marked in units ranging from 0 to 100 and can be used to evaluate relationships. Most relationships fall within the 30 to 60 range of the continuum, indicating that most people can improve the quality of their relationships with family members and with persons outside the family.

Just as coaches and teams experience different and varying levels of functioning, families also do. Some families demonstrate high levels of skills in their relationships; others do not. Families might be compared with the most and least successful teams in a conference of ten teams in which the majority, eight out of the ten to be exact, are in the middle. This type of record is also true of families. While the majority of families may not be ideal, they are they not completely ineffective.

Demonstrating Self-Loving Behavior

In families that are skilled in relationships, feelings are expressed openly and honestly, effective coping skills are practiced, and respect for each family member is evident. A child growing up in this kind of environment can become an independent adult who is able to function responsibly in relationships.

One of the behaviors observed and taught in this kind of family is self-loving behavior. **Self-loving behavior** is behavior that is healthful and responsible and indicates that a person believes himself/herself to be worthwhile and lovable. This kind of behavior is an outgrowth of the way a person is treated within the family by his/her parents or by other significant adults. As the person matures, these traits will become a positive influence in his/her relationships outside the family.

Because the most emotionally influential adults are usually parent figures, the word "parents" will be used in the following discussion. Messages from parents are internalized by children. When they are comforted or when their needs are met by parents, children begin to view themselves as being worthwhile. To a child, a message such as "I'm glad you were born and I am going to take care of you," means "I am worthwhile and my world is safe and secure." Messages and attitudes such as this that indicate a child's worth help the child form a positive self-concept. **Self-concept** is the personal, internal image or feeling a person has about himself/herself.

Feelings of worthiness help children form a positive self-concept. A positive self-concept in turn helps a child desire

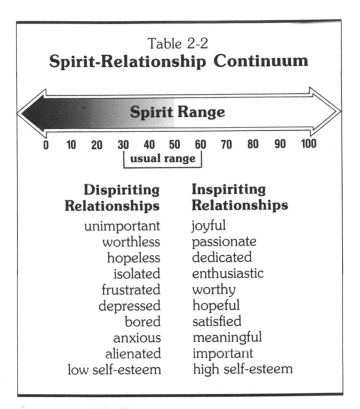

Table 2-2
Spirit-Relationship Continuum

Spirit Range

0 10 20 30 40 50 60 70 80 90 100
usual range

Dispiriting Relationships	Inspiriting Relationships
unimportant	joyful
worthless	passionate
hopeless	dedicated
isolated	enthusiastic
frustrated	worthy
depressed	hopeful
bored	satisfied
anxious	meaningful
alienated	important
low self-esteem	high self-esteem

to behave in self-loving ways and may help the child avoid self-destructive behaviors. As a result of experiencing feelings of worthiness within the family, a child will expect other relationships outside the family to reflect love and respect. If a relationship does not meet the child's expectation, it may become a source of disappointment and frustration.

In training and "coaching" a child, parents have a responsibility to teach a child the difference between the positive effects of self-loving behavior and the negative effects of self-centered behavior. **Self-centered behavior** is behavior in which a person takes actions to fulfill his or her needs and wishes with little or no regard for the needs and wishes of others. Self-centered behavior interferes with a person's ability to form and maintain responsible and satisfying relationships with others both within and outside of a family.

Expressing Feelings in Healthful Ways

How to communicate effectively is an important skill to learn in a family. **Communication** is the sharing of feelings, thoughts, and information with another person. Communication is important in all relationships.

Verbal communication. A responsible way to communicate is to use I-messages. **I-messages** are statements used to express feelings. When a person uses I-messages, (s)he assumes responsibility for sharing feelings. I-messages are statements that refer to the individual, the individual's feelings, and the individual's needs. To have the greatest impact, I-messages must include the following components: (l) a specific behavior, (2) the effect that behavior has on the individual, and (3) the feeling that results.

The opposite kind of message is a you-message. *You-messages* are statements that attempt to blame and shame another person rather than express feelings. For example, an I-message might be "When you picked me up late for the game (specific behavior), we were late for the game (effect), and I was annoyed with you (feeling). The you-message might be "You are always late for everything."

The I-message gives the opportunity for a response without the other person feeling attacked. The you-message puts the other person on the defensive provoking a different kind of response.

Listening is another important skill that is first learned in the family. Learning to listen well is important because it shows interest in another person. One way to be an effective listener is to use active listening. *Active listening* is a type of listening in which a person is reassured that his/her message is heard and understood. Active listening helps clarify what has been said. For example, the active listening response to the sample I-message stated previously might be "I really understand why you are annoyed with me."

Nonverbal communication. Nonverbal communication is the use of behavior rather than words to express feelings. Examples of nonverbal communication are a nod of the head, a hug, a smile, a frown, tapping a foot, or looking away. When verbal and nonverbal communications are used together, it is important that they do not give a mixed message. It would be confusing, for example, if positive words were spoken while the person was frowning. Mixed messages are difficult to understand.

It is possible to communicate messages by behaviors that may be passive, aggressive, or assertive. *Passive behavior* is the holding back of ideas, opinions, and feelings. Persons who demonstrate passive behaviors have difficulty expressing their concerns. Passive verbal behaviors include self-criticism and unnecessary apologies and excuses. Passive nonverbal behaviors might include looking away or laughing when discussing or trying to express serious feelings.

Aggressive behavior is the use of words and/or actions that tend to communicate disrespect toward others.

Aggressive verbal behaviors include name calling, loud and sarcastic remarks, and statements of blame. Interrupting others and monopolizing the conversation are also aggressive verbal behaviors. Aggressive nonverbal behaviors include glaring at another person, using threatening hand gestures, or assuming a rigid posture.

Assertive behavior is the honest expression of thoughts and feelings without experiencing anxiety or threatening others. Assertive behavior is healthier than either passive or aggressive behavior. Assertive behavior promotes high-quality relationships. Persons who demonstrate assertive behavior use I-messages and active listening. Nonverbal assertive behavior includes a confident body posture, hand gestures that complement what is being said, and comfortable eye contact.

Using Stress-Management Skills

Challenges and changes are everyday occurrences, and they make demands on a person. The demands may be physical, such as being involved in running a race. The demands may be mental, such as solving a difficult problem or taking an exam. Meeting someone for the first time may be a social or emotional demand. Whatever the challenge, and whatever the response, the person has experienced stress. *Stress* is the nonspecific response of the body to any demand made on it. Stressors trigger the response. A *stressor* is any demand made on the body, such as the race, the difficult problem, or the first-time meeting. The emphasis should be on the word *any*: unhappy events certainly cause stress but the most stressful responses can be caused by a person's happiest experiences (Cohen & Cohen, 1984).

The symptoms of stress affect all aspects of a person's life. The symptoms may be physical illnesses, such as asthma, arthritis, or hypertension; they may be emotional, depending on how much a person tries to cope with or avoid the stress. Depression, alcohol and other drug abuse, delinquency, suicide, and homicide are common ways teenagers especially show the stress they are experiencing (Gordon, 1990).

Stress can be the result of personal experiences or environmental, social, or economic factors (Gordon, 1992). Gordon also states the following:

Studies done by Sidney Cobb on auto workers who were about to be fired revealed a marked increase in hypertension, ulcers, and arthritis, while Harvey Brenner's epidemiological research showed a consistent correlation between periods of economic recession and the incidence of cardiovascular disease, depression, and alcoholism. (p. 49)

Responses to stressors may be healthful or harmful. A person who has coped well experiences eustress or the feeling of success. **Eustress** is a healthful response to a stressor that produces positive results. For example, if a gymnast were involved in a competition, (s)he might be highly motivated to prepare by eating a balanced diet, getting enough sleep, and practicing the routine over and over. (S)he envisioned himself/herself as a winner. The response was positive and healthful.

A person who does not cope well experiences distress. **Distress** is a harmful response to a stressor that produces negative results. For example, the gymnast might be overwhelmed at the prospect of the competition. (S)he might skip meals, sleep poorly, and be so anxious that (s)he could not perform the routine well. The response was negative and harmful. The same stressor can produce either eustress or distress depending on the person's response.

Hans Selye, a pioneer in the study of stress, referred to the response a person makes to a stressor as the general adaptation syndrome, or GAS. The **general adaptation syndrome, (GAS)**, is the body's response to a stressor that occurs in three stages: the alarm stage, the resistance stage, and the exhaustion stage.

The **alarm stage** is the body's initial response to a stressor. During this stage, adrenocortical hormones in the bloodstream increase; breathing and heart rates increase; and muscles tense. As a result of these physiological changes, the individual experiences quick energy. The alarm and resistance stages of the GAS are illustrated in Fig. 2-3.

The **resistance stage** is the second stage during which the individual's body attempts to regain a state of internal balance, or homeostasis, which is the body's normal state. During the resistance stage, the biochemical effects of the alarm stage are reversed: breathing and heart rate decrease; adrenocortical hormone levels decrease; and muscles begin to relax. In the case of the gymnast who responded positively to the competition, homeostasis would be regained in a short period of time. However, in the case of the gymnast who responded negatively, the resistance stage would be prolonged, and the third stage of GAS, exhaustion, would result.

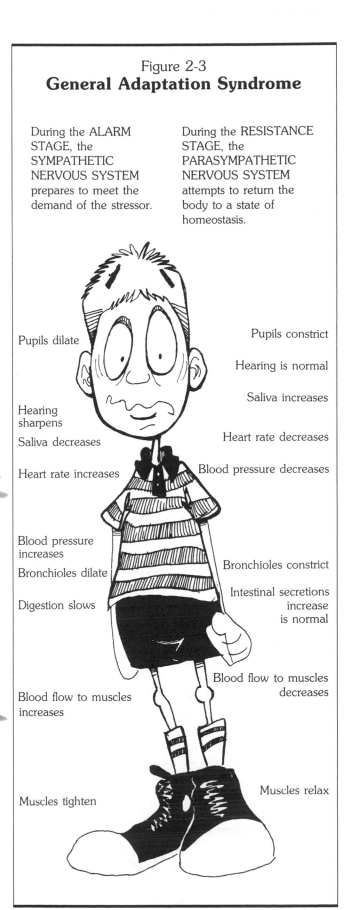

Figure 2-3
General Adaptation Syndrome

During the ALARM STAGE, the SYMPATHETIC NERVOUS SYSTEM prepares to meet the demand of the stressor.

During the RESISTANCE STAGE, the PARASYMPATHETIC NERVOUS SYSTEM attempts to return the body to a state of homeostasis.

Pupils dilate

Hearing sharpens

Saliva decreases

Heart rate increases

Blood pressure increases

Bronchioles dilate

Digestion slows

Blood flow to muscles increases

Muscles tighten

Pupils constrict

Hearing is normal

Saliva increases

Heart rate decreases

Blood pressure decreases

Bronchioles constrict

Intestinal secretions increase is normal

Blood flow to muscles decreases

Muscles relax

The *exhaustion stage* occurs when a period of stress is prolonged and the body experiences burnout, or biochemical exhaustion. The exhaustion stage can result in wear and tear on the body, lowered resistance to disease, and/or death.

For good health, therefore, it is essential to learn skills to manage stress. *Stress-management skills* are techniques used to help cope with and prevent or lessen the harmful effects produced by stress. Problem solving, diet and exercise, and relaxation techniques are examples of stress-management skills.

Problem solving. Problem solving is a series of steps that can be applied to a difficult situation so that a responsible decision can be reached.
1. Identify the cause of the stress and anxiety.
2. Identify ways to cope with the situation.
3. Evaluate each way that could be used to cope with what is happening.
4. Choose a responsible action to cope with the source of stress.
5. Evaluate the choice.
6. Rely on talking with such people as a parent, a significant adult, or a close friend to assist in whatever decision is made.
7. Keep a journal, so that a record of the way in which the problem was solved is available.

Diet and exercise. Eating to maintain an ideal weight and exercising are two very practical ways to cope with stress. Because diet is linked to six of the ten leading causes of death, a healthful diet is essential. It provides the best sources of energy and in the right amounts. In addition, prolonged periods of stress suppress the immune system. A diet high in vitamins C and B is believed to bolster the immune system. Regular exercise uses up adrenaline and sugar in the blood and helps restore homeostasis. It is best to exercise as soon as the effects of stress are felt. However, exercise up to 24 hours after the onset of stressful feelings is beneficial. A regular program of exercise will help a person cope with stressors, since the body releases beta-endorphins after a period of exercise. Beta-endorphins are substances that relieve pain and create a feeling of well-being.

Relaxation response. There are self-induced relaxation techniques that help restore homeostasis to the body. Herb Bensen, a pioneer in relaxation response research in his book, *Beyond the Relaxation Response*, suggests four conditions that are necessary to bring about the relaxation response.

1. A quiet environment with as few distractions as possible.
2. A mental device on which to focus, such as repeating a single-syllable sound.
3. A passive attitude that does not try to judge performance.
4. A comfortable position to remain restful: head and back support; loose clothing; no shoes.

The techniques that can be used under these conditions are meditation, progressive relaxation, autogenic training, and biofeedback. *Meditation* involves controlling thought processes and focusing on the present. Put thoughts of the past and concerns about the future out of mind: listen to music, use guided imagery, or breathing exercises as effective ways to reduce muscular tension and other symptoms of stress (VanWie, 1987).

Progressive relaxation involves relaxing the mind by first relaxing the body. Muscle groups, such as in the hand, are contracted and then relaxed until gradually no tension is felt. This effect can be felt by clinching the fist tighter and tighter, and then relaxing and letting the fingers become loose.

Autogenic training involves a series of exercises to increase muscle relaxation. As a person does these exercises, (s)he focuses on heaviness, warmth, and relaxation of muscles.

Biofeedback is getting information about what is occurring in the body at a particular time, so that a physiological function can be altered. Many functions such as skin temperature, heart rate and nerve impulse patterns within the brain can be monitored electronically. It is possible for a person to learn how to consciously reduce heart rate and blood pressure, for example.

Because all of life is stressful, learning to handle stress should be a priority. And learning to cope is a personal matter. Each person must learn what stressors affect her/him the most, what the early signs of stress are, and ways to break the cycle (Johnson, 1992).

Developing Conflict-Resolution Skills

Just as life without stress is impossible, so is life without conflict. Learning how to come to an agreement about an issue over which there are conflicting opinions is an important skill to learn. Conflicts occur naturally in every area of life, including the family, so it is important for children to learn how to resolve their differences in nonviolent ways.

Children become frustrated when their interests conflict with the interests of others, and because they lack the necessary social skills, they tend to express their feelings in aggressive behaviors (McClure, Miller, & Russo, 1992). In discussing strategies for resolving conflicts among children, McClure, Miller, & Russo discussed the following findings:

Edelson (1981) focused on teaching children the skills necessary for successful conflict resolution. He defined an effective conflict response as one the reduced problems and negative consequences of the solution while producing positive solution consequences. His group therapy technique identifies the child's problem and examines solutions while taking the consequences into account. Shantz (1987) defined *constructive resolution* as resolution that focuses on the issue and ends in mutual satisfaction. She explained that conflict would be viewed as less negative if it occurred in more agreeable interactions. Clark, Willihnganz, & O'Dell (1985) maintained that children could learn the art of persuasion, thereby providing them with communication strategies to handle conflict. Anderson (1980) demonstrated the use of fantasy as a successful technique in helping children release conflict-related emotions. Finally, Maynard (1985) contended that conflict resolution in an organized group structure assists children in developing abilities that could be generalized to other settings. (p. 269–270)

Suggestions for promoting conflict resolution when dealing with children include the following (McClure, Miller, & Russo, 1992):
• allow physical movement,
• be consistent,
• identify the situation that is causing the conflict,
• acknowledge and validate the feelings being expressed.

According to Fisher and Ury (1981), three criteria may be used to judge whether or not a resolution is fair:
1. Is it wise? (A wise agreement meets the interests of both parties.)
2. Is it efficient?
3. Does it improve, or at least not damage, the relationship of the two parties?

Arguing over positions is not an effective way to deal with an issue because the focus is on the position and not on the issue.

In their book, *Getting to Yes*, Fisher and Ury (1981) discuss a method devised by the Harvard Negotiation Project, called principled negotiation, which has the following 4 basic points:

1. **People:** Separate the people from the problem. Conflicting viewpoints often involve people misunderstanding each other and getting angry and upset.
2. **Interests:** Focus on interests, not positions. Persons on each side of the issue have to be open to suggestions and listen to the other side's interests in the matter.
3. **Options:** Generate a variety of possibilities before deciding what to do. It is better to broaden the possible solutions by being creative rather than eliminate possible solutions.
4. **Criteria:** Insist that the result be based on some objective standard.

Being Drug Free

The internal environment of the human body is normally maintained within a narrow range of variables. Anything that upsets this internal balance affects a person's ability to function. Drugs change the chemical balance, mainly affecting the nervous system, which is the body's control center. Drug dependence leads people to behave in ways that are contrary to their values, their judgement, and their common sense.

The nervous system is known as the communication system of the body. The nervous system keeps a person in touch with his/her environment and enables the person to interpret and respond to stimuli of all kinds. The functions of this system include memory, thinking, solving problems, communicating and emotions. In other words, the delicate balance of the body's internal environment is in large part maintained by the nervous system.

A person who uses drugs drastically affects the ability of the nervous system, and especially the brain, to function normally. Drugs interfere with the delicate mechanisms of the nervous system by which information critical to daily existence is processed.

Conversely, a person who is not under the influence of drugs is more likely to:
• be in control of his/her behavior,
• make responsible decisions,
• desire to resolve conflicts in mutually satisfying ways,
• relate well with others,
• express emotions in healthful ways,
• be skillful in managing stress,
• have a positive self-concept.

FACTORS THAT INCREASE THE RISK OF VIOLENCE

Violence is clearly linked to several large-scale social problems. Lack of educational opportunities, poverty, racism, sexism, and unemployment are examples of social problems that correlate with the risk of interpersonal violence (NCEHIC, 1992). Changes in American families have also had their effects. These social ills must be addressed in order to reduce the number of injuries and deaths due to interpersonal violence (Hammond & Yung, 1993). The enormity of violence problems in the United States calls for actions by all segments of society, including schools and teachers, to alleviate these large-scale social problems (Page et al., 1992).

In addition to considering large-scale social problems as causes of violence, a national panel of violence-prevention experts also listed the following as other causal factors of violence (NCEHIC, 1992):

1. ready access of perpetrators to highly-lethal weapons;
2. the demand for crack or other addicting drugs;
3. the illicit trafficking of drugs by gang members;
4. the lack of alternative ways for gang members to develop self-esteem or a sense of belonging;
5. the lack of opportunities for jobs that might build the self-esteem of vulnerable adolescents, might help them resist the lure of drugs, or at least might give them the means to move away from highly-violent neighborhoods;
6. a culture that glorifies violence as a means of attaining desired ends;
7. childhood and family experiences among perpetrators that contribute to the adoption of violence and aggression as appropriate behavior patterns.

This section of the chapter will include a discussion of demographics of perpetrators and victims of violence. It also will include a discussion of the following risk factors characteristic of individuals or environments associated with increased vulnerability to violent behavior (Fig. 2-4): using alcohol and other drugs; being involved in drug sales, purchases, or trafficking; exhibiting antisocial behavior; having an available firearm; being impulsive when arguing; witnessing violence in the family; experiencing poverty and hopelessness; being exposed to violence in the media; belonging to a gang; and belonging to a cult.

Identifying Perpetrators and Victims of Violence

Youth appear to be more vulnerable than adults to violent crime. According to the National Crime Survey, 67 of every

1,000 teenagers experience a violent crime each year. In comparison, that rate for adults is substantially lower, 26 of every 1,000 adults (Whitaker & Bastian, 1991). In one study, 1 in 132 Massachusetts youth (ages 0 to 19) were treated in hospitals for injuries resulting from fights, rapes, child batterings, or other violent assaults each year (Guyer et al., 1989). For each youth homicide victim, there were 534 room visits and 33 hospital admissions.

Perpetrators and victims of violent behavior are very similar in terms of demographic characteristics. Perpetrators, as well as victims, of homicide and many other forms of interpersonal violence are disproportionately young males. Males are the victims of 76 percent of all homicides and are perpetrators of 84 percent of homicides with male victims, and 90 percent of homicides with female victims (U.S. Department of Justice, 1990; NCEHIC, 1992).

Using Alcohol and Other Drugs

The use of alcohol and other drugs appears to be a critically important risk factor of violent behavior and victimization. The book *Anger, Alcoholism, and Addiction* (Potter-Efron & Potter-Efron, 1991) examines several studies showing that alcohol and drug use is associated with various forms of violence and violent situations. The authors point out the following research findings about substance use and violence:

- 72 percent of abused females in a shelter reported that their mates had a drinking problem;
- The actual severity of child battering increases as a perpetrator drinks more;
- Addicted or alcoholic families tend to be violent, even in recovery, especially around issues of control;
- Sibling physical abuse is a problem in alcoholic or addicted families;
- A history of physical or sexual abuse is often linked with alcohol or other drug problems;
- Alcoholic females are more likely to have experienced physical and sexual abuse than other females;
- Daughters of alcoholics are twice as likely as other females to be the victims of incest;
- Females in chemical-dependency treatment are likely to have physically or sexually abused their own children;
- Child neglect and abuse are associated with alcoholic families.

It has been well established that alcohol consumption is disproportionately present among both victims and perpetrators of violence. This association has been well documented because of the common use of blood alcohol tests on homicide victims. However, far less is known about

Figure 2-4
Risk Factors Increase Vulnerability to Violent Behavior

The following factors are risk factors:

* Using alcohol or other drugs
* Being involved in drug sales, purchases, or trafficking
* Exhibiting antisocial behavior
* Having an available firearm
* Being impulsive when arguing

* Witnessing violence in the family
* Experiencing poverty and hopelessness
* Being exposed to violence in the media
* Belonging to a gang
* Belonging to a cult

the association between interpersonal violence and the use of cocaine, marijuana, and other controlled substances.

High rates of interpersonal violence are often attributed to high levels of illicit drug use and drug trafficking. Recent increases in child abuse and neglect appear to be related to increased birth rates of infants born to cocaine-addicted mothers. This correlation raises the concern that such infants may be at increased risk of child abuse or neglect. In many urban city areas, it is not known if increased risk of violence is due to poverty or the effects of drug abuse (NCEHIC, 1992).

Through modifying moods and behavior, psychoactive drugs may directly influence episodes of violent behavior. Less immediate effects may be on moods and psychological states. Depression, paranoia, irritability, and impairment in thinking abilities sometimes follow long-term use of alcohol and other substances. In addition, withdrawal from long-term drug use is sometimes associated with feelings of hostility, irritability, or paranoia. These affective and cognitive states can increase the propensity for interpersonal violence (NCEHIC, 1992).

Alcohol. Alcohol is the drug that is most commonly associated with violence, probably because it is used so widely in our society. Alcohol use appears to foster anger and aggression. Violence can be triggered from alcohol during intoxication as well as during withdrawal (Potter-Efron &

Potter-Efron, 1991). Aggressive feelings and behavior that would normally be controlled, appear to be less controlled when an individual is under the influence of alcohol.

Sedative-hypnotics. The abuse of barbiturates is strongly associated with aggression. Withdrawal of sedative-hypnotic drugs is also strongly associated with interpersonal violence. Sedative-hypnotic drugs rate second only to alcohol as contributors of assaultive behavior. Because sedative-hypnotics reduce normal inhibitions, intoxicated users tend to be irritable and argumentative. Heavy barbiturate users tend to provoke senseless fights with family members and others (Potter-Efron & Potter-Efron, 1991).

PCP. PCP is a drug that is known to be associated with extremely violent behavior. There is evidence that the drug itself is responsible for aggressive behavior. Above a certain dosage level, PCP can produce aggressive effects in most persons. Chronic PCP use is also associated with aggression. Many PCP users become progressively more angry, irritable, and violent over time (Potter-Efron & Potter-Efron, 1991).

Cocaine. Cocaine use is associated with feelings of irritability and paranoia. These feelings do not automatically lead to aggression. Therefore, researchers do not report a strong correlation between cocaine use and violence. However, the propensity for violence and significant psychiatric symptoms is heightened when smoking crack cocaine (Potter-Efron & Potter-Efron, 1991).

Other stimulants. Amphetamine use is associated with feelings of irritability and hostility. Similar to PCP, psychotic reactions can occur in users within a short time. High doses of amphetamines can result in hyperactivity, paranoia, and impulsivity, which can facilitate aggressive or violent behavior. Amphetamine-induced psychosis can remain in a user for months or years after he or she quits taking amphetamines. The propensity for violence is increased when users smoke "ice" or smokable amphetamines (Potter-Efron & Potter-Efron, 1991).

Other drugs. The pharmacological effects of heroin and other opiates rarely result in feelings of anger or aggressiveness. Physically-dependent users going through withdrawal, however, may experience feelings such as irritability, paranoia, and hostility. These feelings may heighten the risk of violent behavior.

Hallucinogens are rarely associated with violence. However, the delusional effects of hallucinogens may occasionally lead to self-directed or interpersonal violence.

Anabolic steroids represent a class of drugs that poses a serious threat of violent behavior. Some experts believe that steroid use can lead to a "bodybuilder's psychosis," which is characterized by aggression and paranoia. However, other experts claim that aggression emanating from steroid use is confined only to individuals who are already prone to aggressive behavior. Whatever the case may be, the potential effects of steroid use on violent behavior must be taken seriously (Potter-Efron & Potter-Efron).

Some studies have concluded that marijuana use is associated with aggressive behavior. Because some people attempt to control aggressive feelings by using marijuana, Potter-Efron & Potter-Efron (1991) make the following comments:

> Others attempt to control their anger and aggression with marijuana, arguing that they are more "mellow" when intoxicated. Although often thought to be virtually harmless, marijuana is hardly a "safe" drug to take, especially if a person has any prior history of paranoia, since chronic marijuana use can increase these symptoms. Additionally, many individuals combine marijuana with other substances, a practice that produces unpredictable and possible anger- or aggression-stimulating responses. (p. 18)

40

Being Involved in Drug Sales, Purchases, or Trafficking

There is no doubt that drugs can directly contribute to violent behavior through their pharmacologic effects. Drugs also serve important roles through their relationship to economic-compulsive violent crime, and systemic violence. **Economic-compulsive violent crime** is crime committed by drug users because of the high cost of some drugs in order to support their continued drug use. **Systemic violence** refers to the heightened risk for both committing violence and being a victim of violence because of participation in the sale and trafficking of illicit substances. Systemic violence serves a variety of purposes such as protection or expansion of drug distribution market share or retaliation against market participants who violate the rules that govern transactions (Goldstein, 1985).

Systemic violence has been prominently featured in the media. Death and bloodshed associated with the drug distribution system take a heavy toll on the market participants themselves. Moreover, this violence often spills beyond those involved in illegal drug transactions and affects nonparticipants directly through injury or death. The proliferation of deadly weapons has made the violence associated with the drug distribution system more lethal and visible. When violence occurs, death and serious injury may be more likely (National Institute on Drug Abuse, 1990).

Exhibiting Antisocial Behavior

The association of antisocial personality and chemical dependency is one of the strongest, most consistent correlations throughout the child development and psychological literature.[1]

Research shows that:
1. Chronic, serious delinquency and adolescent drug use share many common risk factors; nearly 50 percent of serious juvenile offenders in the National Youth Survey report using multiple illicit drugs and over 80 percent report using one illicit drug;
2. Early initiation into alcohol and other drug use (by age 14) predicts early chemical dependency and abuse and is associated with general deviance and other antisocial problems and problem behaviors;
3. As part of a constellation of antisocial behavior patterns, drug use can be predicted by personality/behav-

---

[1]This discussion was adapted from the Office for Substance Abuse Prevention Monograph-5, *Communication About Alcohol and Other Drugs: Strategies for Reaching Populations at Risk.* DHHS Publication No. (ADM) 90-1665.

ior characteristics that can be identified in early childhood and that remain constant over time.

Children who manifest conduct disorders in their early years and antisocial characteristics later are more likely to use alcohol and other drugs early and frequently. These preteen children who have trouble with prosocial bonding to family, school, friends, and society often join other alienated, isolated youngsters in a peer group that shares drinking and other antisocial activities. The personality factors exhibited by these children seem sufficient to explain why they initiate early use of antisocial behaviors. These young people are often rebellious, resist traditional authority and traditional values, and have a high tolerance for deviance and a strong need for independence. It is thought that marijuana-using youth have a sensation-seeking orientation and a willingness to risk injury and illness. Ninth grade drug users perceive their parents as less caring and more rejecting than do nonusers. This suggests a motive for turning from parents to peer influences at an early age.

The literature on alcohol and other drug use reflects the fact that, as part of a constellation of antisocial behavior problems, alcohol and other drug use can be predicted by previous patterns of antisocial behavior. Problematic conduct early in life continues for certain groups of children. A longitudinal study of high-risk, early signs of delinquency (Spivack, 1983) revealed that conduct disturbances in adolescence could be predicted from kindergarten and first grade by the following signs:
1. Acting out,
2. Overinvolvement in socially-disturbing behavior,
3. Impatience,
4. Impulsiveness,
5. Defiance and negativity.

Childhood antisocial behavior is consistently related to later alcoholic outcome, encompassing greater amounts of antisocial and aggressive activity, and more rebelliousness. Boys at the highest risk of developing adolescent drug problems have been found to be aggressive and shy. Boys at somewhat less risk are characterized by aggression without shyness.

Having an Available Firearm

Results from the 1990 Youth Risk Behavior Survey indicate that one in twenty senior high school students carried a firearm, usually a handgun, during the 30 days preceding the survey (Centers for Disease Control, 1991b). A recent study of urban Seattle eleventh grade students reported that 34 percent of students reported easy access to handguns (47 percent of males, 22 percent of females). In addition, 11.4 percent of males and 1.5 percent of females reported owning a handgun. One-third of those who owned handguns reported that they had fired at someone. Nearly one in ten female students reported a firearm homicide or suicide in family members or close friends. Six percent of male students reported carrying a handgun to school sometime in the past. Handgun ownership was associated with gang membership, selling drugs, interpersonal violence, attacking a teacher, being convicted of crimes, and either suspension or expulsion from school (Callahan & Rivara, 1992).

Firearms can be found in about half (46 percent) of all U.S. households and one-fourth of all households have a handgun (Handgun Ownership in America, 1991). Over half of handgun owners report that their guns remain loaded. Further, Weil and Hemingway (1992) found that many loaded weapons are not locked up, even if children are in the household. This poses a serious risk to the lives and health of children when these guns are accessible, particularly when they are loaded.

In Texas and Louisiana, deaths from firearms, for the first time in many decades, surpassed deaths from motor vehicles as the leading cause of injury deaths (Centers for Disease Control, 1992a). The leading cause of death in both African-American and white American males is gunshot wounds (Koop & Lundberg, 1992). From 1979 through 1989, the firearm homicide rate for 15- to 19-year-olds in the United States increased by 61 percent, while at the same time, nonfirearm homicide rate decreased 29 percent (Fingerhut, Ingram, & Feldman, 1992). Other facts to consider about firearms and violence in our nation from the National Center to Prevent Handguns are as follows:
1. Every day 10 children (19 years old and under) are killed in gun accidents, suicides, and homicides; many more are wounded;
2. Gunshot wounds to children 16 years old and under nearly doubled in urban areas between 1987 and 1990;
3. Firearm murders of children and adolescents increased 125 percent between 1984 and 1990;
4. One out of every 12 children who died in 1988 was killed with a gun.
5. Guns are the method used in 65 percent of male teen suicides and 47 percent of female teen suicides.
6. Handguns account for 70 percent of all firearm suicides.
7. In 1970, fewer than one-third of the suicides by young females ages 15 to 24 were committed with guns, compared to 42 percent with drugs. In 1984, more

41

than half were committed with guns and only 19 percent with drugs.

8. Guns are the most lethal suicide method—92 percent of attempted suicides with guns are completed.

9. A suicidal teenager living in a home with an easily accessible gun is more likely to commit suicide than a suicidal teenager living in a home where no gun is present.

10. Most teen suicides are impulsive, with little or no planning, and 70 percent occur in the victims' homes.

11. Suicidal teens who have been drinking alcohol are 5 times more likely to use guns than any other suicide method.

12. More than 1.2 million elementary-aged, latch-key children have access to guns in their homes.

13. A study of 266 accidental shootings of children ages 16 and under revealed that 50 percent of accidents occurred in the victims' homes, and 38 percent occurred in the homes of friends or relatives. The handguns used were most often found in bedrooms. Males were predominately the victims (80 percent) and shooters (92 percent).

14. At least 71 students and teachers nationwide were killed with guns on school campuses between the 1985 to 1986 and the 1989 to 1990 school years. Another 201 were wounded and at least 242 were held hostage at gunpoint.

Being Impulsive When Arguing

Most homicide victims are killed in the course of arguments, usually by people they know—often spouses or other family members. The ready availability of a firearm greatly heightens the risk that the firearm will be used when emotions are running high and/or when one or both parties have been drinking (Weil & Hemingway, 1992). Today, adolescents appear to be more willing to turn to firearms to solve quarrels than in the past. Whereas the former tendency was to fight with fists, or at the very worst knives, the tendency now is to use firearms (Marwick, 1992).

Impulsiveness is also a critical factor in youth suicides, especially those involving firearms. According to Rosenberg and Mercy (1991), many young suicide victims, particularly males, are not generally depressed but act on impulse in response to school, home, or legal difficulties. A recent study showed that the availability of guns in the home, independent of firearms type or method of storage, increases the risk for suicide among adolescents. Guns were twice as likely to be found in the homes of suicide

victims as in the homes of suicide attempters or controlled adolescents (Brent et al., 1991).

Witnessing Violence in the Family

Violent families are likely to produce violent children. The childhood experiences of being abused or witnessing violence increase a person's risk of exhibiting violent behavior at a later time. Exposure to violence also adversely affects children's development in many areas, including their ability to function in school, their emotional stability and orientation to the future (Groves et al., 1993). Of children attending a Boston inner-city hospital pediatric clinic, one of every ten children witnessed a shooting or stabbing before the age of six (Taylor et al., 1992).

Adults who as children witnessed violence in their families are at increased risk of physically abusing their spouses or intimates and children. They also are at increased risk of being victims of physical abuse (Hotaling & Sugarman, 1986; NCEHIC, 1992).

In violent families, children learn to solve their personal conflicts and stresses according to the model set by the parents. Wodarski and Hedrick (1987) state the following about children whose parents model violence as a problem-solving strategy:

> . . . violent children do not learn empathic behaviors nor adequate cognitive strategies for dealing with anger. Likewise, they do not learn to handle stress in a prosocial manner. Thus, violent children are not prepared to deal with stress once they leave protected homes. (p. 31)

Compared to nonabused children, children as young as one to three years of age who have been physically abused at home are at least twice as likely to physically assault classmates and adult caretakers at school (George & Main, 1979). Children identified by court records as abused have been found to be at increased risk of committing violent crimes. Widom (1989) found that abused children were 42 percent more likely to be arrested for a violent crime at some point during their lifetime than those no identified as having been abused.

The lack of appropriate parenting is an important factor in the development of violent behavior. Parental overcontrol as well as undercontrol of monitoring and discipline, inconsistent rule application, and aversive parent-child interactions are more likely to be present among children who exhibit violent behavior than among those who do not (Loeber, 1982; Wodarski & Hedrick, 1987). Family rejection also increases the likelihood of violent behavior in children and adolescents (Patterson & Dishion, 1985).

Experiencing Poverty and Hopelessness

Homicide and other forms of interpersonal violence are closely related to poverty. Youth in the lowest socioeconomic levels of society are the most likely to be victims and perpetrators of homicide. Poor urban and inner-city areas in particular tend to have higher incidences of interpersonal violence than rural and suburban areas (Ropp et al., 1992). Factors such as low socioeconomic levels, poor housing, high unemployment rates, and high population density characterize areas prone to violence. However, it is important to understand that it is the feelings that accompany these conditions that likely account for high violence statistics. In other words, the fact that impoverished urban youth are hopeless about their life options and are angry about poverty and perceived racism increases their risks of violent behavior.

Being Exposed to Violence in the Media

There is a broad consensus that exposure to television increases children's physical aggressiveness. This is evidenced by at least three landmark reports of the effects of viewing television violence. The National Commission on the Causes and Prevention of Violence concluded that viewers of television learn how to engage in violent behavior.

The Surgeon General's Report, Television and Growing Up: The Impact of Televised Violence concluded that fairly extensive experimental evidence exists for short-term causation of aggression among some children. Finally, the National Institute of Mental Health report, Television and Behavior: Ten Years of Scientific Progress and Implications concluded that a causal link between television viewing and aggressive behavior is scientifically established and that television viewing of violence has the potential for creating both immediate and long-term effects. The viewing of television and film violence may produce subsequent violence by providing violent role models, influencing beliefs and attitudes favorable to the use of violence, and by portrayals of violence as an effective means of solving problems (NCEHIC, 1992).

Young children up to approximately age four, are often not able to interpret truth from fantasy in television programs, despite coaching from adults (Flavell, 1986). This is of concern in light of the fact that the average child age two to five watched 27 hours of television per week in 1990 (A.C. Nielson Company, 1990). Centerwall (1992) describes how young children interpret what they view on television:

In the minds of such young children, television is a source of entirely factual information regarding how the world works. Naturally, as they get older, they come to know better, but the earliest and deepest impressions were laid down when the children saw television as a factual source of information about a world outside their homes where violence is a daily commonplace and the commission of violence is generally powerful, exciting, charismatic, and efficacious. Serious violence is most likely to erupt at moments of severe stress—and it is precisely at such moments that adolescents and adults are most likely to revert to their earliest, most visceral sense of what violence is and what its role is in society. Much of this sense will have come from television. (pp. 3059–3060).

In Deadly Consequences (Prothrow-Stith & Weissman, 1991), the following points regarding violence and the media are discussed.

1. Our popular culture is the most violent in the world, showing violent behavior as ordinary and amusing.
2. As a culture and as individuals, we have become desensitized and insensitive to the portrayal of violence before our eyes on the television or film screen.
3. There has been a merging in the media of sex and violence: viewers are barraged with depictions of vicious crimes directed at females with which violence has become "sexualized."
4. Televised news coverage of accident scenes and crimes has become more grisly in its coverage of violent events.
5. "Good guys" are shown to use violence as a problem-solving strategy as a first resort.
6. Television may be as much of an influence on society as school or church, or maybe even more so.
7. The constant exposure of televised violence seems to legitimize violence as an acceptable way to deal with conflict and to avenge oneself.
8. Television often teaches children how to use aggressive behavior for personal gain.
9. Television programs rarely model positive behaviors such as sharing, concern or empathy for others, willingness to delay gratification, compromising.
10. Individuals exposed to lots of television/film violence are more fearful than other people and tend to overestimate the amount of violence in their environments (the "mean world syndrome").

11. Those most vulnerable to television's exposure to violence are children who are poor, those who witness or have been victimized by family violence, and those that lack nonviolent, male role models.

Scott Snyder (1991) reports the following:

One example of these emerging demographics is that preteens, ages 11–14, rent violent horror movies in higher numbers than do any other age group in the U.S., according to the editor of *Video Marketing Newsletter*. This group obtains the R-rated movies through older friends, siblings, unsuspecting or desensitized parents, or apathetic video store employees (*National Coalition on Television Violence News*, 1989). (p. 121)

Lyrics in both rock and rap music can be aggressive, focus on the gruesome, send messages that are sexually explicit, and urge listeners to rebel against authority (Berger, 1989). In her book, *Coping with Cults*, Maryann Miller quotes Dwight Silverman, a journalist in San Antonio:

Heavy metal is a mean-spirited music. In it, women are abused, parents are objects of derision and scorn and violence, education is a foolish waste of time. Rock 'n' roll has always been a music of rebellion and frustration, but never hatred. (pp. 78–79)

Gilda Berger in her book, *Violence and the Media*, concludes that all forms of the media—newspapers, magazines, books, television, movies, cable TV, videotapes, and music records and videos—all expose us daily to violence—murders, assault, stabbing, torture, and rape. A major shift in priorities will have to occur before any solution to the violent influence that the media exert, especially on the young. The solutions will not be easy.

According to the *NAEYC Position Statement on Media Violence in Children's Lives*:

. . . media violence is not just a reflection of a violent society, it is also a contributor. (p. 21)

Belonging to a Gang

Youth gangs are groups of youth who form an allegiance for a common purpose and engage in violent, unlawful, or criminal activity. Gangs usually have names and are usually territorial. They use graffiti to mark their "turf." Gang members associate together and often commit crimes against other youth gangs or against the general population. Most gang members adopt certain colors and/or dress style that is easily recognized and identified with a particular gang. Youth gangs are often composed exclusively of white Americans, African-Americans, Hispanic, or Asian-American members.

Youth and young adult gangs in cities and localities are an accelerating problem and are certainly not confined to major urban areas (Eckholm, 1993; Nielsen, 1992). and to low-income youth (National School Safety Center, 1988). Gangs, which are a prominent part of youth culture, provide opportunity, protection, belonging, inclusion, brotherhood, help to the underdog, and a promise for the future. Gang violence has become increasingly violent (Hammond & Yung, 1993) to the point where violence and death are pervasive involving younger children, including girls (Odum, 1991).

In recent years, the print and electronic media have routinely carried accounts of gang-related activities, such as drive-by shootings. In one six-week period alone in 1991, there were 162 drive-by shootings and 26 gang-related homicides in Los Angeles (Cotton, 1992). Drive-by shootings by young gang members are often the result of gang warfare, drug dealing, or simply random acts of rage. Young muggers, whether they belong to a gang or not, may attack simply to get their victims' sneakers, jackets, or jewelry. Most often, violent youth target their peers. More than any other group of Americans, young people between the ages of 11 and 24 are robbed, raped, and assaulted (Kohl, 1991).

The pervasiveness of gangs is a major force in the chronic, community violence that hundreds of thousands of American children face. For example, in some Chicago neighborhoods, by the time children reach five years of age, virtually all will have first-hand encounters with shootings. In these same neighborhoods, by age 15, 30 percent of all youth have witnessed a homicide and 75 percent have witnessed a life-threatening assault with a knife or gun.

Facing the constant threat of community violence creates enormous challenges for young children and the people who care for them. The threat of violence can produce significant psychological problems that interfere with learning and appropriate social behavior in school and that can interfere with normal parent-child relationships.

The attraction of gangs. Being exposed to violence also makes children prime candidates for involvement in gangs, where the violent economy of the illicit drug trade offers a sense of belonging and solidarity as well as cash income for youth who have few prosocial alternatives for either

44

(Garbarino, 1991). Youth who are economically disadvantaged, who are in trouble academically, who have dropped out of school, and/or who have no job skills are at high risk for gang involvement (Huff, 1989). Activities available through gang membership, such as crime and drug sales, can provide an avenue for the generation of income and status when options through legitimate channels are perceived as unavailable. Other reasons for joining gangs are the excitement of gang activity, peer pressure, attention, "family" tradition, boredom, alienation from families and peers, and a lack of realization of the hazards involved. Because the desire for acceptance is so strong during late childhood and adolescence, vulnerable youth are often attracted to gangs.

Consequences of gang membership. Parents do not often realize that their children are engaged in gang activity. On the other hand, some children have parents who are gang members and who may even expect their children to bring drug money home or face parental punishment. The consequences of gang membership for youth are often serious. Being a member of a gang increases exposure to illicit drugs, alcohol abuse, firearms and other weapons, fighting and altercations, dropping out of school, arrest, and imprisonment. Family members of active gang members may suffer fear for their safety, damage to personal property, personal injury, and/or emotional responses such as trauma and depression from the loss or injury of a loved one because of gang violence.

Types of gangs. There appears to be different types of youth gangs. In a study of Ohio gangs, Huff (1989) identified 3 major types of gangs:

1. **Hedonistic gangs** serve a basic purpose in letting members have a good time around getting high on psychoactive substances. Gang members infrequently participate in violent crimes, but occasionally engage in minor property crimes.
2. **Instrumental gangs** are highly involved in property crimes for economic reasons. Most members use alcohol and other drugs and some may be involved in drug trafficking. However, drug selling is not an organized gang activity.
3. **Predatory gangs** are much more deeply involved in criminal activity and violent behavior than hedonistic and instrumental gangs. They are likely to have committed robberies, street muggings, group rape, and even homicide. Group members are likely to be highly involved in the use and trafficking of illegal drugs, often for the purpose of financing the purchase of sophisticated weapons.

Belonging to a Cult

A cult has been defined as an alternative system of beliefs that is usually the idea of someone who doesn't agree with the way the world is working (Miller, 1990). Some cults solve their problems by destructive means and therein lies the problem. Many young people are attracted to these groups at times in their lives when they are vulnerable and curious. These young people for the most part are intelligent, well-educated, trusting, and indecisive (Miller, 1990). The aim of the cult leaders is to get control of the minds of these young people. They accomplish this by indoctrination techniques.

In her book, *Coping with Cults*, Maryann Miller lists fourteen characteristics that describe destructive cults. The list was developed by Marci Rudin.

1. Members swear total allegiance to an all-powerful leader whom they believe to be the Messiah.
2. Rational thought is discouraged or forbidden.
3. The cult's recruitment techniques are often deceptive.
4. The cult weakens the follower psychologically by making him or her dependent on the group to solve problems.
5. The cults manipulate guilt to their advantage.
6. The cult leader makes all career and life decisions of the members.
7. Cults exist only for their own material survival and make false promises to work to improve society.
8. Cult members often work full time for the group for little or no pay.
9. Cult members are isolated from the outside world.
10. Cults are antifemale, antichild, and antifamily.
11. Cults claim to be the only ones who will survive the soon-approaching end of the world.
12. Many cults follow an "end justifies the means" philosophy.
13. Cults, particularly in regard to finances, are shrouded in secrecy.
14. A feeling of or potential for violence frequently surrounds cults. (pp. 19–20)

TYPES OF VIOLENCE

Violence takes many forms and the effects of it are far-reaching. Not all forms of violence involve death; some forms cause physical injury: other forms result in psychological trauma to individuals and families. In this section of the chapter, the discussion will include homicide, assault injuries, suicide, child abuse and neglect, rape, partner violence, fighting among children, physical fighting among adolescents, and school violence.

Homicide

Homicide is currently ranked as the 10th leading cause of death in the United States (Novello, Shosky, & Froehlke, 1992), accounting for an estimated 24,020 deaths in 1991 (Mason & Proctor, 1992). **Homicide** is defined as death due to injuries purposely inflicted by another person, not including deaths caused by law enforcement officers or legal execution. Males, teenagers, young adults, and minority group members, particularly African-Americans and Hispanics, are most likely to be homicide victims (Hammond & Yung, 1992). Most homicides are committed with a firearm, during an argument, and they occur among people who are acquainted with one another.

Intrafamilial homicide accounts for approximately one of six homicides, primarily among young adults and African-Americans. Approximately half of family homicides are committed by spouses. The risk of being killed by one's spouse is 1.3 times higher for wives than for husbands.

Homicides between intimates, regardless of whether or not the victim is male or female, is often preceded by a history of physical and emotional abuse directed at the female. The prevention of homicides among spouses and intimates is directly linked, therefore, to the prevention of abuse of females. Focusing on abuse only within legally sanctioned marriages, however, will omit abuse that occurs during dating, in nontraditional relationships, and in legal relationships that have been terminated through separation and/or divorce.

The majority of homicide victims under age four, when both the victim and the offender are identified, are killed by a family member or caretaker. Older child victims are murdered by acquaintances or strangers. Child abuse causes about 1,000 deaths annually. Half of these result from physical abuse and half from neglect.

Death rates from homicide among African-American males, females, and children far exceed the rates for other citizens of the same age and gender. Homicide is the leading cause of death for African-Americans ages 15 through 34 (Centers for Disease Control, 1991a). Hispanic and American Indian males also have an elevated risk of homicide compared to non-Hispanic white American males. No cause of death so greatly differentiates African-Americans from other Americans as homicide (USDHHS, 1991). While African-Americans comprise 12 to 13 percent of the U.S. population, they account for 44 percent of all victims of homicide.

Although poverty has been identified as an important factor in homicide, the use, manufacture, and distribution of drugs also are extremely important factors. Violence may occur as a consequence of the pharmacological effects of drugs, of economically-motivated crimes to support drug use, or interactions related to the manufacture, buying, and/or selling of drugs.

Assault Injuries

Each year, 2.2 million people suffer nonfatal injuries from violent and abusive behavior. An **assault injury** is any physical or bodily harm that occurs during the course of a rape, robbery, or any other type of attack on a person. Of those injured, one million receive medical care and 500,000 are treated by emergency medical facilities. However, these figures underestimate the true extent of nonfatal assaultive injuries that occur in the United States.

More than 25 percent of the 10,000 to 15,000 spinal cord injuries each year are the result of assaultive violence. The proportion of permanent disabling injuries resulting from violent behavior is highest in urban areas. In Detroit, 40 percent of all traumatic spinal cord injuries resulted from gunshot wounds. This proportion is particularly high among adolescents.

Suicide

Suicide is the eighth leading cause of death, accounting for approximately 30,000 deaths annually (Shaffer, 1993). Injuries resulting from gunshots cause a majority of suicidal deaths, and much of the increase in suicide rates since the 1950s can be accounted for by firearm-related deaths. Guns were used in 61.2 percent of suicides in 1988 (Mason & Proctor, 1992). Impulsive suicide without associated clinical depression appears to account for a particularly large proportion of youth suicides.

The overall suicide rate has changed relatively little since 1950. However, the rates vary substantially by gender, age, and race/ethnicity. Males are more likely to commit suicide. Rates are generally higher for white Americans and American Indians. Elderly white American males (65 years of age and older) and young, male American Indians are particularly susceptible. Suicide is the third-ranked cause of death in children, with rates for persons aged 15 to 19 years of age nearly doubling over the past two decades (Garland & Zigler, 1993; Mason & Proctor, 1992). The 1989 youth suicide rate was the highest it has ever been (Novello, Shosky, & Froehlke, 1992). As many as 5,000 Americans ages 15 to 24 take their own lives and more than 500,000 others attempt suicide each year (Ackerman, 1993).

Child Abuse and Neglect

Annually, an estimated 1.6 million children nationwide experience some form of abuse or neglect. In addition, 1,100 die as a result of abuse or neglect. Child abuse deaths increased by 10 percent in 1991 over 1990 (Peterson, 1992). **Child abuse and neglect** are terms that refer to physical or mental injury, sexual abuse or exploitation, negligent treatment, or maltreatment of a child by a person who is responsible for the child's welfare, under circumstances that indicate that the child's health or welfare is harmed or threatened (The Child Abuse Prevention, Adoption, and Family Services Act of 1988).

Family members are responsible for 85 to 90 percent of child abuse cases. Parents may be more likely to maltreat their children if the parents:
- are emotionally immature;
- are isolated, with no family or friends for support;
- were emotionally deprived, abused, or neglected as children;
- feel worthless;
- have never been loved or cared about;
- are in poor health;
- abuse alcohol or other drugs (National Center on Child Abuse and Neglect, 1991).

Many abusive and neglectful parents do not intend to harm their children and often feel remorse about the maltreatment. However, their own problems may prevent them from stopping their harmful behavior and may result in resistance to outside intervention.

Children may be at a higher risk of maltreatment if they are unwanted, resemble someone the parent dislikes, or have physical traits or behaviors that make them different or especially difficult to care for. Changes in financial conditions, employment status, or family structure may shake a family's stability. Some parents may not be able to cope with the stress resulting from these changes and may experience difficulty in caring for their children (NCCAN, 1991).

Being abused or neglected as a child increases one's risk for violent behavior as an adult. Abused children are also more likely to fail grades in school, have a difficult time forming friendships, have disciplinary problems at school, exhibit physically assaultive behavior at school and in the home, and be involved in alcohol and other drug use

(Gelles & Strauss, 1988). Children and teenagers who have been abused need help in understanding that parents have no right to abuse them. They need help placing the responsibility for the maltreatment on the adult and not on themselves. They need help in recognizing that other adults can and will protect them. They need to understand that the abuse is not their fault. They need help with developing self-esteem. If they do not develop self-esteem, they are likely to form adult relationships in which they are the abuser or the victim. The pattern is repeated.

Specific types of child abuse. An estimated 358,300 children are physically abused each year (NCCAN, 1991). **Physical abuse** is characterized by inflicting injury by punching, beating, kicking, biting, burning, or otherwise physically harming a child. Although the injury is not an accident, a parent or caretaker may not intend to hurt the child. The injury may result from discipline or physical punishment that is inappropriate to the child's age. Signs of physical abuse include bruises, burns, cuts, missing teeth, broken bones, and head and internal injuries.

Child neglect is failure to provide for a child's basic needs. Neglect can be physical, educational, or emotional. **Physical neglect** includes refusal of or delay in seeking health care; abandonment; expulsion from home, or not allowing a runaway to return home; and inadequate supervision. **Educational neglect** includes permission of truancy, failure to enroll a child of mandatory school age, and inattention to a special educational need. **Emotional neglect** includes such actions as chronic or extreme spouse abuse in the child's presence, parental permission of alcohol or other drug abuse by the child, and failure to provide needed psychological care. Emotional abuse might involve withholding love, or constantly criticizing or ridiculing a child. As a result, the child may suffer from low self-esteem. It is important to distinguish between willful neglect and failure to provide necessities of life because of poverty or cultural norms (NCCAN, 1991).

Mental injury includes acts or omissions by the parent or other adult responsible for the child's care that cause, or could cause, serious behavioral, cognitive, emotional, or mental disorders. An example of an extreme form of mental injury abuse is the parent's or caretaker's use of an extreme or bizarre form of punishment, such as torture or confinement in a dark closet. Less severe acts include such acts as habitual scapegoating, belittling, or rejection (NCCAN, 1991). Any of these acts can be devastating to a child's emotional growth and self-esteem.

Sexual abuse includes fondling a child's genitals, intercourse, incest, rape, sodomy, exhibitionism, and sexual exploitation. To be considered child abuse, these acts have to be committed by a person responsible for the care of a child (a parent, baby-sitter, or day-care provider). Many experts believe that sexual abuse is the most underreported form of child maltreatment because of the secrecy or "conspiracy of silence" that often characterizes these cases. There has been a three-fold increase in the reported incidence of sexual abuse since 1980 (NCCAN, 1991).

Sexual abuse is against the law. Every state has laws that require physicians, other health professionals, and teachers to report cases of child abuse to child welfare authorities. Children who were sexual-abuse victims of fathers or stepfathers, whose molestation involved force, appear to be at especially high risk for severe long-term psychological impacts (Browne & Finklehor, 1986). Females who were sexually abused as children also are at increased risk of later rape and physical abuse by husbands or other adult partners as well as strangers. The risk of substance abuse and developing alcoholism is higher among females who have been sexually abused than for other females.

Rape

Experts agree that cases of rape are vastly underreported. They suggest that the frequency of rape is probably at least twice as high as the number of reported cases. **Rape** is the nonconsensual sexual penetration of an adolescent or adult by physical force, by threat of bodily harm, or when the victim is incapable of giving consent by virtue of mental illness, mental retardation, or intoxication (Searles & Berger, 1987).

Young, unmarried, and low-income females are the most frequent victims of rape and rape attempts. Females between the ages of 12 and 34 are particularly vulnerable, with victimization rates more than twice as high as females in other categories. Most rapists are unarmed and operate alone. Many rapes are committed by acquaintances of the victims. The FBI reports that at least 50 percent of rapes in the U.S. involve alcohol.

Sexual assaults in dating relationships. Many widely-accepted false beliefs exist about rape; for example that forced kissing, fondling, or sexual intercourse is acceptable behavior in the context of dating relationships. This type of belief is an important factor underlying sexual assault in our society. A survey of students in sixth to ninth grades found that 65 percent of boys and 57 percent of girls believed that it was acceptable for a male to force a female

to have sex if they have been dating for more than 6 months. Similarly, 51 percent of boys and 41 percent of girls believed it was acceptable for a male to force a female to have sex if he had spent a lot of money on her.

According to some estimates, more than 1 million teenagers are sexually assaulted each year. Nine of ten teenagers who report rape were raped by someone they knew. In a survey of college students, more than four of ten female students reported that they have experienced some form of sexual assault—completed rape, or other forcible sexual contact (Koss & Harvey, 1991). In another survey, 1 of 12 male college students reported committing acts that met the legal definitions of rape or attempted rape (Wilson, 1990). Most did not believe that they had done anything wrong in their actions of forcing or coercing females into having sex with them.

Alcohol is often a factor in sexual assaults that occur during dating relationships. Alcohol impairs the ability to think clearly and reduces inhibitions and defenses. A male may feel powerful and become more aggressive under the influence of alcohol. He is less able to control himself and is much less aware of the consequences of his actions. A dangerous scenario develops when the psychopharmacological effects of alcohol are combined with feelings of sexual arousal. Having impaired judgment, he may reason that as he makes unwelcome advances, his sexual impulses and actions are not rape.

Females who have been drinking alcohol are more vulnerable to sexual assault than females who have not been drinking. A person under the influence of alcohol has more difficulty sticking to the choices she has made for herself and her body. Alcohol reduces inhibitions that normally help protect against unwelcome advances. The ability to recognize the early warning signs leading to trouble is impaired. Some males are eager to take advantage of alcohol's effects on a female. They may apply pressure to get a female to drink, "loosening her up so she's easier prey for their advances" (Wilson, 1990, p. 14).

Avoiding alcohol can often make the difference for a female between being able to make the decision of doing what she wants to do with her body vs. allowing her date to do what he wants to do with her body. An alcohol-free mind is a protection because a young female can think clearly and is physically capable of coordinating her defenses (Wilson, 1991). When alcohol consumption leads to unconsciousness in a female, the risk of rape increases greatly.

Partner Violence

Although male partners are also abused, females appear to be at greater risk of injury from abuse and are most likely to attack their partners in self-defense. Between two and four million females are physically battered each year by partners including husbands, former husbands, boyfriends, and lovers. Between 21 and 30 percent of all females have been beaten by a partner at least once. In addition, at least 3.3 million children are at risk for witnessing parental abuse each year (Groves et al., 1993).

Once physical violence has occurred in a relationship, it tends to recur and become more severe over time. More than 1 million females seek medical assistance for injuries caused by battering each year, and the vast majority of domestic homicides are preceded by earlier episodes of violence. One analysis found that 21 percent of all females using emergency surgical services were there because of the consequences of domestic violence (Council on Scientific Affairs, 1992).

Females in the United States are more likely to be assaulted and injured, raped, or killed by a current or male ex-partner than by all other assailants combined (Council on Scientific Affairs, 1992). In addition, females are often battered by their partners during pregnancy. From 4 to 8 percent of females going to prenatal clinics have been identified as being abused during pregnancy (Rosenberg, Saltzman, & Shosky, 1992).

Domestic violence is a major context for suicide attempts, substance abuse, and depression among females and 45 percent of the mothers of abused children are themselves battered females. Physical abuse accounts for 25 percent of all female suicide attempts and more than 4,000 homicides per year (Holtz & Furniss, 1991). Females who are killed by a current or former male partner represent over half of all female homicide victims in the United States.

Fighting Among Children

During their normal stages of development, children are learning to balance their desires and needs with requirements that are imposed on them not only by society but also by their own stages of physical, emotional, moral, social, and mental development (Lovejoy & Estridge, 1987). As children seek to attain a sense of self-esteem, they experience some frustration and pain. When two or more children interact, their desires and needs often clash and the result may be a the bullying of one child by the other in order to gain a feeling of supremacy. **Bullying** is an attempt by a stronger student to harm a weaker victim,

presumably in the absence of provocation (Hoover, Oliver, & Hazler, 1992). Victims of bullying may be male or female, and the harassment can be either physical or mental in nature, or both.

Ronald Stephens, Executive Director of the National School Safety Center, explains that schoolyard bullies are often subjected to extensive physical punishment in their own homes. Bullies are also likely to have experienced family rejection in early childhood, inconsistent application of rules and guidelines, and to not be disciplined for their anti-social actions. He also says that although teachers and school officials often can identify potential bullies as early as kindergarten and first grade, little is done to rechannel their energies into positive behaviors. Early aggressive behavior patterns often persist through adolescence into adulthood.

Physical Fighting Among Adolescents

Physical fighting among adolescents is often considered a normal and sometimes necessary part of growing up. The first encounter for many adolescents may be a fist fight. However, if the disagreement is not settled, future encounters may involve firearms. In other words, aggressive, physical confrontations easily escalate to dangerous situations and involve other people. If a person is under the influence of alcohol or another drug, the fighting is likely to get out of control.

Fighting results in hundreds of homicides and uncounted numbers of nonfatal injuries among adolescents each year. Fighting is the most immediate antecedent behavior for a large proportion of adolescent homicides that occur each year. Estimates from the National Adolescent Student Health Survey indicate that 44 percent of eighth grade students and 34 percent of tenth grade students were involved in a physical fight in 1987.

The national school-based Youth Risk Behavior Survey asked a representative sample of 11,631 ninth through twelfth grade students the following question: "During the past 30 days, how many times have you been in a physical fight in which you or the person you were fighting were injured and had to be treated by a doctor or nurse?" Because students were not asked the location of the fights, it was not possible to determine the extent to which physical fights occurred on school premises. About 8 percent of all students in these grades reported that they had been in at least 1 physical fight that resulted in an injury requiring treatment by a doctor or nurse. About 12 percent of all males reported being in a fight: 10.1 percent of white

49

American males; 17.6 percent of African-American males; and 16.2 percent of Hispanic males. As expected, the proportions of females involved in fighting was considerably lower—3.6 percent: 2.4 percent of white American females; 7.7 percent of African-American females; and 4.4 percent of Hispanic females (Centers for Disease Control, 1992b).

A reduction in the incidence of physical fighting may prove extremely important in disrupting the causal mechanisms of homicide and assaultive injury. For this reason, experts in the prevention of violence recommend that emphasis should be placed on helping schools teach nonviolent, conflict-resolution skills as a means of preventing violence. The acquisition of conflict-resolution skills may serve to help adolescents decrease their risk of homicide and assaultive injury victimization and penetration. If adolescents can be taught to avoid violence as a way of solving problems, alternative nonviolent patterns of behavior might be carried throughout life.

One study found that about 10 percent of ninth through twelfth graders could be described as extreme victims of peer abuse (Perry, Kusel, & Perry, 1988). Another study (Hoover et al., 1992) found that 72 percent of female students and 81 percent of male students attending secondary schools in the midwest felt that they had experienced bullying at some point in their student careers. About 14 percent of the students in this study described themselves as experiencing severe reactions to the abuse.

School Violence

Schools are increasingly concerned about the threat of violence (Bushweller, 1993; Sabo, 1993). Almost three million incidents of crime and violence are reported on K–12 campuses annually, or about 1,700 per day (Stephens, 1991). These include reported criminal acts such as robbery, aggravated assault, and violent victimization. Violence in schools affects school personnel as well as students. In 1978, the National Institute of Education conducted the "Violent School-Safe School" study, which found that 5,000 teachers were attacked monthly in U.S. schools. The study also found that 1,000 of these teachers sustained injuries serious enough to require medical attention. Since this study, there have been no national studies conducted on the number of cases of violence against teachers. However, data from local and regional areas suggest that the number of cases of violence directed at teachers persists, or perhaps has increased (Stephens, 1991). The National Education Association estimates that every day 6,250 teachers are threatened with injury and

260 are actually assaulted. Further, 100,000 students carry a gun to class every day (Hull, 1993).

The presence of violence in elementary and secondary schools creates climates of fear. An atmosphere of fear distracts students' minds from learning and teachers' minds from teaching. When personal safety is threatened at school, survival itself becomes the primary objective during the school day.

Strategies of dealing with violence and vandalism must be more than informational programs that recount how many crimes have been committed and what will happen to them if they get involved in those kinds of activities. Most youths, who would be willing to respond positively to rules and regulations, do not know how to react to acts of violence they see. When students have the opportunity to become involved in solutions to vandalism and violence, positive results happen (Diem, 1982).

To summarize, violence is a challenging problem for society and particularly for educators. Awareness of the prevalence of violence and the types of violence forces educators to give violence education a top priority.

PROMOTING NONVIOLENT BEHAVIOR IN YOUTH

Violence reduction has been targeted as a major goal for schools. The National Education Goals call for offering disciplined school environments that are conducive to learning by the year 2000 (National Education Goals Panel, 1991). Goal 6 of the National Education Goals aims to have every school in the United States free of violence and drugs in order to achieve such school environments. Several of the national health objectives for the year 2000 target reductions in violence or risk factors for violence (United States Department of Health and Human Services, 1991). These objectives target:

- reducing the number of homicides in the total population and in such high-risk groups as African-American males ages 15–34, American Indians, and children ages three and under;
- reducing the number of suicides in the total population and in such high-risk groups as youth ages 15–19, white American males ages 65 and older, and American Indians;
- reducing weapon-related deaths;
- reversing the rising incidence of maltreatment of children;
- reducing cases of physical abuse directed at females by male partners;
- reducing the number of assault injuries;

- reducing the number of rapes and attempted rapes among females;
- reducing the incidence of injurious suicide attempts among adolescents;
- reducing the incidence of physical fighting among adolescents;
- reducing the incidence of weapon-carrying by adolescents;
- increasing the proportion of elementary and secondary schools that teach nonviolent conflict-resolution skills, preferably as a part of quality school health education.

How might this overwhelming task be accomplished? What type of educational program might be implemented to promote nonviolent behavior in youth and nonviolent schools? This section of the chapter discusses violence education that focuses on inner well-being and describes the integration of violence education into the drug education curriculum presented in this book.

Violence Education and Inner Well-Being

Violence education must provide skills that enable young persons to become strong, have a sense of self, and resist external pressures. In developing a concrete philosophy for violence education and the violence curriculum, the authors have given much thought as to the integration of violence prevention strategies into the drug education curriculum. The authors believe that the skills young people need to resist drugs and to behave in nonviolent ways enable them to develop inner well-being. As stated previously in Chapter 1, inner well-being is a condition that results from:

- having positive self-esteem,

- managing stress effectively,
- choosing healthful behaviors,
- choosing healthful situations,
- engaging in healthful relationships,
- making responsible decisions,
- using resistance skills,
- demonstrating character,
- participating in the community,
- abiding by laws.

About This Book

This book is designed for drug education professionals who are engaged in helping young persons develop inner well-being and choose a drug-free and drug-informed lifestyle. A discussion of violence and strategies to reduce the incidence of violence and promote respectful, caring, and nonviolent relationships are included for at least two reasons. First, young persons who have respectful, caring, and nonviolent relationships are more likely to choose a drug-free and drug-informed lifestyle. Second, young persons who choose a drug-free and drug-informed lifestyle are more likely to have respectful, caring, and nonviolent relationships. Simply stated, behaviors that reduce harmful drug use are closely connected to behaviors that promote high-quality relationships.

For this reason, the authors have infused totally awesome teaching strategies to promote high-quality relationships and to promote respectful, caring, and nonviolent relationships at every grade level in the drug education curriculum presented in Section V of this book.

BIBLIOGRAPHY

Ackerman, G.L. (1993) A congressional view of youth suicide. *American Psychologist*, 48:183–184.

Berger, G. (1989) *Violence and the Media*. New York: Franklin Watts.

Brent, D.A., Perper, J.A., Allman, C.J., Moritz, G.M., Wartella, M.E., & Zelenak, J.P. (1991) The presence and accessibility of firearms in the homes of adolescent suicides: A case-control study. *Journal of the American Medical Association*, 266:2989–2995.

Browne, A., & Finklehor, D. (1986) The impact of child sexual abuse: A review of the research. *Psychological Bulletin*, 99:66–77.

Bushweller, K. (1993) Guards with guns. *The American School Board Journal*, January, 34–37.

Callahan, C.M., & Rivara, F.P. (1992) Urban high school youth and handguns: A school-based survey. *Journal of the American Medical Association*, 267:3038–3042.

Centers for Disease Control. (1991a) Homicide among young black males: United States, 1978–1987. *Morbidity and Mortality Weekly Report*, 265:183–184.

Centers for Disease Control. (1991b) Weapon-carrying among high school students: United States, 1990. *Morbidity and Mortality Weekly Report*, 40:681–684.

Centers for Disease Control. (1992a) Firearm-related deaths: Louisiana and Texas, 1970–1990. *Morbidity and Mortality Weekly Report*, 41:213–215, 221.

Centers for Disease Control. (1992b) Physical fighting among high school students: United States, 1990. *Morbidity and Mortality Weekly Report*, 41:91–94.

Centerwall, B.S. (1992) Television and violence: The scale of the problem and where to go from here. *Journal of the American Medical Association*, 267:3059–3063.

Children's Safety Network. (1991) *A Data Book of Child and Adolescent Injury*. Washington, D.C.: National Center for Education in Maternal and Child Health.

Cohen, S. & Cohen, D. (1984) *Teenage Stress*. New York: M. Evans and Company.

Cotton, P. (1992) Gun-associated violence increasingly viewed as public health challenge. *Journal of the American Medical Association*, 267:1171–1173.

Cotton, P. (1992) Violence decreases with gang truce. *Journal of the American Medical Association*, 268:443–444.

Council on Scientific Affairs, American Medical Association. (1992) Violence against women. *Journal of the American Medical Association*, 267:3184–3189.

Diem, R.A. (1982) Teaching strategies for dealing with violence and vandalism. *The Social Studies*, July/August, 172–174.

Eckholm, E. (1993) Teenage gangs are inflicting lethal violence on small cities: Mix of guns and crack pushes murder rates to big city levels. *The New York Times*, January 31, volume 142, 1(L).

Fingerhut, L.A., Ingram, D.D., & Feldman, J.J. (1992) Firearm and nonfirearm homicide among persons 15 through 19 years of age: Differences by level of urbanization, United States 1979 through 1989. *Journal of the American Medical Association*, 267:3048–3053.

Fisher, R., & Ury, W. (1981) *Getting to Yes*. Boston: Houghton Mifflin.

Flavell, J.H. (1986) The development of children's knowledge about the appearance-reality distinction. *American Psychologist*, 41:418–425.

Forward, S. (1989) *Toxic Parents*. New York: Bantam Books.

Garbarino, J. (1991) Testimony and prepared statement. In Subcommittee on Juvenile Justice, Committee on the Judiciary. *Senate hearing 102-655: Youth Violence and Gangs* (Serial No. J-102-45). Washington, D.C.: U.S. Government Printing Office.

Garland, A.F., & Zigler, E. (1993) Adolescent suicide prevention: Current research and social policy implications. *American Psychologist*, 48:169–182.

Gelles, R., & Straus, M. (1988) *Intimate Violence*. New York: Simon & Schuster.

George, C., & Main, M. (1979) Social interactions of young abused children: Approach, avoidance, and aggression. *Child Development*, 50:306–318.

Goldstein, P.J. (1985) The drugs-violence nexus: A tripartite conceptual framework. *Journal of Drug Issues*, 15:493–506.

Gordon, J. (1990) *Stress Management*. New York: Chelsea House Publishers.

Groves, B.M., Zuckerman, B., Marans, S., & Cohen, D.J. (1993) Silent victims: Children who witness violence. *Journal of the American Medical Association*, 269:262–264.

Guyer, B., Lescohier, I., Gallagher, S., Hausman, A., & Azzara, C. (1989) Intentional injuries among children and adolescents in Massachusetts. *New England Journal of Medicine*, 321:1584–1589.

Hall, J.R., Reyes, H.M., Meller, J.L., & Stein, R.J. (1993) Traumatic death in urban children revisited. *American Journal of Diseases of Children*, 147:102–107.

Hammond, W.R., & Yung, B. (1993) Psychology's role in the public health response to assaultive violence among young African-American men. *American Psychologist*, 48:142–154.

Holtz, H., & Furniss, K.K. (1991) Getting involved: Health care workers and domestic violence. *USA Today*, March, 88–89.

Hotaling, G.T., & Sugarman, D.B. (1986) An analysis of risk markers in husband to wife violence: The current state of knowledge. *Victims and Violence*, 1:101–124.

Hoover, J.H., Oliver, R., & Hazler, R.J. (1992) Bullying: Perceptions of adolescent victims in midwestern USA. *School Psychology International*, 13:5–16.

Huff, C.R. (1989) Youth gangs and public policy. *Crime & Delinquency*, 35:524–537.

Hull, J.D. (1993) The knife in the book bag. *Time*, February 8, 37.

Johnson, K. (1992) *Turning Yourself Around*. California: Hunter House Publishers.

Jourard, S. (1970) *Transparent Self*. New York: D. Van Nostrand Company.

Kohl, H. (1991) Opening statement. In Subcommittee on Juvenile Justice, Committee on the Judiciary. *Senate hearing 102-665: Youth Violence and Gangs* (Serial No. J-102-45). Washington, D.C.: U.S. Government Printing Office.

Koop, C.E., & Lundberg, G.D. (1992) Violence in America: Public health emergency, Time to bite the bullet back. *Journal of the American Medical Association*, 267:3075–3076.

Koss, M.P., & Harvey, M. (1991) *The Rape Victim: Clinical and Community Approaches to Treatment*. Beverly Hills, CA: Sage Publications.

Loeber, R. (1982) The stability of antisocial and delinquent child behavior: A review. *Child Development*, 53:1431–1446.

Lovejoy, F.H., Estridge, D. (1987) *The New Child Health Encyclopedia*. New York: Dell Publishing Company, Inc.

Marwick, C. (1992) Guns, drugs threaten to raise public health problem of violence to epidemic. *Journal of the American Medical Association*, 267:2993.

Mason, J., & Proctor, R. (1992) Reducing youth violence: The physician's role. *Journal of the American Medical Association*, 267:3003.

McAnarney, E.R. (1993) Life will never be the same: Violence in rural America. *American Journal of Diseases of Children*, 147:264.

McClure, B.A., Miller, G.A., & Russo, T.J. (1992) Conflict within a children's group: Suggestions for facilitating its expression and resolution strategies. *The School Counselor*, 39:268–272.

Miller, M. (1990) *Coping with Cults*. New York: Rosen Publishing Group.

National Association for the Education of Young Children. (1990) NAEYC position statement on media violence in children's lives. *Young Children*, July, 18–21.

National Center for Environmental Health and Injury Control, Centers for Disease Control. (1992) *Position Papers from the Third National Injury Control Conference*. Atlanta: Centers for Disease Control.

National Center on Child Abuse and Neglect. (1991) *Family Violence: An Overview*. Washington, D.C.: National Clearinghouse on Child Abuse and Neglect and Family Violence Information.

National Education Goals Panel. (1991) Measuring progress toward the National Education Goals: Potential indicators and measurement strategies—discussion document. Washington, D.C.: National Education Goals Panel.

National Institute on Drug Abuse. (1990) *Drugs and Violence: Causes, Correlates, and Consequences*. NIDA Research Monograph 103. DHHS Publication No. (ADM)91, 1721. Washington, D.C.: U.S. Government Printing Office.

National School Safety Center. (1988) *Gangs in Schools: Breaking Up Is Hard to Do*. Malibu, CA: Pepperdine University Press.

Nielsen, S. (1992) The emergence of gang activity: One junior high school's response. *NASSP Bulletin*, April, 61–67.

Novello, A.C., Rosenberg, M., Saltzman, L., & Shosky, J. (1992) A medical response to domestic violence. *Journal of the American Medical Association*, 267:3132.

Novello, A.C., Shosky, J., & Froehlke, R. (1992) A medical response to violence. *Journal of the American Medical Association*, 267:3007.

Odum, R. (1991) Testimony and prepared statement. In subcommittee on Juvenile Justice, Committee on the Judiciary, Senate hearing 102 665: Youth Violence and Gangs (Serial No. J-102-45). Washington, D.C.: U.S. Government Printing Office.

Page, R.M., Kitchin-Becker, S., Solovan, D., Golec, T.L., & Hebert, D.L. (1992) Interpersonal violence: A priority for health education. *Journal of Health Education*, 23:286–292.

Patterson, G.R., & Dishion, T.J. (1985) Contributions of families and peers to delinquency. *Criminology*, 23:63–79.

Perry, D.G., Kusel, S.J., & Perry, L.C. (1988) Victims of peer aggression. *Developmental Psychology*, 24:807–814.

Peterson, K.S. (1992) Child abuse deaths up 10 percent in '91. *USA Today*, April 3, 1(D).

Potter-Efron, R.T., & Potter-Efron, P.S. (1991) *Anger, Alcoholism, and Addiction: Treating Individuals, Couples, and Families*. New York: W.W. Norton.

Prothrow-Stith, D., & Weissman, M. (1991) *Deadly Consequences*. New York: Harper Collins.

Ropp, L., Visintainer, P., Uman, J., & Trelor, D. (1992) Death in the city: An American tragedy. *Journal of the American Medical Association*, 267:2905–2910.

Rosenberg, M.L., & Mercy, J.A. (1991) Introduction. In M.L. Rosenberg & M.A. Fenley, (Eds.), *Violence in America: A Public Health Approach* (pp. 3–13). New York: Oxford University Press.

Sabo, S.R. (1993) Security by design. *The American School Board Journal*, January, 37.

Searles, P., & Berger, R.J. (1987) The current status of rape reform legislation: An examination of state statutes. *Women's Rights Law Reporter*, 9:25–43.

Shaffer, D. (1993) Suicide: Risk factors and the public health. *American Journal of Public Health*, 83:171–172.

Snyder, S. (1991) Movies and juvenile delinquency: An overview. *Adolescence*, 26:121–130.

Spivack, G. (1983) *High Risk Early Behaviors Indicating Vulnerability to Delinquency in the Community and School*. National Institute of Juvenile Justice and Delinquency Prevention. Washington, D.C.: U.S. Government Printing Office.

Steck, G.M., Anderson S.A., & Boylin, W.M. (1992) Satanism among adolescents: Empirical and clinical considerations. *Adolescence*, 27:901–912.

Taylor, L., Zuckerman, B., Harik, V., & Groves, B. (1992) Exposure to violence among inner city parents and young children. *American Journal of Diseases of Children*, 146:487.

United States Department of Health and Human Services. (1991) *Healthy People 2000: National Health Promotion and Disease Prevention Objectives*. (Publication No. PHS 91-50213). Washington, D.C.: U.S. Government Printing Office.

United States Department of Justice. (1990) *Federal Bureau of Investigation: Uniform Crime Reports, 1989*. Washington, D.C.: Department of Justice.

VanWie, E.K. (1987) *Teenage Stress: How to Cope in a Complex World*. New York: Julian Messner.

Weil, D.S., & Hemingway, D. (1992) Loaded guns in the home: Analysis of a national random survey of gun owners. *Journal of the American Medical Association*, 267:3033–3037.

Whitaker, C., & Bastian, L. (1991) *Teenage Victims: A National Crime Survey Report* (Publication No. NCJ-128129). Washington, D.C.: U.S. Department of Justice, Bureau of Justice Statistics.

Widom, C.S. (1989) The cycle of violence. *Science*, 244: 160–166.

Wilson, L.L. (1990) Alcohol and date rape: Dangerous liaisons. *Listen*, April, 11–14.

Wodarski, J.S., & Hedrick, M. (1987) Violent children: A practice paradigm. *Social Work in Education*, Fall, 28–42.

DRUGS: A FACTUAL ACCOUNT

DRUG ACTIONS AND REACTIONS

The systems of the human body function together to maintain an internal environment that remains at a relatively constant level. This environment is important not only to the health of the individual but also to the health of each cell in his or her body. This environment is normally maintained within a narrow range of variables such as temperature and chemical content within the body. It is important to be aware of any factors that might upset the delicate balance of the internal environment and thus affect a person's ability to function. In this chapter, drug terminology, the nervous system, methods of drug administration, and factors that determine the effects of drugs will be discussed.

DRUG TERMINOLOGY

To understand how drugs act, it is important to become acquainted with some basic terminology. **Drugs** are substances, excluding food, that alter the function of the body. **Medicines** are drugs that are used to treat, prevent, or diagnose illness. The focus of this book is primarily on psychoactive drugs. **Psychoactive drugs** are substances that are capable of altering a user's moods, perceptions, feelings, personality, or behavior. This section will discuss drug use and drug dependence.

Drug Use

Drug use is the use of drugs (including alcohol) in any form, legal or illegal, whether by prescription or for "recreational" purposes (Trapold, 1990). All drugs, legal as well as illegal, have the potential for misuse or abuse. **Drug misuse** is the inappropriate use of drugs including prescribed or nonprescribed medicines.

Examples of drug misuse include:
• taking medicine leftover from a previous illness,
• driving after taking certain medications,
• drinking alcohol while taking certain medications,
• using another person's prescription drug,
• mixing medications without consulting a physician.

Drug abuse is the use of drugs that results in impairment of a user's ability to function normally or that is harmful to the user or others. It is important to remember that drug abuse can involve both legal and illegal drugs, and that abusers commonly use more than one drug. **Polydrug abuse** is the simultaneous abuse of more than one drug.

Some examples of impairment or harm resulting from drug abuse are:
• scholastic failure or underachievement,
• motor vehicle injuries,
• cirrhosis of the liver (from chronic use of alcohol),
• lack of emotional development,
• suicide or suicide attempts,
• drug overdose,
• social withdrawal,
• fetal alcohol syndrome,
• financial difficulties,
• relationship difficulties,
• loss of self-esteem,
• risk of HIV infection,
• drug dependence.

Drug Dependence

Drug behavior is an all-encompassing term used to describe nonuse and all phases of drug use (Akers, 1992). Drug behavior can be viewed as a continuum ranging from abstinence of a particular substance to drug dependence on the other extreme. Several other terms also describe patterns of drug use, abuse, and dependence. These are described here in ascending order from the least to the most serious (NIDA, 1990).

• **Social-recreational use** is a type of drug use that typically occurs in social settings among friends who are also using for the purpose of experiencing the drug's effects. This type of use tends to be limited to infrequent social situations and to involve small to moderate amounts of the particular drug(s) that is being used.

• **Circumstantial use** is use motivated by a desire to obtain a specific effect that is perceived as desirable within a certain situation. Examples are using a drug to relax after a stressful experience; using stimulants to stay awake all night to study; and taking stimulants to diet.

- **Intensified use** is a pattern of use that occurs when drugs are taken daily or almost daily, usually in low to moderate doses. This level of drug use is usually motivated by an individual's need to achieve relief from a persistent problem, such as anxiety or depression, or to maintain a desired level of performance.
- **Compulsive use** is the daily or almost daily use of high doses of a drug to obtain a desired physical and/or psychological effect. Drug use becomes the most important thing in the user's life, around which all other activities are organized. Compulsive use is the most dangerous pattern of use and is often termed drug dependence. It is the type of use that is the most likely to come to the attention of others at school, home, or work.

Thus, **drug dependence** is compulsive use of a drug (or drugs) despite adverse psychological, physiological, or social consequences. The lives of drug-dependent people become dominated by obtaining and using drugs. Drug dependence leads people to do things that are often contrary to their values, their best judgement, and their common sense in order to use drugs. Drug dependence is an illness that requires treatment (NIDA, 1990). Drug dependence, also known as chemical dependence, is believed to develop in 10–20 percent of those who use mood-altering (psychoactive) drugs (Trapold, 1990).

According to Trapold (1990), an individual is drug dependent if (s)he:
- uses mood-altering drugs,
- suffers serious recurring life problems as a result of that use, and
- nevertheless continues to use drugs.

> Those individuals whose drug use causes problems, but who then curtail their drug use so that the problems cease, are also not chemically dependent. Only those who continue their problem-causing drug use, despite these problems, are chemically dependent. (p. 247)

Drug dependence is further defined by physical and psychological dependence on one or more psychoactive drugs (Fleming & Barry, 1992). **Physical dependence** is a physiological process in which repeated doses of a drug cause the body to adapt to the presence of the drug. In other words, a physically dependent person's body becomes accustomed to having the drug in its system by making physiological adaptations to its presence (NIDA, 1990). Physical dependence includes the development of tolerance or of withdrawal symptoms (Fleming & Barry, 1992).

Tolerance is a condition in which the body becomes adapted to a drug so that increasingly larger doses are needed to produce the desired effect (Levy, Dignan, & Shirreffs, 1992). For example, individuals who were able to "get high" by drinking one can of beer, find that they must drink three, four, five, six, or even more to achieve the same effect. **Withdrawal symptoms** are unpleasant symptoms experienced by individuals who are physically dependent on a drug when deprived of that drug (Levy, Dignan, & Shirreffs, 1992). These symptoms occur in response to a situation in which certain physiological processes that were suppressed by the presence of a drug become hyperactive in its absence. Because withdrawal symptoms are unpleasant, drug use may be continued in order to avoid them. Physical dependence on a drug is not always a prerequisite of chemical dependency (Trapold, 1990).

Psychological dependence is a condition characterized by a pervasive desire or "craving" to achieve the effects produced by a drug. This type of dependence may or may not be accompanied by physical dependence. For example, some people crave heroin and inject it repeatedly, but do not use enough to develop physical dependence. Such people are called "needle freaks." They are generally considered dependent, even though they are not physically dependent. Another example is the person who uses LSD daily or almost daily. LSD does not produce physical dependence, but this level of compulsive use would make most people consider such a person to be dependent. Conversely, a person who becomes physically dependent on narcotics to relieve pain following surgery, and who discontinues narcotic use when the pain disappears, is usually not termed a drug addict or diagnosed as drug dependent because the psychological aspect (psychological dependence) of drug self-administration is not present (NIDA, 1990).

Trapold (1990) stresses the important role of psychological dependency in a drug-dependent person.

> It is psychological dependency that keeps people "locked into" continued drug use and produces most of the deviant behavior in chemical dependency. Psychological dependence is the condition that must be treated if the deviant behavior is to be corrected. Physical dependence may or may not develop contingent on the pattern of drug use and the individual. When physical dependence does develop, it probably serves to strengthen the psychological dependence, but it is not necessary for the definition or diagnosis of chemical dependency. (p. 247).

It is important to conceptualize drug dependence as a disease that is often progressive and fatal (Rogers, Silling, & Adams, 1991). Drug abuse and dependence can lead to overdose, vital organ destruction (i.e., brain, liver, kidneys), and contribute to motor vehicle crashes and other accidents. Other adverse consequences that can occur in drug dependent individuals are:

- marijuana-induced cognitive impairment,
- chest pain while using cocaine,
- family problems,
- child abuse,
- impaired social relationships,
- arrest for drug possession,
- impaired scholastic or job functioning,
- driving under the influence of drugs,
- public intoxication,
- financial problems.

Compared to adults, adolescents and children appear to have an increased susceptibility or vulnerability to drug dependence. However, in contrast to adults, physical dependence, with the development of withdrawal and tolerance, is uncommon in adolescents (Flynn, 1992). Morrison (1991) comments on the nature of drug dependence in young people:

> They also clearly experience a more accelerated progression of the disease process than observed in adults. Because of their age, lack of personality development, dependent family role, immaturity, impulsivity, and acting out of age-related behavioral tendencies, symptoms specific to the adolescent population occur. These symptoms are compounded by the phenomenon of denial which yields a more entrenched and complex delusional system in the adolescent that dictates age-specific intervention and treatment approaches. Polydrug use is more common in adolescents and also complicates the presenting clinical picture. Dual diagnoses are prevalent and in addition to chemical dependence, conduct disorders, depression, anxiety, and organic mental syndromes are most common. Treatment issues offer a challenge as successful treatment and subsequent recovery appear to involve a process of habilitation (initial learning)—not rehabilitation (relearning)—and the use of comprehensive, flexible, multimodality treatment approaches.

THE NERVOUS SYSTEM

The key to how psychoactive drugs produce their powerful effects lies in how they affect the human nervous system. It is important to review the primary structures and functions of this body system in order to understand how drugs cause specific effects. This section will include a discussion of the organization of the nervous system, the brain, and nerve cells and neurotransmitters.

Organization

The nervous system is the body's control system. It is composed of a network of nerve cells, neurons, that carry messages, or impulses, to and from the brain and spinal cord to all parts of the body. The nervous system keeps us in touch with our external environment and allows us to respond to such factors as noises, lights, or changes in temperature. The functions of this system include memory, thinking, solving problems, communicating and emotions. The delicate balance of the internal environment of the body is in large part maintained by the nervous system.

Two branches of the system are the central nervous system and the peripheral nervous system. The **central nervous system** is composed of the brain and spinal cord. The **peripheral nervous system** consists of many pairs of nerves that branch from the brain and spinal cord to the periphery of the body. Twelve pairs of cranial nerves branch from the brain and transmit information to and from the eyes, ears, nose, and tongue. Cranial nerves also control muscles in the face and neck. Thirty one pairs of spinal nerves branch from the spine and transmit information to and from all other parts of the body.

The Brain

The brain can be divided into several large regions, each responsible for some of the activities vital for life. The **brain stem** is the lowest portion and controls basic functions such as heart rate, breathing, eating, and sleeping. When one of these basic needs must be fulfilled, the brain stem structures can direct the rest of the brain and body to work toward that end. While these structures may be simple, they can exert powerful effects on our behavior (Fig. 3-1).

Above the brain stem, encompassing two-thirds of the human brain are the two hemispheres of the cerebral cortex. It is the cortex, the convoluted outer covering of nerve cells and fibers, that is the most recent part of the brain to evolve, developing completely only in mammals. Because they have a cortex, all mammals have more complex behavioral repertoires than creatures with simpler brains, like birds and reptiles. It is the large size and increased complexity of the human cerebral cortex that makes us different from other mammals.

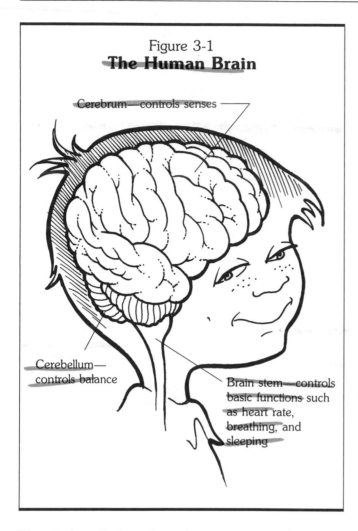

Figure 3-1
The Human Brain

Cerebrum—controls senses

Cerebellum—
controls balance

Brain stem—controls
basic functions such
as heart rate,
breathing, and
sleeping

Though the cells throughout the entire extent of the cerebral cortex are remarkably similar, the cortex can be divided into dozens of specific areas, each with a highly specialized function. It is like a collection of small computers, each working on a different aspect of a large problem. Much of the cerebral cortex is devoted to our senses—enabling us to see, hear, smell, taste, and touch. Other areas give us the ability to generate complex movements; still other regions allow us to speak and understand words, and different regions altogether allow us to think, plan, and imagine.

On top of the brain stem and buried under the cortex, there is another set of more primitive brain structures called the limbic system. The **limbic structures** connect the cortex, which deals mainly with the outside world, with our emotions and motivations, which reflect our internal environment and survival needs. These connections allow us to experience a wide range of feelings and to influence these feelings with our perceptions and actions. They also enable us to use our impressive cognitive abilities to help us do the things we need to do to survive. The **hippo-**

60

campus and the **amygdala** are two large limbic structures that are also critical for memory. Sensory information flows from the cortex to these primitive brain regions, which take into account what is going on inside the brain and the body and then instruct the cortex to store what is important.

One of the reasons that drugs of abuse can exert such powerful control over our behavior is that they act directly on the more primitive brain stem and limbic structures, which can override the cortex in controlling our behavior. In effect, they eliminate the most human part of our brain from its role in controlling our behavior.

Surprisingly, the feelings of pleasure turn out to be one of the most important emotions for our survival. In fact, the feeling of pleasure is so important that there is a circuit of specialized nerve cells devoted to producing and regulating it. One important set of these nerve cells, which uses a special chemical messenger, a neurotransmitter called dopamine, sits at the very top of the brain stem. These dopamine-containing neurons relay messages about pleasure through their nerve fibers to the nerve cells in a limbic structure called the nucleus acumbens. Still other fibers reach to a related part of the frontal region of the cerebral cortex. So, the pleasure circuit spans the survival-oriented brain stem, the emotional limbic system, and the complex information processor called the cerebral cortex.

The reason that pleasure, which scientists call reward, is a powerful biological force for our survival is that pleasure reinforces any behavior that elicits it. If you do something pleasurable, the brain is wired so that you tend to do that again. This is the reason a rat or a monkey so readily learns to press a lever for food. The animal does it because it is reinforcing—pressing the lever gets food and eating the food turns on the pleasure center, an action that helps ensure that the animal will do again what got him food in the first place. And all of this happens unconsciously. We do not have to think about it or pay attention. It is an automatic brain function.

Thus, life's sustaining activities, such as eating a good meal or engaging in sex, activate this pleasure circuit. By doing so, they teach us to do these things again and again. But certain substances, including all the drugs that people abuse, also can potently activate the brain's pleasure circuit. Unfortunately, the more a person learns to repeat the drug-taking behavior the more the brain learns to depend on drugs to evoke pleasure.

This is the key reason that people repeatedly abuse drugs. Drugs make them feel good by directly turning on the pleasure circuit. It also is a reason that drug addiction is so difficult to treat. These drug users find that only drugs can give them pleasure. Drug addiction is a biologically-based disease that alters the way the pleasure center, as well as other parts of the brain, function. By directly turning on our pleasure circuits, many addictive drugs make our brains behave as if these compounds were as important for survival as food, sex, and all the other natural rewards that also turn on the pleasure circuits. Thus drugs pervert to a destructive end a strong emotion that helps to activate one of the brain's most powerful learning mechanisms.

Nerve Cells and Neurotransmitters

To further understand how drugs influence behavior, it is important to understand how nerve cells and the molecules that make up these cells interact with the molecules that make up drugs. A **neuron** is the basic unit of structure and function in the nervous system. Each neuron, or nerve cell, contains three important parts (Fig. 3-2). The central **cell body** (which contains the nucleus) directs all the activities of the neuron. **Dendrites** are sets of branches through which messages from other nerve cells are relayed directly to the cell body. An **axon** is a cable-like fiber through which the cell body sends impulses, or messages, to dendrites of other neurons. However, the axon does not make direct contact with the dendrites of other neurons. A **synapse** is a tiny gap that separates the terminal of an axon from the dendrites of a neuron with which it seeks to communicate. A **neurotransmitter** is a chemical that transmits an impulse across the synaptic gap between two neurons. The neurotransmitter is released at the end of the axon and diffuses across the synapse. **Receptors** are special molecules on the surface of dendrites of adjacent neurons to which the neurotransmitter binds.

When the neurotransmitter couples to a receptor, it is like a key fitting into a lock that starts the process of information flow in that neuron. First, this coupling allows the receptor molecules to link with other molecules that extend through the cell membrane to the inside of the cell. These other molecules cause a change in the cell. This is how the neurotransmitter that can affect only a receptor molecule sitting on the outside edge of the cell can change the way the cell behaves. Once the receptor activates these other molecules, its mission is complete. The neurotransmitter then is either destroyed or sucked back into the nerve cell that released it. **Chemical neurotransmis-**

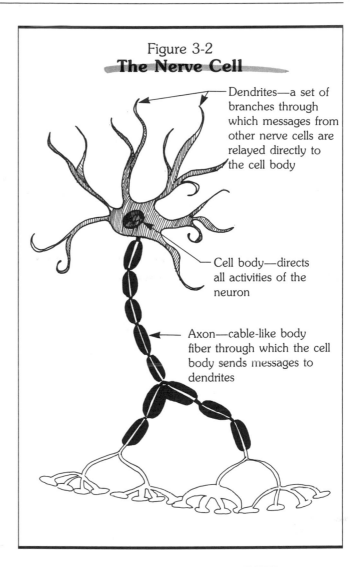

Figure 3-2
The Nerve Cell

Dendrites—a set of branches through which messages from other nerve cells are relayed directly to the cell body

Cell body—directs all activities of the neuron

Axon—cable-like body fiber through which the cell body sends messages to dendrites

sion is the entire process of the effect of the neurotransmitter on a receptor.

Almost all drugs that change the way the brain works do so by tinkering with chemical neurotransmission. Some drugs, like heroin, mimic the effects of a natural neurotransmitter. Others, like LSD, block receptors and thereby prevent neuronal messages from getting through. Still others, like cocaine, interfere with the process by which neurotransmitters are sucked up by the neurons that release them. Others, like caffeine and PCP, exert their effects by interfering with the way messages proceed from the surface receptors into the cell interior.

When drugs interfere with the delicate mechanisms through which nerve cells transmit, receive, and process the information critical for daily living, we lose some of our ability to control our own lives. The continued use of these drugs can actually change the way the brain works. This is the biological basis of addiction.

61

Observations of people and experiments with animals have taught us that addiction begins when a drug is inappropriately and repeatedly used to stimulate the nerve cells of the pleasure circuit of the brain. Rats hooked up to a drug pump will repeatedly press the lever for doses of illicit drugs that activate dopamine-containing nerve cells in the ventral tegmental area or the neurons that these cells end on in the nucleus accumbens and the frontal cortex. In fact, there is a remarkable similarity between the drugs humans like to abuse and the ones that laboratory monkeys will self-administer. Given the opportunity, both monkeys and some humans will use cocaine, amphetamines, heroin, alcohol, phenobarbital, nicotine, and virtually every opiate drug. Hallucinogens seem to be the only class of drugs preferred only by people.

Animal experiments have taught us that cocaine turns on the pleasure circuit by allowing dopamine to accumulate in the synapses where it is released. Because the amount of dopamine is allowed to build up, strong feelings of pleasure, even euphoria, are elicited. Heroin turns on the pleasure circuit by directly activating opiate receptors on other neurons in this circuit. Even drugs like marijuana, which animals do not like to self administer, can make it easier for other drugs or natural pleasures to turn on the pleasure circuit. This may be why people compulsively use even a relatively weak drug like marijuana.

So, people abuse drugs and animals self-administer them because drugs turn on the pleasure center. They do this by altering the normal process of chemical neurotransmission.

METHODS OF DRUG ADMINISTRATION

Drugs produce their effects on very specific tissues. **Sites of action** are limited places in the body where drugs produce their effects. If a drug is not able to effectively get to its specific sites of action, it will have a limited effect.

The method of drug administration has an important effect on how strong a response a drug produces. For example, a method of administration that results in slow absorption of a drug (i.e., swallowing a drug or absorption through the skin) will generally produce a weaker drug effect than a method in which a drug is delivered directly into the bloodstream (e.g., intravenous administration). The manner in which a drug is administered influences how much of the drug gets to its site of action, how fast it gets there, and even whether it gets there in the first place (Fig. 3-3). In this section, the discussion will be concerned with oral ingestion, inhalation, injection, and absorption.

Oral Ingestion

The oral ingestion of drugs is the most common method of drug administration. This is primarily because oral ingestion is the most convenient and simple means of taking a drug for most people. Orally ingested drugs are formulated as tablets, capsules, caplets, and liquid preparations.

The ingested drug enters the stomach and may be completely or partially absorbed into the bloodstream. However, the small intestine is the site where the absorption of many drugs is most efficient. Oral ingestion is the slowest and least predictable method of drug administration.

The presence of strong acids and digestive enzymes can destroy or change the viability of a drug compound's active ingredients. The hallucinogenic drug DMT and insulin, a needed drug for diabetics, are examples of drugs that cannot be effectively taken by oral ingestion. When swallowed, these compounds are destroyed by the digestive juices in the stomach.

Another major factor influencing the absorption rate of a drug is the absence or presence of solid foods in the stomach. Generally, when drugs are taken on an empty stomach, they rapidly pass into the small intestine and are absorbed quickly. The presence of particular foods in the stomach can also interfere with a drug's actions.

Inhalation

There is a rapid absorption of a drug compound into the bloodstream when the drug is inhaled. Specialized for absorption, the lungs are rich with tiny blood vessels called capillaries. Inhaled substances are efficiently absorbed into the bloodstream through these capillaries. The efficiency of this method of drug administration explains why many psychoactive drug users prefer inhaling or smoking their drugs of choice. Commonly used illicit substances such as marijuana, cocaine, and methamphetamine are often taken through inhalation. All of the drugs that we discuss in Chapter 9 are classified as inhalants because their volatile chemical nature favors users to inhale them.

Some drug users inhale drugs by snorting. **Snorting** is the process of sniffing a drug through the nose so that it can be absorbed through the mucous membranes of the upper nasal passages. This is a frequent route for the administration of cocaine.

Drug inhalation can potentially irritate the tissues that line the lungs and throat. Chronic irritation due to inhalation

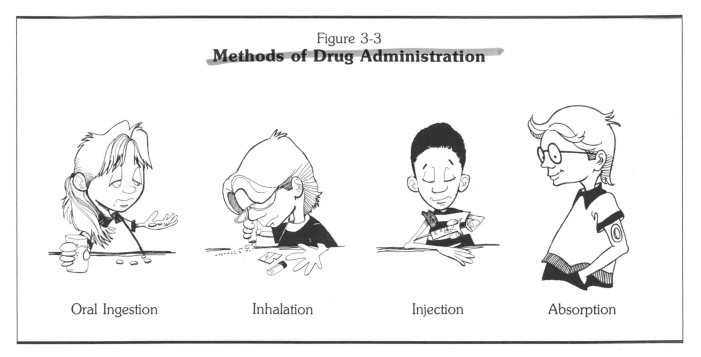

Figure 3-3
Methods of Drug Administration

Oral Ingestion   Inhalation   Injection   Absorption

of some drugs, particularly those that are smoked (e.g., marijuana and tobacco), can damage respiratory tissues. Long-term inhaling of substances may result in respiratory diseases such as asthma, chronic obstructive disease, and lung, throat, and other cancers.

Injection

Parenteral administration is a method of drug administration that involves injecting drugs into the body. Technically, the term parenteral refers to all routes of drug administration that do not involve the digestive system. Drugs must be dissolved into some liquid before they can be injected into the body. Generally a weak salt solution or saline is used. A **subcutaneous administration** is an injection of a drug just beneath the skin. This is sometimes called "skin popping."

An **intramuscular administration** is an injection of a drug into a muscle. The most common sites for intramuscular injections are the buttocks, thigh, or upper arm where a large muscle mass has a rich blood supply.

An **intravenous administration**, **IV**, is an injection of a drug directly into the bloodstream. Intravenous injection is also known as "mainlining" and produces a very rapid response to a drug. The practice of injecting illicit drugs carries significant risk of contamination from viruses and other pathogens such as HIV and hepatitis B when drug users share needles.

Absorption

Many drug compounds applied to the skin or mucous membranes can be absorbed into the bloodstream. **Transdermal administration** is the application of a drug to the skin. Transdermal administration is sometimes accomplished by the use of skin patches. **Skin patches** are worn on the body while a drug compound is slowly absorbed through the skin into the bloodstream. Many people who are attempting to quit smoking are relying on transdermal nicotine patches to help them achieve cessation. Nitroglycerin and scopolamine, an antimotion sickness drug, are also available in skin patches.

A suppository inserted into the anus is an example of a drug that is placed in a body orifice to be absorbed through the wall of a mucus membrane. Other drugs are absorbed through the mucous membranes of the mouth. **Sublingual drug administration** is the absorption of a drug under the tongue. **Buccal administration** is the absorption of a drug between the cheek and gum. All of these mucous membrane areas are effective absorption sites because they are rich in blood vessels that are close to the surface.

FACTORS THAT DETERMINE THE EFFECTS OF DRUGS

We have explained that in order for drugs to produce a reaction, they have to be effectively administered into the body (method or route of drug administration). Once inside the body, a drug compound has to travel to specific areas (sites of action) to produce its desired effect. **Pharmokinetics** is the study of the process of how drugs reach target sites of action. In this section of the chapter, the blood-brain barrier, dosage, the plateauing effect, drug interactions, individual variability, and user expectations will be discussed.

The Blood-Brain Barrier

Most of the drugs of abuse produce their desired effects by working on cells located within the brain. Drugs that produce psychoactive effects readily pass through what is known as the blood-brain barrier. The **blood-brain barrier** is largely composed of fat-covered membranes that surround capillaries in the brain. These capillaries have relatively few pores in comparison to capillaries located elsewhere in the body. Generally, drugs that are fat insoluble have difficulty passing through this barrier; whereas, fat-soluble compounds are less likely to be hindered and have less difficulty diffusing directly through capillary walls. For example, LSD, opiates, barbiturates, tranquilizers, caffeine, nicotine, marijuana, alcohol, and cocaine appear to have no difficulty passing through the blood-brain barrier.

Dosage

An important factor in determining the effect of a drug is dosage. **Dosage** is the amount or quantity of a drug compound that is administered within a specified time period. Many drugs produce dose-related effects. **Dose-related effects** are differing pharmacologic effects that are related to the quantity of a drug that is administered. For example, some drugs stimulate nerve cells when a low dose is administered, but block neurotransmission at higher dose levels. This elicits a depressive effect. Another commonly witnessed example of a dose-related effect is the person who is friendly and seemingly happy after one alcohol drink, but turns belligerent, rude, and perhaps aggressive after four, five, or six drinks.

The Plateauing Effect

With many drugs there is a plateauing of effects such that increasing dosage beyond a certain level does not increase response to the drug. In other words, taking more of a particular drug beyond a certain dosage will not increase the magnitude of its effects. The adage "if one pill is good, then two or more pills is better" does not hold for many drugs. Once a maximum therapeutic or in some cases psychoactive effect has been achieved, taking more of certain drugs will not increase the intensity of the desired effect. LSD provides a good example of this principle. Once a user has achieved a maximal change in perception at a given dose, increasing the amount of the drug will not further alter perception.

The same holds true for a person who has achieved a maximal therapeutic effect of reducing headache pain by taking two aspirin tablets. Doubling the dose to four tablets will not further reduce headache pain. Increasing dosages always increases the risk of side effects.

Alcohol and other sedatives are exceptions to the plateau principle. Increasing the amount of alcohol in the bloodstream progressively increases the depressive effects on the central nervous system. In fact, these depressive effects on the central nervous system continue until there is loss of consciousness, coma, or even death. **Additive effects** are progressive effects that are due to increasing dosages of a drug.

Drug Interactions

Because many people use two or more drugs simultaneously, there is risk of drug interactions. A **drug interaction** is the effect of one drug on the action of another drug or drugs. In addition, some foods interact with drugs by altering their actions. The effects of the interacting compounds can be either enhanced or diminished when taken simultaneously. Interactions can be harmful to a user. One particularly dangerous combination is taking tranquilizers with alcohol. These compounds potentiate each other's depressive effects and greatly exaggerate the risk of respiratory depression.

There is a great deal of individual variability in drug effects. For example, drug effects can be influenced by age, gender, body weight, diet, and expectations. Greater sensitivity to drug effects is more often observed in infants and the elderly than in adults. Females generally react more sensitively to the effects of drugs than males. Heavy people generally experience less drug effect for the same amount of drug than people who are lighter. The presence of food in the stomach at the time a drug is orally ingested tends to slow absorption of some drugs thus reducing drug effects.

User Expectations

One of the most important influences on drug effects are user expectations. If a person believes that a drug will be effective, it may prove to be so. **Placebos** are pharmacologically inert substances, such as "sugar pills." There is some evidence that placebos produce positive effects because user expectations may stimulate the release of endorphins. As we discussed earlier, endorphins are naturally released substances in the body that are similar in chemical structure to morphine and other opiate drugs.

In some research studies, a placebo is given to some of the participants to serve as a comparison to a drug that is under consideration. The **placebo effect** is the resulting effect caused by taking a placebo. Sometimes this result is powerful enough, even in the absence of a pharmacologically active drug, to produce a desired response. Because a specific response to a placebo cannot be anticipated, the process of the placebo effect is not fully understood (Carroll, 1993).

BIBLIOGRAPHY

Akers, R.L. (1992) *Drugs, Alcohol, and Society: Social Structure, Process, and Policy.* Belmont, CA: Wadsworth.

Carroll, C.R. (1993) *Drugs in Modern Society.* Madison, WI: William C. Brown Communications.

Fleming, M.F., & Barry, K.L. (1992). *Addictive Disorders.* St. Louis, MO: Mosby-Year Book.

Flynn, S. (1992) Adolescent substance abuse. In M.F. & K.L. Barry (Eds.), *Addictive Disorders.* (pp. 232–248). St. Louis, MO: Mosby-Year Book.

Levy, M.R., Dignan, M., & Shirreffs, J.H. (1992) *Life and Health: Targeting Wellness.* New York: McGraw-Hill.

Morrison, M. A. (1991) Overview: Kids and drugs. *Psychiatric Annals,* 21(2):72–73.

National Institute on Drug Abuse. (1990) *Drug Abuse Curriculum for Employee Assistance Program Professionals.* DHHS Publication No. (ADM)90-1587. Rockville, MD: National Institute of Drug Abuse.

National Institutes of Health. (1991) *Drugs and the Brain.* Washington, D.C.: National Institutes of Health.

Rogers, P., Silling, S.M., & Adams, L.R. (1991) Adolescent chemical dependence: A diagnosable disease. *Psychiatric Annals,* 21:91–97.

Trapold, M. (1990) Adolescent chemical dependency. In S.W. Henggler & C.M. Borduin (Eds.), *Family Therapy and Beyond: A Multisystemic Approach to Treating the Behavioral Problems of Children and Adolescents.* Pacific Grove, CA: Brooks/Cole.

STIMULANT DRUGS

In Chapter 3, the discussion involved the fact that the key to understanding the powerful effects of drugs is to know how they affect the human nervous system. **Stimulants** are drugs that increase the rate at which organs controlled by the central nervous system function. Stimulants produce a generalized arousal, resulting in an increased sense of alertness, an increase in pulse and blood pressure, an increase in physical activity and strength, a decrease in appetite, and a feeling of well-being that ranges from mild happiness to euphoria. The intensity of the effects depends on the particular stimulant and the dosage. Stimulants come from many naturally-occurring sources, such as cathine and cathinone (derived from khat) and theophylline (found in tea leaves), and also from synthetic sources. In this chapter, pharmacology and the effects of stimulants, medical use of stimulants, cocaine, amphetamines, look-alike drugs, caffeine, other stimulant drugs, and stimulants and sexuality will be discussed. The naturally-occurring stimulant nicotine will be discussed in Chapter 14.

PHARMACOLOGY AND THE EFFECTS OF STIMULANTS

Pharmacology is the study of the action of drugs on the human body. Some stimulants produce effects that last for three to four hours when taken intravenously and eight to twelve hours when taken orally. The effects of cocaine are different and will be discussed later in this chapter. In this section, tolerance and withdrawal, paranoid ideation, seizures, and blood pressure will be the topics of discussion.

Tolerance and Withdrawal

Tolerance to the euphoric effects of stimulants occurs very quickly, especially in the case of cocaine. Combined with the short duration of the effects, drug users often increase their doses rapidly. The most common situation occurs when a person takes several "hits" of cocaine, develops tolerance, and increases the dose to repeat the effect. This sequence recurs until the person is taking very high doses over a short period of time. All these factors, combined with the intense euphoric effect, probably account for the extremely high abuse potential of cocaine and its propen-

sity to turn occasional users into becoming addicted very quickly.

The withdrawal effects of all stimulants are almost mirror images of the drug's initial effects (Fig. 4-1). A person who has been using stimulants and stops will experience irritability, weakness, a marked reduction in energy, hypersomnia, depression, loss of concentration, and increased appetite. The symptoms are more severe in persons who have taken high doses over a long period of time. These symptoms may disappear within two to three days. However, they may sometimes last for a week or more.

Paranoid Ideation

Paranoid ideation is a serious adverse effect of stimulants in which a person becomes suspicious and fears that others are watching or following him/her. This adverse effect may even result in auditory hallucinations (hearing voices) and delusions. For example, the individual may become convinced that someone is plotting to kill him/her. These mental effects are identical to paranoid schizophrenia, a serious mental disorder.

Individuals vary in their susceptibility: some experience these effects from only one or two doses; others become paranoid only after using large doses over a long period of time. Because it is difficult to predict how any one individual will respond to stimulants, they are regarded as very toxic by psychiatrists. It is believed that anyone who takes stimulants can become paranoid if high enough doses are used for an extended time. Paranoid effects usually disappear within 2 to 14 days, but can last much longer.

Seizures

Stimulants can also induce seizures as a result of the stimulation of the nervous system. These seizures can result in sudden death as a result of the effects on the heart such as irregular heartbeat, a heart attack, inflammation of the heart muscle, or even cardiac arrest (a sudden stopping of the heart action). Cardiac arrest appears to have caused the death of Len Bias, the basketball player at the University of Maryland, who died after cocaine use in 1986.

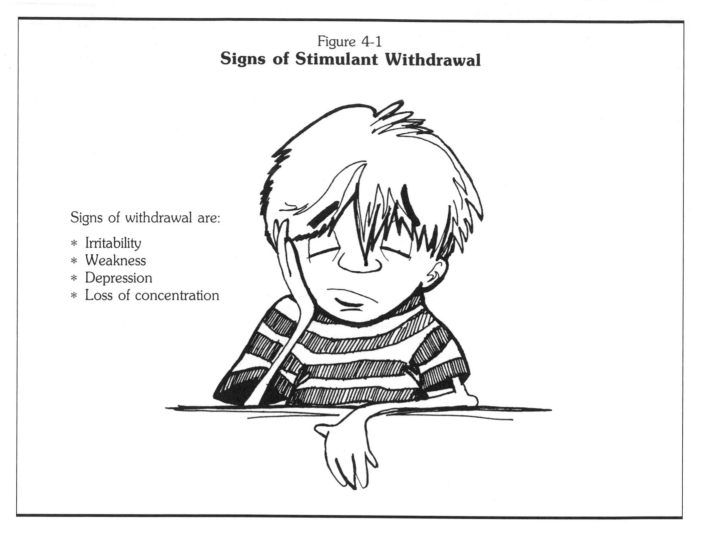

Figure 4-1
Signs of Stimulant Withdrawal

Signs of withdrawal are:

* Irritability
* Weakness
* Depression
* Loss of concentration

It is impossible to predict when cardiac toxicity might occur or how many doses may produce it.

Blood Pressure

Elevated blood pressure is another very serious adverse effect of stimulant use. This may be the underlying cause for the number of cerebrovascular accidents, or strokes, that are being observed with increasing frequency in hospital emergency facilities in association with cocaine use. A stroke involves the rupture of a blood vessel or clotting in a blood vessel or vessels in the brain that results in the death of brain cells. Many cocaine-related cerebrovascular accidents, some resulting in permanent neurological defects or even death, are well documented.

MEDICAL USES OF STIMULANTS

Most stimulants have appropriate medical uses. For example, a legitimate but infrequent medical use of stimulants is in chronically depressed elderly patients, or as an adjunct to a variety of antidepressant treatments in persons who have been unusually resistant to more standard treat-

ments. This type of use, however, is generally seen only in very specialized medical clinics or hospitals. In this section of the chapter, minor surgical procedures, weight reduction, and performance will be discussed.

Minor Surgical Procedures

Cocaine produces numbness when applied to mucous membranes and for that reason it is used often by ear, nose, and throat (ENT) specialists, and occasionally in ophthalmology and urology for minor surgical procedures. Because cocaine constricts blood vessels, it also stops bleeding. This effect adds to its usefulness in ENT surgery, which typically produces considerable bleeding because of the rich blood supply in the areas affected.

Weight Reduction

Stimulant drugs also have been used in attempts to control weight. This is one of their most controversial uses and has led to many abuses and inappropriate prescribing practices. One example is the advertisements about treating obesity by prescribing stimulants (usually Dexedrine or Ritalin). Physicians who have prescribed stimulants to everyone who requests the treatment have often developed huge practices, called fat clinics, with dubious benefits to their many "patients" and often with diversion of stimulant drugs into the illegal market.

A number of studies have shown that stimulants may cause modest weight reduction for some persons over a period of two to four weeks. However, tolerance to the appetite-suppressing effects then develops, and higher doses must be used to obtain the same effect. The general conclusion from a large number of such studies is that the benefits of stimulants for weight reduction are modest and of short duration, and their liabilities are high. Therefore, their use for weight control appears to be inappropriate and unwise. As a result, most physicians will not use them for this purpose, and many states have passed laws that forbid their use for weight reduction.

Performance

Because stimulants temporarily increase alertness and strength, drugs such as dextroamphetamine (Dexedrine) are sometimes used by students to cram for exams, by long-distance truck drivers who need to stay awake at night, and by athletes to improve performance.

Paradoxically, good medical evidence supports the use of stimulants to decrease physical activity and increase attention in children who are hyperactive. Stimulants also help people who suffer from narcolepsy. **Narcolepsy** is a condition in which a person is unable to stay awake. In these cases, the least potent stimulants, such as methylphenidate (Ritalin), are used orally to minimize the chances for abuse or other undesirable side effects.

COCAINE

Cocaine is a strong stimulant that is derived from the leaves of the coca bush. The leaves are typically steeped in sulfuric acid and kerosene until coca paste, consisting of 20 percent to 85 percent of cocaine sulfate, is produced. Hydrochloric acid is added to convert the cocaine sulfate into powdery flakes or rocks of nearly pure cocaine hydrochloride. Cocaine hydrochloride is a colorless or white, odorless crystalline powder. In this section, how cocaine is administered; the initial effects of cocaine use; the long-term effects of cocaine use; crack; particular effects of crack and cocaine on females; and prenatal and early infant exposure to cocaine will be discussed.

How Cocaine Is Administered

Cocaine can be absorbed through any mucous membrane, and is circulated in the blood to the heart, lungs,

and other body organs. Inhaled intranasally, it reaches the brain and neurons of the sympathetic nervous system in three minutes; injected, in fifteen seconds; smoked, in seven seconds.

Many users of cocaine inhale it through the nose, or "snort" it. A small quantity of the powder is placed on a mirror, chopped with a razor blade to remove flakes and lumps, and formed into "lines" or "rails" one to two inches long and one-eighth inch wide. The cocaine is inhaled through a straw or rolled-up currency. Inhaled, the drug's effects peak in 15 to 20 minutes, and disappear in 60 to 90 minutes.

Another way cocaine is administered is by placing a small amount of freebase on a piece of foil, which is heated from below with a match or lighter. **Freebase** is the purified base form of cocaine processed from the hydrochloride salt using volatile chemicals, usually ether. The rising wisps of smoke are inhaled—a practice known as "chasing the dragon" when used with heroin.

Some users inject a cocaine solution under the skin, into a muscle, or into a vein. Intravenous use is often preferred, as it is the only route of introduction yielding 100 percent absorption of the drug. The result is an intense high that crests in 3 to 5 minutes and wanes over 30 or 40 minutes.

The most dramatic cocaine high, and the most dangerous one from a number of perspectives, is smoking "alkaloidal base" or cocaine freebase. It is typically smoked through a water pipe. The typical "hit" involves about 120 mg of cocaine, although the amount that finds its way into the user's system varies greatly. The apex is reached in 90 seconds and effects dissipate within a few minutes.

Initial Effects of Cocaine Use

Cocaine is a vasoconstrictor, narrowing the blood vessels. Heart rate, blood pressure, and respiration are quickened, and the body's metabolism is stepped up. The user's appetite is deadened and he or she cannot sleep while "wired" on the drug. Cocaine stimulates at least two areas of the brain—the cerebral cortex (which governs higher mental activity, such as memory and reasoning), and the hypothalamus (which is responsible for appetite, body temperature, sleep, and certain emotions).

Cocaine is metabolized rapidly by the blood and liver. Its actions on the sympathetic nervous system mimic the body's fight-or-flight response to fear or challenge. The effects are similar to those of amphetamine. In fact, subjects in research studies couldn't distinguish between the effects of the two at lower doses, except that amphetamine's actions are longer lasting.

The extreme euphoria associated with cocaine use resembles that produced by direct electrical stimulation of the reward centers of the brain. However, what goes up must come down. With cocaine, as with other stimulants, the higher the high, the lower the low. The euphoria and excitement of the initial "rush" taper off—gradually when injected or smoked—and the user slides into a physiological depression. This state is characterized by a "let-down" feeling, dullness, tenseness, and edginess.

Long-Term Effects of Cocaine Use

Daily or binge users characteristically undergo profound personality changes. They become "coked out." They are confused, anxious, and depressed. They are short-tempered and grow suspicious of friends, loved ones, and other associates. Their thinking is impaired; they have difficulty concentrating and remembering things. They experience weakness and lassitude. Their work and other responsibilities fall into neglect. They lose interest in food and sex. Some become aggressive, some experience panic attacks. The more of the drug they use, the more profound their symptoms become.

In acute cases, where consumption is frequent and/or the dose is high, users may suffer a partial or total break with reality—"cocaine psychosis." The cocaine psychotic has delusions and may become paranoid, sometimes reacting with violence against those (s)he imagines are persecuting him. Many have visual, auditory, or tactile hallucinations (one of the most common is "coke bugs" or **formication**, the sensation of insects crawling under the skin). Cocaine psychosis can continue for days, weeks, or months. Severe cases require hospitalization and the use of antipsychotic medications.

Those who sniff cocaine regularly experience a constantly running nose, burns and sores on the nasal membranes (sometimes to the point of perforating the septum between the nostrils), sore throats, and hoarseness. Many experience shortness of breath, cold sweating, and controlled tremors as their consumption increase. Long-term use may damage the liver.

Cocaine shares mechanisms with other drugs (such as methamphetamine and MDA) that have been known to cause neural damage. Although there has been insuffi-

cient study to date to determine if cocaine causes neural damage, the common properties it shares with these drugs would lead one to believe that neural damage due to cocaine is highly likely. The drug can injure cerebral arteries. The acute hypertension sometimes brought on by cocaine use has been known to burst weakened blood vessels. The drug can also induce epilepsy even in those with no previous signs of it.

Heavy use can cause angina and irregular heartbeat. It can worsen preexisting coronary heart disease and bring on a heart attack. New studies suggest that cocaine can bring on acute high blood pressure that can cause a blood vessel in the brain to rupture and cause strokes. There is some preliminary evidence that indicates that cocaine can cause spasms of arteries that feed the heart muscle, thus causing a heart attack. Chronic users sometimes report a phenomenon known as "snow lights," which are flashes of light in the periphery of vision; eye specialists have detected small crystals in the retinas of some of these individuals.

Because cocaine reduces appetite, many habitual users suffer from malnutrition and lose significant amounts of weight. This can lower immune defenses and make the user susceptible to tuberculosis, fungal diseases, and other infections. Poor diet results in nutritional deficiencies and a host of other problems, many of which are compounded by lack of sleep and negligent personal hygiene.

Intravenous users risk hepatitis, HIV and other infections from contaminated needles, and freebase smokers risk harm to the lungs (Fig. 4-2). The most common causes of death from cocaine abuse are respiratory paralysis, heart rhythm disturbances, and repeated convulsions, usually from massive overdoses or at the end of a binge. Some users suffocate in the deep stupor that follows an extended period of use; some drown in their own secretions. Still others succumb to allergic reactions.

Death from cocaine overdose comes swiftly. Typically, a user with no apparent symptoms lapses suddenly into grand mal convulsions and high fever, followed in a minute or so by respiratory collapse and death. Often the exact cause of death is difficult to pinpoint. Sudden death is infrequent and appears to be unpredictable, affecting those who may have used as little as 60 mg (two or three lines).

Some people may lack an enzyme that destroys circulating cocaine. Another possible explanation is a kind of reverse tolerance known as "**kindling.**" Users of cocaine sometimes die from doses smaller than they have taken

70

Figure 4-2
Intravenous Cocaine Users Are At Risk for Becoming Infected with HIV

previously with no obvious ill effects. This suggests to researchers that cocaine causes chemical changes that trigger the body to sprout new neural receptors. This might "amplify" the power of the drug and overload the system.

Some users, despondent over their dependence and the problems that dependence creates, turn to suicide as the only obvious solution. Murder is not uncommon in the high-stakes netherworld of cocaine dealing. The drug no doubt also figures in a number of motor vehicle deaths in which it is never implicated. There has also been a dramatic increase in recent years of deaths in which cocaine use is combined with other drugs.

Crack

In 1985, a smokable form of cocaine known as "crack" or "rock" appeared on the drug market in several American cities. Named for the sound it produces when smoked, crack is almost pure cocaine. Crack cocaine use has increased greatly in popularity throughout the United States. Crack has been described as looking like slivers of soap,

but having the general texture of porcelain. It is made by processing the hydrochloride to a base state in a process that uses baking soda and water (as opposed to volatile chemicals as in the case of freebasing). Crack is sold in a form that lends itself to smoking, frequently in a pipe and it is sold in quantities that are relatively inexpensive. Crack is the most easily accessible and powerful form of cocaine.

Since 1985, however, the process of producing smokable cocaine has been simplified, which has reduced its cost and facilitated wider distribution. When smoked, crack-cocaine creates an intense euphoric effect lasting for five to ten minutes. Crack works more quickly than other forms of cocaine, taking about seven seconds to reach the brain instead of three minutes it takes for snorted cocaine. Crack, like other forms of cocaine, acts as a stimulant and as a local anesthetic, inducing a hyper-aroused state in which the user experiences a decrease in appetite, rapid breathing, and tingling in the fingers. The user experiences alertness and a sense of well-being, with a lowering of anxiety and social inhibitions, and heightened energy, self-esteem, sexuality, and emotions. The effects of crack are said to be 10 times greater than snorted cocaine.

The euphoric state, however, is short-lived compared to that of cocaine, which lasts for one to one-and-a-half hours. Instead, within 20 to 30 minutes, the crack "high" is usually followed by just as intense a "crash." After coming down, the user experiences restlessness, irritability and impatience, pessimism or depression, and often a headache and convulsions. In addition, the user typically experiences an insatiable craving for more.

In the brain, crack and other forms of cocaine directly affect the pleasure centers, which are thought to be controlled primarily by the neurotransmitter dopamine. Animal studies have shown that the reinforcing properties of cocaine are enormous, producing a powerful craving that leads the user to abandon all else in a compulsion to obtain more of the drug. Heavy crack cocaine users often forego food and sleep to stay high, and they frequently suffer malnutrition and exhaustion as a result.

Cocaine is capable of producing both a physical and psychological dependency. As tolerance for the drug develops, the user needs more and more crack cocaine to experience the same degree of effects. The effect that crack cocaine produces may be accompanied by confusion, increased heart rate and blood pressure, and sweating. Withdrawal from the drug after prolonged use produces feelings of anxiety, irritability, insomnia, and depression. Some users find these sensations frightening and choose to avoid the drug because of its powerful side effects.

Smoking crack cocaine also heightens certain important effects that are relatively mild when cocaine is snorted—increased heart rate, blood pressure, and temperature—which can lead to seizures, heart attack, stroke, and death. A fatal overdose is possible with even a small amount of crack cocaine at the first use of the drug. Medical effects of crack cocaine use include chronic respiratory problems (most commonly a persistent cough), chronic fatigue, and insomnia. Long-term psychological effects of crack cocaine use include behavior and personality changes including impulsive, even violent, behavior and paranoia. Panic attacks are also occasional reactions to chronic crack cocaine use. All of these effects adversely influence a crack cocaine user's relationships, responsibilities, and overall physical and mental health.

Particular Effects of Cocaine and Crack on Females

A female's attraction to cocaine and crack is of particular concern. Injecting cocaine (or other drugs) poses special

72

dangers of infection with the human immunodeficiency virus (HIV) that causes AIDS. Sharing needles and other injection paraphernalia ("works") carrying HIV-infected blood is a primary mechanism for AIDS-virus transmission. Not only is unsterilized equipment more likely to be shared when drugs impair judgment, but females are very likely to share needles with sexual partners who assist them in shooting up.

In many inner cities, the escalating use of crack has also resulted in increasing numbers of females exchanging sex for drugs. Both needle sharing and unprotected sex with HIV-infected partners have increased the frequency of AIDS among females and their offspring. Nearly three of every four cases of AIDS reported in females (about 73 percent) are directly or indirectly linked to intravenous drug use, and four of every five children (under 13 years of age) with AIDS has a parent who injects drugs.

Evidence suggests that from 30 to 50 percent of pre-natally-exposed babies of HIV-infected mothers are also infected with the virus. It takes as long as 15 months after delivery to confirm if babies' antibodies reflect their own or their mother's infection. The exact mechanisms and timing of mother-to-child viral transmission are not completely established, but prenatal exposure, delivery, and breast-feeding are implicated.

In addition to increasing risks for HIV infection, the sexual promiscuity associated with cocaine use has been blamed for growing numbers of females with other sexually-transmitted diseases. Although more treatable than HIV infection or AIDS, these infections can also be transmitted to the fetus or to the infant at birth. The Centers for Disease Control reports that the current epidemic of syphilis among adults and newborns in many inner cities is strongly linked to cocaine and crack use.

Prenatal and Early Infant Exposure to Cocaine

Cocaine use during pregnancy may be more harmful to expectant mothers and their newborns than other drugs. Females who use cocaine during pregnancy have the poorest maternal and infant health outcomes when compared to either non-drug users or to females dependent on other drugs but not cocaine.

Cocaine crosses the placenta and reaches the fetus, but its dangers probably reflect actions on the cardiovascular systems of the mother and the fetus rather than more direct toxicity. Cocaine constricts the user's blood vessels, reducing blood flow through the placenta to the fetus and diminishing both the oxygen supply and the nutrients reaching the fetus, increasing the risk of miscarriage and malformation of the fetus. The vasoconstrictive properties of the drug also interfere with normal placental functioning and may damage this fetal life-support system. Recent animal research experiments confirm these effects.

Because cocaine is a short-acting drug, with doses repeated at frequent intervals, fetal blood flow reductions due to blood vessel constriction in the mother are likely to be intermittent and potentially disruptive to normal development of fetal tissue. This mechanism would be consistent with recent reports of structural central nervous system abnormalities, intestinal anomalies, and malformations of extremities, as well as urogenital malformations in cocaine-exposed babies.

Females who stop using cocaine by the end of the first three months of pregnancy have improved birth outcomes more than those who continue use throughout pregnancy. Pregnancies are more likely to last nine months, and delivered infants are more likely to be normal weight than infants of mothers who continue using cocaine.

Infants born to mothers who stopped using cocaine before the last trimester of pregnancy also have improved intrauterine growth compared to infants exposed to cocaine throughout their in-utero development. The rate of early placental separation does not decrease, however, even when cocaine use is stopped early in pregnancy. The damage to the placental and uterine blood vessels that results from cocaine use in early pregnancy is apparently nonreversible.

Effects during pregnancy and delivery. The earliest reports of cocaine effects on pregnancy noted a high rate of spontaneous abortion and separation of the placenta from the wall of the uterus (abruptio placentae). The complication of abruptio placentae has now been confirmed in at least five additional studies. In one study of in-utero cocaine exposure, abruptio placentae was also associated with an increased number of stillbirths.

Prenatal cocaine exposure is also associated with an increased rate of premature rupture of membranes, early onset of labor, and preterm delivery. Cocaine apparently causes contractions of the uterus. In fact, it is reported to be common knowledge on the street that crack will induce labor. Some females have used the drug in attempting self-induced abortions. Premature labor is most likely to occur if cocaine is taken during the last three months of

pregnancy. Pregnant mothers should be warned that cocaine use within a few days of delivery can be especially hazardous.

Effects on newborns. Cocaine use during pregnancy is most consistently associated with increased risk among newborns for intrauterine growth retardation. Babies born to cocaine-using mothers are more likely to have significantly lower birth weight and length and smaller head circumferences than newborns of drug-free mothers. The appetite-suppressing characteristics of cocaine cause poor maternal nutrition, which may also contribute to lowered birth weight in prenatally-exposed infants.

Babies born to cocaine-using mothers appear to have fewer clearly discernible withdrawal symptoms than babies exposed to heroin and other narcotics in utero. Although the cocaine-exposed newborns tend to be jittery, to cry shrilly, and to startle at even the slightest stimulation, these effects have generally been attributed to neurobehavioral abnormalities rather than withdrawal. In comparison to infants born to mothers who use cocaine, methamphetamine, heroin, and/or methadone during pregnancy, the newborns exposed to cocaine and/or methamphetamine display such altered behavior patterns as abnormal sleep, poor feeding, tremors, and increased muscle tone. These behaviors represent the direct effects of the drugs, not withdrawal.

Neurological abnormalities among cocaine-exposed newborns, such as impaired ability to orient and to control muscles, have also been measured on the Brazelton Neonatal Behavioral Assessment Scale. This set of tests measures newborns' functioning abilities: how well they respond to people or to the environment, how quickly they stop reacting to selected visual and auditory stimulation, how well they can use their muscles, and how well body temperature is regulated. Persisting abnormalities of muscle tone, reflexes, and volitional movement were also found in 43 percent of otherwise healthy four month old cocaine-exposed babies, using a set of tests called the Movement Assessment of Infants. Some muscle tone and movement problems were still apparent when these babies were retested at eight months. Such movement-related problems in newborns are generally associated with delays or deficits in motor development.

One investigation of newborns prenatally exposed to cocaine found an increased risk for sudden infant death syndrome (SIDS), but subsequent and larger prospective studies failed to confirm this. Several studies have suggested an association between in-utero cocaine exposure and structural birth defects, notably of the genitourinary tract, cardiovascular system, central nervous system, and extremities. Cases have also been reported of cerebral infarctions, central nervous system lesions, and neural tube defects among cocaine-exposed babies. However, although sufficient data for definitive conclusions have yet to be collected in large-scale and well-controlled studies, the risk for major malformations does not appear to be greatly increased among cocaine-exposed babies.

Conclusions about increased risk for structural anomalies are still premature, but preliminary data from a large Centers for Disease Control study of birth defects (as well as findings from earlier studies) indicate that defects in the genitalia and urinary tract may, indeed, be more prevalent among cocaine-exposed babies. Continuing reports of very serious central nervous system malformations, limb anomalies, intestinal impairments, and facial abnormalities are disturbing, but require further confirmation. All of these cocaine-related risks, however, are ultimately so interwoven and confounded by other maternal risk factors that the absolute risk of maternal cocaine use may never be ascertained.

It is too early to know whether or not the neurobehavioral effects identified in cocaine-exposed newborns continue into later childhood and adult life. Very few studies with large populations samples have been completed; more are needed.

Effects on breast-fed infants. Cocaine use by nursing mothers may also pose a threat to their infants. Two case reports illustrate this. In one, marked tremulousness, irritability, startle responses, and other neurological abnormalities in a two-week-old infant girl were traced to cocaine in her mother's milk. The infant's urine still contained a byproduct of cocaine 60 hours after last being breast-fed by her cocaine-using mother. A more recent report describes convulsions in an 11-day-old nursing infant, resulting from the mother's use of cocaine on her nipples to relieve soreness.

AMPHETAMINES

In contrast to cocaine, which is a naturally occurring substance, amphetamine drugs are chemically manufactured drugs that are powerful stimulants of the central nervous system. The use of amphetamines and methamphetamine will be discussed in this section of the chapter.

Use of Amphetamines

Amphetamines were first used medically in the mid-1930s to treat narcolepsy, a condition in which a person has uncontrollable periods of sleep. After the introduction of the amphetamines into medical practice, the number of conditions for which they were prescribed multiplied as did the quantities made available. They were sold without prescription for a time in inhalers and other over-the-counter preparations. Amphetamines became popular as appetite depressants and as a means of staying awake for long periods of time.

Abuse of the inhalers became popular among teenagers and prisoners. "Speed freaks," who injected them, won notoriety in the drug culture for their bizarre and often violent behavior. Whereas a prescribed dose is between 2.5 and 15 mg per day, those on a "speed" binge have been known to inject as much as 1,000 mg every two or three hours. Recognition of the deleterious effects of these drugs and their limited therapeutic value has led to a marked reduction in their use by the medical profession. The medical use of amphetamines is now limited to narcolepsy, hyperactivity in children, and certain types of obesity—as a short-term adjunct to dieting.

The illicit use of amphetamines closely parallels that of cocaine in the range of short-term and long-term effects. Despite broad recognition of the risks, clandestine laboratories produce vast quantities of amphetamines, particularly methamphetamine, for distribution on the illicit market.

Methamphetamines

Methamphetamine is a stimulant drug that falls within the amphetamine family. The use of methamphetamine produces similar behavioral and physiological effects as cocaine and other stimulants. These effects include euphoria, increased alertness, the perception of improved self-esteem and self-confidence, impaired judgment, and impulsiveness. Acute and chronic use of methamphetamine typically results in nervousness, irritability, restlessness, and insomnia. Amphetamine psychosis, a type of paranoia, can also result.

A major difference between cocaine and methamphetamine is duration of action. The half-life for cocaine's euphoric effects is less than 45 minutes; for methamphetamine it is three to six hours. Therefore, one can expect that the period of stimulant-induced euphoria would be much longer in methamphetamine abusers and that likewise the period of impaired judgment will be longer.

Recent research evidence suggests that permanent neurological changes and deficits can result from chronic methamphetamine use. Laboratory research with animals has shown that the long-term administration of methamphetamine results in neurotoxic effects on the brain, permanently affecting levels of the neurotransmitters serotonin and dopamine. Other physiological effects such as increased body temperature and rapid respiration and heart rates have been reported frequently. Death from acute overdose, which is rare, is usually preceded by an elevated body temperature, cardiovascular shock, and convulsions.

Ice. Since 1987, smoking crystals of "ice," which is very pure methamphetamine, has become a common method of taking the drug. As with cocaine, smoking methamphetamines compounds the effects and promotes rapid addiction. Ice, also known as crank, is a much longer-acting drug than crack. Compared to crack, the half-life of ice is 60 times longer. Unlike crack and other forms of cocaine, ice remains largely unchanged when it is excreted from the body. As a result, repeated consumption of ice is associated with significant accumulation of methamphetamine in the body. This accounts for the prolonged high produced by ice, but also poses a serious health threat because dangerously high toxic levels can build up in the body (Labianca, 1992).

MDMA. The term "designer drug" is often associated with MDMA, known to drug abusers as "ecstasy" or "Adam," and other analogs of methamphetamines. By producing a drug that is chemically slightly different and therefore not legally restricted, its producers hope to avoid the legal penalties for distributing a controlled substance. In the case of MDMA, the parent drug is methamphetamine, which was widely abused during the 1960s and is now undergoing a resurgence of use in the form of "ice."

The effects of MDMA have been described by users as resembling those of both cocaine and LSD. Early reports of MDMA suggested that it induced an altered state of consciousness and made psychiatric patients receptive to psychotherapeutic intervention by facilitating communication and heightening empathy. However, MDMA's effectiveness as an adjunct in psychotherapy is supported only by anecdotal reports; there have been no double-blind, dose-response, controlled studies.

As a result of growing concern over its potential for abuse, MDMA and other analogs of controlled substances were included in Schedule I of the Controlled Substance Analogue Enforcement Act, Anti-Drug Abuse Act of 1986 (Public Law 99–570). MDMA has a demonstrated abuse liability both in humans and animals. MDMA has been associated with fatal and near fatal toxic reactions. More information about MDMA is presented in Chapter 8.

LOOK-ALIKE DRUGS

Look-alike drugs are tablets or capsules manufactured to resemble legitimate pharmaceutical products and are frequently sold as appetite suppressants and antifatigue medications. They typically contain caffeine, ephedrine, and phenylpropanolamine, either alone or in combination.

In 1981, the Food and Drug Administration declared the triple combination (caffeine, ephedrine, and phenylpropanolamine) a new drug. As a result, they are able to impose legal restrictions on the manufacture and distribution of these products. This action, along with well-planned raids of known manufacturers, significantly curtailed the distribution of these products. Additional legislation prevents the sale of combinations of two stimulants, so most over-the-counter diet products now contain only caffeine or phenylpropanolamine. An analysis of look-alike products suggests that their toxicity is not significant (Fig. 4-3).

CAFFEINE

Caffeine is the most well known member of the methyl xanthine class of stimulants. Other members of this class are the drugs theophylline and theobromine. Theophylline is found primarily in tea and theobromine is found primarily in chocolate. The sources of caffeine and the effects of caffeine will be discussed in this section of the chapter.

Sources of Caffeine

Caffeine is found in a wide variety of sources—coffee, tea, soda pop, chocolate and chocolate-flavored products, prescription drugs, and over-the-counter drugs such as weight control aids, alertness pills, analgesic compounds, diuretics, and cold/allergy remedies (Fig. 4-4). As a result of its inclusion in so many popularly consumed products, caffeine is the world's most widely used stimulant.

Effects of Caffeine

Caffeine is a powerful central nervous system stimulant, producing the familiar "pick-me-up" effects. Caffeine is capable of stimulating all levels of the brain. Its direct stimulation of the cerebral cortex is associated with greater sensitivity to stimuli, clearer thinking, wakefulness, and better physical coordination (Liska, 1986). Caffeine is known to reduce fatigue and drowsiness.

Caffeine is also a cardiac stimulant causing heart rate to increase and increasing the force of the heart's contrac-

Figure 4-3
Look-Alike Drugs

tions. In some people, caffeine appears to contribute to irregular heart beats and heart rhythms. This can be particularly risky for people with underlying heart disease.

Another important effect of caffeine is its stimulation or excitation of spinal nerves and the areas of the brain that control breathing. Such stimulation accounts for an increase in breathing rate as well as muscle tremors or shakiness (Liska, 1986). Skeletal muscle tension is also associated with the central nervous system stimulation produced by caffeine.

Caffeine and other methyl xanthines are unique from other stimulants in that they cause relaxation of most smooth muscle. Relaxation of smooth muscle results in a dilation of the bronchi of the lungs. This action decreases airway resistance, making it easier for people who suffer from

asthma to breathe. For this reason, theophylline is sometimes prescribed for asthmatics (McKim, 1991).

Caffeine has a powerful diuretic effect. Coffee, tea, and caffeinated soft drink use is often incorrectly assumed to increase urinary output because of the amount of liquid in these drinks. However, the real reason is caffeine's diuretic effect, which causes a loss of even more fluids than were consumed in the caffeinated beverage (Leccese, 1991).

By causing a constriction of blood vessels in the brain, caffeine lessens pain and gives some relief from certain types of headaches. For this reason, caffeine is a common ingredient in many over-the-counter headache remedies. It is interesting that in other areas of the body, such as the heart, caffeine causes dilation of blood vessels (Leccese, 1991).

Figure 4-4
Sources of Caffeine

An important side effect of caffeine is irritation of the stomach. Because caffeine stimulates an increase in the production of stomach acids, consumers often experience upset stomachs. The release of these acids can be particularly troublesome for individuals who are prone to ulcers. It is important to note that decaffeinated coffee also stimulates stomach acid secretions.

Caffeinism is a condition of chronic caffeine toxicity or poisoning associated with very heavy use and preoccupation with caffeine. Carroll (1993) lists several signs and symptoms that are associated with caffeinism:
- disruption of sleep and insomnia
- wakefulness
- mood changes
- anxiety
- restlessness
- irritability
- muscle twitching
- tremulousness

- headache
- sensory disturbances such as ringing in the ears and dry mouth
- lethargy and depression
- palpitations and irregularities in heartbeat
- changes in blood pressure
- diuresis (increased urinary output)
- nausea and vomiting
- stomach pain
- gastric ulcer
- diarrhea
- various body complaints

Over the years, caffeine has been implicated as a potential cause of such ailments as heart disease, osteoporosis, and fibrocystic breast disease. However, current scientific thinking and findings suggest that caffeine does not cause any of these conditions (International Food Information Council, 1992; Nutrition Reviews, 1992). However, scientists believe that excessive caffeine consumption may play a role in aggravating these conditions if they exist in a person (Turner, Sizer, Whitney, & Wilks, 1992). For example, caffeine is known to trigger stress-related hormones, raise blood pressure, and sometimes cause heartbeat irregularities. This could certainly be harmful to an individual who has heart disease.

Caffeine is also believed to intensify fibrocystic breast disease in females with the disease and possibly hasten bone loss (Turner et al., 1992). Research to date does not support connections between caffeine consumption and cancer or birth defects. However, pregnant females should nevertheless be counseled to avoid the use of caffeine containing products until it is known with certainty that caffeine does not cause birth defects.

OTHER STIMULANT DRUGS

Methylphenidate (Ritalin) and Phenmetrazine (Preludin) are also important stimulants. The medical indications, patterns of abuse, and adverse effects compare closely with those of the other stimulants. Methylphenidate is used mainly for treatment of attention deficit disorder in children. Phenmetrazine is medically used only as an appetite suppressant. These stimulant drugs have been subject to abuse in countries where freely available, as they are in localities where medical practitioners write prescriptions on demand.

In recent years, a number of drugs have been manufactured and marketed to replace amphetamines as appetite suppressants. These so-called anorectic drugs included benzphetamine (Didrex), chlorphentermine (Pre-Sate), chlortermine (Voranil), diethylpropion (Tenuate, Tepanil), fenfluramine (Pondimin), mazindol (Sanorex), phendime-trazine (Plegine, Bacarate, Melfist, Statobex, Tanorex), and phentermine (Ionamin, Adipex). They produce many of the effects of the amphetamines but are generally less potent.

STIMULANTS AND SEXUALITY

Cocaine and amphetamines affect sexual functioning similarly. At low doses, cocaine enhances sexual desire and is highly rated as an aphrodisiac in the drug culture, especially by males. This seems to be so because many of the physiological changes produced by these drugs are similar to those experienced during sexual excitement—increases in heart rate, blood pressure, and blood flow to the gen-

itals. However as the dosage increases and use becomes chronic, particularly if the route of administration is freebase smoking or injection, a male may experience impairment of ejaculatory and erectile ability.

Males sometimes value cocaine because of the delayed ejaculation, but often erectile performance is so impaired that erection will not occur. Females may have difficulty achieving orgasm.

High doses of cocaine and amphetamines can facilitate aberrant sexual behaviors such as compulsive masturbation and multipartner sexual marathons.

BIBLIOGRAPHY

Carroll, C.R. (1993) *Drugs in Modern Society.* Dubuque, IA: Wm. C. Brown.

Duncan, D., & Gold, R. (1982) *Drugs and the Whole Person.* New York: John Wiley & Sons.

Fullilove, R.E., Fullilove, M.T., Bonser, B.P., & Gross, B.P. (1990) Risk of sexually transmitted disease among black adolescent crack users in Oakland and San Francisco, California. *Journal of the American Medical Association,* 63:851–855.

International Food Information Council. (1992) Caffeine and women's health: An update. *Food Insight: Current Topics in Food Safety and Nutrition.* May/June, 6–7.

Labianca, D.A. (1992) The drug scene's new "ice" age. *USA Today Magazine,* January, 54–56.

Leccese, A.P. (1991) *Drugs and Society: Behavioral Medicines and Abusable Drugs.* Englewood Cliffs, NJ: Prentice-Hall.

Liska, K. (1986) *Drugs and the Human Body: With Implications for Society.* New York: Macmillan.

McKim, W.A. (1991) *Drugs and Behavior: An Introduction to Behavioral Pharmacology.* Englewood Cliffs, NJ: Prentice-Hall.

National Institute on Drug Abuse. (1985) *Cocaine Use in America: Epidemiological and Clinical Perspectives. Prevention Research Monograph 61.* DHHS Publication No. (ADM)85-1414. Washington, D.C.: U.S. Government Printing Office.

National Institute on Drug Abuse. (1986) *Cocaine Use in America.* DHHS Publication No. (ADM)86-1443. Washington, D.C.: U.S. Government Printing Office.

National Institute on Drug Abuse. (1990) *Drug Abuse Curriculum for Employee Assistance Program Profes-*

sionals. DHHS Publication No. (ADM)90-1587. Rockville, MD: National Institute on Drug Abuse.

National Institute on Drug Abuse. (1991) *Drug Abuse and Drug Abuse Research: The Third Triennial Report to Congress from the Secretary, Department of Health and Human Services.* DHHS Publication No. (ADM)91-1704. Rockville, MD: National Institute on Drug Abuse.

Nutrition Reviews. (1992) Regular or decaf? Coffee consumption and serum lipoproteins. 50:175–177.

Office for Substance Abuse Prevention. (1990) *Alcohol, Tobacco, and Other Drugs May Harm the Unborn.* DHHS Publication No. (ADM)90-1711. Rockville, MD: Office for Substance Abuse Prevention.

Office for Substance Abuse Prevention. (1991) *Crack Cocaine: A Challenge for Prevention, OSAP Prevention Monograph-9.* DHHS Publication No. (ADM)91-1806. Rockville, MD: Office for Substance Abuse Prevention.

Page, R.M., & Goldberg, R. (1986) Practices and attitudes toward caffeinated and non-caffeinated beverages. *Health Education,* October/November, 17–21.

Subcommittee on Human Resources of the Committee on Ways and Means, U.S. House of Representatives. (June 12, 1990) *The Enemy Within: Crack Cocaine and America's Families.* Washington, D.C.: U.S. Government Printing Office.

Turner, L.W., Sizer, F.S., Whitney, E.N., & Wilks, B.B. (1992) *Life Choices: Health Concepts and Strategies.* St. Paul, MN: West.

U.S. Department of Justice, Drug Enforcement Administration. Stimulants. *Drug Enforcement,* July 1979.

Yarber, W.L., & Parrillo, A.V. (1992) Adolescents and sexually transmitted diseases. *Journal of School Health,* 62:331–338.

SEDATIVE-HYPNOTIC DRUGS

Sedative-hypnotic drugs are central nervous system depressants. They have a calming effect on behavior. **Hypnotic drugs** induce drowsiness and encourage sleep. Having useful medical purposes, they are especially dangerous when self-administered, or administered without medical supervision and direction. Like alcohol, which also is a central nervous system depressant, sedative-hypnotics have a high potential for abuse and are associated with both physical and psychological dependence. Alcohol will be discussed in Chapter 13. In this chapter, pharmacology and the effects of sedative-hypnotics, barbiturates, methaqualone, nonbarbiturate sedative-hypnotics, benzodiazepines, abuse patterns, treatment for sedative/anxiolytic drug withdrawal, and sexuality and sedative/anxiolytic drug use will be discussed.

PHARMACOLOGY AND THE EFFECTS OF SEDATIVE-HYPNOTICS

All sedative-hypnotics produce a general and nonspecific depression of physiological functions. The central nervous system is extremely sensitive to the depressant effect of sedative-hypnotics, so drugs of this class can be used in doses that depress the central nervous system without depressing other body functions. This section of the chapter will include a discussion of tolerance, withdrawal, potentiation, and chronic use.

Tolerance

Sedative-hypnotics are often prescribed to produce daytime sedation or sleep. These drugs lose most of their ability to produce sleep after only two or three weeks of regular use. This occurs because the central nervous system develops tolerance to the sedative effects of the drugs fairly quickly. For this reason, and also because of the risk of producing physical and psychological dependence, most physicians have become very conservative in using these drugs. Prescriptions usually are for brief therapy if they are prescribed at all. An example of this would be for inducing rest or sedation immediately before (or after) major surgery.

Though their main effect is one of sedation and drowsiness, sedative-hypnotics also have other effects, one of the most important being impaired coordination. This can be seen, for example, in a person with a staggering gait and slurring of speech, which obviously create serious obstacles to driving or performing other tasks that involve coordination and judgment.

Sedative-hypnotics also have antiseizure effects and can be used to stop convulsions. Finally, some can cause euphoria, especially when used in doses that are higher than recommended.

As in the case of alcohol, these effects may vary not only from person to person, but also from time to time in the same individual. Low doses produce mild sedation. Higher doses, insofar as they relieve anxiety or stress, may produce a temporary sense of well-being; they may also produce depressive moods and apathy. In marked contrast to the effects of narcotics, however, intoxicating doses of sedative-hypnotics invariably result in impaired speech, loss of motor coordination, and disorientation.

Withdrawal

The abrupt cessation or reduction of high-dose sedative-hypnotic intake may result in a characteristic withdrawal syndrome, which should be recognized as a medical emergency more serious than that of any other drugs of abuse. As with other abused substances, the withdrawal effects of all the sedative-hypnotics mirror the acute effects. Unlike narcotics and stimulants, some sedative-hypnotic withdrawal effects can cause death. This makes it essential to identify and treat sedative-hypnotic dependence as soon as possible.

Acute withdrawal effects usually occur one to two days after the sedative-hypnotics are stopped and can last as long as seven to ten days. The early symptoms are uncomfortable but not life-threatening and include increased anxiety, sweating, restlessness, agitation, and tremors of the extremities.

In cases of severe physical dependence, these symptoms can progress to seizures and a toxic psychosis, both of

79

which have been associated with fatalities. The seizures, if they occur, resemble grand mal epilepsy and are characterized by loss of consciousness and generalized tonic-clonic movements of the body and extremities.

A toxic psychosis sometimes follows seizures. This a confused and agitated state in which the person is completely disoriented and often has auditory and visual hallucinations. During a toxic psychosis, blood pressure and pulse rate are elevated and the person is extremely restless and must be restrained. These severe withdrawal reactions usually occur only in people who have been taking sedative-hypnotics in high doses for an extended time. An example would be someone who took 10 to 12 sleeping pills a day for longer than three months.

Treatment of physical dependence on sedative-hypnotics almost always requires hospitalization for gradual reduction of the dose with extended follow-up treatment.

Potentiation

A number of very serious adverse effects can result from sedative-hypnotic use, abuse, and dependence, in addition to those mentioned above. One of the most dangerous is the potentiation of a sedative's respiratory depressant effects when the sedative is used with other depressants such as alcohol. In such a situation, the effects of one drug are not simply additive but enhance and multiply those of the other, resembling a mathematical equation in which 1 plus 1 equals 4 rather than 2.

Potentiation has led to tragic and fatal consequences, even in people who are taking sedative-hypnotics as prescribed, such as someone taking a sedative to help with sleep. An example is a person who takes slightly more sedative than is prescribed after having two or three drinks of alcohol. Neither drug is taken in a particularly high dose, and the person has previously taken each separately in similar doses with no problems. But when taken together, potentiation occurs, respiration is severely depressed, and the person dies while asleep.

Even when taken in recommended doses, sedative-hypnotics, like narcotics, also depress the nerves that control respiration. If taken in sufficiently large doses, these drugs can cause death, even when taken alone. Taking them in combination with another sedative-hypnotic such as alcohol simply multiplies their ability to suppress respiration.

When taken at higher than recommended doses, sedative-hypnotics release inhibitions and can unmask a per-

son's anger. This can present a problem in many situations if the anger is excessive. Some people can become very agitated and belligerent after taking only small doses of sedative-hypnotics. On the other hand, individuals intoxicated with sedative-hypnotics can be extremely disruptive because of their sedated, hostile, and agitated behavior.

Chronic Use

Chronic use of sedative-hypnotics can cause mental depression. This has been documented in studies that have followed chronic sedative-hypnotic abusers over a period of years. The studies have shown that these persons are very likely to develop depressive symptoms, even if they were mentally free of depression when they begin to abuse sedative-hypnotics. Chronic sedative-hypnotic abuse can also cause brain damage, similar to that seen in alcoholics.

A final problem that can result from chronic sedative-hypnotic use is habituation. This can occur when a person takes one or two sedative-hypnotics every night for sleep, and then becomes so mentally accustomed to taking the drug that it is impossible to sleep without it. This is not physical dependence, but it can lead to a medical situation in which it is very difficult to discontinue the sedative-hypnotics.

BARBITURATES

Barbiturates are among the drugs most widely prescribed to induce sedation and sleep. About 2,500 derivatives of barbituric acid have been synthesized, but of these only about 15 remain in medical use. Small therapeutic doses tend to calm nervous conditions, and larger doses cause sleep 20 to 60 minutes after oral administration. As in the case of alcohol, some individuals may experience a sense of excitement before sedation takes effect. If dosage is increased, however, the effects of the barbiturates may progress through successive stages of sedation, sleep, and coma to death from respiratory arrest and cardiovascular complications. In this section of the chapter, the discussion will include the classification of barbiturates, and barbiturate use and pregnancy.

Classification of Barbiturates

Barbiturates are classified as ultrashort-, short-, intermediate- and long-acting. The ultrashort-acting barbiturates produce anesthesia within one minute after intravenous administration. The rapid onset and brief duration of action make them undesirable for purposes of abuse. Those in medical use are hexobarbital (Evipal), methoexital (Brevital), thiamylal (Surital), and thiopental (Pentothal).

Pentobarbital (Nembutal), secobarbital (Seconal), and amobarbital (Amytal) are among the barbiturates classified as short- and intermediate-acting barbiturates. These three drugs are in the category of depressants most sought after by abusers. The group also includes butabarbital (Butisol), butalbital (Lotusate), allobarbital (Dial), aprobarbital (Alurate), and vinbarbital (Delvinal). After oral administration the onset of time of action is from 15 to 40 minutes and duration of action is up to six hours.

Physicians prescribe short-acting barbiturates to induce sedation or sleep. They are abused either orally or intravenously after being dissolved in water.

Long-acting barbiturates, which include barbital (Veronal), phenobarbital (Luminal), mephobarbital (Mebaral), and metharbital (Gemonil), have onset times of up to one hour and durations of action up to 16 hours. They are used medicinally as sedatives, hypnotics, and anticonvulsants. Phenobarbital is used widely in the treatment of epilepsy. Long-acting barbiturates have a greater margin of safety than shorter-acting barbiturates and are rarely abused, probably because their slow onset of action makes it difficult to get high, even from taking large doses. They are sometimes used to detoxify people from physical dependence on other sedative-hypnotics because of their low potential for abuse, higher margin of safety, and long duration of action.

Barbiturate Use and Pregnancy

Long-acting barbiturates, such as phenobarbital, taken as antiseizure medications have been associated with congenital birth defects resembling fetal alcohol syndrome (see Chapter 13). Even short-acting barbiturates, such as Seconal and Tuinal, have been associated with increases in birth defects and are not considered safe for use during pregnancy (Fig. 5-1).

Chronic use of barbiturates during the last months of pregnancy, at doses of 60 to 100 mg per day, has been associated with infant withdrawal symptoms appearing four to seven days after birth. These symptoms typically include high-pitched crying, irritability, tremulousness, and sleep disturbances that can persist for months and can interfere with mother-infant bonding.

METHAQUALONE

Methaqualone is a synthetic sedative-hypnotic chemically unrelated to the barbiturates and other sedative-hypnotics discussed in this chapter. It has been widely abused because it was once mistakenly thought to be nonaddictive and

Figure 5-1
Barbiturate Use During Pregnancy

effective as an aphrodisiac. Hence, it was promoted on the street as the love drug.

Actually, methaqualone has caused many cases of serious poisoning and its supposed power as a love drug was probably due more to its placebo effect than to actual properties of the drug itself (Faulkner, 1991).

81

Although having effects similar to other sedative-hypnotics, methaqualone has stronger euphoria-generating effects. It is administered orally. Large doses cause coma, which may be accompanied by thrashing movements or convulsions. Continued heavy use of large doses leads to tolerance and dependence.

Methaqualone has been marketed in the United States under various brand names such as Quaalude, Parest, Optimil, Somnafac, and Sopor. Counterfeit Quaalude tablets, which do not necessarily contain methaqualone, are prevalent in the U.S. illicit market, similar in appearance to the tablet formerly distributed by a U.S. pharmaceutical company. Because of its strong euphoria-generating effect and the fact that it was widely abused, methaqualone was removed from the market by the Drug Enforcement Agency. This action essentially eliminated methaqualone as a drug of abuse in the United States.

Occasionally, one hears of one taking "ludes," but they are very likely an imitation, perhaps made in a black-market laboratory by using another sedative-hypnotic and packaging it to resemble methaqualone.

NONBARBITURATE SEDATIVE-HYPNOTICS

Chloral hydrate is the oldest of the hypnotic drugs. It was first synthesized in 1862 and soon supplanted alcohol, opium, and cannabis preparations for inducing sedation and sleep. Its popularity declined after the introduction of the barbiturates, but chloral hydrate is still widely used. It has a penetrating, slightly acrid odor, and a bitter caustic taste. Its depressant effects, as well as the resulting tolerance and dependence, are comparable to those of alcohol, and withdrawal symptoms resemble delirium tremens (see Chapter 13).

Chloral hydrate is a liquid, marketed in the form of syrups and soft gelatin capsules. Cases of poisoning have occurred from mixing chloral hydrate with alcoholic drinks. Chloral hydrate is not a street drug of choice. Its main misuse is by older adults.

Meprobamate, first synthesized in 1950, introduced the era of mild or "minor" tranquilizers. Meprobamate is distributed under such brand names as Miltown, Equanil, Kesso-Bamate, and SK-Bamate. Meprobamate is prescribed primarily for the relief of anxiety, tension, and associated muscle spasms. Its onset and duration of action are like those of the intermediate-acting barbiturates. It differs from them in that it is a muscle relaxant, does not produce sleep at therapeutic doses, and is relatively less

toxic. Excessive use, however, can result in psychological and physical dependence.

Glutethimide (Doriden) was introduced in 1954. At that time, it was said to be a safe barbiturate substitute without potential for addiction. However, experience has shown glutethimide to be another central nervous system depressant, having no particular advantage over the barbiturates and several important disadvantages. The sedative effects of glutethimide begin about 30 minutes after oral administration and last for four to eight hours. Because the effects of this drug are of long duration, it is exceptionally difficult to reverse overdoses, which often result in death.

BENZODIAZEPINES

The benzodiazepines are very important nonbarbiturate sedative-hypnotic drugs. They have become synonymous with "tranquilizers" because of their usefulness in reducing anxiety. Their general effects are similar to those of the sedative-hypnotics, but subtle yet important differences have led to their widespread use. This section of the chapter will include a discussion of use of benzodiazepines, pharmacology and effects, and use during pregnancy.

Use of Benzodiazepines

Benzodiazepines have essentially replaced sedative-hypnotics, such as barbiturates and other sedative-hypnotics described in this chapter as antianxiety agents. In addition, some members of the benzodiazepine class have even been used successfully as sleeping pills.

These drugs have become popular because, unlike sedative-hypnotics, which are general depressants and produce considerable drowsiness, benzodiazepines are much more specific for anxiety. This means that they reduce anxiety with fewer of the typical sedative-hypnotic side effects such as impaired coordination. They are also preferred over sedative-hypnotics because they have a much greater margin of safety. Twenty or thirty 100-mg capsules of Seconal or Nembutal can be fatal if taken in a single dose. Benzodiazepines are rarely fatal even if taken in very large doses.

However, benzodiazepines can be dangerous if taken in combination with other sedatives such as alcohol or with narcotics. In addition, benzodiazepines retain their major effect (reduction of anxiety) for a much longer time than any other drug class used for similar purposes. Thus they can be useful for individuals with chronic anxiety or insomnia. For these reasons, the medical profession has shifted away from sedative-hypnotics and toward benzo-diazepines for reduction of anxiety and induction of sleep. Several different benzodiazepines are approved for use in the United States.

Pharmacology and Effects

All drugs of this class have both antianxiety and sedative effects. However, the sedative effect is the most prominent effect. Benzodiazepines are often referred to as **anxiolytics** or drugs that relieve anxiety. They are thought to act on two specific types of receptors within the central nervous system: one that mediates the antianxiety effects and the other the sedative effects.

Tolerance develops quickly (one to three weeks) to the sedative effects, but does not develop to the antianxiety effects. This latter quality makes benzodiazepines useful even when taken for very long periods of time. The same quality differentiates them from sedative-hypnotics, which reduce anxiety only until tolerance develops to their sedative effects. Benzodiazepines are remarkably effective and safe, and this accounts for their wide use.

Though benzodiazepines are useful, they are not without their drawbacks. Two common problems are sedation and impairment in short-term memory. Neither of these problems is considered serious under most conditions, because tolerance develops rapidly to the sedative effects, and the effects on short-term memory last only one to two hours after the drug is taken.

One problem resulting from long-term (greater than four months) use of benzodiazepines is the development of physical dependence from therapeutic doses. Withdrawal effects of benzodiazepines in persons who abuse them by taking very high doses are similar to those that occur when sedative-hypnotics are abused.

However, another type of withdrawal syndrome has been identified consisting of anxiety, restlessness, sweating, dysphoria (opposite of euphoria), hypersensitivity to stimuli such as lights and sounds, muscle twitches, and paranoid ideation. This occurs in persons who abruptly stop therapeutic doses of benzodiazepines. Though seizures and toxic psychoses have been observed during withdrawal from very high doses, these reactions are rarely seen during withdrawal from therapeutic doses. Nevertheless, withdrawal from long-term use of therapeutic doses can produce uncomfortable and persistent symptoms, and some persons have been unable to completely discontinue taking benzodiazepines as a result.

It is possible to become addicted to a drug even when taking it "as medically prescribed." It is important to understand that withdrawal symptoms associated with therapeutic doses of benzodiazepines do not signify abuse or addiction. These symptoms are a form of physical dependency. A person having this problem should not be labeled as being addicted. Current research information indicates that the likelihood of withdrawal varies according to the time over which the benzodiazepines were taken. Forty to forty five percent of persons who take a benzodiazepine regularly for longer than four months develop withdrawal symptoms upon abrupt cessation of the drug. That percentage increases to 80–85 percent in persons who have taken a benzodiazepine regularly for two or more years. A gradual reduction of the drug usually can prevent these symptoms from developing, and most physicians are familiar with the procedures necessary to treat such a withdrawal.

Though benzodiazepines share similar basic effects, they differ in many ways. One difference is in their onset time. Some act more quickly than others, and these are the drugs that are most likely to be abused. A rapidly-acting benzodiazepine, and the one that has generated the most reports of abuse, is diazepam, or Valium. Another, newer drug with rapid onset that also appears to be abused is alprazolam, or Xanax. Almost all reports of benzodiazepine abuse indicate that the abuse occurs almost entirely in individuals who abuse other substances as well.

Another difference among benzodiazepines is their length of action. Some are absorbed, metabolized, and excreted quickly; examples are oxazepam (Serax), lorazepam (Ativan), and triazolam (Halcion). Others are changed into metabolites that are also pharmacologically active and that remain effective in the body for days. Examples are diazepam (Valium) and flurazepam (Dalmane).

The function of active metabolites has been noted to cause problems, especially with flurazepam. This drug is given as a sleeping pill, and it works very well. However, because it is changed into active metabolites, it sometimes causes drowsiness during the following day. This problem led to the development of triazolam (Halcion), which has a very rapid onset of action and no active metabolites, so it does not cause drowsiness during the day. However, this positive quality creates problems of its own because triazolam, with its very short duration of action, occasionally causes a mild withdrawal reaction early the following day, especially after chronic use.

All these problems have led to more efforts to find better antianxiety agents. More drugs with fewer side effects will probably be introduced in the near future.

Use During Pregnancy

All the benzodiazepines (minor tranquilizers) have been associated with increased reproductive risks. Use of tranquilizers by pregnant females may complicate delivery and leave newborns lethargic, with respiratory difficulties, episodes of not breathing, poor muscle tone, and decreased sucking ability. Tranquilizers should be used with caution during labor because a newborn's respiration can be depressed.

Diazepam (Valium) consumed during the first three months of pregnancy has been linked to a fourfold increase in cleft palates, lip anomalies, and malformations of the heart, arteries, and joints. The risk of these congenital defects seems to increase when diazepam is combined with tobacco and alcohol use.

A 1989 Swedish case study of eight offspring of mothers whose excessive use of benzodiazepines during pregnancy was confirmed by blood tests, reported birth defects resembling those seen in fetal alcohol syndrome. All but one infant was also significantly below average in birth weight.

Chlordiazepoxide (Librium) use by females during the first six weeks of their pregnancies has been linked to central nervous system abnormalities in infants.

Diazepam, when used daily for the last two to four months of pregnancy in dosages as low as 10–15 mg, has been found to result in tremulousness and other symptoms of withdrawal in a newborn. Flurazepam (Dalmane), given in 30-mg doses for ten days, has been associated with lethargy and abnormal muscle tone in newborn infants lasting several days after birth. Because diazepam accumulates in breast-fed infants, it and meprobamate (Equanil, Miltown), should not be used by nursing mothers.

ABUSE PATTERNS

Sedative-hypnotics and benzodiazepines have been sold illicitly and used for purposes other than accepted medical uses. Drug abuse of these substances is constituted as nonmedical use because of psychic effects or because of dependence, or in a suicide attempt. The profile of abusers and trends in use will be discussed.

Profile of Abusers

Emergency room data from 1984 to 1987 show a steady decrease in emergency room records for sedative/anxiolytic categories (tranquilizers, nonbarbiturate sedatives, and barbiturate sedatives) compared to more commonly abused drugs such as cocaine and alcohol. The greatest decline was for diazepam (Valium). Diazepam is, however, still the most frequent sedative/anxiolytic agent implicated in emergency room admissions and is mentioned five to six times more frequently than any other sedative/anxiolytic. Approximately 16 percent of all emergency room records are for sedative/anxiolytics. In fact, the number of emergency room admissions resulting from the use of these drugs is higher than that of all other drug classes. The second highest is the opioid analgesic class (narcotics).

The typical nonmedical user of sedative/anxiolytic compounds is white American, female, and between 20 and 40 years old. When these users are admitted to an emergency room, it is usually because of an overdose. Thirty-seven percent of those identified by emergency room personnel as having attempted suicides employed sedatives/anxiolytics, the highest mention of all drugs noted.

However, these drugs are rarely used to achieve a psychic effect or to maintain dependence, as are the other major abused compounds (cocaine, heroin, marijuana). In marked contrast to these other drugs, sedative/anxiolytics are usually obtained legally by prescription. In only a small fraction of emergency room records have the sedative/anxiolytic compounds been obtained by buying the substance on the street.

Sedative/anxiolytics are often used in combination with alcohol, but infrequently with cocaine, heroin, and marijuana. Emergency room admissions and deaths resulting from sedative/anxiolytics are common, especially when the drug involved is used in combination with other drugs.

Data from drug abusers in treatment suggest that sedative/anxiolytics are most frequently used by those who are polydrug abusers. Benzodiazepines, in particular, are usually abused in combination with other drugs and are rarely listed as the primary drug of abuse. There is a high rate of diazepam (Valium) abuse by methadone maintenance patients. Diazepam users tend to use other groups as well, but rarely switch to other benzodiazepines because the others seem to lack any euphoric effects. There is an unconfirmed belief among chemically-dependent persons

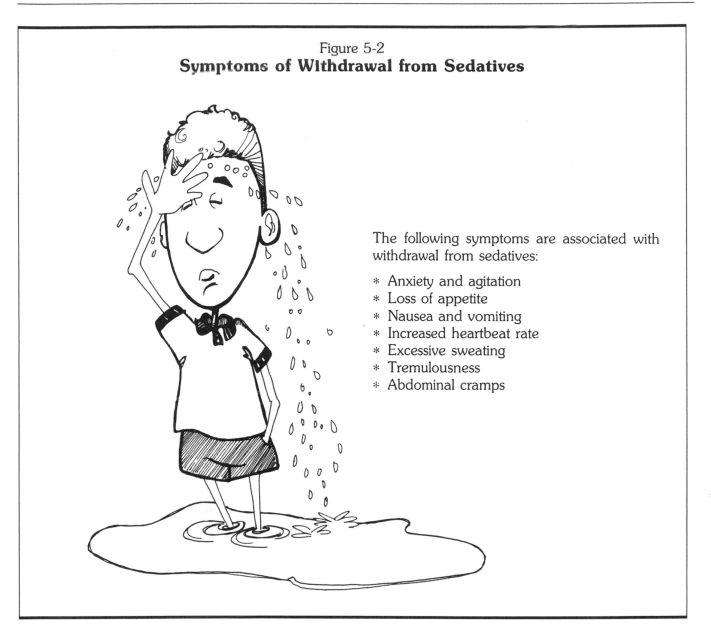

Figure 5-2
Symptoms of Withdrawal from Sedatives

The following symptoms are associated with withdrawal from sedatives:

* Anxiety and agitation
* Loss of appetite
* Nausea and vomiting
* Increased heartbeat rate
* Excessive sweating
* Tremulousness
* Abdominal cramps

that the combination of diazepam and methadone has a heroin-like euphoric effect.

Trends in Use

A long-term gradual decline in barbiturate use began in about 1975 and halted in 1985. The annual prevalence of barbiturate use among high school seniors fell to 3.3 percent, compared to 10.7 percent in 1975. It remained at 3.4 percent in 1990. Annual prevalence of barbiturates is even lower among young adults (1.9 percent), and lower still among college students (1.4 percent).

Methaqualone has shown quite a different trend pattern. Its use rose among high school seniors from 1975 to 1981, when annual prevalence reached 8 percent. It then fell

rather sharply to 0.7 percent by 1990. Use also fell among all young adults and among college students, who had annual prevalence rates of only 0.3 percent and 0.2 percent, respectively, the last year that they were asked about this drug in the Monitoring the Future Study (Johnston, O'Malley, & Bachman, 1991). In recent years, shrinking availability may well have played a role in this drop, as legal manufacture and distribution of the drug ceased.

A long and substantial decline, which began in 1977, has occurred for tranquilizer use among high school seniors. Annual prevalence now stands at 3.5 percent compared to 11 percent in 1977. Annual prevalence has now declined to 3.7 percent for the young adult sample, and to 3.0 percent for the college student sample.

TREATMENT FOR SEDATIVE/ ANXIOLYTIC DRUG WITHDRAWAL

Physical withdrawal from sedative/anxiolytic drugs is a serious and often life-threatening experience for most people. It must be understood that withdrawal from these drugs, particularly barbiturates, is a medical emergency requiring medical supervision and often hospitalization (Carroll, 1993). Withdrawal syndrome should be recognized as a medical emergency more serious than that of other drugs of abuse (Fig. 5-2). Within 24 hours, minor withdrawal symptoms manifest themselves, among them anxiety and agitation, loss of appetite, nausea and vomiting, increased heartbeat rate, excessive sweating, tremulousness, and abdominal cramps. The symptoms usually peak during the second or third day of abstinence from the short-acting barbiturates or meprobamate. The peak may not be reached until the seventh or eighth day of abstinence from the long-acting barbiturates or benzodiazepines. It is during the peak period that the major withdrawal symptoms usually occur. The patient may experience convulsions indistinguishable from those occurring in grand mal epilepsy. More than half of those who experience convulsions will go on to develop delirium, often resulting in a psychotic state identical to the delirium tremens associated with alcohol withdrawal syndrome.

Detoxification and treatment must therefore be carried out under close medical supervision. While treatment techniques vary to some extent, they share common objectives: stabilization of the drug-dependent state to allay withdrawal symptoms followed by gradual withdrawal to prevent their recurrence.

The pharmacological treatment of sedative/anxiolytic withdrawal is often facilitated with the administration of a cross-dependent drug, such as phenobarbital or diazepam. Fleming (1992) outlines the pharmacologic treatment goals of sedative/anxiolytic withdrawal as:

- relieving symptoms (for example, hyperactivity, tremulousness, agitation, anxiety, sleep disturbances);
- preventing severe withdrawal syndrome (delirium tremens);
- preventing seizures;
- reducing the chance of new dependencies on cross-dependent drugs used for withdrawal;
- minimizing the toxicity associated with cross-dependent drugs used for detoxification.

It is essential to realize that successfully eliminating physical dependence is only part of successful treatment. Psychological dependence is, of course, much more difficult and challenging to treat (Witters, Venturelli, & Hanson, 1992). Treatment is compounded when dependent individuals are experiencing several personal and/or emotional problems simultaneously.

After detoxification from sedative-hypnotics, there is no established sedative-hypnotic specific treatment for abusers (McKim, 1991). However, the principles of narcotic and alcohol treatment discussed in Chapter 6 and Chapter 13 generally apply to treatment of sedative/anxiolytic abuse and dependency.

SEXUALITY AND SEDATIVE/ ANXIOLYTIC DRUG USE

The effects of sedative/anxiolytic drugs on sexuality have not been studied in detail (Doweiko, 1993). However, the research that has been conducted generally has shown effects of diminished sexual functioning (White, 1991). These drugs are likely to cause erectile dysfunctions and high-dosage levels may cause impotence in males. Sedative/anxiolytic agents appear to also contribute to loss of sexual drive and difficulty in achieving orgasm. Decreased vaginal secretions before and during sexual intercourse have been noted by females using these agents (White, 1991).

BIBLIOGRAPHY

Carroll, C.R. (1993) *Drugs in Modern Society (second edition)*. Dubuque, IA: Wm. C. Brown Publishers.

Doweiko, H.E. (1993) *Concepts of Chemical Dependency*. Pacific Grove, CA: Brooks/Cole.

Faulkner, R.W. (1991) *Therapeutic Recreation Protocol for Treatment of Substance Addictions*. State College, PA: Venture Publishing Co.

Fleming, M.F. (1992) Pharmacologic management of nicotine, alcohol, and other drug dependence. In M.F. Fleming & K.L. Barry (Eds.), *Addictive Disorders: A Practical Guide to Treatment*. St. Louis, MO: Mosby-Year Book.

Johnston, L.D., O'Malley, P.M., & Bachman, J.G. (1991) *Drug Use Among American High School Seniors, Col-*

lege Students, and Young Adults. 1975–1990. Volume I, High School Seniors. DHHS Publication No. (ADM)91-1813. Rockville, MD: National Institute on Drug Abuse.

Liska, K. (1986) *Drugs and the Human Body: With Implications for Society.* New York: Macmillan.

McKim, W.A. (1991) *Drugs and Behavior: An Introduction to Behavioral Pharmacology.* Englewood Cliffs, NJ: Prentice-Hall.

National Institute on Drug Abuse. (1990) *Drug Abuse Curriculum for Employee Assistance Program Professionals.* DHHS Publication No. (ADM)90-1587. Rockville, MD: National Institute on Drug Abuse.

National Institute on Drug Abuse. (1991) *Drug Abuse and Drug Abuse Research: The Third Triennial Report to Congress from the Secretary, Department of Health and Human Services.* DHHS Publication No. (ADM)91-1704. Rockville, MD: National Institute on Drug Abuse.

Office for Substance Abuse Prevention. (1990) *Alcohol, Tobacco, and Other Drugs May Harm the Unborn.* DHHS Publication No. (ADM)90-1711. Rockville, MD: Office for Substance Abuse Prevention.

U.S. Department of Justice, Drug Enforcement Administration. Depressants. *Drug Enforcement,* July 1979.

White, J.M. (1991) *Drug Dependence.* Englewood Cliffs, NJ: Prentice-Hall.

Witters, W.L., Venturelli, P.J., & Hanson, G. (1992) *Drugs and Society (third edition).* Boston: Jones & Bartlett.

Narcotics

Narcotics refer to a second type of depressants that has an inhibiting effect on one function of the central nervous system—the awareness or perception of pain. Narcotics may be natural or synthetic substances. The medical meaning of the term **narcotic** refers to opium and opium derivatives or to synthetic substitutes. The major therapeutic use for narcotics is **analgesia**, or pain relief. In this chapter, the discussion will include natural narcotics, semi-synthetic and synthetic narcotics, pharmacology and the effects of narcotics, current use patterns, AIDS and intravenous drug abuse, narcotics and pregnancy, narcotics and sexuality, and treatment of narcotic addiction.

NATURAL NARCOTICS

Natural narcotic drugs are also called **opiates** because of their derivation or chemical similarity to opium. This group of drugs includes such substances as the illicit substance, heroin, as well as such known therapeutic medications as morphine, codeine, meperidine (Demoral), oxycodone (Percodan), hydromorphone (Dilaudid), pentazocine (Talwin), and methadone. In this section of the chapter, the source of opiates, opium, morphine, codeine, and thebaine will be discussed.

Source of Opiates

The poppy *Papaver somniferum* is the main source of the natural or nonsynthetic narcotics. There is evidence of its presence in the Mediterranean region as early as 300 B.C. and it has since been cultivated in countries around the world.

Since ancient times, the milky fluid that oozes from incisions in the unripe seedpod has been scraped by hand and air-dried to produce opium gum. A more modern method of harvesting is by the industrial poppy straw process of extracting alkaloids from the mature dried plant. The extract may be either liquid, solid, or powder form. Most poppy straw concentrate made available commercially is a fine brownish powder with a distinct odor. Hundreds of tons of opium or its equivalent in poppy straw concentrate are legally imported annually into the United States.

Opium

Until the early 1900s, patent medicines often contained opium without any warning label. Today there are state, federal, and international laws governing the production and distribution of narcotic substances, and there is little abuse of opium in the United States. A small amount of opium is used to make antidiarrheal preparations such as paregoric.

At least 25 alkaloids can be extracted from opium. These fall into two general categories, each producing markedly different effects. The first, known as the phenanthrene alkaloids, represented by morphine and codeine, are used as analgesics and cough suppressants; the second, the isoquinoline alkaloids, represented by papaverine (an intestinal relaxant) and noscapine (a cough suppressant), have no significant influence on the central nervous system.

Morphine

Morphine, the principal constituent of opium, ranges in concentration from 4–21 percent. It is one of the most effective drugs known for the relief of pain. It is marketed in the form of white crystals, hypodermic tablets, and injectable preparations. Its licit use is restricted primarily to hospitals. Morphine is odorless, has a bitter taste, and darkens with age. It may be administered subcutaneously, intramuscularly, or intravenously, the latter method being the one most frequently resorted to by chemically-dependent persons. Tolerance and dependence develop rapidly in the user. Only a small part of the morphine obtained from opium is used medically. Most of it is converted to codeine and, secondarily to hydromorphone (Dilaudid).

Codeine

Codeine is an alkaloid found in raw opium in concentrations ranging from 0.7 to 2.5 percent. It was first isolated in 1832 as an impurity in a batch of morphine. Although it occurs naturally, most codeine is produced from morphine.

Compared with morphine, codeine produces less analgesia, sedation, and respiratory depression. It is widely

89

distributed in products of two general types. Codeine for the relief of moderate pain may consist of codeine tablets or be combined with other products such as aspirin or acetaminophen (Tylenol).

Some liquid codeine preparations (antitussins) are available for the relief of coughs. Codeine is also manufactured to a lesser extent in injectable form for the relief of pain. It is by far the most widely-used, naturally-occurring narcotic in medical treatment.

Thebaine

A minor constituent of opium, thebaine is the principal alkaloid present in another species of poppy, *Papaver bracteatum*, which has been grown experimentally in the United States as well as other parts of the world. Although chemically similar to both codeine and morphine, it produces stimulant rather than depressant effects. Thebaine is not used in this country for medical purposes, but is converted into a variety of medically important compounds, including codeine, hydrocodone, oxycodone, oxymorphone, nalbuphine, and naloxone.

SEMISYNTHETIC AND SYNTHETIC NARCOTICS

Semisynthetic narcotics are compounds that have been derived by modification of the chemicals contained in opium. Heroin, hydromorphone, oxycodone, etorphine, and diprenorphine are semisynthetic narcotics. In contrast to pharmaceutical products derived directly or indirectly from narcotics of natural origin, **synthetic narcotics** are produced entirely within the laboratory. Semisynthetic and synthetic narcotics are called **opioids**. A continuing search for a narcotic product that will retain the analgesic properties of morphine without the consequent dangers of tolerance and dependence has yet to yield a drug that is not susceptible to abuse. In this section of the chapter, the discussion will include heroin, hydromorphone, oxycodone, etorphine and diprenorphine, meperidine, methadone and related drugs, and narcotic antagonists.

Heroin

First synthesized from morphine in 1874, heroin was not extensively used in medicine until the beginning of this century. The Bayer Company in Germany first started commercial production of the new pain remedy in 1898. While it received widespread acceptance, the medical profession for years remained unaware of its potential for addiction. The first comprehensive control of heroin in the United States was established with the Harrison Narcotic

Act of 1914. Heroin is not approved for any medical use in the United States.

Pure heroin is a white powder with a bitter taste. Illicit heroin may vary in color from white to dark brown because of impurities. Pure heroin is rarely sold on the street. A "bag"—slang for a single dosage unit of heroin—weighs approximately 100 mg and contains about 5 percent heroin. To increase the bulk of the material sold to the heroin user, diluents are mixed with the heroin in ratios ranging from 9 to 1 to as much as 99 to 1. Sugars, starch, powdered milk, and quinine are common diluents. Major medical problems associated with heroin use can occur from injection of these additives into the bloodstream.

Hydromorphone

Most commonly known as Dilaudid, hydromorphone is the second oldest semisynthetic narcotic analgesic. Marketed both in tablet and injectable form, it is shorter-acting and more sedating than morphine. However, hydromorphone's potency is from two to eight times as great as morphine. It is a highly-abused drug. The tablets, stronger than available liquid forms, may be dissolved and injected.

Oxycodone

Oxycodone (Percodan) is synthesized from thebaine. Oxycodone is similar to but more potent than codeine. It is marketed in combination with other drugs for the relief of pain and is effective when taken orally.

Etorphine and Diprenorphine

Etorphine and diprenorphine are both derived from thebaine. Etorphine is more than a thousand times as potent as morphine in its analgesic, sedative, and respiratory depressant effect. For human use, its potency is a distinct disadvantage because of the danger of overdose. Etorphine hydrochloride (M99) is used by veterinarians to immobilize large wild animals.

Meperidine

The first synthetic narcotic meperidine (Demoral) is chemically dissimilar to morphine but resembles it in its analgesic potency. It is probably the most widely-used drug for the relief of moderate to severe pain. Available in pure form as well as in products containing other medicinal ingredients, it is administered either orally or by injection, the latter method being the most widely abused. Tolerance and dependence develop with chronic use, and large doses can result in convulsions.

Methadone and Related Drugs

German scientists synthesized methadone during World War II because of a shortage of morphine. Although chemically unlike morphine or heroin, methadone produces many of the same effects. Introduced into the United States in 1947 as an analgesic and distributed under such names as Amidone, Dolophine, and Methadone, it became widely used in the 1960s in the treatment of narcotic-dependent persons.

The effects of methadone differ from morphine-based drugs in that they have a longer duration of action, lasting up to 24 hours, thereby permitting administration only once a day in heroin detoxification and maintenance programs. Moreover, methadone is almost as effective when administered orally as it is by injection. But tolerance and dependence may develop, and withdrawal symptoms, though they develop more slowly, are more prolonged. Ironically, methadone, designed to control narcotic addiction, has emerged in some urban areas as a major cause of overdose deaths.

The synthetic compound levo-alpha-acetylmethadol (LAAM) is closely related chemically to methadone and has an even longer duration of action (from 48 to 72 hours). This allows a further reduction in clinic visits and the elimination of take-home medication. Its potential in the treatment of narcotic-dependent persons remains uncertain.

Another close relative of methadone is propoxyphene, first marketed in 1957 under the trade name of Darvon for the relief of mild to moderate pain. Less dependence-producing than the opiates, it is also less effective as an analgesic.

Narcotic Antagonists

The deliberate effort to find an effective analgesic that is not dependence-producing has led to the development of a class of compounds known as narcotic antagonists in recent years (Fig. 6-1). **Narcotic antagonists**, as the name implies, tend to block and reverse the effects of narcotics. However, these drugs also produce narcotic effects and are used both orally and by injection to relieve moderate pain. Though they are weaker than morphine, hydromorphone, meperidine, and methadone, they also have abuse potential and have been sold on the street.

Nalorphine, introduced into clinical medicine in 1951 is called a partial antagonist. In a drug-free individual, nalorphine produces morphine-like effects; whereas in an individual under the influence of narcotics, it counteracts these effects. Another partial antagonist is pentazocine (Talwin) which was introduced as an analgesic in 1967.

Relatively pure antagonists have also been developed. Naloxone (Narcan) was introduced as a specific antidote for narcotic poisoning in 1971. It does not have analgesic properties. A number of "pure" antagonists have since been developed that are longer lasting and effective when administered orally. One of them is Naltrexone, which has few side effects and in a single dose can provide narcotic antagonist effects for up to 72 hours. It is sometimes used as an adjunct to narcotic treatment programs.

Pentazocine (Talwin) was probably the most likely narcotic antagonist to be sold illegally. However, the pharmaceutical company that produces pentazocine began mixing small amounts of naloxone in the drug preparation. This caused users who injected pentazocine to have a narcotic withdrawal reaction and appears to have substantially reduced the abuse of this drug.

Buprenorphine is often classified as a mixed agonist/antagonist narcotic. It is used in the United Kingdom as an analgesic and is being tested in the United States as a substitute for methadone in the treatment of narcotic addiction. It is unique because it produces few withdrawal symptoms, even after being administered regularly for long periods of time. It also blocks the effects of other narcotics and has pleasant psychological effects, similar to morphine and other narcotics. It is in an early stage of testing but may become a useful addition to the existing treatment for narcotic addiction.

PHARMACOLOGY AND THE EFFECTS OF NARCOTICS

The drugs we have reviewed have major differences in their potency, the speed with which their effects are produced, the degree to which they are effective when taken orally, and their duration of action. These differences underlie their preference by abusers. When given by injection, fentanyl, hydromorphone, and heroin are the most potent and have the most rapid onset of action; codeine is one of the least potent and among the slowest to take effect. In this section, general and side effects, medical use, and street use will be discussed.

General and Side Effects

An important effect of narcotic use and abuse is often a short-lived state of euphoria. The initial effects, however, are often unpleasant, leading many to conclude that those

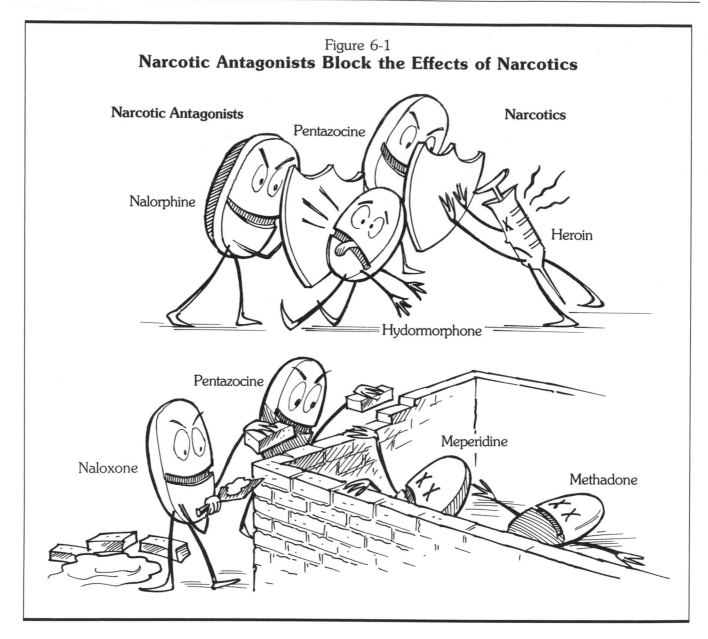

Figure 6-1
Narcotic Antagonists Block the Effects of Narcotics

who persist in excessive or illicit use may have latent personality disturbances.

Narcotics are unique in their ability to reduce or eliminate severe pain, and this is their major use in medical practice. However, they also reduce anxiety and depression, sedate, dry secretions in the nose and mouth, decrease respiration, suppress the cough reflex, and cause constipation (Fig. 6-2). Their ability to suppress coughing and control diarrhea has resulted in the wide use of narcotics for these purposes as well.

Narcotics tend to induce pinpoint pupils and reduced vision, together with drowsiness, apathy, and decreased physical activity. A larger dose may induce sleep, but there is an increasing possibility of nausea, vomiting, and depres-

sion—the major toxic effect of the narcotics. Except in cases of acute intoxication, there is no loss of motor coordination or slurred speech as in the case of depressants.

Several narcotic effects occur during regular use and are considered undesirable, and thus are classified as side effects. The most common of these are sedation and constipation. Tolerance to these effects occurs but is usually not complete, and people who take narcotics for chronic pain often require stool softeners or other laxatives. Cough- and respiratory-suppressing effects, though desirable in some cases, can be dangerous in people who have chronic lung disease, as small doses of narcotics can sometimes cause severe respiratory problems. Occasionally, people are allergic to narcotics and develop a skin rash or some other uncomfortable response.

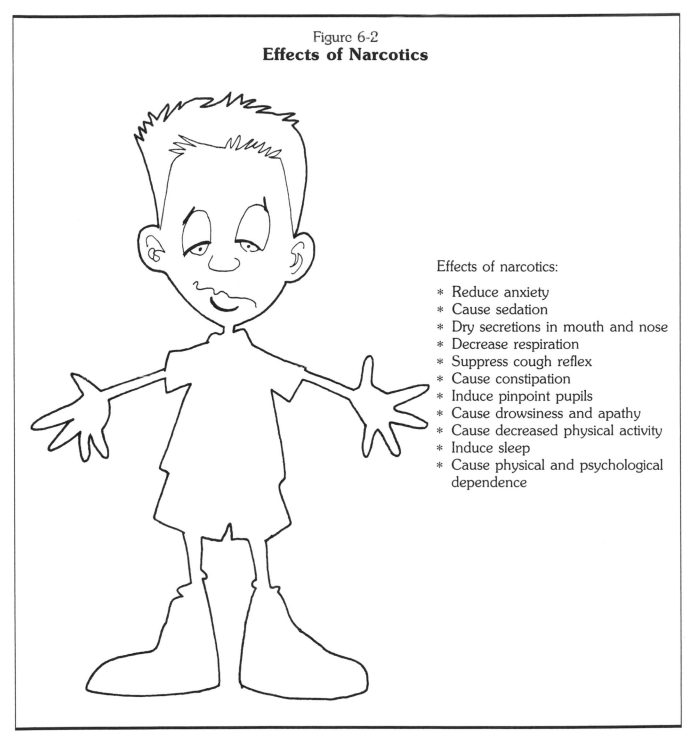

Figure 6-2
Effects of Narcotics

Effects of narcotics:

* Reduce anxiety
* Cause sedation
* Dry secretions in mouth and nose
* Decrease respiration
* Suppress cough reflex
* Cause constipation
* Induce pinpoint pupils
* Cause drowsiness and apathy
* Cause decreased physical activity
* Induce sleep
* Cause physical and psychological dependence

The most serious potential side effect that occurs in people who take narcotics for relief of chronic pain is the development of tolerance and physical dependence, as well as the risk of developing psychological dependence. All these problems can be minimized by careful attention to prescribing practices and patient compliance.

Medical Use

Methadone is the most effective narcotic analgesic when given orally, and it also suppresses narcotic withdrawal symptoms for 24 to 36 hours. It has a significantly longer withdrawal-suppressing effect than any other narcotic and is used for maintenance treatment of narcotic addiction and to control chronic pain.

All the narcotics we discussed are used in medical practice in the United States with the exception of heroin. Those narcotics with the weakest effects are used for the mildest types of pain, such as the pain associated with minor surgery. Examples are codeine or oxycodone (Percodan) for dental extractions. The stronger narcotics such as morphine, meperdine (Demoral), and hydromorphone (Dilaudid) are used for more severe pain such as that involved with bone fractures, cancer, or major surgery.

Methadone is used primarily to control chronic pain and as a substitution therapy for narcotic addiction. Paregoric is used almost exclusively to control diarrhea. Codeine cough syrups are used to suppress coughing. Fentanyl is used only for anesthesia. It is important to emphasize that any narcotic is subject to abuse, even those with the lowest potencies such as codeine, paregoric, and proproxyphene (Darvon).

Street Use

The most commonly used street narcotic is heroin. It is very much desired by narcotic-dependent persons for its potency and extremely rapid effect when taken intravenously or "mainlined." Heroin is occasionally administered by inhalation or smoking. For example, U.S. troop members who used heroin while stationed in Vietnam usually smoked pure heroin, a form of abuse almost unknown in the continental United States. The heroin sold here is usually too weak to be effective when smoked; it must be dissolved and injected for the user to achieve a significant effect. In contrast, the heroin sold in Vietnam was often 90–95 percent pure, which allowed considerable amounts of the drug to get into the body even when it was smoked.

Periodically, more potent heroin or a synthetic narcotic produced in illegal laboratories (designer drugs) are sold to users. This creates a dangerous situation, as persons who are accustomed to using a lower potency narcotic may overdose, sometimes with fatal outcomes. Such cases have been reported, especially with alpha methyl fentanyl, a derivative of fentanyl. This has been sold as "China White" and has caused a number of overdoses from its very high potency.

CURRENT USE PATTERNS

Household surveys do not adequately measure the prevalence of heroin use and are believed to result in significant underestimates, particularly for current use. This discussion will include statistics and chronic and repeated use.

Statistics

The 1988 Household Survey data show that 1.9 million Americans (1 percent) have tried heroin. Rates of lifetime use were highest for males (1.3 percent) and for African-

Americans (2.3 percent). Among high school seniors the annual prevalence of heroin use has been very steady since 1979 at 0.5 percent to 0.6 percent. The heroin statistics for young adults and college students have also remained quite stable in recent years at low rates of about 0.1 percent to 0.2 percent (Johnston, O'Malley, & Bachman, 1991). It has been estimated that there are about 500,000 heroin-dependent persons in the United States (Doweiko, 1993).

The use of opiates other than heroin has been fairly level since 1975. High school seniors have had an annual prevalence rate of 4 percent to 6 percent since 1975. The rate for 1990 was 4.5 percent. Young adults in their twenties have generally shown a similar cross-time pattern (Johnston, O'Malley, & Bachman, 1991).

Chronic and Repeated Use

To the extent that the response to narcotics may be pleasurable, its intensity may be expected to increase with the amount of the dose administered. Repeated use, however, will result in increasing tolerance; the user must administer progressively larger doses to attain the desired psychoactive effects. This reinforces the compulsive behavior known as drug dependence.

Continuous use of narcotic drugs, even for relatively short periods of time, causes physical dependence. As discussed in Chapter 1, physical dependence refers to an alteration of the normal functions of the body that necessitates the continued presence of a drug in order to prevent the withdrawal or abstinence syndrome.

The intensity of physical symptoms experienced during the withdrawal period is related directly to the amount of narcotic used each day. Deprivation of an addictive drug causes increased excitability of those same bodily functions that have been depressed by its habitual use. If untreated, typical flu-like narcotic withdrawal symptoms may result, including chills, gooseflesh, tears, runny nose, yawning, rapid heart rate, high blood pressure, perspiration, irritability, cramping, diarrhea, insomnia, and muscle spasms. For most heroin users, the peak period of discomfort is 48 to 72 hours after the last drug dose.

Without treatment, visible symptoms of withdrawal continue for 7 to 10 days, but may take weeks for the body to return to normal functioning. Although uncomfortable, heroin withdrawal, unlike that from high-dose chronic alcohol or barbiturate dependence, is seldom life-threatening. Craving for heroin or other narcotics is often described by chronic users long after the body has returned to normal. Relapse is common among heroin users, as it is among chronic abusers of tobacco, alcohol, and cocaine.

Since chronic narcotic abusers tend to become preoccupied daily with obtaining and taking drugs, they often neglect themselves and may suffer from malnutrition, infections, and unattended diseases or injuries. Chronic abusers are at risk of hazardous overdose reactions to large amounts of narcotics, with effects ranging from breathing difficulties to coma and possible death, caused by suppression of the brain center that regulates respiration.

Major medical problems associated with heroin addiction are caused by the additives used to cut heroin before street sales and by infections transmitted in unsterile paraphernalia used for injection. The risk of infection with the human immunodeficiency virus (HIV), the virus that causes AIDS, is greatly increased among narcotics abusers who inject drugs and share unsterile paraphernalia.

AIDS AND INTRAVENOUS DRUG ABUSE

Acquired immunodeficiency syndrome (AIDS), the end-stage illness associated with the HIV epidemic, is one of this century's most serious public health challenges. Intravenous (IV) drug-associated transmission is a leading cause of the disease. IV drug abuse or sexual contact with intravenous drug abusers (IVDAs) account for over 80 percent of the cases in females, including those who infect their children with the disease. In New York City, 93 percent of heterosexually acquired infections are associated with having an IVDA for a sexual partner, and 80 percent of pediatric patients with AIDS have an IVDA parent.

Current AIDS surveillance techniques may seriously underestimate the extent of HIV-associated death and illness among IVDAs, since there has been an unexplained increase in infectious disease deaths among IVDAs. Because of the seriousness of AIDS and its association with the use of shared "works" (paraphernalia used in injecting drugs intravenously), preventing this mode of HIV transmission has achieved special urgency.

Listed here are some of the key findings from the *Third Triennial Report on Drug Abuse and Drug Abuse Research to Congress from the Secretary, Department of Health and Human Services* regarding knowledge of this source of HIV infection:

- The first wave of AIDS cases among IVDAs was noted as early as 1982 in New York City, and cases have now been reported from all 50 states, the District of Columbia, and Puerto Rico.
- African-American and Hispanic IVDAs account for disproportionate numbers of the AIDS cases associated with IV drug use—over half are African-American and nearly a third are of Hispanic origins.
- If HIV-associated mortality is adjusted to take into account excess deaths from infectious diseases in IVDAs, more than half (53 percent) of AIDS-related deaths in New York City would be associated with this form of drug use.
- HIV infection may also be responsible for the substantial increases in viral hepatitis among IVDAs because these cases too may be the result of HIV-impaired immune response.
- Studies done in the U.S. and abroad document the potential for rapid increases of HIV infection within the IVDA population.
- Injecting drugs in so-called "shooting galleries," where chemically-dependent persons gather to use drugs and often share works, is a common source of HIV infection.
- Heroin injection alone or in combination with cocaine ("speedballing") has been associated with bacterial endocarditis, types A and B hepatitis, and more recently, HIV infection.
- Drug injection may add to the risk of sexual transmission of HIV infection both by increasing the likelihood of unprotected sex and by increasing the prevalence of sexually-transmitted diseases, which are possible cofactors in HIV infection.
- IVDAs are frequently unaware of the multiple modes of HIV transmission and effective prevention measures.

NARCOTICS AND PREGNANCY

It has long been known that narcotic drugs taken by a female during pregnancy reach the fetus. More recently, it has also been determined that newborn babies suffer withdrawal symptoms if their mothers are chronic heroin users. Studies have confirmed that narcotics cross the placenta and enter the fetal bloodstream, but the level of either heroin or methadone in the fetus remains lower than in the mother. Complications, effects on newborns, effects on breast-fed babies, and effects on the growing child will be discussed.

Complications

A pregnant female's use of narcotics may reduce the oxygen supply to the fetus, a medical condition known as **hypoxia**. Alternating toxic and withdrawal effects experienced by the mother also result in an unstable uterine environment. In addition, heroin and other narcotics suppress maternal appetite and may interfere with the absorption of nutrients from foods by reducing intestinal, liver, and pancreatic functioning.

Pregnancy complications for heroin users include increased risk of abruptio placentae (early separation of the placenta), eclampsia (a serious, sometimes fatal, toxic condition with high blood pressure, swelling, seizures, or coma), placental insufficiency, breech presentations, premature labor and ruptured membranes, and delivery by cesarean section. Ten to fifteen percent of these females develop toxemia that may lead to eclampsia.

Heroin use during pregnancy increases the likelihood of stillbirths and fetal distress, indicated by meconium staining (excreting fecal matter into the amniotic fluid) and aspiration pneumonia in the newborn. These effects are attributed to alternating toxic and withdrawal states in the expectant mother. In addition, nearly half of heroin-dependent females who receive no prenatal care deliver prematurely, often because of infections.

Effects on Newborns

A well-confirmed risk to newborns from their mothers' narcotic use during pregnancy is intrauterine growth retardation (IUGR) and small size for gestational age. Birth weight in narcotic-exposed infants may also be related to the amount of prenatal care their mothers received, as well as to the specific narcotic used.

About 80 percent of babies born to heroin-addicted mothers have such serious medical problems as hyaline membrane diseases (a serious lung disease), brain hemorrhages, and respiratory distress syndrome. The majority of these complications are the result of prematurity (Fig. 6-3).

Infants born to heroin-using mothers are also at risk for perinatally-transmitted HIV infection, later developing into AIDS. Higher death rates among these newborns are attributed to sudden death infant syndrome (SIDS), as well as to poor living conditions in which infections are more likely and more dangerous to premature and/or low birth weight infants.

Although narcotic exposure before birth is not usually associated with an increased risk for physical malformations, one in four infants born to mothers in a methadone-treatment program had strabismus—a visual disorder in which the infant's eyes cannot focus together properly. This is a rate five to eight times higher than that in the general population. Since other psychoactive drugs in

addition to methadone were used by mothers during pregnancy, these findings suggest that maternal drug abuse may predispose infants to strabismus and that health care professionals should examine drug-exposed infants for visual abnormalities.

Dramatic withdrawal symptoms are the most frequently observed consequence to newborns from prenatal narcotics exposure. This neonatal abstinence syndrome has been observed in hundreds of infants born to narcotic-addicted mothers. Restlessness, tremulousness, disturbed sleep and feeding, stuffy nose, vomiting, diarrhea, a high-pitched cry, fever, irregular breathing, or seizures usually start within 48–72 hours. The heroin-exposed infant also sneezes, twitches, hiccups, and weeps. Occasionally, these symptoms do not begin until two to four weeks after delivery. This irritability, resulting from over-arousal of the central nervous system, usually ends after a month, but can persist for three months or more.

Between 60 and 90 percent of newborns prenatally exposed to narcotic drugs develop abstinence signs requiring special, gentle handling and medication after birth. These difficult newborns, like the jittery cocaine babies, are challenging to caretakers. Their agitation may discourage appropriate bonding with their mothers unless appropriate parenting skills are taught and encouraged. Heroin-exposed newborns may also have poorly controlled responses to their surroundings and difficulties directing their attention to sights and sounds.

Effects on Breast-Fed Infants

Heroin, methadone, and other narcotics are transmitted in breast milk. Observers in the early years of this century noted that opium withdrawal symptoms in the newborn could be alleviated by breast milk from an addicted mother and that a breast-fed infant could become narcotic dependent from nursing. More recently, nursing infants whose mothers regularly used propoxyphene (Darvon) and oxycodone (Percodan) showed signs of drowsiness and failure to thrive.

Breast-feeding by motivated mothers in well-supervised methadone-treatment programs should not automatically be ruled out, particularly during the first six to eight weeks postpartum when the greatest immunologic and bonding benefits are likely to result. Some research studies suggest that the newborn would be exposed to very small amounts of prescribed methadone in breast milk, especially when compared to prenatal exposure levels from the same dosage. Before a methadone-maintained mother is encour-

Figure 6-3
Risks to Newborns from Maternal Use of Narcotics

Risks to newborns:

* Low birth weight
* Lung disease
* Brain hemorrhage
* HIV infection
* Sudden infant death syndrome (SIDS)
* Withdrawal symptoms
* Poorly controlled responses

aged to nurse, she should be (1) well controlled on a stable dosage, (2) in good health, with adequate nutrition, (3) not infected with HIV, tuberculosis, or hepatitis B, and (4) not using alcohol and other drugs.

It is important to note that cases of HIV transmission through breast milk have been documented. Furthermore, the amount of methadone transmitted to and consumed by the growing infant, if nursing continues beyond three to six months of age, may make later breast-feeding inadvisable. Close monitoring is needed of the nursing infant's responses and the lactating mother's potential for other illicit drug use.

Effects on the Growing Child

When heroin-exposed babies are followed beyond the withdrawal period, their abilities to adapt to their surroundings and to interact with their caregivers seem to improve. After a month, only subtle differences can be observed between most of these babies and other babies who were not exposed to narcotics in utero. However, the development of muscle control may be uneven and motor coordination more impaired in children who experience severe neonatal withdrawal.

Follow-up studies of babies born to heroin-using or methadone-maintained females have been particularly difficult because of the following: (1) the mothers drop out of the studies and cannot be traced, (2) the babies grow up in very different home environments that make it difficult to differentiate outcomes resulting from drug exposure from those stemming from caretaking variations (especially continuing drug abuse by parents, as well as the presence or absence of the mother), and (3) the mothers have very different lifestyles during pregnancy that also affect outcomes in their infants.

Nonetheless, growth disturbances and other behavioral effects such as hyperactivity, shortened attention spans, temper tantrums, slowed psychomotor development, and impaired visual functioning have been noted in infants and older children born to narcotic-dependent mothers. Several studies have shown problems in speech development. However, test scores measuring these children's physical and psychological development are generally within the normal range.

Many problems associated with prenatal exposure to heroin also occur after prenatal exposure to methadone. These findings regarding prenatal effects of methadone, it should be noted, are complicated by the fact that methadone-dosed mothers are likely to continue using other drugs, including heroin. In general, babies born to methadone-maintained females receiving adequate and consistent prenatal care thrive better and have fewer neurological complications than those whose mothers continue to use heroin or to take methadone in an uncontrolled manner during pregnancy.

Experts generally agree that heroin-affected children have numerous school and behavioral problems, whether they are born to drug-using mothers or raised by drug-using caretakers. This finding has important implications for interventions to (1) improve the home surroundings and day care opportunities of drug-exposed youngsters and (2) enhance the parenting skills of their caretakers.

NARCOTICS AND SEXUALITY

Narcotic use by females increases amenorrhea (cessation of menstrual periods) and menstrual irregularity, thereby interfering with fertility. Many females who use heroin also report a decrease in sexual desire. The sexually-transmitted diseases associated with prostitution and the lifestyles of many heroin users often result in pelvic inflammatory disease (PID). This condition causes scarring of the fallopian tubes and seriously impairs fertility.

Reduced sexual desire (libido) in males is associated with chronic narcotic use. Narcotic drug use is also likely to result in decreased erection and orgasm for males.

TREATMENT OF NARCOTIC ADDICTION

During the 19th century, treatment for narcotic addiction was generally handled by private physicians and usually involved helping the patient through withdrawal. Heroin, which was commercially produced in 1898 as a potent pain killer and cough suppressant, was believed to be nonaddictive. Because it relieved morphine withdrawal symptoms, it was advertised as a cure for morphine addiction. Several years passed before medical authorities discovered that heroin was as addictive as morphine. It was during this time that most physicians regarded drug addic-

tion as a physical disease that could be cured by gradually reducing use of the drug (withdrawal.) The psychological element of addiction was ignored largely and, because very little follow-up was done on patients after treatment, the significance of the problem was not recognized. In this section, the discussion will include hospitalization, methadone maintenance, therapeutic communities, drug-free outpatient treatment, multimodality treatment, narcotic antagonist treatment, and females and narcotic treatment.

Hospitalization

Hospitalization was used to treat drug dependence in the 19th century and was continued in federal drug abuse-treatment clinics that were established in the 1930s. Treatment began with gradual withdrawal of the drug, by decreasing dosage over a period of one or two weeks, until the patient was drug free. Withdrawal was followed by a period of inpatient care, usually lasting several months, during which the patient remained isolated from his or her former environment and from drugs. The patient received psychiatric counseling, psychotherapy, group therapy, or work therapy. The third stage of the hospitalization method consisted of a period of outpatient care in which the patient lived in the community but continued to receive counseling, psychotherapy, or vocational rehabilitation.

The emphasis on security and isolation of the patients from the community resulted in a prison-like atmosphere in many of the facilities. Legal controls were often used to confine patients to hospitals. Hospitalization is the most expensive method of treatment and is generally believed to be the least effective method, in view of the high relapse rates of most hospitalization programs over the years.

Methadone Maintenance

In recent years, methadone maintenance has been the most widely used method for treating narcotic-dependent persons. Most large cities have treatment programs that provide methadone detoxification and maintenance services after a diagnosis of narcotic addiction has been made. Methadone maintenance programs have demonstrated the ability to attract a large number of narcotic-dependent persons and to retain them in treatment. In addition, since most methadone-maintenance programs offer treatment on an outpatient basis, it is a markedly less expensive method than treatment that involves hospitalization or confinement.

The methadone-maintenance technique used by Marie Nyswander and Vincent Dole in the mid-1960s involved sufficient dosage to create a "blockade effect" in patients. In other words, with this technique, patients became tolerant to the euphoric effects of opiates. For example, if a patient used heroin while receiving a large oral dose of methadone daily, he or she would not experience the usual euphoria that accompanies heroin usage. In many patients this "blockade effect" tended to discourage repeated illicit use of narcotics.

Similar successful treatment outcomes for patients using smaller daily doses of methadone have been achieved. For this reason, many maintenance programs today use a lower daily dose of methadone.

Federal regulations require that methadone-maintenance programs provide additional treatment such as group therapy and family counseling. Although the ultimate goal of methadone-maintenance treatment is eventual withdrawal from methadone and elimination of dependence on any drug, for some individuals maintenance may continue for months or years. The general theory behind methadone maintenance is to relieve the craving for heroin while engaging the patient in additional treatment aimed at helping the heroin-dependent person work out a better way of living.

In addition to maintenance, methadone programs also provide outpatient detoxification. This treatment involves administering decreasing doses of methadone over a period ranging from a few days to a few weeks for the purpose of relieving withdrawal symptoms. Some heroin-dependent persons volunteer for detoxification in an attempt to become drug free. However, detoxification alone is rarely successful. Most patients either relapse into heroin use or enter methadone maintenance programs after detoxification has failed.

Critics of methadone maintenance point to the fact that methadone does not cure drug dependence but merely transfers dependence from one drug to another. Another criticism is that some patients begin chronic abuse of other drugs such as alcohol, amphetamines, barbiturates, or cocaine while enrolled in methadone maintenance treatment. In view of these deficiencies, entry into methadone maintenance should be voluntary and offered as an alternative to other forms of treatment.

Therapeutic Communities

Therapeutic communities are residential treatment programs that attempt to deal with the psychological causes of addiction by changing the character and personality of chemically-dependent persons. The first therapeutic community was Synanon, founded in 1959. The techniques used were modeled after those of Alcoholics Anonymous, which involved repeated confessions, group interaction, and mutual support among members.

During the late 1950s and early 1960s, the concept of group therapy grew in popularity throughout the country, and as therapeutic communities developed, they adopted it as a major technique. The growth of therapeutic communities paralleled the growth of communes, and some of the cooperative spirit of the communes was incorporated into them. The idea of a group of people living and working together for their mutual benefit was, and still is, a basic tenet.

Although therapeutic communities are often managed by former chemically-dependent persons and ordinarily do not have mental health professionals on their staffs, the treatment method is based on two techniques of group psychotherapy. The first technique is confrontation, or encounter group therapy, in which the chemically-dependent person is forced to confess and acknowledge weaknesses and immaturity. The second technique is "milieu therapy" in which the dependent person lives and works within a hierarchical social structure and may progress upward in status as he or she demonstrates increased responsibility and self-discipline. The principles of behavior modification, or conditioning, are applied constantly within the community in the form of reinforcement of good behavior and punishment of bad behavior.

The time period for treatment varies from one therapeutic community to another. Synanon is a permanent community where residents may remain for life. Most of these communities require members to stay one or two years. The programs also vary in selectivity. In the older programs, applicants were screened rigorously and only the most highly-motivated individuals were accepted. The older programs also continue to be drug free, whereas some newer programs use methadone maintenance or both methadone- and drug-free therapy.

The problem with therapeutic communities as a treatment method is that they appear to be suitable for very few people. In fact, about 75 percent of those who enter them drop out within the first month. Members who remain in the communities and seem to respond to the treatment regimen are largely white Americans and from middle class backgrounds. Some critics feel that the treatment of residents in a demeaning or punitive way, which is characteristic of many communities, goes against the principles of supportive psychotherapy. Because they are residential, therapeutic communities are more expensive to operate than drug-free, outpatient programs, even though many are operated entirely by members. In terms of results, however, therapeutic communities do not appear to be more effective than other drug-free methods of treatment.

Drug-Free Outpatient Treatment

The treatment method that offers drug-free services entirely on an outpatient basis is referred to as either drug-free outpatient, ambulatory drug free, or outpatient abstinence treatment. Programs vary in the scope or level of treatment they provide, but usually some or all of the following services are included:
- group or individual psychotherapy
- vocational and social counseling
- family counseling
- education
- community outreach

Programs also differ in the degree of patient involvement in treatment. Some programs are social or "rap" centers where patients drop in occasionally. Others are free clinics providing a range of health services. Some programs provide structured methadone detoxification and monitor patient drug use by urine analysis throughout treatment. Most experts believe that these programs do help some people but that the attrition rates are very high. It appears that drug-free outpatient treatment may be more effective with youths who are experimenting with drugs than with hardcore chemically-dependent persons.

Multimodality Treatment

In recent years, some treatment programs have adopted a multimodality approach in their method of treatment. This approach has the advantage of offering patients a choice among alternative treatment regimens. Some patients respond better to a particular method of treatment than to others; and in a multimodality program, patients may be transferred easily from one type of treatment to another. The larger multimodality programs may include methadone maintenance, detoxification services, inpatient and outpatient drug-free treatment, and a therapeutic community.

Narcotic Antagonist Treatment

Narcotic antagonists counteract the effects of narcotic drugs on the body, including euphoria. However, unlike methadone, they do not cause physical dependence. This ability to reverse the effects of narcotic drugs has made them useful in treating overdoses of narcotics.

One problem with narcotic antagonists is that some have unpleasant or possibly harmful side effects. Another problem is that all of them are relatively short acting, and must be administered daily or more frequently. For these reasons, participation in a treatment program using antagonists requires a high degree of motivation.

Scientists are attempting to develop longer-acting antagonists that would be effective for several days or weeks. It is possible that such an antagonist could be very useful in helping dependent persons who have been rehabilitated while on methadone and motivated to be detoxified and remain drug free.

Two kinds of narcotic antagonists are used: partial antagonists and pure antagonists. The partial antagonists are nalorphine (Nalline), pentazocine (Talwin), cyclasocine, and levallorphan. The results of antagonizing the analgesic response to morphine with a narcotic antagonist such as nalorphine are complicated. Studies of nalorphine suggest that it is a competitive antagonist because the degree of antagonism increases to a certain point and then declines with doses beyond that level. Pentazocine is considered a very weak antagonist and has been clinically useful as an analgesic despite its shorter duration and one-half to one-sixth the potency of morphine.

Cyclazocine antagonizes the analgesic effects of morphine but apparently is significantly less effective in antagonizing morphine-induced respiratory depression than either nalorphine or levallorphan. It is also known to antagonize the nausea and vomiting-producing effects of morphine, which may be offset by the fact that it causes constipation in humans. The antagonistic effects of levallorphan are numerous. It has been described as five-to-eight times more effective than nalorphine in antagonizing narcotics-induced respiratory depression. Levallorphan also is an effective antagonist for the morphine's and analgesics' circulatory and hyperglycemic effects, and is completely effective in antagonizing the antidiuretic effects of morphine.

The pure antagonists are naloxone and naltrexone. Naloxone is a relatively short-acting compound, with a narcotic blockade lasting only four to six hours at normal dosages. It is also relatively ineffective when administered orally. The high cost of a single 100-mg oral dose required to block the effects of 40 mg of heroin taken intravenously is prohibitive. Because of its potency, and longer duration of action, and oral effectiveness, naltrexone has definite advantages over naloxone in the treatment of heroin dependence.

100

The antagonists have four basic clinical uses:
- They are useful in the treatment of narcotics addiction.
- They produce analgesia (a state of not feeling pain).
- They can be used to diagnose narcotic dependence.
- They are effective antidotes for narcotic analgesic intoxication (blocking of narcotics).

Females and Narcotic Treatment

The extent of heroin use and abuse among females is unknown. Treatment programs generally serve more males than females, although federally-funded programs report an increase in the proportion of female clients (to 30 percent) in recent years, especially as more appropriate services are provided.

Studies of narcotic-addicted females find numerous health and psychosocial problems that must be addressed during treatment and recovery. Females entering drug treatment usually have more medical problems than do narcotic-addicted males, including anemia, sexually-transmitted diseases, hepatitis, hypertension, urinary tract and other infections, and diabetes. Most come from low socioeconomic backgrounds and are undereducated and unskilled. Many are involved in prostitution and have other criminal histories, such as petty charges for shoplifting and other drug-related activities. Most suffer from low self-esteem and depression. The majority are of childbearing age and already have children, although their parenting skills may be limited, and child neglect and abuse are not uncommon. The lifestyles of heroin-abusing females are typically chaotic.

The many complications of heroin addiction cause additional concerns regarding mothering and risks to offspring. Injection of drugs by the mother or her sexual partner is associated with four in every five pediatric cases of AIDS. The sexually-transmitted diseases found in females who are addicted also threaten their babies. Bacterial endocarditis, a life-threatening infection of the heart's lining associated with intravenous drug use, is an added risk for pregnant females and their offspring.

BIBLIOGRAPHY

Akers, R.L. (1992) *Drugs, Alcohol, and Society: Social Structure, Process, and Policy.* Belmont, CA: Wadsworth.

Doweiko, H.E. (1993). *Concepts of Chemical Dependency.* Pacific Grove, CA: Brooks/Cole.

Fields, R. (1992) *Drugs and Alcohol in Perspective.* Dubuque, IA: Wm. C. Brown.

Johnston, L.D., O'Malley, P.M., & Bachman, J.G. (1991) *Drug Use Among American High School Seniors, College Students, and Young Adults, 1975–1990. Volume I: High School Seniors.* DHHS Publication No. (ADM)91-1813. Rockville, MD: National Institute on Drug Abuse.

Liska, K. (1986) *Drugs and the Human Body: With Implications for Society.* New York: Macmillan.

National Institute on Drug Abuse. (1990) *Drug Abuse Curriculum for Employee Assistance Program Professionals.* DHHS Publication No. (ADM)90-1587. Rockville, MD: National Institute on Drug Abuse.

National Institute on Drug Abuse. (1991) *Drug Abuse and Drug Abuse Research: The Third Triennial Report to Congress from the Secretary, Department of Health and Human Services.* DHHS Publication No. (ADM)91-1704. Rockville, MD: National Institute on Drug Abuse.

National Institute on Drug Abuse. An overview of treatment for opiate and nonopiate dependence. *Drugs in Perspective.* Rockville, MD: National Institute on Drug Abuse.

Office for Substance Abuse Prevention. (1990) *Alcohol, Tobacco, and Other Drugs May Harm the Unborn.* DHHS Publication No. (ADM)90-1711. Rockville, MD: Office for Substance Abuse Prevention.

Schilit, R., & Gomberg, E.L. (1991) *Drugs and Behavior: A Sourcebook for the Helping Professions.* Newbury Park, CA: Sage.

U.S. Department of Justice, Drug Enforcement Administration. Narcotics. *Drug Enforcement*, July 1979.

Marijuana

The hemp plant *Cannabis sativa* grows throughout most parts of the world and grows wild in many tropical and temperate regions. It is a single plant species that has long been cultivated—the tough fiber of the stem for rope; the seed for animal feed mixtures; and the oil for an ingredient of paint. The most common use of *Cannabis sativa* is for its euphoric effects since it contains psychoactive substances, which are most highly concentrated in the leaves and resinous flowering tops. Cannabis products, pharmacology and acute effects, patterns of use, health risks, possible medical uses, and marijuana and sexuality will be discussed in this chapter.

CANNABIS PRODUCTS

Cannabis plant material has been used as a drug for centuries. In 1839, it entered the annals of western medicine with the publication of an article extolling its therapeutic potential, including possible uses as an analgesic and an anticonvulsant agent. This section of the chapter will give a brief history of the use of cannabis, marijuana and THC, hashish, and hashish oil.

History of the Use of Cannabis

The cannabis plant was alleged to be effective in treating a wide range of physical and mental ailments during the remainder of the 19th century. With the introduction of many new synthetic drugs in the 20th century, interest in cannabis as a medication waned. The controls imposed with the passage of the Marijuana Tax Act of 1937 further curtailed its use in treatment, and by 1941 it had been deleted from the U.S. Pharmacopoeia and the National Formulary, the official compendia of drugs.

However advances continued to be made in the chemistry of cannabis. Cannabinoids are unique chemicals found only in cannabis. Among the many cannabinoids synthesized by the plant are cannabinol, cannabidiol, cannabinolidic acids, cannabigerol, cannabichromene, and several isomers of tetrahydrocannabinol, one of which, delta-9-tetrahydrocannabinol (THC), is believed to be responsible for most of its characteristic psychoactive effects.

There has been a resurgence in the scientific study of cannabis, one goal of which has been to develop therapeutic agents which, if used as directed in medical treatment, will not produce harmful side effects. While THC can now be synthesized in the laboratory, it is a liquid insoluble in water, it decomposes on exposure to air and light, and thus it is difficult to prepare in stable dosage units. The possible medical uses of cannabis will be discussed later in this chapter.

Marijuana and THC

The cannabis plant is prepared for consumption in various ways. Three common forms of cannabis are marijuana, hashish, and hashish oil. Having no currently accepted medical use in the United States, all three are considered as controlled or illegal substances.

The term **marijuana** refers to the cannabis plant and to any part or extract of it that produces somatic or psychic changes. The tobacco-like substance is produced by drying the leaves and flowering tops of the plant. Marijuana varies significantly in potency, depending on the source and selectivity of plant materials used. The most selective product is reported to be Sinsemilla (which in Spanish means without seeds), prepared from the unpollinated female cannabis plant. Sinsemilla is one of the most potent varieties of marijuana.

All parts of the cannabis plant contain THC. **THC is the major psychoactive ingredient in marijuana.** The flowering tops and upper leaves of the plant contain the highest concentrations of THC. Other biologically active components as well as additional additives or contaminants may be present. Concentrations of THC in legally-confiscated marijuana have risen from around 1–2 percent in the 1970s to an average of 3–5 percent currently.

In the past few years, there has been evidence of an increasing sophistication on the part of those who grow marijuana in their ability to produce extremely potent material—up to 15 percent THC. Because the potency of street marijuana has increased so markedly, smaller

103

amounts are needed to achieve the effects desired by users. The stronger material may increase the likelihood of undesired adverse psychological effects (e.g., drug-induced anxiety or panic), particularly for inexperienced users. However, the use of higher potency marijuana may also reduce users' exposure to some of the smoke's harmful ingredients because the amount inhaled is also diminished. The drug is usually smoked in cigarettes, pipes, or water pipes for its intoxicating and sensory-distorting "high," although it can be mixed into food and eaten.

Marijuana has a long history and has been smoked or ingested for hundreds of years in many different countries. It has probably been used for as long as alcohol or opium. It has a lower abuse liability than most of the other abusable drugs, and thus most people who use it do so intermittently. However, some people become psychologically (and perhaps physically) dependent and must exert considerable effort or even obtain medical treatment to stop using it. A common term for such people is "potheads." In this regard, marijuana is much like alcohol in that most who use it do so intermittently and in low doses, but a subgroup uses it regularly in high doses and develops significant problems as a result.

Hashish

The major form of cannabis used in the Middle East and North Africa is hashish. **Hashish** consists of the drug-rich resinous secretions of the cannabis plant, which are collected, dried, and then compressed into a variety of forms, such as balls, cakes, or cookie-like sheets. It is frequently smoked, either alone or mixed in with tobacco, as well as baked in cookies or candies (McKim, 1991). Hashish in the United States varies in potency as in appearance, ranging in THC content from trace amounts up to 10 percent. In the Far East, hashish is known as charas.

Hashish Oil

Hashish oil is a variation of hashish, produced by a process of repeated extraction of cannabis plant materials to yield a dark viscous liquid. This extract contains a higher concentration of THC than does hashish, with some samples containing THC concentrations up to 60 percent. In terms of its psychoactive effect, a drop or two of this liquid on a cigarette is equal to a single "joint" of marijuana. In addition to smoking, some users place a drop on hot tinfoil and inhale the smoke (McKim, 1991).

PHARMACOLOGY AND ACUTE EFFECTS

Cannabis products are usually smoked in the form of loosely rolled cigarettes or "joints." They may be used alone or in combination with other substances. They also may be administered orally, but are reported to be about three times more potent when smoked. In this section of the chapter, the general effects, effects on body organs, effects on performance, and tolerance and withdrawal will be discussed.

General Effects

When marijuana is smoked, the effects are felt within minutes, reach their peak in 10 to 30 minutes, and may linger for two or three hours (Fig. 7-1). When eaten, the onset of effects happens more slowly—approximately 30 to 60 minutes after consumption, reaching peak effects in about two to three hours, with effects lasting three to five hours. When cannabis is baked in cakes, brownies, or other foods the high temperatures alter its chemistry producing more potent drug actions (Schilit & Gomberg, 1991). Nausea or vomiting are more likely to occur in the case of oral administration.

Experienced marijuana smokers are often in the practice of holding marijuana smoke in their lungs for several minutes. This allows for more complete absorption of THC, by bringing it in contact with the blood in the alveoli (air sacs).

Effects on Body Organs

Because of THC's high lipid solubility, it is rapidly absorbed (Payne, Hahn, & Pinger, 1991). It tends to be stored in fatty areas of the body, such as the heart, lungs, and liver. Easy crossing of the blood-brain barrier is enhanced because of the high lipid solubility of THC (Leccese, 1991). THC tends to remain for long periods bound to proteins in fatty storage areas of the body. For this reason, THC can be measured in the blood several days or weeks after a chronic user had his/her last "joint" (Schilit & Gomberg, 1991).

The most obvious and verified effect of marijuana on humans is a dose-related, temporary increase in heart rate, as high as 160 beats per minute. In animals, by contrast, heart rate in response to marijuana is often slowed. Blood pressure levels while a user is standing tend to drop but typically remain unchanged or even increase slightly while sitting or reclining. Conjunctival congestion, a reddening of the eyes, is also a common physiological reaction to acute marijuana use. This result is not simply a result of the irritating effects of marijuana smoke. This is indicated by its occurrence even when the drug is orally ingested.

Figure 7-1
Effects of Marijuana

THC is stored in heart, liver, and lungs.

THC remains in the blood for several weeks.

Marijuana:

* Affects memory, thinking, speaking
* Interferes with learning
* Causes eyes to redden
* Fragments speech
* Interferes with reading comprehension
* Impairs communication
* Causes restlessness
* Causes craving for sweets
* Results in rapidly fluctuating emotions
* Alters sense of self-identity

Effects on Performance

While marijuana-intoxicated, a user shows many indications of impaired psychological functioning, including effects on memory, thinking, speaking, various kinds of problem solving, and concept formation. Most of these effects seem to share in common an impairment of short-term memory that leads to fragmented speech, disjointed thinking, and a tendency to lose one's train of thought.

Many specific types of performance are impaired. Examples include digit/symbol substitution, in which the subject is required to replace a series of random digits with symbols representing each digit; the number of orally-presented digits that can be recalled (digit span); serial subtraction, in which the subject subtracts a number repeatedly from an initially large number; and reading comprehension. Time perception is affected also and is reflected in an overestimation of elapsed time intervals. Most users are aware of this tendency to distort time.

As with other drugs, marijuana's effects are dose related. The higher the dose, the more likely that performance disruption will occur. At least with simpler tasks, experienced users become tolerant of the drug's psychological effects and when strongly motivated may be able to attenuate the drug's effects.

Research on the effects of marijuana has been done primarily with young adult males. Systematic research has not been carried out on the effects of marijuana use on much younger users or on how it affects classroom functioning directly. If anything, however, effects on younger users might be expected to be still more disruptive than effects on older users, and the similarity of classroom tasks to those tasks experimentally investigated leaves little doubt that marijuana is likely to interfere with learning. The more complex, unfamiliar, and demanding the task to be performed, the greater the likelihood that being high will cause impairment.

Marijuana use also produces acute effects on perception and social interaction. Perceptually, users typically report a heightened awareness of visual, auditory, and tactual sensations. Despite these reports by users, the enhancement of sensation has not been detected in experimental studies. Although marijuana has a street reputation as a social facilitator, research indicates that even at moderate doses communication is impaired by the intrusion of irrelevant ideas and words and that there is even greater disruption at higher doses.

106

A condensed description of marijuana's acute effects is apt to be inadequate or even misleading because so much depends on the experience and expectations of the individual as well as the activity of the drug. Low doses tend to induce restlessness and an increasing sense of well-being, followed by a dreamy state of relaxation, and frequently hunger, especially a craving for sweets. Stronger doses may lead users to experience shifting sensory imagery, rapidly fluctuating emotions, and a flight of fragmentary thoughts with disturbed associations; an altered sense of self-identity; impaired memory, and a dulling of attention despite an illusion of heightened insight. Higher doses may result in image distortions, a loss of personal identity, fantasies and hallucinations. Very high doses can result in a toxic psychosis.

Tolerance and Withdrawal

As with several other drugs, relatively little tolerance develops to marijuana when doses are small or use is infrequent. Tolerance becomes apparent only after high doses and sustained, prolonged use.

There have been relatively few reports of spontaneous withdrawal symptoms resulting from the sudden interruption of chronic marijuana use. Yet, mild withdrawal symptoms do appear in research subjects who have received large doses of THC for at least several days. Only a small fraction of marijuana users consume this much drug, which probably explains the infrequency of withdrawal symptoms reported.

PATTERNS OF USE

Marijuana is the fourth most commonly used psychoactive substance following alcohol, nicotine, and caffeine. It is the most widely-used illicit drug in the United States. Marijuana has been called a "gateway drug" because its use is associated with the use of other drugs. For example, lifetime cocaine use is rare (less than half of 1 percent) among people who have never used marijuana and the likelihood of having used cocaine increases as marijuana use increases. Current statistics and results of research will be presented in this section of the chapter.

Current Statistics

A third of Americans, almost 66 million people, have tried marijuana one or more times. Four million youths (12–17), 17 million young adults (18–25), and over 45 million adults age 26 and older have used marijuana. Among those who have used marijuana 200 or more times in their life, 77.4 percent have tried cocaine.

In 1988, 5.9 percent (11.6 million) of the population age 12 and older were current marijuana users (that is, had used it in the past month). Current use was higher for males (7.9 percent), for young adults ages 18–25 (15.5 percent), for the unemployed (14.8 percent), and for those living in large (population of 1 million or more) metropolitan areas (6.9 percent). Of the 21.1 million people who had used marijuana in the previous year, almost one-third, or 6.6 million, used marijuana once a week or more.

Among high school seniors, marijuana is by far the most widely used illicit drug with 41 percent reporting some use in their lifetime, 27 percent reporting some use in the past year, and 14 percent reporting some use in the past month. Another important fact is that marijuana is used on a daily or near-daily basis by about 1 in every 45 seniors (2.2 percent). Marijuana consistently has had one of the lowest noncontinuation rates (34 percent) in the senior year of any of the illicit drugs. This occurs because a relatively high proportion of users continue to use it at some level over an extended period. Annual marijuana use is reported by 25 percent of the college-bound seniors vs. 31 percent of the noncollege-bound (Johnston, O'Malley, & Bachman, 1991).

Results of Research

The following are important research findings regarding marijuana use among young people:
- The lower the age of initial use of alcohol and cigarettes, the more likely the individual is to use marijuana;
- Age of first use of marijuana has steadily decreased;
- Daily use (20 or more days per month) is positively correlated with absenteeism and poor school achievement among high school seniors and negatively correlated with involvement in one's faith and plans for college attendance;
- High school seniors who spend little time at home are more likely to be daily users than are those less socially active;
- High school seniors who are daily users of marijuana are much more likely to use other drugs than are less frequent users.

HEALTH RISKS

Widespread use of cannabis, particularly on a habitual basis, is little more than two or three decades old. Initially, use was largely limited to young adults occasionally using marijuana that had a lower potency than that currently being used. The discussion in this section of the chapter will include early health studies, respiratory effects, effects on the immune system, effects on the brain and behavior,

effects on fertility, effects of prenatal exposure, effects during pregnancy and delivery, effects on the newborn, effects on breast-fed babies, and effects on the growing child.

Early Health Studies

Early attempts to determine possible adverse effects of marijuana use compared occasional users collectively with nonusers. Such a comparison was as unlikely to detect marijuana-related health effects as would be a comparison of occasional cigarette smokers with nonsmokers. When intensity of use was taken into account, it was—and still is—usually defined by drug use frequency with little distinction made in the actual quantities consumed. For convenience, marijuana has often been studied in isolation from other drugs. Frequently, its principal psychoactive ingredient, delta-9-tetrahydrocannabinol (THC), is isolated and administered orally to humans or animals. Although there are good arguments for studying marijuana in this way, it is not the way in which cannabis is usually consumed. Marijuana is generally smoked and is quite commonly used concurrently with alcohol, tobacco, and frequently with other illicit drugs as well. This is especially true for the heavy user.

THC is only one of several hundred ingredients in marijuana smoke, and the smoke contains several dozen additional chemical compounds that are unique to marijuana. Much less is known about the action of these other chemicals, although they are thought to modify THC's psychological and toxic effects as well as to have effects of their own (Fig. 7-2).

Respiratory Effects

The smoke from marijuana shares many characteristics with tobacco smoke and presents similar dangers. A comparison of the tars from both drugs has shown that when smoked the same way, marijuana produces more than twice as much tar as a popular brand of cigarette and when inhaled deeply and exhaled slowly—as is usual in smoking this drug—yields nearly four times more tar. Inflammation and other abnormalities in the lungs of marijuana smokers have led to warnings that heavy users are at risk for chronic asthma, bronchitis, or emphysema.

Chemical analysis of marijuana smoke indicates that it contains several chemical compounds similar to those found in tobacco smoke that are known to be carcinogenic. Marijuana smoke residuals, like those of tobacco, cause skin tumors when applied to the shaved skin of experimental animals. The fact that marijuana smokers are also fre-

Figure 7-2
Health Risks of Marijuana Use

This week's Top Ten List of reasons to avoid marijuana use.

Ten health risks of marijuana use:

10. Lung cancer
 9. Chronic asthma
 8. Bronchitis
 7. Emphysema
 6. Acute brain syndrome
 5. Cannabis psychosis
 4. Amotivational syndrome
 3. Temporary sterility
 2. Spontaneous abortion/stillbirth
 1. Carbon monoxide levels to unborn

quently cigarette smokers may well pose an additional risk beyond that of either marijuana or tobacco smoked alone.

The shorter life spans in countries in which the use of marijuana is traditional and lack of research studies of causes of death in these countries may have obscured the possible role of marijuana in lung cancer. Since lung cancer and other chronic lung diseases are usually diseases of later life, many years of exposure to marijuana may be needed before clear evidence of a connection can be demonstrated.

Effects on the Immune System

Currently there is no conclusive proof that marijuana use suppresses the body's immune system, its principal defense against disease. Some animal and human studies provide some evidence of a diminished immune response, but other studies do not. The emergence of the acquired immunodeficiency syndrome (AIDS) epidemic has raised new concerns regarding the immune system. Despite earlier conclusions that marijuana may have little or no effect on

the normal immune system, new concerns are surfacing about the possible effects of drug abuse on an already compromised immune system. It remains to be determined if marijuana plays any role in individual susceptibility to AIDS or in the disease's progression.

Effects on the Brain and Behavior

There is little question that marijuana use interferes with complex mental functioning as well as with skilled performance including driving or piloting a plane. Presently, studies have not confirmed that marijuana use changes the structure of the brain. However, marijuana use does appear to produce persistent changes in brain function. There is clear evidence of disturbed functioning, such as memory defects, despite lack of clear evidence of structural damage to the brain.

A variety of adverse behavioral-psychological effects of marijuana have been described as resulting from acute and chronic cannabis use. Users frequently report reactions that are negative although not severe enough to seek medical or other outside assistance. Transient mild paranoid feelings are common. Such reactions seem to be more frequent in inexperienced users who lose the perspective that what they are experiencing is a drug reaction rather than a basic change in their mental state.

An acute brain syndrome marked by disorientation, confusion, and memory impairment has been reported. These acute reactions may occur when the individual ingests an unexpectedly potent variety of marijuana or uses the drug in larger quantities than usual. These overdose reactions are more likely to occur when the drug is taken orally than when smoked.

In countries such as India, a cannabis psychosis has been described that resembles schizophrenia. It is not clear whether or not this results from the drug use itself or is the product of an underlying schizophrenia that is made worse by the use of the drug. A cannabis psychosis has not been commonly reported in the United States although there have been reports that marijuana use in psychotic patients who were in remission has precipitated a recurrence of their schizophrenia. In a Swedish report, an apparent causal link between heavy hashish use and a schizophrenic-like illness has been found. This illness is characterized by confusion, aggressiveness, and instability of moods in individuals with little evidence of preexisting psychosis. The disorder appeared and disappeared in a period of weeks or months following cessation of cannabis use. The question of whether or not long-term cannabis use produces a loss of conventional motivation and an inability to persist in achieving long-term goals—a so called **amotivational syndrome**—has been raised with respect to traditional use and also with respect to contemporary use.

At one extreme, it appears likely that chronic marijuana intoxication interferes with functioning in this way. The question of whether or not regular, heavy use at levels less than chronic intoxication causes the same interference is more difficult to answer. For some, a lack of strong motivation to pursue long-term goals precedes drug use. However, there are many health professionals who are convinced that these motivational effects are directly related to use and that following cessation of marijuana use normal motivation may return.

There is much concern about the possible effects of frequent marijuana use on the psychological, emotional, and social development of children and adolescents. In this area, firm research evidence is seriously lacking. Much of what is known regarding marijuana's effects on children

is largely based on impressions of health professionals and individual case studies. There is growing consensus among health professionals who see children and adolescents who are frequent users that frequent use seriously interferes with functioning and development.

Further, there are many individual case reports by older users indicating that their marijuana use, frequently coupled with other drug use, has been a seriously disruptive factor in their lives. The question of whether or not it is marijuana use itself that is responsible for this disruption or some combination of drugs and other lifestyle factors is not known. There is good reason to believe that heavy users of marijuana are likely to be multiple-drug users whose lives revolve around drug use. It must be kept in mind that there are some heavy users who continue to function reasonably well despite their marijuana use, as is true of other types of drug use.

Effects on Fertility

Chronic marijuana use can lower sperm counts in males and may affect menstrual cycles and ovulation in females. These effects appear reversible when use stops and, in females, when tolerance is established. Temporary sterility may sometimes result, however, when couples already are marginally fertile. In laboratory animals, marijuana also inhibits the secretion of reproductive hormones, interfering with ovulation in females and sperm production in males. As with humans, hormone levels return to normal as tolerance develops to chronic exposure. Despite earlier speculation and warnings of potential genetic damage, no evidence of chromosome damage to cells incubated with THC has been found in either animals or humans.

Effects of Prenatal Exposure

Although pregnant females are less likely to use marijuana than alcohol or cigarettes, heavy marijuana users are less likely to reduce their marijuana consumption during and after pregnancy than to cut back on drinking and smoking. Marijuana readily crosses the placenta, although transmission is apparently higher in early pregnancy than in the last trimester. The drug level in the bloodstream of a marijuana-smoking pregnant female is generally greater than that of the fetus, ranging from two-and-a-half to seven times higher. Like cigarettes, marijuana increases carbon monoxide levels in the mother's blood; this reduces oxygen availability to the fetus.

Effects During Pregnancy and Delivery

Animal studies suggest that marijuana use may cause spontaneous abortions and stillbirths, though only at much higher doses than those used by most drug abusers. Laboratory studies also suggest that female animals receiving THC produce more male than female babies. One human study had similar findings: the male-to-female ratio of offspring increased if either parent was a heavy marijuana smoker.

Because the research findings regarding marijuana effects on human pregnancy are inconsistent, caution is advised in ascribing adverse outcomes to the drug alone. In larger studies, where other maternal factors that might influence outcomes were controlled analytically, the drug did not consistently increase spontaneous abortions, stillbirths and premature deliveries.

Effects on the Newborn

Increased tremulousness and altered visual-response patterns to a light stimulus have been noted in the newborn infants of mothers who smoked marijuana heavily while pregnant. Although more subtle, long-term consequences cannot be ruled out, these effects usually disappear within 30 days. However, a follow-up study by the same researchers, using a larger sample, found persisting tremors and startles in 30-day-old offspring of mothers who regularly used one or more marijuana joints per week while pregnant. Another study of neonatal sleep found that maternal marijuana use during pregnancy affected sleep and arousal patterns in a newborn. The long-range implications of this finding are not known.

In studying the relationships among fetal marijuana exposure and lowered birth weight, infant length, and shortened gestation only six studies examined sufficient numbers of subjects to control for such potentially complicating factors as maternal smoking, drinking, other drug use, and race/ethnicity. Unfortunately, the collective findings from these studies are conflicting and difficult to interpret. Unlike the research on tobacco smoking, marijuana use during pregnancy is not consistently associated with lowered birth weight, although some individual studies have found some dose-related reductions in gestation, infant length, and birth weight.

Possible reasons for these inconsistent results are (1) likely variations, (2) the problems in teasing out many other maternal factors (health, socioeconomic background, lifestyle), and (3) other methodological issues such as underreporting of marijuana use by pregnant females, compared to alcohol and cigarette use.

Most human evidence suggests that fetal marijuana exposure does not, by itself, produce physical abnormalities. However, marijuana consumption by pregnant females, when combined with other drug use, drinking, malnourishment, and inadequate prenatal care, may increase the chances of negative fetal consequences. A study found that maternal marijuana use was the strongest predictor of newborns with features compatible with FAS (fetal alcohol syndrome). This finding supports a possible synergistic effect of marijuana when interacting with alcohol and other substances.

Effects on Breast-Fed Infants

Marijuana is rapidly transmitted into breast milk and remains there for a prolonged period. Although its effects on nursing infants are unknown, breast-feeding is not recommended for mothers who smoke marijuana and are unwilling or unable to give it up.

Effects on the Growing Child

Evidence of postnatal problems in children prenatally exposed to marijuana is both limited and inconsistent. For example, in one study, prenatally marijuana-exposed youngsters averaging four years of age were slower than matched controls in their visual responsiveness, indicating delayed maturation in this component of the central nervous system. However, these same researchers in an ongoing study of 700 babies found prenatal marijuana exposure not to be associated with diminished mental, motor, or language outcomes or visual responsiveness in one- and two-year-olds. The researchers were not certain if the apparent normal ranges of the toddlers were due to the transitory nature of effects from prenatal marijuana exposure or if any adverse effects are too subtle to be measured in early childhood, but may be manifested by school age.

POSSIBLE MEDICAL USES

For many years, cannabis has been reported to have a variety of therapeutic uses, but until recently, the evidence was little more than anecdotal. With the advent of synthetic analogs, interest in possible clinical uses of cannabis grew. Reports have indicated that one or more of the cannabinoids have analgesic, anticonvulsant, antiglaucoma, antinauseant, and antiemetic (prevent vomiting) effects. Only one of these therapeutic uses to date has been useful in practice. Nabilone, a synthetic cannabinoid, was marketed in Canada in 1981 as an antiemetic adjunct to cancer chemotherapy. The new drug gained little medical acceptance. In 1987, delta-9-THC under the trade name Dronabinol was introduced in the United States as an antiemetic to control the nausea and vomiting accompanying cancer chemotherapy when not relieved by the usual antinauseant drugs. Dronabinol has been well received by physicians in the United States, and there is little evidence that it is being abused.

In 1986, it was reported that cannabidiol, a cannabinoid that does not produce psychoactive effects when taken, reduced involuntary muscle contractions in patients with muscle contraction disorders. There was, however, an increase in parkinsonism-like signs and symptoms.

MARIJUANA AND SEXUALITY

Marijuana has often been touted by some users as having aphrodisiac effects. These subjective effects are probably related to the fact that marijuana reduces behavioral inhibitions and alters time perception (Witters, Venturelli, & Hanson, 1992). Because time seems to pass slower, the pleasurable sensations of sexual activity may be perceived to last longer than they actually do. In contrast, other users report that marijuana use has no effect on sexual desire or performance. Still, other users contend that marijuana use is responsible for their loss of interest in sexual behavior (Carroll, 1993).

In contrast to marijuana's reported effects on sexuality (e.g., that it is an aphrodisiac) are its known physiological effects (Doweiko, 1993). For example, about 80 percent of research subjects who used marijuana prior to sexual intercourse reported that their use of the drug increased their awareness of being touched by their partners. Yet, other research has demonstrated that tactile perception is not impacted by marijuana use. In fact, some research suggests that tactile perception may even be lessened by marijuana use (Doweiko, 1993; Masters, Johnson, & Kolodny, 1986).

A substantial proportion of males who use marijuana have difficulty achieving erections. Masters, Johnson, and Kolodny (1986) found that 20 percent of daily marijuana-using males experience erectile problems. Long-term, high-dosage use leads to a suppression of the testes and subsequent decreased testosterone (the principal male hormone) production. This is believed to be an important factor in the loss of sexual desire in regular users (Doweiko, 1993) and may account for marijuana-associated impotence (Witters, Venturelli, & Hanson, 1992). Male use is also associated with reduced sperm production, abnormal sperm structure, and impaired sperm mobility. Most of these effects are believed to be reversible when the drug is discontinued (Fields, 1992).

Females who use marijuana may experience vaginal dryness, which may account for painful intercourse. There is also some evidence that marijuana use may cause abnormal menstruation, including failure to ovulate (Carroll, 1993).

BIBLIOGRAPHY

Carroll, C.R. (1993) *Drugs in Modern Society* (second edition). Dubuque, IA: Wm. C. Brown.

Doweiko, H.E. (1993) *Concepts of Chemical Dependency*. Pacific Grove, CA: Brooks/Cole.

Fields, R. (1992) *Drugs and Alcohol in Perspective*. Dubuque, IA: Wm. C. Brown.

Johnston, L.D., O'Malley, P.M., & Bachman, J.G. (1991) *Drug Use Among American High School Seniors, College Students, and Young Adults, 1975–1990. Volume I, High School Seniors*. DHHS Publication No. (ADM)91-1813. Rockville, MD: National Institute on Drug Abuse.

Leccese, A.P. (1991) *Drugs and Society: Behavioral Medicines and Abusable Drugs*. Englewood Cliffs, NJ: Prentice-Hall.

Masters, W.H., Johnson, V.E., & Kolodny, R.C. (1986) *Sex and Human Loving*. Boston: Little, Brown, & Co.

McKim, W.A. (1991) *Drugs and Behavior: An Introduction to Behavioral Pharmacology*. Englewood Cliffs, NJ: Prentice-Hall.

National Institute on Drug Abuse. (1984) *Marijuana Overview*. Rockville, MD: National Institute on Drug Abuse.

National Institute on Drug Abuse. (1990) *Drug Abuse Curriculum for Employee Assistance Program Professionals*. DHHS Publication No. (ADM)90-1587. Rockville MD: National Institute on Drug Abuse.

National Institute on Drug Abuse. (1991) *Drug Abuse and Drug Abuse Research: The Third Triennial Report to Congress from the Secretary, Department of Health and Human Services*. DHHS Publication No. (ADM)91-1704. Rockville, MD: National Institute on Drug Abuse.

Office for Substance Abuse Prevention. (1990) *Alcohol, Tobacco, and Other Drugs May Harm the Unborn*. DHHS Publication No. (ADM)90-1711. Rockville, MD: Office for Substance Abuse Prevention.

Payne, W.A., Hahn, D.B., & Pinger, R.R. (1991) *Drugs: Issues for Today*. St. Louis, MO: Mosby Year Book.

Schilit, R., & Gomberg, E.L. (1991) *Drugs and Behavior: A Sourcebook for the Helping Professions*. Newbury Park, CA: Sage.

U.S. Department of Justice, Drug Enforcement Administration. Cannibis. *Drug Enforcement*, July 1979.

Witters, W.L., Venturelli, P.J., & Hanson, G. (1992) *Drugs and Society* (third edition). Boston: Jones & Bartlett.

HALLUCINOGENS

Drugs that create illusions and distort a user's senses are psychedelic or hallucinogenic drugs. **Hallucinogenic drugs** are substances that have the major effect of producing marked distortions in perception (Sikkink & Fleming, 1992). With the exception of phencyclidine (PCP), which was used as an anesthetic until it was discontinued because of hallucinogenic side effects, hallucinogenic drugs have no approved use in general medicine. Peyote and mescaline, which are naturally occurring substances found in certain types of mushrooms, traditionally have been used by American Indians during certain ceremonies. Hallucinogen use and abuse by members of the general population started among college students in the 1960s. These drugs seemed to attract many people who simply were curious about the effects of these powerful and unusual drugs, or who were trying to "expand their consciousness." In fact, hallucinogens were once said to be useful adjuncts to psychotherapy, but studies failed to confirm these claims. In this chapter, hallucinogen use among youth, pharmacology and the effects of hallucinogens, types of hallucinogens, and treatment will be the topics of discussion.

HALLUCINOGEN USE AMONG YOUTH

LSD (d-lysergic acid diethylamide), one of the major drugs comprising the hallucinogen class, showed a modest decline from 1975 to 1977 among high school seniors, followed by considerable stability through 1981. Between 1981 and 1985, however, there was a second period of decline, with annual prevalence falling from 6.5 percent in 1981 to 4.4 percent in 1985. Use has remained fairly level since 1985, with annual prevalence in 1990 at 5.4 percent (Johnston, O'Malley & Bachman, 1991). One bit of encouraging news is that most teenagers who use LSD use smaller doses of the drug than did teenagers who used LSD in the 1960s (Seligmann, 1992).

Prevalence statistics for PCP have shown a very substantial decline. Annual prevalence dropped from 7.0 percent of high school seniors in the class of 1979 to 2.2 percent in the class of 1982. After leveling off for a few years, it has since dropped further to reach 1.2 percent in 1990 (Johnston et al., 1991).

PHARMACOLOGY AND THE EFFECTS OF HALLUCINOGENS

Hallucinogens are usually taken sporadically. Their pattern of use is markedly different from the daily or very frequent patterns that develop with other drugs of abuse such as cocaine, amphetamines, or narcotics, although some individuals occasionally may take hallucinogens daily or almost daily. Because they have no legitimate use in medicine, any use is considered misuse or abuse. The effects on the senses, tolerance, the "bad trip," and flashbacks will be discussed.

Effects on the Senses

All hallucinogens have the major effect of producing marked distortions in perception (Fig. 8-1). These range from a heightened sensitivity to all stimuli (a condition in which sounds and lights appear brighter than they really are), to auditory and visual hallucinations. Hallucinogens also cause euphoria (one of the reasons for repeated use), impair short-term memory, increase pulse, seem to make time to pass very slowly, and produce significant disturbances in judgment. **Synesthesia** is a phenomenon that refers to a crossing of the perceptual senses. A user may speak of "seeing" sounds and "hearing " colors. Hallucinogens are believed to work by mimicking such neurotransmitters as serotonin, acetylcholine, or norepinephrine.

Tolerance

Effects of hallucinogens last from hours to days, depending on the dose and the individual's sensitivity. Tolerance develops to the acute effects of these drugs, but they do not produce withdrawal reactions. Cross-tolerance exists between most of the hallucinogens. Tolerance wears off after only a few days when hallucinogen use is discontinued. Most hallucinogens are ingested by mouth rather than smoked, snorted, or injected. PCP is the exception and can be smoked, snorted, injected, or taken by mouth.

The "Bad Trip"

Hallucinogens have many severe adverse effects, the major one being the "bad trip." Three kinds of bad trips include

Figure 8-1
Hallucinogens Produce Marked Distortions in Perception

Lights appear BRIGHTER

Sounds appear LOUDER

Time passes very SLOWLY

Effects of hallucinogens:

* Impaired short-term memory
* Significant disturbances in judgment
* Euphoria

after it was taken. They usually take the form of visual hallucinations or other disturbances of visual perception such as the intensification of a perceived color, the apparent motion of a fixed object, seeing trails or flashes of colors, seeing positive and negative afterimages, or seeing halos (Nadis, 1990). Flashbacks are generally brief, lasting only a few seconds, but they have been reported to reappear even years after the drug was taken. Very little is known about the physiological mechanisms underlying flashbacks or about the appropriate treatment of them (Nadis, 1990; Sikkink & Fleming, 1992).

TYPES OF HALLUCINOGENS

There are many substances that can cause alteration in users' perceptions of reality and are classified as hallucinogens:

* LSD (d-lysergic acid diethylamide)
* PCP (phencyclidine)
* peyote and mescaline
* psilocybin
* DMT (dimethyltryptamine)
* STP or DOM (2,5-dimethoxy-4-methamphetamine)
* MDA (3,4-methylenedioxy-amphetamine)
* MDMA
* Morning glory seeds
* Nutmeg
* Anticholinergic compounds—scopolamine, hyoscyamine, atropine

acute anxiety reactions or panic attacks; severe depressive episodes; and psychotic breaks that resemble schizophrenia and are characterized by anxiety, delusions, and hallucinations. All these reactions are short-lived, usually ending within 24 hours, though they occasionally last for days, especially in the case of PCP. Treatment usually involves mild sedation, such as an antianxiety agent (tranquilizer) by mouth, placing the person in a quiet place, and observing and talking to the person in a calm and reassuring manner. Hallucinogens rarely produce permanent psychosis.

Occasionally, accidents occur during a bad trip, and some deaths have resulted. For example, someone takes LSD and jumps from a window believing he or she can fly; or someone develops a panic attack and runs into the path of a car.

Flashbacks

A troublesome but less serious side effect is the production of flashbacks. **Flashbacks** are manifestations of one or more of the acute effects of the drug that recur long

In this section of the chapter, the discussion will include LSD, peyote and mescaline, psilocybin and psilocin, synthetic amphetamine- and mescaline-like hallucinogens, PCP, and other hallucinogens.

LSD

LSD is an abbreviation of the German expression for the chemical name for this hallucinogenic drug, d-lysergic acid diethylamide. It is produced from lysergic acid, a substance derived from the ergot fungus that grows on rye or from lysergic acid amide, a chemical found in morning glory seeds. LSD was first synthesized in 1938. Its hallucinogenic effects were discovered in 1943 when a Swiss chemist by the name of Albert Hofmann accidentally took some LSD. As he began to experience the effects now known as a "trip," he was aware of vertigo and an intensification of light; closing his eyes, he saw a stream of fantastic images of extraordinary vividness accompanied by a kaleidoscopic play of colors. This condition lasted for about two hours.

LSD is a clear, tasteless, colorless liquid that usually is taken orally and rapidly absorbed into the bloodstream

(Leccese, 1991). Within 30 to 60 minutes the effects of LSD are noticeable and those effects that develop gradually last for 8 to 10 hours, peaking in 2 to 4 hours. LSD works on the sympathetic nervous system, presumably because of its structural similarity to the neurotransmitter serotonin, causing increased blood pressure, heart rate, body temperature, and sweating. The pupils of the eye dilate and muscle tremor, weakness, nausea, and dizziness also may occur (Schilit & Gomberg, 1991).

LSD is an extremely potent drug: one ounce contains about 300,000 doses (Witters, Venturelli, & Hanson, 1992). A dosage as small as 50 micrograms (0.05 milligrams) can produce a classic LSD "trip" (Doweiko, 1993). However, despite its potency for producing psychoactive effects, LSD is not a very toxic drug. Overdosing is rare; the amount of LSD that needs to be taken to be lethal is more than 200 times the hallucinogenic dosage (Witters et al., 1992). The potency of a typical dose of LSD currently ranges from 20 to 80 micrograms (a microgram is one-millionth of a gram) as opposed to 150–300 micrograms in the 1960s. A shirt button is equivalent to the size of 1 gram of LSD. Thus, 1 microgram of LSD would represent one-millionth the size of a button (Hales, 1992).

When users take several hits, they greatly increase their risk of having a bad trip. A **hit** is a dose of LSD. As with many drug purchases, buyers have no way of knowing how strong the LSD is that they are purchasing. It easily could be two or three times as strong as the last batch they bought.

LSD users usually buy blotter acid. **Blotter acid** is blotter-like paper that has been impregnated with LSD and cut into small squares. The blotter acid is swallowed or chewed briefly. Blotter acid is the medium of choice for most users. It comes decorated in a wide array of designs, some of which are copied from the characters created by Disney and other cartoon studios. Drug enforcement authorities are concerned about the special appeal that blotter acid with pictures of Donald Duck and teddy bears will have for children. Unlike some other drugs, blotter acid is within financial reach of many children at only 3 or 4 dollars a hit. LSD also comes in tablet form. **Microdots** are tablets of LSD that are less than an eighth of an inch in width. **Windowpanes** are tiny, thin gelatin chips of LSD. It would take 10 or more windowpanes to equal the size of an aspirin tablet.

There is a persistent myth that LSD sometimes is bought as a piece of impregnated paper (a "tattoo") that is stuck on the skin allowing the LSD to soak through the skin and produce a hallucinogenic high. Experts note that the paper would have to be treated with a very large and expensive amount of LSD to generate a hallucinogenic effect by this method. The Drug Enforcement Agency finds no evidence that stick-on LSD "tattoos" are being marketed.

There also is no scientific evidence that LSD use causes brain damage or cognitive deficits in users. Neither is there research support for the contention that LSD use damages chromosomes when used by humans and thus causes birth defects. Serious concern was raised about chromosome damage during the 1960s when it was observed that LSD added to a test tube containing white blood cells damaged the chromosomes of these cells (Witters et al., 1992). These studies used doses of LSD that were as much as 100 times the usual dosage used by humans and did not attempt to link these chromosomal damages to birth defects (Leccese, 1991).

Later studies failed to replicate the chromosome damage that was reported in these earlier studies and failed to find chromosomal damage in studies involving laboratory animals. Despite a lack of evidence for LSD as a cause of birth defects, there is ample concern about the use of LSD during pregnancy. LSD easily crosses the placental barrier during pregnancy and could be a potential teratogen (cause of physical defects in a fetus). Research studies have found no evidence of any carcinogenic (cancer-causing) effects of LSD.

Peyote and Mescaline

The primary active ingredient of the peyote cactus is the hallucinogen mescaline, which is native to the deserts of Mexico and the southwestern United States (McKim, 1991). It is derived from the fleshy parts of buttons of this plant and has been used by American Indians in northern Mexico from the earliest recorded time as part of certain traditional rites. A special act of congress legalized peyote for use in certain ceremonies in American Indian churches.

Peyote, or mescal buttons, and mescaline should not be confused with mescal, the colorless Mexican liquor distilled from the leaves of maguey plants. Peyote is usually ground into a powder and taken orally. Mescaline also can be produced synthetically. Mescaline is much less potent than LSD, perhaps 1000 to 3000 times less potent (Schilit & Gomberg, 1991).

A dose of 350–500 mg of mescaline produces illusions and hallucinations lasting from five to twelve hours. Following an oral dose of mescaline, a user typically feels nauseous and shaky and may even vomit. The psychoactive effects are very similar to LSD. Mescaline is believed to produce its hallucinogenic effects by decreasing the levels of norepinephrine (adrenaline) in the brain and altering the function of serotonin (Schilit & Gomberg, 1991). Synthesizing or obtaining mescaline costs more than making LSD; as a result, most of the "mescaline" sold on the streets is actually diluted LSD (Insel & Roth, 1991).

Psilocybin and Psilocin

Like the peyote cactus, *Psilocybe mexicana* mushrooms have been used for centuries in traditional American Indian rites (Fig. 8-2). When they are eaten, these "sacred" or "magic" mushrooms affect mood and perception in a manner similar to mescaline and LSD. Their active ingredients, psilocybin and psilocin, are chemically related to LSD, bearing a structural similarity to serotonin. Thus the hallucinogenic effects of these chemicals are similar to LSD. Psilocybin is more potent and less toxic than mescaline. Users of psilocybin and psilocin also develop cross-tolerance to the effects of LSD and mescaline. Psilocybin and psilocin can be made synthetically, but much of what is sold under these names on the illicit market consists of other chemical compounds. These two drugs are rarely found on the illicit drug market.

Psilocybe mushrooms can be eaten raw, brewed as a tea, or cooked in various recipes. The mushrooms also can be dried and made into a powder to be snorted or taken in a capsule (Gold, 1991). Poisonous mushrooms occasionally are mistakenly eaten by people seeking hallucinogenic experiences. The consequences can be very serious because some mushrooms are highly toxic.

Dimethyltryptamine (DMT)

Dimethyltryptamine (DMT) is not widely used in the United States. It is found naturally in many plants that are native to South America and the West Indies. DMT also can be synthesized in a laboratory. It is ineffective when taken orally, except in the rare case when it is taken at the same time with a monoamine oxidase inhibitor, which is a class of antidepressant drugs (Ray & Ksir, 1993). DMT is mostly smoked, snuffed, or injected. While the effects of DMT are similar to those of LSD, its effects last no more than half an hour (Gold, 1991). Because of the short duration of action, DMT has earned the reputation as the "businessman's trip."

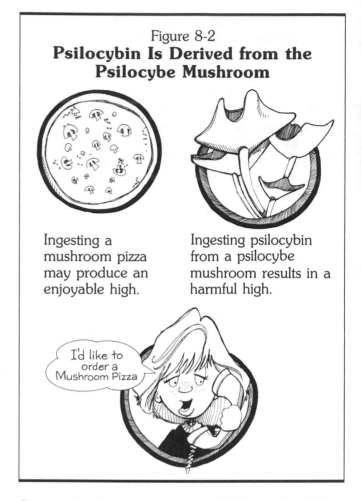

Figure 8-2
Psilocybin Is Derived from the Psilocybe Mushroom

Ingesting a mushroom pizza may produce an enjoyable high.

Ingesting psilocybin from a psilocybe mushroom results in a harmful high.

I'd like to order a Mushroom Pizza

Synthetic Amphetamine- and Mescaline-Like Hallucinogens

An interesting family of substances has evolved that have hallucinogenic properties. McKim (1991) elaborates on the nature and evolution of these drugs:

> The structure of the mescaline molecule has been altered to form a family of drugs that is actually closer to amphetamine. These drugs may be thought of as a cross between amphetamine and mescaline, and many such drugs have been discovered. Much of this research was done in the hope of finding a drug with a medically useful property. Unfortunately, the only use for these new substances has been in the drug subculture, where they are used as hallucinogens. (p. 307)

McKim goes on to describe how the evolution of these drugs was the beginning of drugs known as "designer drugs" and the potential for danger these drugs carry:

> During the heyday of hallucinogens in the 1960s, many synthetics were invented and manufactured in clandestine labs in an attempt to circumvent the law, which

only identified specific chemicals as illegal. They have become known as "designer drugs" and appeared on the street with a bewildering variety of names. Because many were not screened for adverse effects as commercially developed drugs must be, some had extremely toxic effects. One drug specifically destroyed neurons in the basal ganglia and created severe Parkinson's disease. Some of these substances were so toxic that they caused a number of deaths. These drugs are much less common now, but some, like MDMA, are still around and still a source of concern. (pp. 307–308)

Dimethoxymethylamphetamine (DOM) was first synthesized in 1963 and appeared on the streets of Haight-Ashbury in San Francisco in 1967. DOM also was known as STP, after a popular motor additive, but later adopted the acronym of "Serenity, Tranquility, and Peace." It is believed that DOM produces its hallucinogenic effects by depressing the activity of sertonin-containing nerve cells and mimicking the effects of dopamine (Schilit & Gomberg, 1991). Other than PCP, DOM is probably the hallucinogenic substance most likely to produce short- and long-term reactions.

MDA (3,4-methylenedioxyamphetamine) also appeared on the streets in 1967, although it was first synthesized in 1910. This drug is known as the "love drug," presumably because users feel a heightened sense of well-being and tactile pleasure during sexual activity (Witters et al., 1992). However, male and female users of MDA and the related compound MDMA appear to have a difficult time achieving orgasm. These drugs also seem to interfere with erection in males.

Perhaps the most well-known of this class of hallucinogenic substances is MDMA (1–3,4-methylenedioxymethamphetamine). MDMA is shorter-acting and its effects are milder than MDA, but it is perceived to have greater euphoric effects and less side effects than MDA. Schilit and Gomberg (1991) describe the typical MDMA experience:

> Effects generally appear within 20 to 60 minutes when the user experiences a "rush" usually described as mild but euphoric. The "rush" may last from a few minutes to half an hour or not occur at all, depending on the user's mental set, the environment, the dose ingested, and the MDMA's quality. After the rush, the high levels off to a plateau usually lasting from 2 to 3 hours and followed by a gradual "coming down" sensation, ending with a feeling of fatigue. Insomnia, however, may persist long after the fatigue stage, depending on the dosage and the user. (p.99)

MDMA also is known for its ability to lower inhibitions. Because of this property, it has been used to some extent and advocated by some to have a useful adjunct to psychotherapy. Some psychotherapists reported it to be useful because they claimed MDMA enhanced communication with patients. In 1985, MDMA was classified as an illegal substance and its use was banned even for psychotherapeutic purposes (McKim, 1991). Other less familiar drugs included in this class of amphetamine- and mescaline-like hallucinogens are MMDA, MDM, DMA, TMA, PMA, DOET, DOAM, and DOB.

PCP

Phencyclidine, known as PCP, is a synthetic compound that was originally marketed and sold as the anesthetic drug Sernylan. Sernylan had an important advantage as an anesthetic over the barbiturate and opiate anesthetics in that it did not dangerously depress the heart rate, blood pressure, or respiration rate of fully anesthetized patients (Leccese, 1991). However, many Sernylan-anesthetized patients recovering from anesthesia woke to experience states of confusion, agitation, disorientation, delirium, and bizarre behavior lasting several hours. As a result, PCP is no longer allowed to be used as anesthetic for humans. For a period of time it was allowed for animal use, but this use is now prohibited by law. Because Sernylan caused a trancelike state in patients who appeared to be separated from sensory experience, it was classified as a "dissociative anesthetic" (McKim, 1991). One interesting feature of Sernylan was that fully anesthetized patients kept their eyes wide open. PCP is most often classified as a hallucinogen because it is taken for its hallucinogenic and euphoric effects (Akers, 1992). However, PCP is much different from other hallucinogenic drugs because it also has stimulant, depressant, and analgesic properties. A high proportion of users experience negative effects such as restlessness, disorientation, anxiety, perceptual disturbances, and a sense of isolation.

The effects of this unique and complex drug vary greatly according to the dose, manner in which it is taken, and the expectations of the user. In some users, it evokes feelings of power, strength, and invulnerability, followed by depression. PCP may cause agitation and confusion, feelings of grandiosity, impaired coordination, and incoherent speech. Small doses produce a feeling of intoxication, with staggering gait, slurred speech, numbness of extremities, and lowered sensitivity to pain. These symptoms resemble sedative intoxication. Users also may exhibit muscular rigidity, a blank stare, changes in body image, apathy, and disorganized thought processes. Increasing doses can cause

117

a person to become fully anesthetized. Heart rate and blood pressure are elevated, and there may be sweating, nystagmus (side-to-side eye movements), hypersalivation (drooling), fever, and muscular rigidity. At even higher doses, convulsions and coma may occur, as well as heart and lung failure. Delusions and LSD-like hallucinations, especially visual, can occur at any dose.

PCP has the reputation of causing people to be violent. Homicidal and suicidal behaviors have been reported as a result of the aggressive and psychotic-like effects of PCP. Sometimes the effects of PCP mimic symptoms of schizophrenia and result in admission for psychiatric treatment. Chronic use can be quite dangerous in adults and is associated with increased risk for memory and speech problems, hallucinations, paranoia, psychotic episodes, seizures, and death by suicide or other violent means. Severe depression and anxiety also can occur and persist.

For the most part, PCP users are most apt to use the drug in a sporadic fashion, similar to LSD users. However, continuous use is becoming more popular. Daily use of PCP appears to cause tolerance to develop, and there is some evidence of dependence and some withdrawal symptoms (McKim, 1991). Abrupt withdrawal after chronic use results in fearfulness, tremors, and facial twitches.

Acute drug effects of PCP usually last four to six hours, but an unusual feature of this drug is its absorption by fatty tissue and slow release into the bloodstream. This can create a waxing and waning sequence of drug effects as the drug is released, metabolized, and released again. This fat solubility also tends to prolong the drug effects and the drug concentrates in fatty areas of the body, including the brain and lungs. The action of PCP on the brain is very complex. PCP influences nearly every known neurotransmitter and also has been demonstrated to bind directly to specific binding sites in the brain or "PCP receptors" (Leccese, 1991). However, the mechanisms of how PCP creates its various and unpredictable effects remain largely unknown by scientists.

PCP is made rather easily in illegal laboratories, sells at relatively low cost, and comes in liquid, powder, or pill form. It is a tasteless, odorless, and colorless compound. PCP effectively produces a psychoactive effect by any means of administration—oral, injection, smoking, or snorting. It is most often taken orally or mixed with marijuana, parsley, mint, or tobacco and smoked in cigarettes as "superweed." PCP contains many contaminants.

118

Prenatal exposure to PCP. Like most other drugs, PCP crosses the placenta in both animals and humans. In mice, it enters the fetal brain quickly—as early as 15 minutes after the mother is injected—but is not detectable there after 24 hours. In one study, the concentration in fetal body tissue was 10 times higher than in the mother's blood. No byproducts of PCP were found, which suggests that the fetal liver does not break it down.

Very little research has been conducted on the effects of PCP on prenatally-exposed newborns and infants. The first descriptive reports were published in 1980. There have been some animal studies and comparisons between PCP-exposed infants and infants exposed to other drugs. One difficulty encountered by investigators of PCP effects on pregnancy and offspring is the pattern of multiple substance use by virtually all of the mothers. Various combinations of alcohol, cocaine, and marijuana, along with PCP, are reported.

The first case reports of newborn behavior attributed to the mother's heavy and regular consumption of PCP during pregnancy described extreme jitteriness, poor visual coordination, coarse flapping movements in response to very slight touch or sound stimuli, and abnormal muscular tension. Only one of the three first babies studied had physical abnormalities.

A larger study of nine infants whose mothers primarily used PCP during pregnancy found these newborns to be more emotionally unstable and less consolable than infants exposed to other drugs. Although the PCP-exposed babies had rapid state changes (alternating between restlessness and calm), they did not exhibit withdrawal symptoms.

Animal studies suggest that PCP may cause birth defects. Extremely high doses of PCP cause malformations and abnormal behavior in laboratory animals, but these dose levels are far higher than human consumption of the drug. In human studies conducted to date, congenital birth defects have not been found.

Other Hallucinogens

It may be surprising that a chemical compound found in morning glory seeds produces hallucinogenic effects similar to LSD when ingested in high enough amounts. Morning glory seeds contain the chemical ingredient lysergic acid amide, which has a molecular structure quite similar to its cousin lysergic acid diethylamide (LSD). Early use of morning glory seeds for their psychoactive properties has been documented by the Aztecs since at least the early seventeenth century. The use of these seeds by young people carries a very serious health risk because morning glory seeds that are sold by garden seed companies are treated with toxic fungicides and mercury-containing preservatives (McKim, 1991).

Myristicin is a hallucinogenic compound found in the fruit and seeds of the nutmeg tree. Both nutmeg and mace, which come from the tree, contain myristicin. Nutmeg is produced from the seeds of the tree and mace is made from its fruit. Myristicin is not a potent hallucinogen, but can produce visual and auditory hallucinations as well as other psychoactive effects. Those who use myristicin for its hallucinogenic effects, are likely to experience toxic effects that include dizziness, headache, and nausea. Myristicin most closely resembles MMDA (McKim, 1991).

Other infrequently-used hallucinogenic substances that come from natural sources are:

- bufotenine, which is found in the beans of a South American tree, in the flesh of a fish called the dream fish, and in the skin of a species of toad,
- harmine and harmaline, which are found in the leaf of a vine that grows in tropical jungles of South America,
- ibogamine, which comes from the root of a shrub native to Central and West Africa,
- ibotinic acid, which is found in the *Amanita muscaria* mushroom (which grows on all continents except South America and Australia).
- scopolamine, hyoscyamine, and atropine, which are found in such plants and herbs as deadly nightshade, mandrake, henbane, and jimsonweed.

TREATMENT

Dependence on hallucinogenic substances is rare. Although physical dependency does not develop, some people may develop a degree of psychological dependency or develop heavy patterns of use. Because heavy and chronic use of hallucinogens is rare, hallucinogen-specific treatment approaches are not available. Treatment for hallucinogenic users include approaches similar to those for people dependent on other psychoactive substances, such as stimulants or opiates.

Special care is needed to treat people experiencing hallucinogenic drug panic reactions or "bad trips." A person experiencing a "bad trip" may be hallucinating and fearful of losing his or her mind. Management of such an episode should include supportive reassurance that everything will be fine and that the hallucinogen user will recover. Whenever possible, this reassurance should be given by a health professional along with friends or family members. It is important to establish and maintain constant verbal contact with the user within nonthreatening environmental conditions. Medications are usually not needed; but when it is not possible to control someone experiencing a "bad trip," a tranquilizer may need to be administered by a physician. Flashbacks also may require supportive care.

Although overdoses are quite rare, a suspected overdoser of hallucinogens should be monitored closely in an intensive care unit (Sikkink & Fleming, 1992). This should include careful observation and monitoring of vital signs and establishing an airway. In the event of convulsions, which often occur during severe PCP intoxication, treatment with anticonvulsant drugs and tranquilizers may be needed. Blood pressure may need to be supported by certain medications if there are cardiovascular complications.

BIBLIOGRAPHY

Akers, R.L. (1992) *Drugs, Alcohol, and Society: Social Structure, Process, and Policy.* Belmont, CA: Wadsworth.

Doweiko, H.E. (1993) *Concepts of Chemical Dependency.* Belmont, CA: Brooks/Cole.

Gold, M.S. (1991) *The Good News About Drugs and Alcohol: Curing, Treating, and Preventing Substance Abuse in the New Age of Biopsychiatry.* New York: Villard Books.

Hales, D.R. (1992) *An Invitation to Health: Taking Charge of Your Life.* Redwood City, CA: Benjamin/Cummings.

Insel, P.M., & Roth, W.T. (1991) *Core Concepts in Health.* Mountain View, CA: Mayfield.

Johnston, L.D., O'Malley, P.M., & Bachman, J.G. (1991) *Drug Use Among American High School Seniors, College Students, and Young Adults 1975–1990. Volume I, High School Seniors.* DHHS Publication No. (ADM)91-1813. Rockville, MD: National Institute on Drug Abuse.

Leccese, A.P. (1991) *Drugs and Society: Behavioral Medicines and Abusable Drugs.* Englewood Cliffs, NJ: Prentice-Hall.

McKim, W.A. (1991) *Drugs and Behavior: An Introduction to Behavioral Pharmacology.* Englewood Cliffs, NJ: Prentice-Hall.

Nadis, S. (1990) After lights. *Omni,* February, 24–25.

Office for Substance Abuse Prevention. (1990) *Alcohol, Tobacco, and Other Drugs May Harm the Unborn.* DHHS Publication No. (ADM)90-1711. Rockville, MD: Office for Substance Abuse Prevention.

Ray, O., & Ksir, C. (1993) *Drugs, Society, & Human Behavior.* St. Louis, MO: Times Mirror/Mosby.

Schilit, R., & Gomberg, E.L. (1991) *Drugs and Behavior: A Sourcebook for the Helping Professions.* Newbury Park, CA: Sage.

Seligmann, J. (February 3, 1992) The new age of Aquarius. *Time,* pp. 66–67.

Sikkink, J., & Fleming, M. (1992) Adverse health effects and medical complications of alcohol, nicotine, and drug use. In M.F. Fleming & K.L. Barry (Eds.), *Addictive Disorders: A Practical Guide to Treatment.* (pp. 145–168). St. Louis, MO: Mosby.

Ulrich, R.F., & Patten, B.M. (1992) The rise, decline, and fall of LSD. *Perspectives in Biology and Medicine,* 34: 561–578.

U.S. Department of Justice, Drug Enforcement Administration. Hallucinogens. *Drug Enforcement,* July 1979.

U.S. Department of Justice, Drug Enforcement Administration. *It Never Went Away: LSD, a Sixties Drug, Attracts Young Users in the Nineties.*

Witters, W., Venturelli, P., & Hanson, G. (1992) *Drugs and Society.* Boston: Jones and Bartlett.

INHALANTS

There are an almost limitless number of aromatic or gaseous materials that can be inhaled. And, for the most part, inhalants are easily accessible, widely available, and relatively inexpensive substances. In fact, there often is an entire pharmacopeia of inhalant drugs within one's kitchen, bathroom, and/or garage. **Inhalants** are substances that are gases or that emit gases at room temperature (Oetting, Edwards, & Beauvais, 1988). People inhale many different materials for their psychoactive effects. The substances that are used most frequently are gasoline, glues, and paints that can be inhaled and that produce psychoactive effects. The biochemical and psychological effects of these substances differ and inhalant users take specific inhalants depending on availability and their current beliefs about the effects of these drugs. In this chapter, inhalant use among youth and types and effects of inhalants will be the topics of discussion.

INHALANT USE AMONG YOUTH

Because inhalants are so easily accessible and plentiful, they often are one of the first types of drugs to be abused by young people (Oetting et al., 1988). The initial use of inhalants typically starts very young, often preceding the initial use of alcohol or tobacco. The average user is 14 or 15 years of age and male (Sikkink & Fleming, 1992), yet inhalant use prior to age 12 is relatively common and has been reported in children as young as four to six years of age (Westermeyer, 1987). Use is believed to be higher among minority youth and those who do not have the money to buy other drugs (Fields, 1992), especially Hispanic and American Indian youth (Schwartz, 1989). Young people who begin with inhalants are more likely to continue to serious levels of drug involvement than those whose first drug is marijuana (Crider & Rouse, 1988).

Among the graduating class of 1990, 18.0 percent of high school seniors reported using inhalants at some time during their life (lifetime prevalence), with two-thirds of the users beginning before tenth grade. The specific classes of inhalants consisting of amyl and butyl nitrites have been tried by roughly one in fifty seniors or 2.1 percent. Sniffing glue and other aerosols tends to be discontinued at a relatively early age (Johnston, O'Malley, & Bachman, 1991).

Results from the National Adolescent Student Health Survey showed that about one out of every five eighth and tenth grade students report having tried sniffing glue. The percentage of eighth graders sniffing glue in the past month was 7 percent and among tenth graders 5 percent (American School Health Association, Association for the Advancement of Health Education, & Society for Public Health Education, 1988).

Despite the fact that millions of children and adults abuse inhalants, few publications on drug abuse even mention inhalant abuse. This is unfortunate because more people need to be made aware of the extent and consequences of inhalant abuse.

TYPES AND EFFECTS OF INHALANTS

There are two main categories of inhalants—household chemicals and industrial chemicals. They will be discussed in this section of the chapter along with the effects of inhaling household and industrial chemicals, nitrite inhalants, effects and reported effects of nitrite inhalants, sexuality and nitrite inhalation use, nitrous oxide, the effects of nitrous oxide, and how inhalants are administered will be discussed.

Household and Industrial Chemicals

The most commonly used inhalant group consists of a wide range of volatile solvents and aerosols, mostly household and industrial chemicals. Examples of such inhaled substances that are abused for psychoactive effects are:
- glues and contact cements,
- gasoline,
- paint thinners,
- lighter fluid,
- spray-can propellants,
- paper correction fluid,
- dry-cleaning fluids,
- transmission fluids,
- liquid waxes,
- shoe polish,
- fingernail polish remover,

- refrigerants,
- vegetable nonstick fryer sprays,
- air sanitizers,
- hair sprays,
- deodorants and antiperspirants,
- spray paints,
- window cleaners,
- furniture polishes,
- gas jets in school science laboratories,
- marker fluids,
- over-the-counter nasal inhalants.

These substances are inexpensive and readily available to children and adolescents. In most cases they are more accessible than illegal drugs (i.e., cocaine, marijuana) and often alcohol or tobacco. Many of these substances are available right within a young person's home. Others easily can be acquired at grocery stores, hobby stores, hardware stores, gas stations, paint stores, institutional cleaning supply stores, or gasoline tanks (Westermeyer, 1987). In addition, household chemicals can be stored or used in an adolescent's bedroom or at a school locker without arousing suspicion (Schwartz, 1989). Although specific substances may be preferred by some users, household chemicals often are used interchangeably by inhalant users (Oetting et al., 1988). The key factor in choosing a chemical to abuse is usually what is readily available to a young person who wants to get "high."

Occupational accessibility to volatile industrial solvents is a risk factor for inhalant abuse. The following workers are considered to be at a higher than average risk of volatile solvent and aerosol abuse (Schwartz, 1989; Westermeyer, 1987):
- cabinetmakers,
- printers,
- shoemakers,
- dry cleaners,
- hair stylists,
- automotive mechanics,
- medical workers,
- those involved in the refinement of petroleum products,
- those involved in the manufacture of volatile solvents.

Adults who are deprived of their drugs of choice (i.e., because of imprisonment) will frequently turn to volatile solvents to get "high." However, most adults and older adolescents who use inhalants are polydrug users using inhalants as one of many substances of abuse.

122

Effects of Inhaling Household and Industrial Chemicals

Because these chemicals rapidly and easily cross the blood-brain barrier, a very quick "high" is produced, even faster than with alcohol. Their action in the body is very similar to depressant drugs. Users become excited as the vapors rush quickly to the brain. However, the "high" is very short-lived, with intoxication lasting only a few minutes, while some of the effects may be felt for about 30 minutes. Pleasurable effects are frequently followed by nausea, headache, and amnesia (Sikkink & Fleming, 1992). Most episodes of use result in episodes of mild intoxication, similar to that produced from alcohol intoxication. Inhalant-induced psychotic episodes also can occur from inhalation of these substances. Decreased inhibitions and sensation of floating as well as the following feelings or effects can occur during intoxication by volatile solvents:
- feelings of "drunkenness,"
- exhilaration,
- disorientation,
- sedation,
- recklessness,
- grandiosity,
- invincibility,
- omnipotence,
- hallucinations,
- unconsciousness,
- time and space distortions.

It often is perplexing to many people why children and adolescents would want to get "high" on these chemicals. Fields (1992) explains that children become exhilarated with the effect of dizziness as evidenced by their desire to be twirled about by adults and their desire to go on amusement park rides that give feelings of vertigo. Similar to these experiences, inhalant drugs create altered states of consciousness that are reinforcing to many young people. Fields also explains that peer group influence and inhalant use in peer group settings are powerful reinforcements of use of these substances.

Commonly-inhaled volatile solvents and aerosols usually do not cause tolerance or physical dependence (Schilit & Gomberg, 1991). However, inhalation of volatile solvents and aerosols can be very dangerous. Because the abused inhaled products often contain several ingredients in combination, it is difficult to precisely determine the potential for damage of each specific product (Ashton, 1990).

The following adverse effects have been noted from inhalation of a wide range of household and industrial chemicals (Fig. 9-1):

- sudden death due to depression of breathing, liver failure, disturbance of heart rhythm, or suffocation from using a plastic bag over the head to inhale a chemical;
- asphyxia by coating the lungs;
- kidney failure from chronic abuse;
- skeletal muscle weakness;
- accidents;
- aggressive and violent behavior;
- seizures;
- chronic liver and/or heart muscle damage;
- bone marrow suppression;
- reduced blood cell formation;
- loss of appetite leading to nutritional deficiencies;
- leukemia (in benzene users);
- lead poisoning (in gasoline sniffers);
- irritation of oral tissues and eyes;
- ulcers around the mouth and nose;
- freezing of upper respiratory tissue (abusers of pressurized propellants);
- peripheral nerve damage causing numbness and weakness in the extremities;
- short-term memory loss and motor skills impairment;
- brain damage;
- toxic psychoses;
- fetal and infant abnormalities.

Nitrite Inhalants

Amyl nitrite, a clear yellowish liquid with a strong chemical smell, is known for its vasodilation (increase in diameter of blood vessels) effects following inhalation. As a result, its first therapeutic use was for the relief of chest pain known as angina pectoris. The original form of the drug was glass ampules enclosed in mesh, called pearls. When crushed between the fingers, the ampules made a popping or snapping sound. Thus, amyl nitrite earned its nicknames of "poppers" and "snappers."

Butyl nitrite has the same medicinal properties as amyl nitrite, but it has never been used clinically. A third member of this class of compounds **isobutyl nitrite** also produces similar effects (Newell, Spitz, & Wilson, 1988).

Effects and Reported Effects of Nitrite Inhalants

Nitrites exert their vasodilation effects by relaxing the smooth muscles in blood vessel walls. Vasodilation of blood vessels in the brain causes an increase in pressure in the head, producing a euphoric effect or "high." Nitrite inhalant use also is reported by both sexes to enhance sexual performance (Lange, Dax, Haertzen, Synder, & Jaffe, 1988; Newell et al., 1988).

Butyl and isobutyl nitrites do not fit the definition of a food, drug, or cosmetic as specified by the Federal Food, Drug, and Cosmetic Act. Because they are not subject to regulation as drugs by the Food and Drug Administration and are not classified as drugs, they are sold legally in the United States. The labels on butyl nitrites state that they are not to be inhaled (Haverkos & Dougherty, 1988). Because amyl nitrite was no longer available after 1969 without a prescription, there was a proliferation of different brands of butyl and isobutyl nitrite during the early 1970s. Most commercial preparations of these substances

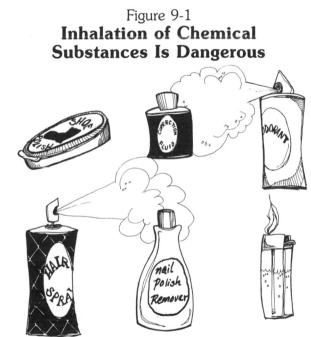

Figure 9-1
Inhalation of Chemical Substances Is Dangerous

Some adverse effects of inhalants:

* Altered states of consciousness
* Changes in behaviors and toxic psychoses
* Seizures and sudden death
* Accidents
* Kidney and liver failure
* Heart muscle damage
* Skeletal muscle weakness
* Irritation in areas exposed directly to inhalants
* Brain and nerve damage
* Bone marrow suppression
* Leukemia (in benzene users)
* Lead poisoning (in gasoline sniffers)
* Fetal and infant abnormalities

contain some of each type, along with unspecified impurities (Newell et al., 1988).

Amyl nitrite was known to have been used recreationally as early as the 1960s. However, the "popper craze" really began during the years of 1974 to 1977. By the end of the 1970s, over five million people in the United States used these drugs more than once a week (Newell et al., 1988). As a street drug, poppers frequently were used on social occasions, often in discotheques, to promote a sense of abandon while dancing, to expand creativity, to stimulate music appreciation, and to enhance meditation. Others used poppers on a more general basis for a euphorigenic rush, an altered state of consciousness, and even as a stimulant. There is no scientific evidence, however, that any of these effects are associated with the use of nitrite inhalants (Lange et al., 1988).

The following acute effects are generally experienced by nitrite inhalant users:
- dizziness,
- rapid pulse,
- feelings of warmth,
- heat loss and subsequent chill,
- throbbing sensations,
- perspiration,
- flushing of the face,
- headache (sometimes called "thunderclap headache"),
- fainting,
- nausea.

The nitrite inhalants also can irritate the skin, particularly the nose and lips if the drug is inhaled directly from a bottle. In fact, a sign of nitrite inhalation abuse is a dermatitis and yellow crusting of the upper lip or nasal passages that may develop through prolonged inhalation of vapors or spilling of the nitrite liquid on these areas (Schwartz, 1989). Allergic reactions also have been known to occur, resulting in itching and wheezing. Because nitrites are flammable and explosive, some cases of burn injuries are known to have occurred. Therefore, the use of these substances when used near ignited cigarettes or other flames is hazardous (Haverkos & Dougherty, 1988). There are serious concerns about the possibility that nitrite inhalants may suppress the immune system, be toxic to body systems, and be potentially carcinogenic. Nitrite inhalants may be particularly dangerous for people with heart disease because they can cause irregular heart beats.

Sexuality and Nitrite Inhalation Use

Since the 1960s, nitrite inhalants have been abused by both sexes in an attempt to augment the physical pleasure

124

of sexual intercourse. Purported sexual attributes include prolongation of penile erection and relaxation of rectal smooth muscle and anal sphincter tone, thus facilitating penetration. Other alleged aphrodisiac drug effects include heightened libido (sexual desire), prevention of premature ejaculation, increased volume of ejaculate, and promotion of a generally intensified or prolonged sexual experience (Lange et al., 1988). As a result, "poppers" have been popular in adult bookstores and gay bars and bath houses (Schwartz, 1989).

In the late 1970s, nitrites were used primarily during sexual activity because they reduce social and sexual inhibitions, heighten sexual arousal, relax the anal sphincter, and are believed to prolong orgasm (Newell et al., 1988). The timing of this increase in recreational use appeared to be connected to the emergence of the AIDS epidemic among young homosexual males during the early 1980s. The first five homosexual males reported to the Centers for Disease Control with AIDS had all used nitrite inhalants, but only one had abused intravenous drugs and only two were reported to be promiscuous (Centers for Disease Control, 1981; Lange et al., 1988). Haverkos and Dougherty (1988) describe the important events of this time period:

> In the 1980s, reports of Kaposi's sarcoma and opportunistic infections among previously healthy men and others led to a search for the cause of a worldwide epidemic, now known as the acquired immunodeficiency syndrome (AIDS). Nitrite inhalants were investigated as a possible cause of AIDS early in the epidemic, partly because of the preponderance of homosexual men who used nitrites among the early patients with AIDS. In 1983 and 1984, a retrovirus, currently named human immunodeficiency virus (HIV), was discovered to be the cause of AIDS. However, concern remains that the use of large quantities of nitrite inhalants may increase the likelihood of development of cancer, Kaposi's sarcoma, after infection with HIV. (pp. 479–480)

More recently, the role of nitrite inhalants has been evaluated in a study of sexual transmission of HIV in homosexual male couples (Seage, Mayer, Horsbaugh, Holmberg, Moon, & Lamb, 1992). Males who "always" used nitrite inhalants during unprotected receptive anal intercourse were 32 times more likely to develop HIV infection than were males who did not engage in unprotected receptive anal intercourse. (Unprotected means having receptive anal intercourse without a condom.) By comparison, males who "sometimes" or "never" used nitrites during unprotected receptive anal intercourse were seven times and nine times more likely to develop HIV infection from their unprotected sexual activity. This study was controlled for such factors as the number of unprotected receptive anal sex partners and history of sexually-transmitted diseases. Thus, this study suggests that nitrite inhalation combined with unprotected receptive anal intercourse increases the risk of HIV transmission more than unprotected receptive anal intercourse alone.

Because nitrite inhalation produces relaxation of smooth muscle and dilation of blood vessels, Seage et al. (1992) propose that nitrites could facilitate the entry of HIV into the bloodstream. They go on to say:

> In turn, traumatized, bleeding anal veins may allow easier passage of HIV into the bloodstream. Nitrites also relax the anal sphincter and so may more readily allow traumatic sexual activity, especially since the receptive partner is high. (p. 9)

Nitrous Oxide

Nitrous oxide is a colorless gas known for its powerful analgesic effect and weak anesthetic effect (Schwartz & Calihan, 1984). Use of nitrous oxide is particularly dangerous when it is not inhaled with supplemental oxygen as often is the case with recreational use. This improper use can lead to hypoxia. **Hypoxia** is a condition of decreased oxygen level in the blood that can lead to permanent brain damage and even death.

Known as "laughing gas," nitrous oxide has a long history of abuse by people in the health professions. Health care professionals have easy access to nitrous oxide because it is used as a general anesthetic in medical and dental care settings for brief surgical procedures. As such, anesthesiologists and other physicians, dentists, medical and dental students, and inhalation therapists are among those at high risk for abuse of nitrous oxide.

Nitrous oxide has been abused by health professionals since the 18th century when it was first introduced into medical practice. Health care professionals also have been at risk of inhalant abuse of other anesthetic drugs such as ether and chloroform. In addition to its use as an anesthetic, nitrous oxide is used as a whipping cream propellant and as a power booster in cars and motorcycles. Nitrous oxide also is abused by young people. The most popular means by which young people obtained nitrous oxide is by the use of "Whippets." Schwartz (1989) explains:

> Users can buy these distinctive battleship gray unmarked cylinders, each of which contains 3.5 liters of the gas, in paraphernalia shops, adult bookstores, bar supply shops, and by mail order. Whippets are sold in boxes of five cylinders, purportedly as a whipping cream propellant. The commercial whipped topping "Reddi Whip" is now enveloped in plastic wrap, in part to prevent adventurous teenagers from tapping off the 1.5 ml (two or three hits) of nitrous oxide when store personnel are not watching. (p. 41)

Effects of Nitrous Oxide

The following sensations and effects are associated with a nitrous oxide "high" (Fig. 9-2), and are well documented (Schwartz, 1989; Schwartz & Calihan, 1984):

- exhilaration,
- sense of warmth,
- light-headedness,
- visual hallucinations,
- detachment from reality, as though flying or floating,
- loss of motivation,
- silliness and giddiness,
- reduced social inhibitions,
- loss of consciousness with continued inhalation,
- loss of motor control.

Accidents do occur among users. Breathing nitrous oxide while standing will cause a user to fall down, possibly causing serious injury. Driving skills also are briefly impaired, thus increasing the likelihood of motor vehicle accidents if used while attempting to drive. As mentioned earlier, hypoxia can result if nitrous oxide is inhaled with insufficient oxygen. People who have abused nitrous oxide for long periods of time may develop nerve damage that may be manifested by weakness of leg muscles, numbness of the toes and fingers, and loss of balance. Other potential effects are (Hecht, 1980; Schwartz, 1989):

- freezing of the mouth and lips from direct inhalation from cylinders,
- respiratory depression,
- coma,
- shortness of breath,
- loss of hearing,
- nausea,
- disturbances in heart rhythm,
- kidney and liver disease,
- spontaneous miscarriage,
- depressed bone marrow function.

Figure 9-2
Inhaling Nitrous Oxide Is No Laughing Matter

The Last Laugh. . . . . . .

Some effects of nitrous oxide:

* Altered states of consciousness
* Changes in behavior
* Respiratory disturbances
* Coma
* Loss of motivation
* Nerve damage
* Loss of hearing
* Heart rhythm disturbance
* Kidney and liver disease
* Depressed bone marrow function
* Spontaneous miscarriage

Nitrous oxide, even among frequent users, does not produce tolerance.

How Inhalants Are Administered

Inhalants can be administered in a variety of ways. The simplest method is to inhale vapors directly from a cup or glass filled with the substance. "Huffing" is sniffing the vapors from a rag or cloth that has been soaked or had a solvent poured on it. "Bagging" is putting the solvent in a bag or spraying an aerosol into a bag, placing the bag over the mouth and nose, and inhaling deeply. This can be risky if loss of consciousness should occur. The user could then be suffocated. Users often place inhalant chemicals into empty soft drink containers to give the appearance of sipping a soft drink (Schilit & Gomberg, 1991).

BIBLIOGRAPHY

American School Health Association, Association for the Advancement of Health Education, & Society for Public Health Education. (1988) National Adolescent Health Survey: Highlights of the survey. *Health Education*, August/September, 4–8.

Ashton, C.H. (1990) Solvent abuse: Little progress after 20 years. *British Medical Journal*, 300:135–138.

Centers for Disease Control. (1981) Pneumocystitis pneumonia—Los Angeles. *Morbidity and Mortality Weekly Report*, 30:250–252.

Crider, R.A., & Rouse, B.A. (1988) Inhalant overview. In R.A. Crider & B.A. Rouse (Eds.), *Epidemiology of Inhalant Abuse: An Update*. NIDA Research Monograph 85, DHHS Publication No. (ADM)88-1577 (pp. 1–7). Washington, D.C.: U.S. Government Printing Office.

Doweiko, H.E. (1993) *Concepts of Chemical Dependency*. Pacific Grove, CA: Brooks/Cole.

Fields, R. (1992) *Drugs and Alcohol in Perspective*. Dubuque, IA: Wm. C. Brown.

Haverkos, H.W. (1988) Epidemiologic studies—Kaposi's sarcoma vs. opportunistic infections among homosexual men with AIDS. In H.W. Haverkos & J.A. Dougherty (Eds.), *Health Hazards of Nitrite Inhalants*. NIDA

Research Monograph 83, DHHS Publication No (ADM)88-1573 (pp. 96–105). Washington, D.C.: U.S. Government Printing Office.

Haverkos, H.W., & Dougherty, J. (1988) Health hazards of nitrite inhalants. *American Journal of Medicine*, 84: 479–482.

Hecht, A. (1980) Inhalants: Quick route to danger. *FDA Consumer*, May, 19–22.

Johnston, L.D., O'Malley, P.M., & Bachman, J.G. (1991) *Drug Use Among American High School Seniors, College Students, and Young Adults, 1975–1990*. DHHS Publication No. (ADM)91-1813. Washington, D.C.: National Institute of Drug Abuse.

Lange, W.R., Dax, E.M., Haertzen, C.A., Snyder, F.R., & Jaffe, J.H. (1988) In H.W. Haverkos & J.A. Dougherty (Eds.), *Health Hazards of Nitrite Inhalants*. NIDA Research Monograph 83, DHHS Publication No. (ADM) 88-1573 (pp. 86–95). Washington, D.C.: U.S. Government Printing Office.

Maickel, R.P. (1988) The fate and toxicity of butyl nitrites. In H.W. Haverkos & J.A. Dougherty (Eds.), *Health Hazards of Nitrite Inhalants*. NIDA Research Monograph 83, DHHS Publication No. (ADM)88-1573 (pp. 15–27). Washington, D.C.: U.S. Government Printing Office.

Newell, G.R., Spitz, M.R., & Wilson, M.B. (1988) Nitrite inhalants: Historical perspective. In H.W. Haverkos & J.A. Dougherty (Eds.), *Health Hazards of Nitrite Inhalants*. NIDA Research Monograph 83, DHHS Publication No. (ADM)88-1573 (pp. 1–14). Washington, D.C.: U.S. Government Printing Office.

Oetting, E.R., Edwards, R.W., & Beauvais, F. (1988) In R.A. Crider & B.A. Rouse (Eds.), *Epidemiology of Inhalant Abuse: An Update*. NIDA Research Monograph 85, DHHS Publication No. (ADM)88-1577 (pp. 172–203). Washington, D.C.: U.S. Government Printing Office.

Schilit, R., & Gomberg, E.L. (1991) *Drugs and Behavior: A Sourcebook for the Helping Professions*. Newbury Park, CA: Sage.

Schwartz, R.H. (1989) When to suspect inhalant abuse. *Patient Care*, 23(10):39–64.

Schwartz, R.H., & Calihan, M. (1984) Nitrous oxide: A potentially lethal euphoriant inhalant. *American Family Physician*, 30:171–172.

Seage, G.R., Mayer, K.H., Horsburgh, C.R., Holmberg, S.D., Moon, M.W., Lamb, G.A. (1992) The relation between nitrite inhalants, unprotected receptive anal intercourse, and the risk of human immunodeficiency virus infection. *American Journal of Epidemiology*, 135:1–11.

Sikkink, J., & Fleming, M. (1992) Adverse health effects and medical complications of alcohol, nicotine, and drug use. In M.F. Fleming & K.L. Barry (Eds.), *Addictive Disorders: A Practical Guide to Treatment*. (pp. 145–168). St. Louis, MO: Mosby/Year Book.

Weil, A., & Rosen, W. (1983) *Chocolate to Morphine: Understanding Mind-Active drugs*. Boston: Houghton Mifflin.

Westermeyer, J. (1987) The psychiatrist and solvent-inhalant abuse: Recognition, assessment, and treatment. *American Journal of Psychiatry*, 144:903–907.

OVER-THE-COUNTER DRUGS

Over-the-counter drugs are big business in the United States. In 1990, about $11 billion dollars were spent on over-the-counter drugs in the United States. By the year 2000, the over-the-counter drug market will reach $19 billion (Segal, 1991). **Over-the-counter drugs** are drugs that are approved for legal purchase and use without a prescription from a doctor. Drug and grocery store shelves are filled with these drugs that, for the most part, are used on a temporary basis and are considered to be relatively safe if used according to the directions provided on the drug label (Carroll, 1993). Over-the-counter drugs are usually self-prescribed and self-administered for the relief of symptoms of self-diagnosed illnesses (Ray & Ksir, 1993). This chapter will include a discussion of the classification of over-the-counter drugs, over-the-counter drug labeling, some common over-the-counter drugs, and over-the-counter drug safety.

CLASSIFICATION OF OVER-THE-COUNTER DRUGS

It is estimated that only about 200 different active ingredients make up the thousands of over-the-counter drugs available on the market. The Food and Drug Administration (FDA) established the following 26 classifications of over-the-counter drugs as part of a massive effort to establish the effectiveness and safety of over 300,000 different nonprescription products on the market:

1. Antacids—used for relief of indigestion, acid stomach, and heartburn (gastroesophageal reflux).
2. Antimicrobials—used to kill bacteria or inhibit their growth; usually found in first aid products.
3. Sedatives and sleep aids—taken to promote sleepiness and drowsiness.
4. Analgesics—taken for the relief of pain.
5. Cold remedies and antitussives—used to relieve symptoms associated with colds and to suppress coughs (antitussive action).
6. Antihistamines and allergy products—taken to control allergic reactions and associated symptoms.
7. Mouthwashes—taken to freshen breath and for antibacterial action in the mouth.
8. Topical analgesics—applied to the skin for the relief of pain.

9. Antirheumatics—used to treat the pain and other symptoms associated with rheumatoid arthritis.
10. Hematinics—preparations of supplemental iron taken to increase hemoglobin in the blood.
11. Vitamins and minerals—taken as supplements to nutrients in the diet.
12. Antiperspirants—used to reduce perspiration secretion.
13. Laxatives—taken to relieve constipation.
14. Dentrifices and dental products—used in cleaning teeth.
15. Sunburn treatments and preventives—used for the relief and prevention of sunburn.
16. Contraceptive products—used to prevent pregnancy.
17. Stimulants—taken to increase alertness and as diet pills.
18. Hemorrhoidals—used for the relief of pain and itching associated with hemorrhoids.
19. Antidiarrheals—used to treat diarrhea (watery stools).
20. Dandruff and athlete's foot preparations—used to treat these conditions.
21. Bronchodilators and antiasthmatics—used to increase air flow in the lungs and relieve the shortness of breath associated with asthmatic conditions.
22. Antiemetics—used to relieve motion sickness and associated vomiting.
23. Ophthalmics—used to treat eye irritation and dryness.
24. Emetics—used to promote vomiting.
25. Miscellaneous internal products—all other over-the-counter preparations that are taken internally and not included in any of the above classifications.
26. Miscellaneous external products—all other over-the-counter preparations that are applied to the skin and not included in any of the above classifications.

OVER-THE-COUNTER DRUG LABELING

By federal law, manufacturers of over-the-counter drugs are required to place specific information on product labels. To insure the proper use, consumers should carefully read labels before using any over-the-counter drug and strictly adhere to directions for use. As formulations occasionally change, consumers should continue to read labels even if they have been using the products for a long time. The

129

following information is provided on over-the-counter drug labels:

- the name and address of the manufacturer, distributor, or packer;
- the lot, control, or batch number;
- the name of the product and what type of drug it is;
- the active ingredients;
- the amount of product contained (e.g., number of tablets or ounces of liquid preparations);
- the symptoms or conditions for which the product should be used (indications for use);
- warnings and cautionary statements (i.e., who should not be taking the drug, adverse reactions that could develop from use, symptoms that signal the need to see a doctor, how long the drug should be taken);
- precautions about interaction with other over-the-counter drugs and alcohol;
- the expiration date (month and year beyond which the product should not be used.

SOME COMMON OVER-THE-COUNTER DRUGS

Although it is difficult to determine accurately, it is estimated that there are about 300,000 different over-the-counter products on the market (Ray & Ksir, 1993). About three-fourths of Americans use over-the-counter drugs (Cornacchia & Barrett, 1993). In this section of the chapter, the discussion will include antacids, analgesics and fever reducers, cold and cough remedies, and laxatives.

Antacids

Nearly $1 billion dollars are spent on approximately 600 different over-the-counter antacid products each year. **Antacids** are compounds that are taken for the relief of indigestion, acid stomach, and heartburn (gastroesophageal reflux). Antacids used in moderation relieve these conditions by neutralizing some of the excess acid in the stomach (Cramer, 1992). Other than this action, antacids do little else for those who turn to them for relief. Antacids do not heal ulcers and their use may contribute to delay in seeking proper medical care.

Sodium, calcium, magnesium, and aluminum are the most often used neutralizing agents in antacids. Sodium bicarbonate (baking soda), found in Bromo Seltzer and Alka Seltzer, is a potent and fast-acting antacid. The relief provided by sodium bicarbonate lasts only for short periods of time. Products that contain sodium bicarbonate are not suitable for repeated use. Repeated use can aggravate high blood pressure for people who are on sodium-restricted diets (Cramer, 1992). Kidney problems also can be aggra-

vated with repeated use. Sodium bicarbonate products should never be used in the following situations:

- to treat an ulcer,
- by females who are pregnant,
- by people who are taking water pills to eliminate excess water (Grogan, 1987).

Alka Seltzer combines sodium bicarbonate with aspirin. It is an especially poor pharmacological combination because aspirin is a stomach irritant that can cause an upset stomach and aggravate ulcers.

Calcium carbonate-containing antacids, such as Tums and Alka-2, are also potent and fast-acting antacids. However, they are longer-acting than the sodium bicarbonate antacids. These products are recommended only for occasional use and not for the treatment of ulcers. Calcium ingestion sometimes causes rebound hyperacidity. **Rebound hyperacidity** is a condition that occurs when calcium (or any other agent) causes the stomach to secrete extra acid (Grogan, 1987). Of course, this action can aggravate ulcers. Another concern about calcium-containing antacids is that they can cause constipation. Kidney stone formation and other kidney disorders also are associated with long-term use of the calcium-containing antacids. The elderly and females who want more calcium because of their concern about osteoporosis may be motivated to take these products regularly. It is important to understand the risks that have been mentioned that are associated with this practice.

Aluminum salts also are used in antacids such as Rolaids and AlternaGel. These are considered to be weak antacids that pose little problem for people with normal-functioning kidneys who use them as directed and only on an occasional basis (Cramer, 1992). High doses, however, can cause aluminum toxicity and may weaken bones by depleting calcium and phosphorus from the body. There also is some concern about aluminum accumulation in the brain. These problems are more likely to occur in people who have kidney problems.

Aluminum often is combined with magnesium salts, because magnesium salts cause diarrhea in most people (Cramer, 1992). The aluminum counteracts this laxative effect because of its tendency to cause constipation. Maalox, Mylanta, Digel, and Riopan are examples of aluminum-magnesium combination antacids on the market. Magnesium salt products without aluminum are also available. One of these is Philip's Milk of Magnesia. Aluminum and magnesium salts are potent and quick-acting antacids.

Analgesics and Fever Reducers

People in the United States spend $2 billion dollars for over-the-counter analgesics, the most advertised category of all over-the-counter products. **Analgesics** are products that are taken to treat aches and pains. The three types of over-the-counter analgesics are aspirin, acetaminophen, and ibuprofen.

Aspirin is an effective anti-pyretic (antifever agent) and pain killer, especially for dull, aching pain. It is often used to treat the pain associated with tension headache, sore muscles, arthritis, or menstrual cramps. Pain relief is accomplished by reducing prostaglandin production in the body. Prostaglandins are hormonelike, regulatory substances produced in the body. While prostaglandins play a role in producing pain, they also serve to protect the lining of the stomach from digestive acids. Therefore, decreased prostaglandin activity produces the most common side effect of taking aspirin—stomach irritation. Aspirin use also can lead to bleeding ulcers, ringing in the ears, allergic reactions, and interference with blood-clotting. Reye's syndrome, a rare but life-threatening condition, has been linked with aspirin use among children who have chickenpox or influenza. As such, parents should be especially cautious in giving aspirin or aspirin-containing products to children (Willis, 1991).

Acetaminophen is a safer alternative than aspirin for relieving flu or cold symptoms in children. Acetaminophen, sold under such names as Tylenol, Tempra, Datril, and Liquiprin, is an effective pain killer for minor pain and a fever reducer. Acetaminophen is not as irritating to the stomach as aspirin, nor does it reduce blood clotting ability. It also can be used safely by individuals susceptible to aspirin-allergic reactions. However, acetaminophen does not reduce inflammation, so it is not a valuable aid to the treatment of arthritis. Another drawback of acetaminophen is the fact that overdoses can be particularly toxic and can destroy liver cells. As few as ten Extra-Strength Tylenol or Anacin-3 tablets can kill a child; as few as 30 can be fatal for an adult (Grogan, 1987).

The newest over-the-counter analgesic is ibuprofen (Advil, Nuprin). Prior to 1984, ibuprofen was available only by prescription. Ibuprofen, like aspirin and acetaminophen, is an effective agent for pain relief of minor aches and pains. People who are allergic to aspirin also may be allergic to ibuprofen. The Food and Drug Administration has approved Pediaprop and children's Advil with pediatric labeling. The FDA was convinced that adequate data to demonstrate safe use for children exist.

Cold and Cough Remedies

The common cold is caused by more than 100 different viruses. No over-the-counter cold remedies do anything to counteract or kill cold viruses. These viruses are capable of causing a variety of symptoms—headaches, stuffed and runny nose, sore throat, coughing, and so forth. Over-the-counter cold remedies treat only the symptoms of a cold. These remedies do nothing to shorten the length or severity of a cold. In fact, some health experts are of the opinion that the use of over-the-counter cold remedies may even prolong and/or increase the severity of a cold.

Nasal decongestants are remedies that are used to temporarily relieve nasal congestion and stuffiness (Fig. 10-1). Decongestants come in a variety of forms—capsules, tablets, liquid preparations, nasal sprays, nose drops, and inhalers. The active ingredients in decongestants cause blood vessels to constrict. This action results in a shrinking of swollen nasal membranes, often leading to temporary relief and improved breathing. Applying decongestants (e.g., nasal sprays) directly to nasal membranes often is associated with a condition known as rebound congestion. **Rebound congestion** is a condition in which nasal membranes become enlarged after repeated doses of topical decongestants. Often the resulting symptoms are even worse than before the medicine was taken. Rebound congestion often is interpreted as the need to increase the dosage, thus compounding the problem. As a result, the use of topical decongestants should be limited to just a few days at a time. The most frequently used decongestants are ephedrine and phenylephrine.

Antihistamines are remedies that are used to treat hay fever and other allergies. Antihistamines produce hay fever and allergy relief by blocking histamine, which is a chemical released in the body when an allergen is present. Although antihistamines frequently are used for treating such cold symptoms as a runny nose and stuffiness, antihistamines have little effect on cold symptoms because histamine is not released during a cold. Thus, antihistamines are of very limited effectiveness in treating cold symptoms.

Antihistamines can be dangerous because they produce drowsiness in users and slight disorientation. Children, on the other hand, are often stimulated by antihistamines. Children who take antihistamines may become irritable and nervous and have a difficult time falling asleep. Antihistamines are dangerous when used in combination with other central nervous system depressants. Antihistamines can lead to tissue irritation because they tend to dry tissue.

131

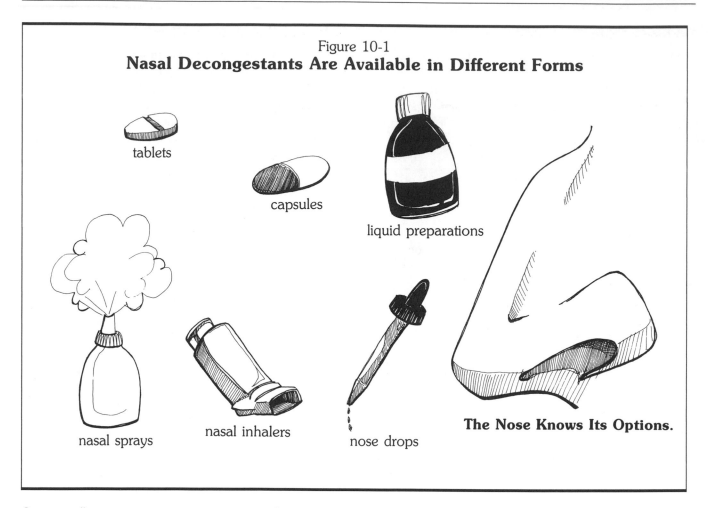

Figure 10-1
Nasal Decongestants Are Available in Different Forms

tablets

capsules

liquid preparations

nasal sprays

nasal inhalers

nose drops

The Nose Knows Its Options.

Occasionally, it is necessary to suppress a dry, hacking, nonproductive cough associated with a cold. In these cases, an antitussive may be warranted. An **antitussive** is a medicine that suppresses coughing. Over-the-counter antitussives contain dextromorphan, a narcotic, which acts by dulling the cough reflex in the brain. However, suppressing a productive cough associated with chest congestion can be harmful. Productive coughing is necessary to bring up fluid or phlegm (mucus) that accumulates in the respiratory tract.

Expectorant cough remedies are medicines that supposedly reduce the thickness of phlegm in respiratory passages, making it easier to cough it up. Unfortunately, widely-used expectorants such as guaifenesin and terpin hydrate have not been judged to work effectively. In fact, drinking adequate amounts of water (six to twelve glasses a day) may be more effective in producing expectoration effects than over-the-counter expectorant preparations. Water also can be used effectively as an expectorant in steam vaporizers and cool mist humidifiers.

Some over-the-counter cold preparations are "shotgun remedies" or combination products that contain several remedies in one capsule, tablet, or liquid preparation. Examples of such products are Contac, Dristan, Coricidin, Comtrex, and NyQuil. Health experts recommend that consumers avoid these products in favor of single remedy products. In other words, a headache should be selectively treated with an analgesic such as aspirin or acetaminophen. Single ingredient decongestants are preferable to multiple combination preparations. One good choice is pseudoephedrine for treatment of stuffy and runny nose.

Laxatives

Laxative use can pose serious side effects, be habit-forming, and delay treatment for serious underlying problems (Cummings, 1991). Laxatives induce bowel movements by stimulating the intestinal tract. Laxatives usually are taken to relieve constipation. Overreliance on over-the-counter laxative products often stems from a belief that a daily bowel movement is essential to good health. Actually, normal ranges for the frequency of bowel movements vary from as few as three a week to as many as three a day. Health experts recommend that constipation or "irregularity" is best treated by increasing fiber and water intake as well as by including exercise in the daily routine.

Laxatives should be used with caution and only under the supervision of a physician. One type of laxative is the bulk-forming laxative. A **bulk-forming laxative** is a product that mimics the actions of fiber in the intestine by creating bulk and increasing the amount of water absorbed into the intestines. These laxatives generally are considered to be the safest laxative type, primarily because they usually do not result in laxative dependence or nutrient absorption. However, they may interfere with the absorption of some of the medications that a user is taking. An infrequent, but potentially serious complication of bulk-forming laxatives is an intestinal obstruction. Examples of bulk-forming laxatives are Metamucil, Serutan, and FiberCon.

Stimulant laxatives are products that work by irritating the linings of the intestines, "causing waves of muscular contractions that expel fecal matter" (Cummings, 1991, p. 34). Stimulant laxatives are the most abused of all the laxative types. Side effects include severe intestinal cramping and nutrient and electrolyte loss. Repeated use of stimulant laxatives can lead to "laxative dependency." The bowel can become conditioned to work only in the presence of a stimulant laxative. Therefore, products such as Ex-Lax and Dulcolax, Castor Oil, and Carter's Little Pills should be used only for the initial treatment of constipation and under physician supervision. The response to these preparations is often unpredictable and could place a user in an embarrassing situation because of uncontrollable bowel movements (Grogan, 1987).

Osmotic laxatives are not much better than the stimulant laxatives. **Osmotic laxatives** are products that work like a "sponge to draw water into the bowel, thereby promoting easier passage of stools" (Cummings, 1991, p. 34). These products can cause a risk of nutrient and electrolye loss and intestinal cramping that often results in diarrhea. Milk of Magnesia is the most popular osmotic laxative.

Another type of laxative is the stool softener. **Stool softeners** or **emollients** are laxatives that work by softening hard stools. Softened stools are able to absorb more liquid. Mineral oil, Colace, Dialose, and Surfak are widely used stool softeners. Among the many side effects of stool softeners is that they can prevent the absorption of fat-soluble vitamins, including vitamin K which is necessary for blood clotting.

OVER-THE-COUNTER DRUG SAFETY

No medication, prescription or over-the-counter, is safe or effective unless it is used responsibly by consumers. In this section, the discussion will include the importance of asking questions, reading labels, and concerns about product tampering.

Asking Questions

Before buying and/or using any over-the-counter product, it is wise to seek advice from a physician or pharmacist about taking the drug. Pharmacists are valuable sources of assistance regarding over-the-counter drugs. They can explain how a product works, its potential benefits and limitations, and possible side effects. Many over-the-counter drugs are contraindicated for use with certain other medications and health conditions. Consulting with health care professionals before over-the-counter drug use is an important safeguard against any potential health-impairing effects and should not be neglected. Always ask questions. It is better to be safe than to suffer an adverse drug reaction.

Those who are elderly or who suffer from specific medical conditions should consult with their physician for any special instructions for taking an over-the-counter drug. Children react differently to medications than do adults. If instructions are not provided for children, consult a pediatrician before administering any over-the-counter drug to a child. Incidentally, it is critical to keep all medications out of the reach of children and to purchase only drug products with child-resistant containers.

Pregnant females (as well as those who plan to become pregnant) need to be especially careful when considering taking over-the-counter drugs. Consult with a physician or pharmacist and carefully check labels for warnings about use during pregnancy before taking any medication. Realize also that some drugs can be passed from a mother to a baby through breast-feeding.

Reading Labels

It is wise to read product labels carefully and to follow directions explicitly. Only the prescribed dosage should be taken. Overdosages can lead to serious health problems. Users of a drug should heed any warnings on a label cautioning against driving or operating machinery while taking a specific drug. Taking a recommended dose of some medicines can impair coordination, make a user disoriented or drowsy, or affect judgment.

Most over-the-counter drugs warn users about possible side effects and how long a person should take the drug before seeing a physician for a particular condition. Side effects can occur from any drug. Not only can active ingredients cause adverse reactions, but so can flavoring, filler, stabilizer, or preservative agents included in products. Use should be discontinued immediately if any adverse reaction to a drug occurs. In such a case, a physician should be contacted. Two or more medications should not be taken simultaneously. Drinking alcohol in combination with many over-the-counter medications is particularly risky.

Product Tampering

In recent years, there have been episodes of over-the-counter drug tamperings. In the state of Washington, two people died after swallowing Sudafed capsules that were laced with cyanide (Cramer, 1991). In 1982, seven people died from taking Extra-Strength Tylenol capsules that were tampered with and laced with cyanide.

Cases such as these prompted the Food and Drug Administration to require tamper-resistant packaging on certain drug and cosmetic products (Fig. 10-2). However, not all products require tamper-resistant packaging. Dentrifices (toothpastes and mouthwashes), lozenges (cough drops), and products applied topically to the skin are notable exceptions to FDA regulations (Cramer, 1991).

Tamper-resistant packaging is not enough to insure the public's safety. Consumers should be alert to signs of tampering and learn to observe signs of tampering before they buy an over-the-counter drug product. In fact, in the case of the cyanide-laced Sudafed capsules that killed two people in Washington, there was plenty of evidence that the product had been tampered with. If the public is not educated about looking for signs of tampering, the public cannot be protected. Cramer (1991) cautions consumers

Figure 10-2
Over-the-Counter Drugs Are Available in Tamper-Resistant Packaging

That's the ultimate tamper-resistant drug package.

Better Safe Than Sorry

that before buying a product they should look for signs of tampering such as broken seals, puncture holes, open or torn boxes, and torn or missing wrappings. Once at home, medicines should be examined specifically for tampering. The label should be read for the product's tamper-evident features and those features should be evaluated. Any products that are discolored, have an unusual odor, or seem altered or suspicious in any way should be avoided. Any product that is suspected of being tampered with should be reported to the retailer where the purchase was made and/or to the local public health department.

BIBLIOGRAPHY

Carroll, C.R. (1993) *Drugs in Modern Society*. Dubuque, IA: Wm.C. Brown.

Cornacchia, H.J., & Barrett, S. (1993) *Consumer Health*. St. Louis, MO: Mosby.

Cramer, T. (1991) Look twice: How to protect yourself against drug tampering. *FDA Consumer*, October, 20–23.

Cramer, T. (1992) A burning question: When do you need an antacid? *FDA Consumer*, January–February, 19–22.

Cummings, M. (1991) Overuse hazardous: Laxatives rarely needed. *FDA Consumer*, April, 33–35.

Grogan, F.J. (1987) *The Pharmacist's Prescription: Your Complete Guide to the Over-the-Counter Remedies That Work Best*. New York: Rawson Associates.

Ray, O., & Ksir, C. (1993) *Drugs, Society, and Human Behavior*. St. Louis, MO: Times Mirror/Mosby.

Segal, M. (1991) Rx to OTC: The switch is on. *FDA Consumer*, March, 9–11.

Willis, J.L. (1991) Using over-the-counter medications wisely. *FDA Consumer*, November, 35–37.

PRESCRIPTION DRUGS

Unlike over-the-counter drugs (see Chapter 10), which are usually self-prescribed and self-administered, prescription drugs require the supervision of a physician or other trained health professional. **Prescription drugs** are drugs that can be legitimately obtained only by a prescription from licensed health professionals (e.g., physicians, podiatrists, dentists) and dispensed by registered pharmacists. Prescription drugs usually are more powerful than over-the-counter drugs and are more likely to cause adverse side effects. In this chapter, the discussion will include drug names, prescriptions and drug labels, using prescription drugs wisely, adverse reactions and interactions, prenatal exposure to prescription drugs, and prescription drug classes and actions.

DRUG NAMES

Prescription drugs are dispensed under either a brand name or a generic name. A **brand name** is a registered name or trademark given to a drug by a pharmaceutical company. A **generic name** is the chemical and/or biological equivalent of a specific brand name drug. A generic name usually is an abbreviated form of the chemical name of a drug. Generic means that a drug is not protected by trademark legislation. For example, many companies manufacture the generic tranquilizer drug diazepam. However, only the Roche company can sell diazepam under the brand name of Valium. Most brand names are capitalized and are created and registered by the manufacturer who owns the trademark. Brand names also are referred to as trade or proprietary names.

Some drugs are sold only under a brand name; many are sold under both generic and brand names. Sometimes a consumer can save money by obtaining a prescription for a generic drug rather than a brand name drug. The savings are often substantial, amounting to as much as 30 to 50 percent. Every state in the United States has a law that allows a pharmacist to fill a prescription with the least expensive equivalent drug product. However, this substitution often must be authorized by a physician before a pharmacist can dispense a generic equivalent for a prescription that specifies the trade name of a drug. In Ohio,

for example, the authorization is implied unless the physician indicates otherwise on the prescription.

In most cases, the bioequivalency of generic and brand names of a particular drug is similar. **Bioequivalency** refers to the ability of one drug to produce similar effects in the body as another drug. This is based on the amount of the drug and the speed by which a drug is absorbed and utilized by the body. The Food and Drug Administration proposes that in most cases there are no substantial differences in the bioequivalency or "therapeutic equivalency" (the way they behave in the body) between generic and trade drugs. However, for a few drugs, the difference may be substantial. Therefore, it is important that a physician or pharmacist advise about the relative advantages and disadvantages of the generic versions of drugs they prescribe. It is important for consumers to realize that because brand name drugs cost more than generic drugs, they bring higher profits to a drug manufacturer. Therefore, consumers should be wary of claims made by drug companies that generic drugs are not as safe or as effective as brand name drugs.

PRESCRIPTIONS AND DRUG LABELS

Detailed information for patients does not have to accompany most prescription drugs. In comparison to over-the-counter drugs, the labels of prescription drugs carry comparatively little information regarding the prescribed drug. The prescription form and patient package inserts will be discussed in this section of the chapter.

The Prescription Form

A **prescription** is a very precise order from a physician or other appropriate health professional to a pharmacist to dispense a certain drug product to a patient. Written on a preprinted form, the first word on the prescription is the name of the drug. Next, is the dosage form (e.g., liquid, capsules, tablets) and the strength (such as 100 mg, or milligrams). Next, the amount (such as 25 tablets or 10 fluid ounces) and directions for use are listed. These are often written by the prescribing physician in Latin abbreviations. For instance, ter in die, written t.i.d., means

135

three times a day. The prescription form also will indicate how many times the prescription can be refilled and if a generic drug may be substituted for a brand name drug.

The pharmacist will translate this information to the label of the drug container. Information that is likely to be on a prescription drug label is the name of the drug, a prescription number, directions for use, date the prescription was filled, and an expiration date. The label normally will also carry identifying information about the dispensing pharmacy, the prescribing health-care professional, and the patient's name, address, and phone number. Whether or not refills are allowable also is indicated on the label. Drugs with high-abuse potential must carry a warning stating that it is illegal to give or sell the drug to anyone other than the person to whom it is prescribed. For a few drugs, such as contraceptives and estrogens, the Food and Drug Administration requires that manufacturers include a leaflet or brochure about the benefits and risks of the products.

Patient Package Inserts

Patient package inserts (PPIs) are supplemental, informational brochures included in prescription drug packages that describe in easy-to-understand language the drug's actions, possible side effects, and interactions. In the early 1980s, Patricia Harris, Secretary for Health and Human Services, announced that PPIs would be required for several drugs. The intention of the Food and Drug Administration was to expand this requirement to include hundreds of different drugs with the passage of time. Unfortunately, drug companies were against the requiring of PPIs, saying that they would be too expensive to print and distribute. Pharmacists complained that stocking and handing out PPIs would be too much burden. What drug companies, pharmacists, and physicians most disliked about the requiring of PPIs was the exercise of authority by the FDA. By 1982, this requirement was cancelled. Today, the American Medical Association sponsors a voluntary program in which information sheets for more than 100 prescription drugs are available for distribution by pharmacists or physicians.

USING PRESCRIPTION DRUGS WISELY

Since each prescription is personalized for an individual's particular needs, it is essential to know as much as possible about the drug being taken. In this section, recommendations for effective use, questions to ask, and adverse reactions and interactions will be discussed.

Recommendations for Effective Use

The following recommendations are guidelines to assist a person in using prescription drugs safely and effectively.

1. If the drug is not accomplishing what it is supposed to for the user, the physician (or other health-care professional) who wrote the prescription should be consulted. A different dosage or a different drug may be prescribed.

2. If there is an unexpected symptom (e.g., a rash, nausea, dizziness, headache), it should be reported to the physician immediately.

3. The use of the drug should not be discontinued just because the user is feeling better. The drug should be used for the prescribed amount of time.

4. Drug labels should be checked for specific instructions or warnings, such as "do not take on an empty stomach" or "do not take with milk."

5. The label should provide any special information about storing the drug. Some drugs must be refrigerated; others must be protected from light.

6. Drugs should be kept out of the reach of children. Even though most prescription drugs come in child-proof containers, children sometimes can open the containers and swallow the contents. (Containers with regular caps can be requested.)

7. Only the person for whom the drug was prescribed should use the drug. Another person's symptoms may seem the same, but (s)he may be suffering from an entirely different problem.

8. The label should be checked each time (especially at night) to make sure the right drug is being taken.

9. Drugs should not be transferred from the original container. These containers are designed to protect the drugs. Fancy pill boxes are not always safe or suitable.

10. Prescription drugs that are no longer needed should be destroyed by flushing them down the toilet and the containers should be disposed of carefully so children can't get them.

11. A list of all drugs a person is taking should be shown to his/her physician and pharmacist.

12. If several different drugs are being taken and it is difficult for the user to remember when and how to take them, a pharmacist may be able to provide a checklist to assist the user.

13. A physician or other health-care professional should never be pressured to prescribe drugs that (s)he does not believe the user should take.

14. Drugs prescribed for one person should not be offered to another person without a physician's counsel.

Questions to Ask

The information on labels of prescription drugs is limited (Fig. 11-1). To get the best results from a drug, it may be necessary to ask the prescribing physician some direct questions such as the following:

1. What is the name of the drug? The user should write it down so s(he) won't forget.
2. What is the drug supposed to do? (Make the pain go away? Get to the cause of the pain? Reduce fever? Lower blood pressure? Cure infection?)
3. How much of the drug should be taken?
4. What side effects might occur?
5. How should the drug be taken? Does "three times a day" mean morning, noon, and night? Should it be taken before meals, with meals, or after meals? If the directions say "every six hours" does that mean getting up during the night to take the drug on time?
6. How long should the drug be taken? If the user stops taking the drug just because s(he) feels good, the symptoms and the disease may recur.

Figure 11-1

Questions to Ask Your Physician About Prescription Drugs

* What is the name of the medicine? Write it down so you won't forget.
* What is the medicine supposed to do? (Make the pain go away? Get to the cause of the pain? Reduce fever? Lower blood pressure? Cure infection?)
* How much of the medicine should be taken?
* What side effects might occur?
* How should you take the medicine? Does "three times a day" mean morning, noon, and night? Should you take it before meals, with meals, or after meals? If the directions say "every six hours," do you have to get up during the night to take the medicine on time?
* How long should you take the medicine? If you stop just because you feel good, the symptoms and the disease may recur.
* Are there other medicines you should not take while you are taking this one?
* Are there any foods, beverages, or activities you should avoid?
* Should you avoid alcoholic beverages while taking the drug?
* Can the prescription be refilled without an appointment or does the doctor need to see you again?
* What should you do if you miss or skip a dose?
* Is the drug available in generic form?
* Is there any written information available about the drug?
* How long should you wait before reporting to your physician if there are no changes in your symptoms?

7. Are there other medications that should not be taken while this particular drug is being taken?
8. Are there any foods, beverages (such as alcohol), or activities that should be avoided?
9. Can the prescription be refilled without another appointment with the prescribing physician?
10. What should be done if a dose is missed or skipped?
11. Is the drug available in generic form?
12. Is there any written information available on the drug?
13. How long should the user wait before reporting to his/her physician if the original symptoms remain?

Adverse Reactions and Interactions

Some drugs can cause side effects. Usually these are mild—a slight rash, mild headache, nausea or drowsiness. Sometimes the side effects are more severe—prolonged vomiting, bleeding, marked weakness, or impaired vision or hearing. These are warning signals that a drug is causing problems. When a reaction is unexpected or severe, a physician should be consulted immediately. Not everyone reacts the same way to medication. One person may experience a reaction to a certain drug, while another may have no problems at all.

Because of the potential for side effects and drug interactions, it is important for a user to tell his/her physician if (s)he:

1. has had any allergic reactions such as rashes or headaches to drugs or food;
2. is taking any medications such as contraceptives or insulin on a regular basis or if (s)he uses any non-prescription drugs on a routine basis;
3. is being treated for a different condition by another physician,
4. is pregnant or breast-feeding,
5. has diabetes, kidney, or liver disease,
6. is on a special diet or is taking vitamin and mineral supplements,
7. uses alcohol or tobacco.

Two or more drugs, taken at the same time, can interact and affect the way one or the other behaves in the body. For example, an antacid will cause a blood-thinning (anticoagulant) drug to be absorbed more slowly, while aspirin greatly increases the blood-thinning effect of such drugs.

Potentiation can occur. **Potentiation** is a greater-than-expected impact that can occur when two drugs with the same effect are taken together. Potentiation can be helpful, as when the antibiotic trimethoprim is used to boost the effect of another antibiotic, sulfamethoxazole, in com-

bating certain infections. Potentiation also can be dangerous, particularly when several central nervous system depressant drugs are involved. Even nonprescription drugs such as antihistamines that are often used to fight colds, can increase the sedative effects of anesthetics, barbiturates, tranquilizers, and some pain killers.

Food and drug interactions. Foods can interact with drugs, making them work faster or slower, or even preventing them from working at all. For example, fatty foods eaten before the antifungal drug griseofulvin is taken can cause the drug levels to rise markedly in the blood. Calcium in dairy products impairs absorption of tetracycline, a widely-used antibiotic. Citrus fruits or juices containing ascorbic acids speed the absorption of iron from iron supplements. Soda pop and fruit and vegetable juices with high acid contents (such as grape, apple, orange, or tomato) cause some drugs to dissolve in the stomach instead of in the intestine where they can be more readily absorbed. Large amounts of liver and leafy vegetables may hinder the effectiveness of anticoagulants because vitamin K in these foods promotes blood clotting.

The most hazardous food-drug interaction is that of foods containing the substance tyramine and drugs sometimes prescribed for severe depression or high blood pressure. The foods involved include aged cheese, Chianti wine, pickled herring, fermented sausages, yogurt, sour cream, chicken liver, broad beans, canned figs, bananas, avocados, and foods prepared with tenderizers. The drugs involved contain monoamine oxidase (MAO) inhibitors (see discussion of antidepressants in this chapter). Mixing the foods listed above with an MAO inhibitor drug can raise blood pressure to dangerous levels.

Food-drug interactions can also go the other way. Oral contraceptives, for instance, are known to lower blood levels of folic acid, a member of the vitamin B family, and vitamin B_6, although depletion usually is not serious enough to cause symptoms. Females who take birth control pills would be wise to include dark green leafy vegetables in their diet. Chronic use of antacids containing aluminum can cause phosphate depletion, leading to weakness, malaise, and loss of appetite.

Drugs and alcohol. Chronic use of alcohol can cause changes in the liver that speed up the metabolism of drugs such as anticonvulsants, anticoagulants, and diabetes drugs. They become less effective because they do not stay in the body as long as they should to be effective.

Prolonged alcohol abuse also can damage the liver so that it is less able to metabolize or process certain drugs. In this case, the drugs stay in the system too long. This is particularly serious when the drugs are phenothiazines (antipsychotic drugs), which can cause further liver damage.

Because alcohol is a central nervous system (CNS) depressant, alcohol taken with another CNS depressant drug can affect performance skills, judgment, and alertness. If the mixture includes overdoses of barbiturates, diazepam (Valium), or propoxyphene (Darvon), the result can be fatal. A person who has developed a tolerance to the sedative effects of alcohol may need larger doses of tranquilizers or sleeping pills to get the desired effect. This can lead to an overdose without a person's being aware of it. Similarly, alcoholics and persons with alcohol in their systems need larger amounts of anesthetics to induce sleep. Once a person is under the influence of alcohol, his or her sleep is deeper and lasts longer.

Drugs and tobacco. Females on birth control pills who smoke cigarettes have an increased risk of heart attack, stroke, blood clots, and other circulatory problems (Fig. 11-2). Nicotine and other tobacco constituents speed up the metabolism of theophylline, an asthma drug, and pentazocine, a pain killer, and to a lesser extent certain tranquilizers, analgesics and antidepressants. Thus, smokers may need larger than normal doses of these drugs. When these persons stop smoking, dosages of these drugs may have to be changed. Smoking also can affect certain diagnostic tests, such as red and white blood cell counts and blood-clotting time determinations.

PRENATAL EXPOSURE TO PRESCRIPTION DRUGS

It is especially important that pregnant females or lactating mothers should report and discuss with their physicians any medications they take, even if these substances have been previously prescribed for them. In this section of the chapter, the discussion will concern categories of pregnancies and risks to infants.

Categories of Pregnancies

The Food and Drug Administration requires manufacturers to describe and categorize what is known about each marketable drug's potential risks to a fetus in cases of various pregnancy categories, balanced against the drug's potential benefit to the patient. This information must be

Figure 11-2

Females Who Smoke Cigarettes and Use Oral Contraceptives Have an Increased Risk of Heart Disease

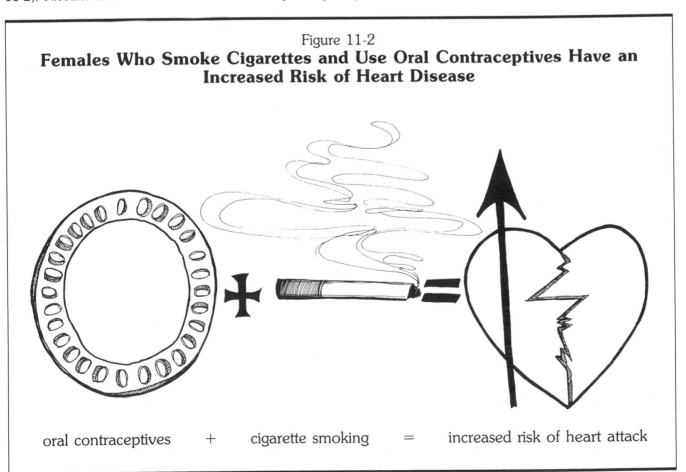

oral contraceptives   +   cigarette smoking   =   increased risk of heart attack

included in a special section of the product-labeling data. The *Physicians' Desk Reference* and several similar, annually-revised publications contain this information for most available drugs.

The pregnancy categories are:

A. <u>*Controlled studies show no risk.*</u> Adequate, well-controlled studies of pregnant females have failed to demonstrate risk to the fetus.

B. *No evidence of risk in humans.* Either animal findings show risk, but human findings do not or, if no adequate human studies have been done, animal findings are negative.

C. <u>*Risk cannot be ruled out.*</u> Human studies are lacking, and animal studies are either positive for fetal risk, or lacking as well. However, potential benefits may justify the potential risk.

D. <u>*Positive evidence for risk.*</u> Investigational or postmarketing data show risk for the fetus. Nevertheless, potential benefits may outweigh the potential risk.

E. *Contraindicated in pregnancy.* Studies in animals or humans or investigational or postmarketing reports have shown fetal risk that clearly outweighs any possible benefit to the patient.

Risks to Infants

Prescription drugs with well-established adverse effects on infants who have been prenatally exposed to them include the following:

- <u>*Accutane*</u> (isotretinoin)—an antiacne medication and vitamin: a derivative that is associated with such major abnormalities in prenatally-exposed babies as microcephalus (small head with severe retardation) and defects of the external ear and cardiovascular system.

- <u>*Antibiotics*</u>—including tetracycline and some sulfanilamides: tetracyclines used during the later half of pregnancy may cause permanent discoloration of a child's teeth.

- <u>*Antimigraine drugs*</u>—those containing ergotamine are not recommended for pregnant females and may cause reactions in nursing infants such as vomiting, diarrhea, weak pulse, and unstable blood pressure.

- <u>*Salicylates*</u>—including Bufferin, Anacin, Empirin, and other aspirin-containing medications, when taken by pregnant females at therapeutic doses close to term or prior to delivery, may cause bleeding in the mother, fetus, or the newborn infant. Regular use of aspirin in high doses during the last six months of pregnancy has been shown to prolong pregnancy and delivery. Aspirin is excreted in human breast milk in small amounts and

may cause metabolic acidosis or a rash or affect the blood.

- <u>*Anticonvulsants*</u>—such as Dilantin (phenytoin) and others have been associated with an increase in heart malformations, cleft lip and palate, microencephaly, mental deficiency, and impaired growth among prenatally exposed babies. Nevertheless, preventive treatment of the mother should not be discontinued during pregnancy, since there is a strong possibility that withdrawal may cause seizures, with resulting oxygen reduction and threat to the fetus. Phenytoin is excreted in low concentrations in human breast milk, and females taking this drug should not nurse.

- <u>*Hormones*</u>—birth control pills should not be taken during pregnancy (especially the first four months) as fetal exposure, even for brief periods, may increase the risk of congenital abnormalities, including heart and limb reduction defects. Exposure to some estrogens during fetal development has been shown to increase the risk for vaginal or cervical cancer among adolescent offspring. There also have been rare reports of breast enlargement in nursing infants exposed to contraceptive pills and of a decrease in the mother's milk production.

PRESCRIPTION DRUG CLASSES AND ACTIONS

There are thousands of prescription drugs available. Nearly 800 million new prescriptions and 800 million refills are filled annually for more than 2,500 different available medications. It is beyond the scope of this book to review all of these drugs. Rather, we will survey some of the important classes of prescription drugs and briefly mention some of the more commonly prescribed and used medications. Detailed information about specific drugs can easily be obtained from consulting a copy of the *Physicians' Desk Reference*. Another excellent resource book on prescription drugs is the 1992 edition of *The Essential Guide to Prescription Drugs* by James W. Long. Copies are available at most public libraries. The information that follows is primarily from these two sources. The discussion in this section of the chapter will cover antiinfectives, nonsteroidal antiinflammatory drugs (NSAIDs), anticonvulsants, gout medications, antihypertensives, lipid-lowering drugs, antiasthmatics, antidiabetic drugs, estrogens, migraine headache medications, antiulcer drugs, and antidepressants.

Antiinfectives

Antiinfectives are drugs that either eliminate or inactivate disease-causing pathogens in the body. The most frequently prescribed medications are antibiotic drugs.

Antibiotic drugs have the ability to inhibit or destroy bacterial growth. They are, however, ineffective in counteracting viruses. Antibiotics must be taken for specific periods of time to be fully effective. Discontinuing use prematurely may result in a relapse bacterial infection. Some bacterial microorganisms are resistant to certain antibiotics. Examples of antibiotics are penicillins, ampicillin, cephalosporins, and erythromycins.

Taking ampicillin or penicillin with milk or antacids can have a neutralizing effect on these antibiotics. Drinking fruit juices with penicillin can inactivate the drug in the stomach. There is much concern about allergic reactions to penicillin. Severe allergic reactions can result in death. Therefore, persons with allergic tendencies, such as eczema or hay fever, or who suspect they have an allergy to penicillin should mention this to their physicians before receiving any medications. As mentioned earlier, tetracycline has been linked to tooth discoloration in children when used by the child's mother during pregnancy.

Antivirals are drugs that are used to fight viral infections. Notable antiviral drugs are amantadine, trifluridine, and acyclovir. Amantadine, sold under the brand names of Symmetrel and Symadine, is an antiviral drug taken for the prevention and treatment of influenza type A viruses. Trifluridine (brand name Viroptic) is prescribed for the topical treatment of herpes infections in the eye. Trifluridine is too toxic to be used as an internal antiviral drug. Oral doses of acyclovir (Zovirax) do not cure herpes, but effectively treat initial episodes and manage recurring episodes of genital herpes. Acyclovir ointment also is available for the treatment and management of genital herpes. In addition to these antivirals that have been approved by the FDA, there are several that are to date only being used experimentally.

Nonsteroidal Antiinflammatory Drugs (NSAIDs)

Nonsteroidal antiinflammatory drugs (NSAIDs) are drugs that are prescribed for the treatment of inflammation associated with arthritis and other inflammatory diseases. Aspirin, as well as several prescription medications, are classified as NSAIDs. (Aspirin is discussed in Chapter 10). NSAIDs suppress the manufacture of prostaglandins in the body, thereby relieving the pain and inflammation associated with arthritis, sprains, and strains. However, prostaglandins also help protect the stomach from irritation from stomach acids. Therefore, NSAIDs often cause stomach ulceration and bleeding.

None of the NSAIDs are more effective antiinflammatory agents than aspirin, but some are better tolerated than aspirin by many people. Therapeutic effectiveness and side effects when taking particular NSAIDs vary greatly from person to person. All NSAIDs produce significant incidences of adverse side effects and reactions. The most serious are aplastic anemia, ulcers, liver and kidney damage, and visual disturbances. Nausea, stomach pain, diarrhea, headaches, fluid retention, skin rashes, allergic reactions, and ringing in the ears may occur. The following NSAIDs are available by prescription:
- indomethacin (Indocin),
- suldinac (Clinoril),
- tolmetin (Tolectin),
- fenoprofen (Nalfon),
- flurbiprofen (Ansaid),
- ibuprofen (Motrin, Rufen),
- ketaprofen (Orudis),
- naproxen (Naprosyn, Naxen),
- suprofen (Suprol),
- piroxicam (Feldene).

Anticonvulsants

Anticonvulsants are drugs that are used to control the symptoms of epilepsy, a disorder characterized by recurring seizures. These medications are helpful only in controlling and preventing seizures. They are not curative. The therapeutic effectiveness of anticonvulsant medications is highly variable from person to person, making the choice of the appropriate medication, dosage, and schedule difficult for prescribing physicians. All anticonvulsants produce toxic effects in high doses and the abrupt withdrawal of these drugs can cause status epilepticus. **Status epilepticus** is a prolonged period of continuous seizures without interruption. Attempts to discontinue anticonvulsants should be done over several months under the supervision of a physician. There also is evidence that certain anticonvulsants may cause birth defects (see the previous section in this chapter on prenatal exposure to prescription drugs). Some of the drugs that are used as anticonvulsants are:
- phenytoin (Dilantin),
- phenobarbital (Luminal),
- carbamazepine (Tegretol),
- primidone (Mysoline),
- ethosuximide (Zarontin),
- valproic acid (Depakene),
- clonezepam (Clonopin).

Gout Medications

Gout or **gouty arthritis** is an inflammatory disease caused by excessive uric acid production. Excessive uric acid in the body causes swelling and pain in the joints and toes. Three drugs are prescribed for reducing levels of uric acid in the blood and tissues: allopurinol (Lopurin, Zyloprim), probenecid (Benemid), colchicine (Colabid, Verban), and sulfinpyrazone (Anturane). Treatment with these drugs is long-term, usually for the life of the patient.

Antihypertensives

Antihypertensives are drugs that counteract or reduce high blood pressure. There are several classes of antihypertensive drugs. **Diuretics** lower blood pressure by promoting the loss of water and salt from the body. A major limitation of a class of diuretic drugs known as the thiazide diuretics is that they deplete potassium levels in the body. Therefore, this depletion often should be compensated by including potassium-rich foods (e.g., orange juice, bananas, apricots) and/or a potassium supplement in the diet.

Beta-blockers are drugs that block certain actions of the sympathetic nervous system, slow the heart rate, and lower blood pressure. **Vasodilators** are drugs that lower blood pressure by causing the blood vessels to dilate, or widen. **Calcium channel blockers** are drugs that inhibit the contraction of the coronary arteries and peripheral arterioles by blocking the normal passage of calcium through vessel walls. This results in blood vessel relaxation and the consequent lowering of blood pressure.

Angiotensin converting enzyme (ACE) inhibitors are drugs that are believed to lower blood pressure by blocking enzyme systems that influence arterial function. These drugs cause the relaxation of arteries thus lowering resistance to blood flow. Other drugs are centrally-acting drugs. **Centrally-acting drugs** lower blood pressure by decreasing the activity of the vasomotor center in the brain. **Peripherally-acting drugs** act directly on peripheral blood vessels. Listed below are several commonly used antihypertensive drugs according to class:

1. Diuretics:
   - thiazides (Anhydron, Duretic, Hydrazide, Oretic),
   - chlorthalidone (Hygroton),
   - quinethazone (Hydromox),
   - metolazone (Diulo, Zaroxolyn),
   - indapamide (Lozol),
   - bumetanide (Bumex),
   - furosemide (Lasix),
   - amiloride (Midamor),
   - triamterene (Dyrenium).

2. Beta-Blockers:
   - acebutolol (Sectral),
   - atenolol (Tenormin),
   - betaxolol (Kerlone),
   - lavetolol (Normodyne, Trandate),
   - metoprolol (Lopressor),
   - nadolol (Corgard),
   - penbutol (Levatol),
   - pindolol (Visken),
   - propranolol (Inderal),
   - timolol (Blocadren),
   - doxazosin (Cardura),
   - prazosin (Minipres).

3. Direct Vasodilators:
   - hydralazine (Apresoline),
   - minoxidil (Loniten).

4. Calcium Channel Blockers:
   - diltiazem (Cardizem),
   - isradipine (DynaCirc),
   - nicardipine (Cardene),
   - nifedipine (Procardia),
   - verapamil (Calan, Isoptin).

5. Angiotensin Converting Enzyme (ACE) Inhibitors:
   - captopril (Capoten),
   - enalapril (Vasotec),
   - lisinopril (Prinivil, Zestril),
   - ramipril (Altrace).

6. Centrally-Acting Drugs:
   - clonidine (Catapres),
   - guanabenz (Wytensin),
   - guanfacine (Tenex),
   - methyldopa (Aldomet).

7. Other Peripherally-Acting Drugs:
   - guanadrel (Hylorel),
   - guanethidine (Ismelin),
   - reserpine (Serpasil).

Lipid-Lowering Drugs

Lipid-lowering drugs reduce the amount of blood fats (lipids) such as cholesterol and triglycerides. These blood fats combine with proteins in the blood to form lipoproteins. **Lipoproteins** carry cholesterol and triglycerides throughout the circulating bloodstream. Drugs such as niacin (Nicotinic acid, Nicobid, Nicotinex) and lovastatin (Mevacor) lower lipid levels by inhibiting cholesterol production and lipoprotein formation. Lovastatin is better tolerated than many other lipid-lowering agents that are currently available. However, the long-term effects are not presently understood. Cholestyramine (Questran), colestipol (Colestid), and probucol (Lorelco) work effectively by hastening the breakdown and elimination of lipoproteins. On the negative side, cholestyramine and colestipol cause severe constipation in one out of five persons who take the drug and also decrease the ability of the body to absorb many other drugs and some nutrients. Probucol often is not a drug of choice because it reduces high-density lipoproteins, which are associated with low heart disease risk. Probucol also has a high frequency of adverse effects such as anemia and diarrhea. A final class of lipid-lowering drugs work by accelerating the removal of lipoproteins in the bloodstream. Drugs in this class are gemfibrozil (Lopid) and clofibrate (Atromid-S). The usefulness of gemfibrozil is limited by its potential for such significant adverse effects as gallstone formation, decreased white blood cell formation, and reduced sex drive in males.

Antiasthmatics

Antiasthmatic drugs work by widening constricted respiratory airways (bronchioles) to relieve breathing difficulty. Commonly- prescribed oral antiasthmatics are theophylline (Bronkodyl, Slo-bid, Theo-Dur), aminophylline (Aminophyllin, Aminodur), and oxtriphylline (Brondecon, Choledyl). Aerosol bronchodilators are pressurized inhalers and include albuterol (Proventril, Ventolin), metaproterenol (Alupent, Metaprel), pirbuterol (Maxair), isoetharine (Bronkometer, Bronkosol), and isoproterenol (Isuprel, Medihaler). Severe acute and chronic asthma that is not controlled by conventional antiasthmatic drugs is sometimes treated by cortisone-like steroids such as beclomethasone aerosol (Beclovent, Vanceril), prednisolone (Delta-Cortef, Sterane), and prednisone (Deltasone, Meticorten). Cortisone-like steroid medications do not directly produce bronchodilation (widening of airways). The primary mechanism by which these drugs function is by reducing inflammation, which is a primary cause of asthma exacerbations.

Antidiabetic Drugs

Persons with Type I diabetes mellitus or insulin-dependent diabetes (IDDM) are characterized by the inability to produce enough insulin. As a result, Type I diabetics must rely on injections of insulin to control their diabetes. **Insulin** is a hormone produced in the pancreas that regulates the level of sugar in the blood and the metabolism of carbohydrates and fats. Insulin facilitates the transport of sugar through cell walls into cells where the sugar can be utilized as fuel for energy. Insulin must be taken to maintain life in Type I diabetics. Use must be carefully regulated because of the potential of insulin to produce serious hypoglycemic (low blood sugar) reactions.

About 85 percent of all diabetics have Type II diabetes mellitus or non-insulin-dependent diabetes mellitus (NIDDM). Type II diabetics often produce normal or partially-reduced amounts of insulin. However, their diabetes is the result of the resistance of body tissues to the insulin they produce. The primary treatment for this form of diabetes is dietary management. In fact, about 75 percent of Type II diabetics can control their condition by diet alone.

When satisfactory control is not achieved by diet alone, oral antidiabetic drugs may be prescribed. **Oral hypoglycemic drugs**, known as the sulfonylureas, are drugs that stimulate the pancreas to secrete more insulin and enhance the utilization of insulin in body tissues. The use of these drugs must be carefully monitored because of their potential to cause hypoglycemia. Commonly used sulfonylureas are:

- acetohexamide (Dymelor),
- chlorpropamide (Diabinese),
- glipizide (Glucotrol),
- glyburide (Diabeta, Micronase),
- tolazamide (Tolinase),
- tolbutamide (Orinase).

Estrogens

Estrogens primarily are prescribed for the treatment of symptoms associated with menopause (i.e., hot flashes, night sweats), postmenopausal atrophy of the genital tissues, and osteoporosis. Estrogens also are used as oral contraceptives. Ovarian failure or removal in younger females and sometimes breast or prostate cancers are treated with estrogen drugs. Estrogens are available in the form of capsules, tablets, vaginal creams, and transdermal patches. Estrogens also are available as combination drug products with mild tranquilizers such as chlordiazepoxide (Librium) and meprobamate (Equanil, Miltown).

There are serious concerns about the use of estrogens among females who smoke cigarettes. Studies have shown that females who smoke more than 15 cigarettes daily in conjunction with estrogen-containing oral contraceptives show increased risk of heart attack. Females who use long-term estrogens should be advised to avoid smoking cigarettes.

Many studies have shown that the long-term use of estrogens (three or more years) increase the risk of cancer of the lining of the uterus (endometrial cancer). Other potentially serious adverse effects include emotional depression, gallstones, liver tumors, uterine fibroid tumors, increased blood pressure, fluid retention, postmenopausal bleeding, and clot formation in the lungs, brain, eye vessels, or coronary arteries. Estrogens taken during pregnancy increase the risk of vaginal or cervical cancer in female offspring. The concurrent use of estrogens alters the effectiveness of many medications.

Migraine Headache Medications

Ergotamine, a vasoconstrictor, is the most effective migraine headache relief medication if taken early during an attack. It is much less effective if taken later. This drug may work by constricting blood vessels in the head thus relieving headaches that are caused by expanded or dilated vessels in the head. Ergotamine medications often are combined with caffeine, which is believed to enhance its absorption. Oral ergotamine preparations are Cafergot and Wigraine. Ergotamine preparations also are available in rectal, sublingual, and inhalant forms. The frequent use of ergotamine should be avoided because it can lead to dependence. Long-term use can cause chronic migraine-like headaches.

Isometheptene (Midrin) is a safer drug than ergotamine and is better tolerated by most persons. Many physicians recommend its use as the first choice in migraine headache therapy. If it is found to be not effective for an individual patient, a stronger drug is often recommended. Other drugs to be considered for relief are aspirin and other nonsteroidal antiinflammatory drugs (NSAIDs) as well as opiod analgesics such as codeine and meperidine (Demerol). Metoclopramide (Reglan) is now available to migraine headache suffers to take with migraine headache relief medications. This drug reduces nausea and vomiting that sometimes accompany the use of relief medications and even enhances the effectiveness of such medications.

Persons who experience three or more migraine headaches a month or who suffer from severe, prolonged migraines may need to consider the use of preventive drugs on a continual basis. Beta-blockers (see section on antihypertensives) are the first choice for long-term preventive management of migraine headache attacks. Propranolol (Inderal) is the most widely-used drug choice for prevention of migraine headaches; nadolol (Corgard) also is frequently used. Beta-blockers used in this manner often can be discontinued or dosages greatly reduced by patients who have achieved headache control. Other choices for the preventive treatment of migraine headaches are: calcium channel blockers such as verapamil (Calan, Isoptin) and nifedipine; antidepressants such as amitriptyline (Elavil, Endep) and desipramine (Norpramin, Pertofrane); lithium; nonsteroidal antiinflammatory drugs (NSAIDs); and methysergide (Sansert). However, the formation of scar tissue in the heart, lungs, blood vessels, and kidneys is associated with the long-term use of methysergide.

Antiulcer Drugs

Ulcers occur when individuals produce excessive amounts of digestive acids or when they have inadequate protection against acid in the tissues that line the stomach and small intestine. Antiulcer drugs are taken to relieve the pain associated with ulcers and to promote healing. **Histamine (H-2)-blocking drugs** work by suppressing the production of excess stomach acid, which is the result of histamine stimulation. Cimetidine (Tagamet) and ranitidine (Zantac) are examples of histamine-blocking antiulcer drugs. Shortly after its appearance on the pharmaceutical drug market in the early 1980s, cimetidine was the single most widely-used of all prescription drugs in the U.S. for a few years. A newer histamine-blocking agent, ranitidine, is better tolerated by most persons and causes less adverse reactions than cimetidine. Many patients find it a convenient drug because it has to be taken only once a day. Another frequently-used antiulcer drug is sucralfate (Carafate), which is believed to form protective coatings over ulcer sites. Sucralfate also may stimulate the healing of ulcers. In terms of effectiveness, this drug is comparable to the histamine blockers.

Antidepressants

Antidepressants are drugs that are used for the treatment of depression. A great variety of these drugs is available. Fluoxetine (Prozac) is believed to relieve depression by slowly restoring levels of the neurotransmitter serotonin in the brain. The restoration of serotonin appears to facilitate nerve impulses. There have been some well-publicized reports that Prozac may create intense suicidal preoccupation in some persons treated with the drug. These reports seem to have been greatly exaggerated in view of the fact that the development or intensification of suicidal thoughts has been documented for several other antidepressant drugs that are widely used. Further, there are several reports of persons who became suicidal while taking other antidepressants. However, when they were switched to Prozac, they experienced an end to preoccupation about suicide and relief for their depressive illness. Because of this, Prozac is suitable for the treatment of major depressive illnesses that have not responded well to other therapies and drug treatments. Prozac is not suitable for the treatment of mild or reactive depression.

The first choice of drug therapy for depression is often the use of a tricyclic antidepressant drug. **Tricyclic antidepressant drugs** relieve depression in some patients by gradually restoring norepinephrine and serotonin in the brain to normal levels. The restoration of these neurotransmitters allows nerve cells to transmit impulses without interruption. The drugs that comprise this class of antidepressants are 60 to 75 percent effective in treating major depression. They may cause drowsiness, particularly during the first weeks of use, and may interact synergistically with alcohol. The abrupt discontinuation of these drugs can cause headaches, anxiety, restlessness, insomnia, muscle aches, and nausea. Therefore, withdrawal should be gradual and under the guidance of a physician. The following drugs are classified as tricyclic antidepressants:
• amitriptyline (Elavil, Endep),
• amoxapine (Asendin),
• desipramine (Norpramin, Pertofrane),
• doxepin (Adapin, Sinequan),
• imipramine (Imavate, Presamine, Tofranil),
• nortripyline (Aventyl, Pamelor),
• protriptyline (Vivactil).

For depressive illnesses that do not respond to tricyclic antidepressants, monoamine oxidase inhibitors are often prescribed. **Monoamine oxidase inhibitors (MAOIs)** are believed to relieve depression by blocking actions of an enzyme (monoamine oxidase type A) in the brain. By inhibiting this enzyme, MAOIs cause levels of certain neurotransmitters to rise in brain tissue, allowing a depressed individual to maintain normal mood and emotional stability.

Those who have been prescribed MAOIs should be careful not to take over-the-counter cold and allergy medications, nose drops, or diet pills. Unfortunately, many drugs and foods can cause adverse interactions with MAOIs. Foods and beverages that contain tyramine should be avoided because its combination with an MAOI can dangerously elevate blood pressure. Chianti and sherry wine, vermouth, and unpasteurized beers are alcoholic drinks that contain tyramine. Some of the foods that contain tyramine include: salami, sour cream, soy sauce, meat tenderizers, raisins, raspberries, meat extracts, pepperoni, herring, liver (particularly if not fresh), canned fish, bologna, and aged cheeses. Commonly prescribed MAOIs are phenelzine (Nardil) and tranylcypromine (Parnate). A variety of other drugs are used to treat depressive illnesses. These include:
• lithium (Eskalith, Lithane, Lithobid, Lithotab),
• methylphenidate (Ritalin),
• trazodone (Desyrel),
• alprazolam (Xanax),
• maprotiline (Ludiomil),
• amoxapine (Asendin).

BIBLIOGRAPHY

Some of the material in this chapter has been adapted from the following government publications:

Office for Substance Abuse Prevention. (1990) *Alcohol, Tobacco, and Other Drugs May Harm the Unborn.* DHHS Publication No. (ADM)90-1711.

U.S Department of Health and Human Services. (1989) *Here Are Some Things You Should Know About Prescription Drugs.* DHHS Publication No. (FDA)89-3124.

ANABOLIC STEROIDS

Steroids are drugs derived from hormones. Testosterone, the major male sex hormone, affects the developing male in two ways: anabolic effects and androgenic effects. **Anabolic steroids** are powerful, synthetic derivatives of testosterone that produce muscle growth by stimulating protein synthesis. The androgenic effect is reflected in the expression of male sexual characteristics. The androgenic effects of steroids include deepening of the voice, growth of facial and body hair, growth of male sex organs, and increase in aggressiveness. In this chapter, the term steroid will be used in connection with the use of anabolic steroids. Anabolic steroids are considered to be ergogenic drugs. **Ergogenic drugs** are drugs that are used to improve athletic performance. The use of anabolic steroids is banned from Olympic athletic events as well as several other athletic events (Kokotailo & Landry, 1992).

In recent years, there have been several revelations of prominent athletes using steroids. Olympic sprinter Ben Johnson was stripped of his gold medal after it was determined that he had used steroids. Former football great, Lyle Alzado, admitted that he frequently used steroids to "bulk up" for professional football. Before his death in 1992, he attributed the brain cancer that killed him to his use of steroids.

Steroid use is not limited to famous athletes. An increasing number of teenagers are using steroids. Although steroids often are taken to improve performance in sports, teenagers are especially drawn to these substances in an effort to enhance their self-image by improving their physiques. Steroid use poses serious hazards to teenagers and others who choose to use them. This chapter will describe the extent of steroid use, the effects of steroid use, and ways of deterring steroid use.

STEROID USE

There are several types of available steroids, with varying combinations of anabolic and androgenic properties. These compounds are often designed chemically to diminish the androgenic or masculinization effects of steroids, while amplifying the potential for anabolic action.

Scientific research has not demonstrated that anabolic steroids increase physical performance. Yet, it is clear that steroids can produce significant increases in lean muscle mass, strength, and muscular endurance when taken in conjunction with physical training and a high-protein and high-calorie diet (American Medical Association Council on Scientific Affairs, 1990). There is some evidence that steroids can lead to more frequent muscular training by shortening recovery time. The ability to train more intensely with shortened recovery periods appears to contribute to the increased frequency of training (Cornacchia & Barrett, 1993).

Steroid use does not appear to benefit cardiorespiratory endurance or agility. Some athletes maintain that anabolic steroids are helpful in speeding recovery from injuries. However, this remains to be scientifically proven. The discussion in this section of the chapter will include medical uses, prevalence of steroid use, sources of steroids, reasons for taking steroids, and patterns of use.

Medical Uses

There are a few legitimate medical uses for which physicians prescribe anabolic steroids to patients. The Food and Drug Administration (FDA) has approved the use of selected anabolic steroids for treating the following conditions (American Medical Association Council on Scientific Affairs, 1990; Payne, Hahn, & Pinger, 1991):

- certain types of anemia,
- some breast cancers,
- osteoporosis,
- severe burns,
- congenital or acquired testosterone deficiency,
- endometriosis,
- hereditary angioedema (a rare disease that causes swelling of various parts of the body).

Although there are claims of anabolic steroid use improving appetite and healing after surgery, the FDA does not approve of such uses.

147

Prevalence of Steroid Use

There is substantial evidence that steroid use appears to be on the increase. A National Institute of Drug Abuse survey showed that 3 percent of high school students reported using steroids at some time in their lives—5 percent of males and 0.5 percent of females. Steroids were used by almost as many students as crack cocaine and by more students than PCP (National Institute on Drug Abuse, 1991). Another study estimated that 5–11 percent of teenage males and 0.5–2.5 percent of teenage females in grades 7–12 have used steroids (Cowart, 1990).

Use among college females also appears to have increased. In a survey of universities in 1984, steroids were reported by females in only one sport—swimming. Four years later, steroid use also was reported by females participating in track and field and basketball (National Institute on Drug Abuse, 1991).

The extent of steroid use among adult or professional athletes has not been well documented. However, there is ample anecdotal evidence supporting wide popularity among football players, weight lifters, wrestlers, and track and field and other athletes.

Sources of Steroids

A major source of anabolic steroids is a highly-organized black market distribution that adds up to millions of dollars in sales each year. Anabolic steroids sold through black markets are frequently produced overseas and smuggled into the United States. Another source is "underground" laboratories in the U.S. Steroids from either of these sources often lack the manufacturing controls of legal pharmaceuticals produced in the U.S. As a result, these steroids carry elevated risks of damaging health because they contain harmful impurities, are improperly formulated, or are mislabeled.

Steroids produced by U.S. pharmaceutical companies sometimes find their way into black markets. This occurs primarily through fraudulent prescriptions and theft of prescriptions. However, increased law enforcement efforts are believed to have decreased the availability of the diversion of legal steroid pharmaceuticals into the black market. These factors are reportedly leading an increasing number of steroid users to legitimate veterinary drugs—alleged to be more effective and cheaper (McConnell, 1991).

Sales of steroids are made in various settings—gyms, health clubs, on campuses, and through the mail. Users report that suppliers may be drug dealers or trainers, physicians, pharmacists, or friends. It is not difficult for users to buy steroids or to learn how to use them. Many users rely on an underground manual on steroids that circulates around the country (NIDA, 1991).

Reasons for Taking Steroids

The primary reason cited by adolescents for taking steroids is to gain an enhanced physical appearance. Achieving positive self-esteem is desired by most people, both adolescents and adults. Although there are many factors that contribute to one's sense of self-esteem during childhood and adolescence, physical appearance has become a prominent factor in today's society. Steroids appeal to young people because they are seen as the pathway to acquiring a more muscular body.

It is difficult to categorize the young people who use steroids: they come from all walks of life. The common link among them is the desire to look, perform, and feel better—almost at any cost. Steroid users, especially young users, are apt to ignore or deny warnings about health risks. If they see friends growing taller and stronger on steroids, they seek the same benefits. They want to believe in the power of the drug.

Some young people maintain the perception that the capacity for athletic success is not achievable without the use of steroids. Weight lifters and body builders are especially attracted to steroids. Weight lifters use steroids to enhance strength and thereby perform better. Body builders, who are judged by muscle size, shape, definition, and symmetry also see a direct correlation between the use of anabolic steroids and success. Participants in the weight events in track and field (hammer, shot put, discus, and javelin) are another group in which steroid use is frequently reported because of the importance of muscular strength in these events. Steroid use also is prominent among football players, sprinters, and swimmers.

Patterns of Use

Anabolic steroids are usually taken in pill form: some that cannot be absorbed orally are taken by injection. The usual prescribed daily dose for medical purposes usually averages between one and five milligrams. On the other hand, some athletes may take up to hundreds of milligrams a day, far exceeding medically-recommended dosages (NIDA, 1991).

Operating on the erroneous more-is-better theory, some athletes indulge in a practice called "stacking." **Stacking** refers to the practice of taking many types of steroids, sometimes in combination with other drugs prior to an athletic event. Many users "cycle," taking steroids for six to twelve weeks or more, then stopping for several weeks before starting another cycle. This may be done in the belief that by scheduling steroid intake, test results can be manipulated and detection avoided. It is not uncommon for athletes to cycle over a period of months or even years (NIDA, 1991).

EFFECTS OF STEROID USE

Steroids pose a special concern for adolescents. Anabolic steroids can halt growth prematurely in adolescents. Because even small doses can irreversibly affect growth, steroids are rarely prescribed for children and young adults, and only for the severely ill. General effects, sexual effects, and steroid dependency will be discussed in this section of the chapter.

Health Effects

Controlled studies on the long-term outcomes of mega-dosing (taking large amounts of steroids) have not been conducted. Extensive research on prescribed doses for medical use has documented the potential side effects of the drug, even when taken in small doses. Reports by athletes and observations of attending physicians, parents, and coaches offer substantial evidence of dangerous side effects. Some effects, such as rapid weight gain, are easy to see. Some effects take place internally and may not be evident until it is too late. Some effects are irreversible (Hough & Kovan, 1990; NIDA, 1991).

For both males and females, continued use of anabolic steroids may lead to health conditions ranging from merely irritating to life threatening (Fig. 12-1). Some effects are:
• acne,
• jaundice,
• trembling,
• swelling of feet or ankles,
• bad breath,
• reduction in HDL, the "good cholesterol,"
• high blood pressure,
• liver damage and cancers,
• aching joints,
• increased chance of injury to tendons.

Persons sometimes take injections of anabolic steroids to augment oral dosages, using large-gauge, reusable needles normally obtained through the black market. If needles are shared, users run the risk of transmitting or contracting HIV infection that can lead to AIDS (Scott, 1989).

Scientists are just beginning to investigate the impact of anabolic steroids on the mind and behavior. Many athletes report "feeling good" about themselves while on a steroid regimen. The downside, according to researchers, is wide mood swings ranging from periods of violent, even homicidal, episodes known as "roid rages" to bouts of depression when the drugs are stopped. Anabolic steroid users also may suffer from paranoid jealousy, extreme irritability, delusions, and impaired judgment stemming from feelings of invincibility.

Sexual Effects

Males who take large doses of anabolic steroids typically experience changes in sexual characteristics. Although derived from a male sex hormone, steroids can trigger a mechanism in the body that can actually shut down the healthy functioning of the male reproductive system. Some possible side effects are:
• shrinking of the testicles,
• reduced sperm count,
• impotence,
• baldness,
• difficulty or pain in urinating,
• development of breasts,
• enlarged prostate.

Females may experience "masculinization" as well as other changes:
• growth of facial hair,
• changes in or cessation of the menstrual cycle,
• enlargement of the clitoris,
• deepened voice,
• breast reduction.

Steroid Dependency

Research studies strongly suggest that the high-dosage, long-term use of steroids may result in addiction (Doweiko, 1993). Steroid users often describe a euphoric state produced by anabolic steroids. Users also claim that steroids function to anesthetize the body. Steroids enable the user to work out intensely without feeling pain. However, when the user stops taking steroids, muscles and especially joints become very sore. Old injuries or strains that were not even noticed before begin to be very painful. The ex-user cannot work out at or near the level (s)he did while taking steroids. It is just too painful and (s)he feels depressed (Fig. 12-2). If the user returns to steroids, the pain disappears, the depression disappears, and the body feels good again. (S)he can resume a full workout regimen.

Figure 12-1
Continued Use of Anabolic Steroids Poses Serious Health Consequences for Males and Females

Health consequences of steroid use:

* Acne
* Jaundice
* Trembling
* Swelling of feet or ankles
* Bad breath
* Reduction in HDLs
* High blood pressure
* Liver damage and cancers
* Aching joints
* Increased chance of injury to tendons

Some users say that feelings of power become so associated with steroid use that they begin to use steroids for social situations in which they feel insecure. For example, adolescents may take steroids before going to a party because they feel nervous, and the steroids give them a sense of being able to handle the situation. In these cases, the drugs address basic feelings of inadequacy.

The culture of the gym itself seems to perpetuate steroid use. The gym culture is very competitive and body build-

Figure 12-2
Discontinuing the Use of Steroids Can Result in Depression

ers are always comparing themselves to others. Those who are developing larger and stronger physiques may feel puny and weak next to someone else who is progressing at a faster rate. In some gyms, the peer pressure to use steroids is very strong.

There is evidence that steroid abuse is sometimes associated with a withdrawal syndrome that is similar to stimulant addiction (Doweiko, 1993). Steroid withdrawal symptoms include (Bower, 1991; Brower et al., 1991; Hough & Kovan, 1990):

- depression and sometimes suicide attempt,
- loss of appetite,
- difficulty sleeping,
- tiredness,
- anxiety and restlessness,
- decreased sexual drive.

DETERRING STEROID USE

Deterring steroid use requires the concerted involvement of many in a community—teachers, coaches, students, parents, law enforcement, media, drug treatment specialists, and medical practitioners. There are several avenues that can be taken to deter steroid use. These include testing, treatment, legislation, and education.

Testing

Testing for steroids is an important step in deterring steroid use among athletes. Currently, many sports associations ban the use of steroids and some have instituted testing programs as part of this enforcement. Testing for steroids is controversial because of the inability of testing programs to accurately detect steroid use. "Masking agents" that help prevent the detection of steroids have come into use. Athletes also are becoming more proficient in timing their use of steroids with the times they are to be tested. Careful scheduling of steroid use before testing periods allows athletes to prevent detection despite using steroids. Despite its shortcomings, testing remains an important strategy in deterring steroid use among athletes. Scientists are working hard to develop more accurate tests for steroids and sports associations are striving to develop more effective testing programs for athletes.

In *Drugs in Modern Society*, (Carroll, 1993) states the following information concerning testing:

The National Football League now includes steroids when testing for drug abuse among its players. The National Collegiate Athletic Conference now tests for both anabolic steroids and chemical "masking agents" that are sometimes taken in an attempt to cover up steroid use. Under new drug-testing measures, first-time offenders could lose an entire year's playing eligibility. Players testing positive for steroids a second time will be banned for life. (p. 46)

Treatment

Because of the high prevalence of steroid use, the need for available treatment services for steroid abuse is increasing. At the present time, little is known about how to best treat steroid abuse. Health professionals are still learning how to best deal with persons who abuse steroids.

The first step in treatment after steroid abuse has been identified is medical supervision and monitoring of detoxification to limit the impact of withdrawal. Most medical problems abate after use is discontinued. However, some side effects may be permanent and require medical intervention (Doweiko, 1993). Because there is evidence of the addictive nature of anabolic steroids, most treatment programs center around the techniques used in traditional substance-abuse treatment programs. Counseling should focus on the self-esteem issues of steroid users and retraining them to accept themselves without resorting to steroids as "crutches." Nutritional counseling also is encouraged so that users can learn how to enhance their physical body without steroids. Support groups also have been shown to be effective in treating steroid abuse (Doweiko, 1993).

Legislation

The distribution or possession of anabolic steroids for nonmedical reasons is a federal offense as a result of the 1988 Anti-Drug Abuse Act. The distribution of anabolic steroids to minors constitutes an offense that may result in being sent to prison. In 1990, legislation was passed by Congress that classified anabolic steroids as a controlled substance. The reclassification of steroids as a Schedule III controlled substance resulted in stricter penalties for those who traffic and use steroids. This law also imposes strict production and record-keeping regulations on pharmaceutical companies that produce steroids as a means of reducing the diversion of steroids onto the black market (NIDA, 1991). As a result of this legislation, enforcement jurisdiction was shifted from the Food and Drug Administration to the Drug Enforcement Administration (Dusek & Girdano, 1993). In addition to federal legislation, a majority of states have passed regulations and laws controlling the abuse of steroids. Other states are considering legislation to control steroid use and abuse.

Education

It is essential that steroid education about steroids is included in any drug education curriculum. Students and educators alike need to recognize that the hazards and risks associated with steroid use are serious and real. Classroom presentations and discussions of these risks are essential. And this is only the beginning. Educators need to recognize that the motives that youth have for taking steroids (e.g., desire to achieve a desirable physical appearance, wanting to improve athletic performance) are powerful reinforcers of behavior. Drug education efforts should assist students in learning to evaluate present motivations regarding steroid use with long-term consequences. This is a challenge for the classroom teacher because adolescents often perceive themselves as immortal and often have difficulty anticipating future consequences. Drug education efforts also should include educating coaches, athletic trainers, parents, and medical practitioners about the hazards that steroids pose, the reasons young people take steroids, and how to recognize steroid abuse.

BIBLIOGRAPHY

American Medical Association Council on Scientific Affairs. (1990) Medical and nonmedical uses of anabolic-androgenic steroids. *Journal of the American Medical Association*, 264:2923–2927.

Bower, B. (1991) Pumped up and strung out. *Science News*, 140:30–31.

Brower, K.J., Blow, F.C., Young, J.P, & Hill, E.M. (1991) Symptoms and correlates of anabolic-androgenic steroid dependence. *British Journal of Addiction*, 86:759–768.

Carroll, C.R. (1993) *Drugs in Modern Society*. Madison,

WI: Brown & Benchmark.

Cornacchia, H.J., & Barrett, S. (1993) *Consumer Health: A Guide to Intelligent Decisions* (5th edition). St. Louis, MO: Mosby.

Cowart, V.S. (1990) Blunting "steroid epidemic" requires alternatives, innovative education. *Journal of the American Medical Association*, 264:1641.

Doweiko, H.E. (1993) *Concepts of Chemical Dependency* (second edition). Belmont, CA: Wadsworth.

Dusek, D., & Girdano, D. (1993) *Drugs: A Factual Account* (fifth edition). New York: McGraw-Hill.

Hough, D.O., & Kovan, J.R. (1990) Is your patient a steroid abuser? *Medical Aspects of Human Sexuality,* 24:24–32.

Kokotailo, P.K., & Landry, G.L. (1992) Drugs in sport. In M.F. & K.L. Barry (Eds.), *Addictive Disorders: A Practical Guide to Treatment.* (pp. 249–269). St. Louis, MO: Mosby/Year Book.

McConnell, H. (1991) Steroid users turn to veterinary drugs for supplies. *Addiction Research Foundation Journal,* 20:39.

National Institute on Drug Abuse Research Monograph 102. Research Report Series. (1991) *Anabolic Steroids: A Threat to Body and Mind.*

Payne, W.A., Hahn, D.B., & Pinger, R.B. (1991) *Drugs: Issues for Today.* St. Louis, MO: Mosby.

Scott, M.J. (1989) HIV infection associated with injections of anabolic steroids. *Journal of the American Medical Association,* 261:1165–1168.

United States Department of Education. (1989) *What Works: Schools Without Drugs.*

ALCOHOL, TOBACCO, AND WELL-BEING

ALCOHOL

The use of alcohol is an ancient practice. Throughout the history of the United States, drinking alcohol as a social custom has been established and accepted by many people. At the same time, many people see the use of alcohol as contributing to many social ills. Alcohol use has been identified as a major national problem (Stoto, Behrens, & Rosemont, 1990) and is by far our number one drug of abuse. About 70 percent of adults use alcohol and approximately eight to nine million have the disease alcoholism. Another seven million abuse alcohol but do not meet the criteria for alcoholism (National Institute on Drug Abuse, 1991).

Adverse consequences from drinking alcohol arise from both single bouts of drinking as well as from long-term use. In addition to automobile accidents, alcohol-involved injuries and deaths, serious medical consequences, and birth defects, alcohol abuse has been implicated as a cause of aggression, crime, marital and family discord, and job loss.

Alcohol-related consequences affect not only drinkers themselves but also their spouses, children, friends, employers as well as strangers. In 1990, alcohol was responsible for more than 65,000 deaths in the United States (Gibbons, 1992). The cost of alcohol abuse and alcohol dependence was estimated to be more than $136 billion in 1990 and is expected to climb to $150 billion by 1995 (Alcohol, Drug Abuse, and Mental Health Administration, 1990). Between 20 and 40 percent of all hospital beds are occupied by people being treated for medical, psychiatric, and traumatic complications of alcohol use (NIDA, 1991). This chapter will include a discussion of pharmacology and acute effects of alcohol, alcohol and adverse consequences, patterns of alcohol consumption, alcoholism: the disease, causes of alcoholism, treatment modalities, and alcohol and youth.

PHARMACOLOGY AND ACUTE EFFECTS OF ALCOHOL

Alcohol is a sedative drug that acts as a central nervous system depressant. The brain and other parts of the cen-

tral nervous system are the organs most sensitive to the effects of alcohol in the body. **Ethanol, or ethyl alcohol,** is a type of alcohol that is formed by the fermentation of fruits, juices, or cereal grains. Known also as grain alcohol, ethyl alcohol is toxic in large amounts. It is the type of alcohol found in alcoholic beverages. The body has effective ways to detoxify and eliminate ethyl alcohol. This is not true of other types of alcohol. **Methyl alcohol,** or wood alcohol, is a type of alcohol that is very toxic and can cause serious damage and even death when consumed. It is found in products such as paint thinner and shellac. A by-product of methyl alcohol metabolism in the body is formaldehyde, which is especially destructive to the eyes and sometimes leads to blindness (Kinney & Leaton, 1991). **Isopropyl alcohol,** commonly known as rubbing alcohol, is another type of alcohol that is not intended to be consumed. This section of the chapter will include a discussion of blood-alcohol concentration, and absorption and elimination of alcohol.

Blood-Alcohol Concentration

Within minutes after alcohol is consumed, it enters the bloodstream and nerve cells are numbed. This action slows nerve messages from the brain to all parts of the body (Gibbons, 1992). Alcohol acts as a relaxant or tranquilizer when one or two drinks are taken. When larger amounts of alcohol are consumed the nerve centers in the brain that govern judgment, memory, speech, reaction time, coordination, muscular control, and brain activity are impaired. The depressive effects of alcohol intensify as the concentration of alcohol in the blood increases. Heavy drinking can result in severe central nervous system depression resulting in sleep, general anesthesia, and eventually coma and death. Death from alcohol overdose occurs due to respiratory failure because of the effects of alcohol on the breathing center in the brain.

Blood-alcohol concentration (BAC) is expressed as a percent and is the ratio of alcohol in a person's blood to the person's total amount of blood. BAC can be measured through urine, breath, or blood samples. Legal levels of intoxication are determined by a person's BAC.

Intoxication is defined in the law as a certain BAC. The legal standard of intoxication in most states is a BAC of 0.10.

The behavioral effects of alcohol depend on the BAC, and there is a progression of effects as BAC increases. A BAC of 0.02, which occurs after one drink for most people, results in feelings of relaxation, feeling "loosened up," and often a slight elevation of mood. At a BAC of 0.05 (2$^1/_2$ drinks), areas of the brain that control judgment and inhibitions are affected and the results are often apparent to others. The drinker will do and say things that normally would be inhibited. There will be a slight decrease in muscular coordination and slight increase in reaction time, making driving dangerous. Feelings of warmth, relaxation, confidence, and being "high" also are likely to be present.

When BAC progresses to 0.10 (the legal level of intoxication in most states), muscular coordination, reaction time, judgment, and perception are seriously impaired, making driving extremely dangerous. Despite these impairments, drinkers with this BAC often claim not to be affected by the alcohol. Drinkers with a BAC of 0.10 usually have consumed five drinks in an hour, have slurred speech, and walk with a stagger. This amount of alcohol in the bloodstream sometimes causes feelings of euphoria, and on the other hand, can also cause feelings of sadness. A BAC of 0.20 causes very erratic changes in emotions and mental confusion. Reflexes also are slowed. A BAC of 0.20 can result from consuming ten drinks.

The most serious acute effects occur when the areas of the brain that control important vital processes are affected. At a BAC of 0.30 there usually is complete loss of coordination and very little sensation. A person in this state of intoxication is stuporous and has only minimal control of mind and body. When the BAC rises to 0.40, a drinker is likely to be unconscious and comatose. Breathing may cease and a drinker may die from respiratory failure. A BAC of 0.50 is a fatal level for many persons and is likely to produce deep coma. The areas of the brain that send impulses to the heart and lungs to regulate the heartbeat and respiration are partially anesthetized (Kinney & Leaton, 1991).

Drinkers can acquire tolerance to some of the psychological and physical effects of alcohol through continued use and drinking experience. Tolerance to physical effects is due to nervous system adaptation to continued drinking, so that larger amounts of alcohol are needed to produce effects that were experienced earlier in one's drinking history. Tolerance to psychological and behavioral effects probably is the result of learned behavior. With experience, drinkers learn to control their behavior so that they do not appear to be affected by alcohol.

Absorption and Elimination

About 80 percent of alcohol absorption occurs in the small intestine, where it passes rapidly into the bloodstream. Approximately 20 percent of a drink is absorbed directly from the stomach, with only minute amounts being absorbed from the mouth and esophagus. Because alcohol must pass through the stomach to reach the small intestine, the presence of food in the stomach can retard absorption of alcohol by diluting the alcohol and extending the time that it takes for alcohol to pass into the small intestine. The presence of fatty foods in the stomach especially slows down the rate of absorption.

Factors that increase absorption rate are: drinking alcohol on an empty stomach, drinking carbonated alcoholic beverages (i.e., beer, sparkling wines, champagne, carbonated mixed drinks), drinking beverages with a high alcoholic content, and drinking alcohol in warm drinks (i.e., hot rum toddy).

Only about 5 percent of consumed alcohol leaves the body unchanged through urine, sweat, or in the breath. Oxidation is the breakdown of alcohol by enzymes in the liver, converting the alcohol into carbon dioxide and water at the rate of about half an ounce of alcohol per hour. Drinking more alcohol than this amount causes the BAC to rise. A **drink** of alcohol is defined as one-half ounce of ethyl alcohol. This roughly is the amount of alcohol in one can of beer, four ounces of wine, or one mixed drink. Generally, the liver can process about one drink per hour. However, the following factors are important influences on blood-alcohol concentration:

- Body size—the larger a person is the more alcohol it takes to get drunk.
- Body composition—body fat does not absorb alcohol as well as lean body tissue.
- Gender—a higher proportion of body fat in females causes BACs to rise faster. Female hormones also seem to make females more sensitive to the effects of alcohol, particularly just before menstruation.
- Race—American Indians and Asian-Americans have more difficulty breaking down alcohol, thus allowing blood-alcohol concentrations to rise quickly.
- Age—the elderly may have a higher propensity for high BACs because of lower volumes of body fluids.

Alcohol and Adverse Consequences

Single episodes of drinking, persistent alcohol abuse, and alcohol dependence can result in adverse consequences. The range of medical consequences of alcohol abuse is immense. Virtually no part of the body is spared the effects of excessive alcohol consumption. The cost of adverse outcomes of alcohol use is high to individuals, families, and society. In addition to physical disease and alcohol-involved motor vehicle crashes, alcohol use and abuse have been linked to other types of accidental injuries and fatalities and also interpersonal violence. Individuals with alcohol-related problems require more general health care, are less productive at their jobs, and also are overrepresented among those who commit acts of interpersonal violence and suicide. The discussion that follows will concern medical consequences—influences on the body, prenatal exposure to alcohol, injuries, suicide, and violence.

Medical Consequences—Influences on the Body

Alcohol-induced liver disorders. Because the liver is the primary site of alcohol metabolism, it can be severely affected by heavy alcohol use. There are three major types of alcohol-induced liver damage: fatty liver, alcoholic hepatitis, and cirrhosis. Fatty liver and alcoholic hepatitis are reversible with abstinence; cirrhosis is not. **Cirrhosis,** which means scarring, is a disease in which alcohol destroys liver cells and plugs the liver with fibrous scar tissue that can lead to liver failure and death (Gibbons, 1992). Among heavy drinkers, 90–100 percent show evidence of some features of fatty liver; an estimated 10–35 percent develop alcoholic hepatitis; and 10–20 percent develop cirrhosis. However, it has been estimated from autopsy studies that 40 percent of cirrhosis cases are not detected during life. The reason that only 10–20 percent of heavy drinkers develop cirrhosis is because they often die from other causes before cirrhosis sets in (Woteki & Thomas, 1992). It may take an average of 25 years of drinking $7^1/_2$ ounces of alcohol a day, about one-third of a bottle of liquor, to produce cirrhosis.

Mortality rates from cirrhosis of the liver have been declining steadily in the United States since 1973. It is now ranked as the ninth leading cause of death, causing more than 26,000 deaths per year. Significant declines in cirrhosis mortality also have been observed in Austria, Canada, France, Greece, Hong Kong, Switzerland, and New Zealand.

The downward trend in cirrhosis mortality is difficult to explain in view of the fact that per capita consumption of alcohol increased in the United States until 1980. Some suggested reasons for the trend are changes in patterns of consumption, earlier diagnosis and treatment, increases in the proportion of alcohol-dependent persons receiving treatment, improved medical management, health promotion efforts, and effective prevention programs.

Cirrhosis death rates for males have been consistently higher than rates for females; in fact, about twice as high. However, females appear to have greater susceptibility to alcohol-related liver damage. Females develop severe liver disease with shorter durations of alcohol use and lower levels of alcohol consumption. Some studies have shown a higher prevalence and greater severity of alcohol-related liver disease in alcohol-dependent females than in alcohol-dependent males. The reasons for this difference in alcohol sensitivity are unknown. They could be related to differences in hormones, immune systems, body weight, or body fluid content.

Over the past two decades, death rates from cirrhosis among African-American and American Indian males have decreased more rapidly than those for white American males. However, current death rates for nonwhite Americans remain almost 70 percent higher than rates for white Americans; the rates for American Indian males are triple those of white American males. These disparities may represent differential access to health care services, differential drinking patterns, or some combination of both (U.S. Department of Health and Human Services, 1991).

Gastrointestinal effects. Alcohol causes significant damage in the stomach, which is exposed to higher concentrations of alcohol than any other site, with the possible exception of the mouth and esophagus. Alcohol slows gastric emptying, interferes with the action of gastroesophageal sphincters, stimulates gastric secretion, and often injures the gastric mucosa (inner lining), especially when combined with aspirin. The use of aspirin by drinkers may increase the likelihood of bleeding from an already-weakened stomach wall, sometimes leading to hemorrhaging.

Regular alcohol consumption may precipitate inflammation of the esophagus and make existing peptic ulcers worse. The risk of esophageal cancer is higher in alcohol abusers, as is the risk of chronic atrophic gastritis, a precursor of gastric carcinoma.

Heavy alcohol consumption also is a leading cause of acute pancreatitis as well as chronic pancreatitis. **Acute pan-**

creatitis is inflammation of the pancreas manifested by severe abdominal pain (usually upper abdominal) often accompanied by nausea, vomiting, fever, and rapid heartbeat. **Chronic pancreatitis** is a condition that typically may occur after five to ten years of heavy alcohol use. By the time alcohol-dependent individuals experience severe abdominal pain, chronic changes already have occurred in the pancreas. These changes disrupt sugar metabolism because the pancreas fails to secrete enough insulin, thus increasing the risk of diabetes. About three-fourths of the cases of chronic pancreatitis in the United States occur in alcoholics. Pancreatic cancer also is seen more often in alcohol-dependent persons than nonalcohol-dependent persons.

Nutritional disorders. Malnutrition resulting from poor eating habits frequently is associated with alcohol dependency. Malnutrition can result from reduced overall food intake as well as from deficiencies of specific nutrients (Reiken, 1991). Alcohol also interferes with the digestion, absorption, and use of many nutrients in food. Deficiencies in the nutrients thiamine, folate, pyroxidine, vitamin A, and zinc are common in alcohol-dependent persons. Alcohol-related nutritional deficiencies can lead to such outcomes as anemia and nervous system damage. **Wernicke's disease** is a condition in which certain areas of the brain are destroyed by the combination of thiamine deficiency and the toxic effects of alcohol. Nutritional deficiencies in alcohol-dependent individuals also may be factors in fetal alcohol syndrome, liver disease, pancreatic disease, and cancer.

Some studies suggest that chronic alcohol use is associated with osteoporosis. **Osteoporosis** is a condition that is characterized by calcium loss and loss of bone density. Persons with osteoporosis are at increased risk of suffering bone fractures. Alcohol-dependent individuals have an increased incidence of fractures when compared to those who are not dependent on alcohol. Studies of alcohol consumption in rats have shown a relationship between bone strength and alcohol consumption. Further, it is known that alcohol stimulates the excretion of calcium from the body. This is critical because calcium is an important ingredient for proper bone and skeletal system development.

Alcohol consumption also may contribute to obesity. Because alcoholic beverages are high in calories, drinking alcoholic beverages may contribute to excess weight gain.

Effects on the cardiovascular system. The long-term use of alcohol can directly damage heart tissue, which can result in abnormal heart functioning (Reiken, 1991; Urbano-Marquez et al., 1989). Alcohol damage to the heart muscle may result in cardiomyopathy and cardiac arrhythmias. **Cardiomyopathy** is a degeneration of the heart muscle. Alcoholic cardiomyopathy or alcoholic heart muscle disease is believed to occur frequently among alcoholics (Kinney & Leaton, 1991). This disease is characterized by severe enlargement of the heart and inability of the damaged heart to pump blood effectively. **Cardiac arrhythmia** is an irregular heartbeat.

During alcohol intoxication, the heart's pumping ability is reduced and heart rate is thus increased (Kelbaek, 1990). Chronic alcohol consumption is associated with a significant increase in high blood pressure and may play a role in ischemic heart disease and stroke. **Ischemic heart disease** is deficient blood circulation to the heart. The type of stroke most associated with heavy drinking is hemorrhagic stroke, which is more often fatal than other types of stroke.

On the other hand, some studies suggest moderate alcohol intake may have a beneficial effect on the development and progression of atherosclerosis by changing the lipid composition of the blood (Weidner et al., 1991). **Atherosclerosis** is the process of fatty build-up in arteries that can lead to a heart attack or stroke. However, medical researchers agree that the bad effects of heavy drinking overwhelm this good effect (Gibbons, 1992). Further, some studies have shown that the risk of coronary heart disease death is increased by heavy drinking. Therefore, it is not clear if the use of alcohol offers any protection against coronary heart disease (Stone, 1990; Alcohol, Drug Abuse, and Mental Health, 1990).

Alcohol and cancer. There is considerable evidence that alcohol abuse is associated with increased risk of certain types of cancer, especially those of the liver, esophagus, and throat. The incidence of these cancers is lower in Mormons and other groups that abstain from alcohol use. The risk of esophageal cancer is much higher when daily drinking is combined with smoking 25 or more cigarettes per day than when either habit is sustained alone.

The relationship between alcohol consumption and cancer of the stomach is inconclusive. Within certain geographic areas, consumption of beer in particular correlates with the appearances of cancers in the lower gastrointestinal tract, suggesting that nonalcohol ingredients or **congeners** may play a role in the development of these cancers. Research evidence from Japan shows that daily drinking consistently elevates the risk of prostate cancer.

At present, there is no definitive evidence linking breast or lung cancer with chronic alcohol use. Some studies have linked alcohol and breast cancer, but have been criticized for methodological shortcomings, inconsistent findings, or only slightly elevated risk for alcohol consumers versus nonconsumers. Further, the amount of alcohol consumed by females with breast cancer was low.

Effects on the immune system. It is difficult to determine the primary effects of alcohol on the immune system in humans because poor nutrition, infection, liver disease, and other disorders may also concurrently affect the immune system. However, there is substantial research evidence that alcohol-dependent individuals are at increased susceptibility to infection and that alcohol can impair normal immune responses (MacGregor, 1988; National Institute on Alcohol Abuse and Alcoholism, 1992; Plant, 1990). Chronic alcohol consumption reduces the number of white blood cells, which are important for fighting infections. Long-term alcohol use also can suppress antibody production, macrophage activity, cell-mediated immunity, and natural killer cells.

There is a high incidence of tuberculosis among alcohol-dependent individuals. The incidence of virus-associated head and neck cancers also is high in alcohol-dependent individuals, suggesting that heavy alcohol use may cause loss of immunity to these viruses.

Alcohol, HIV infection, and AIDS. No evidence exists to indicate a direct association between alcohol use and the development of acquired immune deficiency syndrome (AIDS). However, the risk of infection by the human immunodeficiency virus (HIV) appears to be heightened because alcohol affects judgment and lowers inhibitions, thus increasing the likelihood that individuals will participate in high-risk sexual practices associated with HIV infection at specific sexual encounters (NIAA, 1992; Steele & Josephs, 1990). Alcohol use also may increase the risk of high-risk drug use behaviors such as needle sharing among intravenous drug users.

At least one study has suggested that a single drinking episode can suppress the immune responses of white blood cells taken from healthy volunteers (Bagasra, Kajdacsy-Balla, & Lischner, 1989). Thus short-term and long-term alcohol use may increase the risk of primary infection by lowering resistance to infection when individuals are first exposed to HIV. For individuals already infected with HIV, alcohol use could speed up the progression from asymptomatic to end-stage clinical infection by depressing the immune mechanisms that act to limit the negative impact

of HIV. Alcohol has been shown to impair white blood cell responses to HIV (Nair et al., 1990).

Neurologic disorders. Heavy alcohol consumption is a well-documented cause of brain and other nerve tissue damage. The neurological complications of heavy alcohol consumption include dementia, blackouts, seizures, hallucinations, and nerve destruction throughout the body. Alcohol-related dementia accounts for nearly 20 percent of all admissions to state mental hospitals. Based on neuropsychological assessment, there is evidence of brain dysfunction in 50–70 percent of detoxified, alcohol-dependent individuals who do not have organic brain syndrome. Structural brain damage in alcohol-dependent individuals, which can be seen on autopsy, includes general atrophy (shrinking) as well as specific cell loss in two structures associated with memory disorders. Many other brain abnormalities and impairments of cognitive function and learning have been observed in alcohol-dependent persons. There is some evidence that abstinence may lead to recovery of some cognitive function and learning and to partial recovery from brain atrophy.

Brain impairment in chronic alcohol-dependent individuals may be conceptualized as two organic brain syndromes: alcohol dementia and Korsakoff's psychosis. **Alcohol dementia** is brain impairment characterized by overall intellectual decline with deficits in abstracting ability and problem solving, difficulty in swallowing, difficulty in manipulating objects, brain wave abnormalities, and cerebral atrophy (Fig. 13-1). These characterizations are considered to be direct toxic effects of alcohol on nerve cells. However, they are sometimes difficult to differentiate from symptoms of primary degenerative dementia or Alzheimer's disease. Chronic brain damage by alcohol is second only to Alzheimer's disease as a known cause of dementia in adults. Many of the symptoms of alcohol dementia are similar to those of Alzheimer's disease. Both show brain atrophy, abnormalities in the electrical functioning of the brain, loss of ability to think abstractly, decreased coordination, and difficulty with speech. While Alzheimer's disease is progressive, alcoholic dementia is not necessarily progressive. If the alcohol-dependent person stops drinking, mental deterioration usually stops and significant recovery is possible.

As mentioned earlier, Wernicke's disease is associated with thiamine deficiency and can be reversed by adequate thiamine intake. Wernicke's disease is characterized by eye disturbances, ataxia (loss of coordination and control of movement), and confusion. A related disorder, Korsakoff's psychosis, may appear without being preceded by

161

Figure 13-1
Alcohol-Related Dementia

thiamine deficiency. When it does so, it is not reversed by thiamine supplementation. **Korsakoff's psychosis** consists of a permanent state of cognitive dysfunction and the inability to remember recent events or to learn new information.

Approximately 80 percent of patients with Wernicke's disease who survive will have Korsakoff's psychosis. Many neurologists consider that Wernicke's disease and Korsakoff's psychosis are really the same disorder, with Wernicke's being the acute and Korsakoff's the chronic form. Early treatment may correct critical abnormalities associated with Wernicke's disease, but the mortality rate is 10–20 percent. For alcohol-dependent patients with Korsakoff's psychosis, previously-learned information may interfere with new learning, and it also may be difficult to recall events that occurred before the onset of the dysfunction.

Prenatal Exposure to Alcohol

Numerous animal studies demonstrate that alcohol and its primary metabolite, acetaldehyde, are directly toxic to the developing embryo and fetus and are capable of producing abnormalities. Alcohol also may interfere with the delivery of maternal nutrients to the fetus, impair the supply of fetal oxygen, and disrupt protein synthesis and metabolism.

Pregnant females who are alcohol-dependent have more obstetrical complications (particularly vaginal bleeding),

premature separation of the placenta, and fetal distress. Maternal alcoholism also is associated with high rates of spontaneous abortion and stillbirth. The risk of spontaneous abortions is dose-related: pregnant females who average three or more drinks a day are more than three times as likely to miscarry than nondrinkers. Even females who consume only one or two drinks a day are at increased risk for miscarriage during the second trimester of pregnancy.

Effects on the newborn and fetal alcohol syndrome. Low birth weight and intrauterine growth retardation (IUGR)—shorter length, and smaller head and chest circumference measurements—are the most consistently observed effects of fetal exposure to alcohol. These problems seem more severe among females who drink heavily during the last three months of their pregnancy. Pregnant females who consume one or two drinks per day are twice as likely as nondrinkers to have a growth-retarded infant weighing less than 5.5 pounds. Lowered birth weight and IUGR increase risks for an infant's early death and for respiratory difficulties, feeding problems, serious infections, and long-term developmental problems.

Several additional factors also may contribute to risk of IUGR. Chronic beer drinking during pregnancy appears to be the most significant determinant. Birth weight deficiencies among newborns are associated not only with their beer-drinking mother's lower weight gain during

162

pregnancy, but also her lower weight at conception, and her smoking cigarettes.

Newborns whose mothers drink heavily (an average of five drinks per day, especially during the last three months of pregnancy) may show signs of alcohol withdrawal such as tremors, abnormal muscle tension, restlessness, inconsolable crying, and reflex abnormalities. Heavy maternal alcohol use also is associated with a decreased ability among newborns to tune out inappropriate stimuli, poor sucking abilities, and disturbed patterns of sleep and wakefulness.

More research is needed on the interaction between drinking alcohol and smoking cigarettes. This combination of drug use has been found to reduce the responsiveness of newborn babies whose mothers drank socially and smoked moderately during pregnancy. Even babies whose mothers consumed only one drink a day during the first three months of pregnancy have more erratic sleeping patterns than infants of nondrinking mothers.

Since the beginning of the 18th century, physicians and researchers in England and France have observed and reported harmful effects of maternal alcohol consumption on offspring. In 1973, a group of scientists at the University of Washington labeled the effects as fetal alcohol syndrome. **Fetal alcohol syndrome (FAS)** is a characteristic pattern of severe birth defects present in babies born to mothers who drink alcohol during their pregnancy. Numerous cases of this syndrome have now been reported from all over the world. A conference of research specialists in 1980 outlined standards for FAS diagnostic criteria, which require at least one feature from each of three categories:

1. Prenatal and postnatal growth retardation—with abnormally small-for-age weight, length, and/or head circumference.
2. Central nervous system disorders—with signs of abnormal brain functioning, delays in behavioral development, and/or intellectual impairment.
3. At least two of the following abnormal craniofacial features—small head, small eyes or short eye openings, or a poorly developed philtrum (the groove above the upper lip), thin upper lip, short nose, or flattened midfacial area.

Other abnormalities also have been reported in conjunction with FAS, including cross-eye (strabismus), nearsightedness, malformations of the ears, heart murmurs, liver and kidney problems, retarded bone growth, skeletal defects, increases in upper respiratory infections, undescended testicles, and hernias.

FAS is the leading known cause of mental retardation, surpassing even Down syndrome and spina bifida (Hawkes, 1993). Several investigators have noted that the degree of mental impairment among FAS children correlates closely with the severity of their malformations of the face and head and growth deficiencies. The cognitive functioning of FAS children with the most severe central nervous system involvement does not improve, even with remedial instruction.

It is not known exactly how often FAS births occur. Studies of population groups in the United States have most consistently found rates ranging from one to three cases per 1,000 live births. European cities that have been studied have comparable rates, averaging one case per 650 live births. However, among one American Indian population at particularly high risk for alcoholism, a rate of 9.8 cases per 1,000 births was observed.

Not all alcohol-dependent females who become pregnant deliver babies with FAS. In one study of contributory risk factors, an FAS diagnosis most frequently was associated with the mother's persistent drinking throughout pregnancy, a greater number of alcohol-related problems, and a larger number of previous births. Females with all four characteristics had an 85-percent chance of producing a baby with FAS. In contrast, females with none of these risk factors had only a 2 percent probability for an FAS baby. In another high-risk group, one in four mothers who had already had an alcohol-affected child gave birth to other FAS-diagnosed children. In more recent research, drinking an average of three drinks per day during the period following conception and before pregnancy was confirmed (organogenesis phase) was found to be the threshold at which risk increased for the characteristic head and face malformations that are used to diagnose FAS in newborns. However, taking an occasional drink during the earliest weeks of pregnancy did not increase risk for these alcohol-associated anatomical defects.

Prenatally alcohol-exposed babies with birth defects that do not meet all three criteria for an FAS diagnosis may be categorized as having suspected fetal alcohol effects (FAE). FAEs often include impaired memory, brief attention span, poor judgment and limited capacity to learn from experience. Steinmetz (1992, p. 38) comments about the future of young people who suffer fetal alcohol effects by saying, "Some victims drop out of school in frustration or wind up on the margins of society." These adverse consequences of maternal alcohol use usually include growth retardation and are estimated to be three times more frequent than FAS.

Injuries

In addition to alcohol-involved motor vehicle crashes, alcohol use and abuse have been linked to other types of accidental injuries and fatalities, including drownings, falls, and burns. Alcohol also may increase the severity of trauma incurred in accidents. A recent study found that children whose mothers were problem drinkers had more than two times the risk of having a serious injury than children whose mothers were nondrinkers (Bijur et al., 1992). The risk of serious injury increases to an even greater level when females who are problem drinkers are married to males who are moderate or heavy drinkers.

Motor vehicle crashes. Motor vehicle crashes are the leading cause of injury deaths in the United States and the leading cause of death among persons between 1 and 34 years of age. In 1990, there were 44,529 fatalities on the nation's highways (Marwick, 1992) and 360,000 persons seriously injured in motor vehicle crashes (Gunby, 1992). Since Henry Bliss was struck and killed by an automobile in 1899, nearly 2.8 million people have died as a result of injuries sustained in motor vehicle crashes and collisions in our nation (Gunby, 1992).

The risk of a fatal crash, per mile driven, may be at least eight times higher for an intoxicated driver (BAC of 0.10 or greater) than for a sober one (Fig. 13-2). A BAC of 0.10 significantly affects a person's ability to drive by impairing vision, perception, judgment, reaction time, and the ability to brake and control speed (USDHHS, 1991). When the BAC is above 0.10, drivers have lower divided-attention performance, reduced dynamic visual activity, reduced adaptation to brightness (and glare-resistance recovery), and reduced ability to see flickering lights (e.g., turn signals).

Approximately half of all traffic crashes involve alcohol. During 1990, alcohol-related crashes killed 22,084 people; one-third were innocent victims. In addition to these fatalities, which account for almost two million potential years of life lost, 1.2 million people were injured in alcohol-related crashes. This includes 4,092 people with permanent total disabilities and 43,140 with permanent, partial disabilities (Randall, 1992). Alcohol-related traffic accidents are the leading cause of spinal cord injury for young people. Evans (1991) estimates that 47 percent of all U.S. traffic fatalities would be eliminated if there was no drinking and driving.

The percentage of fatal crashes that involve alcohol declined from 57 percent in 1982 to 49 percent in 1990 (Randall, 1992). The decline is attributed to the emergence of highly-visible, citizen activist groups such as Mothers Against Drunk Driving (MADD), the media attention that such groups generated, and the resulting increases in deterrence activities involving legislation, enforcement (including roadside

Figure 13-2
Drinking and Driving: A Deadly Duo

The risk of a fatal crash, per mile driven, may be at least eight times higher for a drunk driver (BAC of 0.10 or greater) than for a sober one.

sobriety checkpoints), and use of sanctions such as license suspensions and revocations. State laws that uniformly established age 21 as the minimum alcohol purchase age were associated with an overall reduction of nearly 13 percent in the fatal-accident involvement rate for youth under 21 years of age.

Much more, however, needs to be done. Other needed measures include increased media attention to alcohol-impairment driving laws and their enforcement, enforcement of alcoholic beverage control laws regarding access to alcohol by minors, and increased testing of drivers involved in fatal and serious injury cases (USDHHS, 1991).

While deaths from alcohol-related accidents declined in all age groups, the most dramatic declines were among teenagers (Randall, 1992). Still, about 40 percent of all teenage deaths that occur are due to motor vehicle injuries and more than 2,800 teenagers between the ages of 15 and 20 die in alcohol-related motor vehicle crashes each year. The number-one killer of teenagers and young adults is alcohol-related highway accidents. Alcohol is the major cause of fatal and nonfatal crashes that involve teenage drivers (Office for Substance Abuse Prevention, 1991). Because teenagers are especially susceptible to the effects of alcohol, drinking and driving is particularly hazardous for teenage drivers and others who may be riding with teenage drivers (Wilson et al., 1991).

Drinking while under the influence is a practice that is more common among adolescent males than females (Klep & Perry, 1990). However, recent analyses show that the proportion of female drivers involved in fatal crashes and the proportion of those arrested for driving while intoxicated may be increasing (Centers for Disease Control, 1992). This suggests that prevention and intervention programs, which have typically targeted males, should also target females.

Other injuries. Researchers have determined that a history of alcohol problems or alcohol consumption occurs more often in deaths from falls and fires than from traffic accidents. Falls are the most common cause of nonfatal injuries in the United States and the second leading cause of fatal accidents, accounting for approximately 13,000 deaths a year. The risk of falls is 3 times greater for individuals with BACs of 0.05 to 0.10, 10 times greater for individuals with BACs of 0.10 to 0.15, and about 60 times greater for individuals with BACs of 0.16 or higher compared to the risk for individuals with no exposure to alcohol.

Injuries from fires and burns are the fourth leading cause of accidental death in the United States and are responsible for an estimated 6,000 fatalities a year. Researchers found that 48 percent of fatal burn victims are intoxicated (BAC equal to or greater than 0.10). Alcohol exposure is very common among victims of fires caused by burning cigarettes. House fires involving cigarettes account for approximately one-third of all fire fatalities. Thus, alcohol use in combination with cigarette smoking presents a serious risk of fire and burn injuries.

Drownings rank as the third leading cause of accidental death in the United States, and a substantial proportion of drownings are also related to alcohol use, particularly among adolescent and young adult males (Wilson et al., 1991). Research findings suggest that victims have been exposed to alcohol in approximately 38 percent of drowning deaths. A person under the influence of alcohol may be more susceptible to drowning because of disorientation, loss of ability to regulate temperature in a cold environment, impairment of psychomotor skills, and reduced ability for breath holding.

Alcohol use also is an important factor in boating accidents. A survey of boat owners showed that 35 percent drank alcohol while operating their boats on the water. A Coast Guard survey had comparable findings when it found that 40 percent of boaters reported carrying alcohol on boating outings.

Suicide

Alcohol is a very important risk factor for suicide (Shaffer, 1993). Research indicates that 20–36 percent of suicide victims have a history of alcohol abuse or were drinking shortly before their suicides. Alcohol tends to be most associated with suicides that are impulsive rather than premeditated. Suicides are judged to be impulsive if the person who commits suicide is not diagnosed as depressed, is not in poor health, has not made prior suicide attempts, or is not under psychiatric care.

The use of firearms in suicides also is related to alcohol. Suicide victims who have been drinking are more likely to have died from gunshot wounds. This relationship also is true for youth suicides. Researchers found alcohol in the blood of 13 percent of suicide victims from 1968 to 1972, 25 percent from 1973 to 1977, and 46 percent in 1978 to 1983. Youth suicide victims with a detectable BAC at the time of death were almost five times more likely to use firearms as a means of suicide than victims with no detectable BAC. Intoxicated victims (BAC equal

165

to or greater than 0.10) were almost 7.5 times more likely to use firearms.

Violence

In both animal and human studies, alcohol, more than any other drug, has been linked with a high incidence of violence and aggression. Recent studies have associated acute and chronic alcohol consumption with high rates of homicides, suicides, sexual assaults, spouse abuse, and child abuse. Laboratory research has produced evidence of links between the pharmacologic effects of alcohol and aggressive behavior. This relationship is quite complex. The effects of alcohol are influenced by many cultural, environmental, and individual factors.

Alcohol is more likely to contribute to some types of violence than to others. Altercations and arguments that escalate to violence within families and among acquaintances are likely to be precipitated in part by alcohol. Alcohol is less likely to be involved in premeditated homicides and other premeditated acts of violence in which the perpetrator makes careful plans to avoid detection.

PATTERNS OF ALCOHOL CONSUMPTION

Drinkers display many different patterns of alcohol use. This discussion will cover categories of drinkers and similarities and differences in drinking patterns.

Categories of Drinkers

The majority of drinkers are social drinkers. **Social drinkers** are those for whom drinking produces no serious long-term health or social consequences and cessation of alcohol use poses no problem. Although these individuals do not experience the effects of chronic alcohol abuse, they are nonetheless at risk for adverse consequences, such as alcohol-related accidents, arising from even single bouts of drinking.

Alcohol abusers or **nondependent problem drinkers** are persons who experience a variety of social and medical problems as a result of high-risk drinking but who are not dependent on alcohol. Alcohol use by these individuals often leads to problems that arise from impaired judgment, diminished concern about the consequences of behavior, and physical effects of alcohol consumption. Such adverse effects may be the result of a single bout of drinking, or they may represent the effects of persistent high-risk alcohol use.

Finally, there are alcohol-dependent persons. **Alcohol-dependent persons** are persons who experience adverse social and medical consequences from single bouts of drinking and from chronic, high-level alcohol use; they also experience physical and psychological dependence on alcohol that results in impaired ability to control drinking behavior. This impairment in control represents the critical distinction between alcohol abuse and alcohol dependence.

Not all drinkers, however, fit neatly into one category or another, and there is a spectrum of degrees of severity of both alcohol abuse and alcohol dependence. Periodic high-risk drinking by individuals generally thought to be social drinkers can cause serious problems such as alcohol-involved injuries. However, these individuals may not satisfy the clinical criteria that define alcohol abuse. Similarly, persistent and repetitive alcohol abuse that causes severe social and medical problems may be difficult to differentiate from alcohol dependence. The risk for acute alcohol-involved problems varies from setting to setting, so that alcohol use that would create minimal difficulties in one situation may prove deadly in another (e.g., drinking at home then going to bed vs. drinking at a tavern then driving home).

In terms of prevalence, a household survey of persons aged 18 and older found that 34 percent of respondents were nondrinkers; 56 percent were nondependent, nonproblem drinkers (analogous to social drinkers described in preceding paragraphs); 4 percent were nondependent problem drinkers (i.e., alcohol abusers); and 6 percent were alcohol dependent.

Examinations of the similarities and differences between patterns of alcohol use have revealed no unvarying or inevitable sequence of behaviors and symptoms leading from one drinking classification to another. Thus, an individual drinker can display more than one drinking pattern during his/her lifetime, and although many people may drink alcoholic beverages and experience few or no adverse effects from their drinking, some drinkers become alcohol abusers or alcohol dependent. For certain individuals, drinking is problematic from the start. For an unfortunate few, a single exposure to alcohol can herald the onset of addiction. However, for most, alcohol dependence takes a few years to develop.

Not all of those who abuse alcohol become dependent, and some ferry back and forth between periods of nonproblem drinking and periods when alcohol use is problematic. Further, just as an individual can be an alcohol

166

abuser without being dependent, individuals can be alcohol dependent before they manifest alcohol-related social and medical problems.

ALCOHOLISM: THE DISEASE

Alcohol dependence is not an infectious disease, but rather one in which biology and behavior interact in complex ways. In this context, alcohol dependence may represent the end result of an interactive process involving many different social and psychological factors in persons who are physiologically vulnerable. The classification of disease and the characteristics of alcoholism will be discussed.

The Classification of Disease

To be classified as a disease, a disorder must have an identifiable cluster of symptoms that predicts a course and outcome. In terms of meeting these criteria, alcohol dependence is no different from other biologically-based diseases. Alcohol dependence, like hypertension, diabetes, and coronary disease, may be characterized basically as a disease in which a genetic predisposition is activated by environmental factors.

Characteristics of Alcoholism

Alcohol dependence (alcoholism) is a serious disease that affects the health and well-being of millions of Americans. It has been noted that alcoholism fits within the pattern of most other major chronic diseases that are the consequence of environmental factors over time in genetically-susceptible persons. For example, hypertension has been shown to have a strong genetic link, yet to conclude that genetic factors alone are causal would be erroneous because environmental factors such as salt intake and smoking may play important roles in its cause.

Alcohol-dependent persons may experience predictable withdrawal syndromes and intense overwhelming compulsions to drink. Withdrawal and craving may contribute to the development of impaired control over drinking. In addition, alcohol-dependent persons develop an alcohol tolerance, which is a need for increased quantities of alcohol to achieve a pharmacologic effect.

CAUSES OF ALCOHOLISM

Both alcohol abuse and alcohol dependence develop as a result of complex, and as yet incompletely-understood processes. Research has produced evidence that both genetic and environmental factors contribute to alcoholism (Frances & Franklin, 1992), and the interaction of genetics and environment is emerging as a fundamentally-important issue in research in the causes of alcohol prob-

lems (Orford & Vellman, 1991). Some forms of alcohol dependence are highly heritable, while others are less so; there are also instances of alcohol dependence without obvious genetic involvement. Genetics, environment, and the combined effects of those factors will be the topics of discussion in this section of the chapter.

Genetics

Even though the mechanisms of genetic transmission are unknown, evidence of genetically-transmitted vulnerability for alcoholism exists (Frances & Franklin, 1992). Much of this evidence has arisen from adoption studies, but additional support for potential genetic contributions is found in research on markers of inherited susceptibility and in research involving animals.

It is important to note that genetic predisposition does not imply predestination or inevitability. Many persons having family histories indicative of risk do not develop alcohol dependence since it is the interaction of genetic and environmental factors that define vulnerability. Thus, even if facilitative genes are inherited, they may not be expressed in the absence of provocative environmental factors. Although it is estimated that one-third of alcohol-dependent persons have one or more parents who are alcohol-dependent, less than half of the children of parents who are dependent on alcohol develop drinking problems, and only a portion develop alcohol dependence.

Both alcohol abuse and alcohol dependence are more likely to occur among males than among females; young, single males are more likely to be frequent heavy drinkers and to report alcohol dependence and alcohol-related problems. African-American males and white American males have similar drinking patterns overall, although African-American males have somewhat higher abstention rates than white Americans, and white American males are somewhat more likely to be heavier drinkers. However, African-American males appear to experience some types of alcohol-related problems at lower levels of alcohol consumption. Hispanic and American Indian males also have high levels of alcohol use problems. However, the degree of problems varies among different subpopulations of these groups.

Environment

Such psychosocial factors as cultural and group norms, peer influences, and expectancies about alcohol's effects influence drinking behavior. Likewise, subjective experiences related to the pharmacologic effects of alcohol, most notably its euphoriant and anxiety-reducing effects, are

167

reinforcing for some drinkers. The effects of early home environment, including family influences, on drinking behavior and the development of alcohol dependence have been explored, as has the relationship of childhood adjustment problems to later alcoholism.

Combined Effects of Genetics and Environment

Recent studies of twins suggest that the interaction between genetic and environmental influences is implicated in certain drinking behaviors. There are two interesting subgroups of alcohol dependence that show one way in which genetic and environmental influences may interact to produce alcoholism.

Type 2, male-limited alcohol dependence is a subgroup of alcohol dependence that has a high genetic penetrance from father to son and minor environmental association. Onset typically occurs before the age of 25 with drinking patterns characterized by persistent consumption accompanied by aggressive behavior and involvement with the police. **Type 1, milieu-limited alcohol dependence** is a subgroup that shows a more complex interplay between genetic and environmental influences. Onset of type 1 alcohol dependence typically occurs after the age of 25 with a drinking pattern characterized by guilt and periods when control over drinking is severely diminished. Personality characteristics related to three traits—novelty seeking, harm avoidance, and reward dependence—are thought to differentiate the types and to represent key differences in the processes by which individuals respond to the environment.

TREATMENT MODALITIES

Alcohol dependence is a serious disease that affects the health and well-being of millions of people in the United States and elsewhere. About 85 percent of those who are treated for alcohol dependence receive outpatient care; the remaining 15 percent are treated in inpatient or residential settings, including medical detoxification settings, social detoxification units, rehabilitation/recovery programs, and custodial/domiciliary settings. Management of alcohol withdrawal, treatment components, and underserved groups and treatment services will be discussed.

Management of Alcohol Withdrawal

Detoxification is the first step in the treatment of alcoholism. **Detoxification** is the process in which alcohol (or any other drug) is withdrawn from the body. Withdrawal is a highly variable and individualized phenomenon in which

patients may experience none, some, or all of three major symptom types:

1. Autonomic nervous hyperactivity seems to account for signs and symptoms of restlessness, sweating, rapid heart rate, high blood pressure, tremors, and similar characteristics.
2. Excitation of neurons may produce seizures.
3. Distorted perceptions, sensations, or arousal may produce hallucinations, delirium, and disturbed sleep.

Opinions vary on which medications should be used to treat alcohol withdrawal and whether or not detoxification should be conducted in medical settings. The fact that a significant number of patients experience no serious medical complications during withdrawal suggests that medically-oriented inpatient detoxification may be unnecessary for patients who are not severely dependent and who are otherwise in good health. Hospital care often is recommended for alcoholics who lack a reliable support network and who have serious medical, neurological, or psychiatric symptoms and a history of alcohol withdrawal symptoms. Others could be suitably managed in outpatient approaches. The influence of medical (pharmacologic) withdrawal on the acceptance of and participation in continued treatment has not been established.

Several studies indicate that both acute and subacute withdrawal symptoms persist for a number of weeks. Signs and symptoms include physiological and psychological variations such as breathing irregularity and unstable blood pressure, tension, anxiety, insomnia, and depressed mood—findings that indicate that central nervous system hyperexcitability persists long after the removal of alcohol. This constellation of symptoms has been called protracted withdrawal syndrome, subacute withdrawal syndrome, late withdrawal, and "intermediate-duration organic mental disorder associated with alcoholism." It appears to be the same syndrome commonly described as "dry drunks,"—thought and behavior patterns that may precede a relapse into active alcoholism.

During the initial period of abstinence, such symptoms may revive a craving for alcohol and lead to renewed drinking. The physical dependency mechanisms that tend to subside with abstinence can be rapidly reactivated by drinking. In animal studies, central nervous system hyperexcitability readily is activated by exposure to ethyl alcohol, and the same effect is thought to occur in humans. Such findings indicate that some patients may need to be abstinent for at least four to six weeks following alcohol withdrawal in order to achieve the most benefit for participation in a therapeutic program. There is a high relapse rate to drinking among detoxified patients, especially when treatment is limited only to management of alcohol withdrawal.

Treatment Components

A number of alternative treatments are available for alcohol dependence, ranging from pharmacologic therapy to counseling and marital and family therapy. Frequently, two or more treatment modalities are combined in one therapeutic approach.

Individual and group therapy. Psychotherapy and counseling are traditional components of many alcoholism-treatment programs. However, there is little systematic evidence about the effectiveness of counseling alone. Individual psychotherapy seldom is used alone with alcohol-dependent patients but is usually combined with other approaches such as education about alcohol dependence, referral to AA (Alcoholics Anonymous), family intervention, and pharmacologic therapy. Group psychotherapy is a widespread and popular approach in alcoholism treatment. It also is used in conjunction with AA, pharmacologic therapy, vocational rehabilitation, and other methods.

Counseling often includes a confrontational focus, based on the rationale that persons dependent on alcohol must be confronted with the reality of their problem before behavior change can take place. Hostile confrontations, however, may be associated with negative outcomes in changing behavior, especially for alcohol-dependent persons with low self-esteem. The behaviors and attitudes of the counselor may play a critical role in the outcome of counseling. Counselors differ in their abilities to keep patients in treatment, and their own personal characteristics may affect patient outcome. Research in this area is still sparse.

Group therapy has long been an essential component of alcoholism-treatment programs and often is used in inpatient settings. Researchers also have found that supportive group therapy in an outpatient setting is a valuable component of treatment. Social-skills training typically focuses on effective communication skills, assertiveness, and resistance to peer pressure. Group training in social skills appears to produce faster improvement in social skills than individual training, and equivalent reduction in alcohol consumption. Individual and group psychotherapeutic approaches form the basis for the treatment model used in most alcoholism treatment programs. The goal of these rehabilitation programs is to help people with alcohol and other drug dependencies achieve abstinence and improve their lifestyles.

Family and marital therapy. In the past few years, there has been increasing interest in family factors that maintain addictive behaviors and in how the family might be involved in initiating and maintaining changes in these behaviors. Family and marital problems may contribute to the original development of problem drinking. However, problems develop as a result of the drinking and then contribute to its maintenance. Alcohol intoxication may facilitate the expression of certain family interactions while inhibiting others. These changes in relationships may serve as temporary solutions to chronic family problems and thus may stabilize the family system. For example, researchers observed that problem solving was more frequent among some alcoholics and their spouses during drinking episodes, a style of interaction that could have reinforcement value for the marriage that in turn reinforces continued drinking. A number of studies have found moderately better outcomes for spouse- and family-involved treatment for alcohol-dependent persons when compared to individually-focused approaches.

Alcoholics Anonymous. Alcoholics Anonymous (AA) is an important component of alcoholism-rehabilitation efforts and plays a central role in many therapeutic programs, providing support for both alcohol-dependent persons and their families through the related Al-Anon and Alateen programs. There are more than 73,000 AA groups throughout the world. Most members are referred to AA by other AA members and by rehabilitation and counseling programs. The average member attends four meetings a week and 60 percent have had prior counseling. Sixty-six percent of AA members are males and the predominant ages are 31 through 50.

AA, which was founded in 1953, is a self-help group in which members give and receive help. By sharing feelings, perceptions, and problems, group members actively work to bring about positive changes in attitude and behavior aimed toward individual empowerment and self-determination. AA is a 12-step program that stresses powerlessness over alcohol. Meetings are open to anyone with a desire to stop alcohol abuse, require no formal referral, and are free of charge. The only requirement for membership in AA is a desire to stop drinking. Research on the effectiveness of AA has been inadequate, largely because of the anonymous nature of AA (National Institute on Drug Abuse, 1991).

Several other groups have used AA as a model for self-help programs for a wide range of people suffering from physical, psychological, and emotional conditions. These include people with compulsions such as gambling, spending money, overeating, cocaine, narcotics, and marijuana use, work, and sexual activity. There also are self-help groups that use similar principles as AA for survivors of incest and sexual abuse, children (and adult children) of alcohol- or drug-dependent parents, and people (or family members) of people who suffer from specific diseases or disorders (Fields, 1992).

Underserved Groups and Treatment Services

While there are many alcohol-treatment programs in existence, access to these programs often is limited to certain groups of people. Economic, cultural, and linguistic barriers preclude provision of adequate services and thus limit the potential for controlling and reducing alcohol and drug abuse. The following populations have the most trouble getting appropriate treatment (USDHHS, 1991):

- People with low incomes. Coverage for alcohol- and drug-abuse services under private and public financing programs is consistently less in amount and scope than coverage for general health care services. Thus, treatment is greatly dependent on the individual's or family's ability to pay. For the uninsured working population and the homeless population, financing of treatment poses a difficult barrier.
- Females. Females have limited access to alcohol- and other drug-abuse treatment services because of their unique needs, especially pregnant females and mothers with young children. Because of the risks to the fetus of alcohol and drug use during pregnancy, programs that specifically address the needs of pregnant females are needed.
- Youth. Adolescent users of alcohol and other drugs have unique needs and problems that cannot adequately be addressed in programs designed for adults. Treatment models specifically designed to serve the needs of youthful users have only recently begun to be developed but can be expected to expand in the future. Special attention to the treatment needs of the homeless, runaways, and school dropouts is needed.
- Minorities. Nonwhite Americans and non-English-speaking minority populations require treatment programs that take specific cultural influences on alcohol and other drug use into account and that impose no language barriers. Concerted attention should be given to the development of multilingual, multicultural-treatment programs.
- Inmates in correctional facilities. A large proportion of incarcerated offenders have varying degrees of alcohol- and drug-abuse problems. The majority of available treatment programs in prisons, however, are under-funded and understaffed. When offenders are released, there is a great probability that their untreated alcohol-

and other drug-abuse problems will reemerge along with criminal behavior.

Alcohol and Youth

Underage drinking often is a problem that is overlooked in the "War on Drugs," yet it affects millions of teenagers. The discussion will focus on statistics, factors that affect alcohol use by youth, trends in alcohol use by youth, availability and accessibility of alcohol to youth, influences on youth drinking behavior, alcoholism and problem drinking in youth, and children of parents with alcoholism.

Statistics

While the use of marijuana declined by 18 percent and cocaine by 40 percent in recent years among high school seniors, the percent of decline for alcohol use was only 2 percent (Johnston, O'Malley, & Bachman, 1991). The use of alcohol among youth is pervasive; 68 percent of all students in grades 7–12 have had at least one alcoholic drink, and 51 percent (or 10.6 million) have had at least one drink within the past year. Eight million (or 38 percent) of all students in junior and senior high school drink alcohol weekly (Office of the Inspector General, 1991). About nine of every ten high school seniors have tried alcohol, and nearly six out of ten are regular (at least monthly) users of alcohol (Johnston et al., 1991).

The average age that students take their first drink of alcohol is between 12 and 13 years of age. Of students who drink, five out of six report having had their first drink by age 15 (OIG, 1991). Junior and senior high school students drink less than 2 percent of the 62 billion bottles and cans of beer that are consumed annually in the United States. While this percentage appears small, it is staggering when one considers that minors illegally consume 1.1 billion beers (102 million gallons) each year. Even more staggering is the proportion of wine coolers that are consumed by young people. Junior and senior high school students have been estimated to drink 35 percent of all wine coolers sold in the United States, which accounts for more than 31 million gallons of wine coolers annually. Forty-two percent of students who drink choose wine coolers as their favorite alcoholic drink. They are popular choices because they taste good, are fruity, do not have a strong taste of alcohol, and do not contain much alcohol (so they think). Students who choose beer as a favorite alcoholic beverage say that it tastes good, is easy to get, is cheap, and does not intoxicate you as fast as other alcoholic beverages.

Factors That Affect Alcohol Use by Youth

Many teenagers use alcohol as a tool to help them cope with certain feelings and situations. Of the 10.6 million junior and senior students who drink, 31 percent drink alone; 41 percent drink when they are upset because it makes them feel better; 25 percent drink because they are bored; and 25 percent drink to feel high. **Binge drinking** is drinking five or more drinks in a row. Of the 5.4 million students who binge drink, 39 percent drink alone; 58 percent drink when they are upset; 30 percent drink when they are bored; and 37 percent drink to feel high. The fact that a high proportion of teenagers drink alone breaks the old stereotype of party drinking and peer pressure (Novello, 1991; OIG, 1991).

Many youths lack essential knowledge about alcohol and its effects. The minimum age to purchase alcohol in all states is 21. Nevertheless, 1.6 million junior and senior high school students do not know that such a law exists. Many students know about the law, but 5.6 million do not know the minimum age is 21. Many do not know that a person can die from an overdose of alcohol. More than one-third believe that drinking coffee, getting some fresh air, or taking a cold shower will "sober you up." Many also think that wine coolers and beer cannot get you drunk, make you sick, or harm in the ways that other alcoholic beverages do.

Most students do not know the relative strengths of different alcoholic beverages. Almost 80 percent do not know that one shot of whiskey has the same amount of alcohol as a 12-ounce can of beer. Similarly, 55 percent do not know that a 5-ounce glass of wine and a 12-ounce can of beer have the same amount of alcohol. One of three students do not know that all wine coolers contain alcohol. Two of three students cannot distinguish alcoholic beverages from nonalcoholic beverages. Students confuse alcoholic coolers with mineral waters that appear similar in color, labeling, and packaging. While containing no alcohol, mineral water with fruit juice or flavor also has become popular. These beverages offer a variety of fruit flavors in bottles that are very similar to the ones used for alcoholic coolers and fruit-flavored fortified wines. While these alcoholic and nonalcoholic beverages offer a similar sweet, fruity flavor and are packaged and sold in attractively designed four-packs or single 12-ounce bottles, they are in fact very different. Mineral waters offer substitutes for soda pop. The coolers offer similar flavors with 4–6 percent alcohol. Fruit-flavored, fortified wines, such as Cisco, offer the same flavors with 20 percent alcohol.

Trends in Alcohol Use by Youth

Despite the fact that it is illegal for virtually all high school students to purchase alcoholic beverages, experience with alcohol is almost universal (more than 90 percent have tried it) and active use is widespread. There also has been a widespread occurrence of occasions of heavy drinking. Thirty-two percent of high school seniors take part in this kind of drinking (Johnston, O'Malley, & Bachman, 1991).

Since 1980, the monthly prevalence of alcohol use among high school seniors has gradually declined, from 72 percent in 1980 to 57 percent in 1990. Daily use declined from a peak of 6.9 percent in 1979 to 3.7 percent in 1990. The prevalence of drinking five or more drinks in a row in the prior two weeks fell from 41 percent in 1983 to 32 percent in 1990 (Johnston, O'Malley, & Bachman, 1991).

Availability and Accessibility of Alcohol to Youth

Almost two-thirds of junior and senior high school students who drink buy their own beverages. This represents 7 million students. Despite minimum-age laws, students as young as 12 or 13 report that they have no difficulty in buying alcoholic beverages. As students get older, a larger proportion buy alcohol directly. Students may use fake identification, buy from stores known to sell to young people or from stores with young clerks who do not enforce the law. In some areas, underage drinkers rely on black market sources for alcohol. Some students who drink obtain alcohol from their friends. Younger students obtain alcohol from their parents with or without their parents' knowledge.

Almost 65 percent of all students have been to parties where alcohol is served. The number of students attending such parties increases with each grade level. More than 79 percent of high school students in grades 9 through 12 have been to parties where alcohol was served.

The National Minimum Drinking Age Act. At the federal level, the National Minimum Drinking Age Act of 1984 requires all states to raise their minimum purchase and public possession age to 21. States that did not comply faced a reduction in highway funds under the Federal Highway Aid Act. All fifty states are in compliance with this Act.

The National Minimum Drinking Age Act specifically prohibits persons under 21 years of age from the purchase and public possession of alcoholic beverages. The Act does

171

not prohibit persons under 21 (also called youth or minors) from drinking. The term "public possession" is strictly defined and does not apply to possession under the following circumstances:

1. for an established religious purpose;
2. when accompanied by a parent, spouse, or legal guardian age 21 or older;
3. for medical purposes when prescribed or administered by a licensed physician, pharmacist, dentist, nurse, hospital, or medical institution;
4. in private clubs or establishments;
5. in the course of lawful employment by a duly licensed manufacturer, wholesaler, or retailer.

The twenty-first Amendment of the United States Constitution, which repealed prohibition, grants states the right to regulate alcohol distribution and sale. State laws are unique, but each allows local communities to regulate youth access to alcohol through local ordinances and law enforcement.

There are exemptions in the National Minimum Drinking Act and loopholes in state laws that permit underage drinking. Although no states permit vendors to sell to minors, six states and the District of Columbia do not prohibit minors from purchasing alcoholic beverages. However, these states do prohibit minors from using false identification or misrepresenting their age. In 38 states, because of exemptions to the law, possession of alcohol by minors is not specifically illegal. Minors can possess alcohol with parental consent, for religious purposes, in private residences, in public establishments with a parent or spouse of legal drinking age present, and for medicinal purposes. The private residence exception is particularly troublesome because often no parental supervision is required. Five states prohibit minors from possessing alcohol only if they intend to consume it. Because they must prove "intent to consume," law enforcement officials in these states are reluctant to arrest minors for possession of alcoholic beverages. In 21 states, consumption by minors is not specifically illegal. Forty-four states allow minors to sell and serve alcohol without adult supervision in stores or restaurants.

Influences on Youth Drinking Behaviors

One important influential factor that encourages youthful drinking is easy access and availability of alcoholic beverages. Other important factors are parents, friends, and advertisements for alcoholic beverages. Almost two-thirds of all students say their parents do not approve of underage drinking or would punish them if they drank. Many

parents are more lenient. Thirty-five percent of junior and senior high school students who drink say their parents tolerate their drinking under certain conditions. These conditions typically limit the amount, frequency, or location of drinking. Almost 15 percent of the students who drink report that their parents trust them or do not say anything about their drinking.

Youths commonly drink with their friends who, in turn, are the main reasons for drinking. Most drink to have fun and to be social. Others say they drink because their friends drink.

Another profound influence is alcohol advertising. Advertisements for alcohol on television and in magazines effectively portray drinking alcohol as glamorous, "cool," and fun. Surveys show that a high proportion of teenagers like advertisements for alcoholic beverages. What they like the most is that advertisements spotlight attractive people and make drinking look like fun. It is clear that alcohol advertisements target youths. It is ironic that the consequences that alcohol often brings (e.g., traumatic accidents, family violence, alcohol dependency) are so different from the fantasy and fun depicted in the advertisements.

There is an ambivalence about alcohol and drugs in our society. To many people, alcohol is not considered a drug. For example, the "War on Drugs" has largely focused on drugs of abuse other than alcohol. Parents often are upset at the suggestion that their children use drugs such as cocaine or marijuana but show tolerance toward alcohol use. This ambivalence results from the fact that alcohol is a legal drug for adults and that many parents also drank when they were underage. Children also receive mixed messages from parents about alcohol and other drug use when they observe their parents using alcohol.

Alcohol is used to cope with such negative feelings as awkwardness, loneliness and shyness, being upset, hopelessness, and boredom (Page, 1990; Page, 1991). Adolescents are vulnerable to these feelings as part of their development and establishment of a personal identity. Relief from these feelings sometimes is temporarily achieved by drinking alcohol. Social and psychological maturity cannot develop when young people rely on alcohol and other substances to cope with negative feelings. They must learn to deal effectively with emotions and the situations with which they are confronted in order to mature beyond adolescence.

Alcoholism and Problem Drinking in Youth

Alcoholism usually is a progressive disease, which means that its consequences get increasingly worse in the absence of treatment. It also is a complex disease because there are social, family, psychologic, genetic, and physiologic causes of alcoholism and problem drinking. Because drinking often starts early in life, sometimes as early as grade school, it is not uncommon to see alcoholism in middle and high schoolers. An early preoccupation with alcohol may result in physical, academic, social, and/or family dysfunction. An important and frightening aspect of alcohol and youth is that young people are more susceptible to alcoholism than are adults (Morrison 1991; Myers & Andersen 1991). Also, youth alcoholism typically progresses to serious consequences at a faster pace than does alcoholism in adults.

Youth alcoholism includes a constellation of signs and symptoms of problematic drinking behaviors. Drinking no longer is done just for the purpose of having fun or to feel "high," but is done in response to negative feelings—worry, anxiety, depression, tiredness, loneliness, or stress. Feelings of guilt about drinking often develop. With an increase in alcohol consumption and frequency of drinking comes the tendency to drink in secret or to hide one's consumption level. Along with increased consumption of alcohol, increasing tolerance to the effects of alcohol develops. A particularly important sign of problem drinking is the appearance of alcohol blackouts. **Blackouts** are periods of alcohol-induced amnesia.

At parties and other drinking situations, a teenager who is alcohol-dependent often will continue to drink after his/ her friends have quit. In order to get a more dramatic effect from alcohol, a teenager who is developing or has developed alcoholism will often gulp drinks. Muscle tremors may develop when there is little or no alcohol in the system, especially in the morning. This often will motivate the young drinker to start drinking early in the day. Other withdrawal symptoms will emerge as alcohol dependency develops and efforts are made to stop drinking. These symptoms include restlessness, insomnia, depression, mental confusion, and, in severe cases, hallucinations and convulsions.

Behavioral changes are likely to occur as alcoholism develops. Grades often decline and absences and tardiness at school typically increase in frequency. A decreased attention span also may be apparent in the classroom as well as difficulty following through with projects and assignments. Another indicative sign of possible alcoholism is a sudden decrease in handwriting skills.

Other behavioral signs that may indicate drinking problems are:

1. preoccupation with procuring and maintaining a supply of alcohol,
2. difficulty in managing money,
3. changes in eating behavior,
4. impulsive behavior,
5. lying to teachers and parents,
6. inability to cope with frustration,
7. changing from one peer group to another,
8. irritability with others,
9. suspiciousness of others,
10. rebelliousness.

Children of Parents with Alcoholism

The National Health Interview Survey on Alcohol showed that nearly one in five adults lived with an alcohol-dependent person at some time during their childhood (Schoenborn, 1991). The number of children under the age of 18 living with an alcohol-dependent parent is not precisely known but is estimated to be between 7 and 15 million. With such estimates, it is probable that four to six children in a typical classroom of 25 students have a parent who is dependent on alcohol (Towers, 1989).

Alcoholism has tragic effects not only on the dependent person directly involved but also on the children of parents who are dependent on alcohol (Fig. 13-3). Characteristics often seen in families in which one or more parents is alcohol-dependent are:

1. primary needs of children are not met;
2. children feel a great amount of responsibility and guilt for their parent's drinking behavior and the consequences that may result;
3. the family environment is characterized by unpredictability because children are confused by the difference between the intoxicated and sober behaviors of a parent (e.g., promises made that are not kept; actions that are praised one day are ignored or punished the next day);
4. feelings of low self-esteem;
5. insecurity about parents' love;
6. family isolation;
7. denial of the alcoholic parent's drinking behavior.

Children in families in which a parent or other family member is alcohol-dependent often are fearful for their own safety as well as for their dependent family member. The threat of accidents is very real and children can perceive some of the risks of the drunken behaviors of the dependent person. They fear that the person may lose control of the car when driving under the influence or may become injured in some other way. Their own safety and

173

Figure 13-3
Children of Parents with Alcoholism Need Help

security is threatened, knowing, for example, that an intoxicated person may pass out or fall asleep while smoking and that the house could be set on fire. There also is terror associated with the arguments they overhear. The associated tension is very upsetting to children, causing them to fear for their own safety. They may have been victims of incest and child abuse in the past. They may feel anger that they are not protected from the violence of the alcohol-dependent person.

Because children in families with alcoholism grow up in an environment of chaos, unpredictability, anxiety, and denial it is common to see the following characteristics in these children:
• seeking approval,
• fear of personal criticism,

• having an overdeveloped sense of responsibility,
• experiencing guilt feelings when standing up for themselves,
• confusing love with pity,
• hiding true feelings,
• judging themselves harshly because of poor self-esteem,
• being terrified at the thought of abandonment,
• being reactors rather than actors,
• eventually becoming alcohol-dependent, marrying an alcohol-dependent person, or both,
• experiencing depression,
• having headaches, upset stomachs, or insomnia due to distress,
• developing learning disabilities,
• coping with eating disorders,
• behaving in deviant and antisocial ways.

CHAPTER 13

BIBLIOGRAPHY

Alcohol, Drug Abuse, and Mental Health Administration. (1990) *Seventh Special Report to the U.S. Congress on Alcohol and Health.* DHHS Publication No. (ADM)90-1656. Washington, D.C.: U.S. Government Printing Office.

Bagsara, O., Kajdacsy-Balla, A., Lischner, H.W. (1989) Effects of alcohol ingestion on in vitro susceptibility of peripheral blood mononuclear cells to infection with HIV and of selected T-cell functions. *Alcoholism: Clinical and Experimental Research*, 13:636–643.

Bijur, P.E., Kurzon, M., Overpeck, M.D., & Scheidt, P.C. (1992) Parental alcohol use, problem drinking, and children's injuries. *Journal of the American Medical Association*, 267:3166–3171.

Centers for Disease Control. (1992) Trends in alcohol-related traffic, by sex—United States. *Morbidity and Mortality Weekly Report*, 189:195–197.

Evans, L. (1991) *Traffic Safety and the Driver*. New York: Van Nostrand Reinhold.

Fields, R. (1992) *Drugs and Alcohol in Perspective*. Dubuque, IA: Wm. C. Brown.

Frances, R., & Franklin, J.E. (1992) Addiction medicine. *Journal of the American Medical Association*, 268:330–331.

Gavin, J. (1992) The U.S. can put an end to drunk driving. *USA Today Magazine*, March, 66–68.

Gibbons, B. (1992) Alcohol: The legal drug. *National Geographic*, February, 3–35.

Gunby, P. (1992) Seven years before centennial of first U.S. traffic death, toll already has reached nearly 2.8 million. *Journal of the American Medical Association*, 268:306.

Johnston, L.D., O'Malley, P.M., & Bachman, J.G. (1991) *Drug Use Among American High School Seniors, College Students and Young Adults, 1975–1990. Volume 1. High School Seniors.* DHHS Publication No. (ADM)91-1813. Rockville, MD: National Institute on Drug Abuse.

Kelbaek, H. (1990) Acute effects of alcohol and food intake on cardiac performance. *Progress in Cardiovascular Diseases*, 32:347–364.

Kinney, J., & Leaton, G. (1991) *Loosening the Grip: A Handbook of Alcohol Information*. St. Louis, MO: Mosby-Year Book.

Klep, K., & Perry, C.L. (1990) Adolescents, drinking, and driving: Who does it and why? In R.J Wilson & R.E. Mann (Eds.), *Drinking and Driving: Advances in Research and Prevention*. New York: Guilford Press.

MacGregor, R.R. (1988) Alcohol and drugs as co-factors for AIDS. *Advances in Alcohol and Substance Abuse*, 7:47–71.

Marwick, C. (1992) Traffic death toll may be declining, but experts not ready to celebrate. *Journal of the American Medical Association*, 268:301.

Morrison, M.A. (1991) Overview: Kids and drugs. *Psychiatric Annals*, 21:72–73.

Myers, D.P., & Anderson, A.R. (1991) Adolescent addiction: Assessment and identification. *Journal of Pediatric Health Care*, 5:86–93.

Nair, M.P.N., Schwartz, S.A., Kronfol, Z.A., Heimer, E.P., Pottathil, R., & Greden, J.F. (1990) Immunoregulatory effects of alcohol lymphocyte responses to human immunodeficiency virus proteins. *Progress in Clinical and Biological Research*, 325:221–230.

National Institute on Alcohol Abuse and Alcoholism. (1992) *Alcohol Alert*, 15:1–2.

National Institute on Drug Abuse. (1991) *National Conference on Drug Abuse Research & Practice: An Alliance for the 21st Century.* DHHS Publication No. (ADM)91-1818. Washington, D.C.: U.S. Government Printing Office.

Novello, A.C. (1991) Prepared statement of Antonia C. Novello, Surgeon General. In Select Committee on Children, Youth, and Families, U.S. House of Representatives. (1991) *Preventing Underage Drinking: A Dialogue with the Surgeon General*. Washington, D.C.: U.S. Government Printing Office.

Office for Substance Abuse Prevention. (1990) *Alcohol, Tobacco, and Other Drugs May Harm the Unborn.* DHHS Publication No. (ADM)900-1711. Rockville, MD: Office for Substance Abuse Prevention.

Office for Substance Abuse Prevention. (1991) *Too Many Young People Drink and Know Too Little About the Consequences.* Washington, D.C.: Office for Substance Abuse Prevention.

Office of Inspector General. (1991) *General Reports on Youth and Alcohol.* RPO799. Washington, D.C.: United States Department of Health and Human Services. This document includes the following three reports: "Drinking habits, access, attitudes, and knowledge," " Do they know what they are drinking?", and "Laws and enforcement: Is the 21-year-old drinking age a myth?"

Orford, J., & Velleman, R. (1991) The environmental intergenerational transmission of alcohol problems. *British Journal of Medicine and Psychology*, 64:189–299.

Page, R.M. (1990) Loneliness and adolescent health behavior. *Health Education*, 21(5):14–17.

Page, R.M. (1991) Loneliness as a risk factor in adolescent hopelessness. *Journal of Research in Personality*, 25:189–195.

Plant, M.A. (1990) Alcohol, sex and AIDS. *Alcohol & Alcoholism*, 25:293–301.

Randall, T. (1992) Driving while under influence of alcohol remains major cause of traffic violence. *Journal of the American Medical Association*, 268:303–304.

Reiken, G.B. (1991) Negative effects of alcohol on physical fitness and athletic performance. *Journal of Physical Education, Recreation, and Dance*, October, 64–66.

Schoenborn, C.A. (1991) Exposure to alcoholism in the family: United States, 1988. *Advance Data from Vital and Health Statistics of the National Center for Health Statistics*. DHHS Publication No. (PHS)91-1250, No. 205. Hyattsville, MD: National Center for Health Statistics.

Select Committee on Children, Youth, and Families, U.S. House of Representatives. (1991) *Preventing Underage Drinking: A Dialogue with the Surgeon General*. Washington, D.C.: U.S. Government Printing Office.

Steele, C.M., & Josephs, R.A. (1990) Alcohol myopia: Its prized and dangerous effects. *American Psychologist*, 45:921–933.

Steinmetz, G. (1992) The preventable tragedy: Fetal alcohol syndrome. *National Geographic*, February, 36–39.

Stone, N.J. (1990) Diet, lipids, and coronary heart disease. *Endocrinology and Metabolism Clinics of North America*, 19:321–344.

Stoto, M.A, Behrens, R., & Rosemont, C. (1990) *Healthy People 2000: Citizens Chart the Course*. Washington, D.C.: National Academy Press.

Towers, R.L. (1989) *Children of Alcoholics/Addicts*. Washington, D.C.: National Education Association.

United States Department of Health and Human Services. (1991) *Healthy People 2000: National Health Promotion and Disease Prevention Objectives*. DHHS Publication No. (PHS)91-50212. Washington, D.C.: U.S. Government Printing Office.

Urbano-Marquez, A., Estrich, R., Navarro-Lopez, F., Grau, J.M., Mont, L., & Rubin, E. (1989) The effects of alcoholism on skeletal and cardiac muscle. *New England Journal of Medicine*, 320:409–415.

Weidner, G., Connor, S.L., Chesney, M.A., Burns, J.W., Matazarro, J.D., & Mendell, N.R. (1991) Sex differences in high density lipoprotein cholesterol among low-level alcohol consumers. *Circulation*, 83:176–180.

Wilson, M.H., Baker, S.P, Teret, S.P., Shock, S., & Garbiano, J. (1991) *Saving Children: A Guide to Injury Prevention*. New York: Oxford University Press.

Woteki, C.E., & Thomas, P.R. (1992) *Eat for Life: The Food and Nutrition Board's Guide to Reducing Your Risk of Chronic Disease*. Washington, D.C.: National Academy Press.

TOBACCO

There are reports that during the 1500s, tobacco was considered to be a useful herb for the treatment of such ailments as headaches and abscesses. Today, however, tobacco is used primarily as a recreational drug. Because tobacco contains nicotine, a powerfully addictive drug, a user can experience both stimulation and relaxation. The actions of nicotine on the brain and in the body reinforce the continual use of the drug and make quitting very difficult. When tobacco smoke is inhaled into the lungs, nicotine is absorbed into the bloodstream and reaches the brain quickly. Nicotine also is absorbed into the bloodstream and reaches the brain when tobacco is used in the form of chew or snuff, or smoked in pipes or cigars.

The initial effects of tobacco use usually are not serious. However, over time the effects on health can be catastrophic. Cigarette smoking is the major, single, preventable cause of disease and death in the United States as well as in many other nations. Tobacco kills more people than the combined toll of AIDS, cocaine use, heroin use, alcohol use, fire, motor vehicle accidents, homicide, and suicide. Cigarette smoking costs our nation $52 billion a year ($221 per capita) in health care and insurance costs and lost productivity. Discussions in this chapter will include cigarette smoking and youth, trends in smoking, components of tobacco smoke, health effects of tobacco, tobacco and the law, and smoking cessation.

CIGARETTE SMOKING AND YOUTH

More than 3,000 children and adolescents begin using tobacco each day in the United States (Davis, 1991), 750 of whom eventually will die from a tobacco-related disease (Glynn, Anderson, & Schwarz, 1991). Adolescent statistics, trends in smoking, and characteristics of youth smokers will be discussed in this section of the chapter.

Adolescent Statistics

Experimentation with smoking is occurring at younger and younger ages and initiation of smoking occurs almost entirely before or during adolescence. Surveys of high school students find that of those who have smoked, about one-fourth smoked their first cigarette by the sixth grade,

one-half by the eighth grade, three-fourths by the ninth grade, and 94 percent by the eleventh grade (United States Department of Health and Human Services, 1991).

These early initiation rates for smoking underscore the importance of starting smoking-prevention efforts in elementary school. Results from the Youth Risk Behavior Survey, a national survey of high school students in grades 9–12, show that 70.1 percent of all students reported having tried cigarettes. The difference between males and females is very small with 70.6 percent of males and 69.5 percent of females trying cigarettes. Hispanic students were the most likely to have tried cigarettes (75.3 percent) while African-American students were the least likely (67.2 percent). Among white American students, 70.4 percent had tried cigarette smoking (Centers for Disease Control, 1992b).

Frequent cigarette use, defined as smoking cigarettes on 20 or more of the 30 days preceding the survey, was reported by 12.7 percent of students. A higher percent (15.4) of white American students than Hispanic (6.8 percent) or African-American students (3.1 percent) were frequent smokers. Frequent cigarette use increased in the first three high school levels; 8.4 percent of ninth graders, 11.3 percent of tenth graders, 15.6 percent of eleventh, and 15.6 percent of twelfth graders. A slightly higher proportion of males (13.0 percent) than females (12.4 percent) were frequent cigarette smokers (Centers for Disease Control, 1992b).

Another survey that provides information on the smoking prevalence of youth is the Teenage Attitudes and Practices Survey (TAPS). TAPS collects information on all adolescents 12–18 years of age living in U.S. households. The survey includes those who attend school, have graduated, or have dropped out. Overall, 15.7 percent of survey respondents age 12–18 reported smoking on one or more days during the preceding month, and 11.5 percent reported smoking on one or more days during the preceding week. Among 17–18 year olds, 43.3 percent of dropouts reported smoking during the previous week. This was much higher than the 17.1 percent of high school attenders or graduates who reported smoking during the previous week. Among high school attenders or graduates the prevalence of smoking during the previous week was similar; 17.5 percent of males and 16.7 percent of females. However, 51.7 percent of male dropouts compared to 33.3 percent of female dropouts smoked cigarettes in the past week (Centers for Disease Control, 1991b).

Adolescent Trends

The prevalence of smoking among high school seniors declined sharply during the late 1970s when nearly 30 percent were daily cigarette smokers (Johnston, O'Malley, & Bachman, 1991). Glynn, Anderson, Schwarz (1991) make the following observations about adolescent smoking trends:

- Since the 1980s, smoking prevalence has declined very little among youth and rates have remained stable for more than a decade. This suggests that those who currently smoke may be more dependent on tobacco and/ or represent a more difficult group of adolescents to reach.
- In the past, male adolescents were more likely than female adolescents to smoke cigarettes. This trend is now reversed. Currently, smoking rates have become similar for both sexes and, in some studies, a higher proportion of female adolescents than male adolescents smoke cigarettes.
- Smokeless tobacco use has increased among adolescents.
- There is a very high smoking prevalence rate among those who drop out of school. A study by Pirie, Murray, and Luepker (1988) showed that 75 percent of high school dropouts smoke cigarettes. This poses a difficult problem for health professionals because this high-risk group cannot be reached through school-based, smoking-prevention programs.

Research indicates that smoking initiation is more sensitive to intervention than is quitting behavior. Therefore, preventing the initiation of smoking and other forms of tobacco use should be a major focus of efforts to reduce the prevalence of cigarette smoking. The national health-promotion goal regarding youth smoking is to reduce the initiation of cigarette smoking by children and youth so that no more than 15 percent become regular smokers by age 20 (USDHHS, 1991).

Characteristics of Youth Smokers

The Teenage Attitudes and Practices Survey (TAPS) revealed many important findings about youth smokers (Allen, Moss, Giovino, Shopland, & Pierce, 1993). The

habit of smoking among adolescents is strongly correlated with the smoking practices of family and peers. Teenagers who smoke are more likely to have a parent who smokes, to have an older sibling who smokes, and to associate with other smokers rather than with teenagers who do not smoke. Teenagers who smoke compared to teenagers who have never smoked report knowing more people who use chewing tobacco, snuff, marijuana, crack, or cocaine; more people who drink alcohol; and more people who are sexually active. School performance and attitudes about school also are strong correlates of smoking uptake among adolescents. Current smokers, more than teenagers who have never smoked, report liking school less, doing poorly in school, and perceiving what they learn in school as being less useful to them later in life. Current smokers also miss more time from school and cut school more often than nonsmokers.

Teenagers who currently smoke cigarettes are more likely than teenagers who have never smoked to:
- feel tired,
- have trouble sleeping,
- be sad or depressed,
- feel hopeless, tense, or worried,
- be involved in risky behaviors.

For example, teenage smokers are twice as likely to have been involved in one or more physical fights in the past year. Smokers are almost three times more likely than teenagers who had never smoked to rarely or never wear seat belts and six times more likely to have ridden in a car driven by someone who had been using drugs or alcohol.

Estimates from TAPS also show other important differences between teenagers who smoke and those who have never smoked, in terms of social and family functioning. For example:
- Nonsmokers are more likely than smokers to dislike being around people who are smoking and to date nonsmokers.
- Smokers are more likely than nonsmokers to have had a steady boyfriend/girlfriend and to have a boyfriend/ girlfriend who smokes.
- Smokers have more spendable income than teenagers who have never smoked cigarettes.
- Teenagers who smoke are more likely to confide in a friend if they need help with a serious problem; teenagers who do not smoke are more likely to confide in a parent.
- Almost twice as many teenagers who smoke, compared to teenagers who have never smoked, are left alone at

home without parental or adult supervision for 10 or more hours a week.

- Teenage nonsmokers are more likely than teenagers who smoke to attend religious services.

What teenagers believe to be true about smoking clearly is influenced by the benefits they perceive from smoking. Current adolescent smokers are more likely to believe that cigarette smoking helps people when they are bored, helps people relax, helps reduce stress, helps people feel more comfortable in social situations, and helps keep their weight down. For teenagers who smoke, the perceived functional utility of smoking clearly outweighs the risks of smoking (Allen et al., 1993).

TRENDS IN SMOKING

In 1964, the Surgeon General of the United States issued the first report on smoking and health, which had a definite impact on statistics concerning trends. The prevalence of tobacco smoking will be discussed in terms of age, education, occupations, race, and gender.

Age

Among people aged 20 and older, cigarette smoking prevalence declined steadily at a rate of 0.5 percentage points per year from 1965 to 1987 (USDHHS, 1991). From 1987, when overall prevalence among adults was 28.8 percent, to 1990 overall prevalence dropped an average of 1.1 percent annually to 25.5 percent of adults. Based on information collected from the National Health Interview Survey, there were 45.8 million current smokers in 1990; 28.4 percent of all males and 22.8 percent of all females were current smokers (CDC, 1992a).

Excepting 18–24 year olds, the prevalence of smoking is higher among males than among females (CDC, 1991a). The average number of cigarettes smoked per day by current smokers is 19. However, males smoke more cigarettes a day than females (CDC, 1992a). Current trends suggest that overall smoking prevalence will be 22 percent in the year 2000 for adults, above the target of 15 percent (USDHHS, 1991).

Education

The prevalence of cigarette smoking among people with less than a high school education is 34.0 percent and for those with only high school education it is 32.0 percent (CDC, 1991a). The rate of decline in smoking prevalence since 1965 for this group has been approximately 0.2 percentage points per year. If the current trend continues, smoking prevalence among people with a high school

education or less will be approximately 31 percent in the year 2000.

Occupations

Smoking prevalence varies by occupational categories. Smoking prevalence is consistently higher among blue-collar and service workers than among white-collar professionals. Approximately the same percentage of white-collar males smoke cigarettes as white-collar females (26 percent). Also, among blue-collar workers, approximately 36 percent of males and 36 percent of females smoke. The unusual similarity of smoking prevalence rates between males and females within the blue- and white-collar working categories suggests that the work environment is an important influence on smoking status.

The prevalence of smoking has been much higher among military personnel than among the overall population. Smoking is inversely associated with military rank, and is at least twice as high among enlisted personnel as among commissioned officers. Smoking prevalence rates among military personnel have now fallen from 52 percent in 1980 to less than 42 percent. If current trends continue, smoking prevalence among military personnel will be roughly 26 percent in the year 2000.

Race

A higher percentage of African-American adults (31.7 percent) than white Americans (27.8 percent), than Hispanics (28.4 percent), and than persons of other races (23.8 percent) smoke (CDC, 1991a). However, smoking prevalence declined more rapidly among African-Americans than among white Americans from 1974 through 1985, indicating that the gap is slowly closing. Although African-American adolescents are less likely than white American adolescents to smoke, African-American adults are more likely than white American adults to begin smoking after adolescence (Escobedo et al., 1990).

This differential in smoking rates between African-Americans and white Americans may disappear in future years. For example, 47.1 percent of African-Americans and 38.6 percent of white Americans aged 20–24 years of age smoked cigarettes in 1974. By 1988, this differential had decreased to 28.5 percent of African-Americans and 24.8 percent of white Americans (CDC, 1991c).

The prevalence of smoking varies considerably among Native American groups. Smoking prevalence is highest among Northern Plains Indians (42–70 percent) and Alaska Natives (56 percent). American Indians from the South-west report much lower smoking rates, ranging from 13–28 percent.

Smoking prevalence among new immigrant Asian groups may be high, consistent with rates of their country of origin. For example, smoking rates are 55–65 percent for Vietnamese males, 71 percent for Cambodian males, and 92 percent for Laotian males. On the other hand, smoking rates for more established Asian-American groups are relatively low.

Gender

The decline in smoking prevalence has been substantially slower among females than for males. In 1965, about one-third of females (32 percent) smoked, compared to over half of all males (Novello, 1991). In 1990, 22.8 percent of females and 28.4 percent of males smoked (CDC, 1992a). If the decline in female smoking prevalence that has occurred since 1985 continues, a convergence of smoking prevalence for both genders is not inevitable (Gritz, 1991).

COMPONENTS OF TOBACCO SMOKE

The estimated number of chemical compounds in tobacco smoke exceeds 4,000. Many of these compounds are pharmacologically active, toxic, poisonous, or carcinogenic. As many as 400–500 vaporous compounds are emitted into the air from a smoking cigarette. Some of these are nitrogen, oxygen, carbon monoxide, carbon dioxide, ammonia, hydrogen cyanide, methane, benzene, toluene, and formaldehyde. Carbon monoxide is a gas that significantly interferes with the ability of blood to carry oxygen by displacing oxygen from hemoglobin. Two major components of tobacco smoke, tar and nicotine, will be discussed in this section of the chapter.

Tar

The particulate matter of tobacco smoke is composed of tiny particles, called tar, that can irritate the trachea and lungs. Tar is a sticky, dark, mixture of at least 3,500 chemicals in cigarette smoke. Some of these chemical compounds are metals, concentrations of pesticides and other agricultural chemicals, and 11 carcinogenic polynuclear aromatic hydrocarbons. Forty-three different carcinogens have been identified in tobacco smoke.

Nicotine

Nicotine is the most abundant chemical compound found in the particulate matter of cigarette smoke. Nicotine is an odorless and colorless compound, the active psychoactive agent found naturally in tobacco, which is responsible for the addictive behavior of tobacco smokers. When tobacco smoke reaches the alveoli in the lungs, nicotine is rapidly absorbed. Smokeless tobacco users absorb nicotine primarily through the mucous membranes of the mouth and/or nose.

Nicotine enters the blood and is rapidly transported to the brain, which has specific receptor sites for the drug. As a result, the effects of nicotine on the brain and central nervous system occur rapidly after a puff of cigarette smoke or absorption of nicotine from other routes of administration. Levels of nicotine in the blood are similar no matter what form of tobacco is used.

Nicotine is primarily metabolized in the liver and, to a smaller extent, in the lungs. About 10–15 percent of the absorbed nicotine is excreted in urine. A primary by-product of nicotine metabolism is cotinine. Cotinine measurements in saliva, blood, or urine can be used as an indicator of nicotine uptake by cigarette smokers, tobacco chewers, and involuntary smokers. It takes 18–20 hours for a smoker to eliminate half of the cotinine in his/her body. However, for an involuntary smoker there is a considerably slower rate of cotinine elimination.

Nicotine stimulates the adrenal glands and the cerebral cortex of the brain. Nicotine acts first as a stimulant, then as a tranquilizer. Other actions include a dulling of the taste buds, constriction of blood vessels, and an increase in blood pressure and heart rate. After smoking cigarettes or receiving nicotine, users perform better on some cognitive tasks than they do when deprived of nicotine. However, smoking and nicotine do not improve general learning.

All forms of tobacco contain nicotine. Specifically, nicotine is a mood-altering drug that can provide pleasurable effects. Nicotine also can serve as a reinforcer to motivate tobacco-seeking and tobacco-using behavior. Tolerance develops as a result of the actions of nicotine. Repeated use results in diminished effects and can be accompanied by increased intake. Nicotine also causes physical dependence characterized by a withdrawal syndrome that usually accompanies nicotine abstinence.

Nicotine, together with carbon monoxide, is a major contributor to a cigarette smoker's increased risk of heart disease. Nicotine causes a persistent activation of the sympathetic nervous system, which prepares the body for dealing with physical emergencies. This activation may increase risk of heart disease by raising the amount of lipids in the blood, making blood platelets clot blood more easily, causing spasms in coronary arteries, and raising heart rate and blood pressure. These factors may accelerate atherosclerosis or contribute to a heart attack in persons with preexisting atherosclerosis.

HEALTH EFFECTS OF TOBACCO

In 1938, the first scientific study showing increased death rates among smokers was published (Pearl, 1938). Since this study, overwhelming and conclusive evidence that cigarette smoking poses serious health hazards has accumulated. The toll on human health is staggering. More than 434,000 people die each year from smoking-related causes in the United States (CDC, 1991d) and about 2 million die in developed countries (Giovino, Eriksen, & McKenna, 1992). Clearly, the greatest single preventable cause of premature death in our nation is cigarette smoking. Smoking is responsible for more than one in every six deaths in the United States. Every day, 1200 smokers die and another 3,500 stop smoking (Glantz, 1993). Discussions in this section will include the Surgeon General's reports, lung cancer, chronic obstructive pulmonary disease, coronary disease, effects of smoking on nonsmokers, effects on fertility, effects of prenatal and childhood exposure to tobacco, and effects of smokeless tobacco.

The Surgeon General's Reports

The 1964 Surgeon General's Report on Smoking and Health concluded that cigarette smoking increases overall mortality in males, causes lung and laryngeal cancer in males, and causes chronic bronchitis. The Report also found significant association between smoking and numerous other diseases.

Reports of the Surgeon General since 1964 have concluded that smoking increases mortality and morbidity in both males and females. Disease associations identified as causal since 1964 include coronary disease, atherosclerotic peripheral vascular disease, lung and laryngeal cancer in females, oral cancer, esophageal cancer, chronic obstructive pulmonary disease, intrauterine growth retardation, and low birth weight babies. Smoking substantially contributes to chronic illness and disability as well.

The 1979 Report of the Surgeon General found smokeless tobacco to be associated with oral cancer. In 1986, the Surgeon General concluded that smokeless tobacco was a cause of this disease. In 1964, tobacco use was considered to be a habit. Since that time, a substantial body of evidence has accumulated and was summarized in the 1988 Surgeon General's report. This report established that cigarettes and other forms of tobacco are

addicting. Given the prevalence of smoking, tobacco use is the most widespread form of drug dependency.

Cigarette smoking is now considered to be a probable cause of unsuccessful pregnancies, increased infant mortality, and peptic ulcer disease. It is thought to be a contributing factor for cancer of the bladder, pancreas, and kidney and to be associated with cancer of the stomach. Accumulating research has brought to light the interaction effects of cigarette smoking with certain occupational exposures to increase the risk of cancer, with alcohol ingestion to increase the risk of cancer, and with selected medications to produce adverse effects. Cigarette smoking accounts for 87 percent of lung cancer deaths, 30 percent of all cancer deaths, and 21 percent of all coronary disease deaths.

Lung Cancer

Cigarette smoking is the major cause of lung cancer and far outweighs all other risk factors in its effect. Approximately 90 percent of lung cancer cases in males and 79 percent in females are attributable to cigarette smoking. Lung cancer incidence risk is proportional to the amount smoked daily and the duration of time smoked. Smokers who smoke more than two packs per day have death rates from lung cancer 15 to 25 times greater than that of individuals who have never smoked.

Tobacco use is a major risk factor not only for cancer of the lungs but also for cancers of the larynx, pharynx, oral cavity, esophagus, pancreas, and bladder. Cancer is the second leading cause of death in the United States, and more deaths occur from lung cancer than from any other type of cancer. Approximately 143,000 people die from lung cancer in a year (American Cancer Society, 1991). Lung cancer is rare in individuals who have never smoked. Cessation of cigarette smoking results in a gradual decrease in lung cancer risk. After 10–20 years of cessation, lung cancer rates for former smokers approach the rates of lifelong nonsmokers.

Among males, lung cancer death rates began to climb sharply in the 1930s, approximately 20–30 years after males began smoking in large numbers. A nearly identical increase in lung cancer deaths among females began in the 1960s, approximately 20–30 years after the post-World War II surge in female smoking. As a result of the declining prevalence of smoking among males, lung cancer death rates for males have begun to level off and are expected to begin to decline in the 1990s. Among females, lung cancer death rates continue to increase and, in 1986, surpassed breast cancer as the leading kind of cancer death. Females now have an incidence of lung cancer nearly identical to that of males 30 years ago. The rising lung cancer death rate for females is expected to peak around the year 2010.

No effective treatment for lung cancer is available. Nearly 90 percent of lung cancer patients die within five years of diagnosis. Survival improves modestly when lung cancer is detected at an early, localized stage, but few cases are detected early.

Prevention is the key to reducing lung cancer morbidity and mortality. Intensified efforts to prevent the initiation of smoking by youth and to increase cessation among those who currently smoke are the primary ways to reverse the upward trends in lung cancer incidence and lung cancer mortality.

Although cigarette smoking is the major determinant of lung cancer risk, exposure to radon decay products, asbestos, or ionizing radiation also can increase lung cancer risk. The combination of cigarette smoking and asbestos exposure increases the risk of lung cancer fifty fold. Chronic exposure to environmental tobacco smoke also increases the risk of lung cancer in nonsmokers.

Chronic Obstructive Pulmonary Disease

Chronic obstructive pulmonary disease (COPD), which is characterized by permanent airflow reduction, is the fifth leading cause of death in the United States and is a major cause of chronic illness and disability. Nearly 80,000 people die each year from this condition, and cigarette smoking accounts for 82 percent of these deaths. Death rates from COPD have paralleled those for lung cancer and have increased progressively over the last 25 years. Death occurs only after an extended period of disability and many of those disabled by COPD die from other causes. Nearly 13 million people report having COPD, which includes chronic bronchitis and emphysema.

Normally, ventilatory function increases during childhood, reaches a peak during adolescence, then declines with advancing age. In cigarette smokers who develop symptomatic airflow obstruction, a similar loss of function takes place, but at a much more rapid rate, and eventually results in shortness of breath and limitation of activity. Evidence of impairment begins in some cigarette smokers as early as a few years after initiation. With cessation of smoking, the rate of functional loss declines, but lost function can-

not be regained. However, timely smoking cessation can help prevent the development of symptomatic disease.

Coronary Disease

Coronary disease afflicts about seven million people, annually causes over 500,000 deaths, and is the leading cause of death in the United States. Many factors influence not only a person's chances of developing coronary disease but also how rapidly atherosclerosis progresses. Genetic predisposition, gender, and advancing age are recognized factors over which individuals have little or no control. Cigarette smoking as well as high blood cholesterol, high blood pressure, excessive body weight, and long-term physical inactivity are key, modifiable risk factors. Control of each of these factors is important in the prevention of coronary disease.

Cigarette smokers are at increased risk for fatal and nonfatal heart attacks and for sudden death. Smokers have a 70 percent greater coronary disease death rate, a two- to fourfold greater incidence of coronary disease, and a two- to fourfold greater risk of sudden death than nonsmokers. Smoking is estimated to account for 21 percent of all coronary disease deaths and 40 percent of coronary disease deaths in people younger than age 65.

Prospective epidemiologic research studies have documented a substantial reduction in coronary disease rates following smoking cessation. While some studies have shown a benefit within 2 years after quitting, other studies have suggested that coronary disease risk gradually decreases over a period of several years. Reducing the number of youth who start to smoke and encouraging smoking cessation among current smokers are important preventive measures for reducing coronary disease incidence and mortality.

Effects of Smoking on Nonsmokers

Research in recent years has established that involuntary smoking is a cause of disease in healthy nonsmokers, and that the children of parents who smoke have an increased frequency of respiratory infections (Fig. 14-1). **Mainstream cigarette smoke** is the smoke drawn through the tobacco into the smoker's mouth. **Sidestream smoke** is the smoke emitted by the burning tobacco between puffs. **Environmental tobacco smoke** results from the combination of sidestream smoke and the fraction of mainstream smoke exhaled by the smoker.

The comparison of the chemical composition of the smoke inhaled by active smokers with that inhaled by involuntary

Figure 14-1
Warning: Sidestream Smoke Is Harmful to Health

smokers suggests that the toxic and carcinogenic effects are qualitatively similar, a similarity that is not too surprising because both mainstream and environmental tobacco smoke result from combustion of tobacco. Individual mainstream smoke constituents, with appropriate testing, usually have been found in sidestream smoke as well. However, differences between sidestream smoke and mainstream smoke have been well documented.

The temperature of combustion during sidestream smoke formation is lower than during mainstream smoke formation. As a result, greater amounts of many of the organic constituents of smoke, some of which are carcinogens, are generated when tobacco burns and forms sidestream smoke than when mainstream smoke is produced. For example, in contrast with mainstream smoke, sidestream smoke contains greater amounts of ammonia, benzene, carbon monoxide, nicotine, and the carcinogens 2-napthylamine, 4-aminobiphenyl, N-nitrosamine, benzanthracene, and benzopyrene per milligram of tobacco burned.

Perhaps the most common effect of tobacco smoke exposure is tissue irritation. The eyes appear to be especially sensitive to irritation by environmental tobacco smoke, but the nose, throat, and airway also may be affected by smoke exposure. Irritation has been demonstrated to occur at

levels similar to those found in actual environmental situations.

Environmental tobacco smoke (ETS) is a cause of disease, including lung cancer and chronic obstructive pulmonary disease, in healthy nonsmokers. Involuntary smoking is a significant health risk for children. The children of parents who smoke are not only more likely to develop lower respiratory tract infections but also to be hospitalized or to be treated by a physician for these conditions during the first year of life. These children are also more apt than children whose parents do not smoke to develop middle ear infections. Parental smoking may compromise lung function in young children and in the developing lungs of the growing child. Parental smoking also may contribute to the rise of chronic airflow obstruction and asthma later in life. As many as half the infants and children in the United States regularly may be exposed to environmental tobacco smoke (Papazian, 1991).

The major source of smoke exposure for young children is in their homes. Both passive smoking and being nursed by a mother who smokes contribute to the amount of tobacco constituents absorbed by an infant. In the most recent and comprehensive study of passive smoke exposure of infants, the amount of tobacco smoked in the same room or vehicle or even the same house in the presence of the infant was the major predictor of the infant's urinary cotinine levels. Smoking near the infant and putting the infant in a room where smoking occurred recently increased the infant's absorption of environmental tobacco smoke. If persons who have contact with children must smoke, they should smoke outdoors or in areas that do not affect the air that a child is breathing.

The primary source of environmental tobacco smoke exposure for nonsmokers is the workplace, unless there is a smoker in their households. The percent of adults reporting exposure at work is 75 percent (Cummings et al., 1990; Emmons et al., 1992).

More than 80 percent of American adults are of the opinion that environmental tobacco smoke is dangerous to nonsmokers' health, and an overwhelming majority favor measures that will reduce or eliminate the public's exposure (Giovino et al., 1992; Hugick & Leonard, 1991). Policies limiting smoking at the worksite have increasingly become widespread and more restrictive. The changes in worksite policies have largely evolved through voluntary rather than governmental action. In a steadily increasing number of worksites, smoking has been prohibited completely or limited to relatively few areas within the worksite. The creation of a smoke-free workplace has proceeded successfully when the policy has been developed jointly by employees, employee organizations, and management; instituted in phases; and accompanied by support and assistance for the smokers to quit smoking.

Effects on Fertility

Fertility often is impaired in males and females who smoke. Several large-scale studies have found higher infertility rates among smoking than nonsmoking females. One study found that female smokers were 3.4 times more likely than nonsmokers to take a year or longer to conceive a desired child. Females who smoke more than a pack and a half of cigarettes a day had a 43 percent lower fertility rate than nonsmokers. Females who smoke regularly also are more likely than nonsmokers to have menstrual irregularities and amenorrhea (cessation of menses). Among males who smoke, the secretion of male hormones is reduced, sperm production and mobility are lowered, and more abnormal sperm are formed. These effects can cause male infertility, especially among those males who are already only marginally fertile.

Effects of Prenatal and Childhood Exposure to Tobacco

Although nicotine crosses the placenta, its harmful effects primarily are the result of blood vessel constriction in the

mother and the consequent reduced oxygen supply to the fetus. This oxygen reduction (hypoxia) also is increased by carbon monoxide interfering with the blood's ability to distribute oxygen throughout the body.

Effects during pregnancy and delivery. There is a direct correlation between the amount of smoking by the pregnant female during pregnancy and the frequency of spontaneous abortion and fetal death. Pregnant females who smoke also have significant increases in premature detachment of the placenta (abruptio placentae), vaginal bleeding, abnormalities in placental attachment to the uterus (placenta previa), ruptured membranes, and preterm delivery. All these complications of pregnancy carry a high risk of miscarrying the baby during the perinatal period.

Maternal smoking has been implicated in as many as 14 percent of preterm deliveries in the United States. Prematurity increases the risks for early infant death and for respiratory illness. A recent large-scale study of over 30,000 pregnant females in northern California found that preterm births were 20 percent more common among females who smoked a pack a day or more during pregnancy when compared to nonsmokers.

Effects on the newborn. There are conflicting findings regarding an association between smoking and some congenital malformations (most usually heart defects, cleft palate, hernias, and central nervous system abnormalities). This lack of a consistent pattern has led some researchers to conclude that maternal (or paternal) cigarette smoking probably is not the sole cause for these abnormalities. However, recent large-scale studies confirm a positive association between physical defects among newborns and maternal smoking during pregnancy. There are higher rates of abnormalities in a variety of categories for children born to smokers than to nonsmokers.

Females who smoke during pregnancy have babies that are, on average, seven ounces lighter than those born to comparable nonsmoking females. Reductions in infants' birth weights are proportional to the amounts mothers smoke and are independent of other risk factors and gestational age. The earlier in pregnancy that a female stops smoking, the better her chances are for delivering a normal weight baby. Based on a nationwide study, if all females stopped smoking during pregnancy, the frequency of low birth weight infants would decrease by amounts ranging from 35 percent among mothers with less than a high school education to 11 percent among those born to college graduates. Low birth weight babies also are shorter than normal for their gestational age and have smaller head and chest circumferences. Long-term studies, still in progress, provide no indication that these growth-retarded children catch up in later years.

Passive smoking—being exposed to the smoking of others—recently has been indicated as having harmful effects on pregnancy. A study of 500 Danish females found that pregnant nonsmokers married to smoking males consistently had lower birth weight babies than those married to nonsmokers. The infants' weight reduction was only about a third less than if the mothers themselves smoked. Another study of more than 900 nonsmoking females in the United States passively exposed to cigarette smoke during pregnancy found that they had twice the risk of delivering a low birth weight baby compared to mothers not similarly exposed. A third study of over 1,200 non-smoking females, whose passive smoke inhalation during pregnancy was confirmed by blood tests, also found that they gave birth to consistently lower birth weight infants than those not exposed to tobacco smoke.

Three studies found low Apgar scores among babies born to smoking mothers. (Apgar scores evaluate the basic health of newborns at one and five minutes after birth by measures of heart rate, respiration, reflexes, muscle tone, and skin color.) One study involving 43,000 babies reported low scores occurring four times as often among the newborns of mothers who smoked two to three packs of cigarettes per day than occurred among nonsmokers' babies. However, a large Boston city hospital study did not confirm this association when other confounding risk factors were controlled.

Infants born to mothers who smoke are at a higher risk of dying before their first birthday. This risk is related to the amount smoked. A recent four-year study of infant mortality found that females who smoked a pack a day or more had a 56 percent higher rate of infant death among their firstborns than nonsmokers. Firstborn babies of mothers who smoked less than a pack a day were still 25 percent more likely to die within the first year than non-smokers' first offsprings. Smoking by mothers, regardless of the amount, increased the rate of infant deaths among later children by 30 percent. This increase in infant deaths primarily is due to respiratory difficulties and sudden infant death syndrome (SIDS)—the leading cause of death in babies during their first year.

Effects on the growing child. Children of mothers who smoke while pregnant are more likely to have impaired intellectual and physical growth. Maternal smoking also has been associated with such behavioral problems in off-spring as lack of self-control, irritability, hyperactivity, and disinterest. Long-term studies indicate that these children perform less well than matched youngsters of nonsmokers on tests of cognitive, psychomotor, language, and general academic functioning. However, these differences are small when compared to other factors affecting achievement in these areas.

A recent critical review of these studies now questions if there is a causal relationship between maternal smoking during pregnancy and deficits in growth, cognitive development, educational achievement, attention span, and hyperactive behavior among offspring. Potentially-confounding differences between parents who smoke and parents who do not smoke in psychological factors and in the family context of the childrearing environment were not sufficiently controlled in earlier research to attribute differences solely to tobacco's toxic effects.

Maternal smoking does increase a child's chances for developing colds, asthma, and other respiratory problems, although it is not clear if these effects are from fetal exposure to nicotine or from passive inhalation of household smoke after birth. Evidence from both human and animal studies suggests that in utero exposure to nicotine adversely affects fetal lung development. However, young babies living in homes where both parents smoke are more often hospitalized for pneumonia or bronchitis than are babies whose parents do not smoke. They also are at increased risk for middle ear infections.

Effects of Smokeless Tobacco

Smokeless tobacco includes both chewing tobacco and snuff. These products contain tobacco leaf and a variety of sweeteners, flavorings, and scents. In chewing tobacco, the leaf may be shredded (loose-leaf), pressed into bricks or cakes (plugs), or dried and twisted into rope-like strands (twists). A portion is either chewed or held in place in the cheek or between the lower lip and the gum. The two categories of snuff, dry and moist, are made from powdered or finely cut tobacco leaves. In some countries, including the United Kingdom, dry snuff is sniffed through the nose, but in the United States both dry and moist snuff are used in the mouth or "dipped." A small amount (pinch) is usually held in place between the lip or cheek and the gum.

Smokeless tobacco is regaining popularity, especially among young adults. In some parts of the United States, as many as 25 to 40 percent of adolescent males report current use of smokeless tobacco. In some schools, the percentage of males who use smokeless tobacco outnumbers the percent who report regular use of cigarettes. There has been an eightfold increase in the use of moist snuff among 17–19-year-olds since 1970 (American Public Health Association, 1992). Moist snuff use among teenage males is twice that of older males (Marwick, 1993).

There is strong evidence that smokeless tobacco causes cancer of the mouth (Fig. 14-2). The risk is particularly high for parts of the mouth where the tobacco is usually placed. Present data are insufficient to come to any conclusions regarding the relationship of smokeless tobacco use to cancers at other sites. However, nitrosamines chemically related to nicotine occur at high levels in smokeless tobacco and, generally, at lower levels in chewing tobacco. These compounds are highly carcinogenic in animals. The concentrations of nitrosamines in smokeless tobacco are far higher than the levels of these compounds allowed in any food or beverage in the U.S. Besides nitrosamines, other known carcinogens present include polycyclic aromatic hydrocarbons and radiation-emitting polonium (Marwick, 1993).

Smokeless tobacco use increases the frequency of localized gum recession and leukoplakia, but evidence of its relationship to other diseases of the mouth is inadequate. **Leukoplakia** is a condition resulting from direct irritation from tobacco and is characterized by white patches on the lining of the mouth. The presence of lead in smokeless tobacco may pose a special risk for the developing fetus of a pregnant female.

Use of smokeless tobacco releases nicotine into the bloodstream and produces blood levels of nicotine comparable to those produced when tobacco is smoked. The primary behavioral consequence of regular use of smokeless tobacco is long-term nicotine dependence and its associated health risks. Other problems related to smokeless tobacco use are tooth decay and loss, receding gums, abrasions of tooth enamel, and bad breath. Despite the health risks associated with its use, some youth and adults mistakenly believe that smokeless tobacco use is a safe alternative to smoking cigarettes.

Smokeless tobacco manufacturers are now required to place warning labels on product packages. The three warnings required by the Smokeless Tobacco Education Act, which also banned radio and television advertising of smokeless tobacco products, are as follows:
1. This product is not a safe alternative to cigarettes.
2. This product may cause gum disease.
3. This product may cause mouth cancer.

Figure 14-2
Warning: Smokeless Tobacco Is Harmful to Health

My choice is sugar-free gum!

Smokeless tobacco causes oral cancer, leukoplakia, gum recession, abrasions of tooth enamel, and bad breath.

TOBACCO AND THE LAW

Restrictions on tobacco use by children are fewer now than at any time in many past decades, despite what is known about the dangers of tobacco use, its addictive nature, and the early age of initiation. Laws prohibiting the sale and distribution of tobacco to youth and indoor clean air laws will be discussed.

Laws Prohibiting the Sale and Distribution of Tobacco to Youth

Strict observance of prohibitions against the sale of tobacco to minors may be the most powerful means for reducing the initiation of smoking by children. Purchases from retailers or vending machines appear to be their main source of cigarettes. The U.S. Department of Health and Human Services (1991) recommends that all states should have in place and enforce state laws requiring at least age 19 as the minimum age for purchase of tobacco products. This federal agency also recommends an age cutoff of 19, as opposed to younger cutoffs, to facilitate the elimination of tobacco from high schools. Selling or otherwise providing tobacco products to children and adolescents where age verification is difficult or impossible, such as through vending machines, also is not advocated by Health and Human Services.

State laws prohibiting the sale of cigarettes to minors. Currently, 44 states and the District of Columbia have laws that prohibit the sale of cigarettes to minors. The age at which children are no longer considered minors ranges from 15–19, with 18 being the most common. These are not new laws. Most were enacted between 1890 and 1920 as a result of pressure from activists who were trying to prevent young boys from smoking. As recently as 1964, 48 states had laws prohibiting the sale of cigarettes to minors, but some of the laws were repealed because they were considered unenforceable. In at least 11 states, vendors must post signs stating that it is illegal to sell cigarettes to minors (Office of Inspector General, 1990).

Penalties for violation of these laws vary greatly—from a $2 fine in Washington D.C. to a maximum of a $3,000 fine and/or a year in jail in Minnesota. In most states, the penalty is a fine and/or jail. Despite the fact that virtually all states license the sale or distribution of cigarettes, only four have license revocation as a penalty for selling to minors. Most states leave enforcement to local law enforcement officials. However, in Florida and New Hampshire, state taxation agencies have the responsibility; in Massachusetts, it is the state Department of Public Health (Office of Inspector General, 1990).

Indications that enforcement of laws is weak come not only from the observable fact that teens are smoking but also from a number of studies and from controlled purchases or "stings" that demonstrate that children can and do buy cigarettes. Several local "stings" have been run by researchers, local reporters, police, and health departments to test youth access laws. Generally, minors are able to purchase cigarettes illegally about 80 percent of the time (Office of Inspector General, 1990).

Additionally, nearly 90 percent of 10th graders in Minnesota who smoked regularly report that it is "very easy" to obtain cigarettes despite a state law. Results from the National Adolescent Student Health Survey showed that 73 percent of 8th and 10th graders said it was "very easy" to buy tobacco and 13 percent said it was "fairly easy."

Ninety percent of New Jersey high school students who smoked said they could "always" or "nearly always" buy cigarettes (Office of Inspector General, 1990).

Other findings from a study of state laws to prohibit youth access to tobacco conducted by the Office of Inspector General (1990) were as follows:

- Two-thirds of state health department officials indicate that there is virtually no enforcement of their state law. Another one-fifth say that enforcement is minimal.
- Nearly half of state health officials believe the law is not enforced because it is not a priority.
- Of the 44 states with laws prohibiting the sale of cigarettes to minors, only five could provide any statistical information on vendor violations.
- More than three-fourths of law enforcement officials do not think that youth access laws are being enforced in their communities. In fact, 85 percent of law enforcement officials and 88 percent of local public health officials report that they do not know of anyone ever being caught breaking this law.
- 87 percent of children who smoke claim that it is easy to buy cigarettes.
- 91 percent of store clerks, managers, and owners know it is illegal to sell cigarettes to minors.

Model law to control youth access to tobacco. In response to the poor enforcement of minors' access laws, the U.S. Department of Health and Human Services has recommended model legislation to the states to control sales of tobacco products to minors (U.S. Department of Health and Human Services, 1990). The key features of the model law are:

- Create a licensing system, similar to that which is used to control the sale of alcoholic beverages, under which a store may sell tobacco to adults only if it avoids making sales to minors. Signs stating that sales to minors are illegal would be required at all points of sale.
- Set forth a graduated schedule of penalties—monetary fines and license suspensions—for illegal sales so that owners and employees face punishment proportionate to their violation of the law. Penalties would be fixed and credible. Those who comply would pay only a license fee.
- Provide separate penalties for failure to post a sign, and higher penalties for sales without a license.
- Place primary responsibility for investigation and enforcement in a designated state agency, and exclusive authority for license suspension and revocation in that agency, but allow local law enforcement and public health officials to investigate compliance and present evidence to the state agency or file complaints in local courts.

187

- Rely primarily on state-administered civil penalties to avoid the time delays and costs of the court system, but allow use of local courts to assess fines, similar to traffic enforcement. This would provide flexibility to both state and local authorities to target enforcement resources.
- Set the age of legal purchase of tobacco at 19. This is higher than under many existing state tobacco statutes but lower than the age for alcohol. States may wish to consider age 21, because addiction often begins at ages 19 and 20, but rarely thereafter.
- Ban the use of vending machines to dispense cigarettes, parallel to alcohol practice and reflecting the difficulty of preventing illegal sales from these machines.
- Contain the number of features to minimize burdens on retail outlets: require identification only for those who are not clearly above the age of 19; allow a driver's license as proof of age; set a nominal penalty for the first violation; disregard one accidental violation if effective controls are in place; have the state provide required signs; and set license fees lower for outlets with small sales volume.

Indoor Clean Air Laws

Restrictions on smoking in public places and at work are growing in number and comprehensiveness. Although the goal of these restrictions is to protect individuals from the consequences of involuntary tobacco smoke exposure, they also may help reduce smoking prevalence by changing the attitudes and behaviors of current and potential smokers.

Most states have laws restricting smoking in public places. A public place usually is defined as any enclosed area to which the public is invited or in which the public is permitted. This broad definition encompasses a diverse range of facilities that usually includes government buildings, schools, health care facilities, public transportation vehicles and terminals, retail stores and service establishments, banks, restaurants, theaters, auditoriums, sports arenas, reception areas, and waiting rooms. Laws do differ, however, in their definition of public places.

The U.S. Department of Health and Human Services (1991) recommends that state laws should be more comprehensive than those currently in place in most jurisdictions. Recently-adopted laws are showing the following three trends:
1. protection against discrimination for supporters of worksite smoking policies,
2. priority given to the wishes of nonsmokers in any disagreement about the designation of any area as smoking or nonsmoking,
3. more stringent ordinances enacted in cities and counties.

An increasing number of employers have instituted policies to control smoking in the workplace. While some of these policies and control measures have been adopted voluntarily, others have resulted from legislation at the federal, state, or local level that restricts smoking in public and/or private worksites.

SMOKING CESSATION

The 1990 Surgeon General's Report documents the benefits of smoking cessation for all age groups (Fig. 14-3). Recently, scientific studies have linked cigarette smoking to such health conditions as leukemia (Brownson, Novotony, & Perry, 1993), adult suicide (Hemenway, Solnick, & Colditz, 1993), and teenage suicide (Garrison, McKeown, Valois, & Vincent, 1993).

Cigarette smoking is maintained not only by the effects of nicotine on a smoker but also the psychological determinants of smoking. The relative contribution of the pharmacologic effects of nicotine and its psychological determinants vary and are virtually impossible to separate among smokers. These pharmacologic and psychologic factors become closely linked in a conditioning process in which smoking is associated with multiple cues. This discussion will include behavior patterns linked to smoking, the health benefits of smoking cessation, nicotine withdrawal and dependence, and smoking cessation techniques and programs.

Figure 14-3
**Smoking Cessation Programs
Help Crush the Habit**

Behavior Patterns Linked to Smoking

A typical smoker who has averaged 20 cigarettes a day over a 15-year period is likely to have taken more than 1 million puffs during the course of her or his smoking history. The highly-dependent smoker who comes to a smoking cessation program tends to have an even longer and more extensive history of nicotine dependence. The sheer magnitude of these millions of self-administrations of nicotine is unmatched in any other form of drug abuse.

There are many cues associated with smoking. The sight of another person smoking or even an ashtray can elicit strong cravings not only in current and newly-abstinent smokers but also in individuals who have achieved longer-term abstinence. Some cues may be extinguished relatively quickly upon cessation. Others may be more problematic, especially in long-term, dependent smokers. Smokers who reported smoking more when they are angry, frustrated, or unhappy may be especially vulnerable to a crisis that occurs after an extended period of abstinence. Cues associated with smoking that are encountered only infrequently might continue to elicit conditioned cravings over time.

Cigarette smoking is a complex behavior pattern that proceeds through a sequence of phases. The **initiation phase** is the interval when individuals start experimenting with cigarettes. They then move into the transition phase. The **transition phase** is that period in which environmental and psychological factors influence individuals to become smokers or nonsmokers. **Maintenance of the smoking habit**, **cessation**, and **maintenance of cessation** are the three subsequent behavior phases. Since relapse occurs at very high rates among those who have stopped smoking (often as high as 70–80 percent return to smoking within one year), the cessation phase also is a transition phase that influences whether or not a smoker remains an ex-smoker or becomes a recidivist who returns to the old behavior of smoking.

Initiation of smoking is strongly associated with social forces such as peer pressure as well as with psychological factors such as self-esteem and status needs. Once smoking has become part of an individual's lifestyle, social factors seem to play a smaller role. Rather, the habit becomes more and more tied to psychological and physiological needs, becoming an intrinsic part of a person's life and serving many functions. Cessation and maintenance of cessation are affected by a combination of social, psychological, and physiological factors.

Health Benefits of Smoking Cessation

The observed and anticipated health consequences of smoking appear to be influential in persuading millions of people to quit smoking. There is a large body of evidence that clearly indicates that smoking cessation has major and immediate health benefits for people of all ages.

People who quit smoking live longer than those who continue to smoke. There are several factors that determine the extent to which a smoker's risk of premature death is reduced after quitting smoking. These include the number of years of smoking, the number of cigarettes smoked per day, and the presence or absence of disease at the time of quitting. Data from the American Cancer Society's Cancer Prevention Study II (CPS-II) show that persons who quit smoking before age 50 have one-half the risk of dying in the next 15 years when compared with continuing smokers.

Smoking cessation increases life expectancy because it reduces the risk of dying from specific smoking-related diseases. One such disease is lung cancer, the most common cause of cancer death in both males and females. The risk of dying from lung cancer is 22 times higher among male smokers and 12 times higher among female smokers compared with people who have never smoked. The risk of lung cancer declines steadily in people who quit smoking. After 10 years of abstinence, the risk of lung cancer is about 30–50 percent of the risk for continuing smokers. Smoking cessation also reduces the risk of cancers of the larynx, oral cavity, esophagus, pancreas, and urinary bladder.

Smokers have about twice the risk of dying from coronary disease compared with lifetime nonsmokers. This excess risk is reduced by about half among ex-smokers after only one year of smoking abstinence and declines gradually thereafter. After 15 years of abstinence, the risk of coronary disease is similar to that of persons who have never smoked.

Compared with lifetime nonsmokers, smokers have about twice the risk of dying from stroke, the third leading cause of death in the United States. After quitting smoking, the risk of stroke returns to the same level as for people who have never smoked. In some studies, this reduction in risk has occurred within five years, but in others as long as 15 years of abstinence were required.

Cigarette smoking is the major cause of chronic obstructive pulmonary disease (COPD), the fifth leading cause of death in the U.S. Smoking increases the risk of COPD by accelerating the age-related decline in lung function. With sustained abstinence from smoking, the rate of decline in lung function among former smokers returns to that of never smokers, thus reducing the risk of developing COPD.

Smoking cessation substantially reduces the risk of respiratory infections such as influenza, pneumonia, and bronchitis. The risk of peripheral artery occlusive disease, abdominal aortic aneurysm, and ulcers of the stomach and intestine are reduced by quitting smoking.

Benefits of quitting during pregnancy. Females who stop smoking before becoming pregnant have infants of the same birth weight range as those born to females who have never smoked. The same benefit holds true for females who abstain from smoking in the first three to four months of pregnancy and who remain abstinent throughout the remainder of the pregnancy. Females who quit at later stages of pregnancy, up to the 30th week of gestation, have infants with higher birth weight than do females who smoke throughout pregnancy.

Smoking is probably the most important modifiable cause of poor pregnancy outcome among females in the United States. Recent estimates suggest that the elimination of smoking during pregnancy could prevent about 5 percent of perinatal deaths, about 20 percent of low birth weight infants, and about 8 percent of preterm deliveries in the United States. In groups with a high prevalence of smoking, the elimination of smoking during pregnancy could prevent about 10 percent of perinatal deaths, about 35 percent of low birth weight births, and about 15 percent of preterm deliveries.

The prevalence of smoking during pregnancy has declined over time but remains unacceptably high. Approximately 30 percent of American females who are cigarette smokers quit after learning that they are pregnant. However, about 25 percent of pregnant females in the United States smoke throughout pregnancy. A shocking statistic is that about 50 percent of pregnant females who have not completed high school smoke throughout pregnancy. Although many females reduce their daily cigarette consumption during pregnancy, there may be little or no benefit for the fetus. Of the females who quit smoking during pregnancy, 70 percent resume smoking within one year of delivery.

Weight gain. The fear of postcessation weight gain may discourage many smokers from trying to quit. The fear or occurrence of weight gain may precipitate relapse among many of those who already have quit. Although four-fifths

of smokers who quit gain weight after cessation, the average weight gain is only five pounds. The average weight gain among people who continue smoking is one pound. A five-pound weight gain poses minimal health risk. Moreover, there is evidence that this small weight gain is accompanied by favorable changes in blood lipid profiles and in body fat distribution. Not only is the average postcessation weight gain small but also the risk of large weight gain after quitting is extremely low. Less than 4 percent of those who quit smoking gain more than 20 pounds. Increases in food intake and decreases in resting energy expenditure are largely responsible for postcessation weight gain.

Nicotine Withdrawal and Dependence

Nicotine withdrawal symptoms include anxiety, irritability, frustration, anger, difficulty in concentrating, increased appetite, and urges to smoke. With the possible exception of increased appetite and the urges to smoke, these effects soon disappear. Nicotine withdrawal peaks in the first one to two days following cessation and subsides rapidly during the following weeks. With long-term abstinence, former smokers are likely to enjoy favorable psychological changes such as enhanced self-esteem and increased sense of control.

Although most nicotine withdrawal symptoms are short-lived, they often exert a strong influence on a smoker's ability to quit and maintain abstinence. Nicotine withdrawal may discourage many smokers from trying to quit and may precipitate relapse among those who have recently quit.

Tobacco dependence is classified as a substance use disorder by the American Psychiatric Association. The continuous use of tobacco for at least one month accompanied by at least one of the following conditions constitutes the criteria for determining tobacco dependence:

1. serious attempts to stop or significantly reduce the amount of tobacco used on a permanent basis, which have not been successful;
2. attempts to stop smoking that have provoked tobacco withdrawal;
3. the continuing use of tobacco despite a serious physical disorder (e.g., respiratory or cardiovascular disease) that the smoker knows is made worse by tobacco use.

Smoking Cessation Techniques and Programs

There is a wide variety of techniques and programs available to help people stop smoking. However, approximately 90 percent of former smokers report that they quit smoking without formal treatment programs or smoking cessation devices.

Nicotine fading. **Nicotine fading** involves the progressive reducing of nicotine intake by switching to brands with less nicotine and gradually decreasing the number of cigarettes (tapering). This is done with the idea that the smoker will eventually stop altogether or that those unable to stop completely will achieve more control over their smoking behavior. Despite laboratory evidence that smokers compensate for decreased nicotine content by puffing more heavily, research shows that nicotine fading can help increase cessation rates and even reduce tar and nicotine levels for nonabstinent smokers. Nicotine fading, combined with self-management and cognitive behavioral techniques, has been found to yield abstinence rates of 30–46 percent at 6 months and, for nonabstainers, lower tar and nicotine levels.

Tapering off on the number of cigarettes before quitting not only reduces the probability of severe withdrawal but also can permit more heavily-dependent smokers to learn how to suppress smoking urges and to develop other skills that are helpful in quitting. Nicotine fading also is helpful for smokers who may have a difficult time quitting outright. Each degree of success can reinforce an individual's perceived self-efficacy. **Perceived self-efficacy** is the belief a person has in his/her own ability to make a change. Perceived self-efficacy is an important predictor of long-term cessation success.

Aversive techniques. The use of aversive stimuli to promote smoking behavior change has included electric shock, aversive imagery, and aversive manipulation of smoke intake (rapid smoking, satiation smoking, and smoke holding). In addition, maintenance plans may include aversive techniques such as the forfeiture of money if relapse occurs. Most aversive techniques, if used alone, appear to be relatively weak. Electric shock, in particular, has shortcomings and is not often used.

Rapid smoking (inhaling every 6 seconds) and satiation (doubling or tripling daily consumption) have shown positive effects on smoking cessation but these effects are relatively weak. Therefore, they are most effective as one component of a multicomponent smoking cessation program. The disadvantages of these techniques include the necessity of screening potential participants because of the possible health risks involved, and the fact that individuals with smoking-related illnesses are likely to be excluded. Because these techniques increase heart rate, levels of

carboxyhemoglobin and other blood gases, and blood nicotine levels, heart complications are a major concern. One variation of the rapid-smoking technique, smoke holding, minimizes this risk while maintaining its effectiveness.

Hypnosis and acupuncture. Hypnosis has long been advocated as an effective treatment for stopping smoking. The intent of hypnosis as a smoking cessation treatment often is to increase personal motivation to stop smoking. This usually is done by posthypnotically suggesting a link between smoking and unpleasant experiences (e.g., "smoking is a poison"). Many hypnosis techniques are similar to behavioral therapy methods (e.g., relaxation training, increased awareness of smoking cues), making it difficult to distinguish the specific effects of hypnosis. There are two basic approaches to the use of hypnosis in the treatment of smoking. In the first, hypnosis is the focus of a single session in which instructions are often standardized. This approach utilizes health-promoting suggestions and may be offered in a group format. The second approach utilizes hypnosis to explore individualized motives and overcome resistance, and usually incorporates other smoking cessation techniques. The effect of hypnosis, although not clearly understood, appears strong enough to warrant careful and well-controlled research to determine its effectiveness. Such research may dispel the sense of hypnosis as a "magic solution" and delineate its value in smoking cessation.

More recently, acupuncture has been touted as an effective treatment for smoking cessation. Acupuncture involves the use of needles or staplelike attachments placed in the nose or ear. The mechanism by which acupuncture may help a person stop smoking is not clear. Some researchers suggest that acupuncture relieves smoking withdrawal symptoms, although there is little evidence to support this claim. Others suggest that the effect of acupuncture is psychological and depends on personal motivation to stop smoking.

Relaxation training. Progressive relaxation is a popular treatment for anxiety-related disorders. As discussed previously, smokers often use cigarettes to cope with anxiety and stress. A large proportion of smoking relapses occur during negative emotional states. Therefore, relaxation training can provide smokers with a means other than smoking for coping with stress and negative emotion. Relaxation training rarely is used as a sole treatment for smoking cessation and is instead incorporated into multicomponent programs.

Contingency contracting. Operant conditioning techniques have been used in smoking treatments to reward people for not smoking and/or to punish them for smoking. The usual procedure is to collect monetary deposits from smokers early in a cessation program with periodic repayments contingent on client achievement of abstinence goals. Variations include having a smoker pledge to donate money to a disliked organization or individual for every cigarette smoked, or contracting for nonmonetary rewards and punishments based on smoking status.

The rationale behind contracting techniques is that they may bolster commitment to abstinence by providing concrete rewards. Contracts are in effect until withdrawal and until the individual has an opportunity to begin alternative, nonsmoking activities that may be rewarding.

Nonpharmacologic cessation aids. A variety of nonpharmacologic aids have been produced over the years to assist smokers in reducing or stopping smoking, including filter systems, smokeless cigarettes, self-help books, audiotapes, and more recently, videos. Evidence regarding the effectiveness of these cessation aids is extremely limited or nonexistent.

Many companies have developed cigarette filter systems to help people stop smoking. The basic idea behind a filter system as a cessation aid is to reduce the amount of nicotine taken in, allowing smokers to wean themselves from the chemical addiction. One of the most popular filter systems available, One Step at a Time, manufactured by Teledyne Water Pik, was first marketed in 1977 and is sold primarily through chain drugstores and advertised in conjunction with local retailers. The filter system consists of four reusable filters, each of which further reduces the amount of tar, nicotine, and carbon monoxide from cigarette smoke. Each of the filters is to be used for two weeks. The One Step at a Time filter system sells for about $10. Teledyne Water Pik also markets a single filter system called Step Four, which is the fourth filter in the filter system and sells for about $5.

Smokeless cigarettes that simulate the taste of tobacco smoke are another popular cessation aid. E-Z Quit, a smokeless cigarette sold through a mail order company, consists of a plastic cigarette with three menthol flavor capsules. The product sells for about $10 and is widely advertised in popular magazines and newspapers.

Numerous how-to-quit-smoking books have been produced and are available. Many of the books are written by former smokers and psychologists who provide a wide range of suggestions on how to stop smoking. In general, the findings of studies comparing the effectiveness of different quit-smoking books suggest that no one book appears to be better than any other. The addition of a personal contract to the provision of written materials appears to enhance quitting behavior. Many bookstores also sell audiotapes on how to stop smoking.

Nicotine-containing gum. To date, the most successful drug product developed to assist smokers in stopping is nicotine polacrilex gum, a nicotine-containing chewing gum. Nicotine-containing gum was first developed in Sweden in 1971, but early studies with gum showed poor results. However, a carbonate buffer added to improve absorption of nicotine improved cessation rates. The main benefit associated with gum use is the alleviation of withdrawal symptoms. Several studies have demonstrated the effect of nicotine-containing gum in relieving irritability, anxiety, problems in concentrating, restlessness, and hunger. Studies suggest that the gum does not fully replace the nicotine provided by cigarette smoke. Chewing 2-mg nicotine gum on an hourly schedule for ten hours yields blood nicotine levels comparable to one-third that achieved while smoking. Use of a 4-mg nicotine gum causes a greater increase in blood nicotine levels and may increase cessation rates. However, only the 2-mg dose is approved for use in the United States.

The Food and Drug Administration approved the marketing of nicotine-containing gum in the United States as a prescription smoking-cessation aid in 1984. This was the first time that the FDA approved a physiologically addictive substance for the treatment of the same addiction. The gum retails for about $18 for a box of 96 pieces. Surveys of nicotine gum users show that two-thirds of prescriptions are generated by the patient rather than by the physician. Millions of smokers have used the gum.

Not all studies have shown nicotine polacrilex gum to be effective. Long-term cessation rates (over one year follow-up) vary widely from 3 to 49 percent. Nicotine-containing gum has become an increasingly popular adjunct to behaviorally-based cessation programs. Studies suggest that behaviorally-based treatment in conjunction with nicotine polacrilex gum tends to be more effective than the same program without gum, or compared with gum alone.

Most who use the gum are able to withdraw from it easily within three to six months. This is partly because the delivery of nicotine is slow and gradual. It takes 20–30 minutes for the peak effect to occur. This is in sharp contrast to the approximate seven seconds that it takes to deliver a strong pulse of nicotine to the brain after a puff on a cigarette. About 25 percent of gum users experience adverse side effects such as upset stomach or jaw problems.

More recently, another nicotine delivery system has become available to help smokers quit, the nicotine transdermal patch. In 1991, a polyethylene patch that delivers a relatively constant level of nicotine when placed on the skin became available. How well these patches work is questionable. The FDA has ruled that the manufacturer of the patches cannot use the term "effective" in its advertising. Other nicotine delivery system are being studied and may someday become available. For example, nasal droplet solutions have been developed that someday may be available as adjuncts to smoking cessation.

Commercial stop-smoking programs. One of the oldest and most successful commercial cessation programs is SmokEnders, which was started by a former smoker in 1969. Headquartered in New Jersey, SmokEnders has chapters or franchises in many U.S. cities and several foreign countries. The program consists of six, two-hour sessions held over a six-week period of time. Classes are conducted by former smokers who are graduates of the SmokEnders program. The program emphasizes motivation for stopping and brand switching as well as behavioral and cognitive skills for gradually reducing the amount smoked.

In 1985, Comprehensive Care Corporation purchased the license to operate SmokEnders. However, the program is basically the same as the one developed in 1969. The cost of the program varies by location, ranging from $225 to $300. Since SmokEnders was established in 1969, an estimated 600,000 smokers have completed the program.

The Schick Stop Smoking program, started in 1971, was the first well-known commercial program to use counterconditioning techniques to help people stop smoking. The Schick Stop Smoking program includes three phases: a one-week preparation phase, a one-week counterconditioning phase, and a support phase. In the preparation phase, smokers are instructed to keep a record of each cigarette smoked. The counterconditioning phase of the program consists of five one-hour treatment sessions held on consecutive days. Two counterconditioning techniques—mild electric shock to the wrist and quick puffing on a cigarette—are used to attach negative experiences to common cues for smoking. In the support phase, clients return to the center for group counseling, receive weekly telephone contacts, and have one additional counterconditioning session. The program is run by trained nonmedical personnel and treats about 2,000 smokers annually. The cost of the program is about $600.

In 1980, Control Data Corporation began marketing "Stay Well," a health-promotion program designed for businesses. The smoking control component of the "Stay Well" program is called "How to Quit Smoking" and consists of eight, one-hour group sessions conducted over seven weeks. The program emphasizes nicotine fading and behavioral coping skills. In 1982, the "Stay Well" program began licensing hospitals to deliver and market the program. Today there are 50 licensed distributors located in most major population centers. More than 600 corporations have used the "How to Quit Smoking" program. The cost of the program varies by distributor, ranging from $35 to $80 per smoker.

Johnson and Johnson, Inc., has recently begun marketing "Live for Life," a wellness program designed for the workplace. The smoking cessation component of "Live for Life" includes an annual health screen with medical advice on smoking, environmental changes to support nonsmoking, and regularly scheduled stop-smoking classes. Classes consist of fourteen, one-hour sessions held over a three-week period. Smoke holding, group support, relaxation training, and behavioral coping skills are the primary elements of the program.

In 1976, the American Institute for Preventive Medicine began marketing a stop-smoking program called "Smokeless." The program includes five, one-hour sessions held on consecutive days, plus three maintenance classes spread over two weeks. The program instructs smokers in a wide range of behavioral and cognitive coping skills and includes some mild counterconditioning procedures. One of these procedures is "pinky puffing," which is puffing a cigarette while holding it between the pinky and ring finger. Another is smoking cigarettes in which the filters have been dipped in anti-nail-biting solution. "Smokeless" has been adapted into a self-help format that sells for about $40. The self-help program is packaged in an attractive kit with six booklets and a relaxation audiotape. The Institute also markets a guide for establishing a smoking policy in the workplace. "Smokeless" is licensed to hospitals or businesses to use and market program materials. Hospitals, in turn, will offer the program to people in the community. Corporate affiliates offer the program solely to their own employees. Each hospital affiliate is responsible for marketing the program in a defined geographic region. The fee for "Smokeless" varies by affiliate, ranging from $75 to $225 per smoker.

Smoke Stoppers is another commercial, stop-smoking program that licenses hospitals and other outlets to use its materials. The program is marketed by the National Center for Health Promotion located in Ann Arbor, Michigan. The format of the Smoke Stoppers is similar to that of "Smokeless," with five classes in the first week, followed by three maintenance sessions. Outlets certified to conduct Smoke Stoppers programs are given exclusive rights to market the program in a defined geographical region. All Smoke Stoppers instructors are required to be former smokers and must attend a forty-hour training program. The fee charged to smokers varies by outlet, averaging about $150 per person. Smoke Stoppers was established in 1977 and has licensed over 300 outlets to conduct programs.

Voluntary health agency cessation programs. Individuals, hospitals, and employers frequently take advantage of the smoking cessation services and materials offered through voluntary health agencies. The American Lung Association offers Freedom from Smoking that includes:
- group stop-smoking programs;
- home video and audiotape programs;
- self-help guidelines for smokers;
- smoking and pregnancy kits for pregnant females and health care providers;
- smoking-in-the-workplace materials for employers and employees;
- help-a-friend materials for nonsmokers to help support smokers who are trying to quit;
- leaflets on passive smoking, weight control, nicotine addiction, and smokeless tobacco;
- no-smoking buttons, desk cards, posters, and other materials.

The American Heart Association has a worksite, smoking-cessation group program entitled In Control. The American Cancer Society's quit-smoking program is entitled FreshStart. Those who utilize this program have the option of either participating in group sessions led by former smokers or choosing a self-help approach. The American Cancer Society also sponsors the "Great American Smokeout" each year on the Thursday before Thanksgiving. This event involves thousands of other organizations in an effort in which smokers are asked to sign pledge cards indicating that they will not smoke during the "Smokeout" day. Local community events and a media blitz draws attention to the "Smokeout."

BIBLIOGRAPHY

Allen, D.F., Moss, A.J., Giovino, G.A., Shopland, D.R., & Pierce, J.P. (1993) "Teenage tobacco use," Data estimates from the Teenage Attitudes and Practices Survey, United States, 1989. *Advance Data from Vital and Health Statistics*, No. 224, February 1. Hyattsville, MD: National Center for Health Statistics.

American Cancer Society. (1991) *Cancer Facts and Figures—1991*. Atlanta, GA: American Cancer Society.

American Public Health Association. (1992) Position paper—alcohol and tobacco products. *The Nation's Health*, September, 18–20.

Brownson, R.C., Novotny, T.E., & Perry, M.C. (1993) Cigarette smoking and adult leukemia. *Archives of Internal Medicine*, 153:469–475.

Centers for Disease Control. (1991a) Cigarette smoking among adults—United States, 1988. *Morbidity and Mortality Weekly Report*, 40:757–765.

Centers for Disease Control. (1991b) Cigarette smoking among youth—1989. *Morbidity and Mortality Weekly Report*, 40:712–715.

Centers for Disease Control. (1991c) Differences in age of smoking initiation between blacks and whites—United States. *Morbidity and Mortality Weekly Report*, 40:754–757.

Centers for Disease Control. (1991d) Smoking attributable mortality and years of potential life lost—United States, 1988. *Morbidity and Mortality Weekly Report*, 40:62–71.

Centers for Disease Control. (1992a) Cigarette smoking among adults—United States, 1990. *Morbidity and Mortality Weekly Report*, 41:354–355.

Centers for Disease Control. (1992b) Selected tobacco-use behaviors, dietary patterns among high school students—United States, 1991. *Morbidity and Mortality Weekly Report*, 41:417–421.

Connolly, G., Orleans, C.T., & Blum, A. (1992) Snuffing tobacco out of sport: A commentary. *American Journal of Public Health*, 82:351–353.

Cummings, K.M., Markello, S.J., Mahoney, M., Bhargava, A.K., McElroy, P.D., & Marshall, J.R. (1990) Measurement of current exposure to environmental tobacco smoke. *Archives of Environmental Health*, 45:74–79.

Davis, R.M. (1991) Reducing youth access to tobacco. *Journal of the American Health Association*, 266:3186–3188.

DiFranza, J.R., Richards, J.W., Paulman, P.M., Wolf-Gillespie, N., Fletcher, C., Jaffe, R.D., & Murray, D. (1991)

RJR Nabisco's cartoon camel promotes camel cigarettes to children. *Journal of the American Medical Association*, 266:3149–3153.

Emmons, K.M., Abrams, D.B., Marshall, R.J., Etzel, R.A., Novotony, T.E., Marcus, B.H., & Kane, M.E. (1992) Exposure to environmental tobacco smoke in naturalistic settings. *American Journal of Public Health*, 82:24–28.

Escobedo, L.G., Anda, R.F., Smith, P.F., Remington, P.L., & Mast, E.E. (1990) Sociodemographic characteristics of cigarette smoking initiation in the United States: Implications for smoking-prevention policy. *Journal of the American Medical Association*, 264:1550–1555.

Fischer, P.M., Schwartz, M.P., Richards, J.W., Goldstein, A.O., & Rojas, T.H. (1991) Brand logo recognition by children aged 3 to 6 years: Mickey Mouse and Old Joe the Camel. *Journal of the American Medical Association*, 266:3145–3148.

Garrison, C.Z., McKeown, R.E., Valois, R.F., & Vincent, M.L. (1993) Aggression, substance use, and suicidal behaviors in high school students. *American Journal of Public Health*, 83:179–184.

Giovino, G.A., Eriksen, M.P., & McKenna, J.W. (1992) The vital diversity of tobacco control research. *American Journal of Public Health*, 82:1203–1205.

Glantz, S.A. (1993). Removing the incentive to sell kids tobacco: A proposal. *Journal of the American Medical Association*, 269:793–794.

Glynn, T.J., Anderson, D.M., & Schwarz, L. (1991) Tobacco-use reduction of a National Cancer Institute Expert Advisory Panel. *Preventive Medicine*, 20:279–291.

Gritz, E. (1991) Women and smoking: Educating them to stop. *World Smoking and Health*, 16(2):3–7.

Hemenway, D., Solnick, S.J., & Colditz, G.A. (1993) Smoking and suicide among nurses. *American Journal of Public Health*, 83:249–251.

Hugick, L., & Leonard, J. (1991) Despite increasing hostility, one in four Americans still smokes. *Gallup Poll Monthly*, 298:19–27.

Johnston, L.D., O'Malley, P.M., & Bachman, J.G. (1991) *Drug Use Among American High School Seniors, College Students and Young Adults, 1975–1990*. Volume 1. DHHS Publication No. (ADM)91-1813. Washington, D.C.: National Institute on Drug Abuse.

Lipman, J. (1992) Surgeon General says it's high time Joe Camel quit. *Wall Street Journal*, March 10, B1.

Marwick, C. (1993) Increasing use of chewing tobacco, especially among younger persons, alarms Surgeon General. *Journal of the American Medical Association*, 269:195.

National Cancer Institute. (1989) *Cancer Prevention Brief: Tobacco Use*. NIH Publication No. 90-3067. Washington, D.C.: National Cancer Institute.

National Institute on Drug Abuse. (1991) *Drug Abuse and Drug Abuse Research: The Third Triennial Report to Congress from the Secretary, Department of Health and Human Services*. DHHS Publication No. (ADM)91-1704. Rockville, MD: National Institute on Drug Abuse.

National Institutes of Health. (1986) *The Health Implications of Smokeless Tobacco Use*. 0-153-019: QL 3. Washington, D.C.: U.S. Government Printing Office.

Novello, A. (1991) Can we prevent the Virginia Slims woman from catching up with the Marlboro man? *World Smoking and Health*, 16(2):2.

Office for Substance Abuse Prevention. (1990) *Alcohol, Tobacco, and Other Drugs May Harm the Unborn*. DHHS Publication No. (ADM)90-1711. Rockville, MD: Office for Substance Abuse Prevention.

Office of Inspector General. (May, 1990) *Youth Access to Cigarettes*. OEI-02-90-02310.

Office on Smoking and Health. (1986) *The Health Consequences of Involuntary Smoking, a Report of the Surgeon General*. DHHS Publication No. (CDC)87-8398. Washington, D.C.: U.S. Government Printing Office.

Office on Smoking and Health. (1987) *Smoking and Health, a National Status Report: A Report to Congress*. DHHS Publication No. (CDC)87-8396. Rockville, MD: Office on Smoking and Health.

Office on Smoking and Health. (1988) *The Health Consequences of Smoking: Nicotine Addiction, a Report of the Surgeon General*. DHHS Publication No. (CDC)88-8406. Washington, D.C.: U.S. Government Printing Office.

Office on Smoking and Health. (1989) *Reducing the Health Consequences of Smoking: 25 Years of Progress, a Report of the Surgeon General*. DHHS Publication No. (CDC)89-8411. Washington, D.C.: U.S. Government Printing Office.

Office on Smoking and Health. (1990) *The Health Benefits of Smoking Cessation, a Report of the Surgeon General*. DHHS Publication No. (CDC)90-8416. Washington, D.C.: U.S. Government Printing Office.

Papazian, R. (1991) Smoking is dangerous to kids. *Parents*, October, 178–183.

Pearl, R. (1983) Tobacco smoking and longevity. *Science*, 87:216–217.

Pirie, P.L., Murray, D.M., & Luepker, R.V. (1988) Smoking prevalence in a cohort of adolescents, including absentees, dropouts, and transfers. *American Journal of Public Health*, 78:176–178.

Prummel, M.F., & Wiersinga, W.M. (1993) Smoking and risk of Graves' disease. *Journal of the American Medical Association,* 269:479–482.

Severson, R.K., & Linet, M.S. (1993) Does cigarette smoking lead to the subsequent development of leukemia? *Archives of Internal Medicine,* 153:425–427.

Siegel, D., Benowitz, N., Ernster, V.L., Grady, D.G., & Hauck, W.W. (1992) Smokeless tobacco, cardiovascular risk factors, and nicotine and cotinine levels in professional baseball players. *American Journal of Public Health,* 82:417–421.

United States Department of Health and Human Services. (1990) *Model Sale of Tobacco Products to Minors Act: A Model Law Recommended for Adoption by States or Localities to Prevent the Sale of Tobacco Products to Minors.*

United States Department of Health and Human Services. (1991) *Healthy People 2000: National Health Promotion and Disease Prevention Objectives: Full Report, with Commentary.* DHHS Publication No. (PHS)91-50212. Washington, D.C.: U.S. Government Printing Office.

PREVENTION AND TREATMENT OF DRUG ABUSE

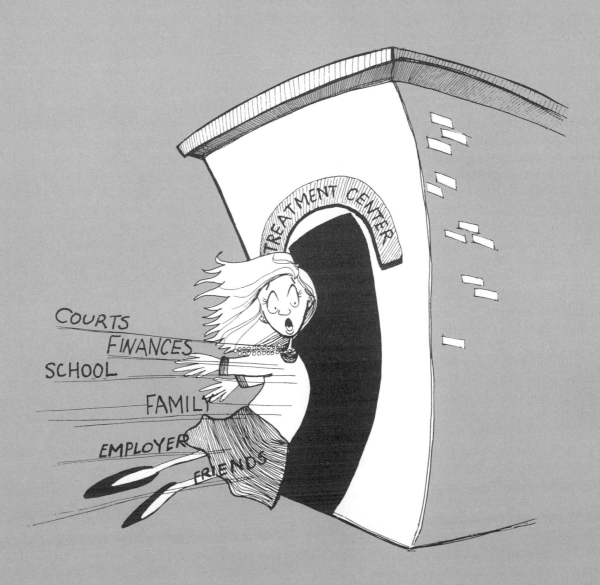

PREVENTION OF DRUG ABUSE

Prevention is a widely-desired goal, but the word is commonly and confusingly applied to many quite different meanings. Drug prevention can mean preventing all initial drug use or stopping all existing use. Prevention can mean reducing not only the demand but also the supply of drugs. Prevention also can focus on the consequences of use and not on the use itself (Office for Substance Abuse Prevention, 1991).

It is important to recognize that prevention alone cannot solve our drug abuse problems. Effective drug treatment is needed for those who are unable to resist the lure of drugs. Treatment for drug abuse will be discussed in Chapter 16. In this chapter, the discussion will include prevention approaches, the historical overview of prevention, what does not work in prevention, community-based drug prevention, parent and family efforts, school-based prevention approaches, and drug prevention in the workplace.

PREVENTION APPROACHES

The family is the first and most important line of defense against drug abuse. The second line of defense must be the community. However, no one sector of the community can be effective alone. When drug abuse is attacked by all sectors of the community—families, schools, businesses, law enforcement, the media, service clubs, recreational programs, and churches—the chances of success are greatly enhanced.

Law enforcement personnel cannot be on every street corner watching for every drug deal. Courts cannot punish every drug offender. Schools cannot monitor young people every minute of the day. However, law enforcement and local education officials can cooperate to keep drug pushers away from school buildings. Local service clubs can join forces with public housing agencies to provide tutors and mentors for high-risk youth. The media can carry antidrug messages and report on community antidrug initiatives. And local businesses and labor groups can team up to sponsor drug-free workplace communities. Citizens and communities can support local drug-abuse

treatment programs and resources (Office of National Drug Control Policy, 1992).

Prevention strategies are essential in combating community drug-abuse problems. Effective law enforcement is needed to deter nonusers from becoming involved with drugs, and to restrict the supply of drugs by disrupting drug-trafficking organizations. Effective interdiction and international efforts are needed to prevent drugs from reaching our borders and to disrupt the transit of drugs. No single part of a drug control strategy can win the war against drugs, nor can we be successful if we neglect any major drug control strategy element (ONCDP, 1992).

Drug prevention and control activities are undertaken by a wide range of community members—legislators, law enforcement officials, health professionals, educators, business leaders, parents, and concerned citizens. Prevention can be applied to any and all drug use such as helping young people avoid alcohol, marijuana, cocaine, or even a form of a particular drug such as crack cocaine. Prevention can be applied to intensified uses or addiction to drugs in general or to a particular drug; for example, stopping cocaine experimenters from going on to everyday crack cocaine smoking. Prevention also can be applied to behaviors and social problems associated with drug use but not to the drug use itself, such as reducing HIV transmission among heroin users.

Earlier chapters have described how illicit drugs are not the only substances that are harmful to adolescents. The use of tobacco and alcohol, as well as the use of steroids, are major national public health problems and, for many, their use is linked to the use of other illicit drugs. For this reason, virtually all prevention programs for young people address alcohol and tobacco.

HISTORICAL OVERVIEW OF PREVENTION

Earlier drug-abuse epidemics in the United States were dealt with primarily through law enforcement approaches relying on tough laws and long sentences to solve drug-abuse problems. In this section of the chapter, the discussion will involve the approaches used in the late 19th and early 20th centuries, the 1960s and 1970s, and the 1980s.

The Late 19th and Early 20th Centuries

The use of cocaine reached epidemic proportions in the late 19th and early 20th centuries, largely as a result of advertisements and depictions by the medical profession of cocaine as a safe, nonaddictive treatment for many common ailments. Cocaine was thought to be so harmless that it could be found in everything from cough drops and skin ointments to tonics and soft drinks. As awareness of cocaine's addictive nature grew, however, citizens began to call for government action to curtail its availability.

This call lead to passage of the Harrison Anti-Narcotics Act of 1914, the first antidrug legislation in U.S. history, which established the regulation of cocaine and other drugs. By the late 1940s, World War II and the disruption of international trafficking organizations had reduced the number of chronic drug users to less than 100,000.

This same approach of drug-use control (government action to curtail availability) by prohibition also was applied to alcohol use between 1919 and 1933. Prohibition curtailed U.S. alcohol consumption but failed to gain sufficient political support (Office for Substance Abuse Prevention, 1991).

The 1960s and 1970s

When the modern drug-abuse epidemic started in the 1960s and drug use emerged throughout our society, the traditional get-tough approach was widely regarded as inadequate and unfair. Severe penalties for marijuana use, in particular, excited popular sentiment that tough laws were the wrong way to prevent drug use.

The popular view held that drug-dependent persons were not criminals at all but sick people who needed treatment, not punishment. The Controlled Substances Act of 1970 codified this attitude by distinguishing between drug users and drug sellers. Drug users got light sentences and drug sellers received relatively harsh sentences. This was the period when, for the first time in U.S. history, "demand reduction" became a significant part of the fight against drug abuse. Although most of the demand reduction efforts in the early 1970s were treatment and not prevention, there was a growing interest in both preventing and treating drug abuse (OSAP, 1991).

200

Because the earlier cocaine epidemic had been so thoroughly suppressed, the general public, as well as educators, legislators, and law enforcement officials, grew complacent about the danger posed by cocaine and other drugs. As a result, throughout the 1950s and 1960s, children received virtually no drug education. The 1960s were characterized by a period of renewed and wide-spread use of addictive and mind-altering drugs, including marijuana, LSD, amphetamines, and heroin. For young people of the 1960's era, drugs became the symbol of generational defiance. By the 1970s, drug use had reached unprecedented levels. The use of drugs became not only tolerated, but also glamorized by many segments of the intellectual, educational, and cultural elite. Movies, television, and popular music portrayed drug use as safe, enjoyable, spiritually enlightening, and a rite of passage for young people.

Many citizens, especially parents, concerned about children's welfare became outraged at the pervasive use of and tolerance for drugs and took action. Antidrug groups of parents began to form around the country. They mounted a massive awareness campaign to teach young people and adults about the destructive nature of drugs, and demanded that authorities enforce existing antidrug laws and pass new, tougher laws. Citizens urged the schools to establish and enforce strict policies against drug use and to implement antidrug curricula. They pressured Hollywood and the media to stop glamorizing drugs and the drug lifestyle. "Just Say NO" became a symbol of our nation's hardening attitudes toward drug use.

The 1980s

The appearance in the early 1980s of a new, potent form of smokable cocaine, popularly called "crack," brought devastating consequences. Crack's highly addictive nature led many of its users to abandon all responsibility and obligation, even to their unborn children. The enormous profits to be made by dealing in crack seduced thousands of young people into a life of lawlessness and turned neighborhoods into battlegrounds. The death of basketball star Len Bias from a cocaine overdose in 1986 gave added impetus to the prevention movement by demonstrating that drug use was not only addictive but also deadly.

Federal, state, and local governments, in response to parents' concerns, began to take action on a variety of fronts—street-level enforcement, education and public awareness, treatment for drug users, border interdiction, and international efforts. The federal government's role in countering illegal drugs expanded greatly in the mid-1980s as several major pieces of legislation were enacted. In addition to stepping up law enforcement and supply-reduction efforts, these acts created a major federal role in drug prevention.

The Office for Substance Abuse Prevention (OSAP) was created within the U.S. Department of Health and Human Services to spearhead federal prevention initiatives. The Drug-Free Schools and Communities Act was passed, providing money to schools and colleges for antidrug programs. The Office of National Drug Control Policy (ONDCP) was established by the Antidrug Abuse Act of 1988 to coordinate national antidrug efforts and oversee Federal antidrug programs.

WHAT DOES NOT WORK IN PREVENTION

Although we do not know with complete certainty which prevention programs work best, we do know, based on research as well as years of experience, a great deal about which prevention programs are ineffective. The following ineffective approaches will be discussed: the information approach, scare tactics, legalization, responsible-use messages, magic bullets, self-esteem exercises, and use of persons recovering from chemical dependency.

The Information Approach

In the 1970s, initial prevention efforts focused on explaining, especially to teenagers, that drugs are harmful. Drug education efforts largely centered around providing young people with specific information on drugs—what they look like and their effects. This approach was based on the assumptions that young people who were exposed to drugs did not know they were harmful and that these young people would not use drugs if they were presented with this information.

An example of a message that was a part of the early efforts was that marijuana use could cause serious problems, such as paranoid reactions. In many cases, curiosity was aroused, and many young people decided to experiment with illegal drugs, using the prevention materials they had been given as a primer on how to use drugs. There was a relentless rise in drug use throughout the United States in the early 1970s, which was the period of time during which schools were relying on the information approach to drug abuse prevention.

A major criticism of the information approach was that the harmful effects of drug use, especially marijuana, were exaggerated while, in fact, the effects of many drugs were poorly understood. In the 1970s, the state of scientific knowledge about drugs was rudimentary by today's standards. Facts that were stressed in drug education may have been myths—leading to lowered credibility of the sources of such information. Another factor that reduced the credibility of drug-education teachers was the fact that during this time all authority was being questioned to an unprecedented degree by young people.

Another important criticism of information programs was that they focused on long-term, negative consequences while the reality is that drugs tend to produce immediate pleasure, not problems. Problems generally occur after a substantial delay. In general, young people are relatively unlikely to consider distant health concerns such as cirrhosis of the liver from chronic drinking or emphysema from smoking. Although some youth appear to be concerned about how drug use can negatively interfere with one's functioning, aspirations, and achievement, others do not show such concern. Those who are least concerned about uncertain and delayed consequences are most vulnerable to drug abuse. Lack of a future orientation is a major characteristic of high-risk youth. The factors underlying this lack of future orientation appear to be fertile ground for drug-abuse prevention efforts.

It is important not to misinterpret the criticisms of the information approach by concluding that the best way to persuade young people not to use drugs is to give them no factual information whatsoever. This would be ill-advised, particularly for the low-risk young person. Providing information to low-risk youth on the health and legal implications of using illegal drugs often is enough incentive for them to avoid using drugs. When low-risk young people really understand the dangers of drugs, they choose to remain drug free. High-risk youth may not be so easily dissuaded from using drugs, and for them additional intervention is necessary.

Information-only approaches also have been highly criticized on the grounds that they ignore the fact that drug use behavior is related to a variety of factors, not simply the absence of knowledge about the health, social, and legal risks (Rhodes & Jason, 1988). This shortcoming for alcohol information approaches is pointed out by Gordon and McAlister (1982):

Probably the most important reason that this type of approach does not have a stronger impact on adolescent drinking is that it does not leave room for discussion of the variety of reasons for which people use alcohol and other mood-altering substances—as a rite of passage to prove sexuality; to relieve boredom; to escape from pressure; to facilitate social interactions; to solve personal problems; to relieve anxiety, depression or fatigue; to satisfy curiosity or need for adventure, conformity, rebellion, or self-exploration; or for pleasure. The emotional and physiological changes of puberty make adolescents extremely susceptible to psychosocial pressures to engage in many high-risk activities in order to achieve status in their peer group, even if the activities have known undesirable health consequence (p. 212).

Scare Tactics

When, in order to deter young people from using drugs, exaggerated or outright erroneous information about drug effects is presented, the credibility of the entire antidrug message is damaged. A prime example of this is the almost comically-exaggerated view of the effects of smoking marijuana portrayed in propaganda such as in the movie "Reefer Madness," which distracted a generation of young people from the drug's very real and very serious medical dangers. Young people should be taught the truth about drugs. The reality of drug use—mental impairment, long-term medical damage, loss of employment, broken family relationships, addiction, and the possibility of an early death—is sobering enough without having to resort to exaggeration or misinformation. Williams et al. (1985) demonstrated that knowledge retention in students is better in a low-fear rather than high-fear appeal and better with a credible communicator.

Legalization

Despite the fact that the use of illegal drugs has decreased significantly over the past several years, there are still those who advocate legalizing drug use. However, if we have learned anything about drug policy, it is that legalization would have catastrophic implications for our efforts to convince young people and others not to use drugs.

Allowing drugs such as cocaine and heroin to be sold openly would undercut and make mockery of society's efforts to convince young people that taking drugs is wrong and harmful. Legalization also would undercut other efforts to reduce the demand for drugs. For example, drug treatment would be much less effective if recovering dependent persons could access readily available, legalized drugs when they leave treatment programs.

One of the chief arguments of legalization proponents is that legalization would eliminate drug-related crime and violence by removing the profit motive for criminals.

However, there is no evidence that legalization would reduce drug use or drug trafficking, and there is plenty of evidence to suggest that both would increase dramatically. Under virtually any of the legalization proposals, drugs would continue to be off-limits for certain groups, such as children and known criminals. This would inevitably give rise to illegal drug markets. Additionally, the easy availability of such drugs as cocaine and heroin would, as experience suggests, lead to more drug use, more dependent persons, and more of the harmful by-products of drug use—crime, violence, family disintegration, impaired infants, and social disruption. In short, the lesson is clear: drugs are not dangerous because they are illegal; drugs are illegal because they are dangerous.

Responsible-Use Messages

Some people have argued that instead of issuing a blanket denunciation of all drug use, educators and government officials should be content with trying to get students to use drugs—including alcohol—responsibly and in moderation. This approach, sometimes referred to as "harm reduction," seeks to reduce problems associated with illegal drug use rather than to prevent such use. Until very recently, a number of widely-used, drug-education curricula incorporated this philosophy. However, the strategy is flawed because of the addictive nature and harmful side effects of illegal drugs. The only responsible use is "no use." By influencing young persons to think otherwise, the "responsible use" approach actually may have encouraged many to experiment with drugs—experimentation that, in many cases, led to regular use and ultimately to addiction.

Magic Bullets

Motivated by an understandable desire to save youth from the ravages of drug addiction, many adults seize upon a variety of antidrug promotional materials as the answer to preventing drug use. The most common are items of clothing bearing antidrug slogans, such as T-shirts, caps, buttons, rings, and headbands. Other items are bumper stickers, posters, antidrug rap songs, school assembly programs, and books or brochures aimed at children. Although such techniques can be helpful in deglamorizing illegal drugs and can provide a forum for young people to express their decisions to lead a drug-free lifestyle, no single "magic bullet" will keep a generation of young people from using drugs. These techniques can be effective only when they are an integral part of a long-term effort to influence the attitudes and behavior of young people.

Self-Esteem Exercises

A widely-used prevention strategy seeks to prevent drug use among young people by reinforcing their self-esteem through a variety of motivational and values-clarification exercises. The rationale behind this approach is that young people use drugs because they have a low opinion of themselves. Consequently, if they can be made to feel good about themselves, they would choose not to use drugs.

The self-esteem argument has an element of validity. However, there is a difference between self-esteem that is earned through an acceptance of responsibility for oneself, one's family and one's community, and the self-esteem promoted by exercises in which young people are told that self-esteem is intrinsic, without any obligations such as to study in school, to stay away from drugs, or to obey the law. It is important that drug-prevention curricula and programs help children gain self-esteem by promoting hard-won accomplishments such as passing a challenging math test, for example, rather than relying on feelings alone.

Use of Persons Recovering from Chemical Dependency

There is an appropriate role in clinical therapy for persons in treatment to learn from the mistakes of other persons recovering from chemical dependency. However, these persons should not use their drug use and recovery experiences to instruct students in prevention programs.

Teenagers are commonly susceptible to feelings of invulnerability. They may miss the recovering person's message of the pain and devastation caused by drugs and may absorb only the idea that anyone can use drugs, recover, and lead a productive life. Teenagers may come to believe that, if necessary, they can always be cured of drug addiction. Recovering, chemically-dependent persons such as rock stars, athletes, and movie actors who are idolized by young people are particularly unacceptable in prevention programs if they claim to have made a glorious recovery. Such messages are unrealistic and can lead young people to assume that they can recover easily from drug addiction—and even subsequently attain affluence, fame, and happiness (ONDCP, 1992).

COMMUNITY-BASED DRUG PREVENTION

The most promising approaches to dealing with alcohol and other drug-abuse problems are comprehensive, self-managed, tailored to the community, and planned to reach every part of the community. Successful prevention programs appear to take the following factors into account:

- society's norms and values,
- state and local laws,
- national policies,
- school policies,
- health professional practices,
- media messages,
- community group activities,
- parents' and children's beliefs, attitudes, and behaviors.

The sharp decrease in alcohol-related traffic deaths in recent years is an example of the results of a comprehensive community-based approach to prevention. This discussion will include community needs and strengths, community coalitions, developing a community prevention plan, utilizing community groups, prevention through mentoring, prevention through media campaigns, and regulation of alcohol use.

Community Needs and Strengths

Each community has different needs and strengths. To create prevention efforts that work and are long lasting, the community itself needs to be involved. Experience has shown that the most successful prevention efforts are those that let the community solve its own problems. Individuals, institutions, and communities must not become dependent on outside professionals or program models whose withdrawal will return the community to its original condition.

When outside professionals are brought in, their role should be to transfer knowledge, skills, and resources to the community. This transfer can be accomplished when the outside professionals form partnerships with identified helpers in the community rather than "do for the community," and when prevention efforts respond to community concerns as they arise rather than to the concerns of the outside "experts." Projects operated by people within the community are the most likely to thrive.

The primary unit of society—the family—exerts a strong influence on whether or not young people develop drug-abuse problems. Strong family bonds and effective communication between parents and children may help protect children from many of the social and emotional factors that trigger alcohol and other substance use. Family-based drug-abuse prevention programs are reviewed later in this chapter.

Schools are concerned about drug use because it has a direct impact on learning. Alcohol and other drug use by students can disrupt academic performance, contribute to vandalism and absenteeism, lead to higher dropout rates, decrease motivation to achieve, and have other harmful consequences. School-based prevention approaches are also discussed in detail later in this chapter.

In addition to the family and school, communities consist of other important groups that have an important part to play in preventing drug use. These include youth and recreational groups, the health care system, the religious community, the business community, civic organizations, media, and the legal system. A discussion of how these groups can be involved follows later in the chapter.

Community Coalitions

The most effective strategies for preventing drug use and keeping drugs out of our schools and neighborhoods are those that mobilize all elements of a community in a coordinated plan of attack. One way for a community to develop and implement that kind of plan is to form a community coalition. Coalitions can be formed in a number of ways. Often an individual—a concerned parent, business leader, school official, or a chief of police—will take the initiative. A coalition enables the community to mobilize all key residents and organizations, including government officials, parents, schools, service clubs, businesses, the media, places of worship, health providers, and law enforcement to forge a broad consensus about how to attack the community's drug problems.

What unites the diverse groups that make up a community coalition is a heightened sense of concern, and even outrage, about what drug use is doing to a community and an urgent commitment to take actions that will be effective. Successful coalitions are able to translate this initial urgency and energy into a process that continually unfolds, generates, and uses new opportunities for action.

Developing a Community Prevention Plan

Some people who are willing to become involved in community efforts to prevent alcohol and other drug problems look on planning as a complex process best suited for professionals. It is true that outside experts can be helpful, but even the most elaborate plans are based on the contributions of local people concerned about the problem of drug abuse. Many effective plans have been developed using only neighborhood volunteers.

In some communities, concerned people have tried to initiate prevention efforts without systematic plans. They want to spend their time doing something about the problem rather than discussing what they should be doing. Too often, however, communities learn that lack of planning results in well-intentioned efforts spread thinly over too many separate activities to make a meaningful difference. Planning a prevention initiative helps communities concentrate on projects that will have the most impact on local alcohol and other drug problems. Planning reduces the frustration and wasted effort that can occur when prevention efforts try to accomplish too much too quickly.

There is another reason that planning is important. Preventing drug-abuse problems costs money, and groups may hope to receive financial support from government agencies, national organizations, and private donors. These funding sources prefer to assist prevention programs that demonstrate specific objectives and measurable accomplishments. Planning helps provide the documentation that groups need to compete for support from funding sources.

Some people think of plans as lengthy, formal documents filled with statistics, charts, and technical terms. At the community level, such elaborate plans usually are unnecessary. A plan for a prevention program can be a brief document written in plain language that defines what the program is designed to do, the resources required, and the measures that will be used to determine if the program is achieving its objectives. The key to success is a systematic, realistic planning effort rather than a glossy, formal planning document.

In general, communities interested in implementing ambitious programs to prevent alcohol and other drug problems are likely to become involved in a more elaborate planning process than those attempting more limited activities. It may be helpful for communities to begin a prevention program or activity with plans for six months or a year and to graduate to more comprehensive programs as they gain planning experience and prevention resources. Whether planning is simple or elaborate, the process generally includes the following nine steps:

1. assessment of the problem,
2. development of goals,
3. development of objectives,
4. identification of resources,
5. identification of funding sources,
6. assignment of leadership tasks,
7. implementation,
8. evaluation,
9. program revision based on evaluation findings.

A final planning document may specifically refer to each of these nine components. Sometimes, the distinctions between goals and objectives or between identifying funding sources and identifying other resources are not explicitly stated. A detailed description of these nine planning steps is included in *Prevention Plus II: Tools for Creating Drug-Free Communities*, which is available from the National Clearinghouse for Alcohol and Drug Information, P.O. Box 2345, Rockville, Maryland 20852.

Utilizing Community Groups

Prevention programs should utilize a wide range of community groups in planning and implementing prevention efforts. The following sections provide some suggestions for utilizing these groups.

Youth and recreation groups. Youth face strong pressure from their peers to use alcohol and other drugs. Teaching young people life skills such as how to cope with uncomfortable emotions, how to make sound decisions, and how to communicate more effectively will help them resist peer and other social pressures to use alcohol and other drugs.

Another prevention strategy is to offer young people alternative after-school and weekend activities and programs such as wilderness challenges and opportunities for meaningful community involvement. Other suggestions are:

- Meet with youth and recreation group administrators to discuss their policies related to substance use.
- Investigate model programs and try to incorporate their success into community efforts to prevent alcohol and other drug use.
- Encourage organizations to distribute prevention materials. Many publications are available free from state and federal agencies.
- Support programs that build self-esteem, improve decision-making and communication skills, and teach resistance skills.
- Contact people who have special skills (such as airplane pilots and mechanics, chefs, and artists) and invite them to get involved in group activities and to serve as role models or mentors.
- Organize fundraisers for community prevention programs or activities.

The health care system. Health care professionals such as doctors, nurses, dentists, and pharmacists can play an important role in prevention strategies. They can serve as information resources by identifying drug-abuse problems among their patients, by referring patients and family members to appropriate treatment programs, and by counseling youth and adults about the risks of drug use. They also can be highly credible advocates for community and state policies, laws, and regulations that promote health and wellness.

The religious community. Many community members look to their churches, synagogues, and other institutions of fellowship for leadership in solving major social problems. These organizations can play a key role in prevention by helping youth and families identify and solve problems before they are compounded by alcohol and other drug use, by referring them to appropriate treatment resources, by sponsoring alcohol and other drug-free social and recreational activities for preteens and teenagers, and by making their facilities available to prevention efforts. Community members can do the following to encourage involvement of these organizations in prevention:

- Encourage the heads of congregations to schedule relevant sermon topics and to tie them into prevention-related community campaigns or special events.
- Volunteer to work with the congregation's youth group.
- Suggest that congregations sponsor training sessions for members to learn how to intervene and how to refer members who need help for a drug-abuse problem.
- Gather materials on preventing alcohol and other drug-related problems for the congregation's library.

The business community. Local businesses have an important role to play in prevention. Businesses can sponsor programs for employees and help reduce the availability of alcohol to minors. In addition, businesses can support local prevention efforts by donating materials and services such as printing and mailing, hosting prevention seminars, and giving their employees incentives for volunteering to work on drug-abuse prevention projects. Community members can consider the following suggestions for involving the business community in prevention efforts:

- Write letters to the local Chamber of Commerce, restaurant associations, and other organizations to seek support for strict enforcement of laws related to selling alcohol to minors.
- Meet with the human resource directors and activities directors of local businesses to discuss taking initiatives such as scheduling lunchtime prevention seminars and providing prevention-related information through company newsletters.
- Contact local businesses about donating resources or materials to help support alcohol or other drug-free youth activities.
- Ask local copy shops or printers to donate services for flyers or brochures about prevention activities.

- Publicize the help and contributions you receive from local businesses by including their names on prevention-promotional materials.

Civic organizations. Civic groups, by their very nature, are committed to improving the health and well-being of the community. Civic groups frequently are action oriented and know how to influence community leaders and obtain resources to get the job done. Many national civic organizations already have joined the prevention bandwagon to support activities to prevent drug-abuse problems. For example, civic groups such as the Junior League, the Lions Club, Service Clubs of America, and the Rotary have sponsored their own alcohol and drug-prevention programs or worked with government officials to enhance the effectiveness of state or national campaigns. Some ideas for involving civic organizations are:

- Meet with members of the program committees of local civic groups and suggest ideas for meetings devoted to prevention.
- Gather prevention information and materials and distribute them at civic group meetings.
- Find out which civic group members are interested in prevention and form a working group to undertake special projects such as creating a treatment-resource directory; monitoring alcoholic beverage sales at local bars, restaurants, and retail businesses; and raising money to support drug-free youth activities.
- Identify a youth group that needs adult volunteers and encourage civic group members to volunteer their time to help the youth group.
- Ask the board of directors of civic groups to proclaim their support for legislation and funding that promote prevention.

The legal system. Community-based prevention programs should assess the following elements of the legal system as they relate to deterring alcohol and other drug use:

- Are local, state, and federal representatives involved in alcohol and other drug prevention? What laws or actions are currently being considered?
- What are the penalties for selling alcohol and other drugs to minors? How are these laws enforced?
- What are the local laws concerning drug dealing and what can community members do to help enforce them?
- What are the laws concerning alcohol and other drug-impaired driving?
- Do police watch for teenagers who park off the road to drink or use other drugs? Is there a Community Watch?
- What is the quality of relations between the law enforcement force and the rest of the community?

- Do law enforcement officials sponsor any prevention activities? Do they coordinate them with the schools or other community groups?
- How are drug-using probationers and parolees handled?
- Are the fines collected from people for driving under the influence or from the taxing of alcohol and tobacco products being used for drug-abuse prevention programs?

The following are suggestions for utilizing the legal system in community prevention efforts:

- Write letters to local, state, and federal officials endorsing crackdowns and stiff penalties for local retailers, restaurants, and entertainment businesses that sell alcohol to minors.
- Report to legal authorities any businesses that sell alcohol to minors.
- Publicize laws related to alcohol and other drug use by writing letters to the editor or by asking local newspaper reporters to cover drug-abuse prevention issues.
- Encourage law enforcement officers and other officials to give prevention talks to classes in local schools.
- Report drug-impaired drivers to the police as soon as possible.
- Suggest that sobriety checkpoints be set up near places at hours associated with heavy drinking.

Prevention Through Mentoring

Many young people, especially those growing up in high-crime, drug-infested neighborhoods, lack a stable, long-term adult presence in their lives. These young people may be completely disengaged from responsible community institutions such as school, church, youth groups, or legitimate employment. Lacking strong adult role models and guidance, they too often succumb to the lure of the drug trade.

Adult mentors can play a vital role in steering such young people away from drugs and crime and toward a productive life (Fig. 15-1). For example, adults and older peers can be organized, trained, and placed in supportive relationships with young people. High school seniors can help incoming freshmen. Professionals, college students, and recent college graduates can volunteer to work with young people. Older parents can be matched with teenage mothers and fathers who may be unprepared for the rigors of parenthood.

An example of an exemplary mentoring program is Baltimore's Choice program. This program works with troubled youths in the city's most distressed neighborhoods. Choice is run by recent college graduates who have agreed

Figure 15-1
Adult Mentors Are Vital Role Models

to spend a year or more working with inner city young people who have been referred by various public agencies. Typically, a Choice worker will see the youth to whom (s)he is assigned three to five times a day, virtually every day of the year. The purpose of the program is to provide intensive attention, guidance, and discipline to adolescents who are used to getting none of these. Choice staff make it their business to know the whereabouts of their young charges at all times, to make sure they attend school, avoid loitering, and stay out of trouble, and to hold them accountable for their missteps.

Prevention Through Media Campaigns

Intensive, well-conceived and sustained media campaigns can help shape public attitudes about drugs. Many people believe that the antismoking campaign of the 1970s had a great deal to do with reductions in teen smoking during that decade. Recently, the same kind of attention has been directed towards drugs. For example, since 1987, the Partnership for a Drug-Free America, a privately-funded initiative of the advertising industry, has conducted an extensive national campaign to encourage negative attitudes towards drugs. The Partnership calls this "denormalizing" drug use, changing the public's attitude from one of acceptance of drug use as normal to one of viewing drugs and the people who use them as abnormal, unfashionable, and unpopular. Survey research conducted in the cities where the Partnership conducted intensive public awareness campaigns has demonstrated a significant impact on public attitudes toward drug use.

In addition to transmitting antidrug messages, it is important that the media refrain from portraying drug use as normal, desirable, or fashionable. Furthermore, the entertainment industry can strengthen society's antidrug messages by producing films that depict drug use realistically— damaging to the users and the users' relationships at work and with family and friends.

Less useful, and perhaps even counterproductive, is the use of sports and entertainment stars who are reformed drug users who tell young people not to do as they have done. While well-intentioned, these stars can carry the unintended message that addiction is not a great risk— you can always recover, go on to become rich and famous, and be a role model for other young people.

Regulation of Alcohol Use

Because alcohol differs from other drugs in legal status, the strategies discussed here cannot be generalized to prevent the use of illegal drugs, except to the extent that those who use alcohol, especially at early ages, are more likely also to use illegal drugs. Communities can influence regulation of alcohol use by young people. Essentially, communities achieve this by increasing public awareness of alcoholic beverage policies that might increase alcohol-related problems, explaining policies that compromise efforts to prevent alcohol use, and persuading public officials to create and enforce laws that promote prevention.

Many community advocacy groups concerned with these issues already are formed. Some groups, such as Mothers Against Drunk Driving (MADD), have been concerned with a single issue, while others have dealt with a combination of issues. In either case, it is important for an advocacy group to familiarize itself with the important agencies and individuals that control policy. Public officials need assistance in understanding the issues; advocacy groups, by planning and timing their efforts, can play a significant role in educating officials and effecting change.

Community groups may want to pursue regulatory prevention strategies as part of their effort to prevent alcohol and other drug use by youth. Instead of focusing on changing individual behaviors, these strategies emphasize changing the environment in which alcohol consumption occurs.

Increasing sales tax on alcohol to raise prices. Research shows that increasing the price of alcoholic beverages will decrease consumption, particularly among young people (Surgeon General's Workshop on Drunk Driving Proceedings, 1989). In some communities, groups have petitioned the appropriate agency to increase the sales tax on alcohol. Groups interested in applying this strategy will need to determine if taxes are applied locally or at the state level. Groups will also need to determine which administrative agency is responsible for taxation. It may be useful to bring your issues to the attention of the Governor, who appoints members to the particular administrative agency. It must be recognized, however, that if consumption goes down, so may revenue for the State. This can be a strong motivation for not raising the price.

Enforcing the minimum drinking age. Increasing the minimum drinking age from 18–21 has proved to significantly decrease alcohol consumption by 18–20-year-olds and to reduce the number of alcohol-related traffic accidents in which youth are involved. Community groups can take measures to see that such a law is strongly enforced. They can petition law enforcement and governing authorities to enforce checking customer-identification cards through surveillance operations and by applying stiff fines to businesses that sell alcoholic beverages to minors. State government identification cards that are difficult to duplicate fraudulently also would enable fewer minors to obtain alcoholic beverages from merchants. Community groups also should encourage local establishments not to serve people who cannot prove their age.

Other strategies might include requiring stiff fines or community service from youth caught purchasing alcohol or drinking. In at least one state, any youth caught drinking in or out of a car is legally required to surrender his/her driver's license. In addition, adults other than merchants

or parents who supply a minor with alcoholic beverages could be more actively prosecuted for contributing to the delinquency of a minor.

Denying or revoking alcohol licenses. Convenience stores and gas stations are often operated by minors who are more willing than adult clerks to sell alcoholic beverages to other minors. Monitoring the sale of alcoholic beverages at stadiums for sports events also is a problem. Generally, multiple bars are set up at these events, and minors find it relatively easy to obtain alcoholic beverages.

Communities can petition the legislature to refuse alcohol licenses to establishments that are known to serve minors. Applying pressure on policymakers to use surveillance operations and applying stiff fines to businesses that sell alcohol to minors are strategies that may be especially useful for discouraging businesses from selling alcoholic beverages to minors.

Identification of underage drinkers. Training for salespeople and servers is now available in many communities. Community representatives can urge business owners to discuss with their employees the seriousness of laws concerning the sale of alcoholic beverages to minors. Community representatives also might urge businesses to create and enforce a policy specifying that employees who neglect to check the identification of customers appearing to be underage will be terminated.

Stricter regulations for alcohol advertising and promotions. Young people and adults see a multitude of advertisements for beer, wine, liquor, and wine coolers. (Advertisements for liquor and cigarettes have been banned from television in the United States because of the health risk associated with these products.) Television, radio, magazines, newspapers, and billboards feature famous former athletes, well-known entertainers, and other attractive people to deliver the message that consuming alcoholic beverages is associated with an athletic, rich, successful, and sexy lifestyle.

The U.S. Department of Treasury's Bureau of Alcohol, Tobacco, and Firearms has a congressional mandate to control alcohol advertising on the national level. This mandate was enacted through the Federal Alcohol Administration Act of 1973 (FAA Act). It does not affect local advertising.

Some states have already adopted the FAA beverage industry codes for local and statewide advertising. Unfortunately, code sections that restrict advertising and promotions are often vague, difficult to monitor, and, as a result, difficult to enforce. Community representatives may therefore choose to develop and enforce restrictions that are much more detailed.

The community can petition lawmakers and policymakers to regulate alcohol advertising more strictly, but achieving change at this level is admittedly difficult. However, while working to change legislation, communities also can work to sensitize local advertisers, retailers, and producers to the health risks of alcohol use and can ask them to make appropriate changes voluntarily. Another useful strategy that can be used by parents, schools, or other community groups is to teach children to analyze alcohol advertising.

PARENT AND FAMILY EFFORTS

In addition to serving as family leaders and nurturers of their children's development, parents can actively take steps to help their children lead drug-free lives. Family experiences have a strong influence on whether or not young people develop drug-abuse problems. The discussion will include actions within the family and suggested interfamily efforts.

Actions Within the Family

Strong family bonds and effective communication between parents and children may help protect children from the many social and emotional factors that trigger alcohol and other drug use. Parents can use the following ten steps to help their children say NO to using alcohol and other drugs:

1. Talk in the family about alcohol and other drugs. Make sure children understand the dangers and problems of alcohol and other drug use.
2. Learn to really listen. Just talking to a child is only half the job. Help keep open the lines of communication by knowing how to listen, and by knowing when to listen and when not to talk.
3. Help them feel good about themselves. Preteens and adolescents often are unsure of themselves. Knowing that their parents have confidence in them and believe in their self-worth is important to them. Communicate this faith in them by giving lots of specific and believable praise and encouragement at appropriate times.
4. Help them develop strong values. A strong value system anchored in a clear sense of right and wrong can give children the courage to make decisions based on facts and sound values rather than on peer pressure.

5. Be a good role model. Children are very aware of habits and spoken and unspoken attitudes concerning alcohol and other drug use. They will tend to follow their parents' example.
6. Help them deal with peer pressure. Children who are taught to be gentle and agreeable also may need skills to resist peer pressure. Help them practice ways they can say NO and feel confident about themselves and their decisions.
7. Set firm rules against alcohol and other drug use. Have clear family rules. Tell children they are not allowed to drink, smoke, use other drugs, or engage in other activities to which you object. Be sure they thoroughly understand the consequences of breaking these rules. Enforce the rules consistently.
8. Encourage healthy, creative activities. Make sure children have enough structure in their daily lives. Create activities for them or encourage them to take part in sports, school programs, or hobbies they might enjoy. Join the children in having fun.
9. Talk with other parents. They're all going through the same experiences. Networking with neighborhood parents and community groups can help. If a child is going to a party or getting together with friends, make sure there is a chaperon and that there will be no alcohol or other drugs present at the party or get-together.
10. Know what to do if you suspect a problem. Learn to recognize the telltale signs of drug use, and get appropriate help quickly from professionals.

Interfamily Efforts

Parents can organize and take action in the fight against drug abuse in a variety of ways. Some parents have organized themselves in drug-prevention efforts in some of the following ways:

Parent support groups. These groups are formed by parents for parents. Through support groups, parents help one another as they cope with the drug and alcohol problems in their homes and neighborhoods. Parent groups often develop guidelines for acceptable behavior such as establishing curfews, chaperoning social events for teenagers, and helping other parents supervise young people's activities to ensure that they are free of drug and alcohol use.

Parent action groups. Parent action groups often grow out of parent support groups to work with federal, state, and local governments, schools, law enforcement agencies, and businesses to influence social policies regarding drug and alcohol use. Examples include modifying school drug and alcohol policies; trying to eliminate sales of drug paraphernalia; demanding stricter enforcement of drug laws and stronger prosecution of offenders; enforcing the minimum purchase age for alcohol; and getting legislation and local ordinances passed that will safeguard children's health and well-being.

Family life skills development. Family life skills programs emphasize important aspects of family health such as positive role modeling and effective problem solving. These strategies enable parents and children to communicate more effectively and learn personal and interpersonal skills. They are effective for both primary prevention and early intervention with drug and alcohol problems.

Parent drug and alcohol education programs. Through drug and alcohol education programs, parents learn about the pharmacology of alcohol and other drugs and the harmful impact they can have on one's health and well-being. Armed with this knowledge, parents can become influential partners with community and school prevention programs in fighting drug abuse.

An excellent resource for parents is *Parent Training Is Prevention: Preventing Alcohol and Other Drug Problems Among Youth in the Family,* which is available through the Office for Substance Abuse Prevention, 5600 Fishers Lane, Rockville, Maryland 20857.

SCHOOL-BASED PREVENTION APPROACHES

One of the six National Education Goals calls for all United States schools to be free of drugs and violence by the year 2000. Because children spend many of their waking hours in the classroom, schools are important sites for drug prevention.

The following discussion will include school standards, assessing drug-use problems in schools, school policies, a comprehensive drug-prevention curriculum, positive peer programs, resistance training, drug-free activities, student-assistance programs, early-childhood programs, working with high-risk students, and in-service training.

School Standards

The best way that a school can prevent students from using drugs is simply to be a good school. This means having a challenging curriculum; high expectations for all students; dedicated, knowledgeable teachers; an energetic

210

principal; involved parents; and an orderly, disciplined learning environment.

An essential component of any school's prevention program is a comprehensive prevention curriculum at all grade levels. Effective prevention curricula emphasize a message of "no use" of alcohol and other drugs, encourage civic responsibility and respect for the law, and teach children the importance of being healthy and drug free. Effective curricula also present accurate information about what drugs can do to young people's bodies and minds, and teach students how to resist peer pressure to use drugs.

Schools should supplement and reinforce their antidrug curricula by establishing and enforcing drug-free school policies. Such policies should provide sanctions or consequences up to and including expelling students who use or sell drugs on school grounds, and also deal firmly with drug use by faculty and other staff members. In addition, schools should vigorously address other problems that are associated with the drug trade, such as the presence of weapons in the school. Schools should offer a student-assistance program and plan drug-free activities for the students. All of these measures—the curricula, the policies, and the programs—are most effective when schools cooperate closely with local law enforcement, community groups, and businesses, and when they work hand-in-hand with parents.

Assessing Drug-Use Problems in Schools

School personnel should be informed about the extent of drug use in their school. School boards, superintendents, and other public officials should support school administrators in their efforts to assess the extent of drug problems and to combat them. To guide and evaluate effective drug-prevention efforts, schools can take the following actions:

- Conduct anonymous surveys of students and consult with local law enforcement officials to identify the extent of drug problems.
- Bring together school personnel to identify areas where drugs are being used and sold.
- Meet with parents to help determine the nature and extent of drug use.
- Maintain records on drug use and sales in the school over a period of time, for use in evaluating and improving prevention efforts. In addition to self-reported drug-use patterns, records may include information on drug-related arrests and school discipline problems.
- Inform the community, in straightforward language, of the results of the school's assessment of alcohol and other drug problems.

School Policies

Clear policies regarding use and possession of alcohol and other drugs, both on and off school property, are critical to all members of the school community. Parents, school officials, students, law enforcement officials, and drug and alcohol professionals should all be involved in the development of the policies to make them most effective. School policies should clearly establish that drug use, possession, and sale on the school grounds and at school functions will not be tolerated. These policies should apply both to students and to school personnel, and may include prevention, intervention, treatment, and disciplinary measures.

School policies should have the following characteristics:
1. Specify what constitutes a drug offense by defining:
   - illegal substances and paraphernalia;
   - the area of the school's jurisdiction; for example, the school property, its surroundings, and all school-related events, such as proms and athletic events;
   - the types of violations (drug possession, use, and sale).
2. State the consequences for violating school policy. Punitive action should be linked to referral for treatment and counseling. Possible measures to deal with first-time offenders include the following:
   - a required meeting of the student and his/her parents with school officials, concluding with a contract signed by the student and parents in which they acknowledge a drug problem and the student agrees to stop using drugs and to participate in drug counseling or a rehabilitation program;
   - suspension, assignment to an alternative school, in-school suspension, after-school or Saturday detention with close supervision, and demanding academic assignments;
   - referral to a drug-treatment expert or counselor;
   - notification of law enforcement agency.

It is important that established policies are enforced fairly and consistently. These should include adequate security measures to eliminate drugs from school premises and school functions. Ensure that everyone understands the policy and the procedures that will be followed in case of infractions. Make copies of the school policy available to all parents, teachers, and students, and publicize the policy throughout the school and community. In addition, strict security measures to bar access to intruders and to prohibit student drug trafficking should be imposed. Enforcement policies should correspond to the severity of the school's drug problem.

Drug testing in schools. Proposals to employ drug testing in schools often create great controversy. Proponents of testing want to identify those who may later experience significant difficulty associated with undetected drug use and to prevent experimentation by those who fear the stigma of detection. Opponents see drug testing in the schools as unnecessary and inappropriate, citing the high costs of testing programs and breach of students' privacy rights, with the added danger that a student may drop out of school to avoid detection. Public concern about adolescent drug use is such that the debate over whether or not to institute drug-testing programs in order to reduce drug use is unlikely to be resolved in the near future.

Comprehensive Drug-Prevention Curriculum

Schools should implement a comprehensive drug-prevention curriculum for pre-kindergarten through grade 12. A model program should have these main objectives:
- to value and maintain sound personal health;
- to respect laws and rules prohibiting drugs;
- to resist pressures to use drugs;
- to promote student activities that are drug free;
- to offer healthy avenues for student interests.

In developing a program, school staff should take the following steps:
- Determine curriculum content appropriate for the school's grade levels and assessed drug problems.
- Base the curriculum on an understanding of the reasons children try drugs in order to teach them how to resist pressures to use drugs.
- Review existing materials for possible adaptation. State and national organizations that have an interest in drug prevention have lists of available materials.

In implementing a program, school staff should take the following steps:
- Include students in all grades. Effective drug education is cumulative.
- Teach about drugs in health education classes, and reinforce this curriculum with appropriate materials in classes such as social studies and science.
- Develop expertise in drug prevention through training. Teachers should be knowledgeable about drugs, personally committed to opposing drug use, and skilled at eliciting participation by students in drug-prevention efforts.

A majority of schools have drug-education and prevention programs, but many programs may be ineffective because they:

- begin too late, long after drug use has started;
- often focus almost exclusively on providing information about drugs;
- are not properly implemented;
- are not based on sound research and evaluation;
- are too narrow and do not relate to other moral, civic, and health issues;
- are not reinforced by policies;
- are not supplemented by other community and school programs and activities.

Positive Peer Programs

Positive peer programs utilize student peers as role models, facilitators, helpers, and leaders for other school-age children, particularly in grades 7–12. Programs such as these can provide help to young people who are having problems, who are undergoing normal adolescent stresses and want to confide in someone, and who want to participate in school and community service activities. School administrators must be prepared to provide extensive support and guidance in order to ensure successful implementation of peer programs.

Resistance Training

Often called "refusal skills training," the strategy of resistance training grew out of successful efforts to teach adolescents how to say NO to smoking (Fig. 15-2). This approach recognizes the enormous role peer pressure plays in influencing a young person's decision to try alcohol or drugs. Resistance training gives children the practical social skills they need to handle such pressure. Unlike some previous school-based approaches, resistance training is predicated on the proposition that using drugs is wrong and harmful and should be resisted. Lately, this training has been further expanded to help youth resist peer pressure to participate in criminal activities.

Drug-Free Activities

If we expect young people to lead drug-free lives, we must provide them with appealing alternatives. Activities ranging from Boys and Girls Clubs to Midnight Basketball leagues can help relieve the boredom that tempts many young people to become involved with drugs, as well as provide them with responsible adult supervision. Another positive aspect of such programs is that they provide young people with a sense of camaraderie and community that can compete with the appeal of youth gangs and drug-trafficking networks.

Other activities also can help fill this need. Many schools have begun to offer alcohol and drug-free after-prom

parties, graduation parties, and other school-based celebrations that allow young people to have fun without exposing them to negative peer pressure. Local businesses are also an excellent source of support for alternative activities such as athletic teams or part-time jobs.

Student Assistance Programs

Student Assistance Programs are modeled after Employee Assistance Programs (EAPs) in business and industry. Teachers and other school personnel are trained to recognize alcohol and other drug involvement or related problems that may interfere with a student's ability to function at school and then to use a referral process for getting appropriate help for the student. Students can also self-refer themselves to program services.

Student Assistance Programs strive to:
1. identify early drug involvement or other problems;
2. refer students to designated "helpers" within the school;
3. provide in-school support and/or counseling services and groups;
4. refer students to outside mental-health, drug-treatment, and family-services organizations and professionals.

The key component in successful student assistance programs is the endorsement, support, and involvement of school officials and administrators, community leaders and organizations, parents, and students.

Early-Childhood Programs

Drug-prevention programs once targeted only high school and junior high school students. However, it is now understood that prevention is most effective when young people are reached at a much earlier age, even as early as preschool, before they are faced with the opportunity to try drugs. Early-childhood programs reach youngsters before they develop bad habits or face negative peer pressure. Effective preschool programs can enhance positive child development as well as work with parents to improve their parenting skills. Research findings suggest that programs can partly counteract the effects of dysfunctional families and exposure to violent surroundings, both of which are associated with adolescent drug use. Early-childhood programs have been shown to reduce the long-term incidence of academic failure, criminal behavior, and other behavioral problems associated with drug use.

Working with High-Risk Students

Schools are not social welfare agencies and should not be expected to provide drug treatment, extended mental-

Figure 15-2
Resistance Skills Help Youth Counter Peer Pressure to Use Drugs

health counseling, welfare, and other services. At the same time, however, schools must become advocates for students who lack adequate support from their families or the community service system. To do this, schools need to move beyond providing educational services and work closely with families and community agencies to coordinate services for students who need them.

Many troubled students, especially those from dysfunctional families, do not receive help that may be available from community services. Community agencies are responsible for addressing students' problems arising from situations such as family drug or alcohol abuse, poor nutrition, mental or physical abuse, and delinquency so that all students can enter the classroom prepared to learn.

In-Service Training

Teachers and counselors are second only to parents and peers in influencing students' knowledge, attitudes, and behavior concerning drugs, including alcohol and tobacco. Teachers and counselors therefore have a special responsibility for drug education, prevention, and intervention. In the classroom, teachers are in a unique position to identify students who have problems that could signal drug use. School counselors also play a key role in intervening with students who come to them with problems or are referred by teachers. Other school staff members also have the opportunity to intervene or counsel students on drug-related matters and should be provided information on identifying and referring students with drug-related problems.

All teachers should be trained in drug prevention so that the school has a unified prevention team, and teachers in all subject areas are prepared to provide students information and support.

In-service training for teachers and counselors should include information on the following:

213

- the laws on all drugs including alcohol and tobacco;
- the school's alcohol and drug policy and implementation;
- the school's drug education and prevention curriculum and programs, and the responsibilities of each teacher and counselor;
- drug use, abuse, and dependency, especially the harmful effects of binge and heavy alcohol drinking and smoking;
- high-risk and protective factors important at different developmental periods;
- influences of family, ethnic, and cultural background, including social drinking by adults;
- ways to identify students with drug problems, and the appropriate time and method to intervene;
- available resources and procedures for referring students with problems;
- ways to communicate with parents;
- ways to motivate students to help solve their own and other students' drug-abuse problems (creating positive peer pressure);
- ways in which teachers and counselors serve as role models for students;
- the relationship between a teacher's general instructional effectiveness and the teacher's role in drug education and prevention.

DRUG PREVENTION IN THE WORKPLACE

Alcohol and other drug abuse in the workplace has become a major national issue. The 1988 Drug-Free Workplace Act requires federal contractors and grantees to provide a drug-free workplace, but it does not require drug testing. Drug-free workplace approaches, drug testing, and a comprehensive drug-free workplace model will be discussed.

Drug-Free Workplace Approaches

Because approximately two out of every three drug users are employed, the workplace is an important focus for drug prevention and intervention. Employees who use drugs are more likely to miss work, to have health problems, and to be involved in accidents and thefts. Many employers have found that comprehensive, drug-free workplace policies can enhance safety, increase productivity, and hold down costs. In the process, a clear message is sent to employees that drug use can endanger their continued employment. Such policies include educating employees about the harmful effects of drugs, training supervisors to recognize and respond to symptoms of drug use, and establishing employee assistance programs to ensure that employees can get the help they need to stop using drugs. In addition, experience has shown that drug testing in the workplace can be an effective deterrent to drug use and a powerful means of identifying drug users in need of treatment.

The Texas Instruments Corporation's program is a good example of what can be provided at the workplace in dealing with drug abuse. Over the last several years, Texas Instruments has implemented an antidrug policy that includes training for managers, education for employees, employee-assistance programs, and a rigorous drug-testing program, including universal testing of all 73,000 employees and new applicants. The corporation has also required that suppliers and contractors who operate on their property have a similarly rigorous program in place in order to do business with Texas Instruments. This practice of using corporate leverage to encourage other businesses to get involved in drug-free workplace activities is a good example of corporate leadership in demanding reduction efforts.

Drug Testing

Periodic, random drug testing is being adopted at an increasing number of workplaces, even as it is being challenged in the courts. It is argued that periodic drug testing is effective in identifying and referring workers whose drug use has not yet caused a significant level of dysfunctional behavior. Drug testing acts as a preventive measure. Discovery of drug use could lead to referral for counseling or other assistance, as well as threaten their jobs or careers. Thus, the high costs of drug use are raised. The infrequent user must consider whether or not the pleasures are worth the costs. The regular user may have to choose treatment or dismissal.

Those who reject random drug testing cite its costs relative to the benefits realized; the likelihood that drug use will eventually affect behavior and come to the attention of supervisors that way; the risk of inaccurate reporting; and the cost to society of breaching an employee's privacy rights for whatever reason. The difference between these two positions is difficult to resolve and promises to be a source of continued conflict.

The U.S. Postal Service conducted a 30-month study to try to determine if preemployment drug testing is related to performance. The Postal Service intended to establish a uniform, national preemployment testing program but needed to determine if there was evidence to support such a program. The study was done because of a lack of information in the available literature.

In this longitudinal study, an applicant with a positive test was not disqualified but was followed, if employed. At the 21 sites where the tests were conducted, 9 percent of those hired tested positive. The data were analyzed three times. The first analysis showed a significantly higher rate of firing for those who tested positive. By the third analysis, the rate of firing had risen even more. Absenteeism showed the same pattern.

A cost-effectiveness analysis projected a savings of $52.7 million for the group hired in the first year of the study over the 10-year average tenure of an employee due to detection of drug use before employment. The projected savings for all persons hired during a 10-year period is more than $270 million.

Comprehensive Drug-Free Workplace Model

A 1986 Executive Order directed each federal agency within the Executive Branch to develop a comprehensive program to address drugs in the workplace. The goal of this effort is to achieve drug-free federal workplaces through a program designed to offer drug users a helping hand by identifying them, making personal counseling and treatment available to them, and returning them to the workplace as healthy, responsible employees.

In response to the Executive Order, a comprehensive drug-free workplace model was developed for the federal workplace. The model provides for:
1. a written policy statement,
2. an Employee Assistance Program,
3. supervisor training,
4. employee education,
5. drug testing.

In addition to a discussion of the agency's philosophy about drugs in the workplace, the policy statement should cover all the model components.

Employee Assistance Programs (EAPs) should provide for counseling and assessment of personal problems and referral of employees to community resources for help. The EAP, through the delivery of training, can and should integrate itself within the organization. The assurance of employee confidentiality is essential to ensure program acceptance by employees. Programs should provide for both self-referral and referral by supervisors.

Supervisor training is necessary to provide each supervisor with the requisite management "tools" needed to exercise a full range of personnel management authority, including authority in the EAP area. Supervisors need to be familiar with the drug-free workplace policy, the EAP, and how the EAP relates to other personnel programs such as discipline, performance appraisal, and awards. Further, supervisors should be trained to identify and document unacceptable performance and to confront employees about poor work and/or conduct. Supervisors also need to be aware of their role as a facilitator in employees' reintegration to the workforce.

Employee education addresses the negative health consequences associated with drug abuse, the symptoms of drug abuse, and the effects of drug abuse on performance. Employees must be told how to use the EAP, what the employer's policy is on drugs at work, the supervisor's role in the policy, and what to expect of the drug-testing program, should one exist.

Drug testing must be done on a carefully controlled and monitored basis. Its primary purpose should be to provide a method of identifying drug users so that they can be counseled by the EAP, referred for appropriate treatment, and subsequently restored to the job as productive workers. Drug-testing categories include applicant testing; testing based on an accident or unsafe practice; testing based on a reasonable suspicion that an employee is under the influence of a drug; testing of employees following their return to work after successful rehabilitation; voluntary testing; and random and universal testing of employees.

BIBLIOGRAPHY

Alcohol, Drug Abuse, and Mental Health Administration. (1983) *Communities: What You Can Do About Drug and Alcohol Abuse.* Washington, D.C.: ADMHA.

Gordon, N.P., & McAlister, A.L. (1982) Adolescent drinking: Issues and research. In T.J. Coates, A.C. Peter-sen, & C. Perry (Eds.), *Promoting Adolescent Health: A Dialogue on Research and Practice.* New York: Academic Press.

National Clearinghouse for Alcohol and Drug Information. (1989) *Surgeon General's Workshop on Drunk Driv-*

ing: *Proceedings*. Rockville, MD: National Clearinghouse for Alcohol and Drug Information.

National Commission on Drug-Free Schools. (1990) *Toward a Drug-Free Generation: A Nation's Responsibility—Final Report*. Washington, D.C.: U.S. Government Printing Office.

Office for Substance Abuse Prevention. (1989) *Prevention Plus II: Tools for Creating and Sustaining Drug-Free Communities*. DHHS Publication No. (ADM)89-1649. Rockville, MD: OSAP.

Office for Substance Abuse Prevention. (1991) *Crack Cocaine: A Challenge for Prevention*. OSAP Prevention Monograph-9. Rockville, MD: OSAP.

Office for Substance Abuse Prevention. (1991) *Turning Awareness into Action: What Your Community Can Do About Drug Use in America*. DHHS Publication No. (ADM)91-1562. Rockville, MD: OSAP.

Office of National Drug Control Policy. (1992) *Understanding Drug Prevention: White Paper*. Washington, D.C.: Office of National Drug Control Policy.

Rhodes, J.E., & Jason, S.A. (1988) *Preventing Substance Abuse Among Children and Adolescents*. New York: Pergamon Press.

United States Department of Education. (1989) *What Works: Schools Without Drugs*. Washington, D.C.: U.S. Department of Education.

Williams, R., Ward, D., & Gray, L. (1985) The persistence of experimentally induced cognitive change: A neglected dimension in the assessment of drug prevention programs. *The Journal of Drug Education*, 15:33–42.

TREATMENT FOR DRUG ABUSE

Drug abuse hurts not only the individuals who use drugs but also their families, businesses, and communities. In addition to suffering from the breakdown of families, society bears a significant financial burden due to drug use in terms of money spent on health care, law enforcement, and loss of productivity in the workplace. This chapter includes a discussion of drug treatments and law enforcement.

DRUG TREATMENTS

Appropriate drug treatment can be cost effective and has been shown to reduce drug abuse, to increase employment, and to reduce costs to society in terms of medical care, law enforcement, and crime (National Institute on Drug Abuse, 1992). In this section of the chapter, the discussions will include the following topics: the need for drug treatment, who needs drug treatment, is drug addiction a disease, getting drug-dependent persons into treatment, treatment approaches, completing treatment, effectiveness of drug treatment, and treatment availability.

The Need for Drug Treatment

Drug use has become a compulsive habit or addiction for many who will not respond to education and prevention efforts. Their lives are centered around acquiring alcohol or other drugs, using them, and then seeking more (Bennett, 1990). Getting these people off drugs is one of the most pressing task in the "war on drugs." Persons dependent on drugs consume a disproportionate amount of alcohol and other drugs. They are a danger not only to themselves but also to virtually everyone with whom they come in contact. They lie to friends. They deceive those who try to help them. They steal—even from family members and neighbors—to support their habit.

The life of drug addiction is often intimately connected with other criminal behaviors. Like the career criminal, the addicted person often risks his/her own life and has little regard for the lives and property of others. That is the reason our response to the problem of heavy drug use has been not only through the health care system but also through the criminal justice system. Although much public debate has framed these two responses as being diametrically opposed to each other, they are not.

The common tendency to think of drug treatment as a soft, nurturing, and easy route away from drugs could not be further from the truth. To the drug-dependent person, genuine drug treatment that works can be demanding, difficult, and physically and emotionally exhausting. Accountability and adherence to rules are important parts of effective drug treatment. Good treatment programs insist on a code of conduct, individual responsibility, personal sacrifice, and sanctions for misbehavior. When drug-treatment programs contain these elements, positive results are attained: addicted persons change their self-destructive pattern of behavior and stop or dramatically reduce drug use. For this reason, drug treatment and criminal justice must be understood as allies in our fight against drug use and abuse (Bennett, 1990).

Drug treatment is a great source of hope in our battle against drug use because it is focused on relieving the most stubborn part of the problem—compulsive, destructive, and dangerous drug use. Those who habitually consume heavy amounts of alcohol and other drugs most often are associated with a wide variety of antisocial behavior that imposes enormous costs on society. Violent crime, loss of employment, broken families, accidents, drug-addicted babies, the transmission of HIV/AIDS, and premature death all can be caused by the problem of drug addiction.

We know on the basis of more than two decades of research that drug treatment can work. It can help turn many addicted persons into productive, law-abiding citizens. However, we cannot be satisfied with the current rates of success in drug treatment. The drug treatment field faces the challenge of improving the quality of treatment, identifying the sorts of treatment that work best with different types of persons, increasing the rates of recovery from addiction, and learning more about what works and why. The treatment of drug addiction is a very crucial part of a broad drug-control strategy that includes law enforcement, prevention, education, border interdiction, and international cooperation.

Who Needs Drug Treatment?

The majority of drug users do not need drug treatment. Treatment is for those drug users who cannot or will not stop their use of drugs without the help of a formal program that may include therapy, counseling, or medication.

Most persons who are not yet addicted are often able to make the decision to stop drug use, and they have the strength to stick with their decision. These are people who use drugs no more than once a month and they don't really need treatment in order to stop doing drugs. But they do need the social climate of intolerance toward drugs and criminal penalties to deter them from becoming habitual users.

Those who use cocaine or heroin at least once a week are more likely to require treatment, but many of them still are able to quit of their own volition. They are apt to grow weary of a lifestyle in which the main satisfaction increasingly comes only from the depressing or stimulating effect of drugs. Other drug users need the persuasion that comes from the threat of social, legal, or employer sanctions—an arrest, an angry spouse, the loss of family, the loss of a job, or deteriorating health. These are the kinds of motivations that provide the bulk of casual but regular drug users with a compelling reason to quit on their own.

Formal drug treatment, on the other hand, is designed for those who have become physically or psychologically dependent on drugs. Without the benefit of a drug-treatment program or the assistance of self-help groups like Alcoholics Anonymous or Narcotics Anonymous, most compulsive drug users find it very difficult to live more than a few days without drugs, no matter what harm they know they are bringing to themselves, their friends, their family, or even an unborn child. Most chemically-dependent persons maintain the delusion that they have a firm grip on their habit, even as they lose control of their drug use and their lives. They are often the last ones to recognize the need for help.

At first, every chemically-dependent person has a "honeymoon" with drugs. For most, it begins at an early age with experimentation with alcohol and cigarettes, which often evolves into regular marijuana use and then into the heavy use of drugs such as cocaine and heroin or heavy alcohol consumption. During this period, (s)he can use drugs while still controlling the level of use. With most

drugs, this "honeymoon" sometimes can last several years before deteriorating into an uncontrollable physical or psychological appetite. **Physical dependence** is the result of frequent and increased use of drugs that literally can change brain chemistry, causing a functional demand for a particular drug. Many drugs, including alcohol, cocaine, and heroin, can cause dependent persons to experience withdrawal symptoms on cessation of drug use. Experiencing withdrawal is evidence that a person is physically dependent on the drug.

The most difficult aspect of addiction to treat, however, is psychological dependence. **Psychological dependence** is a condition evidenced by an altered state of mind on which chemically-dependent persons come to depend. Drug users report taking drugs to enjoy a momentary thrill, to temporarily allay despair, to find a shortcut to success, or just because it feels good. Chemically-dependent persons, on the other hand, frequently report that eventually they take drugs because sobriety itself is uncomfortable or even unbearable. Making a bad situation worse, many chemically-dependent persons like to offset the negative side effects of one drug by the use of another, and they often end up becoming addicted to more than one drug (ONDCP, 1990).

Is Drug Addiction a Disease?

Some scientists, health professionals and social psychologists insist that drug addiction be understood as a disease, though not for the same reasons. Advocates of the "disease model" have theorized that some people have a genetic or hereditary susceptibility to drug dependency—they cannot help getting hooked if they use drugs. Others liken drug addiction to a disease because they see it as a manifestation of underlying psychological problems like depression, childhood trauma, or feelings of despair.

Addiction researchers have provided still further—and different—arguments to support the idea that drug addiction be considered a disease. They have found evidence to suggest that habitual drug use actually can alter brain chemistry, which may make future controlled use extremely difficult if not impossible. At that point, it is argued, the heavy drug user has developed the disease of drug addiction, a disease that requires total abstinence and treatment.

None of these views, however, is without controversy. Critics assert that whether or not these hypotheses are borne out by further research, drug consumption and addiction must be distinguished from illnesses like multiple sclerosis or Alzheimer's disease. Those diseases, they argue, are not dependent on the behaviors and decisions of the individual. By contrast, drug use almost always involves choices.

As long as disagreements over psychological and biological causes of drug dependency and the debate over individual motivations for drug use persist, no single account is likely to prove entirely satisfactory. Yet the controversy continues to ensnare and confound public health officials, insurance companies, and policy makers.

Nevertheless, none of the arguments precludes the need for drug treatment as a major and necessary element in any adequate solution for the problems of addiction. No matter how the issues sort out, the challenge faced by the drug treatment field, and society as a whole, remains essentially the same. Many chemically-dependent persons will not curb their drug consumption even when offered reasonable arguments and passionate pleas from friends and loved ones, or when threatened with arrest, imprisonment, or even death. However the drug problems started, the task of drug treatment is to stop consumption and reverse addiction by laying the groundwork for self-control. For hard-core drug users, drug treatment often is the only avenue available to break what has already become a deeply-ingrained pattern of self-destructive behavior.

Getting Drug-Dependent Persons into Treatment

The notion that all addicted persons eventually will come to their senses and decide on their own to seek treatment is as false as it is widespread. Yet it is in part the basis for the popular cry of "treatment on demand"—a policy prescription aimed at supplying treatment space to whomever asks for it, and whenever they ask for it. Such proposals are undoubtedly well-intentioned, but they address neither the real needs of the treatment system nor the realities of drug addiction and treatment. Research has found that as many as 90 percent of the people undergoing treatment did not seek it on their own, let alone "demand" it. They were compelled to do so by family, legal, or employer pressure, or some combination of the three (Fig. 16-1).

The reasons for avoiding treatment are fairly clear. It is no secret among chemically-dependent persons that quitting drugs is extremely difficult. Treatment programs are often demanding and difficult experiences for which people who have been engaged in a relentless pursuit of the euphoria of drugs scarcely can be expected to volunteer. Drug treatment is directed at denying addicted persons

their single greatest source of pleasure and comfort—something every addicted person knows. One of the chief reasons people do drugs is because it makes them feel very good. Despite all the other destructive and terrible things drugs do to mind, body, and soul, drugs produce temporary states of euphoria, excitement, intoxication, overconfidence, delirium, and a host of other altered states. During the initial period of heavy drug use, few people feel they have a problem with drugs, and those that do repeatedly promise themselves to get help—tomorrow.

The larger problem with the call for treatment on demand is that it ignores the more immediate and fundamental problems that confront the treatment system. While it is certainly true that there are chemically-dependent persons who voluntarily seek treatment, many of these volunteers repeatedly enter and impulsively drop out of treatment. Their goal, unlike the goals of their treatment providers, is to return to "controlled use" or to "stay clean" for a few days to reduce their tolerance so the same high can be achieved from lower and cheaper doses. Others who seek treatment on their own do so only after they have "bottomed-out." They have reached a point where their addiction has so consumed them and devastated their lives that they can no longer function. They cannot care for their children, show up for work, or even associate with people who do not use drugs.

For addicted persons like these, simply providing additional treatment slots does nothing to ensure that treatment generally is made more effective and provided in a more rational way. Even where treatment slots are plentiful, the treatment system still must improve its ability to assess the medical and psychological background of all potential treatment patients, direct them to the most appropriate kind of treatment, provide properly trained staff, and then ensure that dependent persons, once in the system, complete a treatment program.

A policy designed primarily to provide treatment "on demand" would create a costly, unbalanced system that brings no guarantee of higher treatment success rates. Moreover, the call for such a system obscures the far more pressing and practical needs of drug treatment. Addressing those needs requires us to come to grips with the fact that while the need for treatment is high, the actual demand for it is relatively low. The overwhelming majority of dependent persons must be "jolted" into drug treatment and induced to stay there by some external force—the criminal justice system, employers who have discovered their drug use, spouses who threaten to leave, or the death of a fellow drug user.

219

Figure 16-1
Factors That Motivate Persons to Seek Treatment

Treatment and the criminal justice system. Frequently, the jolt that gets dependent persons to enter treatment is trouble with the law. In fact, according to the 1989 Treatment Outcome Prospective Study (TOPS)—one of the most comprehensive evaluations of drug treatment ever conducted—as many as one out of two persons who enter public drug-treatment programs are under either direct or indirect legal pressure to do so. It is becoming increasingly common for arrestees in pretrial detention to be professionally evaluated to determine if they are, in fact, addicted to alcohol or other drugs. If it is determined that an arrestee is drug dependent, the criminal justice system can steer offenders toward drug treatment in a number of circumstances—as a condition for deferred prosecution, in lieu of incarceration, as part of a reduced prison sentence, or as terms for probation or parole.

In all cases, the addicted person diverted into treatment is expected to be accountable for entering and remaining in a treatment program by either a probation office or other authority who, by means of supervision—and in the best cases, urinalysis—keeps the court informed of the addicted person's compliance.

Research has determined that those who enter treatment under some form of coercion are likely to do at least as well as—sometimes better—than those who enter voluntarily. The person who voluntarily enters treatment is always free to drop out of the program when the going gets tough. That is a temptation that every recovering chemically-dependent person must overcome. For those referred to treatment by the courts, whose only other option is imprisonment or further legal sanctions, the incentive to complete treatment is even more powerful. Yet similar incentives exist for anyone whose marriage, family, job, or finances depend on successfully completing a treatment program. That is the reason that those who have a lot to lose are on the whole better candidates for treatment success.

No matter how the addicted person gets to treatment, drug treatment can be a very grueling experience. Getting treatment under the supervision of the criminal justice system often means that a chemically-dependent person will have to complete very difficult treatment regimens, be held accountable for frequent urinalyses as a condition of return to the community, and be closely supervised throughout the process. New York's "Stay 'N Out," like many other prison treatment programs, found that a number of convicted criminals with a history of drug use willingly return to the general prison population after a few weeks in the more demanding treatment unit (ONDCP, 1990).

Treatment for pregnant females and their infants. In the past three decades, the majority of illicit drug users have been males. The arrival of crack cocaine in 1985 has somewhat altered that pattern. The rate of cocaine use is still twice as high for males as females. However, there are now unprecedented numbers of chemically-dependent females, many of them pregnant or of childbearing age. Unfortunately, pregnant addicted females often are among the most reluctant to seek treatment, and many treatment programs are neither equipped nor prepared to accept them.

The number of press stories concerning pregnant females using drugs is not mere sensationalism. Pregnant females and their infants represent an especially difficult problem for which there is no ready answer. The long-term consequences of the problem may become more evident as the first wave of "crack babies" enters our schools. No single phenomenon has demonstrated the destructive power of drugs as vividly as the anguish of newborns who have been exposed to crack and other drugs before birth.

Babies exposed to drugs suffer widely different consequences after birth. Research by a number of pediatricians suggests that babies born exposed to cocaine are more likely to be delivered prematurely, have smaller head circumference, low birth weight, and severe birth defects. Some newborns are born addicted and, because of cocaine withdrawal symptoms, cannot be touched or held for days following delivery. Other babies have been exposed to cocaine in utero, but are not born addicted or obviously afflicted. They may, however, later suffer from hyperactivity, poor attention span, and other learning disabilities. Surprisingly, many drug-exposed babies escape physical and mental harm.

Both addicted and drug-affected infants as well as addicted pregnant females can benefit from treatment. These infants usually require special care immediately after birth. Addicted, pregnant females need treatment that will bring their drug use to an end and allow them to properly care for their children. Many treatment centers already are engaged in ambitious outreach efforts to identify and contact drug-using pregnant females. However, in too many cases, treatment centers are not equipped to respond to the special problems presented by pregnancy, addiction, and females with young children. At the same time, what is true for all addicted persons is true of pregnant females who have serious drug problems. Many of them will not seek treatment on their own, even when it is available. When they do receive treatment, it is often a result of going through the criminal justice system.

Treatment Approaches

Many approaches have been developed to help addicted persons permanently kick their habit, but not all approaches work equally well for each type of dependent person. Unfortunately, the type of treatment a patient receives frequently is determined by the first door on which (s)he happens to knock. If a heroin-dependent person knocks on the door of a therapeutic community program, that's what kind of treatment (s)he will receive. If the dependent person knocks on the door of a methadone maintenance program, (s)he will probably receive methadone.

Most chemically-dependent persons stand a much better chance of success in treatment when aspects such as personality, background, mental condition, and duration, extent and type of drug use are evaluated during a preadmission screening process that places the person in a treatment program that is most likely to meet his/her needs and to produce the best outcomes. If a person is not getting the right kind of treatment initially, the chances for success are diminished until (s)he is redirected or transferred to a more appropriate program. Patients who have a serious mental illness in addition to their addiction—what psychiatrists call "dual diagnosis"—may not be able to recover from drugs without proper attention to their psychological condition, regardless of what sort of treatment they receive.

Descriptions of the principal methods of treatment most commonly found in the United States follow. In practice, of course, each form of treatment will vary with the circumstances and type of patient a particular clinic will encounter. As treatment has expanded, varieties of treatment practice have emerged that borrow elements of two or more different traditional methods (ONDCP, 1990).

Detoxification. Detoxification is often the first stage of the treatment process. Its aim is to stabilize the heavy alcohol or other drug user until his/her body is relatively free of drugs. Detoxification sometimes is essential if the patient is to end immediate drug use and cope with the discomfort of withdrawal from drugs such as heroin, and the craving and depression of withdrawal from drugs such as cocaine. Withdrawal from alcohol and barbiturates can, in some instances, be life threatening. Detoxification is not, however, in and of itself a form of treatment. Detoxification helps people get off drugs—treatment helps them stay off. Although it is not uncommon in our treatment system today for a chemically-dependent person's experience in treatment to begin and end at this stage, experts agree that detoxification does little good unless it constitutes a transition to, or preparation for, a long-term drug treatment program.

No treatment program effectively can work on changing the attitude and behavior of patients who are still in a drug haze, suffering through a painful withdrawal, or having memory trouble after having stopped using the drug (as is sometimes the case with cocaine-dependent persons). Patients go through the detoxification process by remaining completely drug free or with the help of medications that ease withdrawal. Methadone, for instance, can be given in decreasing doses to persons still heroin dependent in order to enable them to avoid the symptoms of heroin withdrawal.

Only a few addicted persons require detoxification inside a hospital (where costs may exceed $500 a day). Some need to be in residential treatment centers (which may cost more than $120 a day). However, the large majority of addicted persons can be detoxified on a far less expensive outpatient basis. Wherever it takes place, there can be complications and challenges when working with those who are still on drugs. With supportive staff, careful supervision, and a number of medications, detoxifying patients generally is a routine task. The hard part comes later— getting chemically-dependent persons to stay off alcohol and other drugs.

Therapeutic communities and residential treatment. Therapeutic communities (TCs) are designed to get patients to face the fact that they are addicted to drugs, and then to foster change in their personalities so they can live without drugs. One of the first such programs, Synanon, was founded in 1958 in California. By the late 1970s, Synanon had developed a controversial reputation and was no longer held in regard. However, the sound and successful concepts in the Synanon model, albeit much improved and modified, remain the foundation of hundreds of TCs in the United States, including some prison programs.

TCs are staffed by both former chemically-dependent persons and professionals who impose personal and community responsibility by means of a rigid hierarchy among staff and patients. Each member of the TC is given a job and is expected to carry his/her own weight. House rules must be strictly observed. The TC staff rewards good behavior with privileges and promotions to positions of more responsibility and punishes bad behavior through "learning experiences"—the suspension of privileges or the assignment of some menial chore. Because patients ascend in the hierarchy by demonstrating their ability to handle increasing responsibility within the community, those near the top are thought to be ready to graduate to a life free of drugs outside the therapeutic community.

Much of what is accomplished in this form of treatment is done through "encounter groups," in which chemically-dependent persons confront each other about their behaviors and shortcomings. These encounter group sessions tend to be confrontational and intense and generally are effective in stripping away the self-deceit, rationalization, and defensiveness common to persons who are dependent on drugs. These persons then are able to begin redressing their weaknesses and rebuilding their self-confidence and motivation.

222

In the later stages of treatment, and when not engaged in encounter groups or other behavior-changing exercises, members of TCs spend time working in the treatment facility and later in the community. The length of stay in a TC ranges from 6 to 24 months, and the cost can range from $1,200 to $2,500 per month. The time commitment, combined with a confrontational and demanding regimen, makes for a very high attrition rate among patients. As many as four out of five patients who begin treatment in a TC drop out or are expelled for violence or drug use before completion of the program. While TCs may be suited for young, old, rich or poor, the program is not appropriate for patients with a serious mental or other illness.

However, therapeutic communities seem especially good for those with a history of criminal behavior or social pathology—people unaccustomed to rules and responsibilities. Overall, TCs have a good record of success, with as many as four out of five patients who complete the program staying drug free several years out of treatment. Research indicates that those who spend more than three months in a TC, even without completing the program, reduce drug use and criminal behavior.

A wide range of hybrid residential programs have evolved from the TC model and are growing in popularity. While borrowing heavily from the TC model, these residential programs usually are less intense and confrontational. They often incorporate more traditional forms of therapy such as professional counseling, drug education, and self-help activities into the treatment regimen. These kinds of residential programs seem to be as effective and generally cost about the same per month as a TC, although the stays are often shorter, ranging from 6 to 12 months.

Minnesota Model and inpatient hospital programs. The "twelve-step" or Minnesota Model approach was developed in the 1950s at Willmar State Hospital in Minnesota for the treatment of alcoholism. However, these programs have recently been used for the treatment of other drug addictions, especially since the onset of the cocaine epidemic. They are residential programs in hospitals or in free-standing facilities, and usually last three of four weeks. The core of the counseling and program activities is derived from the self-help therapy of Alcoholics Anonymous's "twelve-steps to recovery."

The twelve steps prescribe for chemically-dependent persons what some have termed a spiritual or moral awakening. The steps include the admission of addiction, acknowledgement of one's impotence to stop it without the help of a higher power, and the need to confront the harm the person has done. Although scientific outcome data from these programs are scarce, they appear to have helped thousands of individuals.

Other types of inpatient programs in hospitals come closest to what many people imagine when they think of someone getting "psychiatric help." Psychiatric treatment in hospital settings lasts anywhere from 4 to 12 weeks, although longer stays of up to six months for troubled adolescents are common. The programs are usually run by psychiatrists, psychologists, and health professionals who employ a variety of basic clinical approaches, including traditional group, individual, and family therapy. Programs often include training in relaxation, exercise, and coping skills. Special psychiatric attention is given to those persons who have a serious mental illness on top of their drug-addiction problem. Attendance at Alcoholics Anonymous or Narcotics Anonymous often is compulsory, although in psychiatric programs this tends to be an auxiliary rather than a central part of treatment.

Anecdotal evidence suggests that many people have benefited from both the Minnesota Model and psychiatric, inpatient programs. However, with few exceptions, these programs are extremely expensive: a four-week stay can cost anywhere from $6,000 for a nonhospital, not-for-profit "Minnesota Model" program to $30,000 for psychiatric hospital care. For reasons of cost, these programs remain almost exclusively private, and are not part of the publicly-funded treatment system.

Methadone maintenance. **Methadone** is a legally-controlled, synthetic medication. Methadone was developed in Germany during World War II as a substitute analgesic, or pain killer, when morphine was in short supply. Its use as an ongoing (maintenance) treatment for narcotic-dependent persons was pioneered by Vincent Dole and Marie Nyswander at the Rockefeller Institute in 1964. When taken orally in carefully regulated amounts, methadone produces little if any high, yet it relieves the craving and withdrawal symptoms for heroin for about 24 hours. Methadone also prevents dependent persons from feeling the effects of heroin should they happen to take the drug while on methadone. Patients drink a small cupful of methadone diluted in orange juice every day and are able to work, attend school, and take part in family and community responsibilities. The annual cost of a methadone maintenance program can range from $3,000 to $4,500.

Methadone is addictive, but gradual withdrawal from it is much less painful than the discomfort of heroin withdrawal. The greatest benefit of methadone maintenance is that it switches the heroin-dependent person from using an illegal, dangerous, injectable, short-acting drug that produces a sense of euphoria to the supervised use of a relatively safe, orally-administered, long-acting controlled drug that has a minimal euphoric effect. Methadone thus provides an opportunity for chemically-dependent persons to be well enough to receive drug counseling and therapy as well as vocational and other types of training, all of which can play an important role in improving such a person's ability to live in the community free of illicit drug use. Methadone can also be lifesaving in this era of HIV/AIDS, as a number of studies have shown by providing heroin-dependent persons with an alternative to intravenous drug use, which exposes them to the risk of HIV infection.

Methadone maintenance is the most researched and evaluated of all the various treatment methods, and there is considerable evidence that methadone can help addicted persons become more productive citizens. In a properly-run methadone program, most patients markedly decrease their use of illegal drugs, although a minority continue with drug use, especially cocaine. The arrest rates of methadone patients are significantly lower than they were prior to getting the patients on the program. Employment and school records improve. Methadone is mainly appropriate for people who have been on heroin or other opiates for two years or more, and it also is apt to be more effective with older, motivated, chemically-dependent persons who do not have major psychological problems.

There is some quite understandable, philosophical objection to methadone maintenance. Critics argue that it merely substitutes one addicting drug for another, and rarely helps the addicted person become free of the influence of drugs. In support of this view, they cite the example of thousands of Vietnam veterans who were addicted to heroin while in Vietnam, but on returning home were able to kick the habit without resorting to therapy or medication. This history makes a compelling argument about the effect of drug availability on the level of drug addiction. When drugs are plentiful, as they were in Southeast Asia, addiction rates can be high.

However, this case does not provide an argument against the beneficial aspects of methadone. Many heroin-dependent persons benefit greatly from methadone maintenance programs, often after several attempts to quit heroin by other means. Many emerge from this type of treatment completely drug free after one, two, or more years. While still on methadone, addicted persons may not be "cured"

of their dependence on drugs, but they can control the destructive, antisocial habits associated with addiction.

The main problems with methadone involve the difficulty patients have in getting off the drug, and the inadequate administration of some of the programs. In such programs, patients receiving daily methadone get little or no counseling or therapy and virtually no attention to their continued drug use, without which no meaningful changes in the patient's habits and way of life can take place. In these respects, methadone programs need to be improved. However, methadone itself—because it is a powerful and addicting substance—should not be considered as a treatment method of first resort for heroin-dependent persons with a short history of drug use. These persons need to be encouraged to enter a methadone program only after trying other intensive methods first.

Nonmethadone outpatient treatment. Outpatient-treatment programs vary greatly in approach and intensity. Some programs use medications such as naltrexone that blocks the effect of heroin, or various drugs that reduce craving for cocaine as part of the treatment. Others are entirely "drug free." Their common denominator is that they do not use methadone. Operating out of hospital clinics or free-standing facilities, outpatient treatment serves a number of different types of patients with different drug histories: the addicted persons who have never sought treatment before; those who have successfully completed another type of treatment and seek continued support and counseling; and recovering persons who have relapsed from prison or an inpatient hospital stay. While methadone-maintenance programs or therapeutic communities can serve heroin- or cocaine-dependent persons, outpatient treatment can be the main therapy for marijuana, psychedelic, or multidrug users as well.

For these persons, outpatient programs offer a mixture of individual counseling, group counseling, family therapy, and specific relapse-prevention training. Individual and group therapy is used in many programs in an effort to resolve psychological problems that underlie a patient's drug dependence. For those who need habilitation instead of rehabilitation, some programs offer education and vocational training as well. Although programs cannot supervise a chemically-dependent person 24 hours a day, good outpatient programs monitor their patients through infrequent visits (that decrease as patients improve), drug tests, and phone conversations when the patients do not come in for counseling or training. The cost of outpatient treatment can range anywhere from $200 to $600 per month, and can be effective as follow-up not only for those who have already been through another type of treatment program, but also for those in treatment for the first time. Because of the added incentive to remain drug free and enrolled in the program, legal pressure often contributes to treatment success. Outpatient programs generally encourage patients to become involved with self-help groups such as Narcotics Anonymous, both for the insight and the communal support they offer and for the drug-free network of friends they provide.

Despite its success, there remains a great deal of skepticism about the effectiveness of outpatient treatment. Programs have been criticized for leaving addicted persons "on the street," or not being intensive enough to overcome the power of addiction. While it is true that chemically-dependent persons in outpatient treatment do have access to drugs and the free time to associate with those who continue to sell and use drugs, many outpatient programs have had a good record of success. Keeping in contact with patients by phone on the days they don't come in seems to be an important factor. The medications being researched today that may alleviate craving or that may block the effects of drugs will make outpatient treatment increasingly applicable and effective for more patients in the future.

A hybrid of both inpatient and outpatient programs is the partial hospital program, which operates on a day or evening schedule. It provides more intensive intervention in the daily life of an addicted person than outpatient programs, but at a much lower cost than inpatient programs.

Common elements of effective treatment programs. Although the various approaches to drug treatment differ in many ways, there are a few basic elements that are part of most, if not all, good programs. The most fundamental of these is that in treatment, chemically-dependent persons begin to eat and sleep properly, often for the first time since their addiction began. Eating and sleeping on a regular schedule are the minimum requirements for a normal, healthy life. However, to someone coming off a serious drug habit, a regular eating and sleeping schedule constitutes a radical change in behavior. The life of a chemically-dependent person is chaotic. The normal human needs that most people take for granted are foreign to the daily behavior of an addicted person. Because of this, the first step of treatment is often to see that the patients get basic nourishment, medical attention, and rest, thus bringing a degree of order into their lives.

Another common element in treatment is holding those who receive treatment accountable. Accountability means clear expectations for behavior, rewards for meeting them, and certain consequences if they are not met. Treatment is often the first time chemically-dependent persons realize that to be a functioning adult, they must answer to themselves and to others for their actions. Programs hold patients accountable for showing up and being on time to counseling meetings and therapy sessions. Therapeutic communities and residential programs hold residents accountable for a daily set of chores. Most importantly, effective treatment programs hold patients accountable through the use of frequent drug testing to determine if they are, in fact, staying off drugs. If drug use is discovered, programs often impose appropriate sanctions and higher degrees of supervision. Even in treatment, most patients remain ambivalent about their drug use. They want to stop because of the problems their drug use has created, and yet they still wish to return to the "honeymoon" period when they could control their use and simply enjoy the pleasurable effects of drugs. Drug testing within a treatment program therefore becomes a powerful deterrent when temptation occurs. One way or another, accountability measures in treatment encourage patients to make responsible decisions, especially decisions about their use of drugs.

Either implicitly or explicitly, most treatment programs inculcate the concepts of trust, respect, right and wrong—ideas that are essential for human civility but alien to the world of drug addiction. Programs that bring a group of recovering drug users together create an atmosphere of support and friendship. These programs use peer pressure to promote the habits of honesty and responsibility. In a number of programs, this same objective is pursued through what could be described as a spiritual or moral awakening that often includes a strong faith in God or some higher power. Whether through the twelve steps of Alcoholics Anonymous or Narcotics Anonymous, the tenets of a therapeutic community, or the teachings of faith-oriented programs, the effort to get patients to abstain from drugs involves fostering their faith in something above and beyond themselves, and certainly beyond the self-absorbed euphoria of drugs.

Finally, effective treatment programs are managed and staffed by competent people who have the capacity to be both tough and compassionate. Whatever the method, treatment relies heavily on the leadership, skills, personalities, and charisma of the males and females who work every day with persons who are dependent on chemicals.

In building a bridge from the initial cessation of drug use to successful drug treatment, a number of methods have emerged, each claiming to be the "cure" for drug addiction. Some look for new medications to come along and painlessly solve the problems of addiction. Others look to techniques like acupuncture, supplements of amino acids, even the use of psychedelics as the elixir that will provide patients relief from drug addiction. The truth is that new medications, and in some cases acupuncture, can be helpful in relieving some of the painful symptoms persons dependent on chemicals face when they stop their drug use. No medication, however, including methadone, can cure drug addiction. Acupuncture needles, pharmacological agents, or "miracle cures" cannot provide the structure, the discipline, the soul searching, or the reasons to remain drug free that each addicted person must find personally. False, untested claims to the contrary mislead the public and serve only to discredit the legitimate, albeit less sensational, methods of treatment.

Completing Treatment

Patients never emerge from a treatment program completely "cured." In fact, it is only after they leave the relatively protective environment of a treatment program that they face the greatest challenges to their ability to stay off drugs. Unfortunately, former chemically-dependent persons tend to yearn for the days when they could control their use of drugs, and most believe that they can go back to that "honeymoon" period, despite numerous warnings from counselors and former addicted persons. The experience of many recovering addicted persons shows that they can't.

For psychological, social, and perhaps even biological reasons, attempts at moderate drug use after completion of treatment often rapidly lead back to former patterns of compulsive drug use. As a result, most patients go through what treatment professionals call a "relapse"—a return to using the drug on which they are dependent. For some, relapse is merely a temporary falter, a "slip" rather than a "fall," and it serves as a hard lesson that they cannot go back to controlled use. However, for others, relapse leads back to ongoing, compulsive drug use. They need more treatment. If renewed drug use leads to other criminal activity, they need criminal sanctions.

Effectiveness of Drug Treatment

Defining success. It would seem obvious that if on completion of a program a patient no longer uses drugs, then the treatment could be declared successful. However, success often comes only after a relapse into drug use and further treatment, which complicates attempts to measure the efficacy of any single treatment program. Although it

is interesting to examine if former criminals who were also chemically dependent are engaged in criminal activity after treatment, or if former unemployed patients are gainfully employed, these questions are important but not central to the determination of drug-treatment success. Drug treatment may be deemed successful when, three to five years after treatment, a former chemically-dependent person is no longer using drugs.

The ultimate goal of treatment should not obscure the fact that partial success can be found when former, heavy, drug users reduce their consumption of alcohol and other dangerous drugs, decrease their involvement in criminal activity, and generally impose a smaller burden on society. They may still use drugs on occasion, but the damage they inflict on society has been minimized, and that can only be viewed as a benefit.

Who is most likely to succeed in treatment? Research shows that about 50 percent of the persons who go through treatment are drug free or dramatically have reduced their drug use three to five years later. However, it is important to remember that all treatment programs and patients are not equal. Some treatment programs are better managed than others. Some patients have strong friendships and family ties while others do not. Some have the education and background that allow them to reintegrate themselves into society more easily.

Those persons who have something to lose if they don't get off drugs—a job, a family, a house—do much better than those who have nothing to lose. Some who are not successful the first time may seek treatment again, and eventually succeed in kicking their drug habit. The uncomfortable truth that every program can attest to is that some—perhaps as many as one out of four chemically-dependent persons, many of them career criminals—will choose not to live without drugs despite numerous rounds of the best treatment available. These failures are too often cited as "evidence" that treatment can't work. Rather, they are grim reminders that for some people, drugs have so penetrated their lives that no form of treatment can protect them from themselves or protect others from them.

Improving drug treatment. Drug treatment is still a relatively new science. There is much more that can and must be learned in order to do a better job of treating chemically-dependent persons. Research currently is underway that should yield important developments to improve treatment success. For instance, currently there are no reliable data to tell us how many persons who are chemically dependent need treatment, or in what sort of treatment they are and what kind of success they are having. Increased efforts to gather such data are underway, although it will be a few years before we have answers to these questions.

A great deal of research is being done to develop medications to aid in the treatment of cocaine and crack addiction. There is good reason to believe that, in the future, medications will be available that can reduce an addicted person's craving for cocaine. Other medications may be able to prevent these persons from deriving any effects from cocaine. Other medications may help in the treatment of those who have become dependent on both heroin and cocaine. Pharmacological agents such as these will enable more dependent persons to undergo treatment successfully.

Researchers at the University of Washington are conducting studies to develop ways to teach persons who are chemically dependent how better to avoid relapse after leaving treatment. The premise of this research is that if addicted persons can be alert to the warning signs and rationalizations attendant to relapse, they also can learn to buttress themselves against the temptation to use drugs.

All these research efforts and others like them are crucial to the future success of treatment programs. Nevertheless, there are a number of factors we already know are certain to make treatment work better. One is family involvement. When family members become involved in the treatment, the chances for success are significantly greater. Another is making sure appropriate treatment programs have the resources or the ability to tie in with existing community agencies to provide recovering patients with vocational and educational services necessary to compete for jobs in today's job market. The single best way to make treatment more successful is to get people to stay in appropriate treatment long enough. Every treatment program better serves its patients when it establishes both formal and informal rewards and sanctions that induce the patients to complete the program.

Treatment Availability

The national drug-treatment system is divided into two sectors, one private and one public. Private treatment is available at hospitals and free-standing facilities to those able to pay the costs or who possess adequate insurance coverage. The public treatment system, funded by federal, state, and local tax dollars, is intended for those who cannot afford private treatment. Most of the federal money

for drug treatment is allocated by the U.S. Department of Health and Human Services in the form of block grants to the states. Federal funds make up approximately 23 percent of our nation's treatment funding. Other money comes from state and local governments (33 percent), third party insurers (27 percent), and private individuals and charities (17 percent). Over $2 billion is spent annually to treat drug addiction.

The federal government also supports drug treatment at hospitals operated by the Department of Veteran Affairs and a variety of treatment-demonstration projects. In addition, the federal government supports basic research on ways to decrease drug addiction, investigations into the physiological characteristics of addiction, and the development of medications that could be instrumental in treating addiction.

Waiting lists. There is concern over the apparent dearth of available treatment facilities in cities across the country and the long waiting lists reported by many facilities (Fig. 16-2.). It certainly is true that there are many programs—good programs—for which people are waiting for the next available space. Recent substantial increases in federal funding for treatment should help these programs expand their services accordingly.

Figure 16-2
**There Can Be a Waiting Period
to Enter Treatment Programs**

Actual lists of chemically-dependent persons who have sought treatment from one program or another are not the best measure of the extent of the need for treatment. There may be waiting lists for a program in one city, but not in others. In large cities, for example, the existence of a waiting list for a methadone program may only be a function of the demands a particular program makes on a person. Unstructured methadone programs that merely dispense the medication and make few demands on a person will often be oversubscribed, while more rigorous programs that require counseling, therapy, and frequent drug tests may have more vacancies.

In other cases, persons with chemical dependence put their name on one waiting list, unaware that there may be an opening in a program nearby, because no central registry exists. Further, because of a lack of communication among treatment programs, an addicted person can put his or her name on a number of waiting lists, and it is likely to remain there indefinitely, even after a treatment program becomes available.

The bottom line is that all drug-treatment waiting lists tend to be soft. Anyone can put his/her name on a waiting list. The real test of drug treatment is to help someone undergo treatment on the terms set by the program rather than on terms set by the patient. The fact that a chemically-dependent person asks to be placed on a treatment waiting list one day is no guarantee that (s)he will want to make the sacrifices necessary for treatment when space becomes available days or weeks later.

Paying for treatment. When trying to estimate the numbers of chemically-dependent persons and the need for treatment, it is important to keep in mind that, according to the National Institute on Drug Abuse, the largest proportion of drug users are white American males between the ages of 18 and 40. Many of them have health insurance to pay for treatment, and at many publicly-funded treatment facilities a sliding-fee scale is established for patients who are able to pay for some or all of their treatment. At private treatment centers, where these patients usually seek treatment, it is not uncommon to have vacancy rates of 45 percent. For those with adequate insurance or sufficient income, availability is not an issue.

The facilities that receive public support, however, were financially strained during the late 1970s and 1980s, and unprepared for the recent onslaught of patients produced by the crack epidemic. In order to help more people, proposed federal and some state spending has increased in recent years.

Impediments in expanding treatment services. The single greatest impediment to the improvement and expansion of treatment is the lack of trained, quality staff. Although it is useful in policy discussions to talk of the treatment system and effective treatment methods, the truth is that the success of any individual treatment program depends on the training and competence of its staff. Many current programs lack trained professionals, and too often counselors and other staff also have limited or inadequate training. In some cities, salaries often are too low to attract or retain the few who have proper training. New or expanded treatment programs clearly will require many more trained males and females. Training programs are being expanded, and former chemically-dependent persons with years of experience but little formal training can accomplish much in therapeutic communities and similar programs. Nevertheless, it will take some time before there are sufficient numbers of trained or experienced staff necessary to achieve a significant increase in treatment quality and availability.

Another impediment to significant expansion of treatment services is the fact that increased treatment availability requires sites for new facilities, and new sites have been very difficult to find. All too often community resistance prevents the location of new programs in neighborhoods where they are needed most. For instance, Missouri has been unable to spend more than $4 million it had budgeted in the St. Louis area because communities have denied zoning for treatment centers. The same difficulty also has been encountered in New York, California, and many other states.

Community resistance to the location selection of drug-treatment facilities cannot be easily dismissed. Although support for a larger and more effective drug-treatment system is widespread, many city residents share the common and not unexpected fear that the arrival of a drug treatment center will have an adverse effect on their neighborhood—increasing crime, attracting drug-dependent persons from other areas, and lowering property values.

Results from the National Institute on Drug Abuse, however, suggest that these fears are largely unwarranted. The data confirmed what has been the experience of many well-managed treatment centers long in operation; namely, that the establishment of a treatment facility creates no discernible rise in crime and no drop in property values in the surrounding area. Nevertheless, finding suitable sites for treatment facilities remains a major obstacle. One state recently proposed legislation that allows the state government to override local zoning legislation that prohibits treatment facilities. While this solution certainly would solve some legal and bureaucratic problems, it does little to allay the sincerely felt anxiety of local residents. As long as that anxiety exists, the "not in my backyard" problem will persist.

Treatment in prison. In our society, the highest concentration of drug-dependent persons are in our prisons. An estimated 50 percent of federal prison inmates and nearly 80 percent of state prison inmates have had experience with drug use, and many are drug addicted. Most convicts who were once heavily involved with drugs finish their prison terms without having any drug treatment, and many return to a life of drugs and crime on their release from prison.

Prisons are designed to incapacitate criminal offenders and provide just punishment. However, prisons also can provide a useful setting for drug treatment: drugs are harder to come by inside a prison; drug testing and accountability are usually not new to correctional facilities; and inmates preparing for release are sometimes eager to find a way out of the type of behavior that put them in prison in the first place.

A number of states are now working to make drug treatment available in their prisons, and the Federal Bureau of Prisons (BOP) has begun an ambitious drug-treatment program based at a number of federal correctional facilities. The BOP program will include professional evaluation and long-term follow-up to determine the effect of the program on recidivism and future drug use. In the future, a wealth of information will be available on how effective treatment in prisons can be.

LAW ENFORCEMENT

Law enforcement is a predominant feature of U.S. drug-control policy. This response to drug abuse is expressed in laws and government policies and programs intended to reduce the availability of illegal drugs and to penalize drug users and traffickers (Carroll, 1993). Law-enforcement efforts are directed against the growing, processing, and production of illegal substances; the illegal importation and distribution of illicit substances; drug trafficking; and consumption and possession of controlled substances (Akers, 1992). Drug laws and enforcement are considered to be an important part of drug-abuse prevention and control by deterring or incapacitating people from using drugs (Currie, 1993). The discussion that follows includes law-enforcement strategies, the limitations of punitive law-

enforcement strategies, and community action to retake neighborhoods from drug dealers.

Law-Enforcement Strategies

Law-enforcement strategies to control drugs are conducted by federal, state, and local agencies. In the 1980s, as the "war on drugs" escalated (the emergence of the crack cocaine epidemic was a major public concern at this time), an increasing federal emphasis on law-enforcement strategies was witnessed. While the Anti-Drug Abuse Acts of 1986 and 1988 placed greater emphasis on drug prevention, education, and treatment through increased funding and expansion of programs, these Acts also resulted in harsher penalties for illegal activities related to the possession, marketing, and production of illegal drugs (Dusek & Girdano, 1993). Ray and Ksir (1993) specify some of the components and the harshness of penalties of the 1988 Anti-Drug Abuse Act.

There were many components to this new law, involving the registration of airplanes, laundering of money, sales of firearms to felons, and possession of chemicals used to manufacture drugs. One part allowed for the death penalty for anyone who murdered someone or ordered the killing of someone in conjunction with a drug-related felony. Major sections of the law funded treatment and education programs as well. The most noteworthy changes were a toughening of approaches toward drug users, aimed at reducing the *demand* for drugs (as opposed to putting all federal efforts into reducing the *supply* of drugs). Before this law there were few penalties and little federal interest in convicting users for possessing small (for personal use) amounts of controlled substances. Under the new law, here are some of the unpleasant possibilities faced by someone convicted of possession of marijuana:

- a civil fine of up to $10,000;
- forfeiture of the car, boat, or plane conveying the substance;
- loss of all federal benefits, including student loans and grants, for up to 1 year after a first offense and up to 5 years after a second offense.

The 1988 law also removed from public housing the entire family of anyone who engaged in criminal activity, including drug-related activity, on or near public-housing premises (p. 53).

The 1988 Act also created the Office of National Drug Control Policy to be headed by a cabinet level Director of National Drug Policy who reports directly to the president. Popularly referred to as the "Drug Czar," this director under law is responsible for preparing a national drug-control strategy and annual consolidated drug-control budget for all federal agencies involved in drug-control activities (Ray & Ksir, 1993).

In 1990, the Anabolic Steroid Control Act was passed by Congress. This Act reclassified anabolic steroids as controlled substances and increased penalties for the illegal possession, distribution, manufacture, and importation of steroids. Those who possess steroids may be subject to a prison penalty of up to 1 year and a fine of at least $1,000. There are even stiffer penalties for those convicted of trafficking in steroids. In addition to prison and fine penalties, health care professionals who illegally supply these substances face the loss of their licenses to prescribe and dispense drugs (Dusek & Girdano, 1993).

Limitations of Punitive Law-Enforcement Strategies

It is clear that the United States has largely invested its drug-control policy in law-enforcement strategies that aim to fight drug abuse through punitive responses (Currie, 1993). The Acts that have just been discussed are evidence that our nation has intensified its efforts to control drug abuse through such means as instituting harsher penalties and more imprisonment for those who use or traffick illegal drugs. In theory, these punitive law-enforcement strategies "work" by deterrence (persuading people who are tempted to engage in drug use or trafficking by the *threat* of punishment) or incapacitation (making it impossible for people to engage in drug use or trafficking by imprisonment).

Punitive responses have at best only a modest deterrent effect on drug use. Drug users either do not view punishment as a real consequence of their drug use or do not view it as a sufficient reason to stop use. In fact, drug users "often regard conventional punishment as no punishment at all" (Currie, 1993). Also, most drug users and traffickers avoid "getting caught" most of the time they use or sell drugs. Research investigating the reasons addicted persons stop using drugs, shows that very few do so out of fear of legal punishment. More salient reasons for quitting drugs are drug-related physical or family problems, desire to change destructive life patterns, and the expense of maintaining a drug addiction.

Prisons not only fail to deter and incapacitate drug use but also often make matters worse. Currie (1993) calls prisons "schools for advanced drug-dealing connections" that provide drug traffickers with tremendous opportuni-

ties for "networking." Rarely do drug offenders leave prison reformed or rehabilitated. Rather, they often maintain addiction and heavy consumption while imprisoned. Prison frequently facilitates drug dealers and users in identifying and cementing a strong identity with an oppositional drug culture. Imprisonment and a criminal record also destroy prospects of obtaining meaningful employment after prison. Life on the streets often is very punishing in and of itself and some who are convicted of a drug offense (i.e., the homeless, the unemployed) may find imprisonment an improvement over the living conditions to which they are accustomed (Currie, 1993).

Beyond the inadequacy of imprisonment in deterring and incapacitating drug use/trafficking, there simply is not enough room and money to keep drug offenders behind bars. In fact, the U.S. Justice Department is seriously considering drastically reducing drug sentences as an effort to control the soaring federal prison population (Cauchon, 1993). This would be a drastic policy change since the length of drug sentences tripled in 1986 as a result of the Anti-Drug Abuse Act. Without a change in sentencing policy, the federal inmate population will exceed 116,000 by 1999. In addition to federal inmates, 1,000 new convicts enter state prisons every week—most of them sentenced on drug-related offenses (Dusek & Girdano, 1993).

The inability of law-enforcement strategies alone to deter and incapacitate drug abuse and drug dealing call for comprehensive drug-control efforts that balance funding and prioritize prevention, treatment, and law enforcement. The nation and each community in the nation must continue to dedicate itself to stopping drug production at its source; interdicting drugs on their way into our communities; investigating major trafficking organizations; and supporting local law-enforcement efforts, drug treatment, and drug education/prevention efforts. Over time, concentrated and balanced federal, state, and local drug-control programs should reduce drug problems in our communities.

Community Action to Retake Neighborhoods from Drug Dealers

The Select Committee on Narcotics Abuse and Control has provided a community guide to retaking neighborhoods from drug dealers (1993). Local leaders from a variety of backgrounds are stepping forward and are taking action themselves against local drug problems. At first, facing skeptical police and government officials, community groups discovered that they had it within their power to break the connection between drug dealers and their customers and to shut down open-air drug markets. Open-air drug markets expose community residents to constant threats to their personal safety and quality of life. These markets tempt neighborhood youth to try drugs or to become involved with drug dealing. And they attract a continuing stream of drug users from outside the community looking for quick, easy, and anonymous drug sales.

Communities can take action by forming neighborhood patrols, cooperating with community residents and businesses, coordinating closely with police, local government agencies, and the media, and using a variety of legal options. The Select Committee's guide stresses several steps for taking community action:

Getting started. The first step involves finding those in the neighborhood who will join the effort.

- Meet with neighbors to discuss the drug and crime problem, form an organization, choose a name, elect a leader or otherwise divide responsibility, and decide on some first steps such as a rally or a march.
- Remove trash from the neighborhood to send a message to drug dealers that citizens care about their community.
- Contact the local Department of Public Works and demand help in broken street light replacement, pothole repair, street and alley sweeping, rodent control, tree maintenance, and sidewalk repair.
- Conduct a letter-writing campaign to local authorities in concert with local businesses, religious organizations and associations urging that they fix up the neighborhood.
- Stretch antidrug banners across a drug-market entrance or paint antidrug messages on sidewalks or display them on posters. Such messages are referred to as "scarecrows" and can sometimes deter drug customers from entering a neighborhood.
- Ask the phone company to remove public phones or to alter them so that they cannot receive incoming calls or be used with a beeper.

Neighborhood patrols. Following are some suggestions concerning ways to be aware of what is happening in the neighborhood.

- Form a citizen patrol to march through areas used by drug dealers. It is not necessary to patrol all night every night. Patrolling during peak times and peak days for several weeks often is sufficient to break the connection between drug buyers and sellers.
- Videotape or take still photos of drug dealers and customers. Follow guidelines established by law-enforce-

ment authorities and citizen patrol members concerning the use of such videotapes or still photos.

- Have patrol group members carry walkie talkies, bull horns, note pads and whistles—all of which serve as badges of authority intimidating to drug dealers and drug customers.
- Picket march in front of crack houses.
- Sustain support for patrol by distributing flyers or newsletters to residents as well as posting them in stores, places of worship, and schools.

Helping law enforcement help your community. The establishment of a community antidrug/anticrime group can transform the way law enforcement personnel see the neighborhood. This kind of group encourages law enforcement, as well as the local city government, to focus more on the needs of the community. Active neighborhood patrols and other related initiatives send a very clear message that residents in crime-ridden neighborhoods want to make things better and are willing to put in time and effort for the cause. The police have a difficult and dangerous job. Knowing they have the support of the community can improve their morale as well as their effectiveness.

- Meet regularly with police to share information about the drug and crime situation in the community.
- Encourage "community policing" activities such as foot and bicycle patrols and the establishment of local substations.
- Take down license plate numbers of cars driving through open-air drug markets and give the numbers to police. Consider asking police to establish license and registration checkpoints near drug markets.
- Encourage police to trace drivers from licenses and to send them postcards in the mail warning them to avoid drug markets for their own safety.

Using the law against drug criminals. Be informed concerning local and state laws that can be applied to neighborhood efforts.

- Pressure owners of properties used for drug dealing or consumption, such as bars or clubs, to crack down on such activities.
- If businesses refuse to comply, picket the establishments and begin proceedings to revoke their liquor licenses.
- Alert the local media about establishments that allow drug dealing.
- Consider the eviction of tenants engaged in illegal drug activities in their apartments.
- Consider the enactment of local antiloitering ordinances to deter drug dealing. If needed, contact local firms for

pro bono aid in defeating challenges to antiloitering proposals.

- Explore padlock or nuisance abatement laws that would require that a building be sealed if there is evidence it is being used for illegal activities, or ask authorities to bulldoze crack houses.
- Encourage police to seize vehicles of drug buyers and display seized vehicles in the community.
- Encourage police to establish driver's license checkpoints at entrances to drug markets.
- Enact a state or local law outlawing the sale of drug paraphernalia.

Fighting drug dealing in housing projects. Large apartment complexes, including many public-housing projects, have often fallen victim to a serious infestation of drug activities. There are a number of reasons that apartments become vulnerable to drug dealers. The most important factor is that drug dealers are usually able to establish escape routes through the maze of apartment buildings, giving them a sense of security.

- In public housing or other apartment building complexes, restrict access by requiring picture I.D. cards for residents.
- Lobby local housing authority or police to put up gates and fences, limit the number of entrances and exits, trim view-obstructing bushes and trees, and ensure that there is adequate lighting.
- For severe problem areas, initiate a community patrol, hire security guards, or install remote video monitors.
- Work to have problem tenants who protect drug dealers evicted from the property and encourage the careful screening of new tenants before they are allowed to move in.
- Increase the residents' role in managing the building or form civic organizations to acquire and rehabilitate drug-plagued properties or those seized and forfeited to the government.
- Consider working to alter rental rates in public housing projects in order to encourage working people to stay.

BIBLIOGRAPHY

Akers, R.L. (1992) _Drugs, Alcohol, and Society: Social Structure, Process, and Policy._ Belmont, CA: Wadsworth.

Bennett, W.J. (1990) Introduction. In Office of National Drug Control Policy. _Understanding Drug Treatment: White Paper_ (pp. 1–3). Washington, D.C.: Office of National Drug Control Policy.

Carroll, C.R. (1993) _Drugs in Modern Society._ Dubuque, IA: Brown & Benchmark.

Cauchon, D. (1993) Drug jail time may be halved. _USA Today,_ May 19, 1A.

Currie, E. (1993) _Reckoning: Drugs, the Cities, and the American Future._ New York: Hill and Wang.

Dusek, D.E., & Girdano, D.A. (1993) _Drugs: A Factual Account._ McGraw-Hill: New York.

National Institute on Drug Abuse. (1991) _National Conference on Drug Abuse Research and Practice: An Alliance for the 21st Century._ DHHS Publication No. (ADM)91-1818. Rockville, MD: NIDA.

National Institute on Drug Abuse. (1992) _20 Q's & A's About Drug Abuse Treatment._ DHHS Publication No. (ADM)92-1951. Rockville, MD: NIDA.

Office of National Drug Control Policy. (1990) _Understanding Drug Treatment: White Paper._ Washington, D.C.: Office of National Drug Control Policy.

Ray, O., & Ksir, C. (1993) _Drugs, Society, & Human Behavior._ St. Louis, MO: Mosby.

Select Committee on Narcotics Abuse and Control, U.S. House of Representatives. (1993) _Block by Block: A Community Guide to Retaking Our Streets and Neighborhoods from Drug Dealers._ Washington, D.C.: U.S. Government Printing Office.

DRUG EDUCATION: CURRICULUM AND TEACHING STRATEGIES

THE DRUG EDUCATION CURRICULUM

Drug education is the field of study that examines life skills for inner well-being that promote drug-free behavior (the avoidance of harmful drugs) and drug-responsible behavior (the use of legal drugs such as over-the-counter and prescription drugs according to directions) as well as intervention and treatment when appropriate. Drug education also examines self-esteem, relationship skills, and knowledge, attitudes, behaviors, and values that promote drug-free and drug-responsible behavior. Drug education also focuses on making students aware of school policies regarding drug use and on obeying these policies as well as the laws of the community. Because of the close interrelationship between drug use and abuse and the incidence of violence, drug education also includes strategies to promote respectful, caring, nonviolent behavior. This chapter identifies the components needed for a successful drug education curriculum and includes a sample model drug education curriculum.

COMPONENTS IN A SUCCESSFUL DRUG EDUCATION CURRICULUM

The authors of this book have worked closely with thousands of school districts throughout the United States as well as in a myriad of foreign countries to produce curricula that emphasizes individual responsibility. The authors have identified the following components as being necessary in a drug education curriculum that will have an impact on students:

- Goals and Philosophy
- Responsible Decision-Making Model
- Model for Using Resistance Skills
- Life Skills for Inner Well-Being
- Scope and Sequence: Objectives Pre-K through High School

- Totally Awesome Teaching Strategies
- Infusion of Drug Education into Several Curriculum Areas
- Critical Thinking
- Character Education
- Multicultural Infusion
- Inclusion of Students With Special Needs
- Implementation: Parental, School, Community, and Professional Involvement
- Intervention and Treatment Model
- Drug Policy
- Evaluation

A MODEL DRUG EDUCATION CURRICULUM

Rather than including a lengthy discussion on how to develop and implement the drug education curriculum, the authors believed that it would be more valuable to include the model drug education curriculum they have developed. It is the experience of the authors that educators prefer professional experts who "show" them rather than "tell" them how to do something. In other words, providing a model curriculum as a reference usually is the best approach to helping school districts determine their specific curricular needs. The following model drug education curriculum, **The Meeks Heit Drug Education Curriculum**, provides a valuable resource for school districts. Because the pages of this book are perforated, this curriculum can be removed and used "as is" by a school district. Prof. Meeks and Dr. Heit consult with school districts who want to make adaptations to this curriculum. They also train parents, administrators, teachers, and community professionals in implementing an effective drug education curriculum and using totally awesome teaching strategies.

The Meeks Heit Drug Education Curriculum

Prof. Meeks and Dr. Heit
are available to consult with school
districts on the development and implementation of drug education curriculum. They
provide "Totally Awesome Teacher Training." For further information, call **Meeks Heit Publishing Company.**

*Drugs, Alcohol, and Tobacco: Totally Awesome Teach-
ing Strategies* contains teaching strategies
for each of the objectives Pre-K through
high school that are identified
in this curriculum.

Goals and Philosophy.....

Wellness is the quality of life that includes physical, mental-emotional, family-social, and spiritual health. The **Wellness Scale** depicts the ranges constituting the quality of life – from optimal well-being to high level wellness, average wellness, minor illness or injury, and premature death. At least six factors influence health and wellness:

1. the behaviors a persons chooses;
2. the situations in which a person participates;
3. the relationships in which a person engages;
4. the decisions that a person makes;
5. the resistance skills that a person uses;
6. the level of self-esteem that a person develops.

Health status is the sum total of the positive and negative influences of behaviors, situations, relationships, decisions, use of resistance skills, and self-esteem on a person's health and wellness. Each influence that is positive is viewed as a plus (+) while each influence that is negative is viewed as a minus (–). A person's health status fluctuates on the Wellness Scale, depending on these influences.

The goal of drug education is to promote wellness in youth. The philosophy or vision for the drug education curriculum focuses on helping youth choose to be drug free and drug informed. A person is **drug free** when (s)he does not use harmful and illegal drugs. A person is **drug**

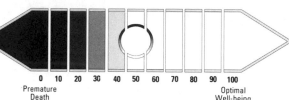

Wellness Scale Factors That Influence Health and Well-Being

Risk behaviors	Wellness behaviors
Risk situations	Healthful situations
Destructive relationships	Healthful relationships
Irresponsible decision making	Responsible decision making
Lack of resistance skills	Use of resistance skills
Negative self-esteem	Positive self-esteem

0 10 20 30 40 50 60 70 80 90 100
Premature Death   Optimal Well-being

Health status is the sum total of the positive and negative influences of behaviors, situations, relationships, decisions, use of resistance skills, and self-esteem.

informed when (s)he follows directions for using over-the-counter and prescription drugs. A person is also drug informed when (s)he makes wise choices in the presence of others who are not drug free (i.e., chooses not to ride in an automobile with them).

A Responsible Decision-Making Model.....

The drug education curriculum helps students learn to make responsible decisions. A decision-making model is applied consistently at every grade level with emphasis placed on making responsible decisions. The steps in the model are as follows:
• Clearly describe the situation.
• List possible actions that can be taken.
• Share the list of possible actions with a responsible adult such as someone who protects community laws and demonstrates character.
• Carefully evaluate each possible action using six criteria.

Six criteria are used to test an action to see if it is responsible. A responsible action is one that is:
1. healthful,
2. safe,
3. legal,
4. respectful of self and others,
5. consistent with guidelines of responsible adults such as parents and guardians,
6. indicative of character.

Model for Using Resistance Skills.....

The drug education curriculum helps students learn to resist harmful peer pressure. A model for using resistance skills or "say NO" skills is applied consistently at every grade level. Youth practice the model as they:
• use assertive behavior,
• avoid saying "NO, thank you" to persons who pressure them to try harmful behavior,

• use nonverbal behavior that matches verbal behavior,
• influence others to choose responsible behavior,
• avoid being in situations in which there will be pressure to make harmful decisions,
• avoid being with persons who choose harmful actions,
• resist pressure to engage in illegal behavior.

Life Skills for Inner Well-Being ....

The drug education curriculum must focus on life skills that enable youth to become strong, have a sense of self, and resist external pressures. **Life skills** are actions that promote optimal well-being and they are learned and practiced for a lifetime. Life skills are stated as "I will…", because they indicate that a person is willingly and willfully choosing to commit himself/herself to doing them. Consistently practicing life skills enables students to experience inner well-being. **Inner well-being** is a condition that results from:

- having positive self esteem,
- managing stress effectively,
- choosing healthful behaviors,
- choosing healthful situations,
- engaging in healthful relationships,
- making responsible decisions,
- using resistance skills when appropriate,
- demonstrating character,
- participating in the community,
- abiding by laws.

. . . .

Protective Factors That Promote Resiliency ....

Drug education must provide young people with armor to protect them or keep them from being vulnerable when they are exposed to situations in which they might use drugs. **Protective factors** are characteristics of individuals and their environments that make a positive contribution to development and behavior. Young people who are armed with protective factors are more likely to resist drugs and demonstrate resiliency. **Resiliency** is the ability to recover from or adjust to misfortune, change, pressure, and adversity. Resilient youth are often described as being stress resistant and invincible in spite of adversity. They are able to cope with misfortune without the use of drugs. Any successful drug education program must focus on protective factors that promote resiliency.

Protective Factors That Serve as a Coat of Armor and Promote Resiliency

Some protective factors are:

- being reared in a loving, functional family,
- being involved in school activities,
- having positive self-esteem,
- having clearly defined goals and plans to reach them,
- having close friends who do not abuse drugs,
- regularly practicing one's faith,
- feeling a sense of accomplishment at school,
- having adult role models including parents who do not abuse drugs,
- having a healthful attitude about competition and athletic performance,
- being committed to following the rules of the community,
- having a plan to cope with life stressors.

Scope and Sequence: Objectives for Grades Pre-K Through 12 ....

The drug education curriculum is organized into a sequential spiral of learning in which life skills for inner well-being are learned, practiced, evaluated, and reinforced at every grade level beginning in pre-kindergarten and continuing through grade 12. The objectives for the curriculum are grouped as follows: Pre-K–grade 2, grades 3–5, grades 6–8, and grades 9–12. For each objective in **The Meeks Heit Drug Education Curriculum**, there is a specific "Totally Awesome" teaching strategy in *Drugs, Alcohol, and Tobacco: Totally Awesome Teaching Strategies*.

OBJECTIVES: Pre-K–2

Students will:

1. describe how they are special;
2. identify features that make them unique;
3. identify different feelings they experience;
4. tell how to share feelings in healthful ways;
5. tell ways to cope with stress;
6. practice making choices that promote health;
7. practice ways to say NO to harmful choices;
8. describe ways in which families and friends influence decisions;
9. describe ways to be a good friend;
10. describe ways medicines can be healthful and harmful;
11. describe the harmful effects of tobacco;
12. describe the harmful effects of alcohol;
13. name illegal drugs and their harmful effects;
14. name responsible adults who protect health, safety, school rules, and laws;
15. tell the difference between loving feelings and loving actions.

Violence Prevention Skills are emphasized within the objectives and throughout the "Totally Awesome" teaching strategies in **The Meeks Heit Drug Education Curriculum.**

OBJECTIVES: Grades 3–5

Students will:

1. practice ways to improve self-esteem;
2. practice healthful ways to share feelings;
3. select healthful ways to manage stress;
4. practice making responsible decisions;
5. practice using resistance skills;
6. differentiate between healthful and harmful relationships;
7. differentiate between the healthful and harmful use of over-the-counter drugs;
8. describe ways alcohol harms physical, mental, and social health;
9. describe ways tobacco harms physical, mental, and social health;
10. identify illegal drugs and ways they harm physical, mental, and social health;
11. describe how the use of alcohol, tobacco, and illegal drugs interferes with reaching goals;
12. follow school rules and laws related to the use of drugs;
13. identify support groups that assist persons and families who need help with alcoholism, smoking cessation, and other drug treatment;
14. interpret messages in the media about drug use;
15. explain why drug use promotes violent behavior.

OBJECTIVES: Grades 6–8

Students will:

1. develop skills that improve self-esteem;
2. develop ways to manage stress;
3. develop skills needed for healthful and responsible relationships;
4. practice responsible decision-making skills;
5. practice resistance skills when pressured to use or abuse drugs;
6. examine the responsible use of prescription and over-the-counter drugs;
7. evaluate the holistic effects of alcohol on health and well-being;
8. evaluate the holistic effects of tobacco on health and well-being;
9. evaluate the harmful consequences that result from using anabolic steroids;
10. evaluate the effects of illegal drugs on well-being;
11. analyze the ways in which the use of alcohol, tobacco, and other drugs interferes with achieving goals;
12. evaluate the benefits of being drug free;
13. describe the relationship between using intravenous drugs and the transmission of HIV;
14. discuss how the use of drugs interferes with making responsible decisions about sexuality;
15. identify school and community resources involved in the prevention and treatment of drugs, alcohol, and tobacco;
16. describe the relationship between heredity and drug dependency;
17. examine the impact of drug dependency on the behavior of family members and friends;
18. analyze the impact of television, movies, videos, and advertising on the use and abuse of drugs;
19. evaluate the impact of drug use on the incidence of violence;
20. examine ways to support law enforcement to eradicate drug trafficking.

OBJECTIVES: Grades 9–12

Students will:

1. engage in activities that promote positive self-esteem and high level wellness;
2. practice stress management skills;
3. select healthful and responsible relationships;
4. differentiate between loving, functional families and dysfunctional families;
5. utilize responsible decision-making skills to remain drug free;
6. practice resistance skills when pressured to use harmful drugs and/or belong to gangs;
7. describe the short-term and long-term effects of harmful drugs on physical, mental, and social health;
8. outline choices that promote the responsible use of over-the-counter and prescription drugs;
9. examine ways in which laws pertaining to the use of alcohol, tobacco, and other harmful drugs help protect personal and community health;
10. examine ways in which the use of alcohol interferes with health and well-being and achieving goals;
11. examine ways in which the use of tobacco interferes with health and well-being and achieving goals;
12. examine ways in which the use of anabolic steroids interferes with health and well-being and achieving goals;
13. examine ways in which the use of illegal drugs interferes with health and well-being and achieving goals;
14. discuss how drug dependency affects family relationships;
15. identify risk factors and protective factors associated with the use of alcohol, tobacco, and illegal drugs;
16. identify risk factors and protective factors associated with violence;
17. describe how to use school and community interventions for the treatment of problems associated with the use of alcohol, tobacco, and illegal drugs;
18. discuss the role citizens can play in eradicating drug sales and trafficking in the community;
19. describe ways in which drug use increases the likelihood of HIV infection;
20. evaluate the effects of using drugs on healthful and responsible sexuality.

Totally Awesome Teaching Strategies.............

Totally awesome teaching strategies are creative ways to involve youth in learning about drugs and in practicing life skills for inner well-being. For each of the objectives identified in the drug education curriculum Pre-K through Grade 12, there is a totally awesome teaching strategy provided in *Drugs, Alcohol, and Tobacco: Totally Awesome Teaching Strategies.*

The design of totally awesome teaching strategies:

- *Clever Title.* A clever title is set in bold-faced type in the center of the page.
- *Designated Grade Level.* The designated grade levels for which the strategy is appropriate appear in the upper left hand corner.
- *Designated Curriculum Objective.* The designated curriculum objective that will be met by using the teaching strategy is identified directly beneath the designated grade level that appears in the upper left hand corner.
- *Infusion into Curriculum Areas.* The strategies are designed to be infused into several curriculum areas other than health education: art studies, language arts, math studies, music studies, science studies, and social studies. The area of the curriculum other than health education into which the strategy might be infused is designated by a symbol to the right of the title of the teaching strategy.
- *Critical Thinking.* Several of the strategies help students develop critical thinking skills. A symbol to the right of the title of the teaching strategy is used to designate critical thinking.

- *Character Education.* Several of the teaching strategies focus on helping students develop character. A symbol to the right of the title of the teaching strategy is used to designate character education.
- *Objective.* The objective for the strategy is listed under this bold-faced subheading. The objective helps the professional focus on what is to be learned and how to measure the learning that has taken place.
- *Life Skill.* The life skill that is reinforced by using this strategy is listed under this bold-faced subheading. Life skills are actions promoting optimal well-being that are learned and practiced for a lifetime as a result of participating in the teaching strategy.
- *Materials.* The materials are items that the professional must gather together in order to do the teaching strategy. They are listed under this bold-faced subheading.
- *Motivation.* The motivation is the step-by-step directions the professional follows when using the teaching strategy. These directions are listed under this bold-faced subheading.
- *Evaluation.* The evaluation is the means of measuring the students' mastery of the objective and/or life skill. The evaluation is described under this bold-faced subheading.
- *Multicultural Infusion.* Suggestions for adapting the teaching strategy in order to incorporate learning about persons of varied cultures are included under this bold-faced subheading.
- *Inclusion.* Suggestions for adapting the strategy to assist students with special learning challenges are included under this bold-faced subheading.

- -

Infusion of Drug Education into Several Curriculum Areas . . . .

The skills for inner well-being and the objectives identified for each grade level are appropriately taught within the health education curriculum. The totally awesome teaching strategies in *Drugs, Alcohol, and Tobacco: Totally Awesome Teaching Strategies* are designed to be taught within the health education curriculum. However, today the trend in education is to infuse learning into many curriculum areas. Thus, the skills for inner well-being, objectives, and totally awesome teaching strategies are designed so that they might be infused or integrated into the following curriculum areas other than health education: art studies, language arts, math studies, music studies, science studies, and social studies.

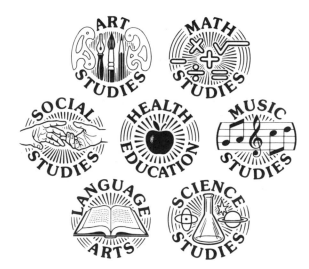

Critical Thinking ....

The drug education curriculum is designed to help students develop critical thinking skills. The skills for inner well-being, objectives, and totally awesome teaching strategies provide an opportunity to examine responsible decision making and to learn to evaluate the consequences of actions.

Character Education ....

The drug education curriculum is designed to help students build character and develop sound moral values. The skills for inner well-being, objectives, and totally awesome teaching strategies provide an opportunity to examine laws and community responsibility. They help students recognize that being responsible and respectful involves choosing actions which are best for the self, others, the environment, and community. Character education promotes citizenship.

Multicultural Infusion ....

A current trend in education is to help students recognize the positive attributes and contributions of persons of many different backgrounds. Many of the totally awesome teaching strategies contain suggestions for infusing multicultural education into the learning experience. This bolsters the self-esteem of students and helps them gain an appreciation for others.

Inclusion of Students with Special Needs ....

A current trend in education is to include students with special needs in the regular classroom. Inclusion is believed to promote learning as well as social development. In order for inclusion to be effective, teachers may need to make adaptations to teaching strategies. These adaptations facilitate learning and bolster self-esteem in students with special needs.

Implementation: Parental, School, Community, and Professional Involvement...

A drug education curriculum advisory team will be formed that includes parents, administrators, teachers, community leaders, and allied health professionals. The advisory team will review the curriculum prior to implementation. A current trend is to schedule a parent meeting in which the goals and objectives of the curriculum are discussed and several totally awesome teaching strategies from *Drugs, Alcohol, and Tobacco: Totally Awesome Teaching Strategies* are presented. Parents are encouraged to discuss topics concerning critical thinking and character education with children. Persons from community agencies and from the allied health professions might present the services they provide. Issues of intervention and treatment will be addressed as well as guidelines regarding the school district's drug policies.

Intervention and Treatment Model ....

A drug education curriculum must address intervention and treatment as well as prevention. Students and their parents need to be aware of the community resources that are available. A current trend is for schools to offer programs such as smoking cessation and to offer support groups for students desiring to change behaviors.

Drug Policy.....................

A drug policy for the school district must be available and must be reinforced. The drug policy might include: rules for student behavior, consequences for breaking rules, procedures for referring students for assessment/treatment, procedures for investigating policy violations, guidelines adhering to due process, guidelines for drug policy dissemination, guidelines for staff training, and guidelines for disseminating the drug policy to students through the drug education curriculum.

Evaluation ....

The drug education curriculum will be evaluated in a variety of ways. The objectives for grades Pre-K through 12 will be used to evaluate youth mastery of learning experiences. Surveys will be used to evaluate short-term and long-term changes in students' behavior. Evaluation will include an examination of the effectiveness of the intervention and treatment models employed.

Meeks Heit Publishing...*producers of quality health education materials and "totally awesome" training packages*

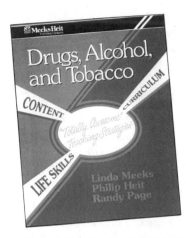

Drugs, Alcohol, and Tobacco: Totally Awesome Teaching Strategies (1994) contains everything needed to implement drug and violence prevention curricula: factual content, goals and philosophy, a responsible decision-making model, model for using resistance skills, life skills for inner well-being, protective factors that promote resiliency, scope and sequence chart with objectives for grades Pre-K through 12, totally awesome teaching strategies, infusion of drug education into several curriculum areas, critical thinking skills, character education, multicultural infusion, inclusion of students with special needs, suggestions for including parents and community leaders, coverage of intervention and treatment, and evaluation. Used for preservice and graduate training at colleges/universities and in-service training provided by school districts, state departments of education, state departments of health, and agencies.

Comprehensive School Health Education: Totally Awesome Strategies for Teaching Health (1992) is the most widely used book in colleges/universities, state departments of education, and school districts for the training of teachers in creative, dynamic, skill-building, health-related teaching strategies. This innovative book is ideal for classroom teachers — novice or experienced. It is used by drug-free and STD and HIV/AIDS coordinators and teachers. This book contains hundreds of "totally awesome," skill-building teaching strategies, curricula, blackline teaching masters, lesson plans, the Year 2000 Objectives for Youth, and up-to-date information on the leading health-related concerns for young children and adolescents.

Education for Sexuality and HIV/AIDS: Curriculum and Teaching Strategies (1993), previously titled **Education for Sexuality: Concepts and Programs for Teaching,** has been the most widely used human sexuality education book in the world for more than twenty years. Published in six languages, this book is used in colleges/universities for preservice through graduate education. It is used in school districts for developing and implementing curricula. A popular resource, it is used in school districts by drug-free coordinators, STD and HIV/AIDS coordinators, and classroom teachers. State departments of education, state health departments, and public health coordinators and nurses continue to find this book "state-of-the-art" for their work in human sexuality.

About The Meeks and Heit "Totally Awesome" Training Packages...

✳ featuring teaching strategies that are dynamic, creative, and easy to use,

✳ building confidence in educators responsible for providing comprehensive school health education, sex education, HIV/AIDS education, violence prevention, and drug education,

✳ involving educators in experiencing teaching strategies that they can use to motivate their students,

✳ providing a personal touch for audiences of 50 through 500.

For further information about Meeks Heit books and/or "Totally Awesome" Training Packages...

Call 1-800-682-6882
    1-614-759-7780 (Ohio)
Fax 1-614-759-6166

Meeks Heit
Publishing Company
P.O. Box 121
Blacklick, Ohio 43004

244

TOTALLY AWESOME TEACHING STRATEGIES

The material in this book is organized and presented within a framework that the authors believe provides the best sequence in which professionals might learn how to educate about drug education. In this sequence, professionals will first study what they need to "know," and then will examine what to "do" with what they have learned. Accordingly, this book is organized into five sections:

Section 1: Drugs and Wellness
Section 2: Drugs: A Factual Account
Section 3: Alcohol, Tobacco, and Well-Being
Section 4: Prevention and Treatment of Drug Abuse
Section 5: Drug Education: Curriculum and Teaching Strategies

The first four sections provide the professional with knowledge and understanding of facts and issues involved in drug education. Section 1, Drugs and Wellness, provides the foundation for the further study of drugs. It also includes a discussion of violence. In this section, the authors present the theme for this book: drug education has as its goal for students to be drug free (avoid the use of harmful and/or illegal drugs) and drug informed (use over-the-counter and prescription drugs according to directions). The background information to support this theme is provided in Section 2, Drugs: A Factual Account; Section 3, Alcohol, Tobacco, and Well-Being; and Section 4, Prevention and Treatment of Drug Abuse. The authors want professionals to have detailed background information before examining ways to implement drug education.

The last section provides the professional with ways in which to implement drug education. Section 5, Drug Education: Curriculum and Teaching Strategies, begins with Chapter 17: The Drug Education Curriculum. This chapter is included to help professionals design an effective drug education curriculum. It includes a model drug education curriculum developed by Prof. Meeks and Dr. Heit. Chapters 18 and 19 complete the task of preparing the professional to implement drug education. Chapter 18, Totally Awesome Teaching Strategies, includes creative strategies that can be used to implement the curriculum. The introduction of the teaching strategies includes a dis-cussion of a philosophy for selecting teaching strategies and for the design of the teaching strategies. Chapter 19, Teaching Masters and Student Masters, contains masters that can be used with the teaching strategies in Chapter 18 as well as by themselves.

A PHILOSOPHY FOR SELECTING TEACHING STRATEGIES

Traditionally, professionals in drug education have relied on the lecture/discussion method and the use of audio-visuals to educate students. This approach was primarily used for two reasons. First, most professionals lacked training in the use of creative teaching strategies. Second, the emphasis in drug education was placed on students learning facts, and facts are easily taught in this manner. Today, however, the philosophy of teaching about drugs has changed. Teachers used to ask, "Could you tell me WHAT I am supposed to teach?" Today this question is quickly followed with, "Could you tell me HOW I am supposed to teach?" In addition, the focus of drug education used to be the acquisition of knowledge. Today, emphasis is placed on building skills for inner well-being. The lecture/discussion method is not as *effective* in skill-building as are methods in which students participate actively. Thus, the authors believe that the content for drug education must be presented through the totally awesome teaching strategies that focus on life skill development that are presented in this chapter. Professionals using this book have permission to use these teaching strategies as they educate others. However, permission is not granted to include these teaching strategies in other publications or in presentations promoting other publications.

THE DESIGN OF THE TOTALLY AWESOME TEACHING STRATEGIES

The Meeks Heit Drug Education Curriculum contains life skills for inner well-being and objectives for grades Pre-K through 12. The totally awesome teaching strategies in Chapter 18 are grouped by grade level beginning with Pre-K and ending with Grade 12. The design of the totally awesome teaching strategies is described in the following discussion.

245

Clever Title. A clever title is set in bold-faced type in the center of the page. The title is meant to be inviting and to impress the teacher that the teaching strategy will involve students actively in the learning process.

Designated Grade Level. The designated grade levels for which the teaching strategy is appropriate appear in the upper left hand corner. Although many of the teaching strategies can be used at more than one grade level, the authors wanted to assure school districts that the drug curriculum would be comprehensive without repeating any of the teaching strategies at more than one grade level.

Designated Curriculum Objective. The designated curriculum objective that will be met by using the teaching strategy is identified directly beneath the designated grade levels that appear in the upper left hand corner. Also, the degree of difficulty for each numbered objective is indicated with a capital letter—A, B, or C—that appears next to the objective number. There is at least one teaching strategy for _every_ objective identified in **The Meeks Heit Drug Education Curriculum**, and for most objectives there are three strategies.

Infusion into Curriculum Areas. The strategies are designed to be infused into several curriculum areas other than health education: art studies, language arts, math studies, music studies, science studies, and social studies (Fig. 18-1). The area of the curriculum other than health education into which the strategy might be infused is designated by a symbol to the right of the title of the teaching strategy.

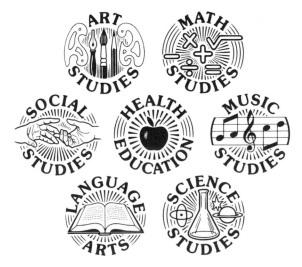

Violence Prevention. Many of the teaching strategies focus on helping students develop violence prevention skills by helping them learn to respect and care for others, manage stress, use conflict resolution skills, obey laws, respect

authority, and recognize the ways in which drug use and drug trafficking contribute to violence. The words "Violence Prevention" are contained within a shaded box to the right of the title of the strategy and to the left of the symbol that designates the curriculum area into which the strategy is infused.

Critical Thinking. A number of the strategies help students develop critical thinking skills. A symbol to the right of the title of the teaching strategy is used to designate critical thinking (Fig. 18-2).

Character Education. A number of the teaching strategies focus on helping students develop character. A symbol to the right of the title of the teaching strategy is used to designate character education (Fig. 18-3).

Objective. The objective for the strategy is listed under this bold-faced subheading. The objective helps the professional focus on what is to be learned and how to measure the learning that has taken place.

Life Skill. The life skill that is reinforced by using this teaching strategy is listed under this bold-faced subheading. Life skills are actions promoting optimal well-being that are learned and practiced for a lifetime as a result of participating in the teaching strategy.

Materials. The materials are items that the professional must gather together in order to do the teaching strategy. They are listed under this bold-faced subheading. The authors designed teaching strategies that require materials that are readily available to teachers.

Motivation. The motivation is the step-by-step directions the professional follows when using the teaching strategy. These directions are listed under this bold-faced subheading. The authors included content within the motivation.

This helps the professional with the wording (s)he uses when asking students to participate in the learning process.

Evaluation. The evaluation is the means of measuring the students' mastery of the objective and/or life skill. The evaluation is described under this bold-faced subheading. The evaluation may also provide the opportunity for infusion into other curriculum areas.

Multicultural Infusion. Suggestions for adapting the teaching strategy in order to incorporate learning about persons of varied cultures are included under this bold-faced subheading.

Inclusion. Suggestions for adapting the teaching strategy to assist students with special learning challenges are included under this bold-faced subheading.

Many of the teaching strategies make use of the full-page teaching masters and student masters in Chapter 19. Some of the teaching strategies also have additional teaching and student masters that can be reproduced and distributed. The choices of teaching strategies selected for use will vary. Many professionals will find that the teaching strategies are suitable for use in adult training sessions. The teaching strategies are easy to adapt for different audiences in different settings. Professionals will find that the teaching strategies convey information, motivate learners, and help build life skills for inner well-being.

Grades Pre-K–2
▪ Objective 1A

| Violence Prevention |

I Am Special

Objective:

Students will describe how they are special.

Life Skill:

I will use my special qualities to show others how I am important.

Materials:

Pencils, crayons, I'm a Winner (page 249), a copy for each student

Motivation:

1 Introduce the word "special" and ask students what they think this word means. After students have shared their meanings, indicate to students that to be special means to be important. Explain that being special can refer to other people. For example, a friend is special; a family member is special. The word special also can refer to talents such as being a gymnast or playing a piano.

2 Indicate that everyone has something about himself/herself that is special. People can feel happy about themselves when they have or do something that is special. Tell students they are going to sing songs that will show just how special they are.

3 Explain that they are going to sing a song about being a winner and that being a winner means they have accomplished something very important. Perhaps they have a skill they do well such as drawing a picture. Emphasize that being a winner is something very special. The following song will use the tune of "London Bridge Is Falling Down." You might select one or more of the following characteristics as being a winner: getting hugs, giving hugs, having friends, doing well in school, and helping at home. Or you may choose to think of other characteristics and use the same tune. The following is an example.

I love getting hugs, getting hugs, getting hugs,
I love getting hugs, every day.

4 Suggest that as students sing the words, they can hug a classmate. Explain that giving hugs is a way to show you like this person. Explain that a person feels good, or feels like a winner, when feelings are expressed in healthful ways.

5 Suggest another example of using the tune of "London Bridge Is Falling Down."
I have very nice friends, very nice friends,
very nice friends.
I have very nice friends, at my school.

6 After students sing this verse, you can ask them to share ways their friends are special. Explain that when friends are special, they help you feel good about yourself and you feel like a winner.

7 Distribute copies of I'm a Winner. Have students print their first name in the blank line. If necessary, you can print the names in pencil on the line and then have students trace each letter with a crayon. Each student is to draw a picture of his/her face in the circle of the ribbon. You can display their ribbons on the bulletin board.

Evaluation:

Using crayons and construction paper, have students draw a picture that shows something they do that makes them feel good. For example, students may draw a picture that shows them riding a bicycle with a family member. Students will then share their pictures and tell why they feel good.

Multicultural Infusion:

This same activity can be adapted by taking a song that reflects a specific culture and using the tune of that song to express how one can feel special.

I'm a Winner

I _____ and I'm a winner!

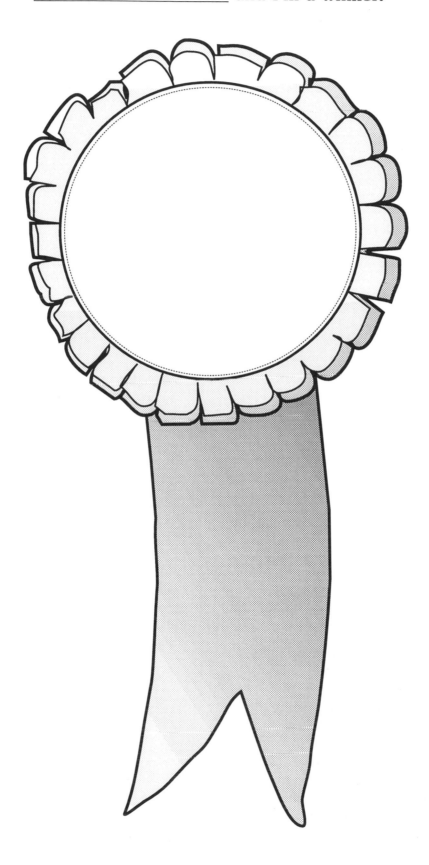

Grades Pre-K–2
▪ Objective 1B

Violence Prevention

PICTURE ME SPECIAL

Objective:

Students will describe how they are special.

Life Skill:

I will behave in ways that show I respect myself.

Materials:

Pencils, crayons, Special Me (page 251), a copy for each student

Motivation:

1 Explain to students that they each have characteristics that show they are special. Write the word special on the chalkboard and ask students what this word means to them. You can begin this activity with your own example. You might say, "I am special because I am a teacher and have such wonderful boys and girls to teach." Or you might say, "I feel special because I jog three miles every day and that helps keep me healthy."

2 Ask students to share ways they are special by telling the class something they do or something they like that helps make them special. In doing this exercise, they are to begin their statements by first telling their names. For example, students will say, "I am John and I am special because I. . . ."

3 After students have shared something special about themselves, distribute copies of Special Me. This master is to represent the cover of a book. Explain to students that the title of the book is their first name. They are to draw a picture on the cover that shows something special about themselves.

4 Have students share their pictures with the class. Then tell students that the picture on the cover of the book represents what might be on the inside of the book. As students show their

covers, have them give a short story about what would be on the inside. For example, a student may have drawn a picture on the cover showing a scene in which (s)he is at a family outing at the zoo. The student might tell why this is a special moment. The student might share reasons why spending time with family members at the zoo makes him/her feel special.

Evaluation:

Have students tell what their definition of the word special means to them and then describe why their pictures show that they are special.

Multicultural Infusion:

Some students may draw pictures that have cultural implications. For example, a family get-together might show family members eating a food that is special to a particular culture. The student can tell the class something about the food.

250

Grades Pre-K–2
- Objective 1C

WHAT DO YOU SEE? IT'S ME

Objective:

Students will describe how they are special.

Life Skill:

I will behave in ways that show self-respect.

Materials:

Shoe box, glue or tape, decorative wrapping paper, pocket mirror

Motivation:

1 Using a shoe box you no longer need, glue or tape a small pocket mirror on the under side of the box cover. Wrap the box and cover separately with decorative wrapping paper. Show the students how attractive the box is. Do not tell students about the mirror.

2 As you hold the box in front of the class, students will be curious about what is inside the box. Ask students if they have ever received a special gift. Have them tell about the special gifts they have received. Have students share why they are excited about receiving special gifts. When students received a special gift, they were probably anxious to open the package in which the gift was enclosed. They wanted to know what was so special about the contents of the box.

3 Tell students that you are holding a gift box. Explain that there is something very special about this box. Tell students that they are going to have the opportunity to view what is inside the box you are holding. Tell the class you are going to hold the box and show it to each student. Emphasize that what they will see is a special gift. As you come to each student, you are going to open the lid of the box and each student can see what is inside the box. (When students open the cover, they will see the reflection of their own face in the mir-

ror.) Ask students to think about what was so special about what they observed in the box.

4 After students have had the opportunity to observe what was inside the box, have them share the special characteristics they observed. Explain that physical characteristics help distinguish people from each other. Explain that people also differ from each other in the special ways they act. Have students share ways they act that demonstrate how they are special. For example, students may share that they choose friends who are always helpful. You can explain that gifts bring happy feelings and that each gift in the box you shared with each student helps make you, the teacher, feel happy. Tell them that each boy and girl in the class gives a gift when (s)he cooperates and is helpful, for example.

5 Have students share gifts they give that are special. The gifts should reflect the student's special characteristics. Students might share as follows:
I give a gift when. . . .
Some examples of completing this sentence are:
> I give a gift when I show others I care about them.
> I give a gift when I am a good friend.

6 After students have shared their statements, you may choose to share some of your gifts. For example, you give the gift of caring about your students. You give the gift of listening to concerns students may have.

Evaluation:

You can assign a partner to each student. Each student is to tell the class something special about his/her partner. Have students tell how they feel when someone says something positive about them.

Grades Pre-K–2
- Objective 2A

A NO-FROWN CLOWN

Objective:

Students will identify features that make them unique.

Life Skill:

I will express my feelings in healthful ways.

Materials:

Scissors, staplers or tape, crayons, construction paper (at least 24 inches square), 2 sheets for each student

Motivation:

1 Explain to students that people have feelings that they show through their facial expressions. Ask students to share if they have ever seen others when they were sad, happy, angry, scared, or surprised. Explain that these are examples of the different kinds of feelings that people have. Tell students that they often can observe how a person feels.

2 Explain to students that they are going to make a face and a hat. Distribute construction paper that is approximately 24 inches square. Help students cut out a circle large enough so that their entire face can show through the opening. They can then design the area of construction paper around the opening by cutting out different designs or by coloring on it. The drawing on this page provides an example. Students might make a clown hat by cutting a cone-shaped "hat" from another sheet of construction paper and securing it by either stapling or taping. To help students understand what is involved, you can make a face and hat for yourself.

3 Explain to students that they are going to be "feeling clowns." Each student is to wear his/her face and hat and display a facial expression that depicts a feeling. For example, a stu-

dent may wear a sad face. This student will come to the front of the room and introduce himself/herself by making up a name such as Terribly Tearful Clown. The student might then tell the class why this clown is sad. For example, the student may say, "I'm Terribly Tearful Clown because my best friend just moved away and that makes me feel sad."

4 For each facial expression, have the student discuss the feeling it displays. If a feeling is one of disappointment, anger, or sadness, discuss how these feelings can be helped. For example, students can be encouraged to talk to their parents or guardians. They can be made aware of sources of help in the school such as a teacher or counselor. If a feeling is one of happiness, you can have other students share what makes them happy. Explain that everyone shows feelings but what is important is how to handle these feelings in healthful ways.

Evaluation:

Have students brainstorm sources of help when they have feelings they need help with so that they can handle the feelings in healthful ways.

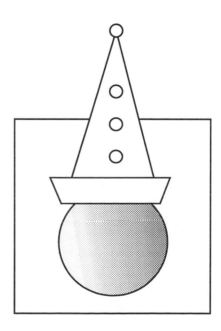

Grades Pre-K–2
Objective 2B

PHYSICAL FEATURES

Objective:

Students will identify features that make them unique.

Life Skill:

I will accept how I look and feel proud about who I am.

Materials:

Pencils, paper, a sheet for each student

Motivation:

1 Explain to students that everyone has physical features that make a person unique. Explain that the word unique means to be "one of a kind" or special. Tell students that physical features are parts of the body that make people look the way they do and that no two people look alike. Provide students with examples of physical features, such as being tall or short, having dark hair or light hair, or having brown eyes or blue eyes. Explain that some people have features that are similar. For example, more than one student in the class may have black hair and more than one student in the class may have brown eyes. However, combinations of features make a student "one of a kind." An example may be a student in the class who is tall and has short brown hair.

2 Explain to students that they are going to be playing a game. Each student is to think about the physical features (s)he possesses and list as many of those features as possible on a sheet of paper. Emphasize that spelling does not count. On the top of the sheet of paper, each student is to print his/her name. Students are to hand their lists to you.

3 Tell the class that you are going to read what is printed on each sheet of paper. You will not indicate the student's name that is on the paper. After you have read what is printed on

each sheet, students are to try to guess which class member fits the physical features that were on the list. In doing this activity, you will find that more than one student will fit some of the descriptors. However, only one student will fit the combination of descriptors on each list.

4 Upon completion of this activity, explain that if enough physical features were described for each person, each person in the class would be the only one with that combination. Explain that most physical features people outwardly display are those with which they were born. Some features such as having short hair or long hair can be changed. However, it is important to emphasize that each person should feel proud about his/her inherited features.

Evaluation:

Have students complete the following sentence by describing a physical feature about which they are proud.
"I feel proud to be me because. . . ."

Multicultural Infusion:

Explain that people of different cultures may have physical features that are unique to their cultures and that help make them special. For example, African-American students usually have dark skin. Hispanic/Latino students usually have black hair. Asian-American students usually have distinctive eyes. White American students have a light skin color. Explain that physical features are inherited from one's parents. Physical features can identify people as belonging to a particular culture. Emphasize that regardless of the physical features people have, they have a right to feel proud about who they are.

Inclusion:

Students can draw a picture of something they have done that makes them feel proud about who they are.

254

Grades Pre-K–2
- Objective 2C

UNIQUE ME

Objective:

Students will identify features that make them unique.

Life Skill:

I will choose actions that show how I appreciate my uniqueness.

Materials:

Markers or crayons, ink pad, index cards, a card for each student

Motivation:

1 Distribute an index card to each student. Ask each student to draw a picture of himself/herself including as many unique features of themselves as possible. The picture is to be a drawing of the body without a head. Have several students share their headless drawings with the class and indicate what is special about their drawings.

2 Have students press their thumbs on the ink pad to make a thumbprint where their heads should be on their pictures. Each student will now have a complete body. Students are to write their names on their cards. Post each card on the bulletin board.

3 Explain to students that the "heads" on the cards may look alike from a distance. However, there is something unique about each of the "heads." Have students closely observe the details of the "heads." Then ask students to indicate what they observed. Students will indicate that each "head" is different because each fingerprint is unique. Explain that no two people have the same fingerprints. Fingerprints are a physical feature that makes one person different from another. Have students share other ways people differ from each other because of their physical features. Emphasize that although people may look similar from a distance, on

closer inspection they are different. For example, thumbprints look alike from a distance but on close inspection, they are different. Explain that people have other unique features with which they were born. A person has no control over these features and it is these unique features that help make everyone special.

Evaluation:

Distribute the cards that were displayed on the bulletin board. Be sure that each student has another student's card. Each student is to go to the student whose card he or she has and tell that student two features observed on the card that make that student special.

Grades Pre-K–2
▪ Objective 3A

IF YOU'RE HAPPY AND YOU KNOW IT

Objective:

Students will identify different feelings they experience.

Life Skill:

I will express my feelings in healthful ways.

Materials:

None

Motivation:

1 Explain that you will be singing a song with the students. Tell the students to make a happy face as they sing the song titled "If You're Happy and You Know It."

> If you're happy and you know it
> Clap your hands.
> If you're happy and you know it
> Clap your hands.
> If you're happy and you know it
> Then your face will really show it.
> If you're happy and you know it
> Clap your hands.

2 You can continue singing this song by substituting other lines for "Clap your hands." For example, you can sing:

> If you're happy and you know it
> Stamp your feet.
> If you're happy and you know it
> Stamp your feet.
> If you're happy and you know it
> Then you're face will really show it.
> If you're happy and you know it
> Stamp your feet.

3 Have students suggest other lines they might insert. Examples might include the following:

> Jump up high.
> Hug a friend.
> Throw a kiss.
> Say, "You're nice."

4 After you have inserted different lines, have students discuss what makes them feel happy. You can review some of the lines you used in your song and ask why these lines would help make someone feel happy. For example, why might hugging a friend help make someone feel happy? You can use this approach to discuss different kinds of situations that help make a person feel happy.

5 Explain to students that their faces showed happiness when they were singing. Ask them to share different facial expressions and have the class guess what feelings are being exhibited by the facial expressions. Some examples of feelings may be happiness, sadness, fear, or surprise. For each expression, have students share what might happen to make a person have this particular feeling.

Evaluation:

You can exhibit different facial expressions for your students. Have students guess what feelings you are exhibiting. For each, ask students to describe what might make you feel that way. In discussing the feelings exhibited, emphasize that it is important to share feelings, especially feelings of sadness, with a trusted and responsible adult. This adult may be a parent, relative, teacher, school psychologist, member of the clergy, or school nurse.

| Violence Prevention |

WEARING A FACE

Objective:

Students will identify different feelings they experience.

Life Skill:

I will express my feelings in healthful ways.

Materials:

Crayons, Wearing a Face (page 258), a copy for each student

Motivation:

1 Explain to students that the feelings people experience can be shown in the facial expressions they exhibit. For example, a person who feels happy might have a smile. Ask students to share an experience that has made them feel happy. For example, a student may state that (s)he has been happy when (s)he received a birthday present. When (s)he felt happy, she showed it in his/her face by smiling. Ask several students to share their experiences.

2 Share different kinds of feelings that people experience. For example, some people may feel sad; others may feel angry. Some people may feel excited; others may feel scared.

3 Using your copy of Wearing a Face as an example, draw a face on the animal. You can draw a face that shows a happy animal. Then show the picture of your animal to the class and tell a story about the animal. For example, you can tell students the following story:

I'm naming my animal Happy Hippo. Hippo has a very happy face. There is a special reason why Hippo is happy. Today is Hippo's birthday. Hippo is six years old and is having a birthday party. Hippo had always wanted a bicycle. And on Hippo's sixth birthday, his family gave him a new bicycle. This certainly was a surprise for Hippo. Hippo showed his

surprise in his face. Hippo was smiling. Hippo even had tears running from his eyes. But these were not tears of sadness. Rather, they were tears of joy. You see, sometimes people cry when they are very happy. Hippo is happy because he knows the many happy times he will spend riding on his new bicycle. You can also see that Happy Hippo is wearing a new helmet. Hippo's parents know that wearing a helmet is important when riding a bicycle. The helmet will help protect Hippo's head if he should fall while riding his bicycle. Hippo appreciates the concern his family has for his safety while riding his bicycle.

4 Provide each student with a copy of Wearing a Face. Tell each student to draw a face on the animal that shows a certain kind of feeling. Students are to draw the face using different colors of crayons. After students complete their drawings, they are to give a name to their animals. They are to take turns giving a story behind the reasons for the facial expressions similar to the sample story you provided.

5 For each story, write a feeling on the chalkboard. After the feelings are listed, have students provide other examples of situations that may cause a person to experience that feeling.

Evaluation:

Explain that there are healthful ways to deal with feelings. Select several feelings that were presented in class and listed on the chalkboard. For example, some feelings may be sadness, loneliness, and fear. Have students share healthful ways to deal with these kinds of feelings. Reinforce the positive ways students indicate they can deal with these kinds of feelings.

Inclusion:

You can have some students share their pictures with a family member and the family member can help develop a story for the picture.

Wearing a Face

| Violence Prevention |

ACADEMY AWARD

Objective:

Students will identify different feelings they experience.

Life Skill:

I will act on my feelings in healthful ways.

Materials:

Sheet of paper, pencil, magazines

Motivation:

1 Explain to students that everyone experiences different kinds of feelings. Happy feelings as well as sad feelings are common experiences that boys and girls exhibit every day. Explain to students that it is important to express feelings in healthful ways.

2 Share with students that they are going to express different kinds of feelings. Their feelings will be expressed nonverbally. Individual students will have an opportunity to come up to the front of the class. You will write the name of a feeling on a sheet of paper and show it to the student in front of the room. Only that student will see the name of the feeling. The student will then act out that feeling for the class nonverbally. Students in the class must guess the feeling being exhibited. Among some of the feelings you can use are sadness, joy, surprise, fear, alarm, fright, and anger.

3 After students have had the opportunity to observe the feeling being exhibited, they are to identify that feeling. For the answer to be acceptable, students are to indicate the clues that provided them with the reason for their answer.

4 After students identify each feeling, they also are to provide a situation that would have been responsible for causing that particular feeling. For example, an argument with a

friend can cause someone to feel anger or sadness. The examples should reflect experiences that are common at their age.

5 Explain that there are healthful ways to act on feelings. Even positive feelings can sometimes be acted on in harmful ways. For example, a person who becomes very happy because (s)he received a good grade on a test may decide not to study for another test the next day. Students need to understand that both positive feelings and negative feelings need to be acted on in healthful ways. For each feeling acted out in class, have students share positive, healthful ways that feeling can be handled.

Evaluation:

Cut out pictures from magazines of people who are showing different feelings. Then have students guess what feelings are being exhibited. Have students describe what might have caused a person to experience a kind of feeling. Then have students identify healthful ways to act on that feeling.

Multicultural Infusion:

Explain that certain events may cause different feelings based on a person's culture. For example, a student may attend a special occasion with his/her family and invite a friend to come along. This may cause the friend to feel anxious because (s)he has never been to such an occasion and wants to know more about it. Emphasize the need for students to be aware of the cultural differences among their peers. Communication and knowledge about cultural differences can help facilitate healthful interactions and thus promote positive feelings. You can have students share tidbits of information with their peers about their cultural backgrounds.

Grades Pre-K–2
- Objective 4A

I FEEL GOOD

Objective:

Students will tell how to share feelings in healthful ways.

Life Skill:

I will engage in healthful activities that make me feel good.

Materials:

Chalk, chalkboard

Motivation:

1 Share with students that many years ago there was a popular song titled "I Feel Good" that was recorded by a singer named James Brown. In fact, this song is still heard today in many different settings such as in commercials and on radio stations. Explain that this song is a very happy song because it describes how one person helps make another person feel good.

2 Share the words of the first chorus of this song with the class. Write them on the chalkboard. The words are:

> I feel good,
> I knew that I would,
> I feel good,
> I knew that I would,
> So good,
> So good,
> 'Cause I've got you.

3 Explain that everyone in the class makes you feel glad that you are a teacher. You can sing the above chorus to the class and, at the end, hold out your hands in a way that shows you feel good about the entire class. Explain to students that you are going to play a special game with this song. Everyone in the class will sing the words of the song. When you get to the last word in the last line, you will point to a student. Everyone must substitute that stu-

dent's name for the last word. For example, you might point to a student named Ann. Everyone in the class will sing "'Cause I've got Ann."

4 After a student is identified, another student in the class is to state a reason why (s)he feels good about Ann. All statements must be phrased as follows: "I feel good about _____ because. . . ." You can continue to do this activity for as many of the students as you wish. The class must repeat the words of the entire chorus for each new student selected.

Evaluation:

After students have had an opportunity to make positive statements about their peers, ask the class to share how they felt about the activity. Students will likely indicate the statements made them feel good.

Inclusion:

You can point to several students in the class and tell why they make you, as a teacher, feel good.

I feel good because I got a new toy.

Grades Pre-K–2
- Objective 4B

THE SHARING TREE

Objective:

Students will tell how to share feelings in healthful ways.

Life Skill:

I will participate in activities that make me feel good.

Materials:

Poster paper, The Me Apple (page 262), a copy for each student

Motivation:

1 Explain to students that everyone does things that help make them happy. When people feel happy, they feel good about themselves.

2 Distribute copies of The Me Apple. Explain that each student will have his/her own "Me Apple." Each "Me Apple" represents its owner. Explain that no two people will have the same apple.

3 Students are to personalize the apple. To do this, each student must print something in the apple that (s)he does to make himself/herself feel good. For example, a student may print that (s)he plays with friends at the end of the day. Each student should print his/her first name on the line inside the apple.

4 You can use a large sheet of poster paper to draw a tree with branches. If you choose not to use poster paper, you can draw this tree on the chalkboard. After the tree is drawn, have each student tape his or her apple to a branch on the tree. As students do this, have them read what they printed on their apples.

5 After students have had a chance to read what other students printed on their apples, summarize the statements by indicating the kinds of things that make students feel good. Then have students share the commonalities that students their age indicate as making them feel good.

Evaluation:

Students will share a number of different activities that help make them feel good. Have students complete the following sentence. "I feel good when. . . ." Students can share their thoughts about feeling good and how feeling good helps them be at their best.

The Me Apple

My Name is...

I'm a Shining Star

Objective:

Students will tell how to share feelings in healthful ways.

Life Skill:

I will show others I feel good about who I am.

Materials:

Flashlight, I'm a Shining Star (page 264), a copy for each student

Motivation:

1 Tell students you are going to turn off the lights in the room. Explain that it will be dark when you do this but that they are to keep silent. After everyone is silent for several seconds while sitting in the dark, turn on your flashlight. Explain that the flashlight represents a shining star. Have students tell you what they know about stars. They may share statements such as, "Stars glow." "Stars light up the sky at night." "Stars are different sizes." "Some stars are brighter than other stars."

2 Tell students they are going to discuss the word star from another context. You can take the definition of star out of the context of science. Provide students with the following statements referring to stars: "Some baseball players are all-stars." "So-and-so is a movie star." "I think so-and-so is a star in school." "So-and-so is the star player on the basketball team." Have students share their definitions of the word star reflecting on these examples. Explain that the word star is most often used to represent something positive, or special.

3 Explain to students that you think each one of them is a star. You might say, "You do your homework on time." "You are helpful to other boys and girls in the class." Distribute copies of I'm a Shining Star. Tell students that they are

to draw a picture of themselves inside the middle of the star. They can draw their face or their entire body. Each student is to show the class his/her shining star and tell why (s)he is a star. You can display your "shining stars" on the bulletin board.

Evaluation:

Have students change the lyrics of "Twinkle, Twinkle, Little Star" to reflect how they are important. They are to use their own words. The following is an example you can share with the class:

I am happy here at school.
I will not break a rule.
I do my homework everyday.
And then, I will play.

I'm a Shining Star

I'm a Shining Star

Grades Pre-K–2
- Objective 5A

| Violence Prevention |

FRIGHTFULLY STRESSFUL

Objective:

Students will tell ways to cope with stress.

Life Skill:

I will handle stress in healthful ways.

Materials:

None

Motivation:

1 Introduce the word stress. Mention that stress is a change in the body that can cause a person to feel upset. For example, a person may not be able to find a toy and become upset. When a person is under stress, that person may feel sick. The heart may beat fast. The person may sweat. The person may feel tired.

2 Explain that everyone experiences stress. Both young people and older people feel the effects of stress. Boys and girls feel stress. Be sure students understand that feeling stress is not an unusual occurrence. Read the following poem to students. The poem is titled "Little Miss Muffet."

> Little Miss Muffet
> Sat on a tuffet,
> Eating her curds and whey.
> Along came a spider,
> And sat down beside her,
> Which frightened Miss Muffet away.

3 Ask students to pretend they are Miss Muffet. Have students describe how they would have felt had they been frightened by a spider. Perhaps they will share their own experiences of being frightened. Students may share that they felt nervous and their hearts began to beat faster. They may share that they wanted to be protected. Explain that this is an example of stress.

4 Ask students to describe what they would do if they felt the effects of stress. You can provide

a situation such as feeling frightened when a person thinks a stranger is following him/her. Explain to the students that they should seek the help of a trusted adult when they feel frightened. Examples of trusted adults may be a parent, teacher, member of the clergy, or a family friend.

5 Explain that there are many other reasons that people feel stress. Ask students to share some reasons they might feel stress.

Evaluation:

Select different reasons for feeling stress that students identified and have them suggest ways to handle them. Some of the kinds of reasons that students identify may be arguments with parents, being pushed by a friend, having a pet die, and so on. Emphasize to students that there are always people in the school or community who are available to offer help.

Grades Pre-K–2
- Objective 5B

| Violence Prevention |

PHYSICAL STRESS

Objective:

Students will tell ways to cope with stress.

Life Skill:

I will handle stress in healthful ways.

Materials:

Inflated balloon, a pin

Motivation:

1 Before the class enters, blow up a balloon and keep it under your desk out of sight of your students. After the students are sitting at their desks and are quiet, reach under your desk. Using a pin, burst the balloon. Obviously, there will be a loud noise and the students will be startled although the feeling will not last long.

2 Explain to students that when the balloon burst, certain things happened inside their bodies. Ask students to share what happened. For example, students may say that their heart rate increased. They may also indicate that they became frightened and perhaps their muscles became tight because they jumped when the balloon burst.

3 Explain that when the balloon burst, they were temporarily stunned and reactions occurred inside their bodies. They were feeling the effects of stress. Explain that certain things like increased heart rates are physical changes that occur with stress. Explain that everyone experiences stress and that the body changes when stress occurs. Other physical signs that indicate a person is feeling stress may be sweating, having a dry mouth, feeling tired, and not being able to go to sleep.

4 Explain that there are many different causes of stress. Have students share ways stress may be caused in their lives. For example, they may have an argument with a friend; they may argue with a family member; their parents may have an argument; they may be moving to another neighborhood; they may be called a name by a friend. These are some reasons that a person may feel stress.

5 Explain that there are ways to deal with stress. How stress is handled may depend on the cause of the stress. For example, if a student has an argument with a friend, (s)he can speak to the friend to settle their differences. A counselor at school may help a student who is feeling the effects of stress. Ask students what they would do if they were called names by friends. Some answers may center around telling a friend that you feel hurt when you are called a name and you would appreciate it if it were stopped. You may choose to discuss other reasons why a person might feel stress and how stress can be handled healthfully.

Evaluation:

Identify different situations that might cause stress for the students. Some examples may be: forgetting to do homework, not having enough money to buy something that is needed, having your feelings hurt by a friend, worrying about a family member who is ill, having a new baby in the family. Have students share ways to deal with each of these stressors healthfully.

Inclusion:

Students can share positive ways people have been nice to them that helped reduce their feelings of stress.

STRESS BOX

Objective:

Students will tell ways to cope with stress.

Life Skill:

I will handle stress in healthful ways.

Materials:

Shoe box with a slit cut in the cover, crayons, notebook paper, a sheet for each student, magazines

Motivation:

1 Distribute a sheet of notebook paper to each student. After reviewing examples of stress such as taking a test or having an argument with another person, ask students to draw a picture of something that can cause stress. They are to use their crayons to color the picture.

2 After students have completed their drawings, have them fold their paper and insert it through the slit in the cover of the shoe box. When all the drawings are in the box, invite each student to take a drawing from the box. They are not to pull their own drawings. (Chances are students will not select their own drawings anyway.) After students have selected a drawing and have returned to their desks, have them look at the drawing they selected for a few moments. Have them think about what they see in the drawings.

3 Ask each student to share what (s)he sees. They are to tell the class what is the cause of stress in the drawing they possess. For example, a student might have a drawing that shows a person got hurt playing on the playground or a person who fell on the stairs. There are many different causes of stress. After each student has described his/her picture, that student is to suggest a way to healthfully handle the cause of the stress.

4 After each student has described his/her picture along with the cause of the stress as well as the solution, have other students in the class discuss additional ways to handle the stress. Emphasize the healthful ways stress can be handled by students.

Evaluation:

Have students find a picture in a magazine that shows a stressful situation. For example, they may find a picture of a baseball player arguing with an umpire or they may find a picture of a child crying because he or she has broken a toy. Have students tell ways that they would handle the stress shown in the picture healthfully.

Grades Pre-K–2
▪ Objective 6A

ILL-EAGLE

Objective:

Students will practice making choices that promote health.

Life Skill:

I will choose actions that are healthful for my body and mind.

Materials:

Pictures of foods from magazines, Ill-Eagle (page 269), a copy for each student

Motivation:

1 Indicate to students that there are certain kinds of substances they can take into their bodies that promote health. For example, many kinds of foods such as fruit juices, fruits, and vegetables can promote health. Many medicines when given by a responsible adult such as a parent, dentist, or physician can help improve a person's health.

2 On the other hand, there are substances that, if taken, will be harmful to a person's health. For example, taking medicines without the supervision of a responsible adult can be harmful to a person's health. Eating too many foods such as cookies that are high in calories or soda pop that is high in sugar can be harmful to a person's health.

3 Hold up pictures of foods you have cut from magazines and ask students which are healthful and which are not healthful. Ask them that if they had to make a wise choice, which foods would they select. Explain to students that some foods may not be healthful if a person eats large quantities of them. This would be true of foods such as potato chips or french fries that have a high fat content.

4 Indicate to students that foods are only one kind of substance that they take into their bod-

ies. Explain that drugs and medicines are other kinds of substances they might take at some time. Emphasize that medicines are drugs. Explain that if they take any kind of medicine without the supervision of a responsible adult, they can become ill. Distribute a copy of Ill-Eagle to each student and explain that this master shows certain kinds of substances that they should not take into their bodies. Among these substances are pills, capsules, liquid medicines, and medicines in syringes. Tell students to place an X through the picture of the medicines they should not take unless given by a responsible adult. Then have students count the number of Xs and write that number in the space provided.

Evaluation:

Review student answers. Have students suggest the names of the healthful products and the products that were not healthful as shown on the master and on the pictures of foods from the magazines.

Multicultural Infusion:

When showing the class different kinds of foods, include some that are common in different countries.

Inclusion:

Identify any of the foods in the pictures and any of the drugs on the master that the students do not recognize.

Ill-Eagle

Grades Pre-K–2
▪ Objective 6B

BEE WISE

Objective:

Students will practice making choices that promote health.

Life Skill:

I will choose actions that help my health.

Materials:

Candy inside an open candy wrapper, picture of a syringe, Bee Wise (page 271), a copy for each student

Motivation:

1 Out of curiosity, students at this age may be tempted to pick up any object they find. For example, a boy or girl may find a candy wrapper with candy inside. (S)he may think it is safe to eat the candy.

2 Tell the class that on your way to school today, you found a bar of candy on the sidewalk. Show the candy with the open wrapper to the students. Ask students, "Would you eat this candy?" Have students share why they made the choices they did. After discussing student answers, stress that they should not eat the candy even if the wrapper was not open. Explain that there is no way that a person could know where the candy came from or why it was on the sidewalk. Emphasize that they should not eat anything that they find on the street. Even if someone offers them candy, they should not take anything from a stranger.

3 Students may find other objects about which they may be curious. For example, they may find a syringe that a drug user has discarded on the sidewalk or in a playground. Show students what a syringe looks like and remind them that when they received an injection in the doctor's office, the doctor or nurse used a syringe. Emphasize that in a doctor's office, a syringe is used only once and then discarded

in such a way that it can never be used again. A syringe should never be touched. A syringe may contain harmful germs. (HIV often is found inside syringes.) Warn students that if they find a syringe they should not touch it. They should tell an adult so that the adult can dispose of the syringe. Students should also be warned to avoid taking any kind of capsule or pill and to avoid tasting any liquid that they find or that is given to them by a stranger. Emphasize that they should take substances only from a parent or guardian, a dentist, a nurse or doctor, or other trusted adult.

4 Distribute copies of Bee Wise. Instruct students to connect the "Nice Bee" to those products that are safe to touch or taste and the "Mean Bee" to those products that are not safe to touch or taste.

Evaluation:

Review the students' answers on the masters and calculate their scores.

Bee Wise

Instructions: Connect the "Nice Bee" to those products that are safe to touch or taste and the "Mean Bee" to those products that are not safe to touch or taste.

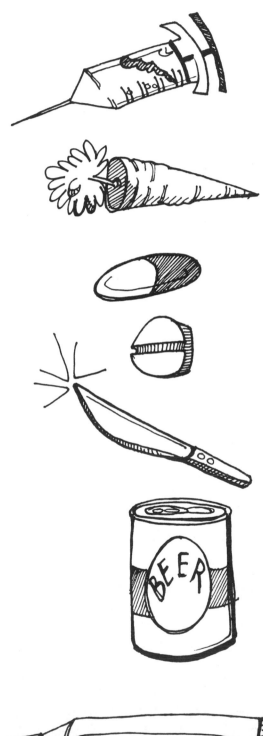

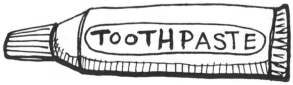

Grades Pre-K–2
▪ Objective 6C

REFUSE TO USE

Objective:

Students will practice making choices that promote health.

Life Skill:

I will be able to support my choices when asked to do something that is not healthful, safe, legal, or is against the wishes of a responsible adult.

Materials:

None

Motivation:

1 Ask students if they have ever been asked to do something they felt was wrong. Have students share how they handled the situation. Students should be able to tell about the pressure of telling a friend they did not want to do something they felt was wrong.

2 Explain to students that it is difficult to say NO to someone when you feel that the person wants you to do something harmful. Have students share if this has happened to them.

3 Explain that sometimes people may try to encourage others to do something harmful by making certain kinds of statements. Tell students you are going to make similar kinds of statements and you want them to reply with a statement that will counteract your statement. Explain what it means to counteract (to counteract means to neutralize or make ineffective.) For example, someone may say, "You're chicken if you don't try this." A statement that would counteract might be, "I don't care if you call me chicken because I don't want to do something that I think is wrong or that would harm my health."

4 The following are examples of statements that students might hear when encouraged to try

something that is harmful, unsafe, illegal, against the wishes of a responsible adult, and shows a lack of self-respect. For each statement, have students come up with a statement that counteracts and that indicates a wise choice.

"Try it. You'll like it."
"Come on. No one will find out."
"Everyone else has tried it."
"It's really fun."
"Everyone will think you're cool."
"If you try it, I'll really be your best friend."

Evaluation:

Have students tell about other similar kinds of statements they have heard used. For each statement they identify, they are to come up with ways to counteract. Students can practice making statements and counteracting them with each other.

Grades Pre-K–2
- Objective 7A

SAY NO

Objective:

Students will practice ways to say NO to harmful choices.

Life Skill:

I will refuse to do things that are harmful to my health.

Materials:

None

Motivation:

1 Explain to students that there are many situations in which they should be prepared to refuse to do anything that can be harmful to their health. Ways to refuse to do something harmful or dangerous need to be demonstrated. Choose a volunteer and ask that student to come to the front of the room. Whisper to the student that you are going to pretend to be a friend. Tell this student that you are going to ask him/her to do something that you know his/her parents would not allow him/her to do. Tell this student to answer NO to what you ask him/her to do. Then aloud say, "Let's cross the street." Have the class observe how the student responded. Most likely, the student responded NO in a low voice, did not look at you, and seemed a bit timid.

2 Emphasize to students that if they are asked to do something that is not safe, they must respond in a way that makes it appear that they mean what they say. They need to show that they are in charge of their decisions. If they do this, it will help keep others from trying to get them to do things that are harmful or dangerous.

3 Explain to students that you are going to make different statements. If the statement is something that would be safe and healthful to do,

the students are to clap their hands once to show their decision and approval. If the statement is something that would be harmful or dangerous to do, the students are to say NO. When saying NO, students are to stand, look at you, and say NO in a loud and firm voice.

4 For each statement, have the students respond as mentioned.

> "Smoke a cigarette." (NO)
> "Read a book." (Clap)
> "Push a friend." (NO)
> "Go with a stranger." (NO)
> "Share your toys." (Clap)

Evaluation:

Review the answers with students and have them share the reasons for their choices. Emphasize the importance of saying NO in such a way that the other person knows they mean it and that they are in charge of their decisions. Have students identify other situations in which they would say NO.

Grades Pre-K—2
- Objective 7B

Violence Prevention

A-PEER WISE

Objective:

Students will practice ways to say NO to harmful choices.

Life Skill:

I will say NO to someone who wants me to do something that could harm my health.

Materials:

None

Motivation:

1 Explain that each day everyone must make choices. Ask students what choices they had to make today. Some students will indicate that they had to choose what to eat for breakfast. Others will indicate they had to decide about what to wear to school. Have students share the choices they made today.

2 After students have shared information about their choices, indicate that sometimes people must make choices about what may be safe and what may not be safe. Read the following poem titled, "Jack Be Nimble."

> Jack be nimble,
> Jack be quick;
> Jack jump over
> The candlestick.

3 Explain to students that Jack may have done something dangerous. If there was a burning candle in the candlestick, Jack could have burned himself. Jack did something that might have been dangerous to his health. Jack made the choice to jump over the candlestick.

4 Have students share situations they know about in which someone was doing something dangerous. They can share something they have seen in a movie or a situation that happened to a friend. After sharing each situation, students are to tell how getting into that situa-

tion could have been avoided. For example, a person who is pressured to cross the street when cars are nearby could say that (s)he would cross only at the corner where there is a light.

5 Tell students they will play a game called "Feeling Proud." Each student will identify a situation that could be harmful to their health and they are to tell how they would avoid that situation. Each student must begin the statement with the words, "I feel proud because . . . ." You can provide the following example. "I feel proud because my friend wanted me to take candy from a stranger but I convinced my friend we should run away."

Evaluation:

After students have identified situations that might be harmful, you can reinforce how dangerous situations can be avoided. Review the importance of learning how to say NO in a firm, loud voice.

Grades Pre-K–2
- Objective 7C

REFUSAL TAG

Objective:

Students will practice ways to say NO to harmful choices.

Life Skill:

I will say NO to situations that can be harmful to my health.

Materials:

Record player and record, or cassette recorder and tape

Motivation:

1 Explain to students that they are going to play a game that will enable them to practice saying NO to unsafe or dangerous situations. The game is going to be called Refusal Tag. This game is similar to Duck, Duck, Goose. Before starting the game, suggest some examples of unsafe or dangerous situations such as taking candy from a stranger, being asked to smoke a cigarette, or being asked to steal something.

2 Have the class sit in a circle on the floor. Everyone faces the center of the circle. You will begin the game by selecting one person to be "It." As you play a song, "It" will walk around the outside of the circle. When you choose, stop the music. When the music stops, "It" must identify an unsafe or dangerous situation. "It" will then tap the closest person on the shoulder and run back to his/her spot in the circle and sit down. The person who is tagged is the new "It." The new "It" must think of a healthful way to handle the unsafe or dangerous situation that was named. For example, if the first "It" said, "Someone wants you to smoke a cigarette.", the new "It" might say,"NO, I don't want to smoke and I never will." Now the new "It" must walk around the circle, wait until the music stops, identify an unsafe or dangerous situation and tap a new "It" on the shoulder.

3 Repeat this process so that the class has identified many unsafe and dangerous situations and students have had the opportunity to identify healthful responses.

Evaluation:

Make a list of the different situations that students identified. Then review the healthful responses. Have students share other responses that could be used in the different situations. Emphasize that there is not just one correct response for each situation.

Grades Pre-K–2
▪ Objective 8A

MY FAMILY

Objective:

Students will describe ways in which families and friends help influence decisions.

Life Skill:

I will follow rules set by responsible family members.

Materials:

Crayons, old magazines, My Family, (page 277), a copy for each student

Motivation:

1 Bring old magazines to class and cut out pictures that show families engaged in healthful activities. Be sure to show different kinds of families such as single-parent families, families with both parents, families with one or several children, families with grandparents, and families of different cultures.

2 Show the class the pictures of families. For each picture, have students tell what they think the people in the family are doing to enjoy themselves and each other. Have students also tell how the families differ.

3 Explain to students that there are many different kinds of families and that all family members can spend meaningful times with each other. Explain that each member of a family has a responsibility to keep other members safe, regardless of the activity the family is enjoying. For example, you might show a family at a cookout and point out that the young children in the family are kept away from the fire so that they do not become harmed.

4 Emphasize that parents or guardians have a responsibility to help protect their children from harm. Children can appreciate the decisions their parents or guardians must make to help keep their children safe.

5 Distribute copies of My Family and have students draw a picture that shows them doing something with one or more of their family members. Emphasize that their pictures should show that they are doing something enjoyable and also safe.

6 After students complete their pictures, have them share what they have drawn. Students should explain not only what they are doing but also why it is safe.

Evaluation:

You may choose to use the word choice instead of decision in the evaluation. Regardless of the word you select, have students share how their family members influence them to make responsible or wise choices. For example, a parent may insist that when riding a bicycle, a helmet must be worn. Thus, when riding a bicycle each time, wearing a helmet becomes an automatic choice. Have students share examples of choices with the class.

Multicultural Infusion:

Have students share activities they do with family members that may be culturally specific. For example, students may go to certain places with family members on special occasions. Have students tell how these are activities that are healthful and how their families encourage them to make wise choices.

My Family

Instructions: Draw a picture of your family being happy and safe.

Grades Pre-K–2
- Objective 8B

| Violence Prevention |

COLOR ME HEALTHY

Objective:

Students will describe ways in which families and friends influence decisions.

Life Skill:

I will follow behaviors set by responsible adults.

Materials:

A dropper, glass of water, red food coloring

Motivation:

1 Show students a transparent glass that has water in it. Explain that the water represents a healthy person. Show the students a dropper that contains a clear liquid (water). Explain that the clear liquid represents healthful choices that a healthy person might choose. Explain that you are going to add drops from the dropper to the water in the glass. Tell students that they are to think of healthful choices that a healthy person might choose. As examples, you can tell students that the liquid you will drop into the water might represent healthful foods, exercises, being friendly to others, or ways to protect themselves, and so on. Specific examples might be eating apples, wearing helmets when riding a bicycle, or saying thank you when others do something nice for you.

2 Ask students to provide comments with each drop you add to the glass. Have them observe what happens to the color of the water in the glass. The water does not change color. Explain that the water is clean and safe. It has not been harmed by anything you added because you added healthful items. Next, fill the dropper with red food coloring. Explain that what is now in the

dropper represents harmful choices. Examples may be harmful drugs, unhealthful foods, and unsafe acts such as running into the street between parked cars. As students share an examples of unhealthful choices, place a drop of food coloring into the glass of water. Explain to students that the color of the water is now changing. The water may not be clean and safe.

3 Reinforce that if you had added only healthful choices to the water, the water would not have been harmed. Explain that you made decisions to cause harm to the water. Explain to students that adults, such as parents and teachers, make decisions to help keep children healthy. But sometimes, people can try to influence others to make decisions that can be harmful to health. Just like the water can be harmed, so can a person be harmed if (s)he make choices that are not healthful.

4 Have students share how they have learned from others to make healthful choices. The others might be family members, teachers, or friends. Explain that when others help them make healthful choices, they are helping them to be healthy. Explain to students that if they are concerned about their health, they might want to share their concerns with a responsible adult, such as a parent or guardian, a teacher, or a school counselor.

Evaluation:

Have students draw a picture of a responsible adult they trust. They can then share their pictures with the class and tell why that person is someone they trust. Explain to students that they can get help from responsible adults if they feel they are in danger or feel threatened. Explain that if they do not get help from the first person they talk with, they can go to another person.

Inclusion:

You can have students take turns placing drops inside the water. Students can observe more closely how the food coloring spreads throughout the water. Be sure students understand the analogy of how healthful choices did not change the color of the water, but unhealthful choices did.

Grades Pre-K–2
▪ Objective 8C

HAPPY GREETINGS

Objective:

Students will describe ways in which families and friends influence decisions.

Life Skill:

I will follow the advice of responsible adults.

Materials:

Construction paper, a sheet for each student, crayons, index cards, a card for each student

Motivation:

1 Ask students if they have ever received a greeting card. Most likely, every student has received such a card. Ask students to remember what the occasion was when they received a greeting card. Most likely, they will remember getting a birthday card. Explain that there are many other occasions besides birthdays when people receive greeting cards. People receive greeting cards when they graduate or when they get married, for example.

2 Inform students that they are going to have the opportunity to make their own greeting cards. But their greeting cards will be for someone in their family. Their cards will have a theme, just like greeting cards they would buy in a store. The theme of their greeting cards will emphasize appreciation to a particular person for helping them stay healthy.

3 Explain that each student will write a poem and draw a picture on his/her greeting card. Distribute sheets of construction paper and instruct students to fold their sheet in half so that it takes the shape of a greeting card. To clarify what the task will be, prepare a sample greeting card. For example, on the cover of your card, it may say "To My Totally Awesome Mother." The inside of the card may have the following short poem:

I just wanted to say,
Having a mother like you,
Makes me feel good today.
You've taught me that keeping my
lungs healthy is no joke.
That's why I will never smoke.
Instead, I will keep my body in shape.
And from exercise, I'll never escape.

4 After students complete their cards, they can share them with the class before taking them home.

5 You can use this activity to emphasize that responsible adults, such as parents and teachers, want young people to take care of themselves and to grow up to be healthy adults. One important aspect of being healthy is to avoid using harmful drugs. Explain that drugs such as tobacco, alcohol, marijuana, and other drugs are harmful and can be dangerous to a person's body and mind.

Evaluation:

Write the following statement on the chalkboard: "I pledge to. . . ." Give each student an index card and have him/her copy this statement across the top of his/her card. Have each student complete the sentence with a healthful choice that a responsible adult would expect of them. For example, a statement may read, "I pledge to avoid ever using drugs that are harmful to me." Have each student sign his/her name on the card. Post these cards on the bulletin board.

280

Violence Prevention

TAIL-OR MADE

Objective:

Students will describe ways to be a good friend.

Life Skill:

I will practice ways to be a good friend.

Materials:

Crayons, Sharing a Tail, (page 282), a copy for each student

Motivation:

1 Explain to students that being a good friend is very important. Good friends help others. Good friends get along well. Good friends share toys. Have students share how they are good friends by asking them ways they show how they have been a good friend. For example, some students may say that they share their toys with others. Some may say they walk to school with a friend. Others may say they play with their friends during recess.

2 Tell students that they are going to have the opportunity to do something nice for a friend. Tell them you are going to assign each student in the class a secret friend. List partner names on a sheet of paper, being sure each student has a secret friend. If there is an odd number of students, you can be a partner to one of the students. As you go around the room, whisper the name of a secret friend to each student. Emphasize that each student is to keep his/her friend's name secret.

3 Distribute copies of Sharing a Tail. Instruct students they are to color the tail in any way they wish. They can make stripes on the tail, use different colors, or make any kind of design they wish. After the entire class has completed this task, each student will give his/her tail to another student. After the tails have been

exchanged, explain that students have shown they are good friends by sharing something with others.

4 Explain that good friends share things with others. It is important to share positive or good things with others. Explain that good friends do not share things that can be harmful to a person's health. For example, good friends would not want others to share in smoking cigarettes or using other harmful drugs. Sharing cigarettes and other kinds of drugs is not something good friends do because drugs can harm a person's health.

Evaluation:

Write the following statement on the chalkboard. "A good friend will not. . . ." Have students complete this sentence by stating something a good friend would not do. For example, "A good friend will not push someone else." Students should be able to differentiate between healthful and harmful behaviors.

Sharing a Tail

• Objective 9B

Violence Prevention

One, Two, A Friend for You

Objective:

Students will describe ways to be a good friend.

Life Skill:

I will practice ways to be a good friend.

Materials:

Paper, pencils

Motivation:

1 Ask students if they have ever heard of the nursery rhyme, "One, Two, Buckle My Shoe." You can tell students the first few lines for this nursery rhyme. It is as follows:

One, two,
Buckle my shoe;
Three, four,
Shut the door;
Five, six,
Pick up sticks;
Seven, eight,
Lay them straight;

2 Tell students that they are going to learn a new version of this nursery rhyme. However, this new version will emphasize the importance of being a good friend. Have students sing the song using the new words. The new words for this song are as follows:

One, two,
I like you;
Three, four,
I'll smile more;
Five, six,
I'll eat a mix;
Seven, eight,
Of foods that are great;

3 Have students number down from one through eight on a sheet of paper leaving some space between numbers. Students are to draw

friendly faces next to each number so that the number of friendly faces matches the number to its left. For example, a student will draw one friendly face next to number one, two friendly faces next to number two, and so on. Collect the papers and check that the numbers match.

Evaluation:

Have each student select a number from one through five. You can have them pick from random numbers in an envelope. For each number, students are to tell ways to be a good friend. For example, a student who selects the number three will tell three ways to be a good friend; a student who selects the number five will tell five ways to be a good friend, and so on.

Grades Pre-K–2
- Objective 9C

| Violence Prevention |

THE FRIEND-SHIP

Objective:

Students will describe ways to be a good friend.

Life Skill:

I will practice ways to be a good friend.

Materials:

Crayons, The Friend-Ship (page 285), a copy for each student

Motivation:

1 Have students define the word friend. Explain that a friend is a person whom you know and like. A friend also is someone who cares about your well-being and wants you to be healthy.

2 Have students identify people whom they would consider to be their friends. These people can be those outside the classroom. Explain that friends do not necessarily need to be someone their age. For example, a teacher may be their friend. The school nurse may be their friend. A firefighter can be a friend. Also explain that friends can be of different cultures. Friends may have different religious beliefs. However, a good friend should always care about you and do things for you that will help keep you healthy and safe.

3 Distribute copies of The Friend-Ship. In each window of the ship, have students draw a face of a person they consider to be a friend. Below each face they are to write who that friend is. They can write the name of the person, such as Donna, or who that person is, such as My Teacher. Have students share their pictures with the class and tell who each friend is.

Evaluation:

Have students tell at least one characteristic about each person they named as a good

friend. For example, "Brad is a good friend because he calls me when I'm absent from school to see if I'm feeling O.K."

Multicultural Infusion:

Have students include one person of another culture in a window of their ship. This person should be a friend. Have students share why this person is a friend. Emphasize that friends of different cultures are the same as other friends.

The Friend-Ship

Grades Pre-K–2
- Objective 10A

WHICH IS HARMFUL?

Objective:

Students will describe ways medicines can be healthful and harmful.

Life Skill:

I will not take a medicine unless it is given to me by a responsible adult.

Materials:

Empty containers of a variety of over-the-counter medicines, old magazines

Motivation:

1 The use and misuse of over-the-counter (OTC) medicines are a major problem for people of all ages, especially young children. Many young children accidentally consume OTC medicines. Perhaps the medicines were not placed out of reach or perhaps they were thought to be candy. Taking medicines accidentally can prove to be harmful, particularly to young children since their bodies are not mature. As a result, the medicine can have an intense effect.

2 Show your students empty containers of different kinds of OTC medicines. Display these on your desk. Also show students other kinds of containers or packages. For example, you may show students food containers or packages of candy. Explain that medicines can be very helpful when taken under the supervision of a responsible adult such as a parent, school nurse, or doctor. But medicines taken without adult supervision can be harmful. They can cause a person to become dizzy and sick, or even to have trouble breathing, if they are not used properly. Even medicines that are used properly can cause a person not to feel well. If this happens, an adult should be told and the medicine no longer should be taken until a doctor has been notified.

3 Place the OTC medicine containers on your desk along with food packages. Ask students to select which are the foods and which are the medicines. Vary the kind and number of food and medicine containers you have on your desk. In addition to having students differentiate between medicines and foods, have them count the number of medicines and foods you lay out on the desk. In this way, you are incorporating math skills with the lesson. Emphasize the dangers of using medicines when not given by a responsible adult.

4 Have students be aware of the danger of taking medicine from another person. Stress that they should not take any medicine except from a parent or guardian, a dentist, a doctor or nurse, or a school counselor.

Evaluation:

You can have students cut out pictures from magazines that show different kinds of products. These products can be OTCs such as aspirin, tablets for upset stomach, or different kinds of first aid products. They also should find pictures of products that are not drugs, such as foods or drinks. Have students select the number of foods or medicines that correspond with a number that you assign to them. For example, you may tell students to cut out three medicines and write the number three. You may then ask students to cut out five foods and write the number five. Review students' completion of this assignment for math skills as well as for skills in being able to differentiate between medicines and products that are not medicines.

Inclusion:

When students count the medicines that are on the desk, you can count with them.

Grades Pre-K–2
- Objective 10B

WHICH IS WHICH?

Objective:

Students will describe ways medicines can be helpful and harmful.

Life Skill:

I will not take something into my body that I know is not safe.

Materials:

Poster paper, glue, four different types of OTC pills/capsules that may also look like candy, four different kinds of candy that can be mistaken as pills/capsules

Motivation:

1 Divide a large piece of poster paper into eight equal sections. In four different sections, glue an OTC pill or capsule. In four other sections, glue a piece of candy. Under each OTC medicine and each candy, write if that product is a medicine or candy. Temporarily, cover what you have written with a strip of paper.

2 Tell students they are going to try to guess which items are medicines and which are candies. Students will find that it may be difficult to distinguish between the two. Hold up each section and, as volunteers guess, remove the strip of paper that indicates a medicine or candy.

3 Review the answers students gave. It will become obvious that students will not always be able to distinguish between what is a medicine and what is a candy. Explain that if they took the medicine and thought they were taking a candy, they might cause harm to their bodies. They might become dizzy. They might feel tired or drowsy. They might experience a rapid heart rate.

4 Stress to students that a person should not distinguish between products like medicines and

candy by appearance only. This is the reason it is important never to take something from another person if there is doubt about what that product is. Suppose a person were to find something in their home, and the person did not know what that product was. That person should not put that product in his/her mouth. The product may be a medicine. Emphasize also that a person should never take something from a stranger. A stranger would not care about the student's health and might give him/her something that could be harmful to the body.

Evaluation:

Suggest different scenarios for the students and ask them what they would do if they were in that situation. For example, while walking in the playground, you find a bottle with what looks like candy inside. What would you do? (Bring it to a responsible adult and do not take what is inside.)

Grades Pre-K–2
- Objective 10C

OK, NOT OK

Objective:

Students will describe ways medicines can be healthful or harmful.

Life Skill:

I will not take anything that is not safe into my body.

Materials:

Pictures from magazines of different medicines and foods, one envelope, one shoe box with the picture of a smiley face glued on it and another shoe box with the picture of a sad face glued on it

Motivation:

1 From magazines, cut out enough pictures of medicines and foods so that each student in the class will have either a picture of a medicine or a picture of a food. Place the pictures in an envelope and pass the envelope around the room. Ask each student to select one picture from the envelope.

2 Explain to students that the box with the smiley face represents a healthy or safe choice. The box with the sad face represents a choice that might not be safe.

3 Emphasize to the students that although some of the pictures are of medicines and that medicines can be healthful and safe, especially when given by a responsible adult, you would like the medicine pictures to be placed inside the box with the sad face. The reason is that the medicine has not been given to them by a responsible adult. The students who have a picture of a food are to place their pictures in the box with the smiley face. The reason is that foods are usually safe to eat and that permission from an adult is not needed in order for a food to be consumed.

4 Ask each student to examine his/her picture and determine in which box the picture belongs. As each student places his/her picture in the box, (s)he is to tell something about the food or medicine in the picture. For example, if a student has a picture of a food, (s)he might indicate if it is a snack food or a breakfast food. You might help a student who has a picture of a medicine by identifying the medicine and reading the label if it is evident. Perhaps the unsafe features of the medicine are listed on the label or on the page on which it was advertised.

Evaluation:

Describe criteria that were used to differentiate between medicines and food. Determine how often students were able to place the items in the appropriate boxes.

Multicultural Infusion:

When selecting pictures of foods, try to include some foods from different cultures. If students are not familiar with a particular food that is pictured, explain about the culture that food represents.

SCIENCE STUDIES

YUCKY BODY

Objective:

Students will describe the harmful effects of tobacco.

Life Skill:

I will not use tobacco products.

Materials:

Two transparencies made from a magazine picture, transparency projector, yellow marker, onion, full-length picture of a person

Motivation:

1 Explain that cigarette smoke is harmful to many parts of a person's body. Through a number of activities, you will demonstrate some of the harmful effects of cigarette smoke.

2 The first demonstration concerns the effect of cigarette smoke on teeth. Select a large photo from a magazine that shows a person with a nice smile. The person's teeth should be visible. Make two transparencies of this picture. Leave one transparency as is, but on the other, color the teeth yellow using a yellow marker.

3 Show the first overlay (the person with the smile but without the yellow teeth) and ask students if they think this person has a nice smile. Ask students why they think this person has a nice smile. Answers will center around the white teeth this person has. Then show the next transparency. Students will notice that this person looks exactly the same except the teeth are different. This person has yellow teeth. Ask students to describe how this person looks. Students will most likely indicate that the person does not look as nice as the first one. This person has yellow teeth. Yellow teeth are not attractive. Indicate that yellow teeth can be caused by smoking cigarettes. Explain that the

harmful ingredients in cigarette smoke causes teeth to become yellow. The ingredients in the smoke also harm the gums around the teeth.

4 Have the students observe you cutting the onion. Be close enough to the students so that their eyes may begin to tear. Ask students what it feels like to have their eyes tear. Explain that when a person smokes, the smoke irritates the eyes and the eyes may begin to tear. This is an annoying experience and causes a person to feel uncomfortable.

5 Explain that these are only two effects of cigarette smoke on a person's body. There are many other effects that are even more dangerous. Explain that cigarette smoking causes persons to have difficulty breathing and that cigarette smoking is damaging to a person's heart. Cigarette smoking is the single most preventable cause of death in the United States. Cigarette smoking is a major cause of cancer.

Evaluation:

Using a full-length picture of a person, have students identify different body parts that are harmed by cigarette smoking. As you point to different body parts, students are to name each. The body parts to which you can point are the eyes, teeth, heart, and lungs. Pointing to the heart and lungs can be confusing. To avoid this, point with one finger to the chest to indicate the heart. Place an open hand on the chest to indicate the lungs.

SMOKING MUDDIES THE WATER

Objective:

Students will describe the harmful effects of tobacco.

Life Skill:

I will not use tobacco products.

Materials:

Large glass of water, large glass of water with soil mixed in it (consistency should be like paste)

Motivation:

1 Show the glass of clear water to the class. Explain that the water in this glass would be safe to drink. To this glass of water, add some of the muddy water from the other glass.

2 Ask the students if anyone would volunteer to come to the front of the class and drink from the first glass of water that had been safe to drink. Of course, no one will volunteer. Ask the class why they would not want to drink the water that is filled with mud. Students will indicate that the water is dirty and that if they consumed it, they might get sick.

3 Praise the students for not wanting to drink the water that would harm their bodies. However, remind students that there are many people who smoke cigarettes. When people smoke cigarettes, they take harmful substances into their bodies. They harm their lungs and other body organs. Explain that the tar in cigarette smoke is somewhat like the mud. Tar may be dark brown and sticky. The tar that is inhaled in smoke affects the linings of the lungs and makes breathing difficult.

4 Have students share why someone would take a harmful substance like cigarette smoke into his/her body. Emphasize the fact that a person need never begin to smoke.

Evaluation:

Have students practice using refusal skills they might use if someone tried to get them to smoke a cigarette. Demonstrate refusal skills such as saying NO in a firm voice and looking directly at the other person. Have students come to the front of the room and practice using refusal skills.

A STIMULATING EFFECT

Objective:

Students will describe the harmful effects of tobacco.

Life Skill:

I will not smoke cigarettes.

Materials:

Watch with a second hand

Motivation:

1 Ask students if they have ever heard of the word stimulant. Explain in simple terms that a stimulant is something that causes the body's activities to increase. For example, while a student is sitting at a desk, his/her heart is probably beating between 60 and 70 beats each minute. To demonstrate what 60 heartbeats per minute is like, use a watch with a second hand and open and close your fist at a rate of one per second. Do this for one minute. Have students count each time you close your fist.

2 Using the watch with a second hand, have students hold one hand up in the air. Have them open and close their fists at a rate of one per second, or 60 times in one minute. As students do this, they are to count. (Students may experience fatigue in their arms and hands doing this exercise.)

3 Now, explain to students that they are going to repeat this activity and pretend they have a drug, like tobacco, that is a stimulant inside their bodies. Explain that when a person smokes, his/her usual heartbeat rate increases about 20 beats per minute. To illustrate this, have students at first open and close their fists 20 times in 15 seconds. Students should be able to appreciate how much faster they had to work to keep up this pace. Encourage students to try to maintain this rate for one minute. Use the second hand of the watch to

make sure the students are opening and closing their fists 20 times every 15 seconds.

4 After one minute of opening and closing their fists 80 times, have students describe how their hands feel. They will most likely indicate that their hands feel tired. Indicate that their heart muscle contracts in a similar fashion. The heart muscle must beat every moment they are alive. Explain that when a person smokes a cigarette, the heart muscle must work harder that it should. This extra work can harm the heart over a period of time. This is the reason that people who smoke have an increased risk of heart disease.

Evaluation:

Have students consider the importance of having a healthy heart and of protecting the heart so that it does not work harder than it should. Ask students to suggest ways that an unhealthy heart might affect their lives. For example, smoking could interfere with the ability to breathe easily, to ride a bike, to run, and to resist disease.

Grades Pre-K–2
- Objective 12A

WHICH IS THE ALCOHOL PRODUCT?

Objective:

Students will describe the harmful effects of alcohol.

Life Skill:

I will not drink alcohol.

Materials:

Empty containers that contained alcohol, empty containers that contained drinks such as fruit juice or soda pop

Motivation:

1 Explain that alcohol is a drug that is harmful to the body. Students should be made aware of the different kinds of products that contain alcohol. Emphasize that it is not legal for people their age to drink alcohol. However, your students may have seen alcohol products in their home or on television.

2 Explain that there are different kinds of products that contain alcohol. Some examples are wine and beer. Explain that some kinds of drinks such as milk and fruit juice are foods. However, although alcohol is a drink, it is not a food. Show students different containers for drinks they enjoy. For example, you can show them a cardboard container for fruit juice, a container for milk, a bottle for soda pop, and a can for fruit juice. Have students observe these containers and identify that their contents were safe to drink.

3 Show students different containers that contained alcohol. Some examples may be a beer can and bottles that contained wine or wine coolers. Point out if the shapes of the bottles that contained alcoholic beverages differ from the bottles that contained fruit juice or soda pop. While your students may not be able to read, they may recognize the word alcohol. Write this word on the chalkboard and point

it out where it is written on the beer cans or othercontainers.

4 Explain that drinking alcohol, especially at their age, is very dangerous. Alcohol is a drug and, like other drugs, it can harm inner body parts. Alcohol also can affect the way a person thinks. Persons who drink alcohol can have accidents and become injured.

5 Line up the different containers on your desk. They should be lined up facing students and should be lined up at random. When you point to a product that is safe to drink, students are to give a thumbs up sign. When you point to a container that contained alcohol, students are to give a thumbs down signal. When students give a thumbs up signal, they are to yell, "Hurrah." When they give a thumbs down signal, they are to yell, "Boo."

Evaluation:

Observe how accurately students differentiate between the products that contain alcohol and those products that do not contain alcohol. Have students indicate why they should not choose drinks that contain alcohol.

SLOW DOWN

Objective:

Students will describe the harmful effects of alcohol.

Life Skill:

I will not drink beverages that contain alcohol.

Materials:

Pencil and paper for each student

Motivation:

1 Explain to the class that alcohol is a dangerous drug. When a person drinks alcohol, many changes occur inside the body. This person cannot think clearly and may become forgetful. Alcohol also slows the way different parts of the body work. The heartbeat slows. A person cannot react to changes quickly. Muscles cannot move body parts the way they normally do.

2 The following experiment will demonstrate how drinking alcohol interferes with the way muscles work. Explain that almost everything we do requires the use of muscles. Even simple tasks like writing require the use of muscles. Have students print their first and last names on a sheet of paper. Then they are to repeat this task by printing their names again using their opposite hand. Thus a person who usually prints with his/her left hand will print with his/her right hand and vice versa.

3 After students have had the opportunity to do this activity, analyze what occurred. Students will indicate that it took longer to print their names and the letters were not as clear when they had to use the hand they usually do not use.

4 Explain that what students experienced was an experiment in which their hand muscles did not work as they usually do when a simple task was performed. By writing with their opposite hand, students could not function as they normally would. If alcohol were inside a person's body, that person would not be able to use his/her body muscles the way they usually work in a smooth and coordinated manner. Explain that this experiment illustrates how alcohol can affect a person's ability to function.

Evaluation:

Have students identify a task they perform each day and then have them imagine how alcohol might interfere with their ability to complete that task in an efficient and safe manner.

Grades Pre-K–2
- Objective 12C

UNCLEAR PICTURE

Objective:

Students will describe the harmful effects of alcohol.

Life Skill:

I will not drink alcohol.

Materials:

A ball made of a sheet of crumpled paper, one sheet of single-ply tissue paper

Motivation:

1 Review some of the physical effects that alcohol has on the body. Examples are blurred vision, slurred speech, poor muscle coordination, lowered heartbeat rate, and loss of body heat due to dilated blood vessels near the surface of the skin.

2 Perform the following activity to show that alcohol can blur vision and interfere with the ability of muscles to function normally. Select two students to come to the front of the class. One student is to stand behind the other and hold a sheet of single-ply tissue paper over the other person's eyes. The person standing behind the other can hold the tissue at two ends to cover the eyes.

3 Stand about ten feet away from the person who has the tissue covering his/her eyes. This person should be able to see you but not clearly. Use a paper ball made from crumpled paper. Tell the person who has the tissue over his/her eyes to try to catch the ball when you throw it. This person may or may not be able to catch the ball. Regardless, this person will feel uncomfortable trying to catch the ball. This person will also appear to be clumsy or uncoordinated.

4 Explain to the class that alcohol produces a similar reaction to that of the person with the

tissue over the eyes. Alcohol can cause blurred vision as well as poor muscle coordination.

Evaluation:

Have students identify tasks people their age perform each day. For example, they may ride bicycles. They may play on playground equipment. They may read books. Have students imagine and describe what might happen if they tried to do the same activities and alcohol was in their body. Emphasize how important it is to be able to think clearly and have good use of their muscles.

Trash That Drug

Objective:

Students will name illegal drugs and their harmful effects.

Life Skill:

I will not use harmful drugs.

Materials:

Empty cigarette packs, empty beer cans, and empty prescription and over-the-counter (OTC) drug containers

Motivation:

1 Students have been exposed to the sight of many illegal drugs on television shows, in the movies, or perhaps in their neighborhood. Explain to students that illegal drugs are those that are not used the way they should be or that are against the law. For example, it is not legal for people their age to drink beer, to smoke, or even to use medicines unless the medicines have been given to them by a responsible adult such as a doctor or a parent.

2 Explain to students that they should not use drugs because they can be harmful. For example, some drugs, like the alcohol in beer, can make a person feel dizzy and sick. The tobacco in cigarettes will make a person cough and cause difficulty in breathing. Certain drugs that are medicines can make a person feel sick if the medicine is taken without the supervision of an adult.

3 Explain that no drug should ever be taken by a student unless that drug is in the form of a medicine given by a responsible adult. Explain that the following game is to help students recognize what certain kinds of drugs look like. Emphasize that tobacco and alcohol are two kinds of drugs. Medicines are drugs. Explain that they are going to play the game "Trash

That Drug." Each student is to come to the front of the room and you will give him/her an empty drug container. As each student takes the drug container, the entire class must say in unison, "Trash that drug." After students make this statement, the student holding the container must throw the drug container in the trash.

4 Do this several times until at least half the students in the class have had a chance to throw a drug container in the trash. You can remove the containers from the trash so that they can be reused.

Evaluation:

Be sure students can differentiate between drugs and other types of products such as bars of soap or packages of tissues. You may choose to show different empty packages of other products and have the class differentiate between drugs and products that are not drugs. This also would be a good time to review with students some of the dangers of the different kinds of drugs. For example, the OTC medicines may have warnings about the possible dangers to a person's health. Review some of these dangers with the class but in terms they will understand. The words you use will depend on the drugs. For example, a medicine label that says, "May cause drowsiness" can be interpreted to mean that the medicine can cause a person to become tired and sleepy when (s)he ordinarily would not be tired and sleepy.

Grades Pre-K–2
▪ Objective 13B

ROW, ROW, ROW YOUR BOAT

Objective:

Students will name illegal drugs and their harmful effects.

Life Skill:

I will not use drugs unless they are medicines that are given to me by a responsible adult.

Materials:

None

Motivation:

1 Have students practice singing the song, "Row, Row, Row Your Boat." The words to the song are as follows:

> Row, row, row your boat
> Gently down the stream.
> Merrily, merrily, merrily, merrily
> Life is but a dream.

2 After students are familiar with the words to this song, tell them that you are going to make up new rhymes. The new rhymes will be about the dangers of using drugs. The tune will remain the same. Write the following new rhymes on the chalkboard.

> Row, row, row your boat
> Gently down the stream.
> Don't use harmful drugs
> So your eyes will keep their gleam.
> Marijuana, marijuana
> You will not think.
> If you try to swim
> You may only sink.
> Alcohol, alcohol
> Do not take a drink.
> You will need a clear mind
> So you'll be able to think.

3 After students have had the opportunity to sing the new rhymes, share with them the dangers associated with the drugs mentioned in the new rhymes. Explain that the drugs are dan-

gerous to a person's health. You can mention that marijuana causes the muscles to not work together well. Some people who use marijuana may experience difficulty in seeing clearly as well as thinking clearly. Alcohol also interferes with the ability to think clearly. People who drink alcohol have many accidents because their muscles cannot work as they should. All drugs can interfere with a person's ability to think clearly and perform tasks safely.

Evaluation:

Have students identify different tasks they perform every day. Then have them identify how these tasks might be more difficult if they had a drug in their body.

HATFUL OF DRUGS

Objective:

Students will name illegal drugs and their harmful effects.

Life Skill:

I will not use illegal drugs.

Materials:

3 × 5 inch index cards, a hat with a band

Motivation:

1 Review different types of drugs with students. Among these can be alcohol, tobacco, marijuana, cocaine, heroin, and LSD. Following is some information you can provide about each of the drugs mentioned:

Alcohol—Alcohol is a drug that slows the actions of the body. Alcohol is a liquid and is found in beer, wine, wine coolers, and hard liquors such as whiskey.

Tobacco—Tobacco is a drug found in cigarettes. The smoke from burning tobacco contains hundreds of harmful ingredients. Tobacco causes diseases like lung cancer and makes breathing difficult.

Cocaine—Cocaine is a dangerous drug that is usually a powder. Cocaine increases the actions of the body to a dangerous level. Cocaine use can result in death because it can cause the heart to stop working.

Heroin—Heroin is a dangerous drug that slows down the actions of the body. Heroin comes from the poppy plant. People often use heroin by inhaling it (snorting) or by taking it through a syringe (needle). Sharing needles to inject heroin can result in the spread of HIV, the virus that causes AIDS.

LSD—LSD is a drug that causes a person to see objects that do not exist.

2 After reviewing this information, play the game "Hatful of Drugs." Ask a volunteer to come to the front of the classroom. Place a hat that has a band on this person's head. On a 3 × 5 inch index card, write the name of one of the drugs already discussed. Stick the card in the band of the hat so the rest of the class can see the name of the drug on the card. The person wearing the hat cannot see the name of the drug. On at a time, the other students will give a one-word clue to the person wearing the hat. Using the clue, the person will try to name the drug that is written on the card inserted in the band of the hat.

3 You can repeat this activity using the names of the other drugs. Select a new volunteer to wear the hat each time.

Evaluation:

You can have the class research information about drugs in the school library. They also can find magazines or books that contain pictures of different kinds of drugs. You can then have each student tell one new fact about one of the drugs described in class.

Inclusion:

Instead of writing the name of the drug on the index card, announce the name of the drug to the class while the volunteer temporarily cannot hear the announcement. Then proceed with the game.

Grades Pre-K–2
- Objective 14A

PROTECTORS

Objective:

Students will name responsible adults who protect health, safety, school rules, and laws.

Life Skill:

I will speak to a responsible adult if I have any questions about my health.

Materials:

Old magazines

Motivation:

1 Explain that there are many persons in a home, school, and community who can help young people if they have any concerns they would like to talk about with someone. These persons are interested in protecting young people from harm.

2 You can explain that a teacher can help protect boys and girls in school. Adults in a family help keep children in the family safe and secure. A teacher helps children learn how to cross the street safely. A teacher also helps children learn how to solve problems by talking with them. A firefighter helps boys and girls be safe from harm by fire and smoke. A police officer helps boys and girls keep safe from others and from danger. A member of the clergy helps boys and girls and their families solve problems.

3 Cut pictures from magazines that show persons in the family, school and community who protect health and safety. You may cut out a picture of a parent and a baby. You may cut out a picture of a school crossing guard guiding children across the street as they walk to school. Cut out several pictures that show different persons helping boys and girls.

4 Show the pictures you have cut out to the class. When you show each picture, have a

volunteer imagine and tell a story about it. The story should include how the picture illustrates a responsible adult who is protecting health, safety, school rules, and laws.

Evaluation:

Have students name a responsible adult in their community who helps protect them and keep them safe. They are to tell how this person helps keep them safe.

Multicultural Infusion:

Show people of different cultures doing something to help protect the health and safety of boys and girls. Explain that no matter what country people come from, there are responsible adults who care about the safety of children.

SHIP AHOY

Objective:

Students will name responsible adults who protect health, safety, school rules, and laws.

Life Skill:

I will speak to a responsible adult if I need help with any kind of problem.

Materials:

Crayons, Ticket to Board (page 300), a copy for each student

Motivation:

1 Emphasize to students that many different people help keep them healthy. Have students share the kinds of people they have seen on television, in the movies, or in books that help keep others healthy. They will identify people such as doctors, nurses, police officers, firefighters, and teachers.

2 Explain to students that *everyone* needs advice or help from another person at times. It is important to get advice or help from people who can really be helpful. Explain that the following activity will help them identify persons in the community who can be helpful. Explain to students that they are going to be taking a trip on a ship. However, in order to board the ship, students need a ticket.

3 Students are going to design a ticket that will get them on board the ship. Distribute copies of Ticket to Board. Explain that students are to draw a picture of a person who they know can help protect their health and safety. They are to color this person and write this person's name on the ticket. Then they are to cut out the ticket (the drawing of the person) and hand it to you. You are to pretend that you are the ticket collector and that you will allow the students on the ship after they have given

you their tickets. Collect all the students' tickets.

4 Have each student share the person whom (s)he identified as being someone who protects health and safety. Have students share how this person protects health and safety.

Evaluation:

Have students brainstorm about the different kinds of people in a community whom they can approach for help. For example, they may identify a parent, the school counselor, or a friend's parent. Summarize the different kinds of people in a community who are helpful.

Ticket to Board

NAME _____

• Objective 14C

Violence Prevention

BE YOUR OWN PILOT

Objective:

Students will name responsible adults who protect health, safety, school rules, and laws.

Life Skill:

I will identify a person I trust whom I would approach if I needed help.

Materials:

Crayons, The Me Plane (page 302), a copy for each student

Motivation:

1 Ask students if they have ever been on an airplane. If there are students who have never been on a plane, ask them if they have seen planes on TV or in a book. All students will have some familiarity with planes.

2 Explain that planes do certain jobs. But a plane cannot perform its job without a crew, persons who know how to operate the plane. Explain that all planes need to be flown by a pilot. The pilot knows how to use controls on the plane so that the plane takes off from the ground, stays in the air during the flight, and lands again. The pilot determines if the plane is going in the proper direction. The pilot also guides the plane so that it will avoid an accident. Without a responsible pilot, the plane would never reach its destination.

3 Explain to students that they are somewhat like airplanes. They have certain goals or destinations they want to reach. These goals need to be healthful and safe. Students need to be guided to grow up to be the very best kind of person they can be. To do this, there are many different people who must serve as their pilots. Their major pilots are their parents. These pilots must protect boys and girls from illness and injury and make sure they are

growing in the proper direction. There are many other individuals at school and in the community who can act as pilots so that boys and girls can grow healthfully throughout life.

4 Distribute copies of The Me Plane. Explain that each student is a "Me Plane." However, they cannot fly their plane because they are too young. They do not have the training to be pilots. Thus, they need persons who can help them grow and learn how to be the pilots of their own lives. As they grow, they need persons who will provide shelter and love. They need persons who will provide understanding. They need persons with whom they can talk. With this in mind, each student is to color his/her plane and write the names of responsible adults who act as pilots for him/her. Students can choose a parent, teacher, or any other person who is important in their lives. After students have completed this task, have them share how the persons they named are like pilots in their lives.

Evaluation:

Using what the students shared, summarize the characteristics of responsible adults who serve as pilots as children are growing.

Inclusion:

If students cannot write the names of specific individuals, they can color their planes and tell about the persons who are their pilots.

The Me Plane

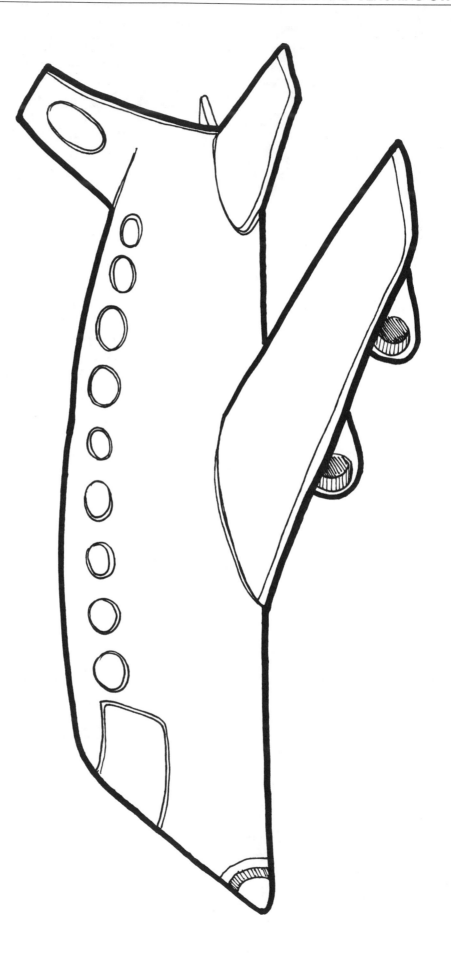

Grades Pre-K–2
- Objective 15A

WARM FUZZY

Objective:

Students will tell the difference between loving feelings and loving actions.

Life Skill:

I will express my feelings in loving ways.

Materials:

Glue, 3 × 5 inch index cards, one for each student, cotton balls, one for each student

Motivation:

1 Tell students that you are going to discuss ways to show others you love them. Explain that when you are kind to others, you express your feelings in healthful ways. Explain that expressing feelings in healthful ways shows others that you care about them.

2 For each student in the class, prepare a fuzzy ball by dabbing glue on a small area of a cotton ball. Attach the glued spot of the cotton ball to an index card. After the glue has dried, the cotton ball will stay attached to the index card.

3 Distribute a card with a cotton ball to each student. Explain that this is a warm fuzzy. Explain that the fuzzy is gentle and kind. The fuzzy also needs attention and love. Explain that if the warm fuzzy falls off the card, it can become harmed. Explain to students that they need to show their warm fuzzies that they like them. Ask students what they would do to keep their warm fuzzies from becoming harmed. Students may say that they will take them wherever they go. They may make sure that the warm fuzzy does not fall on the floor. Have students share other ways they can keep their warm fuzzies safe and protected.

4 Explain that when they care for their warm fuzzies, they are showing loving actions. Explain that some people do not show loving actions. They might let their warm fuzzy fall on the ground. They may kick their warm fuzzy. Explain that they are showing unloving actions when they do these kinds of things. They would not be showing that they care about their warm fuzzies. Explain that sometimes people get upset about something that has happened to them. Sometimes, when people are upset they do things they ordinarily would not do. Their actions may not be loving actions. People who are upset often harm others. Explain that people who engage in unloving actions as well as people who receive unloving actions need help. Emphasize that students need help if they feel they are being harmed.

5 Have students care for their warm fuzzies for the rest of the day. They are to practice showing loving actions to their warm fuzzies.

Evaluation:

Have students share how they can show loving actions to others. Some examples might be hugging a friend, sharing toys with others, telling others you like them, and helping others when they need help.

Grades Pre-K–2
- Objective 15B

PUPPY LOVE

Objective:

Students will tell the difference between loving feelings and loving actions.

Life Skill:

I will express my feelings in healthful ways.

Materials:

A pet that you or a student are allowed to have in the classroom or a stuffed animal

Motivation:

1 If possible, have a student bring a pet such as a dog or a cat to class. If a student can bring a pet to class, be sure that a parent approves and accompanies the pet. The pet also should be a suitable pet to have around other children. You can also use a stuffed animal.

2 Have the class sit in a small circle on the floor. Either you or the parent should hold the pet next to you. Explain that you are going to discuss loving feelings. Ask students to describe how they feel about the pet. They will indicate that they think it is cute. Some might ask to pet the animal. Explain that by wanting to pet the animal and perhaps to hold it, the students in the class are expressing loving feelings. Explain that showing loving feelings to other persons and to pets is important. It shows others you care. Tell the class that when the animal you are holding was born, it received love from its mother. The mother fed the animal. The mother also helped protect the baby animal from harm.

3 Explain to students that everyone may become upset with others at times—even a friend. People become upset with their pets sometimes. Explain that it is OK to be upset, but being upset does not make it all right to show actions that are harmful. For example, if a pet does

something that is upsetting, what might be done? Ask the class what they would do if they had a pet and it chewed on something they wanted to keep. Explain that kicking or punching the pet is not a loving action. Rather than punching or kicking the pet, the pet can be taught not to chew on things. The pet might be kept in a separate part of the house to prevent doing more harm. The people in the family could be careful not to leave things around on the floor that the pet could chew. Although the pet may be punished for its actions, it can be treated in a healthful and loving way. Explain to students that they may do something that their parents do not like and that they may be punished. But even when they are punished, they can be treated in healthful and loving ways.

4 Emphasize that actions such as punching and kicking are violent actions. Violent actions are not healthful ways of acting. Explain to students that if anyone treats them in violent ways, they should tell a responsible adult. Review with the class who responsible adults are in their school and community (family members, a teacher, a school nurse, and so on). Explain to students that if they do not receive help from the first person they ask, they should ask another person.

Evaluation:

Have students share ways they can show loving actions to others. Summarize student responses.

Grades Pre-K–2
- Objective 15C

Violence Prevention

THE LOVING TREE

Objective:

Students will tell the difference between loving feelings and loving actions.

Life Skill:

I will express my feelings in healthful ways.

Materials:

Poster paper, marker, The Loving Tree (page 306), a copy for each student

Motivation:

1 There are many different ways to express loving actions. Loving actions are the ways people express how they care about others. Have students identify some of the ways they show loving actions. They might mention hugging a parent, helping a family member set the table, or picking up something a person has dropped.

2 Explain that when people express loving actions, they not only help others but also help themselves. Helping others brings joy and satisfaction knowing that you've done something kind. On a sheet of poster paper, draw a tree with many branches. Explain to students that this is a Loving Tree but it needs to be decorated. Distribute copies of The Loving Tree. Explain to students that they will make decorations for the tree you have drawn. Instruct students that they are to print a way they show a loving action on each leaf. They do not need to print any lengthy statements—just enough to let others know what they do to show loving actions.

3 After this is completed, have students tape their leaves to The Loving Tree. The Loving Tree will now be complete. Read each loving action to the class. Have the class think about the different loving actions that are mentioned. Perhaps they can then mention other examples of loving actions. Summarize the kinds of loving actions that students identified.

4 Explain that everyone can always be looking for new ways to show loving actions.

Evaluation:

Have students choose a loving action discussed in class that they will show to others. They are to share this with the class.

Inclusion:

Students can be given the option of drawing pictures on the leaves.

The Loving Tree

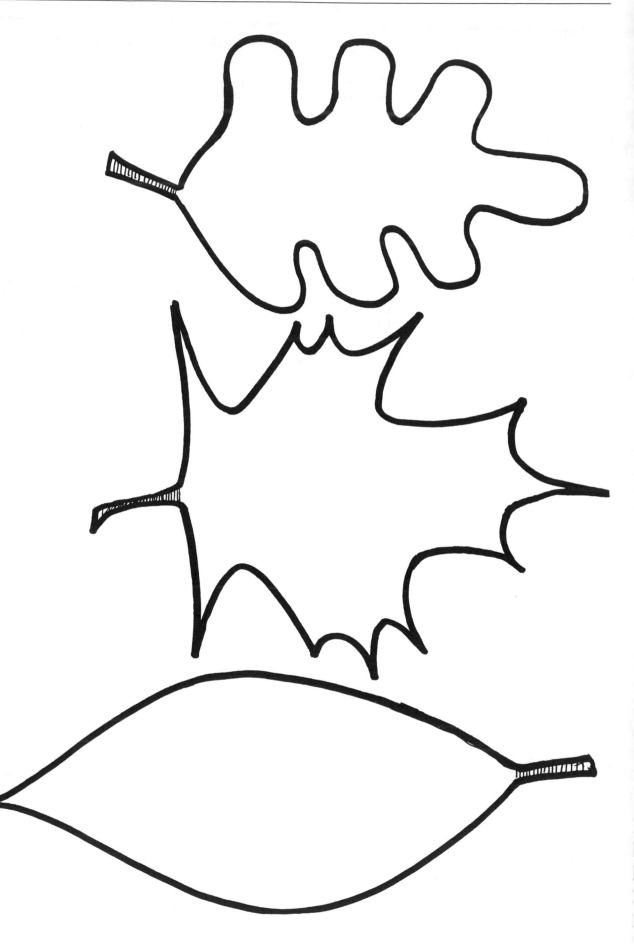

Grades 3–5
▪ Objective 1A

| Violence Prevention |

IT'S A GOAL!

Objective:

Students will practice ways to improve self-esteem.

Life Skill:

I will engage in activities that promote my self-esteem.

Materials:

Large sheet of construction paper labeled "drugs," two movable chairs, a crumpled sheet of paper rolled into a ball, pencils, paper, a sheet for each student

Motivation:

1 Introduce the term self-esteem. Explain that self-esteem is the way people feel about themselves. When people have positive self-esteem, they feel worthwhile and lovable. When they have negative self-esteem, they feel unworthy and unlovable.

2 Introduce and define the word drug. Explain that a drug is any substance other than food that changes how the body works. Explain that medicines are drugs. Medicines are drugs that are used to treat, prevent, or diagnose illness. Medicines are taken under the supervision of a responsible adult and can be healthful. Drugs that are not medicines can be harmful.

3 Place two chairs about six feet apart. The area between the chairs represents the goal, or scoring area. Select a volunteer to be a goalie who will hold a sheet of construction paper with the word "drugs" written on it. The goalie is to stand between the chairs. Ask the students to each think of a goal they wish to accomplish. Then take a crumpled paper ball and tell students that the ball represents their individual goals. Have each student stand ten feet away from the goal area. One student at a

time will name a goal (s)he has. Standing ten feet away from the goal area, that student will then try to reach his/her goal (or score) by throwing the ball between the two chairs without it's being blocked by the goalie, or "drugs." The goalie will try to block the ball from reaching its goal.

4 Explain to students that using harmful drugs will prevent people from reaching their goals. When people cannot reach their goals, their self-esteem is affected. When a student's goal is blocked by "drugs" (the goalie), ask the student how his/her life might be affected by not reaching that goal. For example, a student's goal might be to get good grades. If his/her grades are not good, the student may be discouraged and may be grounded by his/her parents. This can affect the student's self-esteem. Explain that using harmful drugs can interfere with the ability to achieve not only the ability to get good grades but also the ability to reach other goals.

5 Explain that everyone has goals. When people reach their goals, they feel good about themselves. They have positive self-esteem. Using harmful drugs will cause a person to have difficulty reaching his/her goals. Explain that people with negative self-esteem are more inclined to use harmful drugs than people who have positive self-esteem. Avoiding the use of harmful drugs will help people have positive self-esteem and they will be more apt to reach their goals.

Evaluation:

On a sheet of paper, have each student write a goal (s)he wishes to accomplish. This goal should not be a repeat of one (s)he did for the activity. (S)he is not to write his/her name on the sheet of paper. Have students place their papers in an envelope. Redistribute the papers so that everyone has another student's paper. Each student will then read the goal written on the paper that (s)he has. In each case, have students indicate how using harmful drugs would prevent them from achieving this goal and how that might influence their self-esteem.

Inclusion:

To help students who may have trouble identifying a goal, you can suggest some possible goals. List them on a separate sheet of paper so that these students have the opportunity to choose a goal from this list.

| Violence Prevention |

TAKE SHELTER

Objective:

Students will practice ways to improve self-esteem.

Life Skill:

I will use protective factors to improve my self-esteem.

Materials:

Two sheets of construction paper, a large cardboard box, markers, scissors

Motivation:

1 Introduce the term protective factors. Protective factors are characteristics that influence a person's development and behavior in a positive way. Explain to students that their level of self-esteem is related to the protective factors they possess. An environment in which there are many protective factors will increase one's self-esteem. The following are examples of protective factors:
1. being reared in a loving family,
2. being involved in school activities,
3. having friends who do not use drugs,
4. having teachers who help you in school,
5. following rules at school and in the community,
6. being able to handle stress.
You can have your students add more examples of protective factors.

2 Using one sheet of construction paper and a marker, outline and cut out five lightning-shaped streaks, each about one foot in length. On each streak, write the word drug. On another sheet of construction paper, draw a large tree. On a large cardboard box, draw some windows and a door. The cardboard box will represent a house. On different places on the box, write examples of protective factors.

3 Select two volunteers to sit in front of the room; one will hold the picture of the tree; the other will hold the cardboard box. Stand behind the student holding the tree. Tell the class that there is a strong thunderstorm accompanied by lightning. Explain that each streak of lightning represents a drug. Remind students that there is no protection if a person is under a tree during a thunderstorm. Tap some of the lightning streaks against the tree. Ask the class what would happen to a person under the tree. (This person is not protected. There are no protective factors present. This person is susceptible to the lightning (drugs).)

4 Now tap the lightning streaks against the house (the cardboard box). Remind students that the house has several protective factors (written on the house). Explain that when the lightning strikes the house, the person inside is not harmed. This person may know that the drugs are near the house, and the person may have a fear of the drugs, but this person is well protected. Explain that people who surround themselves with protective factors are less likely to use harmful drugs than people who do not surround themselves with protective factors. Emphasize that people who have many protective factors also will have positive self-esteem. And positive self-esteem helps reduce the risk of using and abusing drugs.

Evaluation:

Have students identify additional protective factors and what they might do to help other students who may not have protective factors.

Multicultural Infusion:

Explain that protective factors may be specific to different cultures and customs. Have students share aspects about their cultures that may serve as protective factors.

Grades 3–5
- Objective 1C

PAINTING A POSITIVE IMAGE

Objective:

Students will practice ways to improve self-esteem.

Life Skill:

I will engage in actions that help me feel good about myself.

Materials:

Assorted paints, paint brushes, a brush for each student, paper, a sheet for each student

Motivation:

1 Explain that in this art lesson, students will have the opportunity to paint self-portraits. They are to use bright colors for their portraits.

2 Explain to students that they are to be as creative as possible. Their portraits are to reflect feelings of positive self-esteem. Each student is to think of a situation (s)he experienced that made him/her feel great. Students might think of situations such as a birthday party or being on a team that won a game. Allow students to think for several minutes before starting their portraits. (To set the tone for this project, you can dim the lights in the room.)

3 When students have finished, have them think of a title they would like to give their self-portrait. The title can reflect the situation that made the student feel great. When the portraits and titles are complete, allow students to share both their self-portraits and the experiences they thought about that made them feel good. This activity should be voluntary. Students do not need to share thoughts they feel uncomfortable sharing.

4 After students have shared, summarize the kinds of situations that made them feel good. For example, several students may have indicated that they felt good when they went on a vacation with members of their families.

5 Use this activity to indicate that there are many kinds of situations that can help students feel good about who they are and what they are doing, and can thus influence their self-esteem in positive ways.

Evaluation:

Have students make a list of activities in which they engage that help them feel good. Have them share reasons why having positive self-esteem is important for avoiding drug use.

Grades 3–5
▪ Objective 2A

SHARING FEELINGS

Objective:

Students will practice healthful ways to share feelings.

Life Skill:

I will share feelings with family members.

Materials:

Strips of construction paper that are about six inches wide and twelve inches long

Motivation:

1 Explain to students that it is important to share feelings with responsible adults. Some of the feelings a student might share are being happy, scared, angry, sad, surprised, or excited. Explain that adults such as family members, teachers, school nurses, or clergy can help people when they experience certain kinds of feelings, such as feelings of sadness. Sharing feelings is healthful.

2 On strips of construction paper, write the names of different kinds of feelings. On other strips of construction paper, write very brief scenarios that might cause those feelings. Below are examples of feelings and corresponding scenarios you might use.
sadness—death of a pet
happiness—good grade on a test
uncertainty—first day at a new school
surprise—unexpected birthday gift
anger—being called a name

3 Select five volunteers and give each one a strip of paper that has the name of a feeling written on it. Select five other volunteers and give each one a strip of paper that has a scenario written on it. Have the volunteers match a feeling with a scenario by standing next to each other. Then have the volunteers share why they chose their partners. Have the class discuss how different partners might have

matched up with each other. For example, a happy feeling could have been matched with "good grade on a test" or "unexpected birthday gift."

4 Explain that everyone experiences different kinds of feelings at different times. Ask students how they would respond if they experienced a sad feeling such as having a pet die. Students can share ways they could respond to different kinds of feelings.

Evaluation:

Brainstorm different kinds of feelings that students experience and the different people in the school and community with whom they can share these feelings.

KEEPING IT IN

Objective:

Students will practice healthful ways to share feelings.

Life Skill:

I will share feelings with a responsible adult.

Materials:

Two balloons, marker

Motivation:

1 Before students come to class, inflate two balloons. One balloon should be inflated until it appears almost ready to burst. With a marker, draw a sad face on this balloon. Inflate another balloon but not as full as the first balloon. Draw a happy face on this balloon.

2 Pass each balloon around the class. Have the students observe the face on each balloon as well as how the balloons feel to the touch. Then collect the balloons and have students share what they observed. They will notice that the sad balloon was hard and seemed ready to burst. The happy balloon was softer and did not appear ready to burst.

3 Explain to students that the sad balloon has a lot of pressure inside it. It represents a person who experiences feelings but who does not share his/her feelings. On the other hand, the happy balloon has less pressure in it. It represents a person who shares his/her feelings. Ask students what would happen if the pressure in the sad balloon continued to increase. Students will indicate that the balloon would eventually burst.

4 Use this analogy to discuss how everyone experiences different kinds of feelings. Explain that there are healthful ways and harmful ways to deal with feelings. When a person shares his/her feelings with a responsible adult, it is

healthful. This is especially true when a person experiences feelings such as anger or sadness. If feelings are not expressed or shared, then pressure builds inside a person and the effects can be harmful. Explain that there are some people who choose not to share their feelings and try to escape from their feelings by using drugs. Explain that using drugs does not relieve the pressures a person faces. Rather, drugs increase the pressures because a person does not have the ability to deal with feelings when (s)he is using drugs. Explain that each student has someone with whom (s)he can discuss feelings. When feelings are shared, a student is choosing a healthful solution, and choosing not to let pressures build.

Evaluation:

Have students identify pressures that people their own age may feel. For each pressure, have them identify a healthful way that the pressure can be relieved.

Multicultural Infusion:

Many pressures that students experience can be related to home and community conditions. These pressures may be related to feelings of discrimination or other insensitivities. Discuss ways students can best handle feelings fostered by these concerns.

| Violence Prevention |

A FEELING MESSAGE

Objective:

Students will practice healthful ways to share feelings.

Life Skill:

I will share feelings with responsible adults.

Materials:

Old magazines, a magazine for each student, scissors, a pair for each student, tape, paper, a sheet for each student

Motivation:

1 Share with students that they are going to have the opportunity to be creative. They will create messages that relate to feelings. Their messages are going to reflect an important message about the kinds of feelings that people experience.

2 Distribute an old magazine, a pair of scissors, and a sheet of paper to each student. (S)he is to identify a feeling and write that feeling in large letters in the upper left corner of the paper. The name of the feeling is to be followed by the word "is." For example, a student may select the feeling "love." Thus, "Love is . . ." would be written on the top of the paper.

3 Each student is to find a picture in the magazine that illustrates the feeling (s)he chose. (S)he will cut the picture out and tape it in the center of his/her paper. Under the picture, (s)he is to complete the sentence. For example, a student might find a picture of ducklings following a mother duck across the road. This student would then complete the sentence. For example, "Love is following in the path of people who care about you."

4 When students have completed their messages have them share them with the class. Post

the messages on the bulletin board. After they are posted, have students share why it is important to share feelings.

Evaluation:

For each different feeling identified, have students discuss what factors promote that feeling. Then have students tell healthful ways to express the feeling.

Inclusion:

You can have students work in groups to complete the message. This would give all students an opportunity to contribute to the message.

Love is.....

following the path of people who care about you.

Grades 3–5
▪ Objective 3A

MATHEMATICAL STRESS

Objective:

Students will select healthful ways to manage stress.

Life Skill:

I will use stress-management skills when needed.

Materials:

Pencil and paper

Motivation:

1 Tell the class that they are going to be given a math problem to complete. You are going to present the problem to the class orally and the problem must be completed within 30 seconds. Read the following problem so that you can complete it in about thirty seconds. Students will feel rushed to keep up with you but do not slow down. Read only the equation of the problem, not the answers which are in parentheses for you. For example, just say 4 times 3 and then continue on to the next part. 4 times 3=(12), divided by 2=(6), times 6=(36), minus 20=(16), plus 8=(24), times 2=(48), divided by 8=(6), plus 23=(29), plus 3=(32), divided by 8=(4).

2 After you have completed reading the problem to the students, explain that you are not interested in the correct answer. Rather, you are interested in how they reacted to trying to keep up with you. Have the students share what they felt as they were listening to you. For example, they were conscious of an increase in their heartbeat rates; perhaps they began to perspire; and perhaps they could feel their muscles tightening. Explain that however they reacted to trying to keep up with you, they were experiencing stress.

3 Explain that everyone experiences stress. Sometimes, the effects of stress can be harmful to a person's body. Explain that there are both healthful ways and harmful ways to deal with stress.

4 Review healthful ways to deal with stress. Some examples are talking with a responsible adult, exercising, or engaging in sports. Explain that some people think that drinking alcohol, smoking cigarettes, or using other drugs will help relieve the feelings of stress. (Make sure that students understand that alcohol and tobacco are both drugs.) However, drugs only make a stressful situation more stressful because drugs reduce the ability of a person to manage the situation that caused the stress. And the drugs themselves become an added problem to a person because of the harm they cause his/her body and mind.

Evaluation:

Have students identify situations that cause stress for persons their age. Some examples may be tests at school, arguments with friends, or having a pet die. For each source of stress, have students identify a healthful way to handle that stress.

Inclusion:

If students are to complete the math problem, assign partners so that students can work together.

Grades 3–5
▪ Objective 3B

WHO'S STRESSED?

Objective:

Students will select healthful ways to manage stress.

Life Skill:

I will recognize the physical symptoms of stress and seek healthful ways to relieve these symptoms.

Materials:

Two identical cans of soda pop

Motivation:

1 Before class, loosen the tab on one of the cans (can # 1) so that the pressure inside the can is reduced slightly. So that it does not appear as if the tab had been loosened, press the tab down gently. Leave the other can (can # 2) as is. Give can # 2 a slight shake. Then place both cans on your desk after your class has entered the room.

2 Ask students to think of these cans as two persons. Ask students if they notice anything different about each person. The class should answer "no" as each can is identical. Explain that if two people look alike on the outside, it does not indicate that they are alike on the inside. Explain that in many respects, people are alike on the inside. For example, they all experience the same kinds of feelings. They may even look alike. However, in many respects, people are different on the inside.

3 Tell students that one of these persons (cans) is under a great deal of stress while the other is not. Ask students if they can tell just by looking at the cans which one is under stress (no). Open the tab of can # 2 and have students observe what happens. (A loud fizz was

heard. This is an indication that there was a great deal of pressure or stress inside.) Then completely open the tab of can # 1. Have students share their observations. (There was no sound, indicating that there was very little pressure inside.)

4 Explain that sometimes people may appear as if they are calm and don't have a worry in the world when in effect, these people are under a great deal of stress. Explain that people who are under stress need ways to relieve the causes of the stress. These people may recognize that they are under stress because their muscles may feel tight, they may not be able to sleep well at nights, or they may not be able to concentrate well when trying to complete tasks. Explain that if these people do not handle the causes of their stress, they may develop physical problems such as heart disease.

5 Have the class discuss healthful ways that stress can be handled. Explain that the source of the stress must be identified. The situation that is causing the stress must be dealt with. For example, a person who feels stress because of getting poor grades in school should speak with a teacher and get help with study skills that (s)he needs to learn.

6 Explain that drugs are not a healthful way to handle stress. A physician may sometimes prescribe a medicine to relieve some of the symptoms of stress for some people. However, the actual causes of the stress must still be identified and managed.

Evaluation:

Have students identify some common causes of stress for persons their age. Have them identify some of the signs and symptoms that persons their age may experience. Finally, have students suggest ways to manage some of the causes of stress they have identified.

Multicultural Infusion:

Have students identify some of the causes of stress that may be specific to their communities. Discuss how to healthfully manage some of these causes.

Grades 3–5
- Objective 3C

I AM A RESILIENT PERSON

Objective:

Students will select healthful ways to manage stress.

Life Skill:

I will practice behaviors that enable me to handle stress.

Materials:

Two large rubber bands, scissors

Motivation:

1 Using two large rubber bands, explain to the class that each rubber band represents a person. And like all persons, these two have their share of stress. Attach one end of one of the rubber bands to a knob or something else that is solid and hold the other end. Have the class identify sources of stress that persons their age experience. With each source identified, pull the rubber band more. Stop before it has stretched too far. Then explain that if the causes of stress are not managed, a person may experience great pressures. Making sure that the students are not close to the band, cut the stretched rubber band with scissors. Point out that the rubber band snapped. Some people have been known to "snap" because of the buildup of stress.

2 Repeat the same procedure with the second rubber band and again have the students identify stressors as you stretch the band. Stop before it is stretched too far. However, this time, have students identify healthful ways to handle stress. For example, if a person is pressured to smoke a cigarette, the person can choose to be with friends who do not smoke. As each stress management technique is identified, ease the pressure, letting the band become more loose.

3 Explain that the person (rubber band) who used stress-management techniques handled stress in a healthful way. Explain that the rubber band is resilient. Discuss the term resilient. A person who is resilient has the ability to recover from or adjust to misfortune, change, pressure, or adversity. Persons who are resilient recover more easily from the stress of daily life than persons who are not resilient. Explain that regardless of the stress one endures in life, the ability to bounce back or be resilient is always a possibility. Explain that using drugs to solve problems interferes with the ability to be resilient. Just as the shape of the rubber band was restored when stress-management techniques were identified, so persons can learn how to maintain their well-being by handling stress in healthful ways.

Evaluation:

Have students determine if they think they are resilient. They can identify how they healthfully handled a stressful situation in a way that made them feel good. For example, they may have received a poor grade on a test but they studied hard for the next test and did well.

Grades 3–5
- Objective 4A

Violence Prevention

DON'T GET BAGGED

Objective:

Students will practice making responsible decisions.

Life Skill:

I will make decisions that promote health.

Materials:

Three paper bags, paper

Motivation:

1 Explain to students that there are many different kinds of decisions they must make every day. Have students share what may be involved when they make their decisions. For example, is their decision one that will lead to safe actions, is it healthful, does it follow the rules of a responsible adult, does it encourage self-esteem, and would the decision result in actions that are legal?

2 Explain to students that they are going to participate in an activity that will examine their decision-making skills and their willingness to take risks that would be dangerous to their health. Before class, insert a slip of paper in each of three paper bags. On each slip of paper, write "Your life is ruined because you have chosen to take drugs." Place the three paper bags on your desk, each standing and open at the top. Tell students there is something inside each bag. (They are not to know what is inside each bag.)

3 Select three volunteers to come to the front of the room. Give each a slip of paper that represents a gift certificate. Tell the three volunteers they have a choice of keeping their gift certificates or trading them for what is inside one of the bags. Explain that it is possible that what is in a bag is worth thousands of dollars. On the other hand, there might be something in a bag that is dangerous to their health. Have each

volunteer make a decision about what (s)he will do. Will (s)he trade or keep his/her gift certificate? The rest of the students can try to influence the volunteers' decisions.

4 Have each volunteer describe what (s)he thought about in making his/her decision. If a volunteer decided to keep his/her certificate, what influenced the decision? If a volunteer decided to trade his/her certificate, what influenced the decision? Did the other members of the class influence any of the decisions the volunteers made?

5 Explain to the class that the volunteers were asked to make a decision about an unknown. The volunteers had no information about what was in the bags. If a volunteer made the decision to trade his/her certificate, (s)he took a risk. Discuss the possible problems with taking a risk. Discuss how making a decision to take drugs is making a decision about an unknown. The results could be life threatening.

6 Emphasize that some decisions have long-term effects. How would a volunteer who traded his/her certificate feel? Would it be worth taking a risk and ruining your life? Explain that when people make a decision to use drugs, they do not think about the long-term impact that drugs will have on their lives. Emphasize what the responsible decision would be. A person who makes the decision never to use drugs does not risk his/her health and life.

7 Review the Responsible Decision-Making Model with students.

Evaluation:

Have students describe the factors they think about in making decisions. Have students describe how they would know if their decisions are responsible decisions.

Grades 3–5
- Objective 4B

NAME THE USER

Objective:

Students will practice making responsible decisions.

Life Skill:

I will make decisions that promote my health.

Materials:

Magazines, scissors

Motivation:

1 Ask students how they might identify a person who uses harmful drugs. Some students may suggest stereotypical traits such as appearance or behavior. Explain that it is difficult to identify people who decide to use drugs.

2 Cut pictures from magazines that show different kinds of people, such as athletes, teachers, physicians, business people, and entertainers. Have students indicate if they think any of the people in the pictures might be using drugs. Most students will say that the people in the pictures do not look as if they are using drugs.

3 Explain that some people of all cultures, gender, and occupations decide to use drugs. Explain that at some time in their lives, most people are faced with the decision of whether or not to try a drug. The drug may be alcohol, tobacco, or any kind of illegal drug such as crack, heroin, or marijuana. Regardless of who a person is, how (s)he looks, or what (s)he does, the choice of whether or not to try a drug is something that person must face.

4 Ask students to describe what they would do if they were asked to try a drug. Explain that they have the right to make a responsible decision and that the only responsible decision is to avoid using drugs. Explain that the people in the pictures are no different from anyone in the class. During their lifetime, these people had to make decisions. Point out that if these people had chosen to use drugs, they might not have been able to accomplish whatever success they have enjoyed. Students may indicate that they have seen on TV many successful people who have admitted using drugs. Explain that most people probably regret that they ever used drugs and that, if they had to do it all over again, they would make a decision not to use drugs.

Evaluation:

Provide the class with the following scenario. They are at a party and a friend is pressuring them to drink a beverage such as a wine cooler that contains alcohol. How would they respond to the pressure? Discuss options such as leaving the party, saying NO firmly, or walking away.

Grades 3–5
- Objective 4C

WHAT'S YOUR DECISION?

Objective:

Students will practice making responsible decisions.

Life Skill:

I will make decisions that protect my health.

Materials:

Three numbered keys

Motivation:

1 Tell the class that they must choose one of the keys that you will show to them. They will choose which key will open the door to your classroom. (Or, you might choose to use a bicycle lock.) You may choose to have three keys that look similar or three keys that look completely different. Students can come up close to observe how the keys look or they can observe the keys from where they are sitting. They cannot try any of the keys to see which one works.

2 Number your keys Key #1, Key #2, and Key #3. Have the class vote on which key they think will open the door. Have students explain why they made the choice they did. Were their choices based on how the keys looked? Were their choices based on a guess? Had they observed what key you used in the past? Was there something unique about the key they chose such as a particular mark?

3 Select the right key and use it to show the class that it fits the lock. Now have the class consider the choices they make in choosing friends. Friends are a major factor in whether or not a person will choose to use harmful drugs. How might a person know that another person will be a friend who will encourage healthful behaviors or a friend who will encourage harmful behaviors such as taking drugs? That is difficult. Just like choosing a key, you

cannot know about a person just by appearance alone.

4 Explain that if students recognized the key that opens your classroom door because they had seen you use it, their decision about the key would have been easy. They would have known from past experience which key would work in the lock. In a similar way, some people choose another person to be a friend because they know what this person has been like in the past. Perhaps they observed how this person treated others. Perhaps they have enjoyed being with this person. Perhaps this person helped them. Their experience with this person has been pleasant and positive. They understand that this person would be a good friend.

5 Explain that choosing friends who are responsible and who promote and encourage healthful choices is important in making decisions about drugs. Research shows that persons who choose to be with other persons who use drugs are at an increased risk of using drugs themselves.

Evaluation:

Have students discuss the relationship between having friends who are drug free and making decisions to avoid the use of drugs.

Grades 3–5
▪ Objective 5A

You Can't Convince Me

Objective:

Students will practice using resistance skills.

Life Skill:

I will use resistance skills to avoid engaging in harmful activities.

Materials:

Candy bar

Motivation:

1 Explain that sometimes people are asked to do things that they know they should not do. Students in your class have probably experienced situations in which they were asked to do something that they knew they should not do, something that might be harmful to their health. Have students share some situations in which they have been pressured to engage in an activity that they considered questionable. For each example, have students indicate how they avoided doing what they were being pressured to do. For example, a student may have been pressured to cross the street when (s)he was not allowed to do so. (S)he may have said NO. Share several different scenarios.

2 Explain that you are going to do an experiment with the class. Choose a volunteer to come to the front of the room. Whisper to the volunteer that his/her parents do not allow him/her to eat candy bars at school. Explain to the volunteer that (s)he is to try to resist the pressure to eat a candy bar, but at the same time, make it appear that (s)he really would like to have the candy bar and that the decision not to take it is a difficult one.

3 Tell the class that you have a candy bar and that you are going to try to convince the volunteer to take the candy bar and to eat it. You can make statements such as, "You'll really

like it," "I won't tell your parents," "It is delicious," "No one else will know," "Just take one small bite."

4 Have the class observe the behavior of the volunteer. Did (s)he take the candy? Did (s)he appear as if (s)he would really like to try it? Did the volunteer forcefully show his/her determination not to take the candy?

5 Explain to the class that if someone pressures them to do something they know is not safe, not healthful, not legal, against parental wishes, or something that does not show self-respect, they can use resistance skills. (Refer to the Model for Using Resistance Skills.) Explain that resistance skills are actions that send a clear message that they will not do something that is harmful or something they know they should not do. In using resistance skills, emphasize to students that they must look at the other person directly and say NO in a loud and firm voice. If someone continues to exert pressure, then a person should always walk away from the person who is pressuring.

Evaluation:

Have the same volunteer use resistance skills as described in the Model for Using Resistance Skills to refuse the candy bar. Have students observe the differences in the volunteer's actions.

Inclusion:

Students can sit at their seats and say NO in unison in a firm voice with eyes focused on the teacher.

Grades 3–5
- Objective 5B

| Violence Prevention |

STOP

Objective:

Students will practice using resistance skills.

Life Skill:

I will use resistance skills to avoid harming my health.

Materials:

Stop in the Name of Health (page 323), a copy for each student

Motivation:

1 Students will be asked to imagine that they are in different situations that require them to use resistance skills. Explain that resistance skills, also called refusal skills, are skills to use when a person wants to say NO to an action and/or to leave a situation in which (s)he is being pressured to do something that (s)he does not want to do or something that (s)he knows would be harmful to his/her health. Using resistance skills will enable students to avoid harming their health.

2 Distribute copies of Stop in the Name of Health. If you choose, students can color this sign red to relate with the red stop signs they see at street corners. Indicate to students that you are going to identify different situations: some may be healthful, others may be harmful. When you identify a potentially harmful situation, students are to signify they are using resistance skills by holding up their stop signs. They will not hold up their stop signs if the situation you describe is not a threat to their health.

3 Share the following situations and after each, observe when the students are holding up their signs. You can add your own situations.

1. Your friend wants you to try a cigarette and assures you that your parents will not know if you try it.

2. Your friend wants you to cross the street while there are no cars in sight and the traffic light is red.
3. Your friend wants to do homework with you.
4. Your friend wants you to tell a lie.
5. Your friend wants you to steal something at the store and calls you a chicken if you won't.

4 Observe how the students use their stop signs. Did some not hold up their signs when you think they should have? Did some students wait to see how the other students were going to respond? Discuss student responses to each situation. There may be some students who may be unsure about using resistance skills. Explain that resistance skills are skills they can learn and that resistance skills will help them protect their health.

Evaluation:

Have students describe other situations, and have the class practice using their stop signs and practice using resistance skills for these situations.

322

Stop in the Name of Health

Grades 3–5
- Objective 5C

REFUSE THAT DRUG

Objective:

Students will practice using resistance skills.

Life Skill:

I will use resistance skills in appropriate situations.

Materials:

None

Motivation:

1 Tell students they are going to be working in groups of about five. Each group will be a rap group that will send a message to get boys and girls to use resistance skills to avoid using drugs.

2 Give each group at least 20–30 minutes to develop a rap song that they will present to the rest of the class. This song will have a message about the dangers of using drugs. In addition, the song will have a message that tells students the importance of using resistance skills to avoid using drugs.

3 Tell each group that they are to first develop a group name. Then they are to work on the lyrics of their song. When they present their song to the class, they are to identify their group name and then sing their song. Explain that individuals can sing certain parts of the song or the entire group can sing the words of the song together. Also emphasize that the group name must have a healthful title such as the Resistance Rappers.

4 As each group sings their song, the rest of the students must identify the words in the songs that show the use of resistance skills. For example, words may refer to looking at the person and saying NO. You can also have the class vote on the two best lines of a song. The two lines should send a clear message about

the dangers of using drugs. Remind the groups that they can be creative but that the message is to be serious.

Evaluation:

Have the class remember ten facts that they identified in the songs. The facts can be related to the dangers of drugs or the use of resistance skills.

Multicultural Infusion:

Students can make up words that may be particularly relevant to their cultures and communities.

Don't be a **fool**,
And think you're **cool**;
Resist that **drug**...
Substitute a **hug**.

Grades 3–5
- Objective 6A

Violence Prevention

FRIENDLY FLAKES

Objective:

Students will differentiate between healthful and harmful relationships.

Life Skill:

I will choose friends who support healthful behaviors.

Materials:

Empty cereal boxes (different varieties of cereals), crayons, paper, 2 sheets for each student

Motivation:

1 Write the words "good friend" on the chalkboard. Ask students to share what a good friend means to them. They may identify several different characteristics such as someone who is nice to them, shares with them, plays with them, or keeps secrets. Explain that persons who are not good friends may not have some of these characteristics.

2 Show students the empty cereal boxes you have collected. Talk about the different kinds of information and pictures that decorate these boxes. For example, point out the names of the cereals, the attractive pictures of the cereals, other information about the cereals that indicate why they are good for you, the ingredients in the cereals, and other information that tries to persuade people to buy the cereal.

3 Explain to students that they are going to use the same ideas to design a box for a new cereal. Their cereal will be called Friendly Flakes. They are to design their boxes of Friendly Flakes so that the message is about the kinds of friends they want to have. These friends will promote healthful habits. Students are to design a front and back of a box of Friendly Flakes. On the front of the box, they can feature sayings such as "Great for you!" "Give

you energy!" and "All natural—nothing artificial." The back of the box may have a message that shows two friends having a good time together. The message might be "Friendly Flakes help you care about each other." Ingredients such as: is fun to be with, keeps secrets, helps me with homework, and calls me when I'm sick. These can also be listed on the back of the box.

4 Have students share their designs and messages with the class. Students might do this activity as a homework assignment and attach art and messages to the front and back of an actual cereal box.

Evaluation:

Have the class develop a list of the ten characteristics they feel are most important in a friend based on the information developed in this activity by the students.

Multicultural Infusion:

Students can make their design and copy reflect specific cultures and customs.

Inclusion:

Students can work with a partner or a parent to design a box for the new cereal.

Grades 3–5
- Objective 6B

PRESSURE SENSITIVE

Objective:

Students will differentiate between healthful and harmful relationships.

Life Skill:

I will not be pressured into engaging in activities that are harmful to my health.

Materials:

None

Motivation:

1 Introduce the term peer pressure. Explain that peer pressure is the influence that people of the same age place on one another. Explain that peer pressure can be positive or negative. An example of positive peer pressure is friends who encourage each other to avoid doing anything that would harm their health. An example of negative peer pressure is being with people who are smoking and encouraging someone to also smoke a cigarette, which would be a harmful choice.

2 The following activity will demonstrate how peer pressure works, especially when it is difficult to recognize. Select a volunteer whom you think will go along with decisions made by peers. You will ask a volunteer to wait in the hall while you set up the activity. After the volunteer has left the room, tell the remaining students what you are going to do. You are going to give the class simple math problems such as 10 + 15 = 25. In each case, you will include the answer. Instruct these students that they are to raise their hands for every math problem even if the answer is wrong. Tell them that when the volunteer returns, your instructions will be different, but they are to follow the directions you are giving them now while the volunteer is out of the room.

3 Have the volunteer return to the classroom. Instruct the students (including the volunteer) that you are going to give them simple math problems and that they are to raise their hands when the answer to a problem is correct. Begin giving the problems. Observe what the volunteer does. Most likely, the volunteer will hesitate and probably raise his/her hand even when the answer to the problem is wrong because (s)he sees the other students raising their hands. After giving several math problems, stop the activity. Review what occurred. Explain that peer pressure was at work. If the volunteer raised his/her hand even when the answer was wrong, (s)he probably did so because everyone else raised a hand.

4 Explain that people often are pressured into doing things even when the pressure is not verbal. Relate this to pressure to use drugs. Explain that if someone were at a party and others at the party were using drugs, there would be pressure for that person to do what the others at the party were doing. This is the reason that it is important to choose friends who engage in healthful behaviors instead of harmful behaviors. Explain to students that if they are in a place where drugs are being used, they should leave.

Evaluation:

Perhaps the volunteer did not raise his/her hand when a wrong answer was given. Use this opportunity to discuss how peer pressure did not influence this person. Remind the class how strong peer pressure really is and how it can influence the decisions students make each day.

Grades 3–5
- Objective 6C

YOU'RE IRRESISTIBLE

Objective:

Students will differentiate between healthful and harmful relationships.

Life Skill:

I will not choose friends who promote harmful health habits.

Materials:

Two strips of masking tape (enough to wrap around two wrists), three sheets of paper, pencil

Motivation:

1 This activity will demonstrate how friends can play a role in influencing people to become dependent on drugs. Explain to the class that to be dependent on a drug means to have a strong desire, mental or physical, for that drug.

2 Select three volunteers to come to the front of the room. On Person A, wrap a strip of masking tape around the right hand, leaving a sticky end exposed. On this person's back, tape a sheet of paper on which is written "I am thinking about using drugs." Do not tell this person what it says on his/her back. On Person B, also wrap a strip of masking tape around the right hand, leaving a sticky end exposed. On this person's back, attach a sheet of paper on which is written "I use drugs." Do not tell this person what it says on his/her back. On Person C, tape a sheet of paper on his/her back on which is written "drug free." Do not wrap any tape on this person's hand and do not tell him/her what is on his/her back.

3 Have the class observe what happens next. Ask person A to shake hands with person B. (The exposed ends of tape will probably stick together.) Then ask them to separate their hands from each other. This will be difficult. Read the signs on each person's back to the class. Point out that the person who is thinking about using drugs became attached to the person who uses drugs. Explain that people who are thinking about or are using drugs will become bonded or attracted to others who do the same.

4 Have Person A shake hands with Person C. Tell the class what is written on the backs of these two students. Explain that although Person C may have stuck somewhat to Person A, (s)he did not become bonded or attracted to Person A. (Person C is drug free and will not become attracted or bonded to Person A. However, it is important to note that Person C may feel some pressure from Person A to use drugs, but Person C can make a responsible decision to avoid Person A.)

Evaluation:

Have the students identify characteristics that might bond persons together. Discuss these statements, "People who use drugs are likely to choose friends who use drugs." "People who do not use drugs are likely to choose friends who do not use drugs."

Grades 3–5
- Objective 7A

WHAT'S ON AN OTC DRUG LABEL?

Objective:

Students will differentiate between the healthful and harmful use of over-the-counter (OTC) drugs.

Life Skill:

I will not use over-the-counter medicines without the supervision of a responsible adult.

Materials:

Construction paper, enough sheets to make 14 strips, one red and one blue writing marker

Motivation:

1 Introduce the term over-the-counter (OTC) drugs. Explain that OTC drugs are medications that can be purchased without a prescription. They can be purchased in stores such as drug stores and supermarkets. OTC drugs are generally not as strong or potent as prescription medications.

2 Explain that there are safe and unsafe ways to use OTC drugs. The following activity will enable students to understand OTC drug labels. Emphasize that students should not use OTC drugs without the supervision of a responsible adult. Provide the following information to describe what is on an OTC drug label.
1. The product name, manufacturer, and manufacturer's address.
2. The contents, such as the number of tablets.
3. The ingredients in the product.
4. The directions for safe use of the product.
5. Warnings such as "Consult a physician if symptoms persist."
6. Possible side effects. Examples of side effects are drowsiness, nausea, or rashes.
7. The expiration date or the date after which the drug is no longer effective.

3 On seven strips of paper, write one of the following using a red marker: Smith's High-Powered Aspirin; contains 100 aspirin; hydroxypropyl methylcellulose; take every four hours; see a physician if symptoms persist for more than three days; drowsiness; expires 5/15/99.

4 On seven other strips of paper, write one of the following using a blue marker: name of product; net contents; active ingredients; directions for safe use; warning; side effects; date of expiration. (These items correspond in order to the items listed in step # 3.)

5 Distribute the 14 strips to 14 students. Have each student who has a strip with blue writing match up with the appropriate students who has the matching information written in red. Then review the correct answers with the class.

Evaluation:

Determine how many students were able to match up correctly. You can follow-up with a matching test in which you list the parts of a label in the left column and the corresponding examples in the right column.

Inclusion:

You can read what is written on the labels to the class.

MATHEMATICAL MILLIGRAMS

Objective:

Students will differentiate between the healthful and harmful use of over-the-counter (OTC) drugs and prescription drugs.

Life Skill:

I will not abuse or misuse over-the-counter drugs or prescription drugs.

Materials:

Pencils, one for each student, paper, one sheet for each student

Motivation:

1 Introduce the term dosage. Explain that the dosage of a medicine is the amount of the medicine that should be taken. Dosage for a pill or capsule is identified in units of milligrams (mg) on both OTC and prescription drugs. When a physician writes a prescription, the number of milligrams as well as the number of tablets or pills to be taken is also included.

2 The following activity will allow students to use their math skills. Have each student compute the answers to each of the problems that follow:

1. Levonne was given a prescription by her physician. The prescription read, "take four pills each day." Assuming each pill contains 300 mg, how many mg will Levonne consume in one day? (1200 mg per day.)
2. Bud had a headache. His mother gave him two aspirin in the morning, two at noon, two in the evening, and two before bed. Each aspirin contains 325 mg. How many mg will Bud have in one day? (2600 mg)
3. Brittany was supposed to take one tablet every four hours, not to exceed four tablets in one day. Each tablet is 450 mg. However, Brittany forgot to take one tablet. How many mg did Brittany consume? (1350 mg)

4. Anthony was given special medications by his physician. He was to take two different tablets. One tablet was to be taken twice each day. This tablet contained 400 mg. Anthony also was to take another tablet every three hours or five times a day. These tablets contained 325 mg. Assuming Anthony was taking all of his required medications, how many mg will he consume in one day? (2425 mg)

Evaluation:

You can use the dosage examples on a test or make up new ones. Various math skills can be incorporated depending on the ability of your students.

Inclusion:

You can have students work with a partner in computing the answers to the questions. Ask to see how the partners computed the problems.

Grades 3–5
- Objective 7C

PRESCRIPTION PRECAUTIONS

Objective:

Students will differentiate between the healthful and harmful use of over-the-counter (OTC) drugs and prescription drugs.

Life Skill:

I will follow safety rules when using prescription drugs.

Materials:

Crayons, construction paper, a sheet for each student

Motivation:

1 Define the term prescription drug to students. Explain that a prescription drug is a medicine that can be bought only with a physician's or dentist's written permission. Prescription drugs can be dangerous if they are not used properly. Explain to students that there are many safety rules that promote the safe use of prescription drugs.

2 Write the following list of safety rules on the chalkboard regarding prescription drugs.
  1. Take the exact amount of the medicine as prescribed.
  2. Never take someone else's prescription drug.
  3. Inform your physician about other medicines you are taking.
  4. Understand the directions for taking the medicine.
  5. Inform a physician if side effects occur.
  6. Store medicines in a cool and dry place.
  7. Ask when a medicine should be taken with regard to eating or drinking.
  8. Dispose of all prescription drugs after they are no longer needed.
  9. Know how long the medicine should be taken.
  10. Understand what the medicine is supposed to do.

3 Distribute a sheet of construction paper to each student. Have each student select one safety tip and draw a picture that illustrates that safety tip. You might choose to assign safety tips to students so that they do not all select the same one.

4 Have students share their pictures with the class. The class must guess what safety tip is illustrated. This activity will help reinforce safety tips for taking prescription drugs.

Evaluation:

Erase the chalkboard and have students recall the ten safety tips that had been identified. How many of the ten did they remember?

AL K. HALL

Objective:

Students will describe ways alcohol harms physical, mental, and social health.

Life Skill:

I will not drink products that contain alcohol.

Materials:

Pencil, a pencil for each student, paper, a sheet for each student

Motivation:

1 Explain that there are many ways that alcohol can harm a person's health. Explain that alcohol can interfere with the ability to think, affect the ability of muscles to be well-coordinated, harm the liver, blur vision, interfere with speech, interfere with learning, cause dizziness, and cause the kidneys to overwork, to name a few effects.

2 The following activity will show how alcohol interferes with the ability to be well-coordinated. On a sheet of paper, have each student write in cursive his/her first and last name. Then have each student do the same thing but with the opposite hand—that is, the hand with which they usually do not write.

3 Have students describe what it felt like to write with the opposite hand. They will share that they did not feel as comfortable and it was not as easy. They will indicate that their handwriting was more sloppy and that they wrote more slowly than when they used their usual hand.

4 Explain that, in a way, this activity simulates having a drink of alcohol. The same kinds of changes can also happen after drinking alcohol. With this in mind, have students describe how alcohol might create dangerous situations. For example, you can ask students to describe what might happen if they were riding a bicy-

cle in traffic. Emphasize the risks of having an accident when drinking. Have students share other ways alcohol might interfere with their health and safety.

Evaluation:

Have students identify the actions they do each day. Then ask them how these actions might be affected if alcohol were involved.

Grades 3–5
▪ Objective 8B

I CAN'T UNDERSTAND YOU

Objective:

Students will describe ways alcohol harms physical, mental, and social health.

Life Skill:

I will not drink alcohol.

Materials:

A bag of marshmallows

Motivation:

1 Review some of the possible physical effects that result when a person drinks alcohol. Examples are slurred speech, poor coordination of body muscles, liver damage, inability to think clearly, drowsiness, dizziness, and injury due to increased risk of accidents.

2 The following activity will demonstrate how alcohol affects coordination of body muscles. Select a volunteer to come to the front of the class and read a paragraph aloud from a book that is an appropriate reading level. Ask the class how clear the reading was. Most students should be able to follow what was read.

3 The volunteer will read the paragraph aloud again, but this time (s)he will have a marshmallow in his/her mouth. This student cannot chew or eat the marshmallow; the marshmallow is to remain in the person's mouth. Again, ask the class how clear the reading was. Were they able to understand what the volunteer was reading? Students will indicate that the student was difficult to understand. The words were slurred.

4 Explain that the tongue is a muscle and that there are many muscles that form the mouth. These muscles could not work together in a coordinated fashion. When a person drinks too much alcohol, muscles cannot work in a coordinated manner. Trying to read with a marsh-

mallow in his/her mouth simulated how a person who drinks too much alcohol might sound.

5 You can have the class try another experiment. Have the students pair off. First one partner will try reading to his/her partner with a marshmallow in his/her mouth. Then the partner will take a turn. Students might also remark that they felt frustrated as they tried to read with a marshmallow in their mouths. Explain that drinking alcohol also can cause a person to become frustrated.

Evaluation:

Have students think of other activities requiring the use of coordinated muscles. Then have students share how drinking alcohol combined with activities can be dangerous.

Grades 3–5
- Objective 8C

BLURRED VISION

Objective:

Students will describe ways alcohol harms physical, mental, and social health.

Life Skill:

I will avoid situations where alcohol is being used.

Materials:

Slide projector, a variety of slides including those with a narrative

Motivation:

1 Review some physical effects of alcohol on the body. You will find many of these listed in Objective 8A and Objective 8B, which are related to alcohol use. You can play a game in which each student is to identify an effect of alcohol use. As each student takes a turn, (s)he must identify an effect of alcohol use. No effects can be repeated. Students can repeat an effect only after all effects have been identified.

2 In identifying effects of alcohol use, be sure to identify some social effects. For example, alcohol use can disrupt families and is the cause of many family breakups. Alcohol use also is involved in many acts of violence. And alcohol use can be the cause of many friendships that are broken.

3 After reviewing the effects of alcohol use, focus on one effect—the effect on vision. Show a slide show in which there is a narrative. As the show proceeds, illustrate the effects of alcohol as follows: as you announce that a viewer has had one drink, slightly turn the focus dial of the slide projector. Next, indicate that the viewer has had another drink and turn the dial again. As you announce each additional drink, turn the focus dial so that the pictures become more and more blurred. Have the students

observe how reading what is on the slide becomes more and more difficult.

4 Discuss the implications of having blurred vision when trying to complete certain tasks. Have students identify certain tasks they perform and have them describe what would happen if these tasks were performed under the influence of alcohol.

Evaluation:

Have students identify certain tasks that require their ability to see accurately. Then have then describe how they could become physically harmed if their vision were impaired because of alcohol.

Grades 3–5
▪ Objective 9A

TARRED LUNGS

Objective:

Students will describe ways tobacco harms physical, social, and mental health.

Life Skill:

I will not use tobacco products.

Materials:

Cotton balls, a straw, one plastic sandwich bag, rubber band, cigarette, cardboard pieces, paper, a sheet for each student; optional, cardboard for boxes

Motivation:

1 Emphasize the effects of smoking cigarettes on the body. For example, smoking interferes with normal breathing. It causes the heartbeat rate to increase more than it should. Smoking also causes an increase in the production of acid in the stomach, which can lead to ulcers. Smoking causes lung cancer and emphysema as well as cancer of the throat and many other body parts.

2 The following activity will demonstrate how smoking affects the lungs. Place cotton balls inside a clear plastic baggie. Insert a straw through the top of the baggie. Attach the top of the baggie to the straw with a rubber band. The straw will represent the air passage to the lungs. The baggie represents a lung. The cotton balls represent the alveoli or air sacs in the lungs.

3 Light a cigarette and without inhaling, blow the smoke through the straw into the baggie. Allow the smoke to exit from the baggie. Continue to puff smoke into the baggie several more times. Have the students observe what is happening. They will notice that the cotton balls in the baggie are turning brown. Explain that the brown color is tar, which is a substance in tobacco. When a person smokes, tar covers

the alveoli in the lungs. The exchange of air from the alveoli to the bloodstream becomes difficult. This is one reason that people who smoke cigarettes have difficulty breathing. By observing the cotton balls, it will be obvious that tar was collecting on them. Explain that there also is a relationship between tar and the development of cancer.

Evaluation:

Have students create a jingle in which they describe the dangers of smoking. To make this activity more creative, students can write the jingle and design a cigarette box on which the jingle can be written.

Inclusion:

Students can make a box similar to a cigarette box on which a jingle can be written.

Grades 3–5
- Objective 9B

SMOKELESS AND TOOTHLESS

Objective:

Students will describe ways tobacco harms physical, mental, and social health.

Life Skill:

I will not use tobacco products, including smokeless tobacco.

Materials:

Magazine, scissors, two blank transparencies, yellow marker, black marker, transparency projector

Motivation:

1 Explain that smokeless tobacco is a very harmful product. Many people think that smokeless tobacco is safe because persons who use it do not inhale smoke into their lungs. However, smokeless tobacco is extremely dangerous. Smokeless tobacco is used either as a powder or as ground up tobacco leaves. Because it remains inside the mouth for long periods of time, smokeless tobacco can cause sores in the mouth that can lead to cancer. Smokeless tobacco may contain sand. When the tobacco is in contact with the teeth, the sand wears away the tooth enamel. Smokeless tobacco also contains sugar, which causes the teeth to rot. Users also experience a separation of gums from the teeth, which can cause teeth to fall out.

2 To demonstrate the effects of smokeless tobacco on teeth, cut a picture from a magazine showing a person with a nice smile with teeth exposed. Make two transparencies of this picture. Leave one transparency as is. On the other transparency, color the teeth yellow. Use a black marker to darken some teeth so it appears as if they have fallen out.

3 First show the transparency of the person smiling. Ask the class to describe this person. Then make up a short story about this person. Tell the class that this person began to use smokeless tobacco because his/her friends were all using it. Explain that after a few years, this person's appearance began to change. The smokeless tobacco had an effect on this person's teeth. Then tell the class you would like to show a more recent picture of this person. Now show the other transparency in which the person has yellow and missing teeth. Explain that smokeless tobacco caused this.

Evaluation:

Have the class discuss how smokeless tobacco is harmful to a person. Students are to identify as many harmful effects of smokeless tobacco as they can.

Grades 3–5
- Objective 9C

WHAT DISGUSTING LUNGS YOU HAVE!

Objective:

Students will describe ways tobacco harms physical, mental, and social health.

Life Skill:

I will not use tobacco products.

Materials:

A sheet cake or single-layer cake cut to resemble the shape of a lung, a mixture of soil, dirty oil or other similar substances dissolved in water, a jar, a knife

Motivation:

1 Bring in a sheet or single-layer cake cut in the shape of a lung. Ask students if they would like to have a piece. Of course, most students will indicate they want a taste of the cake. However, before the cake can be eaten, explain that it must be decorated. Before class, mix the soil, dirty oil and water in a jar. (Other substances might be substituted for the dirty oil.)

2 Show the cake to the class. Explain that this cake is in the shape of a lung and is the lung of a person who smoked. Explain that the cake must reflect the effects of being exposed to cigarette smoke over a period of many years. Tell the class you have the ingredients of cigarette smoke in a jar, a disgusting-looking mixture. The odor also will probably be strong. Walk around the room with the jar and allow students to observe and smell the mixture.

3 Return to the front of the room and spread the mixture on the cake. After you have completed decorating the cake, cut several slices of the lung (cake) and ask students if they now want a taste. Students will respond that the cake is disgusting. Ask students why they think the cake is disgusting. Explain that a person who smokes has lungs that are coated in a similar

fashion. Tar from cigarette smoke discolors the lungs.

Evaluation:

Students will be repulsed by what they have seen. Explain that just as a cake must be clean to eat, so must the insides of a lung be clean to function so that a person can breathe normally. Have students describe why they believe smoking is harmful to lungs.

IT'S A DIFFICULT TASK

Objective:

Students will identify illegal drugs and ways they harm physical, mental, and social health.

Life Skill:

I will not use any illegal drugs.

Materials:

One pair of old eyeglasses, petroleum jelly, needle, thread

Motivation:

1 Explain that the use of illegal drugs can be harmful to many parts of the body. Opiates such as heroin and morphine are types of illegal drugs that can be abused. These drugs slow the actions of the central nervous system. Drugs that slow body actions are called depressants. Other drugs called stimulants speed up the actions of the body. Cocaine, amphetamines, and crack are stimulants. Stimulants can speed up actions of the body so much that a person can experience heart failure. Marijuana is a drug that is prepared from crushed leaves of the cannabis plant. People who smoke marijuana may experience amotivational syndrome which is a condition in which people lack a desire to perform common everyday tasks such as doing homework.

2 Explain that many body parts are affected when a person uses illegal drugs. The following activity will demonstrate how drugs affect muscle coordination and the ability of the brain to control muscle activity.

3 Place a light coating of petroleum jelly on the lenses of an old pair of eyeglasses. Select a volunteer to come to the front of the class. Give the volunteer a needle and a piece of thread. Ask the volunteer to try to thread the needle while (s)he is wearing the eyeglasses.

The student will have difficulty performing this task.

Evaluation:

Have the students in the class relate how using drugs might be compared with wearing eyeglasses that are coated with petroleum jelly. Explain that the blurred vision caused by the petroleum jelly prevented the student from threading the needle. (Using illegal drugs can interfere with vision, which makes the completion of simple tasks difficult.)

Grades 3–5
- Objective 10B

DRUGS TAKE AWAY EVERYTHING

Objective:

Students will identify illegal drugs and ways they harm physical, mental, and social health.

Life Skill:

I will not use illegal drugs.

Materials:

Pencils, a pencil for each student, paper, a sheet for each student, tape

Motivation:

1 Give each student a sheet of paper to fold into four parts. The paper should be folded so that there are two parts on the top half and two parts on the bottom half.

2 Have students identify four things in their lives that are important to them. They can identify people, activities, or possessions. Students are to write one item in each of the four parts. Each student is to tape the sheet of paper on his/her chest.

3 Explain that you are going to identify four different drugs. As you name a drug, each student will tear away one of the parts of their papers and place it on his/her desk. The four drugs you will name are marijuana, cocaine, heroin, and crack. After you have named each drug, the students in the class will have removed all four parts of their papers. In essence, they will be left with nothing.

4 Have the students consider how a person loses all his/her important possessions if (s)he uses illegal drugs. Answers will center around families breaking up, crimes being committed to get money to buy drugs, adults losing jobs because they no longer can do their work, and conflicts with family and friends which are difficult to solve.

5 Explain that everyone has conflicts and difficulties at times. People who are resilient can bounce back regardless of the situation. They do not try to escape from their difficulties by taking drugs. Have students identify four ways they would handle problems so that they can bounce back from adversity without taking illegal drugs. Examples are talking with parents, talking with the school counselor or a trusted teacher. As students identify how they would handle their problems, have them tape their "possessions" back on their chests.

Evaluation:

Have students discuss how families and friends of a person who uses drugs might be affected by that person's drug use. Students can identify protective factors that help prevent the use and abuse of drugs.

Violence Prevention

Family Frustration

Objective:

Students will identify illegal drugs and ways they harm physical, mental, and social health.

Life Skill:

I will not use illegal drugs.

Materials:

Two identical textbooks, two coins, one pair of thick gloves, two shoes with laces

Motivation:

1 Inform the class that they are going to play a modified version of Family Feud called Family Frustration. There will be two teams. Select four students for each team. It is important to have at least one person on each team who is wearing shoes or sneakers that have shoelaces. The importance of this will be evident later. Identify one team as the Loving Family; the other team is the Unfortunate Family.

2 Have the two teams come to the front of the room. Explain that the Loving Family is made up of members who support each other, show love in many different ways, and work together. The Unfortunate Family has one member who uses illegal drugs. Explain that one family member from each team will play the game. The other family members will cheer for the team member who is playing.

3 In selecting the player from each team, choose one who is wearing shoes or sneakers that have shoelaces. The player for the Unfortunate Family is to wear thick gloves. The Loving Family member will not be required to wear gloves.

4 The players will be given three tasks to perform. The goal is to complete each task as fast as possible. The player who completes the task first will score a point for his/her team. Two

out of three points wins. Each player will start each tasks at the same time.

5 For the first task, undo each player's shoelaces. At your signal, each player must tie his/her shoelace. Give a point to the player who finishes the task first. For the next task, give the two players identical textbooks and assign a page to which they are to turn. The player who turns to the page in the shortest time will earn a point. For the third task, have each player pick up a coin that you have placed on the floor. The player who is the first to pick up the coin earns a point for the family.

6 After completing the three tasks, it should be evident that the Loving Family is the winner and the Unfortunate Family is the loser. Have students describe why they think the Unfortunate Family failed. Emphasize that when a family member is involved in drug use, the results of his/her actions affect the entire family. Every family member is adversely affected by the drug-taking behavior of one of its members. It was evident in this game that the Unfortunate Family could not function. The Loving Family functioned well.

7 Explain to students that the thick gloves made it impossible for the Unfortunate Family player to do ordinary tasks easily. Explain that when a person uses drugs, (s)he affects the way his/her body works. This person cannot do ordinary things well or the way (s)he would ordinarily do them. Discuss what a family like the Unfortunate Family can do if one of its members is a drug user. One suggestion might be to get counseling for the family member who is using drugs as well as for the other members of the family.

Evaluation:

Have students share what they would do if they knew that a member of their family was abusing drugs and disrupting the family.

Grades 3–5
• Objective 11A

HEALTH IS WEALTH

Objective:

Students will describe how the use of alcohol, tobacco, and illegal drugs interferes with reaching goals.

Life Skill:

I will avoid using drugs so I can reach my goals.

Materials:

Pencils, a pencil for each student, paper, a sheet for each student, index cards

Motivation:

1 Introduce the word goal. Explain that a goal is a desired achievement toward which a person works. A goal can be short-term, something that a person wants to accomplish within a short period of time. An example of a short-term goal might be to get a good grade on a test tomorrow. A long-term goal is something that may take a longer time to reach. For example, a person may have a goal to graduate from high school or college even though that person is still in elementary school.

2 Explain that reaching a goal requires that a person work hard. Sometimes there are obstacles that interfere with persons reaching their goals. One of these obstacles is drugs. Drugs interfere with a person's health. To reach one's goals, one must be healthy. This means that a person's mind and body must be in top working condition.

3 Emphasize that taking care of their health means doing activities that help keep their bodies and minds working as well as possible. On a sheet of paper, have students list ten ways they take care of their health. For example, items they list may include playing basketball, getting enough sleep each night, talking to par-

ents when they have problems, and getting school assignments done on time.

4 On index cards, write the names of different kinds of drugs, one name per card. List such drugs as alcohol, tobacco, LSD, marijuana, heroin, cocaine, crack, and steroids. Select several students to read the lists they developed that emphasize ways they keep healthy. After a students has read his/her list, hand him/her one of the index cards. Then have that student indicate how the drug that is named on the card might interfere with his/her health. For example, drinking alcohol can interfere with the ability to think clearly. It can also cause conflicts within a family, thereby increasing stress. Explain that achieving and maintaining good health takes work. People who are not in good health have difficulties achieving their goals.

Evaluation:

Have students discuss the different ways that their classmates take care of their health. Be sure that students understand that staying healthy involves exercising both the body and the mind. Ask students to list some goals they want to reach and ways they plan to reach those goals. The goals may be short term or long term.

Grades 3–5
▪ Objective 11B

HAVING CLEAR GOALS

Objective:

Students will describe how the use of alcohol, tobacco, and illegal drugs interferes with reaching goals.

Life Skill:

I will set goals for myself and avoid using any drugs that can interfere with my reaching these goals.

Materials:

Poster paper, marker, petroleum jelly, old sunglasses

Motivation:

1 Have students brainstorm goals that they or people their age may have. List these goals on a sheet of poster paper that is taped to the classroom wall where every student can see it.

2 After the list is complete, have students take turns reading each goal. Explain that these goals present a clear picture of what people wish to accomplish. Explain that sometimes people make choices that prevent these goals from being reached.

3 Smear petroleum jelly over the lenses of an old pair of sunglasses. Select a volunteer to wear these sunglasses. Ask this student to read the goals listed on the poster paper. The student will not be able to see clearly and probably will not be able to read the goals. Explain to the class that the petroleum jelly simulated the effect that drugs have on a person's ability to see clearly. Use this analogy to explain that when a person uses drugs, the drugs will prevent that person from seeing his/her goals clearly. A person who does not have clear goals will have difficulty reaching these goals. Using any kind of drug will endanger health and prevent a person from being at his/her

best. When persons are not at their best, they cannot accomplish their goals.

4 Use an example of how a drug can interfere with the ability to reach a goal. A person who drinks alcohol will not be able to think clearly. This person also will not be able to perform tasks efficiently. This person also is more likely to be involved in an accident when drinking, and possibly cause serious injury to himself/herself or to another person. A serious injury can prevent a person from achieving a particular goal.

Evaluation:

Have students provide other examples of how using drugs can interfere with a person's ability to achieve a goal.

Grades 3–5
▪ Objective 11C

STICK TO YOUR GOALS

Objective:

Students will describe how the use of alcohol, tobacco, and illegal drugs interferes with reaching goals.

Life Skill:

I will not use any kind of illegal drug.

Materials:

Felt, six Ping Pong balls, Velcro, marker

Motivation:

1 Cut a circle from a piece of felt. (The circle must be large enough to serve as a target.) Draw a bull's-eye and circles on the felt to resemble a target. On three Ping Pong balls, glue strips of Velcro to cover almost the entire ball. On three other Ping Pong balls, write the name of a drug such as alcohol, marijuana, heroin, or cocaine. On these balls, glue just a small strip of Velcro.

2 Select three volunteers to whom you will give a Ping Pong ball covered with Velcro and three other volunteers to whom you will give a Ping Pong ball that has the name of a drug. The volunteers are to stand a few feet from the felt target. Explain that the target represents a goal. As each volunteer throws a ball toward the target, (s)he will identify a goal (s)he has. Explain that a ball that sticks to the target represents a person who reaches his/her goal. The class will observe that the Ping Pong balls that have the name of a drug written on them and have only a small strip of Velcro most likely will not stick to the target. These balls represent a person who uses drugs. (It is possible that one or two of these balls may stick to the target but the analogy can still be used.)

3 Have the class discuss how drugs interfere with the ability of people to achieve their goals. You may ask questions to stimulate the discussion.

Why didn't the balls with the names of drugs written on them stick to the target? If any of them stuck to the target, why was it possible? Did all the balls have the same chance of sticking to the target?

Evaluation:

Have every student identify a goal and throw the balls at the target. Have the class describe how drugs can prevent a person from reaching his/her goals.

Inclusion:

Help students identify their goals before they come to the front of the room to throw balls at the target.

Grades 3–5
- Objective 12A

Violence Prevention

GOLDEN RULES

Objective:

Students will follow school rules and laws related to the use of drugs.

Life Skill:

I will not break any rules at school.

Materials:

Sticks of uncooked spaghetti, Golden Rules (page 344), a copy for each student, crayons

Motivation:

1 Explain to students that there are rules that everyone must follow in school. As you identify some of these rules, emphasize that these rules are not to be broken. For example, you might say that there is no talking allowed in class. As you state a rule, take a stick of uncooked spaghetti and break it in half. (Breaking the spaghetti is for emphasis: you can break some things, but you should not break a rule.) Identify other rules such as no fighting on school grounds, keeping the aisles in the classroom clear, using certain exits when there is a fire drill, no littering inside or outside the school building, or not leaving the classroom without a pass. Use other rules that are particular to your classroom and to your school.

2 Explain to students that there are rules they must follow regarding drugs. No drugs are allowed in school or on the school property.

3 Explain to students that they are going to design a message that will promote following the rules that pertain to the use, possession, or distribution of drugs at their school. Give each student a copy of Golden Rules. Explain that Golden Rules is a cereal box. Tell students that they are to design their cereal boxes with a message to encourage all students in the school to follow school rules related to drugs.

Their messages can be creative such as writing a jingle or combining a jingle with a picture.

Evaluation:

Have students share their Golden Rules with the class. Review specific school rules pertaining to drugs that students must follow.

Inclusion:

Students can work in teams to perform this task: one person may be skilled in drawing, another in writing.

Grades 3–5
- Objective 12B

Violence Prevention

DRUG RULES

Objective:

Students will follow school rules and laws related to the use of drugs.

Life Skill:

I will follow school rules related to drugs.

Materials:

Paper, pencils, a rule book (such as a sports rule book)

Motivation:

1 Bring a rule book to class. The easiest kind of rule book to find would be one related to sports. Show the book to the class and explain that the book has rules that must be followed in order to play that particular sport. For example, there are rules that protect players from injury, rules about time periods, and rules related to penalties if other rules are violated.

2 Divide the class into groups of about five. Explain that each group represents a special rules committee. This committee is a drug rules committee. Each group will have the responsibility to develop a rule book about drugs. Just as the sports rule book has different categories, so will the drug rules book have certain categories. Rules about the sale, possession, and use of drugs at school, penalties for breaking the rules, who is in charge of the rules, and rules that protect students from possible harm are possible categories. Students may identify others.

3 Allow students about 30 minutes to work in their groups. One person in each group can be designated as the recorder. Encourage input from all students in the group. When the time is up, have each group present the rules they developed.

Evaluation:

Allow students the opportunity to challenge statements made by the groups. Students will begin to see that it is not easy to establish rules about drugs.

Grades 3–5
▪ Objective 12C

DRUG FREE, YOU AND ME

Objective:

Students will follow school rules and laws related to the use of drugs.

Life Skill:

I will not use illegal drugs in my school, home, or community.

Materials:

Paper, a sheet for each student, pencils, crayons

Motivation:

1 Explain to students that they have a right to be drug free as well as to be around others who are drug free. Explain that the school environment is a place where illegal drugs such as alcohol, tobacco, and marijuana are not permitted.

2 Explain that they are going to have the opportunity to encourage everyone in the class to be drug free. Each student is to take a sheet of paper and fold it down the middle from top to bottom. Tell students that they are going to make greeting cards that have the message that everyone in the class has the right to be in a drug-free environment. This includes you, the teacher.

3 Give students guidelines that would be similar to cards they might buy in a card shop. For example, the front of the card might have the beginning of a quote or other statement that is to completed on the inside of the card. Students may write a poem or draw a picture to help them send the message that they have a right to be in a drug-free environment and that others should not use drugs.

4 You can modify this activity by having students work in pairs to complete this task. At the completion of this activity, have students share their cards. You may choose to place some cards on the classroom bulletin board.

Evaluation:

Have students summarize the rules about drugs that have been identified. Which ones do they think are the most important ones? Write these rules on the chalkboard.

Multicultural Infusion:

Students may be able to write statements in another language and read and show them to the class.

Grades 3–5
- Objective 13A

GIVING BACK SUPPORT

Objective:

Students will identify support groups that assist persons and families who need help with alcoholism, smoking cessation, and other drug treatment.

Life Skill:

I will use support groups in my school and community if I need help.

Materials:

A stool that has no back

Motivation:

1 Ask for a volunteer to sit on a stool that has no back while the rest of the class will be seated at their desks. Continue to teach your lesson: ask students (including the volunteer) to be prepared to take notes.

2 About halfway through the lesson, ask the volunteer how (s)he is doing. Ask what it feels like to sit for a period of time on a chair that has no back. Ask the volunteer to explain what it felt like to try to take notes without having a desk or tabletop. The volunteer may express how the lack of support made it difficult for him/her to hold a notebook and write: (s)he may express some frustration or discomfort.

3 Explain to the class that the volunteer had no support. In this case, you are talking about physical support, of course. Explain that another kind of support is the encouragement that other people can provide to assist a person who has problems that need help. Explain that in a similar way, a person who needs support when dealing with a problem may feel frustrated and be unable to function as (s)he should.

4 Explain that everyone has problems at times and that there are always people available to

assist in handling these problems. Explain that parents give support: other relatives may be able to help. In the community, a person might talk to someone at a mental health center, a member of the clergy, or a counselor. In school, a teacher, school psychologist, school nurse, or guidance counselor can give support.

Evaluation:

Have the students help develop a directory of people in the community who serve as support groups. This directory can be made into a resource book.

Grades 3–5
- Objective 13B

| Violence Prevention |

DRUG AID

Objective:

Students will identify support groups that assist persons and families who need help with alcoholism, smoking cessation, and other drug treatment.

Life Skill:

I will identify sources of help in my community for myself and others.

Materials:

Pencil, paper, telephone directory yellow pages

Motivation:

1 Explain to students that you are going to share with them how to use the yellow pages of the telephone directory. Explain that they can find many sources of help if they look under the specific categories or headings such as "Psychologists" and "Mental Health Services." They also will find specific services listed that relate to conditions such as "Suicide Prevention."

2 Using the yellow pages, show students how they could find help for problems related to drug use. Have students take turns finding sources of help that are listed in the yellow pages.

3 Divide the class into groups. Explain that each group will be responsible for developing a song that focuses on resources to help individuals and their families. By looking at some of the ads in the yellow pages, students will be able to gather ideas for the words of their songs. Many of the ads describe specific services that different agencies and organizations offer. The words in these ads can be modified into the words of a song. Give each group about 15–20 minutes to develop their songs.

Evaluation:

Based on the information given by each group, you can list on the chalkboard the names and telephone numbers of the agencies that were identified. Students can copy this information in their notebooks and save it for reference.

Violence Prevention

BLOCKS OF SUPPORT

Objective:

Students will identify support groups that assist persons and families who need help with alcoholism, smoking cessation, and other drug treatment.

Life Skill:

I will use support services in my community if needed.

Materials:

Six toy blocks, paper, pencils, tape

Motivation:

1 Using toy blocks, tape a tag to each. Five tags should have one of the following protective factors listed on it: has someone to talk to; copes with stress; relates well with family members; engages in school activities; follows rules. One tag should have the name of a fictitious person written on it.

2 Stack the blocks on top of each other. The top block should be the one with the person's name on the tag. Explain that the name is for an example only. Explain that the person on the top block is receiving support in the form of protective factors, which enables the person to be drug free. This person knows that if (s)he has a problem, (s)he can find help to handle that problem.

3 Now pull the lower five blocks away from the stack. The person no longer has any support. Without the support of the protective factors, the person cannot cope by himself/herself. The person might be overcome with the temptation to use drugs. Have the class discuss why this person might now be tempted to try drugs.

4 Explain that students can have the opportunity to help this person become resilient again. Have students identify how this person might rebuild his/her protective factors. Students might suggest the following: visit a counselor in the community; participate in activities in school; and participate in healthful activities with family members. As students identify each protective factor, rebuild the stack.

Evaluation:

Have students share how protective factors can help prevent drug use.

Grades 3–5
• Objective 14A

CHECK OUT MY MESSAGE

Objective:

Students will interpret messages in the media about drug use.

Life Skill:

I will differentiate between fact and fiction in messages in the media as they relate to drugs.

Materials:

Old magazines, scissors, a pair for each student, paper, a sheet for each student, glue or paste

Motivation:

1 Introduce the term media. Explain to students that the term media refers to the ways by which information is communicated to people. The media we are referring to are television, radio, videos, records, newspapers, books, and magazines. The media often influence the way people behave.

2 Distribute old magazines to students. They are to find ads such as those for cigarettes or beer. Each student is to cut out an ad and paste it to a sheet of paper. Then each student is to turn the ad into a negative message. They are to find other ads or articles in the magazines from which they can cut out words to create their own negative messages. For example, students may have an ad that shows a person smoking a cigarette. Their negative message might be, "Many people killed." Each student can share his/her ad with the class.

3 You may choose to have small groups work together on this activity. In this way, students can search through more than one magazine at a time to find appropriate pictures and words. Each group can present its ad to the class. The group members can describe the original message in the ad so that students can be aware of the difference.

4 Take each ad and display it on the bulletin board. Students can then review how advertisers promote the use of their products. For example, students can discuss how the people in the ads appear, the activities in which they are engaged, and the background scenes.

Evaluation:

Have students identify advertising techniques that companies use in their efforts to get people to use their products.

MUSIC VIDEO

Objective:

Students will interpret messages in the media about drug use.

Life Skill:

I will not allow music videos to influence me to engage in harmful activities.

Materials:

Pencils, paper

Motivation:

1 Have the students identify some of their favorite music videos. As they name a video, they are to describe what they like about the video. Have students discuss what message is being communicated by the performer(s) in the video.

2 Divide the class into groups of five. Explain to students that they are to develop a video that encourages healthful behaviors. (Students will not actually produce a video but they will create lyrics for a song.) Their lyrics should be at least ten lines in length. In addition to the lyrics, they are to name their group something healthful such as "Dorothy and the Drug Free's."

3 Allow students about 20–30 minutes to develop lyrics to promote a drug-free lifestyle. They will need additional time to practice before they sing their songs for the class. When they come to the front of the room, they are to introduce their group name and then sing their song. Remind the other students to listen carefully to the message being sung.

4 After each group has had the opportunity to present its song, the other students in the class are to identify the antidrug messages in the songs. Students are to make a list of messages that encouraged health and discouraged drug use.

Evaluation:

Students can make posters that display anti-drug messages.

Multicultural Infusion:

Students can develop songs that would be in a style specific to their particular culture.

Grades 3–5
▪ Objective 14C

A POETIC MESSAGE

Objective:

Students will interpret messages in the media about drug use.

Life Skill:

I will not use drugs such as alcohol and tobacco that are advertised in the media.

Material:

Old magazines, pencils, paper

Motivation:

1 Have students look through magazines that have ads for alcohol and tobacco products. In class, discuss with students how the messages in the ads promote the use of a particular product.

2 Assign students to work in pairs. Based on the class discussion about how ads promote the use of a product, have students create poems that might appear in a magazine. Their poems should discourage the use of alcohol or tobacco. The students can cut out an ad that encourages the use of alcohol or tobacco from a magazine and attach their poems to the ad.

3 Provide students with the following example of how this can be accomplished using the following short poem about tobacco.

> Please Don't Smoke.
> If I were you, I'd never smoke.
> The tar and nicotine will make you croak.
> Rapid heartbeats and reddened eyes,
> The pictures you see are a bunch of lies.

This poem might be attached to a picture in an ad that shows persons who look very healthy.

4 Have each pair of students present their poems and ads to the class. Some of the modified ads can be placed on the bulletin board as reminders.

Evaluation:

Have the class analyze each of the ads for ways the media encourage people to smoke or to use alcohol. Have students discuss their reactions to the poems that were added to the magazine ads.

- Objective 15A

| Violence Prevention |

MENDING A BROKEN HEART

Objective:

Students will explain why drug use promotes violent behavior.

Life Skill:

I will seek support from people in the school or community if I feel threatened by violence.

Material:

Pencils, tape, Mending a Broken Heart (page 354), a copy for each student, scissors, a pair for each student

Motivation:

1 Introduce the word violence. Explain that violence is the use of force to harm yourself or another person. There are many forms of violence such as hitting, using knives, or using guns. Explain that drug use plays a major role in violent crimes. People may commit crimes to get money to buy drugs. They may commit crimes because they are dealing in drugs. They may commit crimes because they are under the influence of drugs and cannot think clearly.

2 Explain that many persons become the victims of violence. The person against whom a crime is committed is not the only victim. The family and friends whose lives are affected are also victims.

3 Give each student a copy of Mending a Broken Heart. Have them cut out the heart. Notice that the heart is divided into four sections. In each section, students are to write a reason that an act of violence might be committed. Then they are to tape the heart on their chests. Select students to stand at their seats and to rip each section of the heart as they name the reason that a violent act might be committed. Eventually, the heart will be torn into four sections. Explain that violent acts can tear the heart of a family.

4 Explain that broken hearts can also be repaired. For each reason identified as a cause of a violent act, have students suggest a way this violent act might have been prevented. As each way is identified, have students tape the sections of their heart together. Stress that violent crimes can be prevented.

Evaluation:

Have the class develop a list of actions that would help prevent violent acts. Some examples to suggest are: do not associate with people who use drugs, do not sell drugs, and do not use drugs.

Mending a Broken Heart

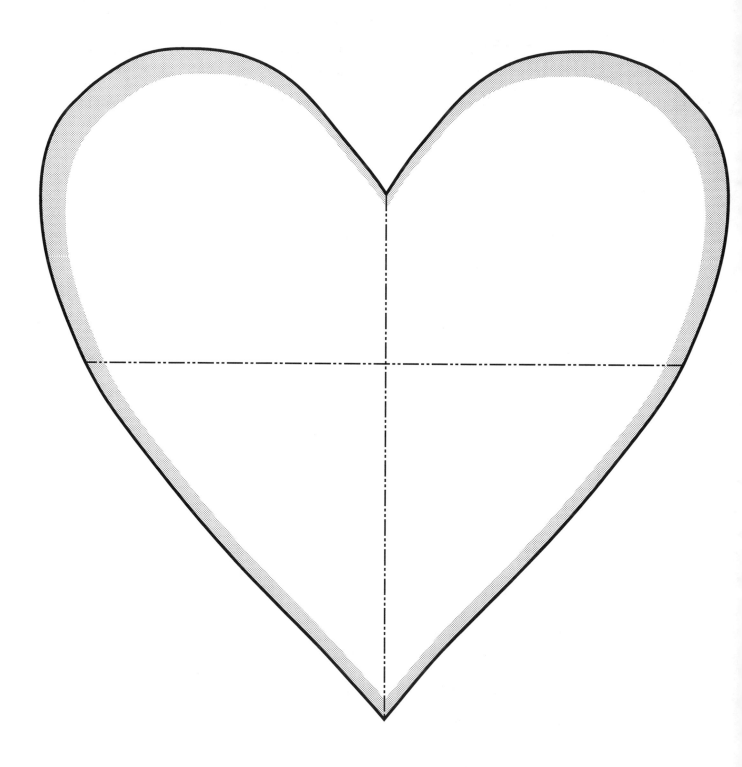

Grades 3–5
- Objective 15B

Cut It Out

Objective:

Students will explain why drug use promotes violent behavior.

Life Skill:

I will use protective factors to prevent being involved in violent behavior.

Materials:

A sheet cake or a one-layer cake, knife, tube of frosting

Motivation:

1 Place the cake on the desk and divide it into ten equal pieces. The pieces should be large enough so that you can "write" on them using a tube of decorative frosting. (These are available in supermarkets.)

2 On each slice of cake, write one of the following abbreviated protective factors: loving family, school activities, positive self-esteem, goals, close friends, faith, success at school, role-model, rules, stress skills.

3 Explain to students that the pieces of cake represent strategies to help prevent violence. A protective factor is written on each piece. Having protective factors reduces the chances of being affected by violence. Explain that most cases of violence involve drugs. By avoiding being around drugs, the chances of being around violence are decreased.

4 Discuss the protective factors that are written on the pieces of cake. Discuss how these factors help prevent violence. For example, having positive self-esteem will enable persons to feel good about themselves and thus not want to destroy themselves by becoming involved with the drug community.

Evaluation:

Have students identify the relationship between each protective factor and how that factor can help reduce the risk of being in a violent situation.

Grades 3–5
▪ Objective 15C

Violence Prevention

DRUGS MAGNIFY PROBLEMS

Objective:

Students will explain why drug use promotes violent behavior.

Life Skill:

I will not engage in violent behavior.

Material:

A magnifying glass, index card with the word "drugs" written on it

Motivation:

1 Ask students if they have ever used a magnifying glass. Explain that a magnifying glass makes an object appear much bigger than it really is.

2 Write the word "drugs" in small letters on an index card. Hold the index card up at the front of the room. Students probably will not be able to see what is written on the card. Tell them that the word "drugs" is written on the card. Tell students that drugs in themselves are a major problem and that, in addition, drugs magnify many situations and make them worse.

3 Pass the index card and the magnifying glass around the class and have students look at the word on the card through the magnifying glass. Explain that the greater the drug problem itself becomes, the greater are the situations or conditions that accompany the use of drugs. One such condition is violence.

4 Have students explain why they feel drugs and violence go hand-in-hand. Students might suggest that drug users need money to buy drugs, that the ability to think clearly is impaired when a person in using drugs, and that gangs are often involved with drugs. Have students describe how violence might be reduced if drugs were not present.

Evaluation:

Have students work in groups to determine a list of school rules they would implement to help reduce the risk of violence.

Grades 6–8
- Objective 1A

| Violence Prevention |

BUILDING BLOCKS

Objective:

Students will develop skills that improve self-esteem.

Life Skill:

I will demonstrate positive self-esteem.

Materials:

Building-Block Pattern (page 359), cardboard, scissors, tape, chalk, chalkboard

Motivation:

1 Discuss self-esteem. **Self-esteem** is the personal internal image that a person has about himself/herself. A person has **positive self-esteem** when (s)he believes that (s)he is worthwhile and lovable. A person has **negative self-esteem** when (s)he believes that (s)he is unworthy and unlovable. Explain that it is important for a person to have positive self-esteem in order to promote health and well-being. The level of self-esteem seems to have a profound effect upon behavior. Persons with positive self-esteem are more likely to avoid self-destructive behavior and to choose self-loving behavior. **Self-loving behavior** is healthful and responsible behavior indicative of a person who believes himself/herself to be worthwhile and lovable.

2 Ask students to brainstorm ways that they might build positive self-esteem. Make a list on the chalkboard. Some suggestions for the list include: developing healthful friendships, setting and working toward goals, helping someone such as a grandparent or neighbor, trying one's best in school, making responsible decisions, saying NO to harmful peer pressure, participating in school activities, practicing one's faith, being honest at all times, spending time with family members.

3 Have students make a building block using the building-block pattern, cardboard, scissors, and tape. Explain that positive self-esteem is a building block for one's life. Explain that there are six surfaces or sides to the building block that they have just made. It is important to have many ways in which you build positive self-esteem. Have students write one way they might build positive self-esteem on each of the six surfaces or sides of their building blocks.

4 Divide the class into groups. Have them create ways to build positive self-esteem combining their building blocks. They will be able to build self-esteem in several ways by rearranging the building blocks several times. Have each group select one combination to share with the class.

Evaluation:

Have students select one new way to build self-esteem in which they currently do not participate. For example, one student might not be involved in school activities. Another student might not help others such as a grandparent or neighbor. Each student is to set a goal and make a plan to participate in this way to build self-esteem. (S)he is to plan to do so within the next week. Then the student is to write a paragraph about how (s)he felt when building self-esteem in this way.

Multicultural Infusion:

When students are writing statements on the six surfaces or sides of their building blocks, ask them to identify something that they do because of their cultural heritage that builds self-esteem. For example, a student who is Jewish might write "I speak Hebrew" on one of the surfaces or sides of the building block. (S)he feels good about himself/herself for having mastered this language.

Inclusion:

Have students with special needs identify something that they have done to adjust to their specific disability that helps them to feel good about themselves. For example, a student in a wheelchair may have learned to play wheelchair basketball. A student with a learning disability may have mastered a difficult assignment with the help of a tutor.

Building-Block Pattern

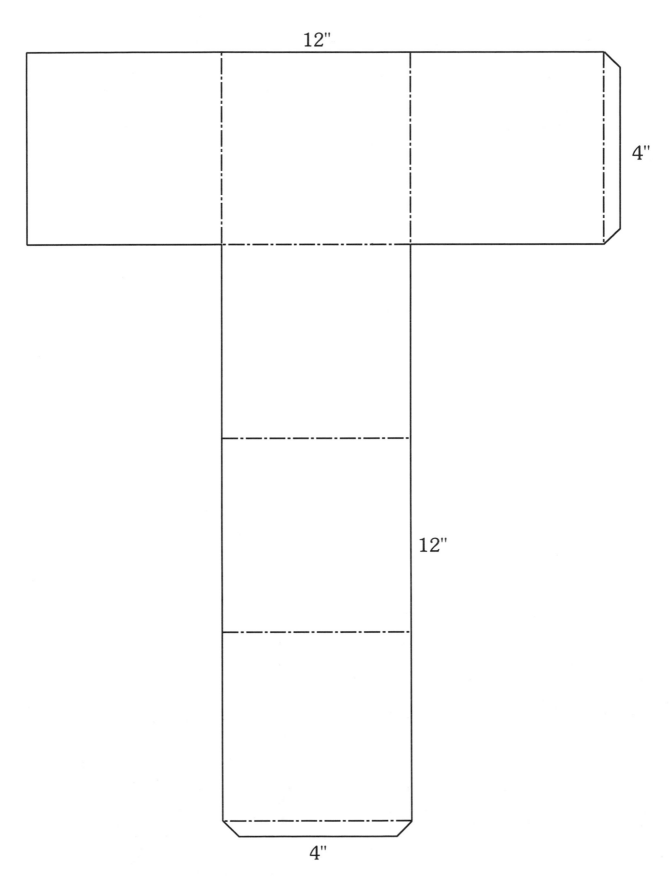

12"

4"

12"

4"

Grades 6–8
▪ Objective 1B

| Violence Prevention |

PAT ON THE BACK

Objective:

Students will develop skills that improve self-esteem.

Life Skill:

I will demonstrate positive self-esteem.

Materials:

Colored construction paper, scissors, masking tape (keep extra on hand)

Motivation:

1 Cut circles with 3-inch diameters from the colored construction paper. You should cut one circle for each student in your class.

2 Discuss self-esteem with your students. **Positive self-esteem** is the feeling of being a worthwhile person. Positive self-esteem is usually the result of a person's having family members who provide support and encouragement, having good feelings about physical appearance and talents, being able to meet challenges, feeling a sense of accomplishment, and having healthful relationships with others.

3 Put a loop of masking tape on the back of each of the circles. Give each student one of the circles.

4 Explain that one way to enhance self-esteem is to listen carefully when you are complimented by others. In this way, you can learn what others see as your strengths and why others appreciate you.

5 You can also learn ways to build self-esteem by paying attention to the compliments you give others. When you do this, you learn what strengths you admire in others and why you appreciate others. Then you can model some of the same behaviors you like in others.

6 Explain to students that they are going to give each other a "Pat on the Back" or a compli-

ment. They are to put the cardboard circle on a classmate's back and identify a strength of the classmate or something the classmate has done that is appreciated. For example, a student might place the circle on a classmate's back and say, "I admire you because you are very honest."

7 The classmate must then remove the circle that is taped on his/her back and place it on his/her front and respond with an acknowledgement message. In this example, the student might say, "Thank you, I value honesty."

8 You can provide other examples to students. For example, a student might give a "Pat on the Back" and say, "I like your sense of humor." The classmate might respond, "Thank you, I never thought of myself as having a good sense of humor."

9 Repeat the "Pat on the Back" several times so that students will interact with at least six classmates giving a "Pat on the Back" and at least six others receiving a "Pat on the Back."

Evaluation:

Discuss this strategy with students. How did they feel getting a "Pat on the Back"? Did they learn anything new about themselves? What did they learn about the values of others? What did they identify as the strengths of their classmates?

Discuss how it feels to get to a positive statement or a "Pat on the Back" from another person.

On the chalkboard, write the following headings: having family members that provide support and encouragement, having good feelings about physical appearance and talents, being able to meet challenges, feeling a sense of achievement, and having healthful relationships with others. On a sheet of paper, have students write one example illustrating these categories to indicate how each category affects a person's level of self-esteem.

Multicultural Infusion:

Discuss different cultures. Explain that your classroom is especially rich because it is made up of students who have different backgrounds. Discuss ways in which having students from varied backgrounds is a strength. Discuss the importance of sharing strengths or "Pats on the Back" with classmates from other cultures. Discuss the importance of listening to classmates who are from different cultures.

Inclusion:

Emphasize the strengths of the students with special needs. Explain that each person has gifts to offer others in a relationship. Some of these gifts might be being a good listener, kind, humorous, compassionate, and honest.

Grades 6–8 Social Studies
- Objective 1C

STAR SEARCH

Objective:

Students will develop skills that improve self-esteem.

Life Skill:

I will demonstrate positive self-esteem.

Materials:

Star Search student master (page 364), one copy; index cards

Motivation:

1 Discuss self-esteem. **Self-esteem** is the personal internal image that a person has about himself/herself. A person has **positive self-esteem** when (s)he believes that (s)he is worthwhile and lovable. A person has **negative self-esteem** when (s)he believes that (s)he is unworthy and unlovable.

2 Explain the importance of having positive self-esteem. A person's self-esteem seems to have a profound effect on behavior. Persons with positive self-esteem are more likely to avoid self-destructive behaviors and to choose self-loving behavior. **Self-loving behavior** is healthful and responsible behavior indicative of a person who believes himself/herself to be worthwhile and lovable. Suppose a person with positive self-esteem is pressured to buy or sell drugs to be a part of a gang. This person is more likely to resist the pressure because (s)he feels lovable. A person with negative self-esteem might choose to sell drugs to gain a sense of belonging that (s)he feels lacking.

3 Give each student an index card. On the index card, the student is to print his/her name and then list at least two things (s)he has done for which (s)he feels worthwhile. Here are some examples: I have a paper route in the morning, I attend worship services regularly, I am a good friend to others, I am the pitcher on the

summer softball team, I care for two children two days a week after school. Collect the index cards.

4 Use the copy of the Star Search student master. After the first statement, draw and initial a star to indicate that the first statement describes you. For each student in your class, select one statement from the index cards you collected. Write a different statement beside each number on the Star Search list. Next to each statement, be certain that there is enough space for a star to be drawn by the student described in the statement. Reproduce enough copies of the completed Star Search list for each student.

5 Have students participate in a Star Search. Each student is to walk up to other students in class and say, "I am conducting a Star Search. Are you the person who...(name one thing listed on the sheet)?" The student might have asked, "Do you have a paper route?" If the student has a paper route, (s)he would draw a star next to this statement on the Star Search copy and place his/her initials inside the Star. If the student does not have this attribute or accomplishment, (s)he would say, "I am a Star in another way." Students are to continue playing Star Search until you say the time is up or until they have an initialed star next to each statement on their copy of the Star Search list.

Evaluation:

After participating in Star Search, students will have learned about the accomplishments and attributes of their classmates. Have them list ten accomplishments or attributes that a person their age can do or acquire to promote positive self-esteem.

Multicultural Infusion:

When students are listing their accomplishments and attributes on the index card, ask them to include something that is culture specific. For example, a student who is American Indian might list that (s)he is able to demonstrate Ceremonial Dances. A student who is Jewish might list that (s)he can read Hebrew. A student who is Hispanic might list that (s)he is bilingual and can speak fluent Spanish as well as fluent English. A student who is Asian-American might be able to prepare a special recipe. A student who is African-American may sing in a Gospel choir. During the evaluation following the Star Search when students are listing the ten accomplishments or attributes that persons their age can do or acquire, have students include at least two multicultural examples.

Inclusion:

This strategy can be used to introduce the differences in students. Explain that all students have accomplishments and attributes that contribute to feelings of self-worth. Further, explain that all students have areas in which they must make adjustments in order to meet their goals. Explain that students with special needs often must make adjustments in order to learn. Yet, these same students have many strengths. Emphasize the importance of being sensitive to persons who are making adjustments in order to learn effectively.

Directions: The following list describes the attributes and accomplishments of your classmates. Introduce yourself to each of your classmates and say, "I am conducting a STAR SEARCH. Have you . . . (repeat one of the statements below)?" If you are correct, your classmate is to draw a star next to the statement and initial it. If you are incorrect, your classmate is to say, "I am a Star in another way." Then your classmate is to tell you which statement describes him/her, draw a star beside it, and initial the star.

1.   I am a very enthusiastic teacher.
2.
3.
4.
5.
6.
7.
8.
9.
10.
11.
12.
13.
14.
15.
16.
17.
18.
19.
20.

Grades 6–8
- Objective 2A

Violence Prevention

STRESS TEST

Objective:

Students will develop ways to manage stress.

Life Skill:

I will manage stress effectively.

Materials:

Ruled paper; pencil; chalk and chalkboard; Health Behavior Contract (page 367), a copy for each student

Motivation:

1 Prior to beginning this strategy, students should not know what topic you plan to cover because the element of surprise is important. As soon as your class begins, place students in the following stressful situation. Ask the students to take out a sheet of ruled paper and a pencil and to number the lines from one to twenty. Explain that you are going to give them a quiz and that the quiz will affect their grade. Begin by asking several very difficult questions regarding the topics that you have recently covered. Ask questions that would be very difficult to answer.

2 Then explain to students that this was only a "Stress Test" that was designed to place them under stress. Ask students to describe changes they experienced in their bodies when they learned that they were having a test. Students will most likely mention increased heart rate, increased respiration, sweating, dry mouth, etc.

3 Define the words stress and stressor. **Stress** is the response of a person's mind or body to stressors. A **stressor** is a physical, mental-emotional, social, or environmental demand. In the illustration that was used, an example of stress was the increase in heart rate. This was one of the body's responses to the stressor. The stressor was the unannounced and difficult test. The test was a mental-emotional demand.

4 Review information regarding the general adaptation syndrome. The **general adaptation syndrome,** or **GAS,** is the body's response to a stressor. During the **alarm stage of GAS**, the body prepares for quick action as adrenaline is released into the bloodstream, heart rate and blood pressure increase, digestion slows, blood flows to muscles, respiration increases, pupils dilate, and hearing sharpens. The body is prepared to meet the demands of the stressor. As the demands are met, the resistance stage of GAS begins. During the **resistance stage of GAS**, pulse, breathing rate, and blood pressure return to normal. The pupils contract and muscles relax. If the demands of the stressor are met unsuccessfully, the GAS continues, and the exhaustion stage of GAS begins. During the **exhaustion stage of GAS**, the body becomes fatigued from overwork and a person becomes vulnerable to diseases.

5 Explain that people respond to stressors in different ways. **Eustress** is successful coping or a healthful response to a stressor. When a person experiences eustress, the resistance stage is effective in establishing homeostasis in the body because the demands of the stressor are met. **Distress** is unsuccessful coping or a harmful response to a stressor. The exhaustion stage often accompanies distress.

6 Emphasize the importance of using stress-management skills. **Stress-management skills** are techniques that can be used to cope with stressors and to lessen the harmful effects of distress. Stress management skills used to cope with stressors include talking with responsible adults about difficult life events and daily hassles, using the responsible decision-making model and resistance skills, and writing in a journal. Exercising, being involved in faith experiences, eating a healthful diet, and spending time with caring persons also help with stress.

7 Outline reasons why using harmful drugs increases stress rather than relieving stress. Harmful drugs such as stimulants increase the body's response to stress. The heart beats faster, respiration increases, digestion slows, and the pupils dilate. Harmful depressant drugs such as barbiturates and alcohol depress the reason and judgment centers of the brain. It becomes more difficult to make choices about what to do about the stressors.

Evaluation:

Have students complete the Health Behavior Contract on the topic of Stress Management.

Multicultural Infusion:

Ask students to describe stressors that they experience and that they believe are specific to their culture. Have the class brainstorm stress management techniques that might be used to alleviate the stress that may be caused by these stressors. How might classmates help students with cultural stressors relieve stress?

Inclusion:

Ask students with special needs to describe stressors that they experience as a result of their specific disabilities. Have the class brainstorm stress management techniques that might be used to alleviate the stress that may be caused by these stressors. How might classmates help students with special needs relieve stress?

HEALTH BEHAVIOR CONTRACT

Life Skill: I will use stress management skills.

Effect on My Well-Being: When I experience a stressor, my body responds with an increase in heart rate, blood pressure, and respiration. My pupils dilate. The blood flow to my stomach is reduced and digestion slows so that blood flow may be increased to the muscles. My liver releases glycogen so that I have plenty of sugar for energy. These bodily changes may be needed to meet the demands of a stressor. However, I want my body to return to normal for good health. Stress management skills protect my body.

My Plan: I will use one or more of the following stress management skills: talk with responsible adults about difficult life events and daily hassles, use the responsible decision-making model, write in a journal, exercise, be involved in faith experiences, eat a healthful diet, and spend time with caring persons.

Evaluating My Progress: I will complete the following chart to indicate stress management skills I used for one week.

Monday	Tuesday	Wednesday	Thursday

Friday	Saturday	Sunday

Grades 6–8
▪ Objective 2B

HEAVY BURDEN

Objective:

Students will develop ways to manage stress.

Life Skill:

I will manage stress effectively.

Materials:

General Adaptation Syndrome transparency (page 538), transparency projector, chair, index cards

Motivation:

1 Explain stress, stressor, the general adaptation syndrome, eustress, and distress using the General Adaptation Syndrome transparency. **Stress** is the response of a person's mind or body to stressors. A **stressor** is a physical, mental-emotional, social, or environmental demand.

2 Use the General Adaptation Syndrome transparency to review the body's response to stressors. Explain that the **general adaptation syndrome** or **GAS** is the body's response to a stressor. During the **alarm stage of GAS**, the body prepares for quick action as adrenaline is released into the bloodstream, heart rate and blood pressure increase, digestion slows, blood flows to muscles, respiration increases, pupils dilate, and hearing sharpens. The body is prepared to meet the demands of the stressor. As the demands are met, the resistance stage of GAS begins. During the **resistance stage of GAS**, pulse, breathing rate, and blood pressure return to normal. The pupils contract and muscles relax. If the demands of the stressor are met unsuccessfully, the GAS continues, and the exhaustion stage of GAS begins. During the **exhaustion stage of GAS**, the body becomes fatigued from overwork and a person becomes vulnerable to diseases.

3 Explain that people respond to stressors in different ways. **Eustress** is successful coping or a healthful response to a stressor. When a person experiences eustress, the resistance stage is effective in establishing homeostasis in the body because the demands of the stressor are met. **Distress** is unsuccessful coping or a harmful response to a stressor. The exhaustion stage often accompanies distress. For this reason, it is important to identify stressors and to know ways to handle them to prevent distress.

4 Ask a student to come forward and to sit in a chair in front of the class. When the student is selected, be certain the student has no neck or upper back problems. Then ask ten other students to come forward. Explain that each student is to name a stressor and then place the palm of his/her hand on the shoulder of the student sitting in the chair. Some of the stressors that students might mention: not having enough money, breaking up with a boyfriend/girlfriend, arguments with family members, giving a report in front of the class, pressure to get good grades, alcoholism in the family, pressure to have sex, pressure to use drugs, divorce of parents, adjustment to a stepfamily, death of a family member, or loss of job.

5 Ask the student in the chair how (s)he feels. The student should feel the heaviness from the weight of the students' hands. Explain that stressors can be a heavy burden unless a person uses stress management skills. Explain that **stress-management skills** are techniques that can be used to cope with stressors and to lessen the harmful effects of distress. Stress management skills used to cope with stressors include talking with responsible adults about difficult life events and daily hassles, using the responsible decision-making model and resistance skills, and writing in a journal. Exercising, being involved in faith experiences, eating a healthful diet, and spending time with caring persons also help.

6 Have each of the students who has a hand on the shoulder of the student sitting in the chair name a stress-management skill and then remove his/her hand.

7 Discuss the importance of practicing stress management skills on a regular basis rather than waiting until a person experiences a stressor.

Evaluation:

Have students keep a journal for one week. In their journals, students are to identify stressors they experienced and the stress-management skills they used. At the end of the week, students are to write a summary paragraph about the stressors in their lives and their ways of managing them.

Inclusion:

Use seven index cards. Print one of the following on each of the index cards: heart rate increases, blood pressure increases, digestion slows, blood flows to muscles, respiration increases, pupils dilate, hearing sharpens. Ask a student with special needs to be the student sitting in the chair. When the students place their hands on this student's shoulders, the student with special needs reads each of the index cards to explain why stressors are a heavy burden.

Ask students with special needs to be the students who name the stressors. Provide them additional help by writing the stressors on index cards. For example, you might print, "I am pressured to drink alcohol," on an index card. The student reads the index card and then places his/her hand on the shoulder of the student sitting in the chair.

Grades 6–8 Language Arts
- Objective 2C

STRESS HOROSCOPES

Objective:

Students will develop ways to manage stress.

Life Skill:

I will use stress management skills when I feel stress.

Materials:

Stress Horoscopes student master (pages 372, 373), a copy for each student; newspaper; paper; markers; pen

Motivation:

1 Discuss stress. **Stress** is the response of a person's mind or body to stressors. A **stressor** is a physical, mental-emotional, social, or environmental demand. According to Hans Seyle, a pioneer in stress physiology, the body responds to stress in three stages. Together, these three stages are called the **general adaptation syndrome (GAS)**. During the **alarm stage of GAS**, the body prepares for quick action as adrenaline is released into the bloodstream, heart rate and blood pressure increase, digestion slows, blood flows to muscles, respiration increases, pupils dilate, and hearing sharpens. The body is prepared to meet the demands of the stressor. As the demands are met, the resistance stage of GAS begins. During the **resistance stage of GAS**, pulse, breathing rate, and blood pressure return to normal. The pupils contract and muscles relax. If the demands from the stressor are met unsuccessfully, the GAS continues and the exhaustion stage of GAS begins. During the **exhaustion stage of GAS**, the body becomes fatigued from overwork and a person becomes vulnerable to diseases.

2 Explain that persons respond to stress in different ways. **Eustress** is successful coping or a healthful response to a stressor. When a per-

son experiences eustress, the resistance stage is effective in establishing homeostasis in the body because the demands of the stressor are met. **Distress** is unsuccessful coping or a harmful response to a stressor. The exhaustion stage often accompanies distress. For this reason, it is important to learn to identify stressors and to know ways to handle them to prevent distress.

3 Ask students to identify life stressors that they believe may result in distress. Research indicates that the life events which are the most severe stressors for young people are death of a parent, death of a brother or sister, divorce of parents, marital separation of parents, death of a grandparent, hospitalization of a parent, remarriage of a parent to a stepparent, birth of a brother or sister, and loss of a job by a parent or guardian. Although these events may elicit distress because of their severity, it is now believed that young people experience distress most of the time from the cumulative effects of daily hassles. The daily hassles include concern about physical appearance, peer acceptance, homework assignments and tests, misplacing or losing belongings, and being the brunt of bullying or criticism.

4 Emphasize the importance of practicing stress management skills. **Stress management skills** are techniques that can be used to cope with stressors and to lessen the harmful effects of distress. Stress management skills used to cope with stressors include talking with responsible adults about difficult life events and daily hassles, using the responsible decision-making model and the model for using resistance skills, and writing in a journal. Each of these techniques helps a person take action to relieve the cause of stress. Stress management skills that protect health include exercising, being involved in faith experiences, spending time with persons who are caring and supportive, watching comedy to elicit laughter, eating a healthful diet containing vitamins B and C, reducing or eliminating caffeine in the diet, practicing breathing techniques, and practicing progressive relaxation in which muscles are tensed and then relaxed.

5 Show students the section of a newspaper that contains horoscopes. Explain to students that they are going to write horoscopes. Give each student a copy of the two-page student master Stress Horoscope. They are to write a horoscope for each month. In each one they are to predict that a stressor(s) will occur and then provide advice for ways to handle the stressor(s). For example, the stress horoscope for Aries might be:

> As an Aries, you are romantic and warm, but this month the object of your desires shows no interest in you. You feel rejected. Focus on spending time with friends who care about you and who are supportive.

An example of a stress horoscope for Virgo might be:

> School has begun and your friends are full of pep and vigor. Unfortunately, news that your parents are separating has dampened your enthusiasm and left you feeling very angry. Focus on sharing your angry feelings with your parents and/or school guidance counselor. Get a well balanced breakfast and plenty of rest and sleep to restore your depleted energy.

6 Display the Stress Horoscopes on a bulletin board in the classroom.

Evaluation

After the Stress Horoscopes have been displayed on the bulletin board for a week, take them down. Give each student a Stress Horoscope other than his/her own. Select three horoscope signs (such as Gemini, Virgo, and Leo) and have students analyze the stressors in the Stress Horoscope they have been given. For evaluation purposes, have students provide other alternatives for relieving the stress.

CAPRICORN (Dec. 22–Jan. 19)

AQUARIUS (Jan. 20–Feb. 18)

PISCES (Feb. 19–March 20)

ARIES (March 21–April 19)

TAURUS (April 20–May 20)

GEMINI (May 21–June 20)

CANCER (June 21–July 22)

LEO (July 23–Aug. 22)

VIRGO (Aug. 23–Sept. 22)

LIBRA (Sept. 23–Oct. 22)

SCORPIO (Oct. 23–Nov. 21)

SAGITTARIUS (Nov. 22–Dec. 21)

Grades 6–8
▪ Objective 3A

GIFT OF FRIENDSHIP

Objective:

Students will develop skills needed for healthful and responsible relationships.

Life Skill:

I will engage in healthful relationships with others.

Materials:

A shoe box for each student, wrapping paper, tape, ribbon, index cards, pens

Motivation:

1 Initiate a discussion about relationships and about friendship. **Relationships** are the connections that people have with each other. Friendship is a special relationship. **Friends** are persons who know us well and care for us. Friends provide a supportive relationship in which we can learn about ourselves and try new ways of interacting in order to grow personally. There are two important ingredients in friendship—affection and respect. **Affection** is a fond or tender feeling that a person has toward another person. It is experienced as emotional warmth or closeness. **Respect** is liking that comes from having esteem for someone's admirable characteristics and responsible and caring actions. In a healthful friendship, there is both affection and respect.

2 Identify some of the admirable characteristics and responsible and caring actions that deem a young person of this age worthy of respect:
- demonstrates self-loving behavior;
- is trustworthy and honest;
- expresses feelings in healthful ways;
- adheres to family guidelines and the principles of his/her faith;
- sets goals and makes plans to reach them;
- demonstrates interdependence;

- demonstrates balance when managing time for family, school, hobbies, and friends;
- avoids abusive behavior;
- is committed to a drug-free lifestyle;
- practices abstinence.

3 Brainstorm other characteristics and responsible and caring actions that are important in friendship. Students may mention behaviors such as "keeps thoughts I share in confidence" and "encourages me to do well in school." Students may also mention qualities that they enjoy in others such as "has a sense of humor" and "has good listening skills." Explain that varied interests are a bonus to friendship. Sharing interests helps bring persons closer together.

4 Give each student a shoe box, wrapping paper, and tape (or have each student bring these items from home). Have students wrap their boxes. They should wrap the top and the bottom of the box separately.

5 Give each student five index cards. Ask students to reflect for a moment on the characteristics and interests that they have that are valuable to a friendship. For example, a student might be a very loyal person. Another student might be a very cheerful person. Another student might have very clear values and behave very responsibly. Another student might be very athletic and enjoy a variety of sports. Another student might be a talented musician. Ask students to make a list of the characteristics and interests that they have that are valuable to a friendship. From this list, they are to select five. Using the index cards, they are to print each of the five items selected on a separate card.

6 Have the students place the index cards in the boxes that are wrapped. Now have students tie a colorful ribbon around their boxes. Collect the boxes and place them in the center of the room.

7 Have each student take a box other than the one that belonged to him/her. Explain that each student has just received a gift. Ask students to describe what is meant by "gift." A **gift** is something special that is given to another person. It involves the act of giving or putting forth effort. A gift is only of value to a person if it is received. So, a gift also involves the act of receiving.

8 Have students open the friendship boxes and read the index cards to learn about the gifts each has received. Then ask students to select one of the five gifts in their boxes. They are to tell the class which gift they selected as most valuable to them and why they would like to receive this gift from a friend.

Evaluation:

Have students identify five gifts of friendship that they have to give and five gifts of friendship that they would like to receive.

Multicultural Infusion:

Initiate a discussion on the importance of having friends from different cultures. Have students share with classmates special gifts they possess because of their cultural heritage. Prior to this sharing, you may want to have students discuss the positive aspects of their cultural heritage with their parents. Students may wish to bring items to share with the class.

Grades 6–8
▪ Objective 3B

THAT'S WHAT FRIENDS ARE FOR

Objective:

Students will develop skills needed for healthful and responsible relationships.

Life Skill:

I will engage in healthful relationships with others.

Materials:

Pie Pattern (page 377), construction paper, scissors, markers or pens

Motivation:

1 Discuss the importance of knowing one's personal strengths. Identify personal strengths that are assets in a relationship. List these strengths on the chalkboard. Some of these personal strengths are: has positive self-esteem, chooses healthful behaviors, makes responsible decisions, resists harmful peer pressure, demonstrates character, follows laws, respects others, has a sense of humor, is a good conversationalist, is loyal, is honest, has a variety of interests, is supportive, is reliable. Students can mention other personal strengths that are an asset to a relationship.

2 Use the pattern of the pie on the next page. Have each student cut out a pie divided into six pieces. The students are to examine the list of personal strengths that are an asset in a relationship. They are to select six of the personal strengths and then write one on each of the six pieces of their pie. Three of the personal strengths selected should be those that the student believes that (s)he possesses. The other three should be personal strengths that the student would like to have or would like to improve. Then they are to cut their pies into six pieces.

3 Explain that students are to keep the pie pieces on which are written personal strengths they would like to improve on or have. However, the students are now allowed to trade the three pieces that describe personal strengths they already have.

4 Have students trade their pieces with classmates in the following manner. The students can circulate around the class and find pie pieces on which are written strengths they value. One student might ask another for a pie piece. For example, a student might want a pie piece that says, "good conversationalist." The student asks the student with this pie piece to make a trade. The student explains why (s)he believes this might be a personal strength in a relationship. The student with this pie piece responds giving the reason that (s)he values this personal strength.

Evaluation:

Have each student describe himself/herself using the six pie pieces. For example, a student might have the following pieces: loyal, good conversationalist, sense of humor, makes responsible decisions, supportive, variety of interests. The student would say, "Hi, I'm Carolyn. I have many personal strengths that improve my relationships. I am loyal and I am a good conversationalist. I will make you laugh. I will be certain that we make responsible decisions. I will support you and share a variety of interests with you." Have students analyze the personal strengths of Carolyn and the benefits of having a relationship with her.

Multicultural Infusion:

Have each student make a pie piece to keep that describes something unique about his/her culture. During the summary of this strategy, discuss the benefits of having friends of different races, faiths, and nationalities.

Pie Pattern

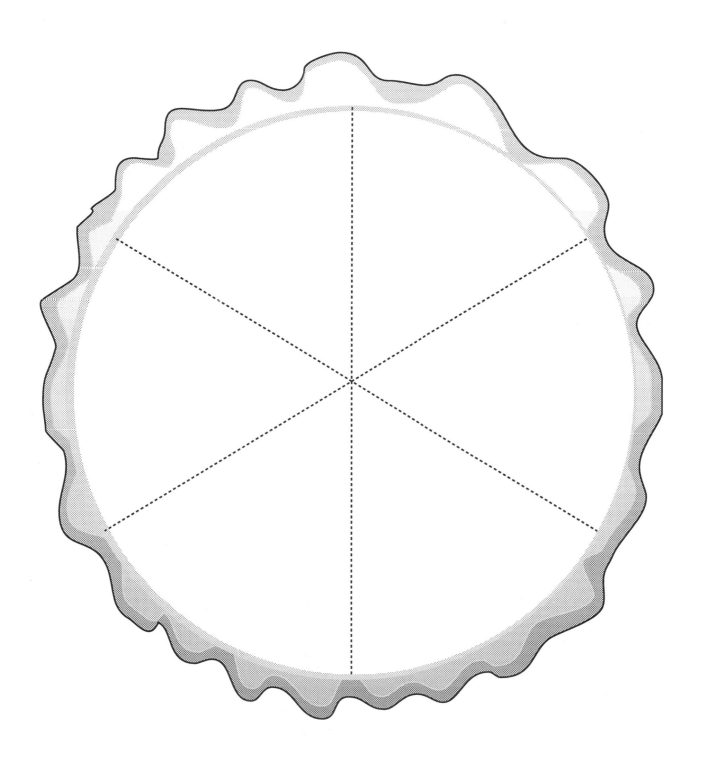

Grades 6–8 Art Studies
- Objective 3C

BUMPER STICKERS

Objective:

Students will develop skills needed for healthful and responsible relationships.

Life Skill:

I will practice skills needed for healthful and responsible relationships.

Materials:

Spirit-Relationship Continuum transparency (page 537), transparency projector, construction paper, markers

Motivation:

1 Discuss relationships with students. **Relationships** are the connections that people have with each other. Explain that the quality of relationships varies. Some relationships are fulfilling; they are a source of happiness and joy. Other relationships are depletive; they are a source of sadness and pain and endanger a person's ability to function.

2 Use the Spirit-Relationship Continuum transparency to differentiate between inspiriting and dispiriting relationships. **Inspiriting relationships** are relationships that lift the spirit and contribute to a sense of well-being. Inspiriting relationships make a person feel worthwhile, important, and high in self-esteem. When a person's spirits are lifted, (s)he experiences joy, enthusiasm, passion, hope, and satisfaction. **Dispiriting relationships** are relationships that lower a person's spirit and make a person feel unimportant, worthless, isolated, and frustrated. They contribute to feelings of low self-esteem.

3 Explain that it is important to learn how to be successful in relationships, to get along well with others, and to respect others' rights. Success in relationships is determined by the skills a person possesses as well as a person's

knowledge, attitudes, values, and behaviors. Skills that enhance relationships include being able to show care and concern for others, to express feelings in healthful ways, to articulate values, to make responsible decisions, and to cope effectively in difficult situations. Additional skills are being able to set goals and to delay gratification if necessary in order to meet those goals. Have students brainstorm a list of additional relationship skills.

4 Provide each student with construction paper. Have markers available for students to share. Have students design bumper stickers that serve as reminders to practice relationship skills. An example of a bumper sticker might be, "Engage in Random Acts of Kindness and Senseless Acts of Caring." This bumper sticker is an alteration of the theme, "Random Acts of Violence and Senseless Acts of Crime."

5 Display the bumper stickers in your classroom to serve as a reminder to practice skills needed for healthful and responsible relationships.

Evaluation:

Have students draw the Spirit-Relationship Continuum. At the end of the Continuum that is labeled "inspiriting relationships," they are to list three skills they can practice to promote healthful and responsible relationships.

Inclusion:

This strategy is ideal for cooperative learning. Pair students with special needs with other students. Each pair of students can work together to design an appealing bumper sticker.

Grades 6–8
• Objective 4A

| Violence Prevention |

ROAD SIGNS

Objective:

Students will practice responsible decision-making skills.

Life Skill:

I will make decisions that result in actions that are healthful and safe, protect the laws of my community, show respect for myself and others, follow guidelines set by responsible adults such as my parents or guardian, and demonstrate that I have good character and moral values.

Materials:

Six broomsticks or six wooden poles, six sheets of poster board, markers, masking tape, Responsible Decision-Making Model transparency (page 524), transparency projector

Motivation:

1 Ask students to brainstorm the various road signs that they have seen that promote highway safety for pedestrians and drivers of automobiles. Examples are as follows: yield, pedestrian crossing, stop, railroad crossing, S-curve in the road ahead, no passing, children at play, school zone, slippery when wet, etc. Explain that these road signs are intended to provide information and directions for pedestrians and drivers so that they know how to react in certain situations.

2 Review the Responsible Decision-Making Model transparency. Focus on step 4, which states, "Carefully evaluate each possible action using six criteria." Draw an analogy between these six criteria and the road signs. Just as the road signs are intended to provide information or directions for pedestrians and drivers so that they know how to react in certain situations, these six criteria provide direction in making responsible decisions in a variety of situations.

In this case, you are in the driver's seat and you are protected when your decisions are:
• healthful
• safe
• legal
• respectful of self and others
• consistent with guidelines set by responsible adults such as your parents or guardian
• indicative of good character and moral values

3 Divide the class into six groups. Give each group a broomstick or wooden pole, a sheet of poster board, markers, and masking tape. Explain to the class that each group is to make a road sign representing one of the six criteria for carefully evaluating each possible action. For example, one group would have the criteria focusing on "safe" actions while another would have "legal" actions. The group having "safe" actions would make a road sign or some kind of symbol illustrating the word "safe." The group having "legal" actions would make a road sign or some kind of symbol illustrating the word "legal." The symbol created by the group would be drawn on the poster board using the markers. It might be cut into a specific shape. Then it would be attached to the broomstick or wooden pole.

4 When the six groups are finished, there will be six road signs to symbolize the six criteria used to evaluate possible actions to ascertain if the actions are responsible. Have the members of each of the six groups stand together in different areas of your classroom with one member of each group holding the road sign the group has created.

5 Read sample scenarios that require a decision to be made. The sample scenarios should be specific to your class and to the types of decisions students living in your community must make. After each scenario is read, each of the six groups is to respond by calling attention to the criteria identified on its road sign. For example, you might read the following scenario:

Two students have invited you to eat lunch with them. One of the students suggests that you go to his/her house because his/her parents are not home. (S)he brags that his/her parents have so much beer in the refrigerator that they would not know if some was missing. Should you eat lunch with these two students?

The group that has the road sign that illustrates "health" would use the criteria on its sign and give input as to whether this would be a responsible decision. This group would say NO because drinking alcohol affects a young person's body in many ways. Specifically, alcohol depresses the function of the brain and this would affect learning after lunch. The group that has "safe" would use the criteria on its sign and give input as to whether this would be a responsible decision. This group would say NO because drinking alcohol increases the likelihood of accidents. It also increases the likelihood of violence. Continue evaluating what to do by having the other four groups use their criteria and provide feedback regarding a responsible decision.

6 Introduce the topic of peer pressure. **Peer pressure** is the influence that persons your age use to encourage you to make decisions they want you to make. Explain that sometimes peers want you to make decisions that follow these road signs. They encourage you to choose actions that are responsible. Yet other times, peers pressure you in other ways and you need to stop and visualize these six road signs before choosing. You are in the driver's seat.

Evaluation:

Write a scenario that requires a decision to be made. Have students list the six criteria to carefully evaluate each possible action and use the criteria to explain what they would decide.

Inclusion:

Before beginning this lesson, obtain a pamphlet illustrating various road signs from your State Department of Highway Safety. Allow students with special needs the opportunity to help you prepare for the lesson. These students might use construction paper, markers, and scissors to copy the illustrations for the different road signs. As you introduce the lesson, these students can share the road signs that they have made.

Violence Prevention

Try It, You'll Like It

Objective:

Students will practice responsible decision-making skills.

Life Skill:

I will make decisions that result in actions that are healthful and safe, protect the laws of my community, show respect for myself and others, follow guidelines set by responsible adults such as my parents or guardian, and demonstrate that I have good character and moral values.

Materials:

Enough small wrapped Tootsie Rolls for two-thirds of the students each to have two, Model for Using Resistance Skills transparency (page 525); Responsible Decision-Making Model transparency (page 524), transparency projector

Motivation:

1 Use the following demonstration to illustrate peer pressure to your students. Divide the class into three groups. The first group is the risk behavior group. Explain that a **risk behavior** is an action that might be harmful to you or others. Give each person in the risk-behavior group a Tootsie Roll. The second group is the risk-situation group. Explain that a **risk situation** is a situation in which another person's behavior threatens your health. Give each person in the risk-situation group a Tootsie Roll. The third group is the healthful-behavior group. No one in this group gets a Tootsie Roll.

2 Now explain peer pressure. **Peer pressure** is the influence that persons your age use to encourage you to make decisions they want you to make. Explain that the members of the first group are to eat their Tootsie Rolls in front

of those in the second group. While they are enjoying eating their Tootsie Rolls, they are to encourage the members of the second group to unwrap and eat their Tootsie Rolls. They are to be as convincing as possible. After several minutes, stop to see if any member of the second group has eaten a Tootsie Roll. Discuss the kinds of pressure the members of the first group used to try to encourage the members of the second group to eat their Tootsie Rolls (engage in risk behaviors).

3 Now have the members of the second group who did not eat their Tootsie Rolls unwrap them and take a small bite. Then they are to hold the remaining part of the Tootsie Roll in their hands near their mouth without eating it. Again, the members of the first group are to pressure the members of the second group to eat their Tootsie Rolls. After several minutes, stop and ask the members of the second group if they were more tempted to eat the Tootsie Roll before they unwrapped it or after they had unwrapped it and had taken a small bite.

4 Take aside the members of the third group so that the members of the first and second groups cannot hear the directions that you are going to give them. Tell the members of the third group to say, "No, I do not want to eat the Tootsie Roll," each time they are pressured by a member of the first or second group. They are not to touch the Tootsie Roll. After they are pressured three times, they are to move away from the person offering them the Tootsie Roll. Now give the members of the first and second groups Tootsie Rolls that they can offer to members of the third group. Instruct them to pressure members of the third group to eat a Tootsie Roll.

5 Discuss the results of the scenario. When members of the first group pressured members of the second group, what convincing techniques were used? After the members of the second group unwrapped their Tootsie Rolls and took a bite, was it more tempting to continue eating the Tootsie Rolls? Explain that it usually is. This is the reason limits need to be set on most behaviors to avoid participating in risk behaviors in which you had previously said you would not participate. For example, taking a sip of beer may lead to drinking, taking a puff of a cigarette may lead to smoking, and petting may lead to sexual intercourse. Discuss what happened when the members of the third group were pressured. The members of the third group avoided the risk behavior by firmly saying NO. Also, this group avoided being tempted by not even touching a Tootsie Roll. Members of the third group left the situation when the pressure continued.

6 Review the Responsible Decision-Making Model transparency. Explain the importance of making decisions that result in actions that are healthful and safe, protect the laws of the community, show respect for self and others, follow guidelines set by responsible adults such as parents and guardians, and demonstrate character.

7 Review the Model for Using Resistance Skills transparency. Emphasize the importance of resisting temptation. Discuss the skills students can use.

Evaluation:

Provide students with the following scenario: You have made plans to go to a friend's house for a party on Friday evening. At lunch, you are sitting with four of your peers who are also planning to go to the party. They mention that there will be a keg of beer at the party. You tell them that you are not allowed to go to parties where there is alcohol or other drugs. They pressure you to go using lines such as, "Your parent(s) won't know," and "You can go and not drink." Have students identify resistance skills they would use to resist the pressure to attend the party.

Violence Prevention

GUIDE LINES FOR DECISION MAKING

Objective:

Students will practice responsible decision-making skills.

Life Skill:

I will make decisions that result in actions which are healthful and safe, protect the laws of my community, show respect for myself and others, follow guidelines set by responsible adults such as my parents or guardian, and demonstrate that I have good character and moral values.

Materials:

Responsible Decision-Making Model transparency (page 524), transparency projector, two ropes, blindfold, sheet of poster board, construction paper, tape, scissors, markers

Motivation:

1. Before beginning this strategy. Divide the class into six groups to make the following props. Each group is to be provided construction paper, tape, scissors, and markers. The directions for the groups are as follows:

Group 1. Select one group member to represent a person who is suffering from health consequences as a result of using drugs. Using the materials, decorate this person appropriately. For example, group members might cut out black eyes to tape over this person's eyes.

Group 2. Select a group member to represent a person who is involved in crime. Using the materials, decorate this person appropriately. For example, group members might cut out a paper knife and tape it to the person.

Group 3. Select a group member to represent a person who is in jail. Using the materials, decorate this person appropriately. For example, group members might cut out jail bars to

tape to the front of the person or make handcuffs out of tape.

Group 4. Select a group member to represent a person who does not respect others. Using the materials, cut out strips of paper and write words that describe a person who does not respect the rights of others. Tape these strips of paper to the person. For example, appropriate words might include abusive and hostile.

Group 5. Select a group member to represent a person who is not close to his/her family. Using the materials, decorate this person appropriately. For example, the group might cut out a broken heart and tape it to the person.

Group 6. Select a group member to represent a person who does not have good character and moral values. Using the materials, cut out strips of paper and write words that describe a person who does not have good character and moral values. Tape these strips of paper to the person. For example, appropriate words might be lies and promiscuous.

2 While the groups are making their props, make a large target from the poster board. At the center of the target, in large letters print RESPONSIBLE DECISION. Tape the target to the chalkboard or wall in the area of the classroom where there is room.

3 When the groups have finished their props, ask the students who are representing their groups to come forward. They are to mingle in the area of the target labeled RESPONSIBLE DECISION.

4 Ask for a student to volunteer. Explain to this student that (s)he needs to make a decision. The decision involves whether or not to use drugs. You might ask the class to brainstorm typical situations in which they have had to make decisions regarding drug use.

5 Explain that the student who volunteered has no guidelines for making a decision. Blindfold the student. Spin the student round and round.

Now have the student walk toward the target labeled RESPONSIBLE DECISION. The other students will be in the path. When the volunteer bumps into one of the other students, the other student is to explain who (s)he is. For example, the Group 1 student might say, "I'm not healthy. I have used drugs. Notice that my eyes are black and I am tired. You have not made a responsible decision." After the volunteer has bumped into a few of the other students representing other groups, have him/her take off the blindfold. Have the remaining students representing groups tell about themselves.

6 Review the transparency of the Responsible Decision-Making Model. Emphasize the importance of carefully evaluating each possible action using the six criteria identified in the model. The criteria are stated as questions:
   a. Will this decision result in an action that will protect my health and the health of others?
   b. Will this decision result in an action that will protect my safety and the safety of others?
   c. Will this decision result in an action that will protect the laws of the community?
   d. Will this decision result in an action that shows respect for myself and others?
   e. Will this decision result in an action that follows guidelines set by responsible adults such as my parents or guardian?

   f. Will this decision result in an action that will demonstrate that I have good character and moral values?

7 Ask for two more student volunteers. They are to hold the two ropes to form a straight path in the direction of the target labeled RESPONSIBLE DECISION. Have the students representing groups stand outside the two ropes. Again, blindfold the other student, but have this student stand inside the ropes and place one hand on each of the two ropes. The student can use the ropes as "guide lines" to walk to the target.

8 Explain to the class that the "guide lines" helped in getting to the target without any serious consequences such as poor health, unsafe actions, ending up in jail, etc.

Evaluation:

One of the goals of this lesson is for students to remember the six criteria or questions that can be used to evaluate an action. Therefore, testing of rote memory is useful. Have students list in writing the six criteria or questions that can be used to evaluate an action.

Grades 6–8
- Objective 5A

Violence Prevention

Stop, Think, Say NO

Objective:

Students will practice resistance skills when pressured to use or abuse drugs.

Life Skill:

I will use resistance skills when appropriate.

Materials:

Red construction paper, tape, scissors, Model for Using Resistance Skills transparency (page 525), transparency projector

Motivation:

1 Review the information on the transparency of Model for Using Resistance Skills. Demonstrate the difference between assertive behavior, aggressive behavior, and passive behavior. Use the following example.

> You (the student) are sitting in the non-smoking section of a restaurant. A person lights a cigarette and begins to smoke. You demonstrate assertive behavior when you ask the person not to smoke and state firmly that this is a nonsmoking section. You demonstrate aggressive behavior when you use words or actions in a disrespectful manner. For example, you might say, "Can't you read? This is a nonsmoking section!" You demonstrate passive behavior when you hold back your feelings. For example, you decide to hold back your displeasure and say nothing.

2 Discuss reasons why it is unwise to say, "No, thank you," when someone pressures you to do something harmful, unsafe, illegal, or disrespectful or that may result in disobeying parents or displaying a lack of character and moral values. You are in no way grateful for the offer.

3 Demonstrate ways in which nonverbal and verbal behavior must match in order to avoid sending a mixed message. The transparency uses the illustration of a person offering you a cigarette. Use the example of a friend offering you a beer.

4 Using the example of a friend offering a cigarette and/or a beer, have students give examples of ways they might influence the friend to choose responsible behavior.

5 Have students think of other situations in which there might be pressure to make harmful decisions. How might they resist or avoid these situations? What might be some of the risks involved in these situations? What would be the advantages of resisting or avoiding these situations?

6 Have students make "stop mittens" (see illustration) using the red construction paper, tape, and scissors. They can make one or two mittens.

7 Explain to students that whenever they are pressured to do something that might be harmful, unsafe, illegal, or disrespectful, or that may result in disobeying parents or displaying a lack of character and moral values, they need to say NO. They can provide a reason. For example, when someone pressures you to smoke a cigarette, you can say "NO, smoking is harmful to health." Suppose someone continues to pressure you. One of the most effective techniques is to repeat what you have just said, "NO, smoking is harmful to health." If the person continues to pressure you, you again repeat, "NO, smoking is harmful to health." The technique you have used is called the broken record technique. You sound like a recording that got stuck because you repeat the same message three times. Each time you repeat the same message, it is more likely to be taken seriously by the person pressuring you. After repeating the message three times, be certain to leave the situation.

8 Explain that the students are going to practice using this technique. Have four students volunteer to role play in front of their classmates. One of the students is to do the pressuring. This student is to try to convince one of the other students to do something harmful such as using smokeless tobacco. Explain that the student being pressured is to "stop, think, and say NO." The student being pressured is to raise his/her stop mitten, take a moment to think, and then say, "NO, smokeless tobacco causes oral cancer." Then the student doing the pressuring continues and gives another reason for using smokeless tobacco. Then the first student being pressured and a second student together raise their stop mittens and say together, "NO, smokeless tobacco causes oral cancer." Repeat a third time. After the student pressures the first student to use smokeless tobacco, all three students raise their stop mittens and say, "NO, smokeless tobacco causes oral cancer." This illustrates how the NO message becomes stronger as it is repeated.

9 Divide the class into groups of four students. Have each group design a role-play situation in which one student pressures another to engage in a behavior that is harmful, unsafe, or illegal, or that is disrespectful of self and others. The behavior might also be against family guidelines and indicate a lack of good character. Each group is to determine a reason for saying NO to this behavior. Then the group is to perform the role play for the class, following the previous guidelines for the performance using the stop mittens and adding an additional person each time for saying NO.

Evaluation

Have students identify the seven suggestions identified on the Model for Using Resistance Skills. Have students describe and/or demonstrate the broken record technique.

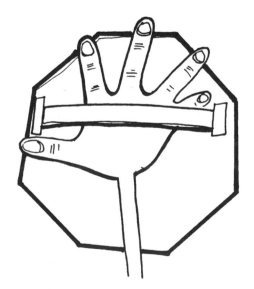

| Violence Prevention |

THE NGUZO SABA
(THE SEVEN PRINCIPLES OF BLACKNESS)

Objective:

Students will practice resistance skills when pressured to use or abuse drugs.

Life Skill:

I will use resistance skills when appropriate.

Materials:

Thirty feet of yarn, sixteen sheets of construction paper, markers

Motivation:

1 For this strategy, you will need to print each of the following terms on a separate sheet of construction paper: UMOJA (Unity), KUJI-CHAGULIA (Self-Determination), UJIMA (Collective Work and Responsibility), UJA-MAA (Cooperative Economics), NIA (Purpose), KUUMBA (Creativity), IMANI (Faith). You will also need to print each of the following on a separate sheet of construction paper: Not close to family; Allow others to make decisions for me; Don't care about my community; Don't set economic goals and work for them; Don't have goals for my future; Don't make the world a better place in which to live; lack faith. Print one of the following on each of the two remaining sheets of construction paper: "Inner Well-Being—Resists Pressure" and "Harmful Peer Pressure."

2 You may want to read *HER STORY: Black Female Rites of Passage* by Mary Lewis, Chicago: African American Images, 1988.

3 Explain the Nguzo Saba, also known as the "Seven Principles of Blackness" (The History of Kwanzaa, *Ebony Jr!* December, 1982, p. 10.).

- *UMOJA (Unity)*—To strive for and maintain unity, with members of a family, community, nation, and race living together in peace and harmony.
- *KUJICHAGULIA (Self-determination)*—To make opportunities to name ourselves, define ourselves, create for ourselves, speak for ourselves, and make our own decisions instead of being named, defined, created, and spoken for by others who make decisions for us.
- *UJIMA (Collective Work and Responsibility)*—To build and maintain our community, with everyone working together; to make our sisters' and brothers' problems our problems, and to solve them together so everyone survives.
- *UJAMAA (Cooperative Economics)*—To build and maintain our own stores, shops, and other businesses, and to share the profits from them.
- *NIA (Purpose)*—To make our collective vocation the building and developing of our community, and to do so in order to restore our people to their traditional greatness.
- *KUUMBA (Creativity)*—To do always as much as we can, in the way we can, to leave our community more beautiful and beneficial than we inherited.
- *IMANI (Faith)*—To believe with all our heart in our people, our parents, our children, our teachers, our leaders, and in the righteousness and victory of our struggle.

4 Explain that these "Seven Principles of Blackness" are intended to empower African-Americans. When a person is **empowered**, (s)he feels strong and has inner well-being. Further explain that these seven principles are important to all persons who are not African-American. Practicing the "Seven Principles of Blackness" helps with empowerment and inner well-being.

387

5 Explain that persons may choose to behave in ways contrary to the descriptors in the "Seven Principles of Blackness." These persons might behave in the following ways: not close to family; allow others to make decisions for me; do not care about my community; do not set economic goals and work for them; do not have goals for the future; do not make the world a better place in which to live; lack faith.

6 Have each of 16 students tape one of the labeled pieces of construction paper to his/her shirt. If there are fewer than 16 students participating in this strategy, students can tape more than one label to their shirts. However, there must be an equal number of students who wear labels with "Inner Well-Being—Resists Pressure" and "Harmful Peer Pressure."

7 Form an imaginary tug-of-war using yarn with these 16 students divided into two teams of equal number and approximately equal size. The student with "Inner Well-Being—Resists Pressure" sheet of paper will hold one end of the yarn and the student with the "Harmful Peer Pressure" sheet of paper will hold the other end. (In order to avoid any possible injury, use yarn instead of rope, and have students imagine instead of actually participating in a tug-of-war.) The seven students with the "Seven Principles of Blackness" on their sheets of paper will line up and form a team with "Inner Well-Being—Resists Pressure." The seven students with the other behaviors on their sheets of paper will form an opposing team with "Harmful Peer Pressure." Have students pretend to proceed with their tug-of-war, imagining that there is about the same amount of pull in both directions.

8 Unbalance the imaginary tug-of-war in favor of "Harmful Peer Pressure." Have three stu-dents who represent the "Seven Principles of Blackness" drop out of the imaginary pull. Explain that if a young person decides not to practice some of the "Seven Princi-ples of Blackness," (s)he is not as empow-ered and may not maintain inner well-being. (S)he has changed the amount of support for a drug-free and drug-informed lifestyle.

9 Unbalance the imaginary tug-of-war in favor of "Inner Well-Being—Resists Pressure." Have each student who represents the "Seven Principles of Blackness" be a part of the imaginary pull. Have five students who represent "Harmful Peer Pressure" drop out of the imaginary pull. Explain that if a young person decides to practice the "Seven Prin-ciples of Blackness," (s)he is more likely to be empowered, maintain inner well-being, and be drug free, drug informed, and nonviolent.

10 End this strategy by asking the students who represent "Harmful Peer Pressure" to drop out of the imaginary pull. The students who represent "Inner Well-Being—Resists Pres-sure" far outnumber the single student with the label "Harmful Peer Pressure."

Evaluation:

Have students write essays on one or more of the "Seven Principles of Blackness" explaining how the principles are empowering and con-tribute to inner well-being. Students should also explain how being empowered and having inner well-being helps a young person resist pressure to use drugs.

Have students identify African-American lead-ers who exemplify empowerment and inner well-being. How have these leaders contributed to a drug-free and drug-informed society?

Grades 6–8 Character Education
- Objective 5C

| Violence Prevention |

PROTECTIVE COAT OF ARMOR

Objective:

Students will practice resistance skills when pressured to use or abuse drugs.

Life Skills:

I will not use harmful and/or illegal drugs. I will avoid being with persons who use harmful and/or illegal drugs.

Materials:

Model for Using Resistance Skills transparency (page 525), Protective Factors That Serve as a Coat of Armor and Promote Resiliency transparency (page 527), transparency projector, construction paper, markers, scissors

Motivation:

1 Discuss resistance skills. **Resistance skills** or **refusal skills** are skills that are used when a person wants to say NO to an action and/or leave a situation. Use the transparency of Model for Using Resistance Skills to examine the various skills young persons can use to resist pressures.

2 Discuss protective factors. **Protective factors** are characteristics of individuals and their environments that make a positive contribution to development and behavior. Protective factors increase the likelihood that a young person will say YES to health and say NO to drugs. Use the transparency of Protective Factors That Serve as a Coat of Armor and Promote Resiliency to review and discuss eleven different protective factors. **Resiliency** is the ability to recover from or adjust to misfortune, change, pressure, and adversity.

3 Have students construct their own shields of armor using construction paper. Their shields should be large enough so that they cover the chest area. To construct their shields, students can make an outline using a marker. The shapes of the shields can vary as long as they can be recognized as shields.

4 Have students review the list of protective factors and decide which of these describe them. Then have students personalize this assignment by making a list of protective factors that describe them. The following list might describe a specific student.

My Protective Factors
I have a loving family. (#1)
I am on the soccer team. (#2)
My two closest friends do not use drugs. (#5)
I belong to a youth fellowship group. (#6)
I study hard and am making good grades. (#7)
I exercise regularly to cope with stress. (#11)

5 Have students draw pictures or write statements on their shields which reflect their list of protective factors that describe them. When they are finished, have the class stand in a circle with each student holding his/her armor in front of him/her. Explain that their armor is their protection from the pressures they will experience to engage in harmful and illegal drug use. Have students share what they have drawn or written on their armor. Emphasize the importance of filling up the armor with as many protective factors as possible in order to have added protection.

6 Cut arrows from construction paper. The arrows can be about two inches wide and from one to two feet in length. The arrows should have statements written on them that describe what peers might say to them to pressure them to use drugs. Using markers, write one statement on each arrow. Here are some suggestions:
- Try it, you'll like it.
- It will make you better in the big game. (steroids)
- Everyone else is doing it.
- Your parents/stepparent will never know.
- Let's do it just once.

7 Call four students to the front of the classroom. Three of these students are to hold their shields in front of them to indicate that they have a protective coat of armor. The fourth student is to stand without his/her shield. Give other students the paper arrows on which statements have been written. Each student is to take his/her paper arrow and strike the shield of one of the students. As each point strikes the shield, the student with the paper arrow is to read what is written on the arrow. The student with the shield is to respond, "I am well-protected from this pressure because . . . (names something that is on his/her shield)." The student then demonstrates a resistance skill.

8 Repeat the same activity, but this time on the student who is not protected with the shield. The student standing without the armor is to respond, "I am without protection so I am tempted to . . . (name a behavior such as smoke a cigarette)."

9 Repeat this activity again, but this time ask the three students with the shields to stand together in front of the class. Ask one of these students to drop his/her shield. Have another student use a paper arrow to try to strike the student who has dropped his/her shield. However, this time have the two students with the shields move their shields in front of the student without the shield. Use this demonstration to discuss the importance of choosing friends who participate in protective factors. By doing so when your guard is down (you have dropped your protective armor), your friends help to defend you from engaging in risk behavior.

Evaluation:

Have students list five to ten responses that might be given when they are pressured to use/abuse harmful drugs.

Inclusion:

Ask students with special learning challenges to be the students who stand in front of the class with and without the shields. On the back of the shields print the responses to be given by the student. For example, on the back of a shield you might print, "I am well protected from this pressure because I spend time with my family." Give student(s) who do not have the shields, an index card that has the desired response printed on it. For example, the index card might read, "I am without protection and I am tempted to smoke a cigarette." Identifying appropriate responses provides students with special challenges the opportunity to be successful when participating in front of peers.

PRESCRIPTIONARY

Objective:

Students will examine the responsible use of prescription and over-the-counter drugs.

Life Skill:

I will follow the directions for using prescription and over-the-counter drugs.

Materials:

Index cards, chalk, chalkboard

Motivation:

1 Explain to students that they will become familiar with information regarding prescription and over-the-counter drugs in a fun and educational way. Tell students they will be playing an adaptation of a game called Pictionary. Students will be required to identify a word or term as a student is drawing a picture related to that word or term.

2 Print the following words on two sets of index cards: prescription drugs, prescription, pharmacist, physician, over-the-counter drug, dosage, side effects, label, warnings, tablets, date of expiration, brand name, generic name, cough syrup, aspirin, decongestant, antihistamine, etc.

3 Divide the class into two equal groups. Give each student in one group the same card as you give a student in the other group. Ask students not to show anyone their cards.

4 Give students ample time to define the term on their cards and to brainstorm a way to illustrate this term on the chalkboard.

5 Have two chairs side-by-side in the front of the room facing the chalkboard. One person from each team will be seated in the chairs. Flip a coin to determine which person will go first. The first person is to begin to draw something on the chalkboard that would help his/her team identify the word or term on his/her card.

6 Each team will be given 30 second to identify the word or term beginning from the time the person begins to draw on the chalkboard. If the team does not identify the correct word or term, the other team will have an opportunity to do so. The team that guesses the word or term will receive one point. When one of the teams guesses the word or term, the second student draws clues for the same word for the class and explains his/her drawing as further review.

7 If neither team guesses the word or term that the first student drew, the second student draws the same word or term. His/her team gets the first opportunity to guess the word or term. If his/her team does not guess correctly, the other team will have an opportunity to do so. The team that guesses the word or term will receive one point.

8 The winning team is the team with the most points.

Evaluation:

Have students make their own Prescriptionary Dictionary. They are to write a definition for each of the words given during the game.

Inclusion:

Provide students with special learning needs additional time to brainstorm ways to do their drawings. You may want to give them their words or terms a class period ahead of the class period in which Prescriptionary will be played.

Grades 6–8
- Objective 6B

SYNERGISTIC EXPLOSIVES

Objective:

Students will examine the responsible use of prescription and over-the-counter drugs.

Life Skill:

I will follow the directions for using prescription and over-the-counter drugs.

Materials:

Two glasses, water, vinegar, baking soda, What You Should Know About Prescription Drugs transparency (page 394), What You Should Know About Over-the-Counter Drugs transparency (page 395), transparency projector

Motivation:

1 Discuss the responsible use of prescription drugs using the appropriate transparency. **Prescription drugs** are drugs that can be obtained only by written permission from a physician or other licensed health-care provider. The written permission is called a **prescription**. Prescription drugs can be sold only by licensed pharmacists.

2 Discuss the responsible use of over-the-counter drugs using the appropriate transparency. **Over-the-counter drugs**, or **OTC drugs**, are medications that can be purchased without a prescription. The major purpose of OTC drugs is to relieve minor symptoms. Before taking any OTC medication, read the label. All OTC labels contain the following information:
- name of the product and the manufacturer's name and address;
- net contents, such as the number of capsules;
- ingredients contained in the medicine;
- directions for safely using the drug, including how often the drug might be taken, how many days the drug is needed, and the dosage for each day;
- cautions or warnings to follow when using the drug;
- side effects that may occur;
- expiration date.

3 Explain drug interactions. **Independent drug reactions** occur when drugs taken together work independently of each other. Neither one affects the action of the other. **Antagonistic drug reactions** occur when drugs taken together interact. The effect of either or both is blocked or reduced. This interaction can be seen in the equation $1 + 1 = 0$ or $1 + 1 = 1$. For example, an antacid may block the effects of an antibiotic. **Additive drug reactions** occur when drugs taken together interact with the net effect being seen in the equation $1 + 1 = 2$. **Synergistic drug reactions** occur when drugs taken together produce an effect that is greater than additive; that is, one drug increases the effects of the other by changing its chemical effects on the body. This interaction can be seen in the equation $1 + 1 = 3$.

4 Demonstrate an additive effect. Pour one cup of water into a glass. Then pour a second cup of water into the same glass and have students observe the level of the water. Explain that one cup of water plus one cup of water produced two cups of water.

5 Demonstrate a synergistic reaction. Place one cup of vinegar in a glass. In a separate container, dissolve two tablespoons of baking soda in one cup of water. Tell students that the vinegar represents alcohol. The water solution represents barbiturates. Now you will add the water and baking soda to the vinegar in the glass. Make sure you have a bowl below the glass or are holding the glass over a sink when you mix the two. When you mix the ingredients from the two glasses, the ingredients overflow. The equation that resulted represented $1 + 1 = 3$.

Evaluation:

Have students write newspaper articles about persons who became ill, injured, or died because they experienced antagonistic, additive, or synergistic effects of drugs.

One cup
white vinegar

+

One cup
water
plus 2 tbs.
baking soda

=

SYNERGISTIC EXPLOSION

WHAT YOU SHOULD KNOW ABOUT PRESCRIPTION DRUGS

- The _name_ of the prescription drug. Write the name on a piece of paper or have your physician write the name clearly.

- The _frequency_ with which the prescription drug should be taken. Be certain to know how many times to take the drug and when to take the drug. Ask what to do if a dose is missed.

- The _results_ the prescription drug is expected to have. Ask if the prescription drug is supposed to relieve symptoms and/or be a cure.

- The _effects if used with another drug._ Ask if the prescription drug can be taken with other drugs. Be certain to tell the physician if you are taking other drugs.

- The _side effects_ that might occur. Contact your physician when side effects occur.

- The _foods to be avoided_ when taking this specific prescription drug. Certain antibiotics are not as effective when taken with milk or other dairy products.

- The _warnings_ to follow when using the prescription drug. Some drugs produce drowsiness, and during their use certain activities may result in an increased risk of accident or injury.

WHAT YOU SHOULD KNOW ABOUT OVER-THE-COUNTER DRUGS

- Always purchase OTC drugs in tamper-resistant packages.

- Do not purchase an OTC drug if its tamper-resistant seal is broken.

- Keep OTC drugs in their original packages.

- Pay attention to the expiration date and do not use after this date as the potency of the drug may have changed.

- Read the directions for use carefully.

- Follow the directions regarding the correct dose.

- Discontinue use of an OTC drug if you experience side effects. Discuss unwanted side effects with your pharmacist and/or physician.

- Consult with your pharmacist and/or physician if you are planning to take an OTC drug at the same time that you are taking another OTC or prescription drug.

- Pay attention to warnings, such as "Do not operate machinery or drive while taking this OTC."

- Remember that OTC drugs should not be taken with alcoholic beverages.

Grades 6–8 Art Studies
▪ Objective 6C

CREATE AN OTC

Objective:

Students will examine the responsible use of prescription and over-the-counter drugs.

Life Skill:

I will follow directions when taking prescription drugs and when using over-the-counter drugs.

Materials:

Questions to Ask Your Physician About Prescription Drugs transparency (page 560), Over-the-Counter Drugs Are Available in Tamper-Resistant Packaging transparency (page 559), transparency projector, samples of over-the-counter drugs, shoe box for each student, white sheet paper, markers, tape

Motivation:

1 Review information pertaining to prescription drugs. **Prescription drugs** are drugs that can be obtained only by written permission from a physician, dentist, or psychiatrist. A **prescription** is the written permission that is used to obtain the prescription drug. It is illegal for a person to obtain a prescription drug without a prescription that is valid. A prescription drug can be sold only by a licensed pharmacist. Review information on the transparency of Questions to Ask Your Physician About Prescription Drugs.

2 Review information pertaining to over-the-counter drugs or OTC drugs. **Over-the-counter drugs** or **OTC drugs** are medications that can be purchased without a prescription from a physician, dentist, or psychiatrist. OTC drugs are usually used to relieve minor symptoms of illness rather than to treat an illness. All OTC drugs contain the following information on the label (list on the chalkboard):

- name of the product and the manufacturer's name and address;
- net contents, such as the number of capsules;
- ingredients contained in the medicine;
- directions for safely using the drug, including how often the drug might be taken, how many days the drug is needed, and the dosage for each day;
- cautions or warnings to follow when using the drug;
- side effects that may occur;
- expiration date.

3 Review information on the transparency of Over-the-Counter Drugs Are Available in Tamper-Resistant Packaging. Show the class examples of containers for OTC drugs. Discuss the tamper-resistant packaging. Discuss the information on the labels.

4 Have students use the shoe boxes, paper, tape, and markers to create fictitious over-the-counter drugs. They should wrap their shoe boxes in the white paper and use the markers to print the necessary information required on the label. They should also figure out a way to keep their shoe-box-OTC drug resistant to tampering.

5 Place all the shoe-box-OTC drugs on a table as if the table were a shelf in a drugstore. Have students browse and examine the different OTCs. They should read the labels and analyze the tamper-resistant packaging.

Evaluation:

Have students list the information that is required on an OTC drug label.

Grades 6–8
- Objective 7A

CREATE A CUBE

Objective:

Students will evaluate the holistic effects of alcohol on health and well-being.

Life Skills:

I will not drink alcohol.
I will not ride in an automobile driven by someone who has been drinking alcohol.

Materials:

How Alcohol Affects Well-Being master (page 401), transparency projector, cardboard, scissors, transparent tape, markers, Create-a-Cube Pattern (page 399)

Motivation:

1 Review definitions of health with students. **Health** is the sum of physical, mental, and social well-being. **Physical health** is the condition of your body. **Mental health** is the condition of your mind and the ways in which you express feelings and make decisions. **Social health** is the quality of your relationships with others.

2 Explain that to be healthy, a person must choose healthful behaviors and avoid risk behaviors. **Healthful behaviors** are actions that promote health and well-being for you and others. **Risk behaviors** are actions that might be harmful to you and others.

3 Explain that all behavior affects us in many ways. **Whole person health**, or holistic health, states that any single behavior affects our total health and well-being. Explain that drinking alcohol is a single behavior that affects total health and well-being. Use the How Alcohol Affects Well-Being master to review the many ways in which alcohol affects health and well-being.

4 Explain to students that they are going to create a cube to show ways in which drinking alcohol affects total health and well-being. Have students create their own cubes using the pattern, cardboard, scissors, and tape.

5 After the students have assembled their cubes, explain that the cube has six sides. Each side or surface of the cube will represent one area of health. Students are to individualize their cubes by selecting six areas of health from the following list:
- mental and emotional well-being
- family and relationship skills
- growth and development
- nutrition
- personal fitness
- substance use and abuse
- diseases and disorders
- consumer health
- safety and injury prevention
- community and environment

6 Using the markers, the students are to write how each of the six areas of health is affected by the single behavior of drinking alcohol. For example, a student may select these six areas: mental and emotional well-being, family and relationship skills, nutrition, substance use and abuse, diseases and disorders, and safety and injury prevention. Each side or surface of this student's cube would represent one of these six areas of health. On the side or surface area of the cube that represents mental and emotional well-being, the student would print one way mental and emotional well-being is affected by drinking alcohol. (S)he might print "interferes with learning." The student would complete the other five sides or surfaces of the cube using the other five areas of health (s)he selected.

7 After the students have finished their cubes, review in the following way. Have students shake and roll their cubes as if they were dice. Explain that drinking alcohol is a risk behavior. The risks to total health and well-being are

397

many. Ask students to share what is printed on the side or surface of their cubes that are facing upwards. Emphasize the many different risks. Shake and roll the cubes again, repeating the review.

Evaluation:

Have students place their cubes in a pile. Then have students select a cube other than the one they created from the pile. Have students examine the cube they selected. Each cube will contain information regarding six areas of health and well-being. Have students list the four areas of health and well-being that are not on the cube they selected. They are to identify one way that drinking alcohol affects each of these four areas of health.

Create-a-Cube Pattern

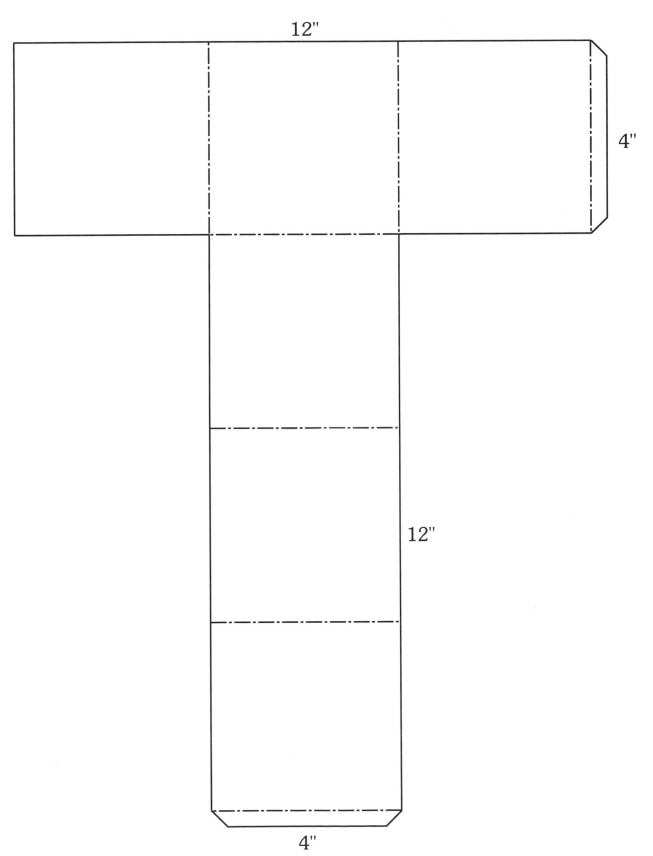

Grades 6–8
▪ Objective 7B

| **Violence Prevention** |

IT COLORS YOUR OUTLOOK

Objective:

Students will evaluate the holistic effects of alcohol on health and well-being.

Life Skills:

I will not drink alcohol.
I will not ride in an automobile driven by someone who has been drinking alcohol.

Materials:

How Alcohol Affects Well-Being transparency (page 401); red food coloring, blue food coloring, two jars (with lids) of water, transparency projector

Motivation:

1 Review definitions of health with students. **Health** is the sum of your physical, mental, and social well-being. **Physical health** is the condition of your body. **Mental health** is the condition of your mind and the ways in which you express feelings and make decisions. **Social health** is the quality of your relationships with others.

2 Explain that to be healthy, a person must choose healthful behaviors and avoid risk behaviors. **Healthful behaviors** are actions that promote health and well-being for you and others. **Risk behaviors** are actions that might be harmful to you and others.

3 Explain that all behavior affects us in many ways. **Whole-person health,** or **holistic health,** states that any single behavior affects our total health and well-being. Use the following demonstration to illustrate this concept. Show the students a container of red food coloring and a container of blue food coloring. Explain that red food coloring represents healthful behaviors. Red has been chosen to represent healthful behavior because it has life-giving associations. Blue food coloring repre-

sents risk behaviors. To one jar of water add a drop of red food coloring. Mention that this drop represents a healthful behavior such as exercising every day. Shake the jar.

4 Ask students what they observe. They will mention that the red has spread and affected the entire jar of water. Explain that a healthful behavior has a total effect also. Give examples. Daily exercise reduces stress, helps control weight, and can be done with a friend.

5 Repeat this demonstration by putting a drop of blue food coloring in the remaining jar of water. The blue food coloring represents a risk behavior such as drinking alcohol. Show students the transparency How Alcohol Affects Well-Being. Review the holistic effects that drinking alcohol has on health and well-being.

Evaluation:

Have students design a graphic to illustrate how alcohol affects well-being using at least five facts from the How Alcohol Affects Well-Being transparency. For example, a student might design a Well-Being Wheel that is pie shaped. The point at the center of the wheel might represent alcohol. The wheel might be divided into five pie shaped pieces. In each of these pieces, a statement might be written telling a way drinking alcohol affects health and well-being.

HOW ALCOHOL AFFECTS WELL-BEING

Mental and Emotional Well-Being:

- Decreases learning and performance in school.
- Intensifies moods and feelings.
- Interferes with responsible decision making.
- Causes various brain disorders including organic mental disorder.
- Intensifies stress.

Family and Relationship Skills:

- Interferes with effective communication.
- Intensifies arguments.
- Increases the likelihood of violence.
- Causes fetal alcohol syndrome (FAS).
- Creates codependence and enmeshment.

Growth and Development:

- Destroys brain cells.
- Decreases performance of motor skills.
- Lowers body temperature.
- Dulls the body senses.
- Increases heart beat rate and resting blood pressure.

Nutrition:

- Interferes with healthful appetite.
- Interferes with vitamin absorption.
- Causes niacin deficiency.
- Causes thiamine deficiency.

Personal Fitness:

- Decreases athletic performance.
- Interferes with coordination.
- Increases likelihood of sports injuries.

Substance Use and Abuse:

- Depresses the brain and respiration center.
- Causes physical and psychological dependency.
- Causes dizziness when combined with tranquilizers.
- Can cause coma and/or death when combined with narcotics.

Diseases and Disorders:

- Causes cirrhosis of the liver.
- Causes heart disease.
- Increases the risk of cancers of the mouth, esophagus, larynx, and pharynx when combined with cigarette smoking.
- Increases the risk of kidney failure.

Consumer Health:

- Is an expensive habit to maintain.
- Is taxed heavily in some states.

Safety and Injury Prevention:

- Is linked to most violent crimes.
- Is linked to most suicides and suicide attempts.
- Increases the risk of being injured, drowning, or falling.
- Is linked to many fires.

Community and Environment:

- Is costly due to increased need for treatment centers and law enforcement.
- Is linked to many missed days of work.
- Contributes to environmental pollution.

Grades 6–8
▪ Objective 7C

PROFILE OF COURAGE

Objective:

Students will evaluate the holistic effects of alcohol on health and well-being.

Life Skills:

I will avoid the use of alcohol.
I will not attend social events in which peers drink alcoholic beverages.

Materials:

Profile of Courage transparency (page 404), transparency projector, paper, markers, pen, computer (optional)

Motivation:

1 Explain that all behavior affects us in many ways. **Whole person health** or **holistic health** states that any single behavior affects our total health and well-being. Explain that drinking alcoholic beverages is a single behavior that affects total health and well-being. Therefore, drinking alcoholic beverages has a holistic effect on health.

2 Review ways in which drinking alcoholic beverages affects health:
- decreases learning and performance in school;
- intensifies moods and feelings;
- interferes with responsible decision making;
- intensifies stress;
- interferes with effective communication;
- intensifies arguments;
- creates codependence and enmeshment;
- dulls the senses;
- interferes with vitamin absorption;
- causes niacin deficiency;
- causes thiamine deficiency;
- decreases athletic performance;
- interferes with coordination;
- increases the likelihood of injuries in sports;
- depresses the brain and respiration center;

- can cause coma and/or death when combined with narcotics;
- causes cirrhosis of the liver;
- causes heart disease;
- increases the risk of cancers of the mouth, esophagus, larynx, and pharynx when combined with cigarette smoking;
- increases risk of kidney failure;
- is an expensive habit;
- is linked to most violent crimes;
- is linked to most suicides and suicide attempts;
- increases the risk of drowning and falling;
- is linked to many missed days of work;
- contributes to pollution.

3 Show students the transparency Profile of Courage. Discuss the information that is presented about Michelle Hwang. Information is provided regarding her likes and dislikes, goals, reading tastes, etc. Discuss reasons why Michelle Hwang avoids the use of alcoholic beverages.

4 Have students develop their own Profiles of Courage. They can draw themselves or they can use a recent picture of themselves for the center of their ads. Some students may want to use markers or pens for writing the information on their ads. Other students may want to use the computer to design their ads.

5 Have students share their Profiles of Courage with the class. As each student shares his/her Profile, (s)he is to explain how drinking alcoholic beverages might affect him/her.

6 Explain that this teaching strategy was titled Profiles of Courage because it takes courage to avoid drinking alcoholic beverages in a society in which drinking alcoholic beverages is glamorized.

Evaluation:

Have students draw a bottle or can representing an alcoholic beverage. Inside the bottle or can have them print at least five ways in which drinking alcohol can affect health and well-being.

Multicultural Infusion:

Have students interview a person from another culture that does not drink alcoholic beverages. Have them design a Profile of Courage for the person interviewed. Have students share these Profiles of Courage with the class.

Profile of Courage

Michelle Hwang

Age: 13
Hometown: Los Angeles, California
Favorite Sport: Soccer
Last Movie Seen: Beauty and the Beast
Favorite Play: My Fair Lady
Favorite Book: Winnie the Pooh
Best Way to Spend Time with Friends: Shopping
Best Reason to Be Drug Informed: Get good grades to be accepted into college
Favorite Drink: Sparkling peach mineral water

Grades 6–8
- Objective 8A

TOBACCO-FREE GETAWAY

Objective:

Students will evaluate the holistic effects of tobacco on health and well-being.

Life Skill:

I will not smoke cigarettes or use smokeless tobacco.

Materials:

Travel magazines, travel brochures depicting desirable islands, paper, markers, colored pencils

Motivation:

1 Review the health consequences of smoking cigarettes and/or using smokeless tobacco. Cigarette smoking has been linked to lung cancer, laryngeal cancer, chronic bronchitis, coronary heart disease, atherosclerotic peripheral vascular disease, oral cancer, esophageal cancer, chronic obstructive pulmonary disease, intrauterine growth retardation, low birth-weight babies, leukemia, unsuccessful pregnancies, increased infant mortality, peptic ulcer, cancer of the bladder, cancer of the pancreas, cancer of the kidney, and cancer of the stomach. Smokeless tobacco use increases the frequency of localized gum recession, leukoplakia, and oral cancer.

2 Show students the travel magazines and travel brochures. Have them discuss where they would like to go on their dream vacation. Have them describe the location in detail. Are there mountains? Is there a beach? What language is spoken? What are the points of interest? What things are there to do?

3 Explain to students that they are going to design a travel brochure for a place that they have created. They are to name this vacation spot, describe it, and draw a picture or other illustration that is appealing. However, there is something unique about this vacation spot—it is tobacco free. No one is permitted to smoke cigarettes or use smokeless tobacco. This unique aspect of this vacation spot is to somehow be described in the travel brochure.

Evaluation:

Have students share their travel brochures with their classmates. After each student describes his/her vacation spot, its name, and the desirable reasons for going there, (s)he is to mention how healthy the inhabitants of this island/place are by saying, "No one who lives at . . . has . . . (identifying one of the diseases that may result from smoking cigarettes and/or using smokeless tobacco)."

Grades 6–8
• Objective 8B

CREDIT ME $$$

Objective:

Students will evaluate the holistic effects of tobacco on health and well-being.

Life Skill:

I will not smoke cigarettes or use smokeless tobacco.

Materials:

Paper, pencil, pocket calculator (optional), chalkboard, chalk, construction paper, scissors, markers

Motivation:

1 Prepare ahead for this strategy by getting the prices of several brands of cigarettes and several brands of smokeless tobacco.

2 Review the health consequences of smoking cigarettes and/or using smokeless tobacco. Cigarette smoking has been linked to lung cancer, laryngeal cancer, chronic bronchitis, coronary heart disease, atherosclerotic peripheral vascular disease, oral cancer, esophageal cancer, chronic obstructive pulmonary disease, intrauterine growth retardation, low birth-weight babies, leukemia, unsuccessful pregnancies, increased infant mortality, peptic ulcer, cancer of the bladder, cancer of the pancreas, cancer of the kidney, and cancer of the stomach. Smokeless tobacco use increases the frequency of localized gum recession, leukoplakia, and oral cancer.

3 Share the price information with students regarding several brands of cigarettes and several brands of smokeless tobacco. Have students compute the following costs: buying one pack of cigarettes every day for a week and buying one package of smokeless tobacco every day for one week. Then have students compute the costs for one month, six months, and one year. Write these figures on the chalk-

board. Then have students compute the costs of buying two packs of cigarettes and the costs of buying two packages of smokeless tobacco every day for one week, one month, six months, and one year. Write these figures on the chalkboard. Repeat the same for buying three packs of cigarettes and three packages of smokeless tobacco every day for one week, one month, six months, and one year. Write these figures on the chalkboard.

4 On the chalkboard, have students list some prices of items they would like to have or of entertainment they would like to enjoy. For example, students might identify a compact disc that is popular. On the chalkboard, they would write the name of the compact disc and the approximate price. Students might enjoy attending a specific concert. They would write the name of the concert group and the price of a ticket for the concert. Students also might identify necessary items they *need* to purchase such as a new coat or soccer shoes.

5 Divide the students into six groups. Give each group a sheet of construction paper, scissors, and a marker. Group 1 represents persons who smoke one pack of cigarettes per day. Group 2 represents persons who smoke two packs of cigarettes per day. Group 3 represents persons who smoke three packs of cigarettes per day. Group 4 represents persons who use one package of snuff per day. Group 5 represents persons who use two packages of snuff per day. Group 6 represents persons who use three packages of snuff per day.

6 Have each group use construction paper, scissors, and markers to make a credit memo for the amount of money that could be saved by not purchasing cigarettes or smokeless tobacco. Then each group is to brainstorm ways that this amount of money might be spent wisely. On the opposite side of the credit memo, each group is to list the purchases that might be made and the prices of each. All purchases must be healthful.

7 Have each group share the amount of money for which their credit memo was made and the purchases that might be made with that amount.

Evaluation:

Have students write a short essay on the cost of smoking and/or using smokeless tobacco. Their essays should address the economic costs as well as the health costs.

Inclusion:

Students who have difficulty with mathematics might use a calculator to compute the costs. Because these strategies foster cooperative learning, it is wise to place these students among the different groups.

Grades 6–8
▪ Objective 8C

SING ABOUT SNUFF

Objective:

Students will evaluate the holistic effects of tobacco on health and well-being.

Life Skills:

I will not smoke cigarettes or use smokeless tobacco.
I will sit in nonsmoking sections of public places in which smoking is allowed.

Materials:

Lunch-size paper sacks, shredded newspaper, markers, white sheets of paper, pencils, pens, stapler

Motivation:

1 Review information about the effects of smoking cigarettes on health and well-being. Cigarette smoking has been linked to lung cancer, laryngeal cancer, chronic bronchitis, coronary heart disease, atherosclerotic peripheral vascular disease, oral cancer, intrauterine growth retardation, low birth-weight babies, leukemia, unsuccessful pregnancies, increased infant mortality, peptic ulcer, cancer of the bladder, cancer of the pancreas, cancer of the kidney, and cancer of the stomach.

2 Initiate a discussion about another form of tobacco: smokeless tobacco—including chewing tobacco and snuff. These products contain tobacco leaf and a variety of sweeteners, flavorings, and scents. In chewing tobacco, the leaf may be shredded (loose-leaf), pressed into bricks or cakes (plugs), or dried and twisted into rope-like strands (twists). A portion is either chewed or held in place in the cheek or between the lower lip and the gum. The two categories of snuff, dry and moist, are made from powdered or finely cut

tobacco leaves. In some countries, including the United Kingdom, dry snuff is sniffed through the nose, but in the United States both dry and moist snuff are used in the mouth or "dipped." A small amount (pinch) is usually held in place between the lip or cheek and the gum.

3 Identify the harmful effects of smokeless tobacco. There is strong evidence that smokeless tobacco causes cancer of the mouth. The risk is particularly high for parts of the mouth where the tobacco is usually placed. Nitrosamines chemically related to nicotine occur at high levels in smokeless tobacco and, generally, at lower levels in chewing tobacco. These compounds are highly carcinogenic in animals. The concentrations of nitrosamines in smokeless tobacco are far higher than the levels of these compounds allowed in any food or beverage in the United States. Besides nitrosamines, other known carcinogens present include polycyclic aromatic hydrocarbons and radiation-emitting polonium. Smokeless tobacco use increases the frequency of localized gum recession and leukoplakia. **Leukoplakia** is a condition resulting from direct irritation from tobacco in which white patches are present on the lining of the mouth. The presence of lead in smokeless tobacco may pose a special risk for the developing fetus of a pregnant female. The primary behavioral consequence of regular use of smokeless tobacco is long-term nicotine dependence and its associated risks with heart disease.

4 Divide the class into groups. Give each group a lunch-size paper sack, shredded newspaper, and markers. Each group is to design a package of smokeless tobacco that highlights the health risks and discourages use. Markers can be used to draw on and label the lunch paper sack. After the design is finished, the group can fill the paper sack with shredded newspaper and staple it shut.

5 Using the sheets of paper and pencils/pens, each group is to compose an eight-line, sing-about-snuff song. Have each group share its design for its bag of snuff and its sing-a-long with the class.

Evaluation:

Explain to the students that they are to be the Surgeon General for the day. They are to write three different warning statements for packages of smokeless tobacco.

Grades 6–8
▪ Objective 9A

| Violence Prevention |

MOVE THOSE MUSCLES

Objective:

Students will evaluate the harmful consequences that result from using anabolic steroids.

Life Skill:

I will not use anabolic steroids.

Materials:

Two balloons, tape, pin

Motivation:

1 Review information about anabolic steroids. **Anabolic steroids**, synthetic derivatives of the male hormone testosterone, stimulate increased muscle growth and when first taken may produce a euphoric state. Users claim that anabolic steroids function to anesthetize the body, allowing the user to work out intensely without feeling pain. Some young persons use anabolic steroids to obtain a temporary euphoric state. They may take these drugs before going to a party to lessen feelings of inadequacy.

2 Explain that there are harmful consequences which result from using anabolic steroids. Take one of the balloons. As you mention each of the following harmful consequences, blow a puff of air into the balloon.

After discontinuing use:
• feelings of depression,
• pain in muscles and joints,
• old injuries and strains reappear,
• feelings of anxiety are heightened,
• feelings of inadequacy are heightened.

Use in males:
• shrinking of the testicles,
• reduced sperm count,
• impotence,

• baldness,
• difficulty or pain in urinating,
• enlargement of breasts,
• enlarged prostate.

Use in females:
• growth of facial hair,
• changes in or cessation of the menstrual cycle,
• enlargement of the clitoris,
• deepened voice,
• breast reduction.

Use in males and females:
• acne,
• jaundice,
• trembling,
• swelling of the feet or ankles,
• bad breath,
• reduction in HDL (good cholesterol),
• high blood pressure,
• liver damage,
• liver cancer,
• aching joints,
• increased chance of injury to tendons,
• halt growth prematurely in adolescents,
• mood swings ranging from periods of violent, even homicidal, episodes known as "roid rages" to bouts of depression,
• paranoid jealousy,
• extreme irritability,
• delusions,
• impaired judgment stemming from feelings of invincibility.

3 After you have mentioned several of the harmful consequences, use the pin to prick the balloon to make it burst. Indicate that anabolic steroids are extremely dangerous and may cause death.

4 Take the second balloon. Explain that young persons often use anabolic steroids for one of two purposes. The first purpose is to obtain a euphoric state to compensate or overcome feelings of anxiety and inadequacy. Ask students to share healthful ways that a person

might use instead to overcome feelings of anxiety and inadequacy and build positive self-esteem. As they mention each way, blow a puff of air into the second balloon. They might say:
- talk with trusted adults,
- practice stress management skills,
- journal,
- talk with close friends,
- participate in school activities.

5 Mention that the second purpose for using anabolic steroids focuses upon increasing muscle growth and improving athletic performance or enhancing appearance. Ask students to identify different exercises that can be used instead to enhance muscle growth. For each exercise mentioned, blow another puff of air into the second balloon.

6 After this balloon is filled with air, tie it in such a way as to prevent the escape of air. With the balloon out of the view of the students, place a piece of transparent tape on the balloon.

7 Show the students the balloon. Take the pin and prick the balloon through the transparent tape. The balloon will not burst. Explain to stu-

dents that there are no harmful consequences from the behaviors they just mentioned. These are healthful ways to cope with anxiety and inadequacy and to increase muscle growth.

Evaluation:

Have students write answers to the following letter.

Dear Helper:
I am very small for my age. I want others to notice me, but I usually shy away from others. I am embarrassed about my size and imagine that others are making fun of me. I am frightened around girls. My buddy told me about some pills I can take to fill out. He said they'll make me feel invincible with girls. He gets into a lot of trouble and makes a number of false promises. Is this for real?

Sincerely,
Concerned

Grades 6–8
▪ Objective 9B

| Violence Prevention |

OUTLINE OF AN ATHLETE

Objective:

Students will evaluate the harmful consequences that result from using anabolic
steroids.

Life Skill:

I will not use anabolic steroids.

Materials:

Large sheets of brown butcher paper that are
the size of the human body, markers, tape

Motivation:

1 Review information about anabolic steroids.
Anabolic steroids, synthetic derivatives of
the male hormone testosterone, stimulate
increased muscle growth and when first taken
may produce a euphoric state. Users claim that
anabolic steroids function to anesthetize the
body, allowing the user to work out intensely
without feeling pain. However, when the user
stops taking the anabolic steroids, muscles and
especially joints become very sore. Old injuries
or strains become painful. Psychological feelings of depression may be experienced. Some
young persons use anabolic steroids to obtain
a temporary euphoric state. They may take
these drugs before going to a party to lessen
feelings of anxiety or inadequacy. However,
when the user stops taking anabolic steroids,
feelings of anxiety or inadequacy return and
may be heightened.

2 Review the health consequences of anabolic
steroid use. Although anabolic steroids are
derived from a male sex hormone, they can
trigger a mechanism in the body that can
actually shut down the healthy functioning of
the male reproductive system. Some possible
side effects include: shrinking of the testicles,
reduced sperm count, impotence, baldness, difficulty or pain in urinating, development of

breasts, enlarged prostate. Females may experience "masculinization" as well as other problems: growth of facial hair, changes in or cessation of the menstrual cycle, enlargement of the
clitoris, deepened voice, breast reduction. For
both males and females, continued use of anabolic steroids may lead to health conditions
ranging from merely irritating to life threatening:
acne, jaundice, trembling, swelling of feet or
ankles, bad breath, reduction in HDL (good
cholesterol), high blood pressure, liver damage,
liver cancer, aching joints, increased chance of
injury to tendons. Anabolic steroids can halt
growth prematurely in adolescents. The use
of anabolic steroids has been associated with
wide mood swings ranging from periods of
violent, even homicidal, episodes known as
"roid rages" to bouts of depression when the
drugs are stopped. Anabolic steroid users
may also suffer from paranoid jealousy, extreme irritability, delusions, and impaired judgment stemming from feelings of invincibility.

3 Divide students into five groups. Have each
group select a different sports program. Be certain that there is a balance of gender in the
sports programs selected. For example, the five
sports programs selected might be: soccer,
football, ice hockey, gymnastics, track, and
wrestling. Give each group a large sheet of
brown butcher paper and markers. Each group
is to outline a life-size body of a person participating in a sport. For example, a group might
outline the body of a female gymnast. Then
the group is to draw body organs such as the
liver, heart, breasts, ovaries, brain, and so on,
inside the outline of the body. Last, the group
is to label the outline with the possible dangers
of using anabolic steroids. For example, in the
case of the female gymnast, the group might
include the following when labelling: acne, high
blood pressure, aching joints, liver damage,
swelling of ankles, growth of facial hair, deepened voice, breast reduction, cessation of menstrual period, jaundice.

412

4 Tape each of the outlined bodies of athletes to the chalkboard so that students can examine the labels. Review the dangers of using anabolic steroids.

Evaluation:

Have students remain in the same five groups. Have each group prepare a five-minute presentation to be given to a sports team by a coach outlining the dangers of using anabolic steroids and the consequences of breaking school rules. The groups should represent the sports teams previously selected. For example, the group who outlined the female gymnast would prepare a five-minute speech for the female gymnastic team given by the coach of that team. Each speech should contain at least five dangers associated with anabolic steroid use.

Grades 6–8
- Objective 9C

MESSAGE FROM THE NCAA

Objective:

Students will evaluate the harmful consequences that result from using anabolic steroids.

Life Skill:

I will not use anabolic steroids.

Materials:

Athletic clothing such as football jerseys

Motivation:

1 Review information about anabolic steroids. **Anabolic steroids** are synthetic derivatives of the male hormone testosterone that stimulate increased muscle growth and when first taken may produce a euphoric state. Users claim that steroids function to anesthetize the body, allowing the user to work out intensely without feeling pain. However, when the user stops taking the steroids, muscles and especially joints become very sore. Old injuries or strains become painful. Psychological feelings of depression may be experienced. Some young persons use steroids to obtain a temporary euphoric state. They may take steroids before going to a party to lessen feelings of anxiety or inadequacy. However, when the user stops taking the steroids, feelings of anxiety or inadequacy return and may be heightened.

2 Review the health consequences of anabolic steroid use. The effects on the male characteristics and reproductive system include: shrinking of the testicles, reduced sperm count, impotence, baldness, difficulty or pain in urinating, development of breasts, enlarged prostate. The effects on the female characteristics and reproductive system include: masculinization of features, growth of facial hair, changes in or cessation of the menstrual cycle, enlargement of the clitoris, deepened voice, breast reduc-

tion. Both males and females may also experience the following after continued use of anabolic steroids: acne, jaundice, trembling, swelling of feet or ankles, bad breath, reduction in HDL (good cholesterol), high blood pressure, liver damage, liver cancer, aching joints, increased chance of injury to tendons.

3 Examine the effects of anabolic steroid use on psychological well-being. The use of anabolic steroids has been associated with wide mood swings ranging from periods of violent, even homicidal, episodes known as "roid rages" to bouts of depression when the drugs are stopped. Anabolic steroid users may also suffer from paranoid jealousy, extreme irritability, delusions, and impaired judgment stemming from feelings of invincibility.

4 On the chalkboard, list sports that students enjoy or sports in which they participate. Divide the class into groups with students who share a common interest in a particular sport being in the same group. Ask students if they have watched a sports event on television in which a college athlete did a commercial in which (s)he discussed the dangers of drug use. Explain that each group is to make a similar commercial. The group is to select a college or university, identify a specific sports program, and make up a fictitious person who is an athlete. Group members are to research some information about the college or university selected. In this way, this teaching strategy infuses career education. Group members are to write the script for the athlete who will do the commercial on the dangers of using anabolic steroids. The group member who will role play the athlete is to practice the commercial with his/her group. Another group member will present information about the college or university as an introduction.

5 By assigning the commercials to be presented on the following day, the group might also decide upon props to be used in the commercial. For example, the group member who is presenting information about the college or university as an introduction might be holding a banner or poster from that school. The group member who is the athlete might dress a specific way.

6 Have the athlete from each group perform his/her commercial for the class. If possible, repeat the presentations for another class or for a school assembly.

Multicultural Infusion:

Ask some students to select colleges and universities that have a specific mission. For example, one group might choose a college or university for African-Americans. Another group might choose a college or university for women. Again, one member of the group would present information on the college or university selected. Another member of the group would role play the athlete and would provide a message warning about the dangers of using anabolic steroids.

Inclusion:

Ask students with special learning challenges to select a college or university that is known for having special programs to meet the needs of special learners. Again, one member of the group would present information on the college or university selected. Of particular importance would be the sharing of information with the class as to the specifics of the special programs. This sharing would help students without special learning challenges appreciate the special needs of others. Another member of the group would role-play the athlete and would provide a message warning about the dangers of using anabolic steroids.

Grades 6–8
- Objective 10A

Violence Prevention

OBITUARY

Objective:

Students will evaluate the effects of illegal drugs on well-being.

Life Skills:

I will not use illegal drugs.
I will choose friends who are drug free and drug informed.
I will avoid persons who engage in drug purchases, sales, or trafficking.

Materials:

Section of the newspaper containing the obituaries, paper, pencil or pen

Motivation:

1 Explain the meaning of obituary. An **obituary** is a notice of a person's death, usually with a short biographical account of the person's life. An obituary may include information about a person's family. For example, it might tell whether or not the person was married, if (s)he had children and grandchildren, and if (s)he had brothers and/or sisters. In the case of a young person, the obituary might state if his/ her parents are living. An obituary might also include information about where a person worked and for how long. It might identify community activities in which the person was involved. An obituary might also describe a person's accomplishments.

2 Read several obituaries that have appeared recently in your local newspaper.

3 Have students write an obituary. They are to imagine a person who lived life to the fullest. They are to give the length of this person's life and the many rewarding events that occurred. They might mention the meaningful relationships that this person had. They are to describe the occupation of this person and the community activities in which (s)he was

involved. They are to imagine that this person's highest goals were accomplished. For example, a student might write an obituary that states this person played professional basketball and was a member of the All-Star team. Another student might state that this person won the Nobel Peace Prize or a prestigious community service award.

4 Have students share the obituaries they have written. Explain that these obituaries reflect the hopes and dreams of people they encounter in everyday life. These hopes and dreams are often attainable with hard work and with support from family and friends.

5 Have students write another obituary. This obituary is to be for another fictitious person. This person was involved in using illegal drugs and/or purchasing illegal drugs and/or drug trafficking. The cause of death is to be either a disease or condition linked to the use of harmful drugs. For example, the cause of death might be liver cancer resulting from the use of anabolic steroids. The cause of death might be a result of violence from being involved in drug sales and/or drug trafficking. For example, the cause of death might be from a gunshot wound that occurred during an argument following a drug sale. The cause of death might also be suicide or a drug overdose. The obituary is to include the difficulties the person experienced in his/her life. These difficulties are to be job-related and family-related.

6 Have students share the obituaries they have written. Contrast these obituaries with the other set of obituaries that were written. Emphasize the effects that illegal drugs have on a person's lifestyle. Evaluate the benefits of being drug-free.

Evaluation:

Have students fold a sheet of paper into three columns. In the first column, they are to list ways that illegal drugs might affect their physical health. In the second column, they are to identify the goals they have for themselves that might not be reached if they use illegal drugs. In the third column, they are to list important relationships that might be jeopardized by using illegal drugs.

Inclusion:

Have students with special needs work with a parent or other caring adult to write the fictitious obituaries.

Grades 6–8
▪ Objective 10B

| Violence Prevention |

DRUG BUG

Objective:

Students will evaluate the effects of illegal drugs on well-being.

Life Skills:

I will not use illegal drugs.
I will choose friends who are drug free and drug informed.
I will avoid persons who engage in drug purchases, sales, or trafficking.

Materials:

Construction paper, scissors, tape, markers

Motivation:

1 Divide the class into groups of five or six students. Give each group several sheets of different colored construction paper, scissors, markers, and tape. Give each group a label. Half of the groups will be labelled drug free and half of the groups will be labelled drug bugs.

2 The directions for the groups that are labelled drug free are as follows: each group is to select one student to decorate symbolically as being drug free using the construction paper, markers, and tape. For example, the group might make a smiley face for the person and tape it to the person to show that the person is happy. Or the group might make dollars bills and tape them to the person to indicate that the person has money because (s)he does not spend it on drugs. They might make any kinds of signs, a hat, jewelry, and so on. The decorations should all be symbolic. The person in the group who is being decorated will later have to introduce himself/herself to the class and explain each of the ornaments that were selected by the members of the group.

3 Directions for the groups labelled as drug bugs are as follows: each group is to select one student to decorate symbolically as being a drug bug who uses and abuses harmful drugs. The groups will use the construction paper, scissors, and tape. For example, the group might cut out a gun to show that violence is often associated with illegal drug use. The group might make paper chains and place them around the wrists and ankles to indicate the grip that drugs can have on a person. The person in the group who is being decorated will later have to introduce himself/herself to the class and explain each of the ornaments that were selected by the members of the group.

4 After the groups have finished decorating their selected persons, have each of these persons stand in the front of the class. The drug-free students should stand together in a group while the drug bugs also stand together. Explain that these are several students enrolled in your school who are now going to introduce themselves and be interviewed. Have the drug-free students introduce themselves first. For example, a student might say, "Hi, I am Monica and I am drug free. You notice that I have a smiley face because I feel good about myself. I am wearing a school letter because I participate in sports and other school activities. I have a telephone in my hand because my friends call me. I am wearing a heart because I am close to my family."

5 After all the drug-free students have introduced themselves, have the students who are drug bugs introduce themselves. For example, a student might say, "I am Lorenzo and I am into drugs. Notice the chains around my wrists and ankles. Drugs have a hold on me. Notice the bruises under my eyes. I get in fights when I drink too much. I am wearing an "F" on my back because I am failing in school. I just don't seem to be able to concentrate."

6 Review what each of the students has said. Describe the effects of illegal drugs on wellness.

Describe the benefits of being drug free. Explain the importance of being drug free and choosing friends who are drug free. Have one of the decorated, drug-free students take off some ornaments and stand with the group of drug-bugs. Have each of the drug bugs take off a drug-bug ornament and place it on the drug-free student. Explain that when a person who is drug free chooses friends who are drug bugs (s)he is at risk for choosing similar risk behaviors.

Evaluation:

Make a drug-bug bulletin board. Each student is to make a large bug from construction paper. The student is to write on the bug at least five effects of illegal drugs on wellness and place his/her bug on the bulletin board.

DRUG FREE

DRUG BUG

Grades 6–8
▪ Objective 10C

DRUG JEOPARDY

Objective:

Students will evaluate the effects of illegal drugs on well-being.

Life Skills:

I will not use illegal drugs.
I will choose friends who are drug free and drug informed.
I will avoid persons who engage in drug purchase, sales, or trafficking.

Materials:

Large sheet of poster board, colored construction paper, markers, index cards, tape, pocket calculator (optional)

Motivation:

1 Design a Drug Jeopardy board as illustrated. Colored construction paper and markers can be used to write the dollar amounts. The dollar amounts can be taped over the questions that have been printed on index cards. As a variation, the questions might be printed on the poster board itself.

2 The questions and categories are as follows:

Stimulants

1. Question: Define stimulants.
   Answer: The class of drugs that increase the rate at which organs controlled by the central nervous system function.
2. Question: Derived from the leaves of the coca bush, daily or binge users of this drug undergo profound personality changes.
   Answer: Cocaine
3. Question: A smokable form of cocaine that can be fatal even in small amounts.
   Answer: Crack

4. Question: The drug of choice of "speed freaks" who often have violent and bizarre behavior.
   Answer: Amphetamines
5. Question: A pure crystal form of methamphetamine that is smoked.
   Answer: Ice

Sedative-Hypnotics

1. Question: The class of drugs that induce drowsiness and sleep.
   Answer: Hypnotics
2. Question: Unlike narcotics and stimulants, what withdrawal symptom can result from the abrupt cessation of sedative-hypnotics?
   Answer: Death
3. Question: A sedative-hypnotic used to induce sedation and sleep that has been associated with congenital defects when taken during pregnancy.
   Answer: Barbiturate
4. Question: A sedative-hypnotic with a nickname of "ludes" that has a strong euphoric effect.
   Answer: Methaqualone
5. Question: Antianxiety drugs that are dangerous when taken with alcohol.
   Answer: Benzodiazepines

Marijuana

1. Question: The hemp plant from which marijuana is derived.
   Answer: Cannabis sativa
2. Question: The major psychoactive ingredient in marijuana.
   Answer: THC
3. Question: The most obvious effect of marijuana in humans.
   Answer: Temporary increase in heart rate as high as 160 beats per minute.
4. Question: The effects of marijuana on memory.

Answer: Marijuana impairs short-term memory leading to fragmented speech, disjointed thinking, and a tendency to lose one's thought.
5. Question: Marijuana produces more than as much tar as a popular brand of cigarettes.
   Answer: Marijuana contains more than twice as much tar and when inhaled deeply produces nearly four times more tar.

Hallucinogens

1. Question: What are hallucinogens?
   Answer: Hallucinogens are drugs that have the major effect of producing marked distortions in perception.
2. Question: What is a flashback?
   Answer: Flashbacks are manifestations of one or more of the acute effects of the drug that recur long after it was taken.
3. Question: Tiny, thin squares of LSD in the form of gelatin.
   Answer: Windowpane
4. Question: A hallucinogen derived from a mushroom that affects mood and perception.
   Answer: Psilocybin and psilocin
5. Question: Violent, homicidal, and suicidal behavior may occur from taking this hallucinogen.
   Answer: PCP

Steroids

1. Question: Define anabolic steroids.
   Answer: Anabolic steroids are powerful, synthetic compounds that are closely related to the male sex hormone testosterone.
2. Question: What are ergogenic drugs?
   Answer: Drugs that are used to improve athletic performance.
3. Question: What is stacking?

Answer: A dangerous practice in which steroids are taken in combination with other drugs such as stimulants, depressants, pain killers, antiinflammatories, and other hormones.
4. Question: The effects of anabolic steroids on the male reproductive system.
   Answer: Shrinking of the testicles, reduced sperm count, impotence, baldness, difficulty or pain in urinating, development of breasts, and enlarged prostate.
5. Question: The effects of anabolic steroids on the female reproductive system.
   Answer: Growth of facial hair, changes in or cessation of the menstrual cycle, enlargement of the clitoris, deepened voice, and breast reduction.

3 Have students play Drug Jeopardy. Select a host for the show. Divide the class into two teams. Toss a coin to determine which team goes first. The team is to arrange itself in order so that the host will be able to call on the first team member, second team member, third team member, etc. The first team member from the team that goes first selects one of the five categories: stimulants, sedative-hypnotics, marijuana, hallucinogens, or steroids. This person then selects an amount of money. The host removes the amount of money from the Drug Jeopardy board and asks the question that appears. The team member answers the question. If the team member is correct, his/her team wins this amount of money and the next member of this team selects a category and amount of money. This procedure continues until the team answers a question incorrectly. Then the other team has the opportunity to select a category and an amount of money using the same procedure. When all questions have been answered correctly and there is no money left on the Drug Jeopardy board, the team with the most money wins.

4 Divide the class into five groups. Assign each group one of the five classifications: stimulants, sedative-hypnotics, marijuana, hallucinogens, steroids. Have each group write five questions and answers to be used for a new game of Drug Jeopardy.

5 Collect the questions and answers from each group and play Drug Jeopardy a second time. Explain to students that they are not allowed to select the category that is the same category as the group of which they were a member.

Inclusion:

Have students with special learning challenges help you prepare the first Drug Jeopardy board. They might copy the questions and answers from this book for you. This helps them review this material and reinforces learning. It better prepares them for the actual game with their classmates. One or more of these students may be appointed as scorekeeper and can use a pocket calculator to tabulate the scores of each team.

Evaluation:

Have students write short essays explaining why the use of illegal drugs is playing jeopardy with health. Students are to provide at least five dangers of using illegal drugs in their essays.

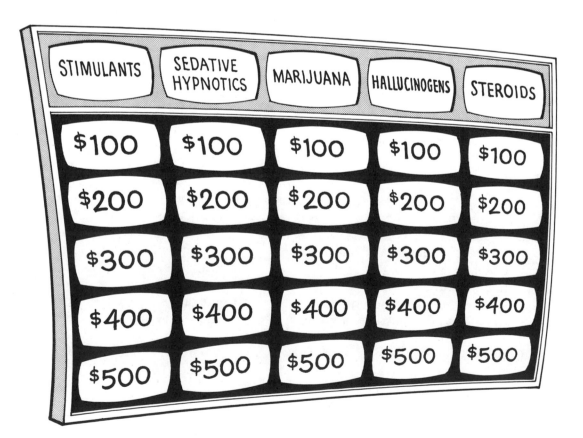

Grades 6–8
- Objective 11A

STEPPING STONES

Objective:

Students will analyze ways in which the use of alcohol, tobacco, and/or other drugs interferes with achieving goals.

Life Skills:

I will set goals and make plans to reach them. I will remain drug free and drug informed in order to meet my goals.

Materials:

Sheets of various colors of construction paper, markers, scissors, tape.

Motivation:

1 Define goal. A **goal** is something desirable toward which you work. It is always important to have goals and to make plans to reach them. Setting goals and working toward their accomplishment helps a person to have positive self-esteem. **Positive self-esteem** is the feeling of being a worthwhile person.

2 Explain that it is important to set goals in several areas of one's life. Some of these areas might include:
- education
- athletics
- community involvement
- school activities
- family life
- friendship

3 Have students brainstorm goals that they have in each of the areas identified in the list. For example, a student might have a goal to become a member of the soccer team. With regard to friendship, a student might have a goal of becoming a better listener. Cut out large circles from the construction paper. Write each of these goals on one of the circles.

4 Have students brainstorm ways that using alcohol, tobacco, and other drugs interferes with the areas of life previously identified. For example, drinking alcohol would make a person ineligible for playing on an athletic team. Smoking cigarettes would offend some friends. Using illegal drugs would interfere with following parental guidelines. Write the statements from the students on other large circles cut from construction paper.

5 Cut two more large circles from construction paper. On one of the circles, print SET GOALS. On the other circle, print SUCCESS.

6 Place the circles on the floor as follows. The circle labeled SET GOALS should be placed down first. Then each of the circles with goals printed on them should be placed in a row with one large step in between them. At the end of the row, place the circle that says SUCCESS. The circles that state the harmful effects of drugs should be scattered around with no definite pattern (see illustration). Tape the circles to the floor.

7 Ask for a student volunteer. Have the student stand on the circle that says SET GOALS. Then have this student step from goal to goal to reach the circle that says SUCCESS. Explain the importance of having stepping stones to self-esteem. These stepping stones are also stepping stones to success.

8 Have this student step on the circles that are labeled with the effects of drugs. The volunteer now represents the student who is headed nowhere. There is no direction or purpose in his/her life. (S)he has stepped off the path to success.

9 Have the student continue to step from one problem to another. Then ask the student to stop on one of the circles. Ask the class to explain what this student will need to do to step back on the path to success.

Evaluation:

Have students do an art project in which they design a layout on a sheet of construction paper to illustrate their paths to success. Their paths must be labeled with goals they plan to reach.

Grades 6–8
- Objective 11B

THIS IS YOUR LIFE

Objective:

Students will analyze ways in which the use of alcohol, tobacco, and/or other drugs interferes with achieving goals.

Life Skills:

I will set goals and make plans to reach them. I will remain drug free and drug informed in order to meet my goals.

Materials:

Pencils and paper

Motivation:

1 Several years ago, there was a television program called, "This is Your Life." A guest on the show would be introduced and then during the remainder of the show there would be vignettes of the person's life. For this strategy, students are to be divided into groups to create the scripts for a similar television program.

2 Divide the class into several groups. Explain to students that each group is to create a television program called, "This is Your Life." The group's television program is to be a series of vignettes. There is to be a vignette for each person in the group. Each person is to make a list of what is to be included in his/her vignette. The vignette is to describe at least two goals the person hopes to achieve by the age of 30. There might be a description of the person's family and job. For example, one group member might have the goal of being a physician who works in a small town. This same person might have the goal of marrying and having two children. During this group member's vignette, other members of the group might pretend to be former patients. The former patients are on the show to tell how much they respect the physician. They might even share humorous stories about their visit to

the physician. Other group members might pretend to be the physician's family. The groups should decide how to present their shows. For example, who will be the host? How will each guest be introduced? Have the groups rehearse their shows.

3 Have each group make one commercial for their show. The commercial should promote a lifestyle without the use of alcohol, tobacco, and/or other drugs.

4 Have each group present their show, "This is Your Life," including their commercial for a lifestyle without the use of alcohol, tobacco, and/or other drugs. After the shows, discuss the goals that different students had selected for themselves. Discuss the impact of using alcohol, tobacco, and other drugs on achieving goals.

Evaluation:

Have students write a paper in which they state one of the goals they want to accomplish by age 30. In their paper, they are to describe three steps they will take toward accomplishing their goal. They are to describe ways in which the use of alcohol, tobacco, and other drugs might interfere with achieving this goal.

Multicultural Infusion:

Have students select a person they admire from their same culture. Have students research this person's accomplishments. Students can share short reports about the person they selected. The class can discuss how the use of alcohol, tobacco, and other drugs might have interfered with the goals that this person accomplished.

Grades 6–8
▪ Objective 11C

OPRAH DRUG-FREE SHOW

Objective:

Students will analyze ways in which the use of alcohol, tobacco, and other drugs interferes with achieving goals.

Life Skills:

I will set goals and make plans to reach them. I will remain drug free and drug informed in order to meet my goals.

Materials:

Chairs, any props students want to use to make a mock television host show

Motivation:

1 Review what it means to be drug free and drug informed. A **drug-free** lifestyle refers to a lifestyle in which young persons do not use harmful and illegal drugs. A **drug-informed lifestyle** refers to a lifestyle in which young persons use legal drugs such as over-the-counter drugs and medicines according to directions.

2 Divide the class into groups of ten. Each group is to produce an Oprah Drug-Free Show for the class. The show is to have a host and three to five guests. Each guest is to be a teenager who is to share an important goal that (s)he has and tell the audience his/her plan to reach this goal. For example, a guest might have the goal of being a teacher. The guest would then explain that (s)he will need to graduate from college as well as from high school. The guest will discuss the importance of studying. The guest might also share volunteer opportunities or job opportunities such as child sitting that (s)he chooses in order to help prepare for the important goal of being a teacher. Finally, the guest must tell the importance of being drug free and drug informed.

3 Explain to the class that they are to produce at least two commercials for their shows. One of the commercials is to sell the audience on the importance of being tobacco free while the other is to sell the audience on beverages that are healthful as an alternative to alcoholic beverages.

4 After the class has been provided enough time to produce their television host shows with commercials, have them perform them for the class. The class will be the audience. The host will call on persons from the audience to ask the guests questions.

Evaluation:

Have students make a list of the top ten reasons they will remain drug free and drug informed.

Grades 6–8
- Objective 12A

DRUG-FREE CALENDAR

Objective:

Students will evaluate the benefits of being drug free.

Life Skill:

I will not drink alcohol, use tobacco, or use other harmful drugs.

Materials:

Rolls of white sheet paper, rulers, stapler, markers, paints, sample calendar, scissors

Motivation:

1 Divide the class into groups. Show the class a sample calendar. Explain to the class that each group is going to design a calendar that illustrates the benefits of being drug free. Each group is to design a layout for the calendar. The layout is to include space for an illustration, a caption for the illustration, the name of the month, the days of the week, and the dates. Students can use the rulers to measure the sheets for each month and to design the layout.

2 The illustration or cartoon for each month must illustrate and/or address the benefits of being drug free. For example, the layout for January might include an illustration of a snow-covered mountain. The caption might be, "A mountain climber takes one step at a time to reach his/her goal. Being drug free allows the mountain climber to head in the right direction." The layout for February might include an illustration of a female athlete jumping a hurdle. The caption might be, "It is easier to jump the hurdles in life when a person is drug free."

3 After each group has completed copy for each of the 12 months in a calendar year, the stapler can be used to staple the copy together to make the calendar.

4 Ask teachers in other classrooms in your building if they would be interested in having one of the groups bring a calendar to their classroom to share with their students. This sharing session might be done with students at younger grade levels. The group would share the illustrations and captions for each of the twelve months. Then the group would give the calendar to the students to display in their classroom.

Evaluation:

Have students write letters to the students in the classrooms that were used for the sharing sessions. Each student is to write a letter providing reasons why (s)he is committed to being drug free. At least five reasons should be given.

Multicultural Infusion:

There are at least two ways that this lesson might be adapted to provide for multicultural infusion. First, some of the students of a particular culture may decide to work in the same group to design a culture-specific calendar. Their illustrations would represent their culture only. There may be specific sayings that they have learned. Second, each of the groups might be asked to designate two or three of the months to be culture specific. For example, one of the months might focus upon American Indians. The illustration might depict something specific about this culture, and the saying might depict something specific as well.

Grades 6–8
- Objective 12B

Violence Prevention

POSITIVELY NEGATIVE

Objective:

Students will evaluate the benefits of being drug free.

Life Skill:

I will not drink alcohol, use tobacco, or use other harmful drugs.

Materials:

Copies of the message "Positively Negative"

Motivation:

1 Make copies of the following message or copy the following message on the chalkboard:

Positively Negative

We drank for joy and became miserable.
We drank for sociability and became argumentative.
We drank for friendship and made enemies.
We drank for sleep and awakened exhausted.
We drank for strength and felt weak.
We drank for "medicinal purposes" and acquired health problems.
We drank to get calmed down and ended up with shakes.
We drank for confidence and became afraid.
We drank to diminish our problems and saw them multiply.
We drank to cope with life and invited death.

Author Unknown

2 Discuss the many facts that are identified in the message of "Positively Negative." After discussing the facts, have students write an adaptation titled "Positively Drug Free and Drug Informed" using the first person. Their adaptations should contain at least ten statements beginning with I. Examples of some possible lines for their adaptations might be as follows.

Positively Drug Free and Drug Informed

I sit in nonsmoking sections of restaurants and avoid lung cancer.
I store medicine out of reach of younger brothers and sisters and keep them safe.
I refuse to ride in an automobile with someone who has been drinking and protect myself from injuries.
I avoid drinking alcohol and using marijuana and keep my brain sharp for schoolwork.
I stay away from person's who use harmful drugs and protect myself from violence.

3 Have students read their "Positively Drug Free and Drug Informed" adaptations. After the adaptations have been read, have students comment on each other's statements with regard to the benefits of being drug free and drug informed. Which benefits were expressed most often? Ask individual students to share a benefit that a classmate mentioned that was not one they mentioned that they believed to be important.

Evaluation:

Give students a quiz in which they are asked to list 10 benefits of being drug free and drug informed.

WANTED: DRUG-FREE YOUTH

Objective:

Students will evaluate the benefits of being drug free.

Life Skill:

I will not use alcohol, tobacco, or other harmful drugs.

Materials:

Want ads from the newspaper, sheets of white paper, markers, pen or pencils

Motivation:

1 Discuss what it means to be drug free. A **drug-free** lifestyle refers to a lifestyle in which young persons do not use harmful and illegal drugs. Have students brainstorm the benefits of choosing a drug-free lifestyle: protecting personal health, avoiding situations that might become violent, avoiding drug dependence, following parental guidelines and laws, staying eligible for school sports and activities, etc.

2 Show students the Want Ad section from your local newspaper. Discuss how potential employers write Want Ads to attract a specific type of person for a job. The employer believes that a person who fits the description will be the most suitable for the tasks that (s)he has in mind.

3 Explain to students that they are each to write a Want Ad, but their Want Ads will be for drug-free youth. Here are examples:

Wanted: Teenager for Childcare.
Looking for a teenager to care for my child after school three days a week. Must enjoy playing with four year old. Must have references from other childcare experiences. Smokers need not apply.

Wanted: Eighth Grade Females for Soccer Team.
Looking for eighth grade females who will play on the school soccer team. Must be in good condition and able to run at least two miles. Must have good grades in school and be able to manage time effectively. Females who are experimenting with cigarettes and/or alcohol need not apply.

Wanted: Teenager to Mow Lawn.
Looking for a responsible teenager to mow my lawn at least twice a week. Must be drug free to operate my power mower safely.

Wanted: Drug-Free Friend
I am new to this school and am looking for a friend with whom I can have fun and share school activities. This friend should be drug free, attend drug-free parties, and introduce me to other classmates who are drug free.

4 Have students read their Want Ads to classmates. Discuss the options and opportunities that are available to students who remain drug free.

Evaluation:

Have the class sit in a circle. Begin with the first student. This student says, "I want to be drug free so that I can play soccer." The next student says, "I want to be drug free so that I can play soccer and get good grades." The third student repeats what the first two students said and adds an additional benefit, "I want to be drug free so that I can play soccer, get good grades, and keep my lungs clean." Continue around the circle with each student repeating the entire list of benefits of being drug free and adding an additional benefit.

Inclusion:

Allow students with special needs extra support in recalling what classmates have said. These students can keep notes in the form of symbols. For example, the students might draw the following on a sheet of paper: soccer ball, large A, lungs. Then when they are called upon to repeat the entire list of benefits of being drug free and add an additional benefit, they can refer to the symbols to help them with recall.

Grades 6–8
- Objective 13A

CHAIN OF HIV INFECTION

Objective:

Students will describe the relationship between using intravenous drugs and the transmission of HIV.

Life Skills:

I will not use intravenous drugs.
I will avoid being around persons who use intravenous drugs and/or who sell intravenous drugs.

Materials:

Red construction paper ($8\frac{1}{2} \times 11$), 2 sheets; tape; scissors; red ballpoint pen with a spring-activated retractable point

Motivation:

1 Make the following preparation for the lesson without students seeing what you are doing. Cut the two sheets of red construction paper into a total of eight strips that are eleven inches long and two inches wide. (You will be able to cut four strips out of each sheet of paper.) Tape the two ends of one of the strips together so that it resembles a link of a chain.

2 Define HIV, AIDS, and intravenous drug use. **HIV**, the **human immunodeficiency virus**, is a pathogen that causes AIDS. **AIDS**, or **acquired immune deficiency syndrome**, is the final stage of HIV infection during which there is a significant decrease in the disease-fighting cells inside the body. **Intravenous drug use** refers to the injection of a drug into a vein. Explain that persons sharing needles for intravenous drug use are engaging in a risk behavior for becoming infected with HIV.

3 Discuss the transmission of HIV through intravenous drug use. The transmission of HIV through intravenous drug use occurs when drug users share needles. The sharing of needles, whether used for anabolic steroids or

narcotics, increases the risk of HIV infection. The process in which the needle is used, whether it be through skin popping or subcutaneous, intramuscular (such as injecting steroids), or mainlining (directly into a vein), makes no difference in a person's chances of becoming infected with HIV. HIV can enter the syringe when the drug user draws back on the plunger to see if the needle is inside the vein. A drug user knows if a vein is tapped when blood is easily drawn into the syringe. Even if only a small amount of blood is trapped inside the syringe, this blood can contain a large amount of HIV when drawn from an infected person. Even if this blood is "shot up," there will remain traces of HIV. If another person uses the same syringe, there will be a high probability that HIV will be transmitted and thus cause infection. One of the reasons for the high probability of infection is the fact that HIV is pumped directly into the bloodstream rather than through the skin.

4 Use the red ballpoint pen to demonstrate what happens when a needle is shared. Click the pen so that the point of the pen is showing. Explain that the point is the needle and that you are using it to inject a substance into your vein or muscle. Then click the pen so that the point does not show. Explain that some traces of blood may now be within the syringe and/or on the needle. Click the pen so that the point is showing. Write HIV with it on a sheet of paper. Since it is a red ballpoint pen, HIV will be written in red. This represents the traces of blood that were on the needle.

5 Ask eight students to volunteer to stand in front of the class and simulate the sharing of an infected needle. Hand the ballpoint pen to the first student. Have this student click the pen so that the point is showing to indicate that (s)he is using the needle and write HIV on a sheet of paper. Again, HIV will be written in red. Explain that this student is now infected with HIV from your blood. Hand the student the red construction paper chain link. Then

431

have the student hand the red ballpoint pen to the next student. Repeat the same demonstration.

6 After this student has written HIV using the red ballpoint pen, take another strip of red construction paper and place it through the chain link of the first student. Close it into another chain link by taping it. Now the first two students are linked together. Repeat the same demonstration with the next six students. Eventually all eight students will be holding a link for a chain and they will be linked together.

7 Explain that this link of infection can be traced back to you. Your blood containing HIV infected the next person and so the chain of infection continued.

Evaluation:

Have students write slogans to warn others about the consequences of sharing a needle/syringe/injection equipment.

Inclusion:

Have students with special needs who want to practice their measuring skills cut out the eight $2'' \times 11''$ strips from the red construction paper.

Grades 6–8
- Objective 13B

Violence Prevention

Stuck for Life

Objective:

Students will describe the relationship between using intravenous drugs and the transmission of HIV.

Life Skills:

I will not use intravenous drugs.
I will report others who use intravenous drugs.

Materials:

Two apples—one shiny and one bruised, a needle, red food coloring

Motivation:

1 Make the following preparation for the lesson without students viewing what you are doing. Place the needle into the container of red food coloring. After removing the needle from the container, some of the red food coloring should remain on it. Then stick the needle into the shiny apple. Be certain that some of the red food coloring gets inside the apple.

2 Define HIV, AIDS, and intravenous drug use. **HIV**, the **human immunodeficiency virus**, is a pathogen that causes AIDS. **AIDS**, or **acquired immune deficiency syndrome**, is the final stage of HIV infection during which there is a significant decrease in the disease-fighting cells inside the body. **Intravenous drug use** refers to the injection of a drug into a vein. Explain that persons sharing needles for intravenous drug use are engaging in a risk behavior for becoming infected with HIV.

3 Show students the two apples—one shiny and one bruised. Explain that each of the apples represents a person. Ask the class which one they believe is infected with HIV. In many cases, most students in the class will say that they believe the bruised apple is the one infected with HIV. Explain that appearance alone will not indicate whether or not a person

is infected with HIV. It is not a person's appearance, or gender, or race, or faith, or sexual orientation that puts a person at risk. Rather, it is a person's behavior.

4 Cut off a piece of the shiny apple near the spot where you inserted the needle with the red food coloring on it. Explain what you had done earlier; that you stuck the apple with the needle that had previously been in the container of food coloring. Further explain that you did this to demonstrate what happens when persons share needles for intravenous drug use.

5 Discuss the transmission of HIV through intravenous drug use. The transmission of HIV through intravenous drug use occurs when drug users share needles. The sharing of needles, whether used for anabolic steroids or narcotics, increases the risk of HIV infection. The process in which the needle is used, whether it be through skin popping or subcutaneous, intramuscular (such as injecting steroids), or mainlining (directly into a vein), makes no difference in a person's chances of becoming infected with HIV. HIV can enter the syringe when the drug user draws back on the plunger to see if the needle is inside the vein. A drug user knows if a vein is tapped when blood is easily drawn into the syringe. Even if only a small amount of blood is trapped inside the syringe, this blood can contain a large amount of HIV when drawn from an infected person. Even if this blood is "shot up," there will remain traces of HIV. If another person uses the same syringe, there will be a high probability that HIV will be transmitted and thus cause infection. One of the reasons for the high probability of infection is the fact that HIV is pumped directly into the bloodstream rather than through the skin.

6 Explain that in the case of the apple that was stuck with red food coloring, enough of the apple might be cut off to get rid of the food coloring. But, this is not true of persons who are stuck with an HIV-infected needle. Once a person is infected with HIV, (s)he is infected for life.

7 Cut off pieces of the bruised apple in several places. Explain to students that even though the bruised apple did not look as healthful or appealing as the shiny apple, it is not infected with HIV.

8 Discuss the importance of persons who have shared needles and/or other injection equipment for intravenous drug use being tested for HIV infection. The test most commonly used to detect HIV infection is called the ELISA test. **ELISA** is a test that detects antibodies developed by the human immune system in response to the presence of HIV. The **Western Blot Test** is a blood test that is used to confirm the results of a positive ELISA.

Evaluation:

Have students write a paper with the following theme—Stuck for Life. Students should include a discussion of how HIV transmission occurs when needles and/or injection equipment is shared. They should explain that once a person is infected with HIV (s)he will always be

infected. Students should also explain why appearance, race, religion, and sexual orientation are not risk factors, rather it is a person's behavior choices. They also should explain the importance of HIV testing for persons who have engaged in risk behavior.

Inclusion:

Have students write a paper including at least ten sentences with the following theme—Stuck for Life. Provide these students with the following list of facts to include in their papers:
1. Intravenous drug use is a risk behavior for HIV infection.
2. A needle that is shared may have droplets of HIV-infected blood on it.
3. You cannot tell by appearance if a person is infected with HIV.
4. A person is not HIV positive because of his/her race, faith, or sexual orientation.
5. A person who has engaged in risk behavior should be tested for HIV.
6. There are two tests for HIV—ELISA and Western Blot.
7. If a person is infected with HIV, (s)he will always be infected.

Sharing HIV

Objective:

Students will describe the relationship between using intravenous drugs and the transmission of HIV.

Life Skills:

I will not use intravenous drugs.
I will avoid persons who use intravenous drugs.

Materials:

Two plastic cups, red food coloring, water, eyedropper

Motivation:

1 Introduce the topic of intravenous drugs. **Intravenous drugs** are drugs that are injected into a vein. Explain that in a large number of cases HIV transmission is related to injecting drugs. The prevalence of HIV infection among intravenous drug users has been on the rise. As the number of intravenous drug users continues to increase, so do the chances that an intravenous drug user will use an infected needle. For example, a ten percent prevalence of HIV infection among drug users in a city results in a one in ten chance another drug user will become infected with HIV if a needle is shared. If the prevalence of HIV infection among drug users is 80 percent, there is an almost certain chance HIV infection will result if unsterilized needles are shared frequently.

2 Pour water into the two plastic cups. Add a drop of red food coloring to one of the cups of water. Allow the food coloring to mix with the water so that the water turns red. Explain to the class that the cup of water that is red represents a person who is HIV positive. Now take the eyedropper and place it into this cup of water. Squeeze some of the red water into the eyedropper. Pull the dropper out of the red water. Place the eyedropper over the cup

and allow the red water to squirt back into the cup. However, leave a drop of the red water in the eyedropper. Explain to the class that this person who is HIV positive has just injected a drug intravenously using a syringe.

3 Now explain that the person who is HIV positive is going to share the syringe with someone who is HIV negative. Place the eyedropper into the colorless water and allow the drop of red food coloring to enter the water. This illustrates that the infected blood from the person who is HIV positive has entered the bloodstream of the person who was previously negative. Now this person is infected with HIV.

4 Provide more facts about HIV transmission. The transmission of HIV through intravenous drug use occurs when drug users share needles. The sharing of needles, whether used for steroids or narcotics, increases the risk of HIV infection. The form through which the needle is used, whether it be through skin popping or subcutaneous, intramuscular (such as injecting steroids), or mainlining (directly into a vein), makes no difference in a person's ability to become infected with HIV. HIV can enter a syringe when the drug user draws back on the plunger to see if the needle is inside the vein. A drug user knows if a vein is tapped when blood is easily drawn into the syringe.

5 Further explain that even if only a small amount of blood is trapped inside the syringe, this blood can contain a large amount of HIV when drawn from an infected person. Even if this blood is "shot up," there will remain traces of HIV. If another person uses the same syringe, there will be a high probability that HIV will be transmitted and thus cause infection. One of the reasons for the high probability of infection is the fact that HIV is pumped directly inside the bloodstream rather than through the skin.

6 Students might ask why intravenous drug users would share needles when so much information is available regarding the risk of HIV infection. Explain that persons who are dependent upon narcotics have a craving for the next fix that interferes with good judgment.

Evaluation:

Have students take a sheet of paper and fold it into thirds to make a pamphlet. Then have students design a pamphlet that provides information about HIV infections and intravenous drug use.

Inclusion:

Rather than designing pamphlets upon which to be evaluated, ask students with special learning challenges to duplicate the demonstration you performed using the two plastic cups, red food coloring, and water. As they do this demonstration for you, they are to explain how HIV can be transmitted through intravenous drug use.

Grade 6–8
- Objective 14A

DROWSY BRAIN

Objective:

Students will discuss how the use of drugs interferes with making responsible decisions about sexuality.

Life Skill:

I will not use harmful drugs that impair my thinking.

Materials:

Tape recorder, blank cassette tape, plastic cup filled with water, red food coloring

Motivation:

1 Prepare for this teaching strategy by following the directions for recording three messages on the blank cassette tape.

Recording 1: (This message should be recorded clearly.)
I am your thinking and reasoning brain. I am in full control of the decisions you make. I am drug free. I have a carefully integrated value system. I have information that tells me that being sexually active is not in my best interest. Sexual involvement does not follow the guidelines of my family. It may lead to an unwanted pregnancy or infection with an STD or HIV. Although I might be tempted, I am in control. I can use this information to say NO to tempting situations and pressures.

Recording 2: (This message is somewhat muffled.)
I am your brain. You have put a chemical in me. This chemical has blocked some of the information that I relied on to make decisions. I cannot think as clearly. I am retrieving messages about sexual decision-making. I am getting some information that tells me that being sexually active is not in my best interest. But, I am not getting the information about ways to resist peer pressure and get out of tempting sit-

uations. The messages I am getting are confused. Some of the messages are coming from my body now.

Recording 3: (This message is very muffled.)
I am your brain. I am getting very drowsy now. It is difficult for me to stay awake and concentrate on all the decisions I have to make. I think I'll doze off for awhile. Hope the body makes good decisions while I nap.

2 Discuss blood alcohol level. **Blood alcohol level, or BAL,** is the amount of alcohol in a person's blood. Blood alcohol level is usually expressed as a percentage. As the blood alcohol level increases, changes occur in the body. The changes occur because alcohol is a depressant. This means alcohol depresses or slows down the functioning of body organs, especially the brain. Several factors influence the blood alcohol level:

- *Amount of alcohol consumed.* The more alcohol consumed, the higher the BAL and the greater the depressant effects. The alcoholic beverage consumed does not make a difference.
- *Rate of consumption.* The liver oxidizes alcohol at the same rate regardless of how fast a person drinks. When a person gulps drinks, BAL increases quickly.
- *Rate of absorption.* Alcohol passes through the stomach and is absorbed by the small intestine. Having food in the stomach slows down absorption.
- *Rate of oxidation.* Heredity plays a factor in the rate of oxidation. Normally, the liver oxidizes about a half ounce of alcohol per hour. Persons with chemical dependency in their families oxidize alcohol more slowly, giving alcohol a more long lasting effect.
- *Body size.* Alcohol will affect a person of lower body weight faster than someone who is heavier.
- *Mood and emotions.* Persons who are depressed may experience more severe depression as BAL increases.

3 Explain that as BAL increases, the depressant effects on the brain increase. Because the brain is the control center for reasoning and judgment, a person begins to experience difficulty in making wise decisions. In other words, the brain becomes drowsy and may doze off when needed. The brain normally relies upon information it has to make responsible decisions about sex. This information includes carefully integrated values that send messages. Play the first recording that you made. Emphasize how clear the messages were because the brain was alert.

4 Take the cup of water. Place a drop of red food coloring in the water. Explain that this is an alcoholic beverage. It is being absorbed by the body and will affect all body organs. It affects the brain. Play the second recording that you made. Emphasize the changes that have occurred because the brain is drowsy.

5 Repeat. Place another drop of food coloring in the cup of water. Explain that the brain now needs a nap. The messages controlling decision making are now coming from the body instead of the brain.

6 Have students summarize what they have learned. They should state that if they want to be in control of decisions regarding sexuality, they need to avoid drinking alcoholic beverages and using other drugs.

Evaluation:

Have students write a script for their brain about sexuality. Their script should include the messages that their brain plays when they are not under the influence of drugs. The messages should include ways to adhere to a value system in which students are not sexually active.

DRUGS + DULL THINKING = SEX

Objective:

Students will discuss how the use of drugs interferes with making responsible decisions about sexuality.

Life Skill:

I will not use harmful drugs which impair my thinking.

Materials:

Sheet of paper, pen or pencil

Motivation:

1 Discuss the effects of drugs on decision making. Most harmful drugs affect the thinking and reasoning functions of the brain. Use alcohol as an example. Alcohol is a depressant drug that depresses or slows down the part of the brain that is used for reasoning and judgment. Suppose a person has decided that (s)he does not want to be sexually active. This same person has made the decision that (s)he should not engage in heavy petting, intimate touching, in order that (s)he might stick to this decision. Now suppose this person drinks an alcoholic beverage. The alcohol depresses the part of the brain that is used for reasoning and judgment. Before drinking the alcoholic beverage, this person was clear that (s)he would not engage in heavy petting. Now (s)he is not as clear.

2 To demonstrate to students how a drug such as alcohol can affect decision making, use the following activity. First, have students write, "I will not engage in heavy petting," in script on a sheet of paper. After they have done this, ask students to hold one foot straight out in front of them. They are to hold out the foot that corresponds to the hand they use for writing; i.e., a right-handed person will extend the right foot.

3 Have students turn their extended foot in a clockwise, circular pattern. While doing this, they are to write, "I will not engage in heavy petting," in script under the previous writing. When doing this, students will find that it is difficult to maintain a circular motion with the extended foot. They should also compare the two messages they wrote before and after extending and performing circular motions with their feet.

4 Have students share what they experienced. Use this information to have students discuss how being under the influence of alcohol and/or other drugs can affect responsible decision making regarding sexual behavior.

Evaluation:

Have students draw a bottle of an alcoholic beverage. They are to make a warning label on the bottle that makes a specific statement about the effects of drinking alcohol on responsible decision making about sexual behavior.

Inclusion:

Allow students with special needs the opportunity to obtain extra credit for finding advertisements for alcoholic beverages in magazines that focus on sexuality. The students should share the message that is portrayed in the advertisement of their choice.

Grades 6–8
▪ Objective 14C

BALANCING ACT

Objective:

Students will discuss how the use of drugs interferes with making responsible decisions about sexuality.

Life Skills:

I will choose abstinence.
I will not drink alcoholic beverages.
I will not use harmful drugs.

Materials:

Poster board, scissors, markers, string, two small clothes pins, 10 index cards

Motivation:

1 Use one of the sheets of poster board to create the bar shown in the illustration. At one end of the bar, draw the brain and print on it "reasoning" and "judgment." On the other end of the bar, print the following: HIV, gonorrhea, syphilis, chlamydia, HPV, herpes, pregnancy, parenthood. In the middle of the top of the bar, attach a string for holding the bar. Attach string at each end of the bar and allow it to hang down. At the end of each of the strings, attach small clothes pins.

2 Use the ten index cards. Print one of the following statements on each of the ten index cards:
  • Being involved in activities that promote self-worth.
  • Establishing goals.
  • Developing loving family relationships.
  • Being assertive and using decision-making skills.
  • Establishing relationships with trusted adults.
  • Selecting friends who choose abstinence.
  • Dating persons who have chosen abstinence.
  • Avoiding situations that are tempting.
  • Abstaining from the use of alcohol and other drugs.

  • Selecting entertainment that promotes sex within a monogamous marriage.

3 Using the other sheet of poster board, cut an outline of a beer can, wine bottle, and hard-liquor bottle. Use the markers to make these look as real as possible.

4 Initiate a discussion of responsible sexual behavior. **Abstinence** is choosing not to have sexual intercourse. Explain that there are many benefits that adolescents can derive from choosing abstinence. Abstinence is healthful and safe. Adolescents who choose abstinence won't have to worry about gonorrhea, syphilis, chlamydia, HPV, herpes, unwanted pregnancy, teenage parenthood, child abuse, and neglect. Neither will they have to worry about HIV as long as they also abstain from intravenous drug use. Abstinence protects the laws of the community. Adolescents won't have to worry about breaking the law and having sexual intercourse prior to the legal age of consent. Abstinence shows respect for self and others. Adolescents can maintain a good reputation. Abstinence follows guidelines set by responsible adults such as parents and/or guardians. Abstinence demonstrates good character and moral values.

5 Explain that there are many life skills that adolescents can practice to support abstinence. Show the students the bar you have created. Pass out the ten index cards. Have students who have been given an index card come forward, read what is on their card, and put the card inside the clothes pin on the side of the bar that says HIV, etc. This will make the other side of the bar swing up. Explain that when these life skills are practiced, reasoning and judgment are at their best and an adolescent makes wise decisions about his/her sexuality. Remove the index cards.

6 Give three different students the outlines of the beer can, wine bottle, and hard-liquor bottle. Have these students attach these to the clothes

440

pin at the end of the bar (brain) labeled reasoning and judgment. This will lower this end of the bar and cause the side labeled HIV, pregnancy, parenthood to rise. Explain that drinking alcoholic beverages lowers reasoning and judgment and increases the risk of becoming sexually involved. Sexual involvement may cause a rise in HIV, gonorrhea, syphilis, chlamydia, HPV, herpes, unwanted pregnancy, teenage parenthood, child abuse, and neglect.

Evaluation:

Have students write a short paper that identifies reasons why it is important to avoid drinking alcoholic beverages and to practice abstinence. Have them think of a clever title such as, "You're Not Thinking When You're Drinking."

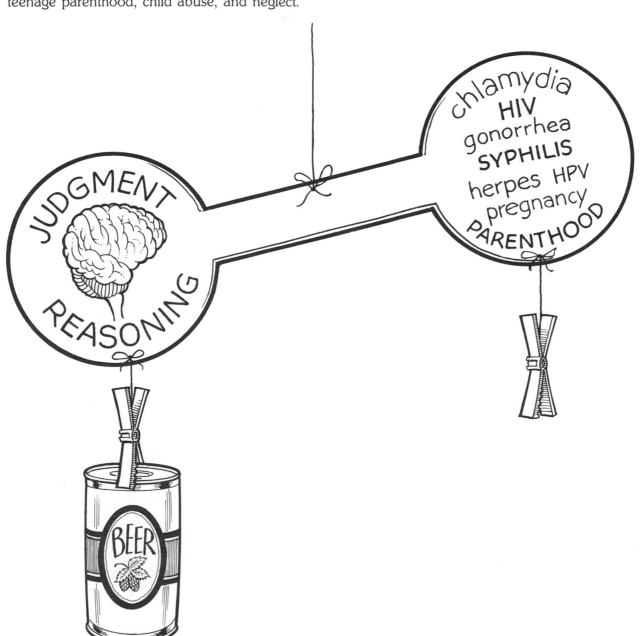

Grades 6–8
▪ Objective 15A

REHAB RAP

Objective:

Students will identify school and community resources involved in the prevention and treatment of drug, alcohol, and tobacco use.

Life Skills:

I will be aware of the school and community resources that help in the prevention and treatment of drug, alcohol, and tobacco use.
I will use school and community resources for the prevention and treatment of drug, alcohol, and tobacco use when needed.

Materials:

Pamphlets describing community resources (including guest speakers) that help with the prevention and treatment of drug, alcohol, and tobacco use; information on speakers bureaus; paper; pencils; index cards; tape; red pen or marker; black pen or marker

Motivation:

1 Discuss the school and community resources that help in the treatment and prevention of drug, alcohol, and tobacco use. If available, invite guest speakers representing community resources to discuss their services with your students. Providing students with pamphlets is helpful.

2 Prepare the index cards as follows without showing them to the students in advance. There are six categories of drugs with examples of each listed below. With a red marker or pen, print the name of each drug category on a separate index card. With a black marker or pen, print the name of each example on a separate index card.

Narcotics
heroin
opium
codeine
morphine
methadone
talwin
percadan
darvon

Hallucinogens
mescaline
LSD
PCP
psilocybin

Stimulants
amphetamines
diet pills
speed
cocaine/crack
coffee
tea
nicotine

Inhalants
glue
nail polish remover
spot remover
aerosol sprays
cleaning fluid
lacquer
liquid correction fluid

Cannabis
marijuana
hashish
hash oil

Depressants
barbiturates
tranquilizers
alcohol

3 Shuffle the cards and place them into a pile face down. Have students form a line. Give each student a card and a piece of tape. The student is to tape his/her card on his/her clothing as if it were a name tag.

4 Explain to the class that there are six categories or families of drugs. These are the red name tags. Then there are drugs that belong to each of these categories or families. These are printed in black. Without speaking, they are to form six groups or families. They are to stand in a specific location with the head of their family and all other family members.

5 After students have formed their groups and you have checked to see that they are in the correct groups, give the following directions. Explain that persons who abuse any of these six families of drugs will need rehabilitation. The class has previously discussed school and community resources that are available. Each group will have fifteen minutes to write a rehab rap that tells about getting help for drug abuse. The rehab rap should be at least ten lines long and contain the names of at least three community resources. The group may want to practice its rehab rap. The group might practice accompanying dance steps and/or hand motions to make the rehab rap as lively as possible.

6 Have the groups perform their rehab raps. Review the information in the raps, paying particular attention to the three community resources mentioned in each.

Evaluation:

Have students write a want ad for a job opening for a person who works in a community agency that helps in the prevention and treatment of drug, alcohol, and tobacco abuse. The job description should be detailed and explain exactly what responsibilities will be included in performing this job.

Grades 6–8
▪ Objective 15B

LET'S PLAY SORRY

Objective:

The students will identify school and community resources that help in the prevention of drug, alcohol, and tobacco abuse and also identify school and community resources available for treatment.

Life Skills:

I will be aware of the school and community resources that help in the prevention and treatment of drug, alcohol, and tobacco use.
I will use school and community resources for the prevention and treatment of drug, alcohol, and tobacco use when needed.

Materials:

Pamphlets describing community resources that help with the prevention and treatment of drug, alcohol, and tobacco use; six sheets of cardboard poster paper, markers, 210 index cards, scissors, game board for "Sorry," guest speaker(s) representing school and community resources

Motivation:

1 Discuss the school and community resources that help in the treatment and prevention of drugs, alcohol, and tobacco. If available, invite guest speakers representing community resources to discuss their services with your students. Providing students with pamphlets is helpful.

2 Show students the game board for "Sorry" made by Parker Brothers. Review the directions for playing the game. Read students some of the cards. Explain to students that they are going to be divided into groups to make game boards for a similar game. Their game boards are going to identify community

resources for the prevention and treatment of drug, alcohol, and tobacco use.

3 Divide the class into six groups. Give each group a sheet of cardboard poster board, markers, index cards, and scissors. Have each group make a game board. Instead of the four designated places for "home," students are to have four different community resources for the prevention and treatment of drug, alcohol, and tobacco use.

4 Each group is to use index cards to draw as they play the game. Students can brainstorm directions to be written on the cards. Fifteen of the index cards should identify healthful behaviors and decisions and instruct the player to move forward. For example, an index card might say, "You attended a drug-free party, move forward three spaces." Another index card might say, "You followed the directions for your prescription medicine, move forward two spaces." Another index card might say, "You keep medicine in a safe place away from children, move forward one space."

5 Fifteen of the index cards should identify risk behaviors and irresponsible decisions and instruct the player to move backwards. For example, an index card might say, "You rode in an automobile that was driven by someone who was drinking, move backwards three spaces." Another index card might say, "You took your sister's medicine, move back two spaces." Another index card might say, "You smoked a cigarette, move back three spaces."

6 Five of the index cards should be "sorry" cards and instruct the player to start from the beginning again. These cards indicate that a person has not adhered to a plan for recovery. For example, an index card might say, "You skipped your AA meeting, SORRY, go back to start." Another index card might say, "You quit smoking and then sneaked a cigarette, SORRY, go back to start."

7 Have each group identify a leader. There will be six stations in the classroom. Each station will have the leader with his/her group's game board. The rest of the members in each group will go to one of the other five stations to play the game. Four students can play at a time while the leader supervises play.

Evaluation:

Have students make their own pamphlets that summarize the community resources that help in the prevention and treatment of drugs, alcohol, and tobacco use.

Grades 6–8
▪ Objective 15C

BREAKING THE CHAIN

Objective:

Students will identify school and community resources involved in the prevention and treatment of drug, alcohol, and tobacco use.

Life Skill:

I will use school and community resources for the prevention and treatment of drug, alcohol, and tobacco use when I, my family, or friends need assistance.

Materials:

Colored construction paper, markers, several pairs of scissors, tape, staplers, rulers, literature such as pamphlets and brochures that detail community resources for prevention and treatment of drug, alcohol, and tobacco use

Motivation:

1 Review various treatment approaches for drug dependency: smoking cessation programs, detoxification, therapeutic communities, residential treatment, Twelve-Step Programs, inpatient hospital programs, methadone maintenance, outpatient treatment. Smoking cessation programs are available from the American Cancer Society, American Heart Association, American Lung Association, and a variety of private organizations. Smoking cessation programs are designed to help a person modify behavior. Detoxification is a treatment process that is used to help a drug-dependent person withdraw from the effects of drugs. Therapeutic communities are designed to get patients to take responsibility for their behavior and to make modifications. Residential treatment usually involves living in a therapeutic community for approximately six to twelve months. Twelve-Step Programs involve groups who meet regularly with the following agenda:

admission of drug dependency, acknowledgment of the inability to stop drug use without the help of a higher power, the need to confront the harm done to others, and the need to modify behavior. Inpatient hospital programs involve treatment for health problems and counseling within the hospital setting. Methadone maintenance involves taking this drug in order to relieve the craving and withdrawal symptoms for heroin. Outpatient treatment programs offer a mixture of individual counseling, group counseling, family therapy, and specific-relapse prevention training.

2 Identify community resources for the prevention and treatment of drug, alcohol, and tobacco use. Share literature about these resources with students. If available, invite professionals responsible for treatment services to share information with the class.

3 Divide the class into several groups of students. Give each group of students several different colored sheets of construction paper, scissors, tape, ruler, and stapler. Students are to cut at least ten strips of construction paper. Each strip should measure eleven inches by two inches. On each of the ten strips of construction paper, they are to write the name of a treatment approach for drug dependency or the name of a community resource that is involved in treatment.

4 Have each group make loops from their paper strips and link the ten strips together to make a chain. Then have each group select one student in the group to represent a person who is drug dependent. The group is to use their chain to chain this person's hands or feet together. Then the group is to select another student who is representing a concerned friend or family member who wants to assist this person in getting treatment for drug dependence.

5 Have each of these pairs of students stand in front of the class. Each pair is to do the following. The drug dependent student is to introduce himself/herself and explain that (s)he wants to "break the chain" of drug dependence. The partner explains that there are effective ways to "break the chain." The partner begins to tear each link from the chain. As each link is removed, the partner reads what is printed on it. For example, the partner might tear off a link that says, "Twelve-Step Programs." The partner then says, "There are Twelve-Step Programs in which persons who have problems with drug dependency can admit that they are dependent, acknowledge their need for a higher power, begin repairing the harm they have done to others, and gain the support of a group." The partner then continues by tearing off another link and reading what is written on it. It might say, "Bay View Hospital has both inpatient and outpatient treatment for drug dependency."

6 Repeat this procedure until each pair has proceeded to "break the chain" of drug dependency by using community resources for drugs, alcohol, and tobacco.

Evaluation:

Have students respond to the following letter to Dear Helper, providing at least three types of treatment and three community resources involved in treatment for drug, alcohol, and tobacco dependency.

Dear Helper,
My brother cannot control his drinking. I know that he is drinking alcohol during the lunch break. He hides cans of beer in his room and drinks by himself at night. We have just moved to this community. Are there community resources that might help my brother and my family? What are some treatment approaches?

Sincerely,
Concerned

Grade 6–8
- Objective 16A

WHAT'S IN YOUR JEANS?

Objective:

Students will describe the relationship between heredity and drug dependency.

Life Skill:

I will obtain information about my family history with regard to drug dependency.

Materials:

Magazines, scissors, poster board, construction paper, markers, tape, index cards

Motivation:

1 For this teaching strategy, you will need to prepare four jean pockets. You may choose to do this yourself or you may want to ask a student(s) to do this for you. Use the four sheets of poster board to cut out the bottom of four pairs of jeans (see illustration). Use the construction paper to cut out the pockets. Tape the pockets to the jean bottoms, leaving the pocket open.

2 Prepare the index cards in four piles as follows:
Pile 1: On one index card, print "high blood pressure." On three index cards, print "no family history of high blood pressure."
Pile 2: On one index card, print "diabetes." On three index cards, print "no family history of diabetes."
Pile 3: On one index card, print "chemical dependency." On three index cards, print "no family history of chemical dependency."
Pile 4: On one index card, print "breast cancer." On three index cards, print "no family history of breast cancer."

3 Divide the class into groups. Explain that each group will have five minutes to brainstorm the names of various brands of blue jeans. They are to include the brand names of jeans that are popular as well as the

brand names of jeans that are not as popular with their peers.

4 After five minutes have passed, have the groups share the brand names that group members identified. Select four of these names. Print the name of each one on one of the pockets of the blue jeans. Explain to the class that there is a person wearing each of the four pairs of blue jeans. Each of these persons has inherited what's inside his/her jeans/genes.

5 Review information about heredity and genes. **Heredity** is the transmission of characteristics and features from one generation to the next. **Genes** are the material through which the hereditary material is passed. Each person gets many genes from his/her biological parents. Sometimes the characteristics and features that are passed are obvious in the person getting them. For example, when a person has brown eyes, others can see this characteristic. And the person knows that there is information about brown eyes in his/her genes. This would be true of height and skin color as well. Since a person gets his/her genes from biological parents, (s)he will have many of the same observable features.

6 Explain that sometimes a person inherits a tendency toward something from his/her biological parents. Some of these tendencies have to do with how well the organs work and with body chemistry. For example, a person's biological parents may have high blood pressure. This person gets information in his/her genes that says, "You have a tendency toward developing high blood pressure." This person may not have high blood pressure but knowing this information is helpful. (S)he can choose behavior that will help him/her keep normal blood pressure. Exercising every day, eating a low fat diet, getting rest and sleep, and controlling stress will help.

7 Provide other examples in which a tendency toward a disease or condition may be inherited. Explain that the tendency toward diabetes is inherited. Eating a healthful diet and controlling weight and stress help prevent the onset of diabetes. There is also a family tendency for breast cancer. Females whose mother and/or sister have had breast cancer are more likely to have breast cancer. Eating a low fat diet and exercising regularly are good health habits for females with this family history. When females become forty years of age, they need regular mammograms to screen for breast cancer.

8 Further explain that the tendency toward chemical dependency is inherited from biological parents. It is important to know one's family history. Does a parent(s) have chemical dependency? Biological aunts or uncles? Brothers or sisters? Grandparents?

9 Take the four piles of index cards. Shuffle each pile and place one of the cards from each pile into each of the jean pockets. There should be four index cards in each of the jean pockets.

10 Explain that it is important to know what's in your genes/jeans because it might influence the behaviors that you choose for good health. For example, suppose you are overweight and eat a high fat and high sugar diet. These behaviors are not healthful for anyone, but they are particularly risky for persons who have a tendency toward diabetes or high blood pressure in their genes/jeans.

11 Have a student select a pair of jeans and remove the index cards from the pocket. Discuss what is "in the genes/jeans" for this person. The index cards might or might not make mention of high blood pressure or diabetes.

12 Discuss chemical dependency. Suppose a young person begins to experiment by drinking alcohol. This is not a healthful

behavior for any young person but it is particularly risky for those who have a tendency toward chemical dependency in their genes/jeans. Have a student select one of the pairs of jeans and remove the index cards from the pocket. Discuss what is on these index cards. The family tendency toward chemical dependency might not be on the cards, but it is not healthful for young persons to experiment with drinking alcohol.

13 Have a student remove the index cards from the other pairs of jeans. One of the pairs of jeans will have an index card that states a family tendency toward chemical dependency. Explain that persons do not always know what is "in their jeans." They need to obtain information about their family history with regard to chemical dependency. And if they have a family history of chemical dependency, they should never drink alcohol.

Evaluation:

Have students write a short summary regarding the link between heredity and chemical dependency. Explain that their short summaries are going to be used for television. They will be used by a news announcer who interrupts a regular program to say, "We interrupt this program to bring you information that researchers have gathered regarding heredity and chemical dependency . . . (students finish the statement)."

Multicultural Infusion:

Students can examine their cultural heritage to determine conditions that might be more or less prevalent in their ancestors. For example, sickle cell anemia is more prevalent in African-Americans and Tay-Sachs syndrome is more prevalent in persons of Jewish and Mediterranean descent.

449

Inclusion:

Students with special needs might help you with this lesson by going through magazines and cutting out pictures of advertisements for different brands of blue jeans. You can explain to these students that all the blue jeans are similar but different. The designer had his/her special label to indicate that his/her jeans are unique. Compare this idea to families. Persons are all similar but different. In very general ways they are similar, but their genetic makeup is different. This is what makes persons unique.

Grades 6–8
- Objective 16B

It's in the Cards

Objective:

Students will describe the relationship between heredity and drug dependency.

Life Skill:

I will attain information about my family history with regard to drug dependency.

Materials:

24 index cards, markers

Motivation:

1 Make six sets of four index cards with one of the following terms written on each as follows: Set one—black hair, brown hair, red hair, blonde hair; Set two—drug dependency, no drug dependency, no drug dependency, no drug dependency; Set three—tall, short, average height, average height; Set four—large frame, small frame, average frame, average frame; Set five—average coordination, average coordination, low coordination, high coordination; Set six—curly hair, curly hair, straight hair, straight hair.

2 Explain to the class that you are going to discuss heredity. **Heredity** is the transmission of characteristics/features from one generation to the next. With the class, identify some characteristics/features that are known to be inherited. Mention the following: color of hair, height, frame, coordination, curly or straight hair.

3 Explain to the class that you are going to do a demonstration to show the characteristics/features that are "in the cards" for four persons. Shuffle the six sets of index cards. Then deal them into four piles. You will have four piles of six cards each.

4 Select four students. Give each of these students a pile of cards. Each student is to read what is written on his/her cards in the follow-

ing manner, "Hi, I am . . . and I have received the following characteristics/features from my family. . . ."

5 One of the students will identify "drug dependency" as a characteristic/feature. Ask the class if this student did anything special in order to get this card. The students will respond NO. Explain that some persons inherit a body chemistry that affects their reactions to drugs. They have an increased likelihood for drug dependence *if they ever use/abuse certain drugs.* **Drug dependence** is the state of psychological and/or physiological need that can occur in a person who uses drugs. Just as a person may have a tendency for heart disease and diabetes if his/her parents has these diseases, a person also can inherit a body chemistry that makes him/her prone to drug dependency.

6 Emphasize two points. A person has no control over an inherited tendency. It is "in the cards" for some persons. And, a person who has been dealt drug dependency "in the cards" will not become drug dependent if (s)he does not use/abuse drugs.

7 Use alcoholism to discuss the family connection. Approximately 12 percent of the population has the disease known as alcoholism. If a male has a close blood relative with alcoholism, his risk of alcoholism is four times greater. If a female has a close blood relative with alcoholism, her risk of alcoholism is three times greater.

8 Discuss ways in which this information is useful. It is important to know one's family history with regard to drug dependence. This includes all drugs, not just alcohol. For example, a person may have family members who are dependent on nicotine from smoking cigarettes. When a person knows his/her family history of drug dependence, choices become even more important and clear. When there is drug dependence in the family, the best advice is never to try drugs. Drinking a can of beer and/

or smoking a cigarette is very risky for a person who has drug dependence in his/her family. Initial experimentation may be the first step toward drug dependence.

Evaluation:

Have students make creative warning labels for drugs such as cigarettes, beer, and wine. Their warning labels should include at least two health risks plus a warning about the increased risk of drug dependency for persons who have family members who have drug dependency.

Inclusion:

Ask a student(s) with special needs to label the index cards for you. In this way, the student(s) can feel that (s)he is helping you, and his/her thinking will be reinforced that drug dependency is "in the cards."

HATS OFF TO HEREDITY

Objective:

Students will describe the relationship between heredity and drug dependence.

Life Skill:

I will obtain information regarding my family history with regard to drug dependency (alcoholism).

Materials:

Four hats, paper, markers, masking tape, index cards, clear tape

Motivation:

1 Design four hats for this demonstration. Use paper, markers, and masking tape. Cut a strip of paper and write "1 X" on it. Use the masking tape to tape it to the front of the first hat. Cut a strip of paper and write "2 X" on it. Use the masking tape to tape it to the front of the second hat. Repeat, having "3 X" on the third hat and "4 X" on the fourth hat.

2 Explain to the class that you are going to discuss heredity. **Heredity** is the transmission of characteristics/features from one generation to the next. With the class, identify some characteristics/features that are known to be inherited. Mention the following: color of hair, height, frame, coordination, curly or straight hair, right or left handedness.

3 Further explain that the tendency toward having certain health conditions may be inherited. For example, persons with parents who had high blood pressure are more likely to have high blood pressure than others. Emphasize two points. First, a person has no control over this increased tendency. And second, a person may be cautious and choose certain behaviors to promote health. In this situation, a person whose parents had high blood pressure would choose behaviors to decrease the likelihood

that (s)he would have high blood pressure. For example, (s)he would exercise regularly and maintain ideal weight.

4 Give students an index card and provide markers for them to use. On the index card, they are to design a caution sign. Collect the index cards.

5 Select four students. Have them sit in chairs in front of the class. Each is to wear one of the hats that you have labeled with "1 X" or "2 X" or "3 X" or "4 X." Give each of the students one fourth of the index cards that have caution signs on them and make the clear tape available. Each student is to tape the caution signs on his/her body.

6 Explain to the class that some persons inherit a body chemistry that affects their reactions to drugs. They have an increased likelihood for drug dependence *if they use/abuse certain drugs.* **Drug dependence** is the state of psychological and/or physiological need that can occur in a person who uses drugs. Just as a person may have a tendency for high blood pressure, a person also inherits a body chemistry that makes him/her prone to drug dependency. Therefore, it is important to know one's family history with regard to drug use. One's family history helps someone to know if (s)he needs to act with even greater caution.

7 Explain that you are going to use the disease of alcoholism as an example of the family connection. Approximately 12 percent of the population has the disease known as alcoholism. That means that out of every 100 persons, 12 have alcoholism. Explain that if a male has a close relative with alcoholism, his risk of alcoholism is 4 times greater. Have all four students who are wearing the hats labeled "1 X" and "2 X" and "3 X" and "4 X" stand. Have students multiply "4 X" the 12 to learn that this male's risk increases to 48 out of 100 from 12 out of 100. Point out the caution signs. Emphasize that a male who has a close relative with alcoholism needs to act with even greater caution. Choosing not to drink is the best way to avoid ever having alcoholism.

8 Have the four students wearing the hats sit in their chairs. Now explain that if a female has a close blood relative with alcoholism, her risk of alcoholism is 3 times greater. Have the three students wearing "1 X" and "2 X" and "3 X" stand. Have students multiply "3 X" the 12 to learn that this female's risk increases to 36 out of 100 from 12 out of 100. Point out the caution signs. Emphasize that a female who has a close relative with alcoholism needs to act with even greater caution. Choosing not to drink is the best way to avoid ever having alcoholism.

Evaluation

Have students draw a can or bottle to represent an alcoholic beverage. Then have them write a warning statement on the beverage container. The warning statement must contain a fact regarding heredity and alcoholism.

THE MANY FACES OF COA

Objective:

Students will examine the impact of drug dependency on the behavior of family members and friends.

Life Skill:

I will seek help from a family member or other trusted adult if I am a member of a family in which there is drug dependency.

Materials:

Construction paper, tape, scissors, clown hat and/or mask, pompoms, picture of goat (optional)

Motivation:

1 Explain that children of parents with alcoholism are often referred to as COAs or children of alcoholics. Because there are so many children of alcoholics, attention has been paid to their characteristics and behaviors. Children of alcoholics often:
- guess what it means to be normal;
- have difficulty setting goals and following through on plans to reach them;
- seek approval and affirmation from others;
- take themselves too seriously;
- fear failure, yet sabotage their success;
- try to keep peace and avoid conflict at any price;
- have difficulty being spontaneous and having fun;
- are either overly responsible or overly irresponsible;
- judge themselves harshly;
- fear rejection and abandonment;
- tell lies when it would not be difficult to tell the truth;
- seek relationships that involve crisis;
- deny their feelings;
- overreact to changes;

- are loyal in situations in which loyalty is not deserved;
- are critical and judgmental of others;
- seek immediate gratification;
- are unable to delay gratification;
- have difficulty being intimate.

2 Explain that you have just described behaviors of children of alcoholics. These children or youth behave in these ways because they are adjusting or attempting to cope with what is happening in their families. Part of this adjustment may be taking on a certain role. There are at least four roles that children of alcoholics may choose.

3 Divide the class into four groups. Give each group an index card upon which the following is written:
Group 1: Family Hero
The family hero attempts to provide self-worth and pride to the family. (S)he is a high achiever and may work very hard in school, sports, and other activities. Achievement is seen as a way to get approval from others. (S)he is overly responsible and seems very mature for his/her age.
Group 2: Mascot
The mascot provides humor and fun. (S)he is usually very immature and others have difficulty taking him/her seriously. (S)he will do anything to get attention and does not care if others laugh at him/her. (S)he often appears to be hyperactive.
Group 3: Scapegoat
The scapegoat provides a safe focus for anger. (S)he is a very low achiever and gets attention as a result of failing. Attention may be obtained from failing at school, running away, becoming a teen parent, or getting into trouble with the law. (S)he is antisocial and a behavior problem.
Group 4: Lost Child
The lost child provides relief. (S)he can be described as "invisible." (S)he prefers to spend time with things such as computers, books, pets, etc., rather than with people.

(S)he has little interaction with others. When interacting with others, (s)he is easily influenced and is a follower. Most of the time, (s)he is withdrawn, aloof, shy, and quiet.

4 Ask each group to use the appropriate props (clown hat, pompoms) and construction paper, scissors, and tape to dress one group member to represent the person described on the index card. For example, the group that is the clown might use the clown mask and hat. Then out of the construction paper, they might draw and cut big feet or something that a clown might wear or have. The person who is going to be the clown tapes on the feet. The group given the card with the lost child might use construction paper to make several books. The group member who is going to be the lost child would carry the books.

5 Explain to the groups that after they have had time to dress one of their group members to represent what was on the card, you are going to introduce this group member to the class.

6 Have the four students representing the groups come forward. Explain that these are four students in your school and each lives in a family with alcoholism. Each of these students is a child of an alcoholic. Explain that you are going to introduce each and tell something about him/her.

7 Introduce the family hero. Explain that the family hero often becomes a school leader. (S)he uses accomplishments to cover up feelings of inadequacy. Have the family hero tell about himself/herself, referring to what was written on the index card.

8 Introduce the mascot. Explain that the mascot is often the school clown. This person is very fearful and insecure and jokes around in order to deny these painful feelings. Have the mascot tell about himself/herself, referring to what was written on the index card.

9 Introduce the scapegoat. The scapegoat is often the school troublemaker. The scapegoat feels rejection and becomes angry with others and acts out and attacks. Have the scapegoat tell about himself/herself, referring to what was written on the index card.

10 Introduce the lost child. The lost child is often the school day dreamer. (S)he feels unimportant and withdraws in most situations. Often people are unaware of his/her presence. Have the lost child tell about himself/herself, referring to what was written on the index card.

11 Explain that children of alcoholics often need help in learning healthful ways to cope. They need help giving up the roles the class has just seen them play. Discuss sources of help such as Alateen, Alanon, COA groups, and mental health clinics.

Evaluation:

Have students design pamphlets in which they identify characteristics of children of alcoholics and places where these children can obtain help.

Grades 6–8
- Objective 17B

THE FIRE OF CODEPENDENCE

Objective:

Students will examine the impact of drug dependency on the behaviors of family members and friends.

Life Skill:

I will seek help from a family member or other trusted and responsible adult if I am experiencing signs of codependence.

Materials:

Construction paper, scissors, tape, markers

Motivation:

1 Explain that the relationships among members of some families are not loving, healthful, and responsible. A **dysfunctional family** is a family in which the emotional, physical, and social needs of family members are not met in healthful ways. Professionals who worked with families in which there was chemical dependency have discovered that all persons within the family usually have difficulty functioning especially in relationships.

2 Explain that persons who belong to a dysfunctional family often suffer from a condition known as codependence. **Codependence** is a condition in which a person becomes so dependent on another person that (s)he loses touch with personal thoughts and feelings. A person who suffers from codependence is called **codependent**. Some of the characteristics of persons with codependence are:
- accepts abuse from others,
- clings to others,
- has difficulty sharing feelings,
- criticizes others,
- makes up excuses for poor behavior of others,
- feels afraid,
- does not tell the truth,
- does not trust others,

- becomes the family hero,
- becomes the family clown.

3 Use the construction paper and markers to make the fire and logs depicted in the illustration. The fire should be made of red construction paper. On the flames of the fire, print the names of drugs whose abuse might lead to drug dependency: alcohol, crack, cocaine, marijuana, heroin, amphetamines, barbiturates, and so on.

4 Use the construction paper and markers to make logs to place under the fire. On separate logs write: accepts abuse from others, clings to others, feels afraid, excuses the poor behavior of others, does not tell the truth, does not trust others, becomes the family hero, becomes the family clown.

5 Tape the fire on the chalkboard with the logs placed under it. Discuss the relationship between the two. The fire is the person(s) in the family who is drug dependent. For example, the fire might represent a mother who is dependent on crack or a father who has alcoholism. The logs represent the behaviors of the persons who belong to the family. These persons begin to show ways of coping that do not promote healthful relationships. For example, in the family where the mother is dependent on crack, the father and children demonstrate some or all of the behaviors on the logs. The father might begin to make excuses for the mother's behavior. He might call her place of work and lie about her reasons for absence. Her children may become distrustful. One of the children may become perfectionistic and excel in many ways in order to be the family hero. This child may mistakenly believe that (s)he can change the mother's behavior by being extra "good." Another child may begin to accept abusive behavior from others.

6 Discuss the relationship between the fire and the logs. The fire and the logs depend on each other. The logs add fuel to the flame. Begin to take the logs away and discuss what happens.

In the example given, if the father no longer makes excuses for the mother at her place of work she will have to suffer the consequences. Discuss what might happen if the flames in the fire die down. In the example given, the family members who behaved as caretakers will no longer have the role to fulfill. Whenever one or more family members in a dysfunctional family changes codependent behavior, the functioning of the family unit is affected.

Evaluation:

Use the following short answer quiz: (1) Define dysfunctional family. (2) Name drugs whose abuse may result in drug dependency. (3) List five characteristics of codependence. (4) Describe the ways in which family members who are drug dependent interact with other family members.

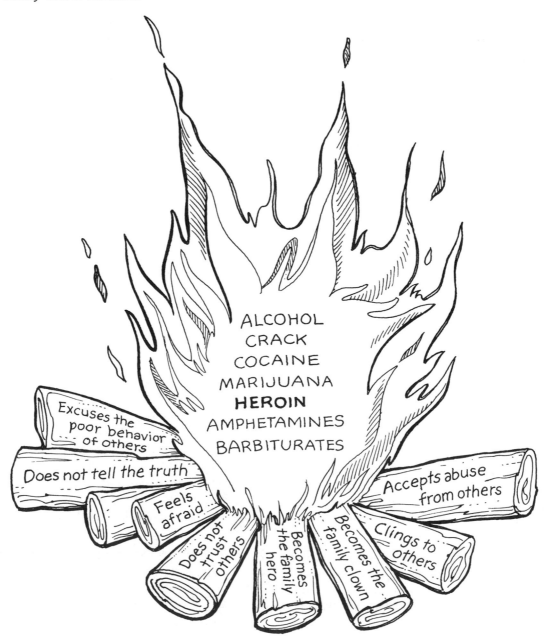

Violence Prevention

RELATIONSHIP SCULPTURE

Objective:

Students will examine the impact of drug dependency on the behavior of family members and friends.

Life Skill:

I will communicate in healthful ways with family members and friends.

Materials:

Spirit-Relationship Continuum transparency (page 537), transparency projector

Motivation:

1 Use the transparency of the Spirit-Relationship Continuum to help students differentiate between dispiriting and inspiriting relationships. **Relationships** are the connections that people have with each other. **Inspiriting relationships** are relationships that lift the spirit and contribute to a sense of well-being, enthusiasm, passion, hope, and satisfaction. Inspiriting relationships make a person feel worthwhile and contribute to feelings of positive self-esteem. **Dispiriting relationships** are relationships that are characterized by a state of low spirits. Dispiriting relationships can be described as being "sick" relationships. Young persons have probably said or heard someone say, "(S)he makes me sick." They are describing a relationship that is dispiriting.

2 Elaborate on this discussion by further differentiating between inspiriting and dispiriting relationships. Begin with a discussion of inspiriting relationships. In inspiriting relationships, there is interdependence. **Interdependence** is a condition in which two persons depend upon one another, yet have separate identities. There are boundaries separating the identities of the two persons involved in the relationship.

3 Demonstrate interdependence by making a relationship sculpture. Have two students come in front of the class. Each of the students should join one of his/her hands to a hand of the other. Each of the students should wave the hand that was left free. Explain that these two persons are interdependent. They are joined in a relationship and can depend upon one another. Yet, each is separate and is able to join the free hand to other things and people. This relationship might be that of a mother and daughter. It might also be two friends. This relationship sculpture might have encompassed an entire family or several friends. In this case, all members would join one hand in the center and leave another hand free.

4 Explain that persons who use drugs often exhibit codependence rather than interdependence within their relationships. **Codependence** is a mental disorder in which persons lose personal identity, have frozen feelings, and cope ineffectively. A relationship in which there is codependence is dispiriting. Research into these relationships indicates that persons in these relationships have certain feelings and behaviors in common. Although the general population demonstrates many of these behaviors, persons with codependence tend to have a higher incidence of them. Some of the characteristics are (list on the chalkboard):
- They often isolate themselves because they are fearful and uneasy around others.
- They are desperate for approval and often do foolish things so others will like them.
- They often are loyal in relationships which are hurtful or "sick."
- They are insecure.
- They are intimidated by persons who are angry and critical.
- They often love persons they can pity.
- They may try to rescue others or take care of them.
- They feel guilty when they stand up for themselves.

- They have a strong need to be in control.
- They are very dependent.

5 Demonstrate codependence by making a relationship sculpture. Have two students come in front of the class. The students are to join each of their two hands to the two hands of the other. Ask the class to differentiate between this relationship sculpture and the relationship sculpture that characterized interdependence. It will be easy for the class to describe the difference. In the second sculpture, both hands are joined. The two persons involved have lost the freedom to maintain personal identity. **Enmeshment** is a condition in which the identities of two persons in a relationship have blended into one whereby at least one of the persons cannot see himself/herself as a separate identity. This person becomes confused and is unable to identify personal thoughts, feelings, and needs.

6 Divide the class into several groups. Explain to the class that you are going to ask them to be creative and to design other relationship sculptures. Half of the groups are to design relationship sculptures that illustrate relationships with interdependence. The other half of the groups are to design relationship sculptures that illustrate relationships with codependence. You may want to assign some of the groups to form relationship sculptures depicting family members and other groups to form relationship sculptures showing a group of friends.

7 Have each group form their relationship sculpture in front of the class. As they form the rela-

tionship sculpture, they are to announce whether the sculpture depicts a family or group of friends. They are not to provide any additional information. Have students describe what they see. After several students have contributed their ideas, the group can explain their relationship sculpture.

8 Have students discuss reasons why they believe it is healthful and responsible to develop interdependence rather than codependence within relationships. Have students brainstorm reasons why persons who use drugs often develop codependence.

Evaluation:

Have students write short stories in which one or more of the characters are involved in harmful drug use. They are to describe the codependence that develops between the characters. You may want to select one of the short stories and have your class enact the story as a play.

Inclusion:

Have students complete the evaluation as a cooperative learning assignment. Pair two or three students together to write a short story. Pair students with special learning challenges with a student or students who have strengths in language arts. The students with special learning challenges might illustrate the story with art.

CHANNELING MESSAGES

Objective:

Students will analyze the impact of television, movies, videos, and advertising on the use and abuse of drugs.

Life Skills:

I will not use illegal drugs.
I will not be swayed by subtle messages in the media to use and abuse drugs.
I will choose entertainment that promotes healthful behavior.

Materials:

A very large box (one for a refrigerator, television, etc.), scissors, paper, pen, classroom set of copies of the student handout Channeling Messages (page 463)

Motivation

1 Construct a replica of a television set using the large box and the scissors. There should be an opening that students can stand behind to simulate being on television.

2 Give students a copy of the handout Channeling Messages. Explain that the handout indicates the possible channels on the homemade television set that you have constructed. The channels are as follows:
- The News Channel
- The Sports Channel
- The Family Channel
- The Violence Channel
- The Tobacco Channel
- The Alcohol Channel
- The Stimulant Channel
- The Narcotic Channel
- The Over-the-Counter Drug Channel
- The Prescription Drug Channel

3 Explain that the first three channels—news, sports, and family—contain healthful and responsible messages about life. These chan-

nels educate persons in positive ways. The next seven channels each contain programming in which negative behavior is portrayed. Of these seven channels, the first five—violence, tobacco, alcohol, stimulant, narcotic—each contain messages that are subtle, but violence and drug use are part of the plot in the programs on these channels. The final two channels—over-the-counter drug and prescription drug—are channels that contain only advertisements. The advertisements on these channels are blatant and try to sway persons to purchase and use specific drugs.

4 Divide the class into ten groups. Each group is to select or be assigned one of the ten channels. The ten groups are asked to do the following:
The News Channel: Develop an advertisement to promote a new series that spotlights local, state, or world events that promote good health.
The Sports Channel: Develop an advertisement to promote a new series that showcases individuals who or sports teams that have experienced success without the use of drugs.
The Family Channel: Develop an advertisement to showcase a new family sitcom that will air soon. The sitcom should be one that promotes family values and character. Give the sitcom a clever name.
The Violence Channel: Develop an advertisement to showcase a new action series that will air soon. This action series should be one that emphasizes violence. Give the series a name that represents the violent content.
The Tobacco Channel: Develop an advertisement to showcase a soap opera in which the actors and actresses use tobacco products. The use of the tobacco products should be subtle. Give the soap opera a clever name which indicates that tobacco products are used.
The Alcohol Channel: Develop an advertisement to showcase a soap opera in which the actors and actresses drink alcohol. The consumption of alcohol should appear to enhance masculinity and/or femininity. Give the soap

opera a clever name to indicate that alcohol is used.

The Stimulant Channel: Develop an advertisement to showcase a soap opera that will air soon. At least one of the actors or actresses on this program abuses stimulants. Give the soap opera a clever name to indicate that stimulants are used.

The Narcotic Channel: Develop an advertisement to showcase a soap opera that will air soon. At least one of the actors or actresses on this program is dependent upon narcotics. Give the soap opera a clever name to indicate that narcotics are used.

The Over-the-Counter Drug Channel: Develop an advertisement in which viewers are encouraged to purchase an over-the-counter drug. The advertisement should be as persuasive as possible.

The Prescription Drug Channel: Develop an advertisement in which viewers are encouraged to ask their doctor to prescribe a specific prescription drug. The advertisement should be as persuasive as possible.

5 Students should be provided ample time to prepare their advertisements for new programs or for over-the-counter or prescription drugs. After ample time has been allowed, each group can present its advertisement using the mock television set.

6 After students have viewed all ten advertisements, have them refer to the student handout on Channeling Messages. Have them discuss which channels they believed offered programs with healthful and responsible messages. Have them discuss which channels they believed contained messages that might encourage the use and abuse of drugs. Emphasize the importance of selecting programs for viewing that promote healthful and responsible behavior.

Evaluation:

Have students make a "Top Ten List of Reasons" why it is in their best interest to view television programs and movies and to listen to music that contain messages which promote family values, discourage violence, and discourage drug use.

Inclusion:

Have students with special needs bring the entertainment section of the newspaper to class. Have them peruse the entertainment section and select three programs which they believe contain messages that promote family values, discourage violence, and discourage drug use. Have them share their choices with their classmates.

Channeling Messages

The News Channel

The Sports Channel

The Family Channel

The Violence Channel

The Tobacco Channel

The Alcohol Channel

The Stimulant Channel

The Narcotic Channel

The Over-the-Counter Drug Channel

The Prescription Drug Channel

Grades 6–8
▪ Objective 18B

I'VE GOTTEN USED TO SEEING IT

Objective:

Students will analyze the impact of television, movies, videos, and advertising on the use and abuse of drugs.

Life Skills:

I will not use illegal drugs.
I will not be swayed by subtle messages in the media to use and abuse drugs.

Materials:

Sheets of construction paper: black, grey, brown, yellow, orange, green, blue

Motivation:

1 Use the following demonstration to illustrate how a person gets less discriminating when (s)he is bombarded with the same messages over and over. Show the class four sheets of construction paper: black, grey, brown, and yellow. Ask the class to tell you which sheet of construction paper is the brightest. The class will respond, "yellow."

2 Now show the class the following colors of construction paper: black, grey, brown, yellow, orange, green, and blue. Ask the class to tell you which sheet of construction paper is the brightest. Students in your class may not be in agreement. Several of the sheets of construction paper might be similar in their degree of brightness.

3 Explain that you used this demonstration to illustrate a point about the use of drugs in the media. The bright sheets of construction paper represent programming in which drugs were used and abused. In the first demonstration, the class viewed four programs: black, grey, brown, and yellow. The yellow program included the use and abuse of drugs. When viewing these four programs, it was easy to pick this out. However, in the second demon-

stration, yellow, orange, green, and blue contained variations of brightness. Each represents programming that contained a degree of use and abuse of drugs. It was more difficult to focus on the use and abuse of drugs because there was more of it.

4 Explain that drugs are used and abused often in the media. During programming, viewers receive subtle messages. For example, if two persons on a television program are celebrating an event, they toast each other with champagne. On a soap opera, a person might stop over at another's house to discuss a difficult event in the middle of the afternoon. One person offers the other a drink. During a television advertisement, two persons who are in love might share a beer. During another television advertisement, two very athletic men might have a beer. The subtle messages are: 1. Celebrate with drugs; 2. Use drugs when a difficult situation arises; 3. Use drugs when in a romantic mood; 4. Use drugs to show that you are masculine.

Evaluation:

Have students analyze the messages regarding drugs in the media. For one week, students might keep a journal of the television programs, advertisements, videotapes, and movies they watch. They are to record the situations in which drugs are used and/or abused. Then they are to brainstorm ways in which the same situation might have been portrayed without the use or abuse of drugs.

Grades 6-8
• Objective 18C

SOLID GOLD

Objective:

Students will analyze the impact of television, movies, videos, and advertising on the use and abuse of drugs.

Life Skill:

I will choose entertainment and music that portray healthful behavior.

Materials:

Compact disc player, popular compact discs to which students listen, paper, pencil, lyrics of a popular song that promotes healthful living

Motivation:

1 Ask students to bring in compact discs to which they enjoy listening. Make a list of their favorite songs that appear on these discs. Play some of the songs for the class. After each song is played, have students summarize the song in one sentence. For example, a few years ago a popular song was *That's What Friends Are For*. Students might summarize the message in this piece of music by saying, "Friends support you in both good times and bad times."

2 Discuss the importance of listening to music whose lyrics support healthful living and positive moral values. Emphasize that when listening to songs students often memorize the lyrics and that, in doing this, they are memorizing messages that promote their health and encourage positive moral values. They are filling their minds with positive health.

3 Have students examine the list of songs that they believed to be popular and the messages that they wrote for each. Which of these songs promoted messages that encouraged healthful living and positive moral values? Which of these songs promoted a drug-free lifestyle? Which of these songs contained lyrics that suggested a lifestyle involving the use of harmful drugs?

4 After students have identified songs that contain lyrics that suggest a lifestyle involving the use of harmful drugs, divide the class into five groups. Each group is to write new lyrics for one of these songs. The new lyrics should focus on the benefits of being drug free. Ask each group to give itself a name and to practice singing its song with the new lyrics. Encourage the group to develop dance steps to accompany its song.

5 Have a "solid gold" television or radio show in the classroom. Allow each group to state its name and sing its song with the new lyrics.

Evaluation:

Have students write a short essay in which they identify a current popular song that promotes healthful living. They are to refer to specific lyrics from the song that remind them of the benefits of choosing a healthful lifestyle.

Inclusion:

Obtain a copy of the lyrics from a popular song that promotes healthful living from a local music store. Provide the copy of the lyrics to students with special needs to assist them in the aforementioned evaluation assignment.

Grades 6–8 Critical Thinking
• Objective 19A

Violence Prevention

RISING TENSIONS

Objective:

Students will evaluate the impact of drug use on the incidence of violence.

Life Skills:

I will not use illegal drugs.
I will abide by the laws in my community.
I will avoid being around persons who use illegal drugs.
I will treat others with respect and avoid violence.

Materials:

A fastener clip of some sort, a yard of twine, tape, a weight such as a heavy metal nut that can be tied to one end of the twine, tape, poster board, markers

Motivation

1 Discuss violence. **Violence** is the use of force with the intent to harm oneself or another person. Violence takes many forms including homicide, suicide, assault, rape, and child abuse. Violence may also include acts such as burglary or the destruction of property in which a person is harmed because his/her possessions are taken or destroyed. Explain that violence is more likely to occur when a person has used alcohol and illegal drugs. In fact, most persons who commit crimes that are violent were drinking alcohol before or during the time the crime took place.

2 Review information about alcohol and about blood alcohol levels. **Alcohol** is a psychoactive drug that depresses the central nervous system. It depresses the activity of the nerve cells of the brain. As the blood alcohol level increases, this depressant effect increases. **Blood alcohol level**, or **BAL**, refers to the amount of alcohol in a person's blood.

Understanding the depressant effects of increasing blood alcohol levels helps explain why drinking alcohol contributes to violence.

3 Explain that other drugs besides alcohol also have a depressant effect on the brain. Narcotics depress the activity of the nerve cells of the brain. Thus, both alcohol and narcotics depress the part of the brain that influences reasoning and judgment.

4 Other drugs stimulate the central nervous system and increase the activity of the brain. Drugs classified as stimulants, such as amphetamines, intensify mood because of this increased activity. Intensified feelings may also interfere with reasoning and judgment.

5 On the chalkboard, list the following crimes: homicide, suicide, assault, rape, child abuse, burglary, and destruction of property. Explain that most persons who respect the rights of others agree that these behaviors are not appropriate. If asked if they would engage in such behavior, they would say NO. However, if the reasoning and judgment part of their brain was under the influence of alcohol, their ability to make decisions about such behaviors might be influenced.

6 The following pendulum-type setup can be used to demonstrate how drinking alcohol depresses brain functions and affects a person's ability to handle conflict in a nonviolent way (see illustration). Using the markers, draw an arc on the poster board. Label the poster board: 3 drinks, 2 drinks 1 drink, resolution zone, tension 1, tension 2, tension 3. Use a clip to attach one end of the twine to the top of poster board. Attach the weight to the other end of the twine.

7 Perform the demonstration as follows. Move the weight to the left but keep it within the "resolution zone." Then let it go. Tilt the board forward a little so that the weight does

466

not rub against the board. The weight will swing to the right but stay within the "resolution zone." Explain that when persons disagree or have conflict, tension is created. However, if they have not used alcohol or other drugs, their reasoning and judgment can help them resolve their disagreement.

8 Now repeat the demonstration, only this time move the weight farther to the left to the area labeled "one drink." Then let the weight go. It will have more momentum and it will swing farther to the right. It may move as far as "tension 1." Explain that drinking alcohol depressed the brain center and intensified mood, increasing the level of tension between the two persons.

9 Now repeat the demonstration, only this time move the weight even farther to the left to the area marked "two drinks." Then let the weight go. It will have more momentum than before and it will swing even farther to the right. It may move as far as "tension 2." Explain that drinking alcohol depressed the brain center and intensified mood, increasing the level of tension between the two persons.

10 Now repeat the demonstration, only this time move the weight all the way to the left to the area marked "three drinks." Then release the weight. This time it will have still more momentum and it will move still farther to the right. It may move as far as "tension 3" or it may stay within "tension 2." Explain that increased consumption of alcohol further depressed the brain center and intensified mood, increasing the level of tension between the two persons.

11 Discuss the importance of removing oneself from a situation in which a person(s) is using alcohol and other drugs. This life skill is important because it helps to reduce the likelihood of being harmed.

Evaluation:

Have students create a "violence prevention tip for the week." Compile their tips and send the tips to a local radio show, requesting that they be aired.

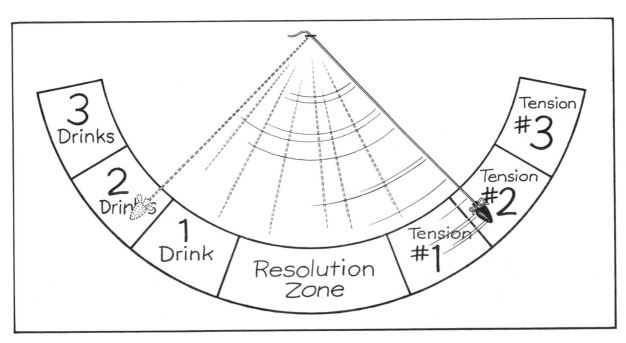

Grades 6–8
▪ Objective 19B

| Violence Prevention |

READY TO FIGHT

Objective:

Students will evaluate the impact of drug use on the incidence of violence.

Life Skills:

I will not use illegal drugs.
I will abide by the laws of my community.
I will avoid persons who use illegal drugs.
I will treat others with respect and avoid violence.

Materials:

None are needed

Motivation:

1 Discuss violence. **Violence** is the use of force with the intent to harm oneself or another person. Violence takes many forms including homicide, suicide, assault, rape, and child abuse. Violence may also include acts such as burglary or the destruction of property in which a person is harmed because his/her possessions are taken or destroyed. Explain that violence is more likely to occur when a person has used illegal drugs. In fact, most persons who commit crimes that are violent were drinking alcohol before or during the time of the crime.

2 Review information about alcohol and about blood alcohol levels. **Alcohol** is a psychoactive drug that depresses the central nervous system. It depresses the activity of the nerve cells of the brain. As the blood alcohol level increases, this depressant effect increases. **Blood alcohol level**, or **BAL**, refers to the amount of alcohol in a person's blood. Understanding the depressant effects of increasing blood alcohol levels helps explain why drinking alcohol contributes to violence.

3 On the chalkboard, list the following crimes: homicide, suicide, assault, rape, child abuse, burglary, destruction of property. Explain that

most persons who respect the rights of others agree that these behaviors are not appropriate. If asked if they would engage in such behavior, they would say NO. However, if the reasoning and judgment part of their brain was under the influence of alcohol, their ability to make decisions about such behaviors might be influenced.

4 The following demonstration illustrates how drinking alcohol depresses brain functions and affects a person's ability to make responsible decisions. Divide the class in half. One half of the class will represent the brain and the abilities of reasoning and judgment. Ask this half of the class to shout NO loudly when they are requested to answer a question. Explain that their NO represents their response to the question, "Would you engage in any of the crimes listed on the chalkboard?" The other half of the class will represent increasing blood alcohol levels. Ask this half of the class to softly say YES when they are requested to answer a question. Explain that their YES represents their response to the same question, "Would you engage in any of the crimes listed on the chalkboard?"

5 Extend the demonstration to illustrate that reasoning and judgment are in control of a person's decisions when there is no presence of alcohol. Explain to the class that the person in question has not been drinking alcohol. Now, ask both groups to respond simultaneously to the same question in the manner that they previously responded. They will notice that the NO from the reasoning and judgment half of the class drowned out the YES from the half of the class that represented the blood alcohol level. This is because the blood alcohol level was 0 because the person had not been drinking.

6 Continue this demonstration to illustrate what happens as the blood alcohol level increases and starts affecting reasoning and judgment. Explain that you are going to give different amounts of alcohol consumed: 0 alcoholic beverages, 1 alcoholic beverage, 2 alcoholic beverages, 3 alcoholic beverages, 4 alcoholic beverages, 5 alcoholic beverages. As you increase the number of alcoholic beverages, the half of the class representing reasoning and judgment is to respond with NO with less and less force. However, the half of the class representing the blood alcohol level is to respond YES with more and more force. Begin the demonstration saying no alcoholic beverages, one alcoholic beverage, two alcoholic beverages, three alcoholic beverages, four alcoholic beverages, and five alcoholic beverages.

7 Have the class discuss what they heard when the group representing the reasoning and judgment part of the brain and the group representing the blood alcohol level responded at the same time. They should notice that with increasing blood alcohol levels, the reasoning and judgment part of the brain that was saying NO was drowned out.

8 Have students discuss the way that the following drugs affect the reasoning and judgment part of the brain: stimulant drugs, sedative-hypnotic drugs, narcotics, marijuana, hallucinogens, inhalants, anabolic steroids. Which drugs might interfere with reasoning and judgment and result in actions that are violent?

Evaluation:

Divide students into groups to make television and/or radio commercials to warn audiences that drinking alcohol is associated with violence. Explain that the groups must include at least two facts in their commercials.

Grades 6-8
▪ Objective 19C

BOILING OVER

Objective:

Students will evaluate the impact of drug use on the incidence of violence.

Life Skills:

I will not use illegal drugs.
I will treat others with respect and avoid violence.
I will avoid being in situations with persons who are using drugs.

Materials:

Risk Factors Increase Vulnerability to Violent Behavior transparency (page 539), transparency projector, chalkboard, chalk, four tall clear glasses, water, white vinegar, baking soda, bowl

Motivation:

1 Introduce the topic of violence. Violence is the use of force with the intent to harm oneself or another person. Identify types of violence: homicide, assault injuries, suicide, child abuse and neglect, rape, partner violence, physical fighting, etc.

2 Ask students to predict risk factors that increase a person's vulnerability to becoming violent. List these risk factors on the chalkboard. Review risk factors using the transparency of Risk Factors Increase Vulnerability to Violent Behavior.

3 Ask students to predict how the use of alcohol and other drugs might influence a person's vulnerability to becoming violent. Use the following experiment to demonstrate. Take two tall glasses. Place one cup of water in each. Explain to students that each glass represents the angry feelings of each of the two persons. Further explain that these two persons begin to

argue. Pour the one glass of water into the other. Explain that this illustrates their tempers rising.

4 Now demonstrate the experiment with modifications using the other two glasses. Place one cup of white vinegar in a glass. Explain that the white vinegar represents the angry feelings of one of the persons. Place one cup of water in the remaining glass. Explain that the water represents the angry feelings of the other person. Now add two tablespoons of baking soda to the water. Explain that each of the tablespoons represents an alcoholic beverage that the person consumed prior to the disagreement.

5 Explain that the tempers of the two persons in the first heated disagreement stayed in check. That is, tempers rose, but the two were able to control their behavior. Now add the glass containing the water and baking soda to the glass of vinegar. Make sure you have a bowl below the glass or do the experiment over a sink. When you add the water and baking soda to the glass of vinegar, the ingredients will bubble up and overflow.

6 Explain that this experiment illustrates what happens when persons drink alcohol and/or use other drugs and have a disagreement. Often angry feelings "boil over" and result in violent actions.

Evaluation:

Have students cut out articles from the newspaper that report violent actions that have occurred while someone was under the influence of alcohol or other drugs. Collect the articles. Share several of the articles with the class. Have students write an editorial for the newspaper concerning drug use and violence in the community. The editorial must address the interrelationships between drug use and violence.

Grades 6–8
- Objective 20A

SAFETY NET

Objective:

Students will examine ways to support law enforcement to eradicate drug trafficking.

Life Skills:

I will not purchase or sell illegal drugs.
I will avoid being with persons who purchase or sell illegal drugs.
I will avoid being in situations in which illegal drugs are purchased or sold.

Materials:

Large ball of yarn, chalk, chalkboard

Motivation:

1 Introduce the topic of drug trafficking. **Drug trafficking** involves purchasing or selling illegal drugs. Drug trafficking is a crime and is associated with increased incidence of violence. Often innocent bystanders are harmed.

2 Ask students to brainstorm a list of ways that they can support law enforcement and eradicate drug trafficking in their community. List these on the chalkboard. Some suggestions might be: be aware of laws, be respectful of police officers, avoid using drugs, avoid being around persons who use drugs, avoid being around persons who sell drugs, avoid being near places where drugs are purchased or sold, spend time with caring adults, know where help is available for persons who abuse drugs, encourage friends to be drug free, encourage friends to avoid being around persons who sell drugs, encourage friends to avoid being near places where drugs are purchased or sold. It may be possible to discuss specifics for your community such as places to avoid.

3 Explain to students that the behaviors that are listed on the chalkboard are responsible and they help to protect them. Erase the list that the students made.

4 Have students form a circle. Take the ball of yarn. Wrap the end of the string loosely around your index finger. Mention one of the ways that a person can support law enforcement and eradicate drug trafficking in the community. Then toss the ball of yarn to a student in the circle. This student wraps a piece of the yarn loosely around his/her index finger and states another way a person can support law enforcement and eradicate drug trafficking in the community. Then this student tosses the ball of yarn to another student. Continue this same process until all students have participated. As students toss the ball of yarn to one another, it works best for them to toss the yarn under the net that is being formed. This keeps the yarn from becoming tangled within the net.

5 Ask the student what the ball of yarn has done. They will most likely say that the ball of yarn has connected everyone in the circle. Explain that everyone in the circle is part of the community and can participate in forming a safety net to support law enforcement in the effort to eliminate drug trafficking.

Evaluation:

Invite a law enforcement officer to class to discuss efforts to eradicate drug trafficking. Have students each list five ways that they can support these efforts. Have students share their list of ways with the law enforcement officer.

Grades 6–8
• Objective 20B

Violence Prevention

DRUG-FREE ZONE

Objective:

Students will examine ways to support law enforcement to eradicate drug trafficking.

Life Skills:

I will not purchase or sell illegal drugs.
I will avoid persons who purchase or sell illegal drugs.

Materials:

Large sheets of brown butcher paper, markers, magazines, newspapers, masking tape

Motivation:

1 Have a class discussion about drug trafficking. Explain that **drug trafficking** involves the purchasing and selling of illegal drugs. Drug trafficking is a crime and is associated with increased incidences of violence.

2 Divide students into five groups. Give each group a large sheet of brown butcher paper, markers, magazines, newspapers, and masking tape. Each group is to use markers to draw a fictitious community in which drug trafficking exists. The group might draw houses, cars, guns, and so on, to represent events that occur in the community. The group can peruse the magazines and newspapers for articles about drug busts and violence, cut the articles out, and tape them to the large sheet of brown butcher paper. They are to give their community a name that indicates it is not a safe or healthful community.

3 After the groups have completed their drawings and decided on a name for their communities, have them tape their sheets of paper in designated places in the classroom. A spokesperson for each group can describe the community and the events that occur there.

4 Have each group design a plan to make their fictitious community a drug-free zone. Examples might include: having a raid on crack houses, having neighborhood recreational programs during after-school hours, having safe homes for young persons who are threatened by violence, and so on. The groups should write their plans on paper. One person in each group should be selected as a community leader who is going to present the plan to interested citizens in the community. This person can share the group's plan with the class.

Evaluation:

Have a contest for students in which each writes an essay describing ways to keep his/her community a drug-free zone or to restore his/her community to a drug-free zone. Invite a panel of concerned citizens from your community to be the judges of the contest. Ask local business owners to donate a prize(s) for the winning entree(s).

Violence Prevention

YOU BE THE JUDGE

Objective:

Students will examine ways to support law enforcement to eradicate drug trafficking.

Life Skill:

I will avoid situations in which there is illegal drug use and/or drug trafficking.

Materials:

Copy of the laws of your community (state and local) pertaining to drug trafficking, index cards

Motivation:

1 Discuss drug trafficking with students. Explain that drug trafficking is illegal and is associated with economic-compulsive violent crime and systemic violence. **Economic-compulsive violent crime** is crime committed by drug users because of the high cost of some drugs in order to support their continued use. **Systemic violence** refers to the heightened risk for both committing violence and being a victim of violence because of participation in the sale and trafficking of illicit substances.

2 Discuss examples of systemic violence that have appeared in the media. Death and bloodshed associated with drug distribution systems take a heavy toll on the market participants themselves. Moreover, this violence often extends beyond those involved in illegal drug transactions and affects nonparticipants directly through injury or death. The proliferation of deadly weapons has made the drug distribution system violence more lethal and visible. When violence occurs, death and serious injury may be more likely.

3 Have each student write a short newspaper article that describes a crime involving drug trafficking and economic-compulsive violent

crime and/or systemic violence. The following might serve as an example:

Four Year Old Killed Playing on Porch.
Juan Ramirez, four years old, was the victim of a stray bullet fired at a teenager by a man driving a red car on Mulberry Street about nine o'clock last night. One witness told police he had seen the man arguing with the teenager earlier in the evening. Another witness told police that the man was known as "Sparky" and that he sold marijuana to teenagers who in turn sold it at the high school. Later, the teenager was apprehended and had possession of marijuana at the time of the arrest.

4 After students have completed their newspaper articles, collect them and redistribute them so that students each have an article that is not their own. Give students several index cards. Explain that one or more of the persons described in the newspaper article that they now have has been arrested and has been found guilty. Explain "you be the judge;" that is, students are to write the sentence for the crimes. They should refer to the local and state laws when determining the sentence. They can write the sentence(s) for each crime on one of the index cards. For example, "Sparky" was guilty of first degree murder and he was sentenced to life in prison. The teenager was found guilty of possession of an illegal substance as well as drug trafficking. The teenager was sentenced by the juvenile court and will be sent to a facility for juvenile detention.

5 Have students return the newspaper articles to their classmates who wrote them. Each student is to read the newspaper article that (s)he wrote and play the role of a prosecutor. Stage a court room scene. There is to be a prosecutor, defendant, and judge. The prosecutor is to announce the offenses for which the defendant is charged. Then the student who played judge for each specific newspaper article is to ask the defendant how (s)he pleads. The defendant pleads guilty. Then the judge reads the sentence that (s)he has imposed on the defendant according to local and state laws. The judge may choose to impose a stricter penalty. The judge is to provide his/her rationale for the penalty.

Evaluation:

Have students identify at least five local and state laws that pertain to drug trafficking. Have students identify at least two reasons why it is important for them to support drug laws and to avoid situations involving illegal drug use and/or drug trafficking.

Violence Prevention

RESILIENCY: LAYERS OF PROTECTION

Objective:

Students will engage in activities that promote positive self-esteem and high-level wellness.

Life Skill:

I will practice protective factors that promote resiliency.

Materials:

Artichoke; Protective Factors That Serve as a Coat of Armor and Promote Resiliency transparency (page 527), transparency projector

Motivation:

1 Discuss resiliency. **Resiliency** is the ability to recover or adjust to misfortune, change, pressure, and adversity. Resilient youth are often described as being stress resistant and invincible in spite of adversity. They are able to bounce back from misfortune. Ask the class why they believe some youth are resilient while others are not.

2 Explain that there has been much research done on resiliency. There are many protective factors that tend to increase the likelihood that a young person will develop resiliency.

3 Take the artichoke. Explain that the artichoke represents a resilient youth. This youth has many layers of protective factors that strengthen him/her inside. **Protective factors** are characteristics of individuals and their environments that make a positive contribution to development and behavior. Use the transparency of Protective Factors That Serve as a Coat of Armor and Promote Resiliency. As you discuss each of the 11 protective factors, peel a leaf from the artichoke. Explain that each protective factor promotes high-level wellness and discourages drug use.

Protective factor 1: Being reared in a loving, functional family. A **loving, functional family** is a family in which feelings are expressed openly and honestly, effective coping skills are practiced, and members show respect for one another. In a loving, functional family, children observe and are taught important lessons that serve as protective factors:
- self-loving behavior;
- healthful attitudes toward sexuality;
- healthful attitudes and practices regarding drug use;
- healthful ways to express feelings and to communicate;
- faith and moral values;
- responsible decision-making skills;
- coping skills with the ability to delay gratification when necessary.

Protective factor 2: Being involved in school activities. There are at least two reasons that involvement in school activities is beneficial in protecting against the pressures to use drugs in irresponsible and harmful ways. First, participation in school activities takes time, leaving youth with less idle time. This prevents boredom and monotony. Second, schools usually have eligibility guidelines for participation in school activities. Youth who enjoy these activities do not want to lose the privilege of participation.

Protective factor 3: Having positive self-esteem. Youth with positive self-esteem are more likely to avoid self-destructive behavior and to choose self-loving behavior. They do not want to harm themselves.

Protective factor 4: Having clearly-defined goals and plans to reach them. A **goal** is a desired achievement toward which one works. Goals add meaning and purpose to life. They provide a link from the present to the future. When youth have goals, they are more likely to evaluate the consequences of their actions in terms of the future as well as the present.

Protective factor 5: Having close friends who do not abuse drugs. Friends are especially helpful as protective factors by providing an armor to shield against the pressures to engage in harmful and irresponsible drug use. Suppose you temporarily drop your armor. Your friends can shield you with their armor. When in the presence of friends who are drug free, youth are less tempted to try drugs.

Protective factor 6: Regularly practicing one's faith. Faith is the belief system that guides a person's behavior and gives meaning and purpose to life. There appear to be important commonalities among the various faiths and belief systems. In each, self-discipline, loving behavior, obedience, and respect are emphasized. Each of these traits plays a role in deterring irresponsible and harmful drug use.

Protective factor 7: Feeling a sense of accomplishment at school. School affords an opportunity to test one's beliefs about himself/herself. Mastering school work provides a sense of accomplishment. It reinforces the attitude that "I know I can succeed if I put forth my best effort."

Protective factor 8: Having adult role models including parents who do not abuse drugs. When youth admire adults who do not abuse drugs, they are better able to screen out and and resist risk-promoting messages provided on television, in the movies, and in advertising.

Protective factor 9: Having a healthful attitude about competitive and athletic performance. Using one's talents to the best of one's abilities and accepting the results is a prerequisite for healthful competition. It enables youth to keep a healthful perspective about winning. Youth with a healthful attitude about competition and athletic performance focus on their talents and developing these talents. They are not swayed to

win at all costs and to use drugs to enhance performance.

Protective factor 10: Being committed to following the rules of the community. A **commitment** is a pledge to do something. When youth are committed to following the rules of the community, they pledge to keep the community safe from drug trafficking and drug abuse that harms individuals.

Protective factor 11: Having a plan to cope with life stressors. All youth experience stress, but youth who regularly use stress-management skills have a plan to dissipate the effects of the stress. As a result, these youth have more balanced lives. They are prepared to deal with difficult situations and are not tempted to use and abuse drugs to temporarily lessen the effects of stress.

4 You have now removed 11 leaves from the artichoke. Explain to the class that you have removed several layers of protection from the artichoke. The artichoke is now more exposed. If this were a person, (s)he would be more exposed or vulnerable without the layers of protection. Emphasize the importance of these protective layers. By making protective factors part of one's life, a person promotes resiliency.

Evaluation:

Have students write a Recipe for Resiliency. They must include the ingredients needed for resiliency. For example, they might have a cup of stress management skills, three tablespoons of adult role models who do not abuse drugs, etc.

Multicultural Infusion:

Explain to African-American students that a study was done comparing African-American youth who were in an environment in which high expectations were set for them by family members, teachers, and significant others in their environment with African-American youth in which low expectations were set. Those African-American youth who received the message, "You are a bright and capable person," tended to become resilient and to develop a sense of purpose and a bright future (Bonnie Benard, "Fostering Resiliency in Kids: Protective Factors in the Family, School, and Community," *Drug-Free Schools and Communities*. Office of Public Instruction and the Montana Board of Crime Control, Western Regional Center for Drug-Free Schools and Communities).

Inclusion:

Discuss the importance of resiliency with students with special needs. Explain that they demonstrate resiliency when they make adjustments. These adjustments are related to managing the school day and managing to learn in nontraditional ways. Emphasize that they are more likely to be resilient if they practice the protective factors that were discussed.

Grades 9–12
- Objective 2

Staying Afloat

Objective:

Students will practice stress management skills.

Life Skill:

I will practice stress management skills.

Materials:

Bowl of water, bar of soap that floats, bar of soap that does not float, construction paper, markers, General Adaptation Syndrome transparency (page 538), transparency projector

Motivation:

1 Before beginning this lesson, unwrap the two bars of soap and rewrap them with construction paper. On the construction paper wrapping for the bar of soap that floats, print the following: exercise, vitamins B and C, journaling, watching comedy, reduced caffeine, and caring friends. On the construction paper wrapping for the bar of soap that does not float, print: no stress management skills. If possible, these two bars of soap should be different colors.

2 Define stress and stressor. **Stress** is the response of a person's mind or body to stressors. A **stressor** is a physical, mental-emotional, social, or environmental demand.

3 Define the general adaptation syndrome. The **general adaptation syndrome** or **GAS** is the three stages of stress identified by Hans Seyle, a pioneer in stress physiology. The three stages are: the alarm stage, the resistance stage, and the exhaustion stage.

4 Explain that during the **alarm stage of GAS**, the body prepares for quick action as adrenaline is released into the bloodstream, heartbeat rate and blood pressure increase, digestion slows, blood flows to muscles, respiration increases, pupils dilate, and hearing

sharpens. The body is prepared to meet the demands of the stressor. As the demands are met, the resistance stage of GAS begins.

5 Explain the resistance stage. During the **resistance stage of GAS**, pulse, breathing rate, and blood pressure return to normal. The pupils contract and muscles relax. If the demands from the stressor are met unsuccessfully, the exhaustion stage of GAS begins.

6 Explain the exhaustion stage. During the **exhaustion stage of GAS**, the body becomes fatigued from overwork and a person becomes vulnerable to disease.

7 Explain that persons respond to stress in different ways. **Eustress** is successful coping or a healthful response to a stressor. When a person experiences eustress, the resistance stage is effective in establishing homeostasis in the body because the demands of the stressor are met. **Distress** is unsuccessful coping or a harmful response to a stressor. The exhaustion stage often accompanies distress. For this reason, it is important to learn to identify stressors and to know ways to handle them to prevent distress.

8 Ask students to identify life stressors that they believe result in distress. Research indicates that the life events which are the most severe stressors for young people are: death of a parent, death of a brother or sister, divorce of parents, marital separation of parents, death of a grandparent, hospitalization of a parent, remarriage of a parent to a stepparent, birth of a brother or sister, and loss of a job by a parent or guardian. Although these events may elicit distress because of their severity, it is now believed that young people experience distress most of the time from the cumulative effects of daily hassles. The daily hassles include: concern about physical appearance, peer acceptance, homework assignments and tests, misplacing or losing belongings, and being the brunt of bullying or criticism.

9 Discuss the need to practice stress management skills. **Stress management skills** are techniques that can be used to cope with stressors and to lessen the harmful effects of stressors. Stress management skills used to cope with stressors include: talking with responsible adults about difficult life events and daily hassles, using the responsible decision-making model and the model for using resistance skills, and writing in a journal. Each of these techniques helps a person take action to relieve the cause of stress. Stress management skills that protect health include: exercising, being involved in faith experiences, spending time with persons who are caring and supportive, watching comedy to elicit laughter, eating a healthful diet containing vitamins B and C, reducing or eliminating caffeine in the diet, practicing breathing techniques, and practicing progressive relaxation in which muscles are tensed and then relaxed.

10 Fill the bowl with water. Show the students the two bars of soap and the messages on their wrappings. Explain that one of the bars of soap represents a person who practices stress management skills. The other bar of soap represents the person without stress management skills. Place both of the bars of soap in the bowl of water. The bar of soap

representing the person who did not use stress management skills sank. When stressors were present, this person drowned in stress. The bar of soap representing the person who practiced stress management skills stayed afloat. When stressors were present, this person stayed afloat. This person has buoyancy or resiliency. **Resiliency** is the ability to recover or adjust to misfortune, change, pressure, and adversity. Resiliency is the ability to stay afloat during stressful periods.

Evaluation:

Have students keep a Stress Journal for one week in which they identify stress management skills they used to stay afloat when they experienced stressors.

Inclusion:

Have students with special needs keep a Stress Journal for one week in which they identify stressors that they experienced associated with learning. Have these students identify ways that they might manage learning stressors. Have these students share their journals and plans with a counselor or other school person involved in helping students with special needs.

Grades 9–12
▪ Objective 3

| Violence Prevention |

THE PERFECT MATCH

Objective:

Students will select healthful and responsible relationships.

Life Skill:

I will choose healthful and responsible relationships.

Materials:

Roots and Characteristics of Codependence transparency (page 530), transparency projector, red and green construction paper (four sheets of each color), patterns for red circles (page 484), patterns for green circles (page 483), black felt tip pen, scissors

Motivation:

1 For this activity, you will need to cut a total of eight circles from construction paper. You should cut four red circles and four green circles, each with a diameter of eight inches. Copy the sentences shown on each of the patterns onto the corresponding colored circle. Then place red circle #1 on top of green circle #1, match the cut lines, and cut them into two parts as shown in the illustration. Do the same for red and green circles #2, #3, and #4.

2 Tell students that you are going to discuss relationships. **Relationships** are the connections that people have with each other. Explain that some people choose healthful and responsible relationships. Persons who choose healthful and responsible relationships are usually trustworthy, honest, dependable, sincere, kind, straightforward, committed, and comfortable sharing feelings. They usually have a good self-image and are involved in school activities and in family life. Other persons may not have healthful and responsible relationships. Some persons may have codependence. **Codependence**

is a mental disorder in which a person loses personal identity, has frozen feelings, and copes ineffectively. Persons who have codependence have certain feelings and behaviors in common. Although the general population demonstrates many of these behaviors, persons with codependence tend to have a higher incidence of them. Persons who have codependence are called **codependent**. Persons with codependence may have some of the following characteristics: low self-esteem, fear, desperate for approval, intimidated by angry persons, attracted to persons who are abusive and/or emotionally unavailable, feel guilty, repress their feelings, overly dependent on others, controlling, moody, promiscuous, and jealous.

3 Give each of eight male students a red circle half. Give each of eight female students a green circle half. The students should hold the circle half so that the blank side is facing them and they should not read the side with words printed on it. If you do not have enough male or female students, ask a student to volunteer to represent a person of the opposite sex.

4 Explain to students that they are going to find their match. They are going to seek out someone who will be compatible with them. Before you begin this strategy, you might ask them to tell you what they believe a good match might be.

5 Have students circulate around the room until they find someone whose circle half fits theirs. When they find a "match," they are to move to a place in the classroom that you have designated and wait for other students to find their matches. After all students have found a match, they can turn their circles over and see what number they are.

6 Ask the couple with circle halves labeled 1A to come forward. Have each partner in this pair read what is written on his/her circle half. The female will say, "I am open, loyal, involved in school activities, and genuine." The male will say, "I am sensitive, kind, trustworthy, and share feelings." Indicate that this is a match. Have this pair show the circle that their combined halves make to the class. The class will see that the two pieces of the circle are equal, but not alike. Explain that in a healthful and responsible relationship, both persons are equal although they are not alike. Ask the couple with circle halves labeled 1B to come forward. Have each partner in the pair read what is written on his/her circle half. The female will say, "I am close to my family, honest, and reliable." The male will say, "I am respectful, self-confident, and have good values." Discuss why these two persons make a match.

7 Repeat this procedure with the couple who are 2A. The female will read what is on her circle half, "I am the child of an alcoholic, overly responsible, and like to rescue others." The male will read, "I am angry and moody and drink too much." Have them show classmates how their circle pieces fit together. Have the class discuss why they might have formed a match. Repeat this procedure with the couple who are 2B. The female will say, "I am angry and moody and drink too much." The male will say, "I am the child of an alcoholic, overly responsible, and like to rescue others." Point out to the class that, in a relationship, either a male or female may demonstrate certain behaviors. In the illustration of couple 2A, the male drank too much and the female was the one who played the role of rescuing. However, in the illustration of couple 2B, the female drank too much and the male was the one who played the role of rescuing. Sometimes, there is the misconception that the female is always doing the rescuing. This is not the case in codependence. A male may also play this role. The same is true for drinking. In a relationship, it may be the female or the

male who drinks too much or both may drink too much.

8 Repeat the procedure using the couple who are 3A. The female will say, "I am argumentative, critical, and abusive." The male will say, "I have low self-esteem, am submissive, and I was emotionally abused by my mother." Ask the students why they believe this couple chose to be a match. Explain that a person who is abused at home often selects a partner who will continue the abuse. Repeat this procedure with the couple who are 3B. The female will say, "I was physically abused by my stepfather and I am submissive." The male will say, "I have a violent temper, am dominant and controlling, and physically abusive." Again, explain to the class that both males and females can be abused or be abusive in a relationship. Also, have students observe the shape of the circles. The abusive partner has a larger half of the circle. This indicates that (s)he is in control of the relationship.

9 Repeat this procedure with the couple who are 4A. The female will say, "I will do anything not to lose my boyfriend. I feel unloved. My parents are never home." The male will say, "If you love me, you will. I am self-centered and make false promises." Discuss how codependence operates in this relationship. The female is fearful of being abandoned because she does not feel loved at home. The male takes advantage of this situation and pressures her by saying, "If you love me, you will." Repeat this procedure with the couple who are 4B. The female will say, "I am promiscuous, possessive, and jealous." The male will say, "I am not involved in school activities. I fear abandonment and am easily pressured." Explain that either a male or female can fear abandonment and make compromises because of this feeling. In this case, it is the male who fears abandonment and who is pressured to be sexually active to say in the relationship.

481

10 Explain to the students that if more students had participated, more than one student would have had a circle half that would have been a match for their circle half. Often a person in a relationship recognizes that the relationship is not healthful. (S)he may break off the relationship and look for a new relationship. But, suppose (s)he does not change what is on his/her half of the circle. Most likely, (s)he will end up with someone who was similar to the previous person. Have the students who had 1A or 1B on their circle halves hold them up. Explain that in order to be in a healthful and responsible relationship, it is first necessary to work on your circle half.

11 Use the Roots and Characteristics of Codependency transparency to review the causes of dysfunctional families and the characteristics of persons who are codependent.

Evaluation:

Have students write a want ad for a date in which they describe a person who is healthful and responsible. Then have students write a want ad for a date that has the characteristics of codependence. Place the want ads on the bulletin board and give each a number. Have students list the numbers. Next to each, they are to indicate whether the want ad describes a person who is healthful and responsible or a person who is codependent.

Patterns for Green Circles
(females)

Circle #1

1A
I am open, loyal, involved in
school activities, and genuine.

1B
I am close to my family,
honest, and reliable.

Circle #2

2A
I am the child of an alcoholic,
overly responsible, and like to
rescue others.

2B
I am angry and moody and
drink too much.

3A
I am argumentative, critical,
and abusive.

3B
I was physically abused by my
stepfather and I am
submissive.

Circle #3

4A
I will do anything not to lose
my boyfriend. I feel unloved.
My parents are never home.

4B
I am promiscuous, possessive,
and jealous.

Circle #4

Patterns for Red Circles
(males)

Circle #1

1B
I am respectful, self-confident, and have good values.

1A
I am sensitive, kind, trustworthy, and share feelings.

Circle #2

2B
I am the child of an alcoholic, overly responsible, and like to rescue others.

2A
I am angry and moody and drink too much.

3B
I have a violent temper, am dominant and controlling, and physically abusive.

3A
I have low self-esteem, am submissive, and I was emotionally abused by my mother.

Circle #3

4B
I am not involved in school activities. I fear abandonment and am easily pressured.

4A
If you love me, you will. I am self-centered and make false promises.

Circle #4

Grades 9–12
- Objective 4

FAMILY SCULPTURES

Objective:

Students will differentiate between loving, functional families and dysfunctional families.

Life Skill:

I will share feelings in healthful ways with family members.

Materials:

The Family Continuum transparency (page 529), transparency projector

Motivation:

1 Contrast the loving, functional family with the dysfunctional family using The Family Continuum transparency. A **loving, functional family** is a family in which feelings are expressed openly and honestly, effective coping skills are practiced, and members show respect for one another. In a loving, functional family, children observe and are taught important lessons that serve as protective factors:
- self-loving behavior;
- healthful attitudes toward sexuality;
- healthful attitudes and practices regarding drug use;
- healthful ways to express feelings and to communicate;
- faith and moral values;
- responsible decision-making skills;
- coping skills with the ability to delay gratification when necessary.

2 A **dysfunctional family** is a family in which feelings are not expressed openly and honestly, coping skills are inadequate, and members are distrustful of one another. In contrast, the loving, functional family might be depicted as the ideal family in which children observe and are taught the skills needed to resist harmful and irresponsible drug use. Children reared in dys-

functional families may exhibit one or more of the following:
- self-destructive behavior;
- confused attitudes regarding sexuality;
- irresponsible and harmful drug use;
- difficulty communicating and expressing feelings in healthful ways;
- confused value system;
- inadequate decision-making skills;
- inadequate coping skills and reliance on instant gratification.

3 Explain to students that you are going to have them form family sculptures to depict the communication styles of families. The first family sculpture will represent the communication in the loving, functional family. Have five students volunteer to form the family sculpture. Explain that the five students are a family. Have the class identify who the family's members are. The five family members might be a mother, stepfather, grandmother, stepsister, and stepbrother. Have the five students stand in a circle. Each of them is to put one arm into the middle of the circle. All five of them are to join hands. This family sculpture depicts five members of a family who are interdependent. Each is standing by himself/herself, yet each is joined to the others. This represents healthful communication because each family member has a separate identity, yet each feels connected to the family.

4 Explain to students that you are going to have them form another family sculpture. This family sculpture will represent communication in the dysfunctional family. Have four students volunteer to form the family sculpture. One of the students will be the mother, one will be the father, and two will be siblings. Have the student who is the mother and the student who is the father stand back to back. Then have the two students who are the siblings stand facing the mother. Ask students to describe the communication that they observe in this family. In this family, the father is not facing the family and this depicts his failure to communicate. It may be that the mother is shielding the father from communication. For example, the father may have alcoholism. The mother stands between the children and the father. The children do not share their feelings about the father's behavior with him. They keep their feelings inside.

5 Divide the class into groups of four or five students. Each group is to work together to make a family sculpture. Group members must first decide what family members will be depicted. They are to decide on a situation that they want to depict. Explain that the family that they depict may have a blend of communication skills. The family does not have to be one

extreme (loving, functional family) or the other extreme (dysfunctional).

6 Have each group form its family sculpture for the class. Have other students describe the type of family communication that they believe is depicted. Then the group will share the type of family communication it had intended its family sculpture to convey.

Evaluation:

Have students draw and label a Family Continuum. On each end of their Family Continuum, they are to write descriptors of the extremes of types of families.

MUSIC STUDIES

Violence Prevention

RESPONSIBILITY RAP

Objective:

Students will utilize responsible decision-making skills to remain drug free.

Life Skill:

I will use responsible decision-making skills in remaining drug free.

Materials:

Pencil, paper, Responsible Decision-Making Model transparency (page 524), transparency projector, tape recorder, blank tape

Motivation:

1 Discuss responsible decision-making and the Responsible Decision-Making Model. The **Responsible Decision-Making Model** is a series of steps to follow to assure that the decisions a person makes lead to actions that promote health, promote safety, protect laws, show respect for self and others, follow guidelines set by responsible adults such as parents and guardians, and demonstrate good character and moral values. Use the transparency of the Responsible Decision-Making Model to review.

2 Divide the class into groups. Each group is to pretend that it is a popular rap group. The group is to give itself a name. Then the group is to write a ten line rap that contains a message about the importance of making responsible decisions regarding the use of drugs and/or participation in violence. For example, a group might name itself "The Violence Vigilantes," and their hit rap might be "Keepin' the Peace." A group might be "The Vocal Locals," and their hit rap might be "Crackin' Down on Drug Use." Allow the groups at least twenty minutes to write and rehearse their raps. Encourage students to have dance steps and hand motions to accompany their raps.

3 Explain that there is going to be a recording session. Someone from each group must introduce the group, telling its name and the hit rap that will be performed. Record the introductions and raps from the groups. After the recording session, ask students to review the responsibility messages that were contained in the raps. Play the tape recording for parents at the next parent teacher association meeting.

Evaluation:

It is important for students to memorize the six questions to ask to carefully evaluate each possible action when making a responsible decision. Have students list in writing these six questions.

Grades 9–12
• Objective 6

| Violence Prevention |

Candies

Objective:

Students will practice resistance skills when pressured to use harmful drugs and/or belong to gangs.

Life Skill:

I will use resistance skills when appropriate.

Materials:

Candy (red, orange, yellow, brown, tan, green), Model for Using Resistance Skills transparency (page525), transparency projector

Motivation:

1 If you have several large bags of candy, the entire class might participate. If not, ask for six volunteers. Give one-third of the class or two volunteers a handful of candies. Each of these persons should have several of each color—brown, tan, green, yellow, orange, and red. They are to place the candies on their desks in view. They are designated as group #1. Give another one-third of the class or two volunteers 12 pieces of candy. They are to be given two pieces of each color—brown, tan, green, yellow, orange, and red. They are to place the candies on their desks in view. They are designated group #2. Explain to the final one-third of the class or two volunteers that they will not have the candies. They are designated as group #3.

2 Explain to students that they are not allowed to eat the candies. These candies represent drugs that are harmful to their health. Ask students which group will have the least difficulty resisting the temptation to eat candies or, in this case, to experiment with harmful drugs. They will select group #3. The persons in group #3 are practicing a

resistance skill. These persons "avoid being in situations in which there will be pressure to make harmful decisions."

3 Explain to students that they are now going to be given another situation. The students who are in group #1 belong to a gang. They have a variety of candies. These candies have not been counted. This indicates that there are no rules. The students in group #2 do not belong to a gang. However, they are in situations in which violence may exist. They have two each of the different colors of candies. These candies have been counted so that the students in this group know that if they eat any of them they are accountable. The students in group #3 avoid being in situations in which there is violence. Ask the class which students are least likely to be victims or participants in violent acts. They will select group #3. Emphasize that anyone might be a victim of a violent action; however, this group is least likely. This group practices a resistance skill to the best of its ability. Student in #3 "avoid being with persons who choose harmful actions." Then ask if students in group #1 or group #2 are least likely to be participants or victims of violence. They will select group #2. Group #2 has rules. They must be accountable for following these rules.

4 Now divide the students in group #3 into two groups—#3A and #3B. The students in group #3A are to pressure the students in group #1 to eat their orange candies. The students in group #3B are to encourage the students in group #2 to stay away from the orange candies. Allow the students three to five minutes to play their roles.

5 Ask students which group, group #1 or group #2, was more likely to resist the temptation to eat the orange candies. The students will select group #2 because those students were encouraged by the students in group #3B. The students in group #3B also practiced a resistance skill as they "influenced others to choose responsible behavior."

6 Now give students in group #3 some candies, but give them only the following colors—brown and tan. Explain that the different colors of candies represent the following behaviors:
- brown—arguing
- tan—shouting
- green—pushing
- yellow—shoving to the ground
- orange—striking with an object
- red—striking with intent to injure

7 Explain that students in all three groups were involved in disagreements. Students in group #1 belonged to a gang in which all six colors of candies were acceptable. Students in group #2 were in a situation in which there were clear rules about the appropriateness of different behaviors; however, they still had all six colors of candies in their presence. Students in group #3 had only the brown and tan candies. They would leave the situation after the brown and tan candies were eaten.

8 Ask students in group #1 to shut their eyes and grab two candies to eat. Ask students in group #2 to select two candies to eat. Explain that they will be disciplined according to what color(s) they select. Now ask students in group #3 to select two candies to eat. Of course, they can only select from the two brown and two tan pieces.

9 Ask which students are least likely to become victims or participants in violence. They will select group #3. Students in this group could only choose brown and tan. They always left a situation that accelerated beyond brown or tan. Students in group #2 would be next. They were clear as to the consequences of their behavior. However, they were at greater risk because they were in situations in which other ways of working through disputes might be used. Students in group #1 were at greatest risk. They were involved in a gang. Rather than being individually accountable for behavior, they entered the situation blind to what might happen if they were caught up in the emotion of the situation.

10 Summarize by emphasizing the importance of practicing resistance skills when pressured to use drugs an/or belong to gangs. Use the Model for Using Resistance Skills transparency to review and practice resistance skills.

Evaluation:

Have students write essays in which they clearly describe situations in which peers might become involved in violence. Students are to identify resistance skills that might be used to deal with the situations.

Grades 9–12
- Objective 7

Violence Prevention

EYES ON MY FUTURE

Objective:

Students will describe the short-term and long-term effects of harmful drugs on physical, mental, and social health.

Life Skill:

I will not use harmful drugs.

Materials:

Broomstick

Motivation:

1 Select a student to do a demonstration for classmates. Placing the tip of the stick end of a broomstick on the finger. This student is to try to balance the broomstick while looking down where the stick rests on the finger.

2 Now have the student repeat this demonstration, only this time the student should look about two-thirds of the way toward the top of the broomstick while trying to balance it. The broomstick should balance for a longer time period while the student looks about two-thirds of the way toward the top rather than when (s)he looks down where the stick rested on the finger.

3 Explain that looking at the bottom of the broomstick is similar to making decisions based upon the present without keeping one's eyes on the future. For example, a person might smoke cigarettes and drink alcohol today without examining ways in which these behaviors might affect the future. The person who behaves in these ways is like the person who tries to balance the broomstick while looking down at the point where the stick rests on the finger. The person will lose control. Soon, there will be undesirable consequences.

4 Explain that keeping the eyes about two-thirds of the way toward the top of the broomstick

is similar to making decisions in which present needs are examined in view of goals that have been set for the future. For example, the person who avoids going to parties where alcohol is served and where persons are smoking cigarettes recognizes that these behaviors interfere with future goals. This person keeps his/her eyes toward the top of the broomstick because future goals are important to him/her. Just as it is easier to balance the broomstick by looking ahead, so it is easier to reach goals when current decisions are examined in view of long-term goals.

5 Have students give examples of goals that they have for their future. Some of these goals might be to attend a vocational school or college, to get a good job, to support themselves financially, to graduate from high school, etc. Discuss ways in which drug use interferes with these goals. Identify short-term and long-term effects of harmful drugs on physical, mental, and social health.

Evaluation:

Have students design cards appropriate for being sent to a student about to graduate from high school. They must include a congratulatory message in their cards. On the back of their cards, they are to write at least five short-term or long-term effects of drugs that interfere with physical, mental, and social health. Have students share the congratulatory messages they have written. Discuss reasons why it is important to graduate from high school. Have students share their lists of ways in which drugs interfere with physical, mental, and social health.

PRESCRIPTION AND OTC CALLIGRAPHY

Objective:

Students will outline choices that promote the responsible use of over-the-counter and pre-scription drugs.

Life Skill:

I will follow the directions for using prescription and over-the-counter drugs.

Materials:

Paper, ink, calligraphy pen (might also use medium-tip black markers), Calligraphy Alphabet student master (page 493), Over-the-Counter Drugs Are Available in Tamper-Resistant Packaging transparency (page 559), Questions to Ask Your Physician About Prescription Drugs transparency (page 560), transparency projector, examples of OTC drugs (optional)

Motivation:

1 Review information about over-the-counter drugs. **Over-the-counter drugs** are drugs that are approved for legal purchase and use without a prescription from a doctor or other licensed health professional. Drug and grocery store shelves are filled with these drugs that, for the most part, are used on a temporary basis and are considered to be relatively safe if used according to the directions provided on the drug label. Over-the-counter drugs are often self-prescribed and self-administered for the relief of symptoms of self-diagnosed illnesses. The label of an OTC contains the following:
- the name and address of the manufacturer, distributor, or packer;
- the lot, control, or batch number;
- the name of the product and what type of drug it is;
- the active ingredients;
- the amount of product contained (e.g., number of tablets or ounces of liquid preparations);
- the symptoms or conditions for which the product should be used (indications for use);
- warnings and cautionary statements (i.e., who should not be taking the drug, adverse reactions that could develop from use, symptoms that signal the need to see a doctor, how long the drug should be taken);
- precautions about interaction with other over-the-counter drugs and alcohol;
- the expiration date (month and year beyond which the product should not be used).

2 If possible, show students several examples of OTC drugs. Use the transparency of Over-the-Counter Drugs Are Available in Tamper-Resistant Packaging. Explain the following. In recent years, there have been episodes of over-the-counter drug tampering. In the state of Washington, two people died after swallowing Sudafed capsules that were laced with cyanide (Cramer, 1991—see Chapter 10 Bibliography). In 1982, seven people died from taking Extra-Strength Tylenol capsules that were tampered with and laced with cyanide. Cases such as these prompted the Food and Drug Administration (FDA) to require tamper-resistant packaging on certain drug and cosmetic products. However, not all products require tamper-resistant packaging. Dentifrices (toothpastes and mouthwashes), lozenges (cough drops), and products applied topically to the skin are notable exceptions to FDA regulations (Cramer, 1991—see Chapter 10 Bibliography).

3 Review information about prescription drugs. **Prescription drugs** are drugs that can be legitimately obtained only by a prescription from licensed health professionals (e.g., physicians, podiatrists, and dentists) and dispensed by registered pharmacists. Prescription drugs usually are more powerful than over-the-counter drugs and are more likely to cause adverse side effects. Prescription drugs are dispensed under either a brand name or a generic name. A **brand name** is a registered name or trademark given to a drug by a pharmaceutical company. A **generic name** is the chemical and/or biological equivalent of a specific brand-name drug. A **prescription** is a very precise order from a physician or other appropriate health professional to a pharmacist to dispense a certain drug product to a patient. **Patient package inserts (PPIs)** are supplemental, informational brochures included in prescription drug packages that describe in easy-to-understand language the drug's actions, possible side effects, and interactions. The information on labels of prescription drugs is limited. To get the best results from a drug, it may be necessary to ask the prescribing physician some direct questions. Use the transparency of Questions to Ask Your Physician About Prescription Drugs.

Evaluation:

Distribute copies of the student master of Calligraphy Alphabet to students. Give each student a white sheet of art paper. If you have calligraphy pens and ink available, allow students to share these materials. If not, have students use medium-tip black markers. Have them write at least three important life skills regarding OTC drugs and prescription drugs in calligraphy. Examples might be: I will check the tamper-resistant package before purchasing an OTC; whenever possible, I will purchase generic brands to save money.

Alphabet Calligraphy

Aa Bb Cc Dd Ee Ff Gg
Hh Ii Jj Kk Ll Mm Nn
Oo Pp Qq Rr Ss Tt Uu
Vv Ww Xx Yy Zz

Grades 9–12
- Objective 9

| Violence Prevention |

ADDING UP THE LOSSES

Objective:

Students will examine ways in which laws pertaining to the use of alcohol, tobacco, and other harmful drugs help protect personal and community health.

Life Skill:

I will obey laws pertaining to the use of alcohol, tobacco, and other harmful drugs.

Materials:

A sheet of construction paper for each student, markers

Motivation:

1 Give each student a sheet of construction paper. Ask them to divide the paper into ten sections. They can fold the paper into ten sections or they can divide the paper using a marker. In each of the ten sections, they are to print PERSONAL AND COMMUNITY HEALTH.

2 Explain to the class that they are going to add up the potential losses to personal and community health that can be attributed to using alcohol, tobacco, and other harmful drugs. You will identify ten losses. Each time you identify a loss, the students are to tear one of the sections from their construction paper to indicate the loss. The losses are as follows:

- *Personal injury.* Someone is visiting your house and drinks alcohol. This person falls down the stairs and is injured. There are many cases of personal injury that result from drinking alcohol.

- *Fire.* At a local hotel, a person falls asleep while smoking a cigarette. The mattress on his/her bed catches fire. The person is injured and the hotel is damaged. Many fires are the result of persons who are smoking carelessly. This problem is magnified if a person drinks and smokes.

- *Drowning.* Two local teenagers have been drinking and then decide to swim in a NO SWIMMING area. They drown. Many accidents resulting in deaths due to drowning are associated with drinking. In fact, 72% of those who drown had been drinking alcohol.

- *Acquaintance rape.* A local teen has charged another teen with acquaintance rape. The female claims that the male had been drinking and forced her to have sex. The male claims that the female was drinking and accompanied him to his bedroom while his parents were not at home. He feels that she led him on. She claims he raped her. Many rapes involve alcohol or other drugs that affect decision-making.

- *Burglary.* Several houses in the community have been burglarized. The burglar seemed to want cash and jewelry. When apprehended, the suspect was high on drugs. (S)he began to suffer from withdrawal. Burglarizing homes was a way for the burglar to obtain money for drugs. Often, persons who become dependent on drugs become involved in crime in order to support their habit.

- *Homicide.* Newspaper headlines in the community say, "Toddler killed in drive-by shooting." Drug trafficking is associated with violence in communities. Often, innocent persons become the victims of violence associated with drug trafficking. There are numerous cases where small children have been killed by stray bullets.

- *Child and spousal abuse.* The local shelter for battered spouses and their children is full. Drug use intensifies feelings. Persons who have a tendency to be abusive and to physically harm others are much more dangerous when using drugs. The children and spouses of such persons suffer losses in self-esteem and may also be injured.

- *Lung cancer and other diseases.* The obituary section of the newspaper describes a woman who died in her fifties leaving a spouse, several children, and grandchildren.

494

This family and friends of this family feel the loss.

- *Automobile accidents.* A family of four was killed when a drunk driver swerved out of his/her lane, crossed the median, and crashed head-on into an oncoming vehicle. Most fatal traffic accidents involve a driver who has been drinking.
- *Birth defects.* Your neighbor has a baby born with fetal alcohol syndrome (FAS). Many birth defects are attributed to a mother's health habits. Drinking alcohol during pregnancy may result in a baby born with FAS. Using crack or cocaine may result in a baby being born addicted. There is much loss of human potential.

3 Explain that laws pertaining to the use of alcohol, tobacco, and other harmful drugs help protect personal and community health. They help protect against the losses that have been explained.

Evaluation:

Have students identify a law pertaining to the use of alcohol, tobacco, and other harmful drugs. Have them explain how this law protects personal and community health. Which losses does it protect against?

Grades 9–12
• Objective 10

JELLY GENES

Objective:

Students will examine ways in which the use of alcohol interferes with health and well-being and achieving goals.

Life Skills:

I will not drink alcohol.
I will learn my family history with regard to chemical dependency.

Materials:

Four bowls, 4 small paper lunch sacks, 3 red jelly beans, 1 yellow jelly bean, 3 green jelly beans, 1 white jelly bean, 3 black jelly beans, 1 orange jelly bean, 3 pink jelly beans, 1 purple jelly bean, chalkboard, chalk

Motivation:

1 Place the following in the four paper lunch sacks:
Sack #1: 3 red jelly beans, 1 yellow jelly bean
Sack #2: 3 green jelly beans, 1 white jelly bean
Sack #3: 3 black jelly beans, 1 orange jelly bean
Sack #4: 3 pink jelly beans, 1 purple jelly bean

2 Discuss heredity and inherited tendencies. **Heredity** is the transmission of characteristics/features from one generation to the next. With the class, identify some characteristics/features that are known to be inherited. Mention the following as examples: color of hair, height, frame, curly or straight hair, right or left handedness.

3 Explain that the tendency toward developing certain diseases is inherited. For example, persons with parents who had high blood pressure are more likely to develop high blood pressure. Persons with parents who

had diabetes are more likely to develop diabetes. Persons with parent(s) who had chemical dependency are more likely to develop chemical dependency. Persons with parents with colon cancer are more likely to develop colon cancer.

4 Explain that you are going to do a demonstration to show how family genes, in this case jelly genes, may influence a person's health. Explain that the jelly genes are going to represent family genes that can be passed to offspring. On the chalkboard, write the following to indicate the information contained on the different colors of jelly genes:
• red—no family history of diabetes
• yellow—family history of diabetes
• green—no family history of high blood pressure
• white—family history of high blood pressure
• black—no family history of chemical dependency
• orange—family history of chemical dependency
• pink—no family history of colon cancer
• purple—family history of colon cancer

5 Ask for four volunteers. Give each one a bowl. Explain that you are going to place some genes in each of their bowls. These genes come from their biological parents. Emphasize that none of these students has control over which genes (s)he will get.

6 Take sack #1 with the jelly genes containing information regarding diabetes. Place one jelly gene in each of the students' bowls.

7 Take sack #2 with the jelly genes containing information regarding high blood pressure. Place one jelly gene in each of the students' bowls.

8 Take sack #3 with the jelly genes containing information regarding chemical dependency. Place one jelly gene in each of the students' bowls.

9 Take sack #4 with the jelly genes containing information regarding colon cancer. Place one jelly gene in each of the students' bowls.

10 Allow the students to look at the four jelly genes that are in their bowls. Ask them what they know about themselves. Explain that they cannot see the health information contained in our genes. There may be two ways to learn about this information. In some cases, there is genetic testing. However, in most cases there is not. The most important way to predict the information contained in our genes is to obtain a family history. A person might gather a family history regarding the incidence of diabetes, high blood pressure, chemical dependency, and colon cancer. A family history is obtained from biological parents and other close blood relatives.

11 Have the student who has the orange jelly gene show it to the class. Explain that this student has a family history of chemical dependency. Perhaps a biological parent has chemical dependency. Perhaps a grandparent also had chemical dependency. Perhaps an older brother or sister has chemical dependency.

12 Give this student two options. (S)he can place this orange jelly gene back in the bowl to indicate that (s)he will never experiment with alcohol or (s)he can eat the orange jelly gene to indicate that (s)he consumed an alcoholic beverage. Remind the student that (s)he had no control over getting the jelly gene, but (s)he does have control over whether or not (s)he chooses to drink.

13 Have students brainstorm ways that drinking alcohol interferes with physical, mental-emotional, and social health. Examples might include: impairs motor ability (physical health), interferes with learning (mental-emotional health), and increases violence (social health).

Evaluation:

Have each student share a personal goal and tell at least one way that drinking alcohol might interfere with the achievement of that goal.

Grades 9–12
- Objective 11

GASPING FOR AIR

Objective:

Students will examine ways in which the use of tobacco interferes with health and well-being and achieving goals.

Life Skill:

I will not smoke cigarettes or use other tobacco products.

Materials:

Straws covered with wrappers, straw-type coffee stirrers, white paper, tape, balloons

Motivation:

1 Provide each student with a straw. Each straw should be wrapped in its original paper.

2 After students have their straws, ask them to remove the wrapping. Explain that students are going to participate in an activity that simulates how difficult it might be to breathe in certain situations. Ask students with respiratory conditions such as asthma to observe rather than participate in this activity. Then ask the rest of the students to pinch their nostrils closed so that they cannot inhale or exhale through their nose. Ask each student to place a straw in his/her mouth. Each student is to keep his/her nostrils pinched closed while inhaling and exhaling through the straw. Explain that if any difficulty exists with breathing, they can stop the activity at any time. Students are to breathe through the straw for one minute.

3 Ask students to describe what it was like to breathe through the straw. Students will explain that it was difficult. In order to inhale the same amount of air that they normally inhale each minute, they needed to inhale more often. This raised the heart beat rate and became tiring. Explain that this is what happens when a person smokes cigarettes. Often, young persons have the impression that the

harmful consequences from smoking cigarettes are experienced only after many years of smoking. Explain that smoking cigarettes can interfere with short-term goals. Performance in athletic activities is decreased by the effects of cigarette smoking.

4 Provide each student with a coffee stirrer. Hand the stirrers to each student rather than passing them around in order to avoid germs. Repeat the strategy. Again, caution students with respiratory conditions such as asthma to observe rather than to participate in this strategy. Ask students to pinch their nostrils closed so that they cannot inhale or exhale through their nose. Ask each student to place a stirrer in his/her mouth. Each student is to keep his/her nostrils pinched closed while inhaling and exhaling through the stirrer. Explain that if any difficulty exists with breathing, they can stop the activity at any time. Students are to breathe through the stirrer for one minute.

5 Explain that the long-term effects of smoking cigarettes are very serious. They have just experienced what it is like to have chronic obstructive lung disease. **Chronic obstructive lung disease** or **COLD** is characterized by progressive limitation of the flow of air into and out of the lungs. Emphysema and chronic bronchitis are two examples of chronic obstructive lung diseases. **Emphysema** is a type of COLD in which the limitation of airflow results from changes in the smallest air passages and the walls of the alveoli, the tiny air sacs of the lungs. These tiny air sacs are destroyed from smoking cigarettes. Then it becomes difficult for the lungs to bring in oxygen and remove carbon dioxide. The heart must then work harder to get oxygen to the cells. **Chronic bronchitis** is a type of COLD in which the bronchial tubes in the lungs become inflamed. The walls of the bronchial tubes become thickened and there is increased production of mucus. This narrows the air passages.

6 Explain that cigarette smoking has also been linked to lung cancer, laryngeal cancer, coronary heart disease, atherosclerotic peripheral vascular disease, oral cancer, esophageal cancer, intrauterine growth retardation, low birth weight babies, leukemia, unsuccessful pregnancies, increased infant mortality, peptic ulcer, cancer of the bladder, cancer of the pancreas, cancer of the kidney, and cancer of the stomach. Smokeless tobacco use increases the frequency of localized gum recession, leukoplakia, and oral cancer.

Evaluation:

Give each student a white sheet of paper. Have them write at the top of the paper, "BEST TIP YET: DON'T SMOKE OR CHEW." Then they are to list at least five reasons why it is harmful to use tobacco products. Have them roll their papers in the shape of a cigarette. Tape them together so they look like paper cigarettes. Collect the paper cigarettes. Distribute them to the class, giving each student a paper cigarette other than his/her own. Have students take turns reading what is written on their cigarette tips.

Inclusion:

Have students with special needs blow up balloons. Tie them together. Explain that this clump of balloons looks like the alveoli or the air sacs in the lungs. Break several of the balloons to show that cigarette smoking destroys these air sacs, making it more difficult to inhale and exhale air.

Grades 9–12
▪ Objective 12

ATHLETIC POISON

Objective:

Students will examine ways in which the use of anabolic steroids interferes with health and well-being and achieving goals

Life Skill:

I will not use anabolic steroids.

Materials:

Two plastic cups half-filled with water, red and blue food coloring

Motivation:

1 Define healthful behaviors, risk behaviors, and the holistic effect. A **healthful behavior** is an action that enhances self-esteem; promotes health; prevents illness, injury, and premature death; and improves the quality of the environment. A **risk behavior** is a voluntary action that threatens self-esteem; harms health; increases the likelihood of illness, injury, and premature death; and destroys the quality of the environment. The **holistic effect** means that a behavior affects a person's total health. When a person engages in a risk behavior, (s)he will experience many harmful consequences. These consequences are harmful to physical, mental-emotional, family-social, and spiritual health in a variety of ways. When a person engages in a healthful behavior, (s)he will experience many positive consequences. The consequences contribute in a positive way to physical, mental-emotional, family-social, and spiritual health.

2 Initiate a discussion of athletic performance. Discuss the need to train well to perform well during sports/athletics. Explain that exercising to promote physical fitness is an example of a healthful behavior. **Physical fitness** is the condition of the body in which there is muscular endurance, muscular strength, flexibility,

cardiovascular endurance, and a lean body composition. **Muscular strength** is the amount of force that a person's muscles can exert against resistance. **Muscular endurance** is a person's ability to continue using muscular strength. **Flexibility** is a person's ability to move his/her body through a full range of motion. **Cardiovascular endurance** is a person's ability to sustain vigorous activity that requires increased oxygen intake for an extended period of time. A **lean body composition** is a body composition in which there is a decrease in fat tissue and an increase in lean tissue. The percentage of body fat is usually 16 to 19 percent for males and 22 to 25 percent for females. Reducing this percentage is healthful.

3 Explain that persons who participate in athletics/sports may want to increase muscular strength, decrease the percentage of body fat, and increase the lean tissue. There are many exercises that accomplish these benefits. These exercises also have other benefits.

4 Take one of the plastic cups of water. Show students the red food coloring. Explain that the red food coloring represents healthful behavior. Explain that you have selected the red food coloring because red is a life-giving color. Each of the benefits is life-giving because it enhances health and well-being. Regular exercise that promotes physical fitness is healthful behavior. Explain that you are going to place a drop of red food coloring in the cup for each of the benefits derived from regular exercise that promotes physical fitness. When you exercise regularly to promote physical fitness, you:
• develop muscle tone,
• reduce the percentage of body fat,
• feel good about your body,
• are more likely to be at a healthful weight,
• have strong bones,
• reduce the likelihood of premature coronary heart disease,
• increase cardiac output (the amount of blood pumped with each heart beat),

- have a more healthful appearance,
- perform better in athletics/sports,
- tire less easily,
- are less likely to feel depressed,
- lower resting heart beat rate and blood pressure,
- have fewer injuries from muscle soreness and strain,
- have better digestion and more regular bowel movements,
- reduce the risk of obesity-related diabetes,
- increase lung capacity.

5 Review information about anabolic steroids. **Anabolic steroids**, synthetic derivatives of the male hormone testosterone, stimulate increased muscle growth and, when first taken, may produce a euphoric state. Users claim that anabolic steroids function to anesthetize the body, allowing the user to work out intensely without feeling pain. Some young persons use anabolic steroids to obtain a temporary euphoric state. They may take these drugs before going to a party to lessen feelings of inadequacy.

6 Take the other plastic cup of water. Show students the blue food coloring. Explain that the blue food coloring represents risk behavior. Risk behavior is not life-giving. When you participate in risk behavior, you are saying NO to health and well-being. The use of anabolic steroids is risk behavior. Explain that you are going to place a drop of blue food coloring in the cup for each of the risks associated with the use of anabolic steroids. The risks are:
- shrinking of the testicles (males),
- reduced sperm count (males),
- impotence (males),
- baldness (males),
- difficulty or pain in urinating (males),
- development of breasts (males),
- enlarged prostate (males),
- growth of facial hair (females),
- changes in or cessation of the menstrual cycle (females),
- enlargement of the clitoris (females),
- deepened voice (females),

- breast reduction (females),
- acne,
- jaundice,
- swelling of the feet or ankles,
- bad breath,
- reduction in HDL (good cholesterol),
- high blood pressure,
- liver damage,
- liver cancer,
- aching joints,
- increased chance of injury to tendons,
- halt growth prematurely in adolescents,
- mood swings ranging from periods of violent, even homicidal, episodes known as "roid rages" to bouts of depression,
- paranoid jealousy,
- extreme irritability,
- delusions,
- impaired judgment stemming from feelings of invincibility.

7 Further explain that persons who use anabolic steroids over a period of time and then stop this practice suffer additional consequences:
- feelings of depression,
- pain in muscles and joints,
- old injuries and strains reappear,
- feelings of anxiety are heightened,
- feelings of inadequacy are heightened.

8 Have students differentiate between the two cups of water. One of the cups of water is a vibrant red. This represents the behavior of a person who says YES to health and chooses to exercise. The other cup of water is a vivid blue. This represents the behavior of the person who says NO to health and uses anabolic steroids. Have students explain why it would be more difficult to achieve future goals for the person who has filled his/her body with the conditions signified by the blue food coloring.

Evaluation:

Have students pretend that they are a coach for one of the male or female athletic teams at your high school. They are to prepare a short speech on the dangers of using anabolic steroids to deliver to the participants on the team they coach. They must mention at least five health consequences. You may want to ask for volunteers to deliver their speeches to the class.

eral index cards. Print the health dangers derived from anabolic steroid use on several index cards. Have students with special needs read these lists while you place the red and blue food coloring in the plastic cups. This provides these students with extra reinforcement in learning the benefits of regular exercise and the risks associated with the use of anabolic steroids.

Inclusion:

Print the health benefits derived from regular exercise that promotes physical fitness on sev-

SOAKING UP THC

Objective:

Students will examine ways in which the use of illegal drugs interferes with health and well-being and achieving goals.

Life Skills:

I will not use illegal drugs.
I will not smoke or eat marijuana.

Materials:

Bowl of warm water, extra bowl, an orange, blue food coloring

Motivation:

1 Cut the orange in half and place it in the bowl of warm water. Explain to students that this is a section of their brain. Further explain that this is the brain of a student who uses the illegal drug marijuana. **Marijuana** refers to the cannabis plant and to any part or extract of it that produces somatic or psychic changes. Place several drops of the blue food coloring into the warm water. Explain that the blue food coloring is THC. **THC** is the major psychoactive ingredient in marijuana. The flowering tops and upper leaves of the plant contain the highest concentrations of THC. Explain that concentrations of THC in legally-confiscated marijuana have risen from around one to two percent in the 1970s to an average of three to five percent currently.

2 Explain that THC has high lipid solubility, and it is absorbed rapidly. It tends to be stored in fatty areas of the body such as the heart, lungs, and liver. Have students observe how the blue food coloring is being absorbed in the different sections of the orange. Explain that THC easily crosses the blood-brain barrier because of the high lipid solubility. It causes an increased heart beat rate.

3 Take the orange out of the bowl of warm water that contains the blue food coloring. Explain to students that the person who has been using marijuana stops. However, THC tends to remain for long periods bound to proteins in fatty storage areas of the body. For this reason, THC can be measured in the blood several days or weeks after a chronic user had his/her last joint. Squeeze the juice of the orange into the clean bowl. Have students notice that the juice of the orange is tainted blue. Explain that because THC remains in the blood several days or weeks after a chronic user had his/her last joint, learning may be affected during this time. THC affects memory, thinking, and speaking. Many specific learning skills are affected. Examples include digit/symbol substitution, in which the subject is required to replace a series of random digits with symbols representing each digit; the number of orally-presented digits that can be recalled (digit span); serial subtraction, in which the subject subtracts a number repeatedly from an initially large number; and reading comprehension.

4 Squeeze the juice from the half of the orange that was not placed in the warm water with the added blue food coloring. Explain that there is no THC in the blood that crosses the blood-brain barrier. Ask students to explain why a person who does not use marijuana has a greater likelihood of achieving short-term and long-term goals. Students should mention the effects that the THC has on learning. Impaired learning affects the ability to get the best education possible. Education is a key to the future.

Evaluation:

Assign students other illegal drugs and/or drugs that can be abused: heroin, opium, morphine, talwin, percadan, darvon, mescaline, LSD, PCP, psilocybin, barbiturates, tranquilizers, amphetamines, speed, cocaine, and crack. Have students research the effects of the assigned drug and determine how use of this drug interferes with short-term and long-term goals. Then have students design their own experiments to demonstrate the effects of their assigned drug.

Inclusion:

Make the evaluation a cooperative learning assignment in which students with special needs are paired with students who learn more easily.

MUSIC STUDIES

FAMILY DANCE STEPS

Objective:

Students will discuss how drug dependency affects family relationships.

Life Skill:

I will seek help for codependent behaviors.

Materials:

Recording of slow music for dancing, tape/CD player, Roots and Characteristics of Codependence transparency (page 530), transparency projector

Motivation:

1 Contrast the loving, functional family with the dysfunctional family. The **loving, functional family** is a family in which feelings are expressed openly and honestly, effective coping skills are practiced, and members show respect for one another. In a loving, functional family, children observe and are taught important lessons that serve as protective factors:
- self-loving behavior;
- healthful attitudes toward sexuality;
- healthful attitudes and practices regarding drug use;
- healthful ways to express feelings and to communicate;
- faith and moral values;
- responsible decision-making skills;
- coping skills with the ability to delay gratification when necessary.

2 Explain that males and females reared in a loving, functional family have learned dance steps that help them dance through life sharing their feelings and being spontaneous. Have two males and two females volunteer to be persons who were reared in loving, functional families. Have these persons come in front of the class to dance to slow music. The couples will assume the traditional style for dancing. The

females will extend their right arms sideways and place their left hand on the shoulder of their male partner. The males will extend their left arms sideways and place their right hand at their female partner's waist. As the music begins, the two couples are to dance several steps.

3 Describe the dysfunctional family. A **dysfunctional family** is a family in which feelings are not expressed openly and honestly, coping skills are inadequate, and members are distrustful of one another. Children reared in dysfunctional families may exhibit one or more of the following:
- self-destructive behavior;
- confused attitudes regarding sexuality;
- irresponsible and harmful drug use;
- difficulty communicating and expressing feelings in healthful ways;
- confused value system;
- inadequate decision-making skills;
- inadequate coping skills and reliance on instant gratification.

4 Explain that persons reared in dysfunctional families learn a special dance called codependence. Use the transparency of Roots and Characteristics of Codependence for review. **Codependence** is a mental disorder in which a person loses personal identity, has frozen feelings, and copes ineffectively. Persons who have codependence are called **codependent**. Review some of the characteristics of codependence that appear on the transparency.

5 Explain that children who are reared in families in which adults are chemically dependent and codependent may copy this behavior. They learn the family dance steps of codependence.

6 Have two males and two females volunteer to be persons who were reared in dysfunctional families. Have these persons come in front of the class to dance to slow music. The couples will assume a different position for dancing. The females will extend their left arms sideways and place their right hand on the waist of their partner. The males will extend their right arms sideways and place their left hand on the shoulder of their partner. As the music begins, the two couples are to dance several steps. The dancing is more awkward than the first demonstration of dancing.

7 Now have other males and females dance in the traditional style. Play the music and have them dance several steps. Stop the music and have every one change partners. The four students from dysfunctional families have not learned the same dance style as the other students in the room.

8 Discuss the options of the students who were from dysfunctional families and who danced differently than others. There appear to be at least two options. The two couples could switch partners so that they would dance with another dysfunctional partner. The two couples, or four students, could learn to dance differently.

9 Explain that persons with codependence need to learn a new style of dancing in order to have healthful relationships with others. There is individual counseling for these persons. There are a variety of Twelve Step Programs available. The Twelve Step Programs help persons with codependence by teaching them healthful and spontaneous ways to dance through life and interact with others.

Evaluation:

Have students make a list of creative names for codependent dances. For example, they might name some of the following dances: "the enmeshment dance," "the pity prance," "the rescue rap." Have each student name a dance and discuss why the dance interferes with healthful living.

Grades 9–12
• Objective 15

BOUNCING BACK

Objective:

Students will identify risk factors and protective factors associated with the use of alcohol, tobacco, and illegal drugs.

Life Skills:

I will practice protective factors that promote resiliency.
I will not use alcohol, tobacco, or illegal drugs.

Materials:

Tennis balls (some of which are new and have a bounce to them and others of which are old and depressurized), yardstick, Protective Factors That Serve as a Coat of Armor and Promote Resiliency transparency (page 527), Risk Factors That Make Young Persons Vulnerable to Drug Use transparency (page 528), transparency projector, black markers

Motivation:

1 Have several students stand in front of the class. Give each a tennis ball. Have students hold the tennis balls waist high and allow them to bounce from the floor. They are to catch the tennis ball. Repeat.

2 Ask students what they observe. They will most likely say that some of the tennis balls bounce back farther than others. Have one of the students with a pressurized tennis ball hold the ball waist high and allow it to bounce. Use the yardstick to measure how far it bounces back. Then have one of the students with a tennis ball that has lost its pressure drop the tennis ball from the waist. Use the yardstick to measure how far it bounces back. As a math activity, have students compute the difference.

3 Focus class discussion on the difference between the tennis balls. The tennis balls each had a different amount of bounce to them. Some bounced back with a lot of spring.

Others had less bounce. Still others had very little bounce. Relate this to the ways that young persons function in their personal lives. Some young persons bounce back or have resiliency while others lack the ability to bounce back. They have very little resiliency. **Resiliency** is the ability to adjust to misfortune, change, pressure, and adversity. Resilient youth are often described as being stress resistent and invincible in spite of adversity. They are able to bounce back from misfortune.

4 Explain that protective factors help promote resiliency in youth. **Protective factors** are characteristics of individuals and their environments that make a positive contribution to development and behavior. Use the Protective Factors That Serve as a Coat of Armor and Promote Resiliency transparency to initiate discussion of the benefits of each of the following:
• being reared in a loving, functional family,
• being involved in school activities,
• having positive self-esteem,
• having clearly defined goals and plans to reach them,
• having close friends who do not abuse drugs,
• regularly practicing one's faith,
• feeling a sense of accomplishment at school,
• having adult role models including parents who do not abuse drugs,
• having a healthful attitude about competition and athletic performance,
• being committed to following the rules of the community,
• having a plan to cope with life stressors.

5 Explain that some youth lack resiliency. They are like the depressurized tennis balls. They are unable to bounce back. Youth who lack resiliency have often experienced risk factors. Use the transparency of Risk Factors That Make Young Persons Vulnerable to Drug Use to discuss the negative contributions of each of the following:
• being reared in a dysfunctional family,
• having negative self-esteem,

- being unable to resist peer pressure,
- having difficulty mastering developmental tasks,
- being economically disadvantaged,
- lacking faith experiences,
- having a genetic background with a predisposition to chemical dependency,
- experiencing family disruption,
- experiencing depression,
- experiencing pressure to succeed in athletics,
- having difficulty achieving success in school,
- having attention deficit hyperactive disorder,
- having immature character disorder,
- having borderline personality tendencies.

Evaluation:

Have students create mobiles that illustrate at least three to five protective factors that promote resiliency.

Inclusion:

Give students with special needs the tennis balls and black markers. The students who are given the new tennis balls that have a lot of bounce to them are to use the black markers to write some of the protective factors on the ball's surface. The students who are given the depressurized balls that have lost their bounce are to use the black markers to write some of the risk factors on the ball's surface. This exercise will help students review the protective and risk factors that influence resiliency.

| Violence Prevention |

VIOLENCE-PROOF VEST

Objective:

Students will identify risk factors and protective factors associated with violence.

Life Skill:

I will practice protective factors to reduce the likelihood that I will be a participant or victim of violence.

Materials:

Vests (bring any vests you have and ask students if they have vests or a parent has a vest they can borrow); index cards

Motivation:

1 Print the following types of violence on index cards:
- Burglary
- Acquaintance rape
- Homicide
- Suicide
- Gunshot wound
- Assault
- Child abuse
- Drug trafficking
- Fighting
- Carrying a weapon

2 For this strategy, obtain vests for up to half of the class. If possible, have half of the students in your class wear vests. If this is not possible, the strategy can still be done with one, two, or three vests.

3 Select five students. Give each of these students two of the index cards on which you have printed a type of violence. Explain to them in confidence that when you ask the other students to walk around the room they are to walk up to students who are not wearing a vest and hand these students one of the cards.

4 Have the class stand. Explain that the classroom is the community in which they live. Have the students who have vests wear them. They are to roam around the community. Explain that there is a gang in the community. This gang engages in random acts of violence. **Violence** is the use of force with the intent to harm oneself or another person. Explain to students that some of them may become victims of violence as they roam through the community. Others may become engaged in acts of violence. Allow students to roam for three to five minutes.

5 Have students form a circle. Explain that some of the students met up with gang members and became victims of violence or became engaged in acts of violence themselves. Ask the class which students were affected by violence and which seemed to be protected. They will recognize that the students wearing vests were not given the index cards.

6 Explain that some of the students were wearing violence-proof vests. Although the violence-proof vests are not a guarantee that they will not be victims or participants in violence, the vests afford some protection. The violence-proof vests indicated that the students wearing them:
- have good relationship skills;
- demonstrate self-loving behavior;
- express feelings in healthful ways;
- use stress-management skills;
- use conflict-resolution skills;
- are drug free;
- have positive self-esteem;
- choose healthful behaviors;
- engage in healthful relationships;
- make responsible decisions;
- use resistance skills when appropriate;
- demonstrate character;
- participate in positive ways within the community;
- abide by laws;
- avoid persons who engage in harmful and violent behavior;
- avoid risk situations.

509

7 Explain that the students who did not wear vests were at risk. These students participated in risk factors and were thus vulnerable to violence. Some of the risk factors in which they participated were the following:
- using alcohol and other drugs;
- being involved in drug sales, purchasing, or trafficking;
- exhibiting antisocial behavior;
- having an available firearm;
- being impulsive when arguing;
- having witnessed violence in the family;
- experiencing poverty and hopelessness;
- having been exposed to violence in the media;
- belonging to a gang;
- belonging to a cult.

8 Summarize by emphasizing the need to protect oneself from violence. Several years ago, the frequency of violence in the United States was approximately 1 incident per 1,000 persons. Today, the frequency is nearly 75 incidents per 1,000 persons. Avoiding risk factors and practicing protective factors is responsible behavior.

Evaluation:

Have students write pamphlets titled, "Are you at risk?" in which they identify ten risk factors that increase the likelihood of becoming a victim or participant in violence.

Violence Prevention

PULLING AWAY

Objective:

Students will describe how to use school and community interventions for the treatment of problems associated with the use of alcohol, tobacco, and illegal drugs.

Life Skills:

I will gain information about places that offer intervention and treatment for problems associated with the use of alcohol, tobacco, and illegal drugs.
I will seek help for myself, family members, or friends when problems with the use of alcohol, tobacco, or illegal drugs exist.

Materials:

Paper, pencil, wrist bands, velcro, needle, thread, name tags

Motivation:

1 Prepare for this lesson as follows. Obtain a wrist band for each student in your class. Ask a local sporting good store to supply them at no charge. On half of the wrist bands plus 10%, sew a piece of velcro.

2 Divide the class into two equal groups. Give group #1 a wrist band with velcro attached to it. Ask these students to wear the wrist band with the piece of velcro facing outward on the outer wrist (see illustration on next page). Give each of these students a name tag. They are to write the name of a drug on the name tag and wear it. Names for drugs might include: alcohol, cigarettes, smokeless tobacco, cocaine, crack, marijuana, heroin, amphetamines, barbiturates, hashish, etc.

3 Give each student in group #2 the remaining wrist bands to wear. Some of these students will have wrist bands with velcro while others will not. Those who have the wrist bands with velcro are to wear the wrist band with the

piece of velcro facing outward on the outer wrist.

4 Explain to students that they are going to circulate around the room. Those students who are drugs are going to introduce themselves to the other students. When a student from group #1 introduces himself/herself to a student in group #2, (s)he is to press her outer wrist (where the wrist band is worn) to the outer wrist of the other student (where his/her wrist band is worn.) If the wrist bands attach securely to one another, the students are to keep them that way. If the wrist bands do not attach, the students in group #2 are free to move away.

5 Explain that some of the students in group #2 became attached to a drug. In other words, they became dependent and could not move freely away. At first, every drug-dependent person experiences a honeymoon with drugs. During the honeymoon period, the drug user can still control the level of use of the drug. But then there becomes an attachment or dependence on the drug. **Physical dependence** is the result of frequent and increased use of drugs, and it can result in changes in brain chemistry causing a functional demand for a particular drug. Many drugs, including alcohol, cocaine, and heroin, can cause dependent persons to experience withdrawal symptoms on cessation of drug use. Experiencing withdrawal is evidence that a person is physically dependent on the drug.

6 Explain psychological dependence. **Psychological dependence** is a condition evidenced by an altered state of mind on which chemically-dependent persons come to depend. Drug users report taking drugs to enjoy a momentary thrill, to temporarily allay despair, to find a short cut to success, or just because it feels good. Chemically-dependent persons frequently report that eventually they take drugs because sobriety itself is uncomfortable and unbearable.

7 While the students are attached, explain that persons who are chemically dependent are usually in a state of denial. They do not admit that they have an attachment to harmful drugs. Intervention often means getting professional help. A confrontation may be arranged. During a **confrontation**, persons who know and are affected by the person meet together face-to-face with the person to describe the effects that his/her drug use is having. The purpose of the confrontation is to get the person to admit that (s)he has a problem that must be treated.

8 Have students pull away from the velcro attachment. Explain that the first step in pulling away during treatment is often undergoing detoxification. **Detoxification** is the process in which a chemically-dependent person withdraws from drugs. The person who is chemically dependent is given assistance with the craving and depression that usually accompan-

ies this withdrawal. Detoxification helps people get off drugs, and treatment keeps them off.

9 After detoxification, persons who are chemically dependent need to use school and community resources to stay drug free. On the chalkboard, list specific resources that are available for such persons:
- school counseling or support groups
- hospitals
- therapeutic communities
- AA
- Alateen
- Alanon

Evaluation:

Students will design pamphlets describing school and community resources available for treatment of problems associated with the use of alcohol, tobacco, and illegal drugs.

Violence Prevention

MOST-WANTED LIST

Objective:

Students will discuss the role citizens can play in eradicating drug sales and trafficking in the community.

Life Skills:

I will follow laws regarding the use of harmful drugs.
I will not purchase or seek illegal drugs.
I will avoid being with persons who purchase or sell illegal drugs.
I will avoid being in situations in which illegal drugs are purchased or sold.
I will support laws related to abuse, purchase, and sale of illegal drugs.

Materials:

Paper and pencil

Motivation:

1 Introduce the topic of drug trafficking. **Drug trafficking** involves purchasing or selling illegal drugs. Drug trafficking is a crime and is associated with increased incidence of violence. Often, innocent bystanders are harmed.

2 Ask students to brainstorm a list of ways that they can support law enforcement and eradicate drug trafficking in their community. List these on the chalkboard. Some suggestions might be: be aware of laws, be respectful of police officers, avoid using drugs, avoid being around persons who use drugs, avoid being around persons who sell drugs, avoid being near places where drugs are purchased or sold, spend time with caring adults, know where help is available for persons who abuse drugs, encourage friends to be drug free, encourage friends to avoid persons who sell drugs, and encourage friends to avoid being near places where drugs are purchased or sold. It may be possible to discuss specifics for your community such as places to avoid.

3 Ask students if they have ever seen or read a "Most-Wanted List." There may be such a list in your newspaper. The list will contain the names and/or pictures of persons who are wanted for serious crimes such as drug trafficking, homicide, assault, etc. Ask students why law enforcement authorities want to apprehend these persons as soon as possible. Why do these persons pose a threat to the community?

4 Explain that the class will now develop a "Most-Wanted List." Each student will write a description of a person for this list. However, this list will be somewhat different from the list you have just discussed. This "Most-Wanted List" will include descriptions of citizens who play a role in eradicating drug sales and trafficking in the community. Students have a variety of options when writing their descriptions of a citizen who qualifies for this list. For example, a police officer might be engaged in activities that help eradicate drug sales and trafficking. A student writing a description of a police officer for the "Most-Wanted List" might describe the specific duties of the police officer. A student might select a parent in the community who displays a SAFE HOME sign in his/her window as a person who plays a role. The student might describe how young persons might seek safety in this home. Encourage students to select from a variety of roles that citizens play: responsible parent, coach, teacher, police officer, juvenile detention officer, rehabilitation person, judge, citizen who is on a jury, etc.

5 After students have written their descriptions of citizens to be placed on a "Most-Wanted List," have them share them with the class. Pretend that you are having a television show to inform the community of persons on the "Most-Wanted List."

Evaluation:

Explain to students that each of them has been nominated for the "Most Wanted List" for citizens who play a role in eradicating drug abuse and trafficking in the community. They are to write a paragraph in which they explain, "I qualify for being selected as a citizen on the 'Most-Wanted List' for playing a role in eradicating drug sales and trafficking because. . . ."

Multicultural Infusion:

Explain that the community in which you live is made up of citizens of a variety of ethnic backgrounds. Have students of the same background work together to identify a person in the community who is a model citizen. Have them describe the role this person plays in keeping the community safe. They are to write a nomination for this person to be recognized as an exemplary citizen. Have the groups share the nominations they have written. Emphasize the importance of recognizing and affirming persons of different backgrounds.

Grades 9–12
• Objective 19

HIV FOOTBALL

Objective:

Students will describe ways in which drug use increases the likelihood of HIV infection.

Life Skills:

I will not use illegal drugs.
I will avoid being around persons who use illegal drugs.

Materials:

Five sheets of red poster board cut out in the shape of t-shirts, eight sheets of white poster board cut out in the shape of t-shirts, marker, string

Motivation:

1 On each of five sheets of red poster board, outline a t-shirt with a marker. Punch two holes in the "t-shirt" on each side of the neck and insert string through each hole so that the "t-shirt" can be worn like a billboard. On the front of each of the "t-shirts" in large letters should be written one of five terms. The five terms are: skin, helper T cell, B cell, antibody, and macrophage. Written on the back of each t-shirt should be information about each term. For skin, you may state, "I'm the first line of defense." Helper T cell will state, "I send a signal to B cells to tell them to make antibodies." B cell will state, "I produce antibodies." Antibody will state, "I destroy pathogens so that macrophages can digest them." Macrophages will state, "I will surround pathogens and digest them." Be sure to number each "t-shirt" so it looks authentic. You can number them as follows: skin, #40; helper T cell, #58; B cell, #60; antibody, #65; and macrophage, #72.

2 On each of eight sheets of white poster board, outline a t-shirt with a marker following the same directions as in step 1. On the front of these t-shirts in large letters should be written the following eight terms: pathogen, HIV, HIV, HIV, HIV, AIDS dementia complex, Kaposi's sarcoma, and pneumocystis carinii pneumonia. Written on the back of each t-shirt should be information about each term. For pathogen, you may state, "I am a disease-causing germ." For each of the four t-shirts with HIV, you may state, "I am a virus that destroys infection-fighting helper T cells." AIDS dementia complex will state, "I am a mental disorder caused by the destruction of brain cells." Kaposi's sarcoma will state, "I am a type of cancer." Pneumocystis carinii pneumonia will state, "I am a type of pneumonia."

3 Select thirteen students to play HIV football. Five students will be wearing the red t-shirts. They will be the defensive unit on a football team. Ask the class to name a team of its choice. Eight students will wear the white t-shirts. They will be the offensive unit on a football team. Have each team huddle and then break out of the huddle.

4 Explain that you are a sportscaster at a big game today. You are going to introduce the two teams that will play for the championship. First, introduce the team that will defend the body. Introduce them in order—skin, helper T cell, B cell, antibody, and macrophage. As you introduce each student, (s)he is to tell what (s)he will do in today's game. For example, you will say loudly, "First, we have #40—SKIN." The student wearing this t-shirt will respond, "I'm going to be tough in today's game. I'm the first line of defense." Second, introduce the offensive team that will destroy the body in order—pathogen, HIV, AIDS dementia complex, Kaposi's sarcoma, and pneumocystis carinii pneumonia. As you introduce each student, (s)he is to tell what (s)he will do in today's game. Mention that the offensive team brought some extra HIV players for today's game in anticipation of risk behaviors during the contest.

5 Now the game begins. Have the defensive unit line up in order—skin, helper T cell, B cell, antibody, and macrophage. Explain that the body is very healthy because of healthful behaviors. Have the pathogen approach the skin. The student who is the skin has his/her arms spread wide. Indicate that the skin has protected the body. There are no breaks in the skin and pathogen cannot enter.

6 Now have the pathogen approach the skin again. Explain that the body is run down and that pathogen gets past the skin. Have the student who is the pathogen approach the student who is the helper T cell. Helper T cell says loudly, "I am going to send a signal to B cell." Then the student who is B cell says, "I am going to make antibodies." Then the student who is antibody says, "I am going to destroy pathogens so that macrophages can digest them." Then the student who is macrophage puts his/her arms around pathogen and says, "I will surround pathogen and digest pathogen."

7 Explain that this is what happens to most pathogens that are on the offense against the body's defense system. But, usually they are unable to score a disease because of the way the defense works together. However, there is a very special pathogen called HIV. Have the student who is HIV explain what HIV does. Explain that the only way the body's defense can protect HIV from scoring is to avoid risk behavior. One kind of risk behavior is sharing a needle, syringe, and/or injection equipment to inject drugs. This is a risk behavior because traces of blood containing HIV from a person who has injected drugs can be left on the needle, syringe, and/or injection equipment that was used. When another person uses the needle, syringe, and/or injection equipment with traces of blood containing HIV on it, the HIV gets into his/her body.

8 Have one of the persons wearing an HIV t-shirt approach the body's defense team. Explain that there was no risk behavior. As a result, there is no break in the skin through which HIV can enter the bloodstream. The body is protected.

9 Now explain that risk behavior has taken place. Have skin step aside as the student with HIV approaches. This time the student who is HIV will approach the helper T cell. Explain that (s)he will put his/her arms around helper T cell to indicate that HIV is attaching to helper T cell. Have the three other students who are HIV enter the body. Explain that HIV is multiplying inside the body and that the number of helper T cells is being reduced. As the number of helper T cells is lowered, the body becomes susceptible to opportunistic infections. Have the students who are AIDS dementia complex, Kaposi's sarcoma, and pneumocystis carinii pneumonia enter the body. As each enters the body, (s)he should state what (s)he is. For example, the student who is AIDS dementia would say, "I am a mental disorder caused by the destruction of brain cells."

10 You may want to repeat HIV football for added comprehension.

Evaluation:

Have students make two diagrams to illustrate the body's defenses and how they work when 1) a pathogen enters the body, and 2) HIV enters the body.

Inclusion:

Have students with special needs help you make the t-shirts. Labeling the backs of the t-shirts may provide extra opportunity to study the vocabulary words for the immune system and for the opportunistic infections.

THE DATING GAME

Objective:

Students will evaluate the effects of using drugs on healthful and responsible sexuality.

Life Skills:

I will not drink alcohol or use other harmful drugs.
I will abstain from sexual intercourse.

Materials:

Three scripts written for students who are the bachelors, one script written for the bachelorette, four scripts written as introductions to the audience, index cards

Motivation:

1 For this teaching strategy, you will be the host/hostess for The Dating Game. Prepare four index cards that you can use to introduce the bachelorette and three bachelors. The descriptions for each are as follows:

Bachelorette: Our bachelorette is Camille. Camille is a high school student from. . . . (provide the name of your high school). She is not involved in school activities. Camille frequently skips school and has been expelled for drinking alcohol during lunch period. Camille is somewhat confused about male/female relationships as she lives with her mother and her mother's boyfriend, and they frequently argue. Her mother's boyfriend drinks often and is physically abusive toward Camille's mother. Camille has difficulty relating to men. She wanted to play The Dating Game to meet someone to date.

Bachelor #1: Bachelor #1 is Robert. Robert is president of the senior class at. . . . (provide name of your high school). He is a leader in the school. One of his hobbies is music and he plays in the school band. Rob has many

friends as he is outgoing, warm, and friendly. He has a part-time job and is saving money for college. Rob would like to meet a female who is a warm, caring classmate.

Bachelor #2: Bachelor #2 is Ricardo. Ricardo just moved to this school. He has joined two school clubs in order to become involved in school activities. At his previous school, Ricardo held the school record for number of take-downs in a single season of wrestling. He works out daily to stay in top condition for the wrestling season. He is being recruited by several colleges. Ricardo enjoys dancing. He wants to meet a female who enjoys dancing and has many friends.

Bachelor #3: Bachelor #3 is Gregory. Gregory is not involved in school activities. In fact, Gregory is often truant from school. He spends time with two friends who have dropped out of school. They enjoy drinking and trying to get into bars with fake IDs. When Gregory drinks, he becomes very loud and argumentative. He likes to be in charge. Gregory wants to meet a female who will cater to his demands. He thinks a real man is in control.

2 You will need to prepare index cards for the bachelorette and three bachelors. The bachelorette will ask the bachelors the following questions and the bachelors will give the following responses.

Bachelorette:
Question 1. What is your best personality characteristic?
Question 2. What are you looking for in the ideal date?
Question 3. What is your idea of fun on a date?

Bachelor #1:
Response 1. I am reliable. You can depend on me. I always tell the truth and follow through on what I say I will do.

Response 2. I am looking for a female who is honest and loyal. I like someone who takes care of herself and has an attractive appearance. She has to understand my busy schedule with band practice and my job.

Response 3. I love music and I would like to take you to a concert. Or, we could get some ice cream and you could come over to my house and listen to CDs.

Bachelor #2:

Response 1. I am fun. My friends at my other school always said I have a great sense of humor. I also like to treat ladies well.

Response 2. I am looking for someone who likes to have fun and wants a guy who can be a good friend. It would be an added plus if she enjoyed watching me wrestle. I would also like for her to play sports. You know, volleyball, lacrosse, softball, or something. I would watch her too.

Response 3. I would like to dance with you. I know all the latest steps. If you aren't hot at dancing, I can teach you. I also like movies. We could go to the video store and check one out that we both like. My mother makes a mean pizza that we could share while we watch a movie. Besides, she always likes to meet my new friends.

Bachelor #3:

Response 1. I am a take-charge guy. No one messes with Gregory and no one is going to mess with my woman. I am tough.

Response 2. I want a real good-looking woman to be seen with. I want her to tell me how great I am. And, I want her to be available

when I want to be with her. Her school activities cannot interfere.

Response 3. I know a bar where I can get you in and we can get some drinks. You can get loosened up. Then we can go back to my house. I live with my dad. He has the night shift so he won't be there. Get the idea?

3 Play The Dating Game. Remind the students who have volunteered to be the contestants to stick to the scripts and the roles they are to play. Explain that they can use their own words.

4 Tell the class that you are going to play The Dating Game. Introduce the three bachelors. Then introduce the bachelorette. If possible, separate them in front of the class so they are not looking at each other.

5 Ask each of the bachelors to say "Hello" to Camille. Then ask Camille to begin asking her questions to each of the bachelors. She is to ask Question #1 to each of the bachelors before asking Question #2, and then ask Question #2 before asking each bachelor Question #3.

6 When the questioning is completed, ask the class which bachelor they believe Camille will select—bachelor #1? bachelor #2? or bachelor #3? Have the class give reasons for the selection.

7 Have Camille announce her selection. She chose bachelor #3. She says she likes a man who is in control. He sounds powerful and masculine. Explain that her choice should not be a surprise. Camille is confused about male/female relationships. Her frequent drinking interferes with her ability to make responsible decisions. She has observed her mother's relationship with her boyfriend. The mother's boyfriend is controlling. He drinks too much. Bachelor #3 also has a habit of drinking. He likes being in control. He also perceives that getting Camille to drink would "loosen her up" up" for the time he planned to spend alone with her.

8 Discuss how drinking alcohol "loosens someone up" and interferes with decision-making. Explain that alcohol is a depressant. It depresses the parts of the brain responsible for reasoning and judgment. Suppose a young person wants to follow specific guidelines and adhere to specific values. This might include abstaining from sexual intercourse. It becomes more difficult to do so after a person has been drinking alcohol.

9 Discuss the importance of selecting friends of the opposite sex as well as of the same sex who avoid drinking alcohol and who have set guidelines for their sexual behavior. Have the class examine the qualities possessed by the two bachelors whom Camille did not select. Why would these two bachelors be better choices for Camille?

Evaluation:

Have students pretend that they are going to be one of the contestants on The Dating Game. They are to describe their good qualities, the qualities they look for in someone else, and the activities that they enjoy. The activities must be drug free and must not facilitate sexual involvement.

TEACHING MASTERS AND STUDENT MASTERS

In writing *Drugs, Alcohol, and Tobacco: Totally Awesome Teaching Strategies*, the authors had two types of audiences in mind—the educator and the learner. The educator might be a professional educator, a community leader, a parent, a person with a religious affiliation, or another responsible person charged with the task of drug education. For the educator, it is the desire of the authors to provide knowledge and understanding of drug education in spiritual, mental, psychological, and physical terms along with a curriculum framework and means for delivering this education. Most books present only facts and figures. For the learner, it is the authors' desire to accommodate a variety of learning modalities in terms and ways that meet the needs and interests of students of a variety of age spans.

To enhance both the presentation and learning of the materials included in this book, the authors provide materials in visual formats as well as in written formats. These specially designed figures and tables are included throughout the book where the related written materials are presented, visually reinforcing factual information, key concepts, and strategies. The figures and tables in Chapters 1 through 16 that the authors deemed appropriate for the classroom are reproduced as full-page masters in this chapter.

USING TEACHING MASTERS AND STUDENT MASTERS

The masters in Chapter 19 can be reproduced as transparencies and used with a transparency projector, or they can be reproduced as handouts. In any case, these visuals can be used in a variety of ways, depending on the presenter and the nature of the audience. The presenter might be a professional educator working with students, a school administrator meeting with parents and families to share background information and knowledge of the curriculum, or another responsible adult presenting the theme and an overview of the drug education curriculum.

Even within the classroom, these masters can be used in a variety of ways. They may be used to introduce topics, to reinforce concepts, and to summarize ideas. They also may be used for evaluation purposes. Tests can be designed around these visuals. Also, students may be asked to demonstrate their comprehension of concepts by using the masters as the basis for a summary presentation to the class.

Some general guidelines should be considered in using these masters in presentation situations. Students and other members of the audience should be seated in such a way that they are able to view the projected materials. If the group is especially large, the master should be reproduced in such a way that the type or other visual material is large enough to be read and distinguished by everyone present. When the figures and tables are reproduced as transparencies or handouts, the copyright information must be included on the page. Professionals using these masters in any form in presentations with other professionals should credit the source of the material. Reproduction of this part of the book in another book or as part of a curriculum is prohibited without the written consent of the publisher.

Figure 1-1
Wellness Scale Factors That
Influence Health and Well-Being

Risk behaviors	Wellness behaviors
Risk situations	Healthful situations
Destructive relationships	Healthful relationships
Irresponsible decision making	Responsible decision making
Lack of resistance skills	Use of resistance skills
Negative self-esteem	Positive self-esteem

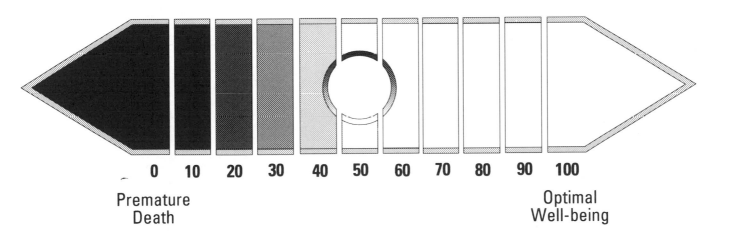

Premature Death

Optimal Well-being

Health status is the sum total of the positive and negative influences of behaviors, situations, relationships, decisions, use of resistance skills, and self-esteem.

Table 1-2

Responsible Decision-Making Model

1. **Clearly describe the situation you face.**
   If no immediate decision is necessary, describe the situation in writing. If an immediate decision must be made, describe the situation out loud or to yourself in a few short sentences. Being able to describe a situation in your own words is the first step in clarifying the question.

2. **List possible actions that can be taken.**
   Again, if no immediate decision is necessary, make a list of possible actions. If an immediate decision must be made, state possible actions out loud or to yourself.

3. **Share your list of possible actions with a responsible adult such as someone who protects community laws and demonstrates character.**
   When no immediate action is necessary, sharing possible actions with a responsible adult is helpful. This person can examine your list to see if it is inclusive. Responsible adults have a wide range of experiences that can allow them to see situations maturely. They may add possibilities to the list of actions. In some situations, it is possible to delay decision making until there is an opportunity to seek counsel with a responsible adult. If an immediate decision must be made, explore possibilities. Perhaps a telephone call can be made. Whenever possible, avoid skipping this step.

4. **Carefully evaluate each possible action using six criteria.**
   Ask each of the six questions to learn which decision is best.
   a. Will this decision result in an action that will protect my health and the health of others?
   b. Will this decision result in an action that will protect my safety and the safety of others?
   c. Will this decision result in an action that will protect the laws of the community?
   d. Will this decision result in an action that shows respect for myself and others?
   e. Will this decision result in an action that follows guidelines set by responsible adults such as my parents or guardian?
   f. Will this decision result in an action that will demonstrate that I have good character and moral values?

5. **Decide which action is responsible and most appropriate.**
   After applying the six criteria, compare the results. Which decision best meets the six criteria?

6. **Act in a responsible way and evaluate the results.**
   Follow through with this decision with confidence. The confidence comes from paying attention to the six criteria.

Table 1-3
Model for Using Resistance Skills

1. **Use assertive behavior.**

   There is a saying, "You get treated the way you 'train' others to treat you." Assertive behavior is the honest expression of thoughts and feelings without experiencing anxiety or threatening others. When you use assertive behavior, you show that you are in control of yourself and the situation. You say NO clearly and firmly. As you speak, you look directly at the person(s) pressuring you. Aggressive behavior is the use of words and/or actions that tend to communicate disrespect. This behavior only antagonizes others. Passive behavior is the holding back of ideas, opinions, and feelings. Holding back may result in harm to you, others, or the environment.

2. **Avoid saying, "NO, thank you."**

   There is never a need to thank a person who pressures you into doing something that might be harmful, unsafe, illegal, or disrespectful or which may result in disobeying parents or displaying a lack of character and moral values.

3. **Use nonverbal behavior that matches verbal behavior.**

   Nonverbal behavior is the use of body language or actions rather than words to express feelings, ideas, and opinions. Your verbal NO should not be confused by misleading actions. For example,

   if you say NO to cigarette smoking, do not pretend to take a puff of a cigarette in order to resist pressure.

4. **Influence others to choose responsible behavior.**

   When a situation poses immediate danger, remove yourself. If no immediate danger is present, try to turn the situation into a positive one. Suggest alternative, responsible ways to behave. Being a positive role model helps you feel good about yourself and helps gain the respect of others.

5. **Avoid being in situations in which there will be pressure to make harmful decisions.**

   There is no reason to put yourself into situations in which you will be pressured or tempted to make unwise decisions. Think ahead.

6. **Avoid being with persons who choose harmful actions.**

   Your reputation is the impression that others have of you, your decisions, and your actions. Associate with persons known for their good qualities and character in order to avoid being misjudged.

7. **Resist pressure to engage in illegal behavior.**

   You have a responsibility to protect others and to protect the laws of your community. Demonstrate good character and moral values.

Figure 1-4
Model of Health and Well-Being

Physical Health

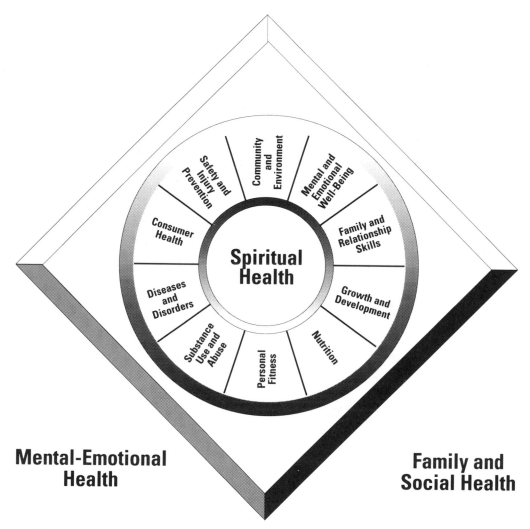

Mental-Emotional Health

Family and Social Health

Health and well-being depend on:

* Choosing healthful behaviors
* Participating in healthful situations
* Developing healthful relationships
* Making responsible decisions
* Using resistance skills
* Developing positive self-esteem

Figure 1-5
Protective Factors That Serve as a Coat of Armor and Promote Resiliency

Protective factors that promote resiliency are:

* Being reared in a loving, functional family
* Being involved in school activities
* Having positive self-esteem
* Having clearly defined goals and plans to reach them
* Having close friends who do not abuse drugs
* Regularly practicing one's faith
* Feeling a sense of accomplishment at school
* Having adult role models including parents who do not abuse drugs
* Having a healthful attitude about competition and athletic performance
* Being committed to following the rules of the community
* Having a plan to cope with life stressors

Figure 1-6

Risk Factors That Make Young Persons Vulnerable to Drug Use

Risk factors are:

* Being reared in a dysfunctional family
* Having negative self-esteem
* Being unable to resist peer pressure
* Having difficulty mastering developmental tasks
* Being economically disadvantaged
* Lacking faith experiences and fellowship
* Having a genetic background with a predisposition to chemical dependency
* Experiencing family disruption
* Experiencing depression
* Experiencing pressure to succeed in athletics
* Having difficulty achieving success in school
* Having attention deficit hyperactive disorder
* Having immature character disorder
* Having borderline personality tendencies

528

Table 1-7
The Family Continuum

The Family Continuum depicts the degree to which a family promotes skills needed for loving and responsible relationships.

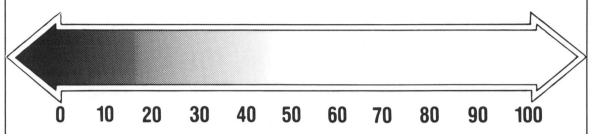

| 0 | 10 | 20 | 30 | 40 | 50 | 60 | 70 | 80 | 90 | 100 |

Dysfunctional Families
- Self-destructive behavior
- Confused attitudes regarding sexuality
- Irresponsible and harmful drug use
- Difficulty communicating and expressing feelings in healthful ways
- Confused value system
- Inadequate decision-making skills
- Inadequate coping skills and reliance on instant gratification

Loving, Functional Families
- Self-loving behavior
- Healthful attitudes toward sexuality
- Healthful attitudes and practices regarding drug use
- Healthful ways to express feelings and to communicate
- Faith and moral values
- Responsible decision-making skills
- Coping skills with the ability to delay gratification when necessary

Figure 1-8
The Roots and Characteristics of Codependence

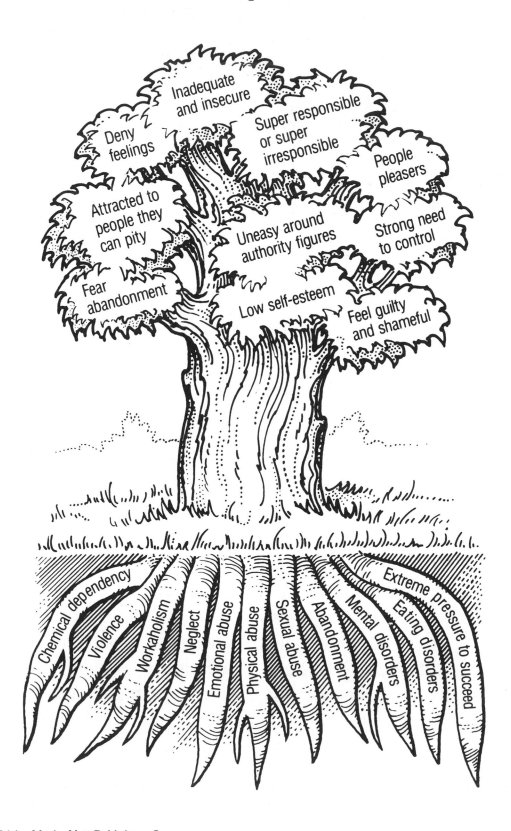

Table 1-9
High School Students* Reporting Lifetime Use of Substances by Gender and Grade—1990 Youth Risk Behavior Survey

Student Category	Substance		
	Alcohol (%)	Marijuana (%)	Cocaine (%)
Gender			
Male	89.5	35.9	8.1
Female	86.7	27.0	5.2
Grade			
9th	82.6	20.6	3.6
10th	87.0	27.9	5.8
11th	90.1	34.7	7.6
12th	92.4	42.2	9.3
Total	88.1	31.4	6.6

Source: Centers for Disease Control. (1991). Alcohol and other drug use among high schools students—United States, 1990. *Morbidity and Mortality Weekly Report*, 40:776–777.

*Unweighted sample size = 11,631 students in grades 9–12.

Table 1-10

High School Students* Reporting Current[a] Use of Substances by Gender and Grade—1990 Youth Risk Behavior Survey

Student Category	Substance			
	Alcohol (%)	Heavy Drinking[b] (%)	Marijuana (%)	Cocaine (%)
Gender				
Male	62.2	43.5	16.9	3.3
Female	55.0	30.4	11.1	1.0
Grade				
9th	50.1	27.7	9.5	1.1
10th	57.0	35.7	13.5	2.4
11th	61.2	39.6	13.9	2.5
12th	65.6	44.0	18.5	2.3
Total	58.6	36.9	13.9	2.1

Source: Centers for Disease Control. (1991). Alcohol and other drug use among high schools students—United States, 1990. *Morbidity and Mortality Weekly Report*, 40:776–777.
*Unweighted sample size = 11,631 students in grades 9–12.
[a]Use during the 30 days preceding the survey.
[b]Consumed five or more drinks on at least one occasion during the 30 days preceding the survey.

Table 1-11

Use of Alcohol, Marijuana, and Cocaine in the Past 30 Days by Male High School Seniors*

Group	Substance			
	Alcohol (%)	Heavy Drinking[a] (%)	Marijuana (%)	Cocaine (%)
White American Males	72.3	48.1	25.0	5.6
African-American Males	49.2	24.0	18.5	2.6
Mexican-American Males	65.0	45.3	22.0	8.2
Puerto Rican & Other Latin-American Males	55.4	31.4	18.9	8.1
Asian-American Males	43.7	19.4	9.7	1.8
American Indian Males	69.0	48.1	27.6	7.3

Source: Adapted from Bachman, J.G., Wallace, J.M., O'Malley, P.M., Johnston, L.D., Kurth, C.L., and Neighbors, H.W. (1991) Racial/ethnic differences in smoking, drinking, and illicit drug use among American high school seniors, 1976–89. *American Journal of Public Health,* 81:372–377.

*The sample for this data consists of 73,527 high school seniors from the Monitoring the Future project conducted by the University of Michigan's Institute for Social Research. This data reflects the results of annual, nationally representative surveys conducted 1985–1989.

[a]Had five or more drinks in a row in the last two weeks.

Table 1-12

Use of Alcohol, Marijuana, and Cocaine in the Past 30 Days by Female High School Seniors*

Substance

Group	Alcohol (%)	Heavy Drinking[a] (%)	Marijuana (%)	Cocaine (%)
White American Females	66.6	31.3	19.8	4.1
African-American Females	32.8	9.3	9.9	1.3
Mexican-American Females	50.5	23.6	13.6	3.0
Puerto Rican & Other Latin-American Females	43.0	14.5	9.6	2.9
Asian-American Females	34.2	10.7	8.1	2.6
American Indian Females	60.2	33.7	23.9	9.2

Source: Adapted from Bachman, J.G., Wallace, J.M., O'Malley, P.M., Johnston, L.D., Kurth, C.L., and Neighbors, H.W. (1991) Racial/ethnic differences in smoking, drinking, and illicit drug use among American high school seniors, 1976–89. American Journal of Public Health, 81:372–377.
*The sample for this data consists of 73,527 high school seniors from the Monitoring the Future project conducted by the University of Michigan's Institute for Social Research. This data reflects the results of annual, nationally representative surveys conducted 1985–1989.
[a]Had five or more drinks in a row in the last two weeks.

Figure 1-13
Drug Education and Inner Well-Being

Inner well-being is a condition that results from:

* Having positive self-esteem
* Managing stress effectively
* Choosing healthful behaviors
* Choosing healthful situations
* Engaging in healthful relationships
* Making responsible decisions
* Using resistance skills when appropriate
* Demonstrating character
* Participating in the community
* Abiding by laws

Figure 2-1
Protective Factors Motivate Persons to Strive for Respectful, Caring, and Nonviolent Relationships

The following skills serve as protective factors:

* Identifying high-quality relationships
* Developing relationship skills
* Demonstrating self-loving behavior
* Expressing feelings in healthful ways
* Using stress-management skills
* Developing conflict-resolution skills
* Being drug free

Table 2-2
Spirit-Relationship Continuum

Spirit Range

| 0 | 10 | 20 | 30 | 40 | 50 | 60 | 70 | 80 | 90 | 100 |

usual range

Dispiriting Relationships	Inspiriting Relationships
unimportant	joyful
worthless	passionate
hopeless	dedicated
isolated	enthusiastic
frustrated	worthy
depressed	hopeful
bored	satisfied
anxious	meaningful
alienated	important
low self-esteem	high self-esteem

Figure 2-3
General Adaptation Syndrome

During the ALARM STAGE, the SYMPATHETIC NERVOUS SYSTEM prepares to meet the demand of the stressor.

During the RESISTANCE STAGE, the PARASYMPATHETIC NERVOUS SYSTEM attempts to return the body to a state of homeostasis.

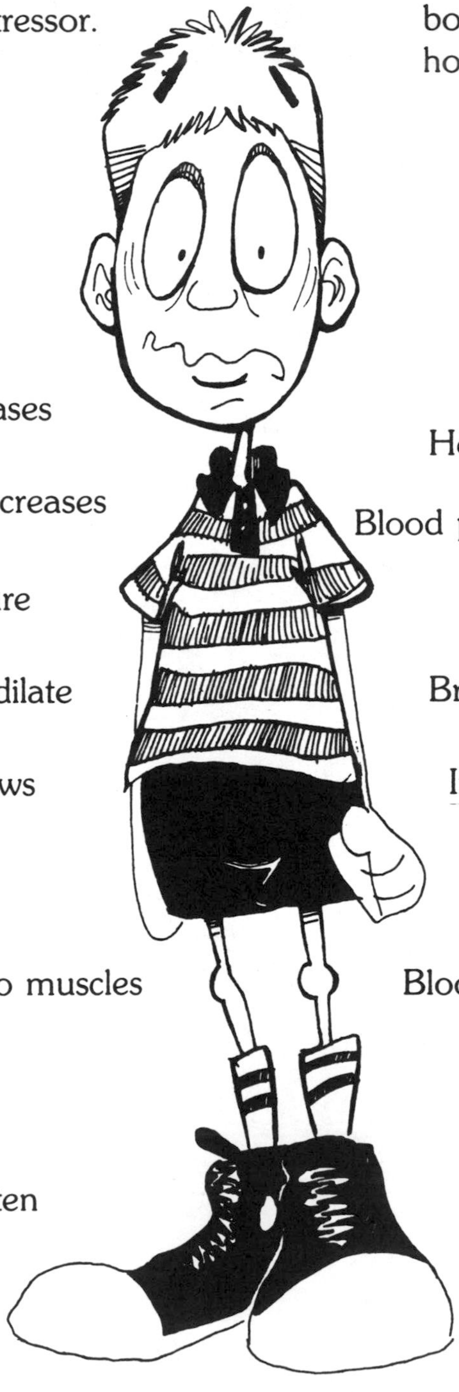

Pupils dilate

Pupils constrict

Hearing sharpens

Hearing is normal

Saliva decreases

Saliva increases

Heart rate increases

Heart rate decreases

Blood pressure increases

Blood pressure decreases

Bronchioles dilate

Bronchioles constrict

Digestion slows

Intestinal secretions increase is normal

Blood flow to muscles increases

Blood flow to muscles decreases

Muscles tighten

Muscles relax

Figure 2-4
Risk Factors Increase Vulnerability to Violent Behavior

The following factors are risk factors:

* Using alcohol or other drugs
* Being involved in drug sales, purchases, or trafficking
* Exhibiting antisocial behavior
* Having an available firearm
* Being impulsive when arguing
* Witnessing violence in the family
* Experiencing poverty and hopelessness
* Being exposed to violence in the media
* Belonging to a gang
* Belonging to a cult

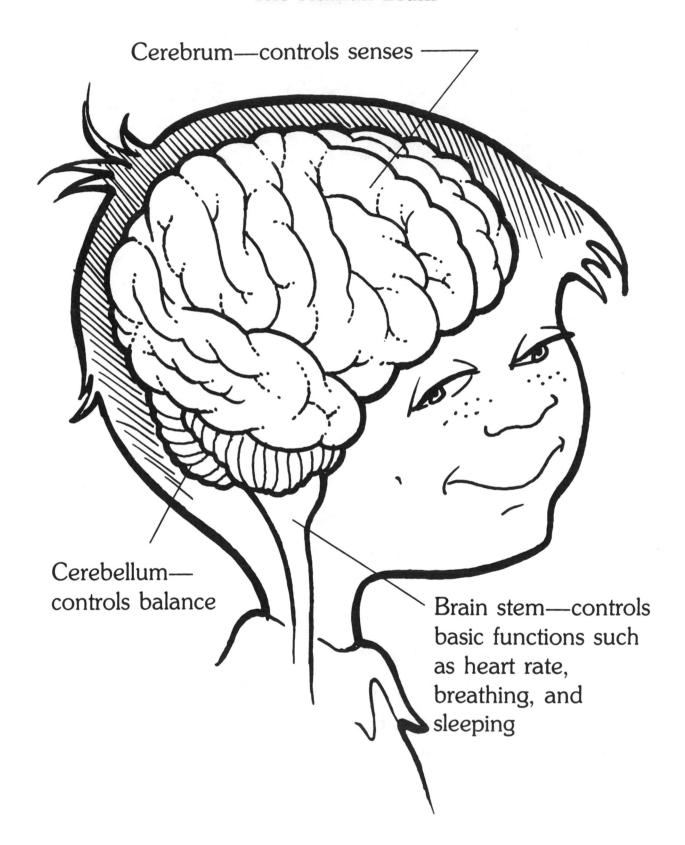

Figure 3-1
The Human Brain

Cerebrum—controls senses

Cerebellum—
controls balance

Brain stem—controls
basic functions such
as heart rate,
breathing, and
sleeping

540

Figure 3-2
The Nerve Cell

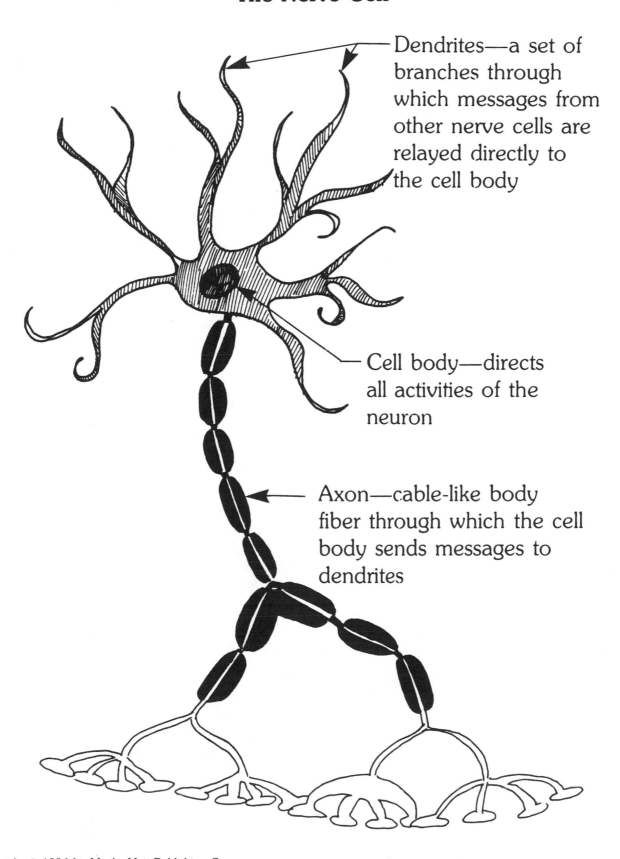

Dendrites—a set of branches through which messages from other nerve cells are relayed directly to the cell body

Cell body—directs all activities of the neuron

Axon—cable-like body fiber through which the cell body sends messages to dendrites

Figure 3-3
Methods of Drug Administration

Oral Ingestion

Inhalation

Injection

Absorption

Figure 4-1
Signs of Stimulant Withdrawal

Signs of withdrawal are:

* Irritability
* Weakness
* Depression
* Loss of concentration

Figure 4-2
Intravenous Cocaine Users Are At Risk
for Becoming Infected with HIV

Figure 4-3
Look-Alike Drugs

Figure 4-4
Sources of Caffeine

Figure 5-1
Barbiturate Use During Pregnancy

Figure 5-2
Symptoms of Withdrawal from Sedatives

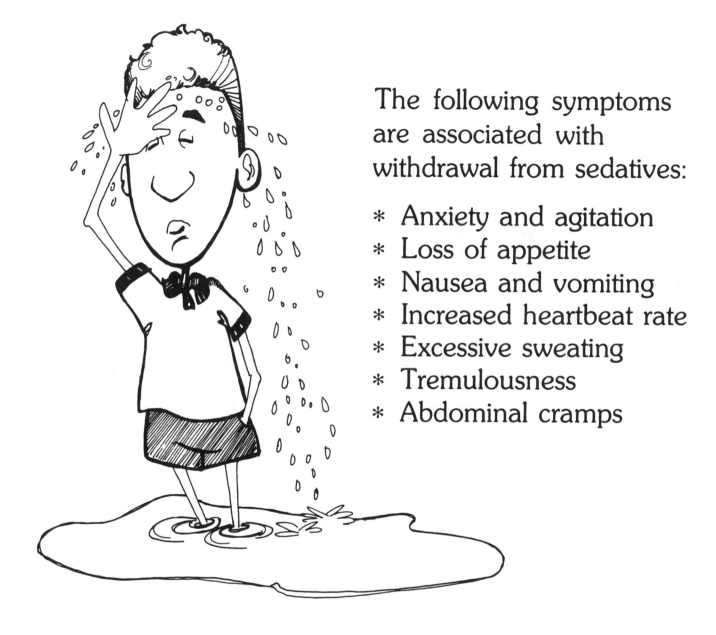

The following symptoms are associated with withdrawal from sedatives:

* Anxiety and agitation
* Loss of appetite
* Nausea and vomiting
* Increased heartbeat rate
* Excessive sweating
* Tremulousness
* Abdominal cramps

Figure 6-1
Narcotic Antagonists Block the Effects of Narcotics

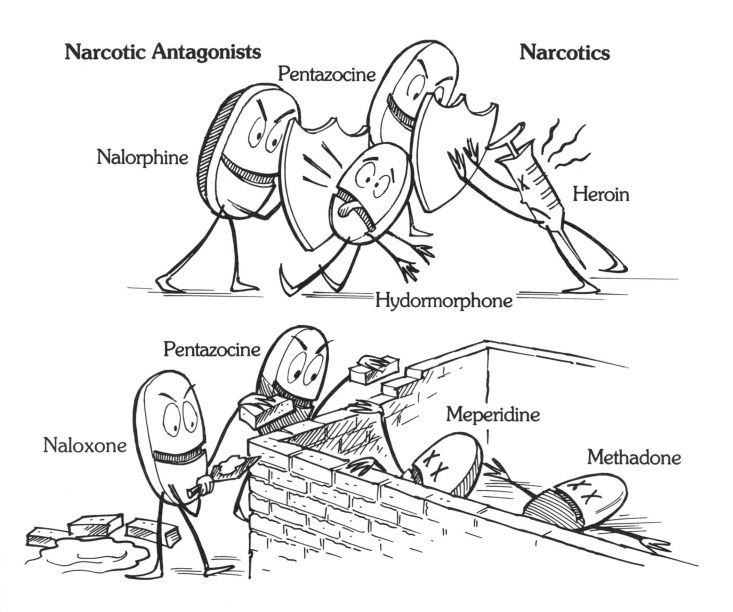

Figure 6-2
Effects of Narcotics

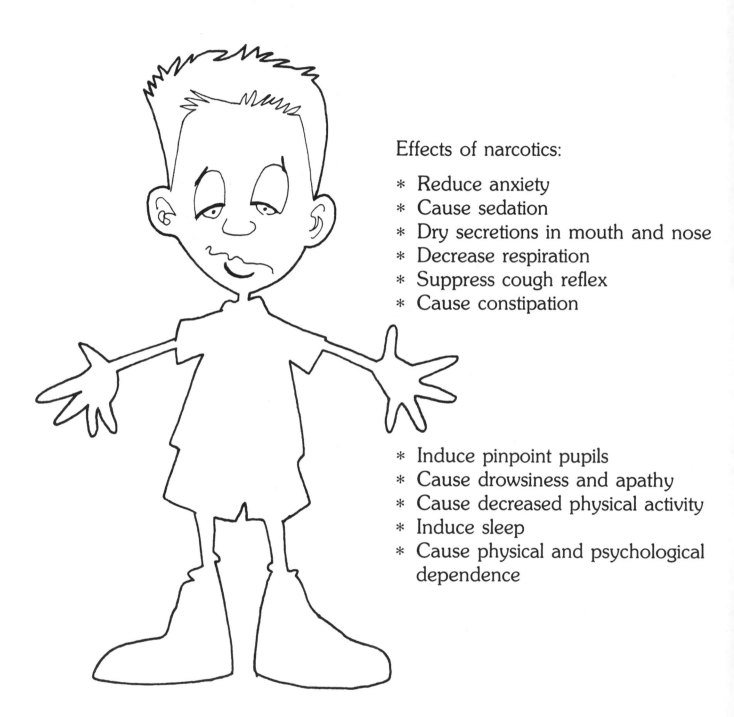

Effects of narcotics:

* Reduce anxiety
* Cause sedation
* Dry secretions in mouth and nose
* Decrease respiration
* Suppress cough reflex
* Cause constipation

* Induce pinpoint pupils
* Cause drowsiness and apathy
* Cause decreased physical activity
* Induce sleep
* Cause physical and psychological dependence

Figure 6-3
Risks to Newborns from Maternal Use of Narcotics

Risks to newborns:

* Low birth weight
* Lung disease
* Brain hemorrhage
* HIV infection
* Sudden infant death syndrome (SIDS)
* Withdrawal symptoms
* Poorly controlled responses

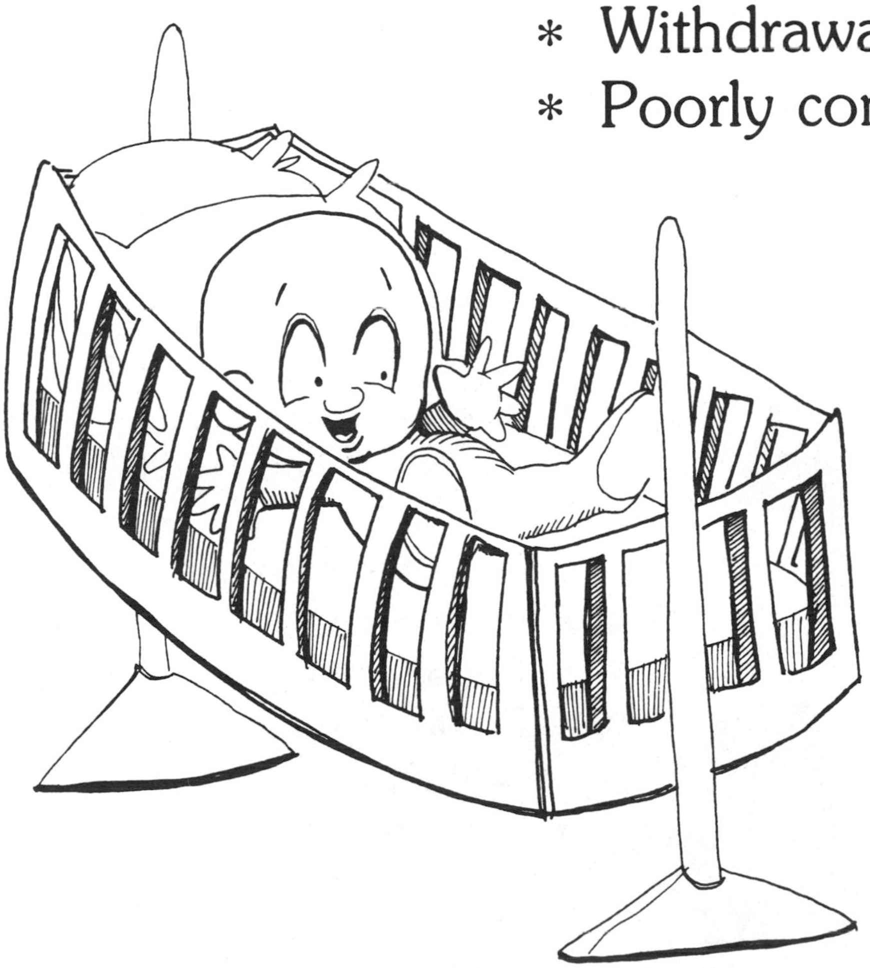

Figure 7-1
Effects of Marijuana

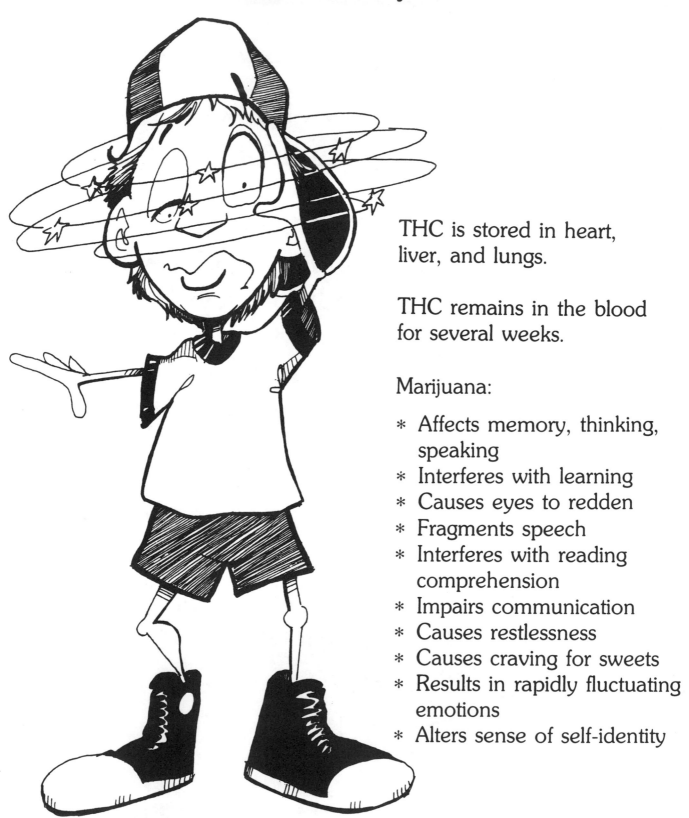

THC is stored in heart, liver, and lungs.

THC remains in the blood for several weeks.

Marijuana:

* Affects memory, thinking, speaking
* Interferes with learning
* Causes eyes to redden
* Fragments speech
* Interferes with reading comprehension
* Impairs communication
* Causes restlessness
* Causes craving for sweets
* Results in rapidly fluctuating emotions
* Alters sense of self-identity

Figure 7-2
Health Risks of Marijuana Use

Ten health risks of marijuana use:

10. Lung cancer
9. Chronic asthma
8. Bronchitis
7. Emphysema
6. Acute brain syndrome
5. Cannabis psychosis
4. Amotivational syndrome
3. Temporary sterility
2. Spontaneous abortion/stillbirth
1. Carbon monoxide levels to unborn

Figure 8-1
Hallucinogens Produce Marked Distortions in Perception

Lights appear BRIGHTER

Sounds appear LOUDER

Time passes very SLOWLY

Effects of hallucinogens:

* Impaired short-term memory
* Significant disturbances in judgment
* Euphoria

Figure 8-2
Psilocybin Is Derived from the Psilocybe Mushroom

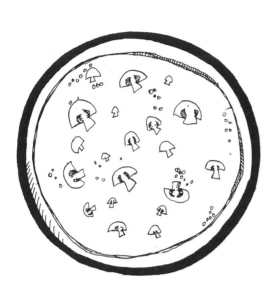

Ingesting a mushroom pizza may produce an enjoyable high.

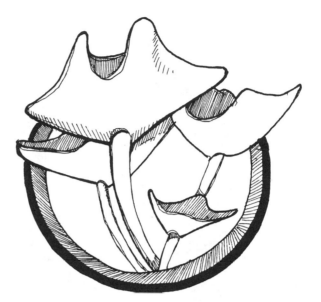

Ingesting psilocybin from a psilocybe mushroom results in a harmful high.

Figure 9-1
Inhalation of Chemical
Substances Is Dangerous

Some adverse effects of inhalants:

* Altered states of consciousness
* Changes in behaviors and toxic psychoses
* Seizures and sudden death
* Accidents
* Kidney and liver failure
* Heart muscle damage
* Skeletal muscle weakness
* Irritation in areas exposed directly to inhalants
* Brain and nerve damage
* Bone marrow suppression
* Leukemia (in benzene users)
* Lead poisoning (in gasoline sniffers)
* Fetal and infant abnormalities

Figure 9-2

Inhaling Nitrous Oxide Is No Laughing Matter

The Last Laugh.........

Some effects of nitrous oxide:

* Altered states of consciousness
* Changes in behavior
* Respiratory disturbances
* Coma
* Loss of motivation
* Nerve damage
* Loss of hearing
* Heart rhythm disturbance
* Kidney and liver disease
* Depressed bone marrow function
* Spontaneous miscarriage

Figure 10-1
Nasal Decongestants Are Available in Different Forms

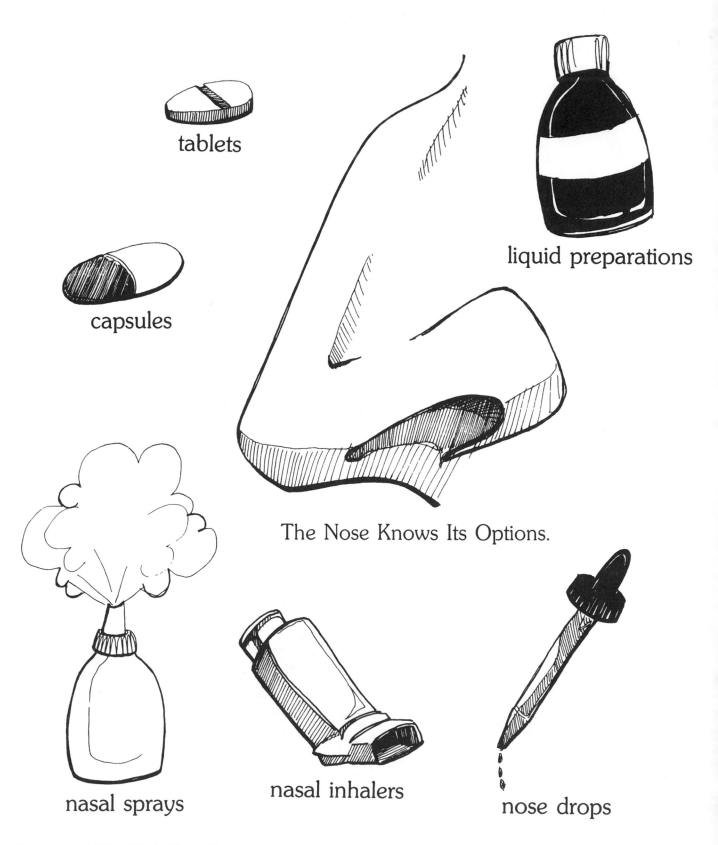

tablets

capsules

liquid preparations

The Nose Knows Its Options.

nasal sprays

nasal inhalers

nose drops

Figure 10-2
Over-the-Counter Drugs Are Available in Tamper-Resistant Packaging

Better Safe Than Sorry

Figure 11-1

Questions to Ask Your Physician About Prescription Drugs

* What is the name of the medicine? Write it down so you won't forget.

* What is the medicine supposed to do? (Make the pain go away? Get to the cause of the pain? Reduce fever? Lower blood pressure? Cure infection?)

* How much of the medicine should be taken?

* What side effects might occur?

* How should you take the medicine? Does "three times a day," mean morning, noon, and night? Should you take it before meals, with meals, or after meals? If the directions say "every six hours," do you have to get up during the night to take the medicine on time?

* How long should you take the medicine? If you stop just because you feel good, the symptoms and the disease may recur.

* Are there other medicines you should not take while you are taking this one?

* Are there any foods, beverages, or activities you should avoid?

* Should you avoid alcoholic beverages while taking the drug?

* Can the prescription be refilled without an appointment or does the doctor need to see you again?

* What should you do if you miss or skip a dose?

* Is the drug available in generic form?

* Is there any written information available about the drug?

* How long should you wait before reporting to your physician if there are no changes in your symptoms?

Figure 11-2

Females Who Smoke Cigarettes and Use Oral Contraceptives Have an Increased Risk of Heart Disease

oral contraceptives + cigarette smoking = increased risk of heart attack

Figure 12-1

Continued Use of Anabolic Steroids Poses Serious Health Consequences for Males and Females

Health consequences of steroid use:

* Acne
* Jaundice
* Trembling
* Swelling of feet or ankles
* Bad breath
* Reduction in HDLs
* High blood pressure
* Liver damage and cancers
* Aching joints
* Increased chance of injury to tendons

Figure 12-2

Discontinuing the Use of Steroids Can Result in Depression

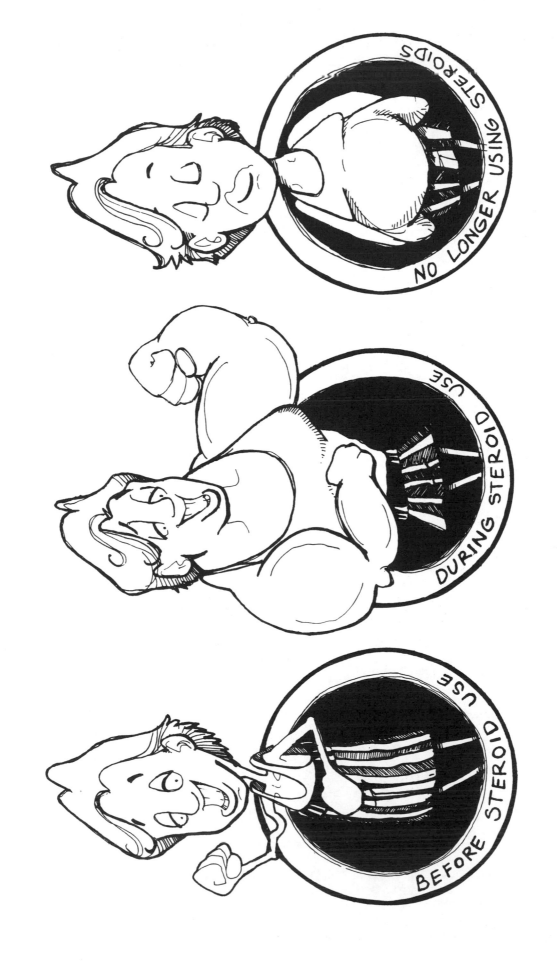

Figure 13-1
Alcohol-Related Dementia

Figure 13-2

Drinking and Driving: A Deadly Duo

The risk of a fatal crash, per mile driven, may be at least eight times higher for a drunk driver (BAC of 0.10 or greater) than for a sober one.

Figure 13-3

Children of Parents with Alcoholism Need Help

Figure 14-1
Warning: Sidestream Smoke Is Harmful to Health

567

Figure 14-2
Warning: Smokeless Tobacco Is Harmful to Health

Smokeless tobacco causes:

* Oral cancer
* Leukoplakia
* Gum recession
* Abrasions of tooth enamel
* Bad breath

Figure 14-3
Smoking Cessation Programs Help Crush the Habit

Figure 15-1
Adult Mentors Are Vital
Role Models

Figure 15-2
Resistance Skills Help Youth Counter Peer Pressure to Use Drugs

Figure 16-1
Factors That Motivate Persons to Seek Treatment

Figure 16-2
There Can Be a Waiting Period to Enter Treatment Programs

GLOSSARY

GLOSSARY

A

able learners: young persons who are able to master academics in standard ways without special help

ACE inhibitors: *see* angiotensin converting enzyme inhibitors

active listening: a type of listening in which a person is reassured that his/her message is heard and understood

acute pancreatitis: inflammation of the pancreas manifested by severe abdominal pain (usually upper abdominal) often accompanied by nausea, vomiting, fever, and rapid heartbeat

additive effects: progressive effects that are due to increasing dosages of a drug

ADHD: *see* attention deficit hyperactive disorder (ADHD)

aggressive behavior: the use of words and/or actions that tend to communicate disrespect toward others

alarm stage: the body's initial response to a stressor; the first stage of the general adaptation syndrome

alcohol abusers: persons who experience a variety of social and medical problems as a result of high-risk drinking but who are not dependent on alcohol

alcohol dementia: brain impairment characterized by overall intellectual decline with deficits in abstracting ability and problem solving, difficulty in swallowing, difficulty in manipulating objects, brain wave abnormalities, and cerebral atrophy

alcohol-dependent persons: persons who experience adverse social and medical consequences from single bouts of drinking and from chronic, high-level alcohol use

amotivational syndrome: a loss of conventional motivation and an inability to persist in achieving long-term goals

amygdala: large limbic structure in the brain that is critical for memory

amyl nitrite: a clear yellowish liquid with a strong chemical smell; known for its vasodilation (increase in diameter of blood vessels) effects following inhalation

anabolic steroids: powerful, synthetic derivatives of testosterone that produce muscle growth by stimulating protein synthesis

analgesia: pain relief; therapeutic use of narcotics

analgesics: products that are taken to treat aches and pains

angiotensin converting enzyme (ACE) inhibitors: drugs that are believed to lower blood pressure by blocking enzyme systems that influence arterial function

antacids: compounds that are taken for the relief of indigestion, acid stomach, and heartburn

antiasthmatic drugs: drugs that widen constricted respiratory airways (bronchioles) to relieve breathing difficulty

antibiotic drugs: drugs that have the ability to inhibit or destroy bacterial growth

anticonvulsants: drugs that are used to control the symptoms of epilepsy, a disorder characterized by recurring seizures

antihistamines: remedies that are used to treat hay fever and other allergies

antihypertensives: drugs that counteract or reduce high blood pressure

antitussive: a medicine that suppresses coughing

antivirals: drugs that are used to fight viral infections

assault injury: any physical or bodily harm that occurs during the course of a rape, robbery, or any other type of attack on a person

assertive behavior: the honest expression of thoughts and feelings without experiencing anxiety or threatening others

atherosclerosis: the process of fatty build-up in arteries that can lead to a heart attack or stroke

attention deficit hyperactive disorder (ADHD): a disorder characterized by difficulty in focusing attention, high levels of distractibility, problems with filtering out background stimuli, impulsivity, difficulty in delaying gratification, and frequent overarousal

autogenic training: a series of exercises to increase muscle relaxation

axon: a cable-like fiber through which the cell body sends impulses to dendrites of other neurons

B

BAC: *see* blood-alcohol concentration

beta-blockers: drugs that block certain actions of the sympathetic nervous system, slow the heart rate, and lower blood pressure

binge drinking: drinking five or more alcoholic drinks in a row

bioequivalency: the ability of one drug to produce similar effects in the body as another drug

biofeedback: the technique of getting information about what is occurring in the body at a particular time, so that a physiological function can be altered

blackouts: periods of alcohol-induced amnesia

blood-alcohol concentration (BAC): expressed as a percent, the ratio of alcohol in a person's blood to the person's total amount of blood

blood-brain barrier: largely composed of fat-covered membranes that surround blood capillaries in the brain

blotter acid: blotter-like paper that has been impregnated with LSD and cut into small squares

borderline personality tendencies: a condition in which young persons do not have a stable identity and, as a result, feel an internal void accompanied by deep depression

brain stem: the lowest portion of the brain; controls basic functions such as heart rate, breathing, eating, and sleeping

brand name: a registered name or trademark given to a drug by a pharmaceutical company

buccal administration: the absorption of a drug between the cheek and gum

bulk-forming laxative: a product that mimics the actions of fiber in the intestine by creating bulk and increasing the amount of water absorbed into the intestine

bullying: an attempt by a stronger person to harm a weaker victim, presumably in the absence of provocation

butyl nitrite: compound that has the same properties as amyl nitrite, but has never been used clinically

C

caffeinism: a condition of chronic caffeine toxicity or poisoning associated with very heavy use and preoccupation with caffeine

calcium channel blockers: drugs that inhibit the contraction of the coronary arteries and peripheral arterioles by blocking the normal passage of calcium through vessel walls

carbon monoxide: a gas that significantly interferes with the ability of blood to carry oxygen by displacing oxygen from hemoglobin

cardiac arrhythmia: irregular heartbeat

cardiomyopathy: degeneration of the heart muscle

cell body: directs all the activities of the neuron; contains the nucleus

centrally-acting drugs: drugs that lower blood pressure by decreasing the activity of the vasomotor center in the brain

central nervous system: composed of the brain and spinal cord

cessation: a subsequent behavior phase in the complex behavior pattern of smoking cigarettes

characterological depression: an emotional state characterized by an overriding negative view of the self, others, and life events; a lifestyle depression

chemical neurotransmission: the entire process of the effect of the neurotransmitter on a receptor

child abuse and neglect: terms that refer to physical or mental injury, sexual abuse or exploitation, negligent treatment, or maltreatment of a child by a person who is responsible for the child's welfare, under circumstances that indicate that the child's health or welfare is harmed or threatened

child neglect: failure to provide for a child's basic needs

chronic obstructive pulmonary disease (COPD): characterized by permanent airflow reduction: the fifth leading cause of death in the United States; a major cause of chronic illness and disability

chronic pancreatitis: condition that typically may occur after five to ten years of heavy alcohol use

circumstantial use: use motivated by a desire to obtain a specific effect that is perceived as desirable within a certain situation

cirrhosis: a disease in which alcohol destroys liver cells and plugs the liver with fibrous scar tissue that can lead to liver failure and death

codependence: a mental disorder in which a person loses personal identity, has frozen feelings, and copes ineffectively

codependent: one who has a mental disorder, loses personal identity, has frozen feelings, and copes ineffectively

commitment: a pledge to do something

communication: the sharing of feelings, thoughts, and information with another person

comorbidity: a term used by mental health professionals to indicate the presence of drug abuse in combination with a psychiatric illness

compulsive use: the daily or almost daily use of high doses of a drug to obtain a desired physical and/or psychological effect

congeners: nonalcohol ingredients that may play a role in the development of some cancers

COPD: see chronic obstructive pulmonary disease

D

delayed gratification: allowing oneself to struggle in the present so that a desirable benefit will be achieved in the future

dendrites: sets of branches through which impulses, or messages, from other nerve cells are relayed directly to the cell body

denial: a condition in which a person refuses to recognize what (s)he is feeling because it is extremely painful

depression: an emotional state characterized by a dysphoric mood, sleep disturbance, withdrawal of interest in environment, feelings of guilt, lack of energy, poor concentration or memory, loss of capacity to experience pleasure, appetite disturbance, and suicidal ideations

depression resulting from chemical dependency: a kind of depression that surfaces during the recovery process

destructive relationships: relationships that threaten self-esteem, are disrespectful, indicate a lack of character, threaten health, and foster irresponsible decision-making; harmful relationships

detoxification: the process in which alcohol (or any other drug) is withdrawn from the body

dispiriting relationships: relationships that lower a person's spirit and make a person feel unimportant, worthless, isolated, and frustrated

distress: a harmful response to a stressor that produces negative results

diuretic: drug that lowers blood pressure by promoting the loss of water and salt from the body

dosage: the amount or quantity of a drug compound that is administered within a specified time period

dose-related effects: differing pharmacologic effects that are related to the quantity of a drug that is administered

drink: defined as one-half ounce of ethyl alcohol

drug abuse: the use of drugs that results in impairment of a user's ability to function normally or that is harmful to the user or others

drug behavior: an all-encompassing term used to describe nonuse and all phases of drug use

drug dependence: compulsive use of a drug (or drugs) despite adverse psychological, physiological, or social consequences

drug education: the field of study that examines life skills for inner well-being that promote drug-free behavior (the avoidance of harmful drugs) and drug-informed behavior (the use of legal drugs such as over-the-counter and prescription drugs according to directions) as well as intervention and treatment when appropriate

drug free: condition characterized by one who does not use harmful and illegal drugs

drug-free lifestyle: a lifestyle in which persons do not use harmful and illegal drugs

drug informed: condition characterized by one who takes over-the-counter drugs and/or prescription drugs to promote health

drug-informed lifestyle: a lifestyle in which persons use legal drugs such as over-the-counter drugs and medicines according to directions

drug interaction: the effect of one drug on the action of another drug or drugs

drug misuse: the inappropriate use of drugs including prescribed or nonprescribed medicines

drugs: substances, excluding food, that alter the function of the body

drug use: the use of drugs (including alcohol) in any form, legal or illegal, whether by prescription or for "recreational" purposes

dysfunctional family: a family in which feelings are not expressed openly and honestly, coping skills are inadequate, and members are distrustful of one another

E

economic-compulsive violent crime: crime committed by drug users because of the high cost of some drugs in order to support their continued drug use

educational neglect: permission of truancy, failure to enroll a child of mandatory school age, and inattention to a special educational need

emollients: laxatives that work by softening hard stools

emotional neglect: actions such as chronic or extreme spouse abuse in the child's presence, parental permission of alcohol or other drug abuse by the child, and failure to provide needed psychological care

endogenous depression: an emotional state that results from physiological changes in the body; physiological depression

environmental tobacco smoke: the combination of sidestream smoke and the fraction of mainstream smoke exhaled by a smoker

ergogenic drugs: drugs that are used to improve athletic performance

ethanol: *see* ethyl alcohol

ethyl alcohol: a type of alcohol formed by the fermentation of fruits, juices, or cereal grains; also known as ethanol

eustress: a healthful response to a stressor that produces positive results

exhaustion stage: prolonged period of stress producing burnout, or biochemical exhaustion; third stage of the general adaptation syndrome

F

faith: the belief system that guides a person's behavior choices and gives meaning and purpose to life

family: a system consisting of interconnecting people in which each person affects the others in profound and hidden ways

FAS: *see* fetal alcohol syndrome

fetal alcohol syndrome (FAS): a characteristic pattern of severe birth defects present in babies born to mothers who drink alcohol during their pregnancy

flashbacks: manifestations of one or more of the acute effects of a drug that recur long after it was taken

formication: the sensation of insects crawling under the skin

freebase: the purified base form of cocaine processed from the hydrochloride salt using volatile chemicals, usually ether

G

GAS: *see* general adaptation syndrome

general adaptation syndrome (GAS): the body's response to a stressor that occurs in three stages: the alarm stage, the resistance stage, and the exhaustion stage

generic name: the chemical and/or biological equivalent of a specific brand name drug

goal: a desired achievement toward which one works

gout: an inflammatory disease caused by excessive uric acid production

gouty arthritis: *see* gout

H

hallucinogenic drugs: substances that have the major effect of producing marked distortions in perception

harmful behaviors: voluntary actions that threaten self-esteem, harm health, increase the likelihood of illness, injury, and premature death, and destroy the quality of the environment; risk behaviors

harmful relationships: relationships that threaten self-esteem, are disrespectful, indicate a lack of character, threaten health, and foster irresponsible decision making

harmful situations: circumstances that threaten self-esteem; harm health; increase the likelihood of illness, injury, and premature death; and destroy the quality of the environment; risk situations

hashish: the drug-rich resinous secretions of the cannabis plant, which are collected, dried, and then compressed into a variety of forms, such as balls, cakes, or cookie-like sheets

hashish oil: a variation of hashish, produced by a process of repeated extraction of cannabis plant materials to yield a dark viscous liquid

healthful behaviors: actions that enhance self-esteem; promote health; prevent illness, injury, and premature death; and improve the quality of the environment; wellness behaviors

healthful relationships: relationships that enhance self-esteem, foster respect, develop character, and promote health-enhancing behaviors and responsible decision making

healthful situations: circumstances that enhance self-esteem; promote health; prevent illness, injury, and premature death; and improve the quality of the environment; wellness situations

health knowledge: facts that are needed to evaluate behaviors, situations, and relationships, to make responsible decisions, to use resistance skills, and to promote positive self-esteem

health status: the sum total of the positive and negative influence of behaviors, situations, relationships, decisions, use of resistance skills, and self-esteem on a person's health and wellness

hedonistic gang: type of gang which serves a basic purpose in letting members have a good time around getting high on psychoactive substances

hippocampus: large limbic structure in the brain that is critical for memory

histamine (H-2) blocking drugs: drugs that work by suppressing the production of excess stomach acid, which is the result of histamine stimulation

hit: a dose of LSD

holistic effect: the effect that a behavior, situation, relationship, decision, resistance skill, and level of self-esteem in any one of the ten areas will have on the other areas and the four dimensions of health

holistic health: the connectedness of the six factors that influence health status with the ten areas of health and the four dimensions of health

homicide: death due to injuries purposely inflicted by another person, not including deaths caused by law enforcement officers or legal execution

hypnotic drugs: drugs that induce drowsiness and encourage sleep

hypoxia: the reduction of the oxygen supply in the blood that can lead to permanent brain damage and even death: especially dangerous to a fetus as a result of a pregnant female's use of narcotics

I

I-messages: statements used to express feelings; a person who uses I-messages assumes responsibility for sharing feelings

immature character disorder: a condition in which young persons display maladaptive personality characteristics as indicated by a chronic history of antisocial behavior, difficulty maintaining close, compassionate relationships, and refusal to accept the responsibility for the consequences of their behavior

inhalants: substances that are gases or that emit gases at room temperature

initiation phase: the first interval in the complex behavior pattern of smoking cigarettes when an individual starts experimenting with cigarettes

inner well-being: a condition that results from having positive self-esteem, managing stress effectively, choosing healthful behaviors, choosing healthful situations, engaging in healthful relationships, making responsible decisions, using resistance skills when appropriate, demonstrating character, participating in the community, and abiding by laws

inspiriting relationships: relationships that lift the spirit and contribute to a sense of well-being

instant gratification: choosing a benefit now rather than waiting until a more appropriate time

instrumental gang: type of gang that is highly involved in property crimes for economic reasons

intensified use: a pattern of use that occurs when drugs are taken daily or almost daily, usually in low to moderate doses

intramuscular administration: an injection of a drug into a muscle

intravenous administration (IV): an injection of a drug directly into the bloodstream

ischemic heart disease: deficient blood circulation to the heart

isobutyl nitrite: substance that produces effects similar to amyl nitrite

isopropyl alcohol: another type of alcohol that is not intended to be consumed; rubbing alcohol

IV: *see* intravenous administration

K

kindling: lack of an enzyme that destroys circulating cocaine; a reverse tolerance

Korsakoff's psychosis: a permanent state of cognitive dysfunction and the inability to remember recent events or to learn new information

L

learning disabled: condition in which one has difficulty learning a basic scholastic skill because of a disorder that interferes with the learning process

leukoplakia: a condition resulting from direct irritation from tobacco; characterized by white patches on the lining of the mouth

life skills: actions that promote optimal well-being and are learned and practiced for a lifetime

lifestyle depression: an emotional state characterized by an overriding negative view of the self, others, and life events

limbic structures: brain structures that connect the cortex, which deals mainly with the outside world, with our emotions and motivations, which reflect our internal environment and survival needs

lipoproteins: drugs that carry cholesterol and triglycerides throughout the circulating bloodstream

look-alike drugs: tablets or capsules manufactured to resemble legitimate pharmaceutical products; frequently sold as appetite suppressants and anti-fatigue medications

loving, functional family: a family in which feelings are expressed openly and honestly, effective coping skills are practiced, and members show respect for one another

M

mainstream cigarette smoke: the smoke drawn through the tobacco into the smoker's mouth

maintenance of cessation: a subsequent behavior phase in the complex behavior pattern of smoking cigarettes

maintenance of the smoking habit: a subsequent behavior phase in the complex behavior pattern of smoking cigarettes

major depression: an emotional state that is usually a response to trauma, to a stressor, or to a significant loss

MAOIs: *see* monoamine oxidase inhibitors

marijuana: any part or extract of the cannabis plant that produces somatic or psychic changes

medicines: drugs that are used to treat, prevent, or diagnose illness

meditation: controlling thought processes and focusing on the present

mental injury: acts or omissions by a parent or other adult responsible for the child's care that cause, or could cause, serious behavioral, cognitive, emotional, or mental disorders

methadone: a legally-controlled, synthetic medication, developed in Germany during World War II as a substitute analgesic, or pain killer, when morphine was in short supply

methanol: *see* methyl alcohol

methyl alcohol: a type of alcohol that is very toxic and that can cause serious damage and even death when consumed; also known as wood alcohol

microdots: tablets of LSD that are less than an eighth of an inch in width

Model for Using Resistance Skills: a list of suggested ways for effectively resisting pressure to engage in actions that threaten health

monoamine oxidase inhibitors (MAOIs): drugs that are believed to relieve depression by blocking actions of an enzyme (monoamine oxidase type A) in the brain

N

narcolepsy: a condition in which a person is unable to stay awake

narcotic: opium and opium derivatives or their synthetic substitutes

narcotic antagonists: compounds that tend to block and reverse the effects of narcotics

nasal decongestants: remedies that are used to temporarily relieve nasal congestion and stuffiness

negative self-esteem: belief that one is unworthy and unlovable

neuron: the basic unit of structure and function in the nervous system

neurotransmitter: a chemical that transmits an impulse across the synaptic gap between two neurons

nicotine: an odorless and colorless compound; the active psychoactive agent found naturally in tobacco that is responsible for the addictive behavior of tobacco smokers

nicotine fading: the progressive reducing of nicotine intake by switching to brands with less nicotine and gradually decreasing the number of cigarettes (tapering)

nondependent problem drinkers: persons who experience a variety of social and medical problems as a result of high-risk drinking but who are not dependent on alcohol

nonsteroidal antiinflammatory drugs (NSAIDs): drugs that are prescribed for the treatment of inflammation associated with arthritis and other inflammatory diseases

NSAIDs: *see* nonsteroidal antiinflammatory drugs

O

opiates: natural narcotics because of their derivation or chemical similarity to opium

oral hypoglycemic drugs: the sulfonylureas; drugs that stimulate the pancreas to secrete more insulin and enhance the utilization of insulin in body tissues

osmotic laxative: product that works like a sponge to draw water into the bowel, thereby promoting easier passage of stools

osteoporosis: a condition characterized by calcium loss and loss of bone density

over-the-counter drugs: drugs that are approved for legal purchase and use without a prescription from a physician

oxidation: the breakdown of alcohol by enzymes in the liver, converting the alcohol into carbon dioxide and water at the rate of about half an ounce of alcohol per hour

P

paranoid ideation: a serious adverse effect of stimulants in which a person becomes suspicious and fears that others are watching or following him or her

parenteral administration: a method of drug administration that involves injecting drugs into the body

passive behavior: the holding back of ideas, opinions, and feelings

patient package insert (PPI): supplemental, informational brochure included in prescription drug packages that describes in easy-to-understand language the drug's actions, possible side effects, and interactions

peer pressure: the pressure that persons exert on other persons to encourage them to make similar decisions or behave in similar ways

perceived self-efficacy: the belief a person has in his/her own ability to make a change

peripherally-acting drugs: drugs that act directly on peripheral blood vessels

peripheral nervous system: many pairs of nerves that branch from the brain and spinal cord to the periphery of the body

pharmokinetics: the study of the process of how drugs reach target sites of action

physical abuse: abuse characterized by inflicting injury by punching, beating, kicking, biting, burning, or otherwise physically harming a child

physical dependence: the physiological process in which repeated doses of a drug cause the body to adapt to the presence of the drug; the result of frequent and increased use of drugs that literally can change brain chemistry, causing a functional demand for a particular drug

physical neglect: refusal of or delay in seeking health care; abandonment; expulsion from home, or not allowing a runaway to return home; and inadequate supervision

physiological depression: an emotional state that results from physiological changes in the body; endogenous depression

placebo: pharmacologically inert substance, such as "sugar pills"

placebo effect: the resulting effect caused by taking a placebo

polydrug abuse: the simultaneous abuse of more than one drug

positive self-esteem: belief that one is worthwhile and lovable

potentiation: a greater-than-expected impact that can occur when two drugs with the same effect are taken together

PPI: *see* patient package insert

predatory gang: type of gang that is more deeply involved in criminal activity and violent behavior than hedonistic and instrumental gangs

prescription: a very precise order from a physician or other appropriate health professional to a pharmacist to dispense a certain drug product to a patient

prescription drugs: drugs that can be legitimately obtained only by a prescription from licensed health professionals (e.g., physicians, podiatrists, dentists) and dispensed by registered pharmacists

progressive relaxation: relaxing the mind by first relaxing the body

protective factors: characteristics of individuals and their environments that make a positive contribution to development and behavior

psychoactive drugs: substances that are capable of altering a user's moods, perceptions, feelings, personality, or behavior

psychological dependence: a condition characterized by a pervasive desire or craving to achieve the effects produced by a drug; a condition evidenced by an altered state of mind on which chemically-dependent persons come to depend

R

rape: the nonconsensual sexual penetration of an adolescent or adult by physical force, by threat of bodily harm, or when the victim is incapable of giving consent by virtue of mental illness, mental retardation, or intoxication

rebound congestion: a condition in which nasal membranes become enlarged after repeated doses of topical decongestants

rebound hyperacidity: a condition that occurs when calcium (or any other agent) causes the stomach to secrete extra acid

receptors: special molecules on the surface of dendrites of adjacent neurons to which the neurotransmitter binds

refusal skills: skills that are used when a person wants to say NO to an action and/or leave a situation; resistance skills

relationships: the connections people have with each other

resiliency: the ability to recover from or adjust to misfortune, change, pressure, and adversity

resistance skills: skills that are used when a person wants to say NO to an action and/or leave a situation; refusal skills

resistance stage: the second stage of the general adaptation syndrome during which the individual's body attempts to regain a state of internal balance, or homeostasis, which is the body's normal state

Responsible Decision-Making Model: a series of steps to follow to assure that the decisions a person makes lead to actions that promote health for self and others

risk behaviors: voluntary actions that threaten self-esteem, harm health, increase the likelihood of illness, injury, and premature death, and destroy the quality of the environment; harmful behaviors

risk factors: characteristics of individuals or environments associated with increased vulnerability to problem behaviors

risk situations: circumstances that threaten self-esteem; harm health; increase the likelihood of illness, injury, and premature death; and destroy the quality of the environment; harmful situations

role model: a person who is influential and whose behavior and attitudes are learned and copied

S

sedative-hypnotic drugs: central nervous system depressants

self-centered behavior: behavior in which a person takes actions to fulfill his/her needs and wishes with little or no regard for the needs and wishes of others

self-concept: the personal, internal image or feeling a person has about himself/herself

self-destructive behavior: behavior irresponsible and/or harmful to the self and that indicates a person does not believe himself/herself to be worthwhile and lovable

self-discipline: the effort or energy with which a person follows through on what (s)he intends or promises to do

self-esteem: the personal internal image that a person has about himself/herself

self-loving behavior: healthful and responsible behavior indicative of a person who believes himself/herself to be worthwhile and lovable

semisynthetic narcotics: compounds that have been derived by modification of the chemicals contained in opium

sexual abuse: fondling of a child's genitals, intercourse, incest, rape, sodomy, exhibitionism, and sexual exploitation

sexuality: the feelings and attitudes a person has about his/her body, sex role, and sexual orientation as well as his/her feelings and attitudes regarding the bodies, sex roles, and sexual orientation of others

sidestream smoke: the smoke emitted by the burning tobacco between puffs

sites of action: limited places in the body where drugs produce their effects

skin patches: patches worn on the body while a drug compound is slowly absorbed through the skin into the bloodstream

snorting: the process of sniffing a drug through the nose so that it can be absorbed through the mucous membranes of the upper nasal passages

social drinkers: those for whom drinking produces no serious long-term health or social consequences and cessation of alcohol use poses no problem

social-recreational use: a type of drug use that typically occurs in social settings among friends who are also using for the purpose of experiencing the drug's effects

spirit-relationship continuum: a set of values that includes a range of dispiriting descriptors at the lower end and a range of inspiriting descriptors at the higher end

stacking: the practice of taking many types of steroids, sometimes in combination with other drugs prior to an athletic event

status epilepticus: a prolonged period of continuous seizures without interruption

stimulant: drug that increases the rate at which organs controlled by the central nervous system function

stimulant laxative: product that works by irritating the linings of the intestine, causing waves of muscular contractions that expel fecal matter

stool softener: laxative that works by softening hard stools

stress: the nonspecific response of the body to any demand made on it

stress-management skills: techniques used to help cope with and prevent or lessen the harmful effects produced by stress

stressor: any demand made on the body, such as a race, a difficult problem, or a first-time meeting

subcutaneous administration: an injection of a drug just beneath the skin

sublingual drug administration: the absorption of a drug under the tongue

synapse: a tiny gap that separates the terminal of an axon from the dendrites of a neuron with which it seeks to communicate

synesthesia: a phenomenon that refers to a crossing of the perceptual senses

systemic violence: the heightened risk for both committing violence and being a victim of violence because of participation in the sale and trafficking of illicit substances

T

THC: delta-9-tetrahydrocannabinol; the major psychoactive ingredient in marijuana

therapeutic communities: residential treatment programs that attempt to deal with the psychological causes of addiction by changing the character and personality of chemically-dependent persons

tolerance: a condition in which the body becomes adapted to a drug so that increasingly larger doses are needed to produce the desired effect

"totally awesome" teaching strategies: creative ways to involve youth in learning about drugs and in practicing life skills for inner well-being

transdermal administration: the application of a drug to the skin

transition phase: that period in the complex behavior of smoking cigarettes in which environmental and psychological factors influence individuals to become smokers or nonsmokers

tricyclic antidepressant drugs: drugs that relieve depression in some patients by gradually restoring norepinephrine and serotonin in the brain to normal levels

Type 1, milieu-limited alcohol dependence: a subgroup of alcohol dependence that shows a more complex inter-play between genetic and environmental influences

Type 2, male-limited alcohol dependence: a subgroup of alcohol dependence that has a high genetic penetrance from father to son and minor environmental association

V

value: something of great importance to a person

vasodilators: drugs that lower blood pressure by causing the blood vessels to dilate or widen

violence: the use of force with the intent to harm oneself or another person

W

wellness: the quality of life that includes physical, mental-emotional, family-social, and spiritual health

wellness behaviors: actions that enhance self-esteem; promote health; prevent illness, injury, and premature death; and improve the quality of the environment; healthful behaviors

Wellness Scale: the ranges constituting the quality of life—from optimal well-being to high level wellness, average wellness, minor illness or injury, major illness or injury, and premature death

wellness situations: circumstances that enhance self-esteem; promote health; prevent illness, injury, and premature death; and improve the quality of the environment; healthful situations

Wernicke's disease: a condition in which certain areas of the brain are destroyed by the combination of thiamine deficiency and the toxic effects of alcohol

windowpanes: tiny, thin gelatin chips of LSD

withdrawal symptoms: unpleasant symptoms experienced by individuals who are physically dependent on a drug when deprived of that drug

wood alcohol: see methyl alcohol

Y

you-messages: statements that attempt to blame and shame another person rather than express feelings

INDEX

INDEX

Meeks Heit Publishing...*producers of quality health education materials and "totally awesome" training packages*

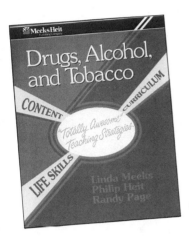

Drugs, Alcohol, and Tobacco: Totally Awesome Teaching Strategies (1994) contains everything needed to implement drug and violence prevention curricula: factual content, goals and philosophy, a responsible decision-making model, model for using resistance skills, life skills for inner well-being, protective factors that promote resiliency, scope and sequence chart with objectives for grades Pre-K through 12, totally awesome teaching strategies, infusion of drug education into several curriculum areas, critical thinking skills, character education, multicultural infusion, inclusion of students with special needs, suggestions for including parents and community leaders, coverage of intervention and treatment, and evaluation. Used for pre-service and graduate training at colleges/universities and in-service training provided by school districts, state departments of education, state departments of health, and agencies.

Comprehensive School Health Education: Totally Awesome Strategies for Teaching Health (1992) is the most widely used book in colleges/universities, state departments of education, and school districts for the training of teachers in creative, dynamic, skill-building, health-related teaching strategies. This innovative book is ideal for classroom teachers — novice or experienced. It is used by drug-free and STD and HIV/AIDS coordinators and teachers. This book contains hundreds of "totally awesome," skill-building teaching strategies, curricula, blackline teaching masters, lesson plans, the Year 2000 Objectives for Youth, and up-to-date information on the leading health-related concerns for young children and adolescents.

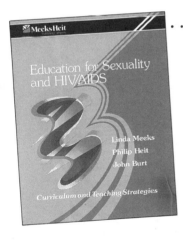

Education for Sexuality and HIV/AIDS: Curriculum and Teaching Strategies (1993), previously titled **Education for Sexuality: Concepts and Programs for Teaching,** has been the most widely used human sexuality education book in the world for more than twenty years. Published in six languages, this book is used in colleges/universities for pre-service through graduate education. It is used in school districts for developing and implementing curricula. A popular resource, it is used in school districts by drug-free coordinators, STD and HIV/AIDS coordinators, and classroom teachers. State departments of education, state health departments, and public health coordinators and nurses continue to find this book "state-of-the-art" for their work in human sexuality.

About The Meeks and Heit "Totally Awesome" Training Packages...

* featuring teaching strategies that are dynamic, creative, and easy to use,

* building confidence in educators responsible for providing comprehensive school health education, sex education, HIV/AIDS education, violence prevention, and drug education,

* involving educators in experiencing teaching strategies that they can use to motivate their students,

* providing a personal touch for audiences of 50 through 500.

For further information about Meeks Heit books and/or "Totally Awesome" Training Packages...

Call 1-800-682-6882
    1-614-759-7780 (Ohio)
Fax 1-614-759-6166

Meeks Heit
Publishing Company
P.O. Box 121
Blacklick, Ohio 43004